SUPPORT AT *every step*

FOR STUDENTS

Effective, efficient studying.

Connect helps you be more productive with your study time and get better grades using tools like SmartBook 2.0, which highlights key concepts and creates a personalized study plan. Connect sets you up for success, so you walk into class with confidence and walk out with better grades.

Study anytime, anywhere.

Download the free ReadAnywhere app and access your online eBook or SmartBook 2.0 assignments when it's convenient, even if you're offline. And since the app automatically syncs with your eBook and SmartBook 2.0 assignments in Connect, all of your work is available every time you open it. Find out more at **www.mheducation.com/readanywhere**

> *"I really liked this app—it made it easy to study when you don't have your text-book in front of you."*
>
> - Jordan Cunningham, Eastern Washington University

Calendar: owattaphotos/Getty Images

No surprises.

The Connect Calendar and Reports tools keep you on track with the work you need to get done and your assignment scores. Life gets busy; Connect tools help you keep learning through it all.

Learning for everyone.

McGraw-Hill works directly with Accessibility Services Departments and faculty to meet the learning needs of all students. Please contact your Accessibility Services office and ask them to email accessibility@mheducation.com, or visit **www.mheducation.com/about/accessibility** for more information.

SOC 2020

SIXTH EDITION

Jon Witt
Central College

McGraw Hill

WITT: SOC 2020, SIXTH EDITION

Published by McGraw-Hill Education, 2 Penn Plaza, New York, NY 10121. Copyright © 2020 by McGraw-Hill Education. All rights reserved. Printed in the United States of America. Previous editions © 2018, 2016, and 2015. No part of this publication may be reproduced or distributed in any form or by any means, or stored in a database or retrieval system, without the prior written consent of McGraw-Hill Education, including, but not limited to, in any network or other electronic storage or transmission, or broadcast for distance learning.

Some ancillaries, including electronic and print components, may not be available to customers outside the United States.

This book is printed on acid-free paper.

1 2 3 4 5 6 7 8 9 LWI 24 23 22 21 20 19

ISBN 978-1-260-07531-1 (bound edition)
MHID 1-260-07531-1 (bound edition)
ISBN 978-1-260-39845-8 (loose-leaf edition)
MHID 1-260-39845-5 (loose-leaf edition)

Author: *Jon Witt*
Field Correspondent: *Richard T. Schaefer*
Executive Portfolio Manager: *Claire Brantley*
Product Development Manager: *Dawn Groundwater*
Lead Content Project Manager, Core: *Susan Trentacosti*
Content Project Manager, Assessment: *George Theofanopoulos*
Content Project Manager: *Sandra Schnee*
Senior Buyer: *Laura M. Fuller*
Design: *Matt Diamond*
Content Licensing Specialist: *Sarah Flynn*
Cover Image: *goodluz/Shutterstock*
Compositor: *SPi Global*

All credits appearing on page or at the end of the book are considered to be an extension of the copyright page.

ISSN: 2164-0696

The Internet addresses listed in the text were accurate at the time of publication. The inclusion of a website does not indicate an endorsement by the authors or McGraw-Hill Education, and McGraw-Hill Education does not guarantee the accuracy of the information presented at these sites.

In memory of Megan Sloss

Sociology, Class of 2014, Central College

Be Bold. Dive Deep. Converse.

Name: *Jon Witt (though my mom always called me Jonathan)*

Education: *I got my BA from Trinity College in Deerfield, IL, and earned my PhD from Loyola University in Chicago.*

Occupations: *Sociologist, father, and Corgi-walker*

Hobbies: *I like reading, writing, and messing around on computers—and I'm addicted to my iPhone and iPad.*

Childhood ambition: *To be a printer like my dad until I decided to become a teacher like my mom.*

Family: *Lori and I have been married for 35 years, and we have two daughters, Emily and Eleanor.*

Best recent book read: *The Overstory by Richard Powers*

Favorite recent film: *Apollo 11 took my breath away*

Favorite soundtrack: *I am loving the Dear Evan Hansen soundtrack*

Quote: *There may be fields of sociological science quite beyond the average mind, and rightly left to the learned specialist; but that is no reason why we should not learn enough of the nature and habits of society to insure a more profitable and pleasant life.*
—Charlotte Perkins Gilman, Human Work, 1904

Social Media: *Twitter @soc101*

BRIEF CONTENTS

WHAT'S NEW IN SOC

Helping Students Succeed with Connect®

McGraw Hill connect®

McGraw-Hill Connect® is an integrated educational platform that includes assignable and assessable quizzes, exercises, and interactive activities, all associated with learning objectives for *SOC 2020*. Videos, interactive assessments, links to news articles about current issues with accompanying questions ("NewsFlash"), and scenario-based activities engage students and add real-world perspective to the introductory sociology course. In addition, printable, exportable reports show how well each student or course section is performing on each course segment.

Here are some of the media-rich activities that will help your students succeed in the introductory sociology course:

In Their Shoes. In Their Shoes develops students' sociological imagination by walking them through the situation, challenges, and crises in the character's life. Covering topics such as "Deviance and Social Control," "Racial and Ethnic Inequality," and "Socialization and the Life Course" students explore and navigate life choices.

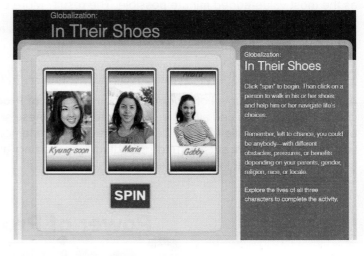

Peathegee Inc/Blend Images LLC
Yellow Dog Productions/Digital Vision/Getty Images
PeopleImages.com/Digital Vision/Getty Images

Applying the Perspectives. In Applying the Perspectives, students examine a problem—global inequality, gender stratification, or family and intimate relationships—from three sociological perspectives and apply their critical thinking skills to align theories with the appropriate perspective.

Concept Clips. Concept Clips are animations designed to engage students and walk them through some of the more complex concepts in the course and conclude with assessment questions to demonstrate their understanding. Topics include research variables, functions of religion, and power and authority.

Concept Clip: Sociology as a Science

Watch the Concept Clip and then respond to the following questions.

Put students first with Connect's intuitive mobile interface, which gives students and instructors flexible, convenient, anytime-anywhere access to all components of the Connect platform. It provides seamless integration of learning tools and places the most important priorities up front in a new "to-do" list with a calendar view across all Connect courses. Enjoy on-the-go access with the new mobile interface designed for optimal use of tablet functionality.

Provide a Smarter Text and Better Value with SmartBook

■I SMARTBOOK° Available within Connect, SmartBook® makes study time as productive and efficient as possible by identifying and closing knowledge gaps. SmartBook identifies what an individual student knows and doesn't know based on the student's confidence level, responses to questions, and other factors. It then provides focused help through targeted learning resources (including videos, animations, and other interactive activities).

SmartBook builds an optimal, personalized learning path for each student, so students spend less time on concepts they already understand and more time on those they don't. As a student engages with SmartBook, the reading experience continuously adapts by highlighting the most impactful content a student needs to learn at that moment in time. This ensures that every minute spent with SmartBook is returned to the student as the most value-added minute possible. The result? More confidence, better grades, and greater success.

New to this edition, SmartBook is now optimized for phones and tablets and accessible for students with disabilities using interactive features.

Prepare Students for Higher-Level Thinking

Aimed at the higher level of Bloom's taxonomy, **Power of Process for Sociology** helps students improve critical thinking skills and allows instructors to assess these skills efficiently and effectively in an online environment. Available through Connect, pre-loaded readings are available for instructors to assign. Using a scaffolded framework such as understanding, synthesizing, and analyzing, Power of Process moves students toward higher-level thinking and analysis.

Also at the higher level of Bloom's, McGraw-Hill's **Application-Based Activities** are highly interactive, automatically graded, online learn-by-doing exercises that provide students a safe space to apply their knowledge and problem-solving skills to real-world scenarios. Each scenario addresses key concepts and skills that students must use to work through and solve course-specific problems, resulting in improved critical thinking and development of relevant workplace skills. Twenty-one Application-Based Activities are new to this edition of *SOC.*

A Revision Informed by Student Data

From the start, Connect Sociology has collected data anonymously on students' performance on specific learning objectives. These aggregated data, displayed in the form of heat maps, graphically identify challenging "hot spots" in the text, helping guide the revision of both core content and assessment activities for the Sixth Edition. This student-directed revision is reflected primarily in Chapters 9, 11, 13, and 15.

Chapter Changes

The following is a list of chapter-by-chapter content changes:

CHAPTER 1: The Sociological Imagination

- New opening vignette on rural life and inequality based on Sarah Smarsh's memoir *Heartland*
- Updated the data on unemployment as an example of a public issue versus private troubles
- Revised the discussion of the sociological imagination to reinforce it usefulness when making decisions about the future
- Updated the CEO-to-average-worker pay ratio data
- Updated the 5 Movies feature to include *Lady Bird* and *Black Panther*
- Updated the film gender wage gap example with Claire Foy's experience on *The Queen*
- Updated data on gender wage gap and race/ethnicity wealth gap
- Revised the discussion of free agency in the NBA to update information and clarify its significance
- Revised the discussion of Comte to clarify three significant contributions he made to early sociology
- Classified Martineau's contributions into three specific areas for the sake of clarity
- Updated graphs and map presenting suicide data
- Added new information about the increasing rates of suicide and the resulting public health concern
- Updated the Going Global feature on the World Happiness Report
- Revised the Three Sociological Perspectives table to increase clarity
- Revised the definition of *personal sociology*
- Replaced the existing Personal Sociology feature with new text
- Updated the Sociology Degrees Conferred in the United States graph
- Revised the discussion of Applied Sociology to include a reference to the Obama administration's Social and Behavioral Sciences Team

CHAPTER 2: Sociological Research

- Revised the Finding Information infographic
- New Did You Know? feature on polling projections and the 2016 presidential election
- Revised the section on common sense to more clearly identify four of its limitations
- Added a consideration of the danger of common sense including a reference to Lazarsfeld's example of the limits of "obvious" explanations for human behavior
- Updated the Did You Know? feature on degree attainment percentages
- Updated the Degree Attainment and Income graph to include new data and a third column representing those whose highest degree attainment is some college/associate's degree
- Updated the Presidential Approval Ratings graph with new data
- Updated the Going Global: Research Abroad feature on the annual Afghanistan national survey with new data
- Updated data on popular baby names as a sign of cultural shifts
- Updated the 5 Movies feature to include *Science Fair* and *Monrovia, Indiana*

CHAPTER 3: Culture

- Updated the opening vignette Improv Everywhere and breaking norms to include the most recent No Pants Subway Ride event and other updated missions from Improv Everywhere
- Moved the introduction of the three-step model of the social construction of reality from Chapter 5 to Chapter 3 in order to set the stage for the next three chapters as corresponding to the three stages of that model
- Added *social construction of reality* as a key term
- Edited the PopSoc feature on Columbusing for greater clarity
- Updated section on diffusion regarding the number of McDonald's and Starbucks locations around the world

- New Did You Know? feature on the invention of the steam engine
- Updated data from Ethnologue on the number of living, endangered languages, and extinct languages
- Updated the Going Global feature on the region of origin of the world's living languages and contrasted that with the number of speakers
- Updated examples of new words for 2018 added to the *Merriam-Webster Collegiate Dictionary*
- Revised the discussion on invented languages for the sake of clarity and to emphasize the three different eras
- Updated the PopSOC feature on Dothraki and the increasing popularity of the name Khaleesi
- Revised the discussion of the Sapir-Whorf hypothesis for greater clarity
- Revised and updated data and graph regarding the values of first-year college students using data from the annual HERI survey
- Updated the 5 Movies feature on U.S. culture feature to include *Sorry to Bother You, If Beale Street Could Talk, En el Séptimo Día (On the Seventh Day),* and *The Rider*
- Revised the discussion of sanctions to clarify the distinction between internal and external policing
- Updated the 5 Movies feature on cultures outside the United States to include the films *Roma* and *Shoplifters*
- Revised the discussion of subcultures to include a consideration of divisions between Republicans and Democrats in the United States
- Edited the discussion of ethnocentrism

CHAPTER 4: Socialization

- Added a discussion linking this chapter to the three-step model of world construction which was introduced in Chapter 3
- Updated the discussion of Dani's story in the Extreme Childhood Isolation section
- Revised and streamlined the discussion of Mead's theory on I, Me, significant other, and generalized other
- Revised the definition of Mead's *generalized other*
- New J. K. Rowling feature quote on the importance of agency
- Added a new subsection on W. I. Thomas in the Sociological Approaches to the Self section
- New graph showing average media use time per week by age groups

- Updated the SOCthink to focus on smartphone use among young adults
- Updated the Telephones and Cell Phones by Country per 100 People graph
- Updated data on mobile phone ownership in Africa and added the term *leapfrogging*
- Updated data on the number of jobs held between 18 and 50
- Revised the 5 Movies feature on socialization to include the films *Eighth Grade, Welcome to Marwen,* and *Three Identical Strangers*
- Updated data on U.S. and global life expectancy
- New graph on living arrangements by age for those 65 and older
- Updated data on Social Security and poverty for those over 65
- Revised the 5 Movies feature on aging to include *Beginners* and *Our Souls at Night*

CHAPTER 5: Social Structure and Interaction

- Revised the Social Interaction section to establish the connection of the material in this chapter to the three-step model of world construction, which is now introduced in Chapter 3 rather than here
- Revised the definition of *secondary groups*
- Revised the discussion of primary and secondary groups for greater clarity
- Added a new discussion on college student friendship networks based on Janice McCabe's research highlighting three types: tight-knitters, compartmentalizers, and samplers
- Updated the Going Global feature on Internet access and social networking use in various countries around the world
- Revised the discussion of images under Postmodern Life to increase clarity
- Updated the Going Global feature on U.S. favorability ratings around the world
- Updated the 5 Movies feature to include *The Greatest Showman, District 9,* and *The Green Book*
- Updated the Pop Quiz feature

CHAPTER 6: Deviance

- Revised and updated the chapter opening on mass shootings to include the Marjory Stoneman Douglas high school shooting in Parkland, Florida, and the Las Vegas concert shooting
- Updated and revised the Binge Drinking on Campus graphs

- Updated data on the correctional population in the United States including updating the U.S. Incarceration Rates graph
- Moved the discussion of marijuana to the Crime section where it was also discussed
- Updated data on piracy as a form of deviance
- Updated the 5 Movies feature on deviance to include *The Purge, Liar, Liar,* and *I Am Not a Witch*
- Updated data on cosmetic surgery by both women and men in the United States
- Revised the discussion of crime for the sake of greater clarity and accessibility
- Updated the data on trends in crime including the crime clock
- Updated the FBI Uniform Crime Reports Data table with latest UCR data on crime rates and trends along with clearance rates
- Revised the definition of *victimization surveys*
- Updated data and graph on victimization survey data showing percentage of crimes reported to police
- Updated the 5 Movies feature on crime to include *Three Billboards Outside Ebbing, Missouri, Charm City,* and *The Shawshank Redemption*
- Revised the definition of *white-collar crime* and streamlined the discussion of the topic
- Revised the discussion of victimless crimes
- Updated the Marijuana Laws by State map
- Updated and moved the Marijuana Legislation graph to the victimless crimes discussion
- New PopSOC on films dealing with Wall Street
- Updated Going Global graph on international incarceration rates
- Updated the Did You Know? feature on drug arrests in the United States
- Added *broken window hypothesis* as a new key term
- Added a new featured quote from Dostoevsky and prisons
- Updated data on death penalty cases, DNA exonerations, and race in the United States
- Updated map with latest data on executions in the United States
- Updated the gender discussion to include changes internationally regarding the loophole in which rapists can avoid prosecution by marrying their victims

CHAPTER 7: Families

- Updated the chapter opening on online dating apps/sites including Jessica Carbino, Bumble's in-house sociologist
- Updated Did You Know? feature on U.S. marriage rate compared to Las Vegas and Hawaii

- Revised the substantive definition of families
- Revised the definition of extended families
- Updated and streamlined the discussion of family types, marriage types, and kinship patterns under the substantive definition of *families*
- Updated the U.S. Households by Family Type graph
- Updated data on the number and ratio of stay-at-home moms to stay-at-home dads
- Updated graph showing median age for first marriage for women and men from 1890 to 2018
- Updated data on age differences between marital partners
- Updated data, table, and graph on interracial marriage
- Revised the definition of *homogamy*
- Revised the discussion of parenting and social class
- Made *concerted cultivation* and *accomplishment of natural growth* key terms
- Updated the Living Arrangements of Children graph on the percentage of children living with two parents versus one parent by race and ethnicity and over time
- Revised and expanded the discussion on parenting, race, and ethnicity
- Updated the 5 Movies feature to include *Instant Family, Leave No Trace,* and *Mudbound*
- Reorganized and retitled sections for better flow including Dating, Mating, and Parenting and Modern Families
- Added a new section covering birth rates and average number of children including a discussion of the impact education and geographic region have on age prior to the section on parenting
- Updated data on international adoption by U.S. parents including overall numbers, top three source nations, and median cost of adoptions from China
- Updated data on the number of children in foster care and awaiting adoption
- Updated data on dual-income families
- Updated data on attitudes regarding same-sex marriage
- Updated the Approval of Same-Sex Marriage by Age graphs showing differences by generations
- Updated data on single-parent families
- Updated data on stepfamilies
- Updated data on multigenerational families
- New graph showing percentage of multigenerational families over time
- Revised the definition of *cohabitation* to make it more inclusive

- Updated data on cohabitation
- Updated data on remaining single
- Updated data on remaining child-free
- Updated data on divorce
- Updated the Trends in Marriage and Divorce in the United States graph to reflect recent rate changes

CHAPTER 8: Education and Religion

- Revised the chapter opening to focus on two students from the Bronx who struggle to make education work as a pathway to opportunity
- Revised the Education in Society section to highlight the importance of principle and practice when it comes to assessing educational outcomes
- Revised the Education in Society section to include a number of subsections, including Education and Opportunity, Educational Attainment, Community Colleges, Teaching as a Profession, and Homeschooling (these last three were moved from another section)
- Updated data on community college enrollments
- Updated the Net Price Cost of College graph showing the net price (tuition, fees, room, and board minus grants) cost of two-year and four-year colleges over time
- Updated the Average Salaries for Teachers map
- Revised the Teaching as a Profession section to also address adjunct/contingent professors
- Updated the Did You Know? feature on college enrollment rates
- Updated the Educational Attainment in the United States graph showing high school and college completion rates from 1910 to 2017
- Revised the Going Global: Educational Attainment of 25- to 34-Year-Olds graph to include percentages for three levels of educational attainment: less than upper-secondary, secondary, and tertiary
- Streamlined the discussion of functions of education, added soft skills to the heading and discussion, and completely reworked the Cultural Innovation subsection
- Updated data in the Child Care subsection on the percentage increase of three- to five-year-old children in preschool and kindergarten over time
- Updated the Education Pays graph on the relationship between education level and income for 25- to 34-year-olds
- New feature quote from Malcolm X on education
- Updated data for Did You Know? feature regarding family income level and likelihood of going directly to college after high school

- Restructured the Sociological Perspectives on Education section including the addition of a new interactionist perspective subsection
- Revised the discussion of the correspondence principle and hidden curriculum and made them part of their own subsection
- Updated Did You Know? regarding Harvard's acceptance rate
- Updated data on student loan debt
- Updated the College Majors by Gender, Percent Female graph to show the percentage of female bachelor's degree recipients for a variety of majors
- Revised 5 Movies feature on education to include *Dead Poets Society, Night School,* and *The Perks of Being a Wallflower*
- Updated SOCthink on women's participation levels in high school and college athletics
- Revised the discussion of a substantive definition to enhance clarity
- Revised the discussion of the functional definition of religion to highlight three functions: encouraging social integration, enforcing existing beliefs and practices, and providing a sense of meaning and purpose
- Added a new subheading for functional equivalents of religion and revised the discussion for greater clarity
- Updated the Major World Religions graph and table with current data
- Revised 5 Movies feature on religion to include *First Reformed* and *Noah*
- Updated the data on women clergy and theological students

CHAPTER 9: Economy and Politics

- Revised the structure of the chapter to improve flow and create a better narrative
- Updated the chapter opening regarding Trump voters' continued support for him
- Revised the introductions to capitalism and socialism to improve clarity
- New Did You Know? feature on attitudes toward capitalism and socialism in the United States
- Revised the discussion of mixed economies including more information about China
- Updated the International Economic Growth, 1980–2017 graph
- Streamlined the discussion of the Great Recession to make it part of the mixed economy discussion
- Revised the discussion of the three economic sectors to make it more accessible
- Added a new subsection Economic Globalization to include the economic accomplishments of capitalism and placed the

- discussion of the more recent challenges of deindustrialization, outsourcing, and offshoring here
- Created a new 5 Movies feature focusing solely on the economy and added *The Big Short* and *The Price of Everything*
- Introduced *polity* as a key term in place of *political system* to describe that social institution
- Added a new Did You Know? feature on the most admired man and woman in America to go along with charismatic authority
- Added a new 5 Movies feature focusing only on politics, and added *RBG, The Post,* and *Cold War*
- Created a new subsection focusing on the relationship between capitalism and democracy including an enhanced discussion of Okun's tension between equality and efficiency and Marshall's discussion of social rights
- Updated the Public Trust in Government graph
- Added a discussion on voter identification
- Updated the What's Your Party? graph on political party identification
- Updated data on voter participation, including a consideration of the 2018 midterm elections
- Updated the Voter Turnout Worldwide graph
- Updated the Reasons for Not Voting graph
- Updated the (Under)Representation in Congress graph to reflect the 2018 midterm results for the 116th Congress
- Added a discussion about the increasing diversity of Congress due to the 2018 midterms
- Updated the Women in National Legislatures graph
- Updated the U.S. Public Opinion on Defense Spending graph
- Updated data on terrorist attacks in 2017
- Updated and revised the Pop Quiz to reflect the new structure and content

CHAPTER 10: Social Class

- Updated data on human trafficking in the United States
- Updated the Did You Know? feature on the Global Slavery Index
- Revised the discussion on income to clarify the varieties of ways sociologists explore income inequality including the importance of the distinction between median and mode, changes in relative income shares by quintile over time, changes in absolute income over time by quintiles, and the Gini index
- Updated median and mean income in the United States
- Updated data on quintile distribution including the Percentage Share of Total Income graphs

- Updated Average Household Income by Quintile graph with the latest data
- Updated Gini index data for income
- Added a new Average Hourly Income, 1964–2018 graph showing both constant and current dollars
- Updated data on wealth distribution and added the Gini index for wealth
- Updated the Did You Know? feature on consumer expenditures by the top quintile
- Updated the Child Poverty Rates around the World graph
- Updated data for table Who Are the Poor in the United States? percentage of population overall versus percentage of poverty population
- Updated the People below Poverty Level map showing variation in poverty levels by state
- Updated data on percentage of health care spending provided by government for select nations
- Revised the discussion on the importance of parents' resources when it comes to children's mobility
- Updated the Education Pays graph of the relationship between education and income for full-time, year-round workers
- Revised and updated the Did You Know? feature on the highest-paid CEOs
- Updated the 5 Movies feature on Social Class to include *The Florida Project* and *Generation Wealth*
- Added a new feature quote on wealth

CHAPTER 11: Global Inequality

- Renamed the opening section Global Interdependence and revised the discussion in that section to emphasize that theme as a bridge to why people should be interested and concerned
- Provided new examples of global production chains
- Updated the Going Global feature showing Human Development Index scores for a variety of nations
- Renamed the second section Sociological Perspective on Globalization to clarify the purpose of the section
- Revised the discussion of modernization theory and clarified its connection to the functionalist perspective
- Revised the discussion of dependency theory and world systems analysis and clarified their connection to the conflict perspective
- Clarified how the discussion of multinational corporations fit into the sociological theories

- Updated Going Global feature contrasting corporate revenue of the top 10 multinational corporations to the GDP of comparably sized nations
- Renamed the third section Economic Inequality around the World
- Split up the discussion of income and wealth into separate subsections and streamlined the discussion of both to avoid overwhelming students with too much detail
- Moved the discussion and map of gross national income to this section instead of appearing earlier
- Updated data on income inequality
- Updated the Quintile Distribution of Income graph showing percentage of income earned by the top and bottom quintiles
- Updated data on wealth inequality
- Updated and revised the Global Wealth Distribution graph
- Updated the Wealth Concentration graph
- Updated data on poverty around the world
- Updated the Living on Less Than $1.90 a Day graph regarding extreme poverty
- Updated the Share of Global Poor graph showing the distribution based on region
- Streamlined the discussion of the Millennial and Sustainable Development Goals
- Revised the Did You Know? feature about what women garment workers in Bangladesh earn compared to CEOs of garment companies
- Updated the discussion of Mexico as a case study, including providing historical context for Mexico
- Revised the discussion of Mexico's income, wealth, and poverty data to bring it into alignment with the previous section and added more data regarding each
- Updated the Did You Know? feature on the number of undocumented workers entering Mexico
- Revised the discussion of indigenous people in Mexico with additional context and data
- Updated data on the status of women in Mexico
- Updated data for the Borderlands map showing apprehensions and remittances
- Revised the discussion regarding emigration to the United States from Mexico with additional information and context
- Updated the 5 Movies feature on Global Inequality to include *Icebox, On Her Shoulders,* and *Capernaum*
- Connected the discussion of human rights to the earlier points about interdependence
- Updated the Human Trafficking Report table showing tiers for countries
- New example of Yemen as a challenging context for human rights abuses
- Updated information on Doctors Without Borders to include statistics on various procedures performed
- Updated the Pop Quiz

CHAPTER 12: Gender and Sexuality

- Updated the chapter opening on Sheryl Sandberg and LeanIn.org with new data
- Revised the structure to include separate sections on sex, gender, and the gender spectrum; moved the discussion of transgender to the beginning of the section and added the discussion about gender binary versus gender spectrum to the end of the section
- Updated data on gender representation in children's books
- Updated data on stay-at-home moms and dads
- Updated data on educational participation and attainment for women
- Updated data on Americans' attitudes regarding abortion
- Created a new subsection highlighting intersectionality
- Added a new photo with caption tying the #MeToo movement to intersectionality
- Updated the U.S. Attitudes about Homosexuality graph
- Updated data on sexual orientation hate crime statistics
- Updated data on teens' age at first sexual intercourse experience and added information on the nature of their relationship with their first partner and reasons for those not having had sex
- Updated data on international contraception use rates
- Updated the Labor Force Participation Rates graph for men and women
- Updated the Women's Representation in U.S. Occupations table showing underrepresentation and overrepresentation in occupations
- Updated data for men and women on median income for full-time, year-round workers
- Updated data on occupational segregation and its relationship to the wage gap
- Updated the Gender Wage Gap by Education table
- Updated data on the gender wage gap by age
- Updated discussion on housework to include its impact on relationship satisfaction and sexual intimacy
- Updated data on women's representation in government after the 2018 midterm elections

- Updated the 5 Movies on gender and sexuality to include *Love, Simon, What Men Want,* and *Transformer*
- Updated the criminal victimization rates on rape and sexual violence
- Updated the data on high school girls' experience of violence and physical coercion

CHAPTER 13: Race and Ethnicity

- Completed an overhaul of the chapter to place greater emphasis on the sociological analysis of race and ethnicity, including more historical context regarding the social construction of race and highlighting the consequences of these constructs
- Updated the opening vignette addressing cases of police killings of African American males
- New section highlighting race as a social construct growing out of particular historical contexts from Linnaeus's racial categorization, through the era of racial pseudoscience, to the post–WWII reconsideration of race as a social construct from both a social and biological perspective
- Revised the definition of *race*
- Revised the definition of *ethnicity*
- Updated statistics in the Racial and Ethnic Groups in the United States table including both numbers and percentage of population
- New PopSOC feature on the work of Brazilian artist Angélica Dass matching Pantone color codes to skin tone to highlight the gradational nature of human variation
- Added a discussion of the role the *Plessy v. Ferguson* case to show its significance in the maintenance of systemic racial inequality
- Added a new PopSOC feature on Denmark's "Do It for Denmark" campaign designed to increase birthrates in the country
- Added a discussion of the eugenics movement in the United States
- Added a Did You Know? feature linking a Frederick Douglass quote regarding the biology of race from the 1850s to the civil rights movement claims 100 years later
- Added a discussion of the UNESCO statement after World War II, led by anthropologist Ashley Montague, advocating the use of ethnicity in place of race
- Added a discussion on the Most Recent Common Ancestor research which shows the degree of shared human ancestry
- Revised the Sociological Perspectives section to include a more fully developed discussion of the role theories can play in our understanding

- of issues related to race and ethnicity and also made the links to the three perspectives more explicit
- Added a discussion of Roth's multidimensional typology to highlight the complexity of race in practice
- Updated the 5 Movies feature to include *Get Out, The Hate U Give,* and *Crazy Rich Asians*
- Added *passing* as a key term to highlight the multidimensionality of race
- Added a discussion of transracial adoption to highlight the multidimensionality of race
- Added a discussion on the function of racial distinction as a foundation for group solidarity
- Revised the definition of *contact hypothesis*
- Modified the definition of *affirmative action*
- Updated the PopSOC feature on racial and ethnic representation in films
- Updated the Median Income by Race, Ethnicity, and Gender graph
- Revised the definition of *institutional discrimination*
- Revised the discussion of racism, including a new definition, to highlight the fact that racism involves more than just how people think and linked it to systemic patterns of inequality
- Updated the Hate Crime Offenses graphic
- New PopSOC feature on Colin Kaepernick's NFL protest regarding racial injustice
- Streamlined and reorganized the discussion on patterns of intergroup relations
- Updated the Racial and Ethnic Groups in the United States graph
- Streamlined the discussion of various racial and ethnic groups in the United States to highlight the consequences of difference and updated data for all groups on income, education, poverty, and so on along with emphasizing degrees of difference within each race/ethnicity category
- Updated the Poverty by Race and Ethnicity graph
- Updated the discussion on African Americans to highlight distinctions within this community, including more recent immigrants from Africa and the Caribbean
- Updated the Age Variation by Race and Ethnicity graph
- Updated the Major Hispanic Groups in the United States graph
- Updated data on immigration, including the Legal Immigration to the United States graph
- Updated the discussion of immigration policies
- Moved the discussion of privilege to the end of the chapter
- Updated the Pop Quiz

CHAPTER 14: Population, Health, and Environment

- Updated data for the United States, world, and select nations for total fertility rate and replacement fertility rate
- Updated the Total Fertility Rates graph showing changes in the average number of births per woman over time for various countries
- Updated data for the United States, world, and select nations for crude death rate, infant mortality rate, and life expectancy
- Updated the Life Expectancy graph showing changes in average number of years a newborn is expected to live over time for various countries
- Updated the Global Migration, 1950–2015 map
- Updated the U.S. Foreign-Born Population graph
- Updated data on source country and state residence of foreign-born population in the United States
- Updated data on immigration categories including lawful permanent resident, naturalization, refugee/asylum, and apprehension.
- Updated World Population Growth graph with new projections
- Updated the Afghanistan and United States Population Pyramid graphic
- Updated data on availability of skilled health care professionals per 10,000 people in the United States versus select nations
- Updated data for the Infant Mortality Rates in Selected Countries graph
- Updated the 5 Movies feature on health and medicine to include *The Big Sick, Unrest,* and *Head Full of Honey*
- Updated data on prevalence and incidence of HIV and AIDS in the United States
- Updated the HIV Prevalence and Mortality graph on cases around the world
- Updated the Percentage of People without Health Insurance graph for people in the United States for both income and race/ethnicity
- Updated the Infant Mortality Rates in the United States graph showing rates by race/ethnicity
- Updated life expectancy by race and gender
- Updated the Smoking Rates by Gender graph showing smoking percentages for men and women over time
- Updated data on prevalence of Alzheimer's disease
- Updated the Health Insurance Rates by Age graph
- Updated the Availability of Physicians by State graph

- Updated data on health care expenditures, including the Total Health Care Expenditures graph
- Updated data on Medicare and Medicaid recipients
- Updated the current state of the Affordable Care Act
- Updated the U.S. Uninsured Rate, 1997–2018 graph
- Updated the Did You Know? feature on bottled water consumption in the United States
- Updated the Did You Know? feature on the amount of Brazilian rain forest lost each year
- Updated the Public Perception of Environmental Issues graph
- Updated data on air pollution deaths
- Updated the 5 Movies on the Environment feature to include *Anthropocene* and *Rodents of Unusual Size*
- Updated data on access to safe drinking water and modern sanitation facilities
- Updated the Global Temperature graph showing the recorded history of average global temperature per year
- Updated the CO_2 Emissions per Capita graph with data for select nations
- Updated the Threatened and Endangered Species graph
- Updated the environmental issues survey results for whether or not they should be a top priority for Congress
- Updated the Perceptions of Global Climate Change among select nations graph
- Updated U.S. policy regarding the Paris Agreement regarding climate change

CHAPTER 15: Social Change

- Made substantial revisions to the structure and content throughout
- New opening vignette on student social movements and standing up for change
- Moved the discussion of social movements to the beginning of the chapter and revised how it gets presented
- Revised the definition of *social movements*
- Added a discussion of crowd theory that emphasizes emotions and the roles of leaders
- Revised the definition of *resource mobilization* along with the discussion of the theory including a consideration of the importance of mobilizing media resources and using technology to do so
- New discussion of the role emotions play in people's participation based on recent sociology of emotions theories

- New feature quote from Anna Lappe
- Revised the structure of the discussion of social change based on three parts: material, social, and cultural resources
- Updated the Social Change in the USA table to include recent data
- Streamlined the discussion on technology to fit it into the context of social change
- Updated the Internet Use and Penetration by World Region graph
- Updated the cloning milestones to include monkeys

- New section on social networks and social change with an emphasis on the importance of diversity
- New section on cultural resources and social change with an emphasis on the importance of expanding knowledge
- Updated the 5 Movies feature to include *BlacKkKlansman* and *An Inconvenient Sequel: Truth to Power*
- New Personal Sociology feature on living in the past, present, and future
- Revised and updated the Pop Quiz to match the new structure and content

Table of Contents

Manny Carabel/Getty Images

James Kirkikis/Shutterstock

©Emmanuele Contini/NurPhoto/Getty Images

Marco Secchi/Awakening/
Corbis/Getty Images

Monkey Business Images/Shutterstock

Jim Watson/AFP/Getty Images

Yu Chun Christopher Wong/ S3studio/Getty Images

Ilene MacDonald/Alamy Stock Photo

Spencer Platt/Getty Images

Bill Sikes/AP Images

Viviane Moos/Corbis Historical/Getty Images

12 > Gender and Sexuality   268

Allison Shelley/Getty Images

Kim Kim Foster/The State/MCT/Getty Images

13 > Race and Ethnicity   294

Michael Nigro/Pacific Press/LightRocket/Getty Images

Anadolu Agency/Getty Images

Manny Carabel/Getty Images

The Sociological Imagination

MY HOMETOWN

Sarah Smarsh was born in the middle of nowhere, smack dab in the heartland of the USA. Raised mostly by her grandmother, Betty, who was herself only 34 when Sarah was born, hers is a tale of opportunity and obstacle, success and failure, hope and despair.

The women and men in her life constantly struggled to find a stable financial footing while maintaining their dignity. Day after day and year after year, Sarah's family members worked to the point of exhaustion and physical frailty, but when it was all said and done, most had little to show for it.

Sarah's story, by contrast, represents the embodiment of the American Dream. Born into a world of rural Kansas poverty, she might have expected little more than to share the fate of her mother, grandmother, and many other women in her life. These women became mothers in their teens, faced limited opportunities, dealt with various addictions, and experienced persistent discrimination. Sarah, on the other hand, overcame numerous obstacles to become the first in her family to go to, and graduate from, college. She went on to work in a

series of professional jobs, including, for a time, as a college professor. Sarah tells her story in her book *Heartland: A Memoir of Working Hard and Being Broke in the Richest Country on Earth* (Smarsh 2018).

But Smarsh refuses to let the American Dream narrative alone win the day. She fully affirms that hers is the story of an outlier, the exception to the rule, in which the luck of having the right person intervene at the right times significantly boosted her odds. Just as important to her, if not more important, is the dominant narrative of those in her family and community. They, too, were smart, innovative, entrepreneurial, passionate, and, perhaps most of all, hardworking. Yet they never experienced the social mobility that she did.

Lack of opportunity due to larger economic trends explains much of what made life difficult for so many in her community. In the 1980s, for example, the farm crisis resulted in many farm foreclosures. Starting in 2008, more people were forced out, or gave up, as a result of the global recession. Crises such as these just exacerbated the general economic decline these communities faced. As Smarsh puts it, "All around us things were closing: the small-town department store, the hardware store with its tiny drawers stretching to the ceiling, the local restaurant. Lawyers took down their small-town shingles and doctors moved to cities" (2018:88). Rural and small-town life became less and less viable. Many people who had invested their lives in the land over multiple generations wanted to make it work. But their economic success seemed beyond their control.

Sociology enables us to better understand the interplay between individual initiative and structural obstacles. Success does depend on the choices we make, but the opportunities to succeed are not equally distributed among us all. When it comes to understanding our outcomes, we must take seriously the ways in which the positions we occupy in society impact the ways we think, act, and feel.

As You READ >>

- **What is sociology?**
- **How do sociologists look at the world?**
- **How might someone practice sociology?**

>> What Is Sociology?

We need one another. We may like to think that we can make it on our own, but our individualism is made possible by our interdependence. We praise the Olympic gold medalist for her impressive skill, dedicated training, and single-minded determination. Yet, if it hadn't been for her mom driving her to the pool every day, for the building manager waking up at 4:00 a.m. to make sure the pool is open, for the women working overnight to make sure the locker room is clean and safe, and so many others who fade into the background in such moments of glory, she would never have had that chance to shine.

The people on whom we depend are often unknown and invisible to us. Even though we may never meet them, we rely on farmers, truck drivers, secretaries, store clerks, custodians, software engineers, scientists, assembly-line workers, teachers, police officers, inventors, politicians, CEOs, and a whole host of others. Yet we mostly take their contributions for granted without fully appreciating the degree to which they make our lives possible.

Sociologists seek to reveal the full extent of our interdependence. They explore the intimate connection between self and society, placing that relationship at the heart of sociology's definition. **Sociology** is the systematic study of the relationship between the individual and society and of the consequences of difference. We examine the various components of that definition in the "Defining Sociology" section, after first considering ways in which the sociological imagination shapes how we see the world.

Sociology The systematic study of the relationship between the individual and society and of the consequences of difference.

Sociological imagination Our exploration of the interdependent relationship between who we are as individuals and the social forces that shape our lives.

THE SOCIOLOGICAL IMAGINATION

American sociologist C. Wright Mills ([1959] 2009) proposed that we think of sociology as a tool that enables us to better understand why we think the way we think and act the way we act. He proposed we use our **sociological imagination** to explore the interdependent relationship between who we are as individuals and the social forces that shape our lives. To put it another way, practicing sociology involves recognizing the powerful intersection between history and biography. We are products of our times and places. Our thoughts, actions, even our feelings are shaped by our social contexts. For example, you chose to go to college, but you didn't do so in isolation. Factors such as your age, family background, geographic location, friendship networks, and available income played a role in your decision to go and what school you chose.

In addition to more immediate influences on our choices, the sociological imagination calls us to also consider the role larger social forces may play. Take unemployment as an example. A person might lose their job for a variety of reasons. A worker who is foolish, selfish, and careless may get fired because they make a lousy employee. But it's also possible for a worker to lose their job due to social forces beyond their control, regardless of how effective they may be as a worker. Using the sociological imagination enables us to recognize that our likelihood of keeping our job rises and falls depending on what is happening in the larger economy. For example, when the economy nosedived in the 2000s, the unemployment rate rose from 4.8 percent in February 2008 to a peak of 10.1 percent in October 2010. Many wise, dedicated, and careful workers lost their jobs in the process.

Analyzing how rates change over time allows us to see patterns we might miss when focusing only on individuals.

U.S. Employment Trends

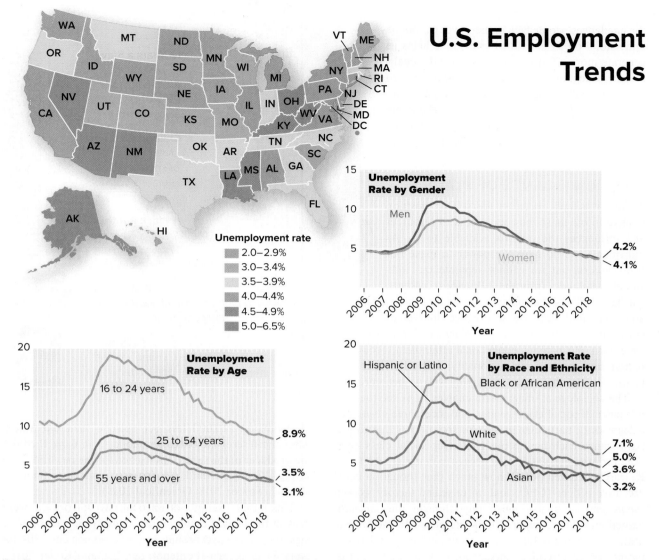

Unemployment rate
- 2.0–2.9%
- 3.0–3.4%
- 3.5–3.9%
- 4.0–4.4%
- 4.5–4.9%
- 5.0–6.5%

Unemployment Rate by Gender
- Men
- Women — 4.2%, 4.1%

Unemployment Rate by Age
- 16 to 24 years
- 25 to 54 years — 8.9%
- 55 years and over — 3.5%, 3.1%

Unemployment Rate by Race and Ethnicity
- Hispanic or Latino
- Black or African American
- White
- Asian — 7.1%, 5.0%, 3.6%, 3.2%

Note: The unemployment rate includes people 16 years and older who are available for work but do not have a job and who have actively looked for work within the previous four weeks.

Sources: Bureau of Labor Statistics 2016a and 2016b.

The sociological imagination enables us to see that people in similar positions experience similar outcomes. Sticking with the unemployment example, as the "U.S. Employment Trends" map and graphs demonstrate, a person's likelihood of experiencing unemployment varies by the person's social location, which includes geographic location, age, gender, race, and ethnicity. Geographically, for example, unemployment was more likely in the Southwest than in the upper Midwest. The level for young people was, and continues to be, substantially higher than for those who are older. Men experienced a more significant jump in joblessness during 2008's Great Recession than did women. Rates for African Americans and Latinos were, and are, significantly higher than those for Whites.

To assist us in understanding the role social forces can play, Mills distinguished between private troubles and public issues. **Private troubles** are problems we face in our immediate relationships with particular individuals in our personal lives. Explanations for such troubles are particular to the individuals involved. For example, you lose your job because you failed to show up for work, disobeyed direct orders from your boss, took money from the cash register, and so forth. The sociological imagination focuses instead on the importance of analyzing **public issues** which are problems we face as a consequence of the positions we occupy within the larger social structure. Private troubles are personal problems, but public issues are social problems.

Analyzing data—such as unemployment rates, divorce rates, and poverty rates—enables us to see influences that might otherwise be invisible to us.

The sociological imagination enables us to make more informed decisions regarding our futures. Understanding that

Private troubles Problems we face in our immediate relationships with particular individuals in our personal lives.

Public issues Problems we face as a consequence of the positions we occupy within the larger social structure.

the challenges people face in their lives cannot be understood on an individual level alone helps us generate more effective solutions. As individuals, we can make more informed choices about how to proceed by taking the social context into account. At a more collective level, political and economic leaders can enact policies geared toward altering the social landscape in more positive directions.

THE SIGNIFICANCE OF PLACE

To put it simply, place matters. Our position relative to others shapes our access to resources and influences the options available to us. As individuals, we do have the power to make our own choices, but we cannot separate our individual preferences from the influence of parents, teachers, friends, coworkers, politicians, the media, and even total strangers whose decisions enable or constrain opportunities for us. Where and when we were born; our parents' educational attainment, occupation, and income; our nationality; and other such factors all play major roles in shaping who we become.

The sociological imagination enables us to see the influence of social class, gender, and race, three positional categories of particular interest to sociologists due to the significance each has in our lives. Our social class position, for example, shapes our access to material resources. Researchers asked people how much they thought a chief executive officer (CEO) and an unskilled factory worker *should* earn and how much they thought they *actually* earned and then compared these numbers. In the United States, respondents said CEOs should earn about 7 times more than an unskilled worker, but they guessed that the real gap was 30 to 1. It turns out that the average yearly compensation for a CEO at a Standard & Poor's (S&P) 500 company in 2017 was $13.9 million, approximately 361 times the $38,613 an average worker in a nonsupervisory role receives (Quinnell 2018; Kiatpongsan and Norton 2014). This suggests that social class differences, such as that between a CEO and an unskilled worker, are even greater than we think.

Turning to gender, sociologists find a persistent wage gap between men and women. For example, English actor Claire Foy played the part of Queen Elizabeth II in the Netflix hit series *The Crown,* which, over the course of six seasons, tells the story of the entirety of the queen's reign. English actor Matt Smith played the part of Prince Philip, the queen's husband. In spite of the fact that Foy, in the title role, is the centerpiece of the series and has substantially more screen time, at £29,000 ($40,000) per episode, she earned

5 Movies on THE SOCIOLOGICAL IMAGINATION

12 Years a Slave
An 1840s African American man is kidnapped and sold into slavery.

Children of Men
A dystopian vision of society where humans can no longer reproduce.

Black Panther
The African civilization of Wakanda might just save the world.

Philomena
A mother's search for the child she gave up for adoption.

Lady Bird
On the path to adulthood, a young woman navigates the obstacles life puts in her way.

an estimated £10,000 less per episode than did Smith. After the discrepancy became public, Left Bank Pictures, the producer of the series, apologized for the pay difference saying, "Going forward, no one gets paid more than the Queen" (Fowler 2018; Greenfield 2018).

This public example of unequal pay mirrors the wage gaps in the United States. When comparing average earnings for full-time, year-round workers, women earn 80¢ for every $1 men earn (Fontenot, Semega, and Kollar 2018). Race and ethnicity also shape likely outcomes. Being born into a White family in the United States significantly

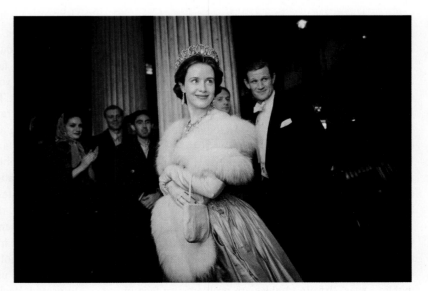

Women actors, such as Claire Foy, regularly receive less pay than do their male counterparts. Left Bank Pictures/Sony Pictures TV Prod UK/Album/Newscom

increases your odds of having access to money. In a study on the distribution of wealth, researchers found that median wealth of $171,000 for White, non-Hispanic households was 9.7 times greater than the $17,600 for African American households and 8.3 times greater than the $20,700 for Hispanic households (Bricker et al. 2017).

Place is important because it shapes how we think, act, and even feel. For example, when computer giant Hewlett-Packard was trying to figure out ways to get more women into upper-level management positions, it found that women applied for promotion only when they thought they met 100 percent of the qualifications for the position, whereas men applied when they believed they met 60 percent (Kay and Shipman 2014). When asked, at the end of his presidency, how Barack Obama would go down in history, 75 percent of African Americans said Obama would be remembered as outstanding or above average, compared to 38 percent among Whites (Pew Research Center 2016f). When it comes to analyzing such patterns, our tendency is to take sides, but the interesting sociological question is why such significant differences form in the first place.

A HAMBURGER IS A MIRACLE

To more fully appreciate how dependent we are on others, imagine that you have to make something completely from scratch but that you must do so without relying on any knowledge, skills, tools, or resources obtained from anyone else. How hard could that possibly be? Let's take a hamburger for example. First, you'll need beef to make the burger, which means you'll need to find a cow. But buying one from a farmer is off limits because doing so means relying on the efforts and abilities of others. So a wild cow it is. Assuming you can find one roaming around somewhere, you need to kill it, perhaps by bashing it over the head with a large rock or running it off a cliff.

Once you've got yourself a dead cow, you need to butcher it, but cowhide is tough. Imagine what it takes to produce a metal knife (finding ore, smelting, forging, tempering, and so on). Perhaps a sharp rock will do. Assuming you come up with a cutting tool, you can carve out a chunk of raw meat. Given that it's hamburger you're after (though you might be ready to settle for steak at this point), you'll need to grind up the meat. You might use a couple of those rocks to pulverize it into something of a meat mash. A meat grinder would work better, if only it weren't so hard to make one. In any event, at last you have a raw hamburger patty.

To cook your burger, you will need fire. But where does fire come from? Perhaps you could strike two rocks together or rub two sticks together. After trying this for a while, you may decide it would be easier to wait around for lightning to strike a nearby tree. However you accomplish it, after you get fire, you still have to cook the meat. No frying pans are available, so either you make one or perhaps cook it on that handy rock you used to kill the cow.

Assuming you are successful, you now have a cooked hamburger patty. But you aren't close to done. You still need to complete many other steps. You need to bake a bun, which involves figuring out how to come up with flour, water, salt, oil, sugar, yeast, and an oven. What about condiments such as ketchup, mustard, pickles, and onions? What if at the end of all that you decide to make it a cheeseburger? You killed the cow! Did you remember to milk her first?

Making something that seems so simple—that we can get for a dollar at McDonald's—turns out to be quite complicated. The resourcefulness necessary to acquire and prepare all the ingredients in a hamburger are beyond the capacity of most of us. Yet if we eat a burger, we seldom consider its complexity. If, instead, we exercise the sociological imagination, we may come to see that a hamburger is a miracle.

Did You Know?

. . . Andy George explores the intricacies of the production process in his YouTube series "How to Make Everything" (www.makeeverything. tv/). For example, he set out to make a grilled chicken sandwich completely from scratch. He grew his own wheat, milked a cow, evaporated ocean water for salt, slaughtered a chicken, and much more. It took him six months and cost him $1,500. The taste-testing verdict? Meh. Other products he makes using the raw ingredients he tracks down include chocolate bars, coffee, glass bottles, and a suit.

Photo: ©G.K. & Vikki Hart/Photodisc/ Getty Images

Not literally, of course, because nothing supernatural is happening, but figuratively, as a symbolic representation of all the knowledge and skill that come together in this one meal. And it's not just hamburgers. All the products we make and use—veggie burgers, books, backpacks, shirts, cars, houses, smartphones—point toward a hidden infrastructure comprising our collective wisdom and ability.

The irony of modern society is that we depend on one another now more than ever, but we realize it less. We embrace individualism, and think we are masters of our own fates. Yet we lack the basic skills necessary for self-sufficiency. Sociology provides us with tools that enable us to more fully understand and appreciate our interdependence.

> The function of sociology, as of every science, is to reveal that which is hidden.
>
> Pierre Bourdieu (1998b)

DEFINING SOCIOLOGY

Sociologists are committed to investigating, describing, and explaining such interrelationships. A more detailed breakdown of the four components of the definition of sociology helps reveal how they go about doing so.

Systematic Study Sociologists are engaged with the world, collecting empirical data through systematic research. Relying on such data means that sociologists draw their conclusions about society based on experiences or observations rather than beliefs or the authority of others. If they want to understand why the average age for first marriage keeps rising or why people commit crimes, they must gather data from those involved in these activities and base their conclusions on that information.

Sociological research historically has involved both quantitative and qualitative approaches to data collection.

Agency Our freedom as individuals to think and act as we choose.

Society The structure of relationships within which culture is created and shared through regularized patterns of social interaction.

SOCTHINK

What do you see as your biggest accomplishment in life so far? What people in your life were most directly responsible for helping make it happen? Given that we rely on others who are often unknown and invisible to us, what other people made indirect but essential contributions to your success?

Quantitative approaches emphasize counting things and analyzing them mathematically or statistically to uncover relationships between variables. The most common way to collect this type of data is through surveys. In contrast, qualitative approaches focus on listening to and observing people and allowing them to interpret what is happening in their own lives. The most common way to collect this type of data is through participant observation, in which the researcher interacts with those she or he studies. In practice, sociologists often draw on both techniques in conducting their research. We investigate these research techniques, along with others, in more detail in Chapter 2.

The Individual Although sociology is most commonly associated with the study of groups, there is no such thing as a group apart from the individuals who compose it. As individuals we are constantly choosing what to do next. Most of the time, we follow guidelines for behavior we have learned from others, but we have the ability to reject those guidelines at any time. A term sociologists use to describe this capacity is **agency,** meaning our freedom as individuals to think and act as we choose. In professional sports, for example, we use the term *free agent* to describe a player who has the power to negotiate with whatever team he or she wishes. We, too, have such freedom. We could choose not to go to class, not to go to work, not to get out of bed in the morning, not to obey traffic signals, not to respond when spoken to, not to read the next sentence in this book, and on and on.

As we saw with the significance of place, the positions we occupy relative to others shape the choices we make. In the NBA, LeBron James has repeatedly exercised his right as a free agent to move from NBA team to NBA team: from Cleveland, to Miami, back to Cleveland, and then to Los Angeles. Signing with the NFL's Green Bay Packers or Major League Baseball's Chicago Cubs was not really an option for him because he lacked the kinds of skills those organizations reward. His choices, like ours, were constrained by both his abilities and the opportunities available to him. The value of the skills and abilities we have depends on our being in a social context that recognizes and rewards them. When we choose, we usually follow "paths of least resistance"—accepted and expected actions and beliefs—but the choice of whether to continue to follow them is ours every second of our lives (A. Johnson 1997).

Society The study of society is at the heart of sociology. Although we will spend most of this book describing various aspects of society, we can begin by thinking of it as our social environment. **Society** consists of the structure of relationships within which culture is created and shared

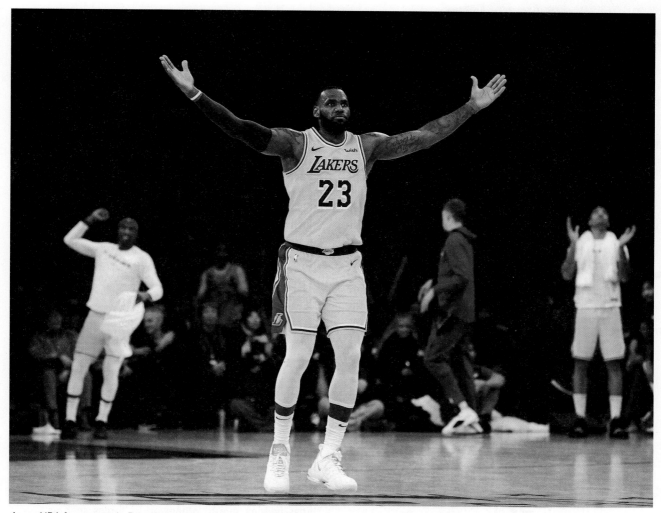

As an NBA free agent, LeBron James moved from the Cleveland Cavaliers to the Miami Heat, back to Cleveland, and then on to the Los Angeles Lakers. Harry How/Getty Images

through regularized patterns of social interaction. The framework it provides is analogous to a building: The structure of a building both encourages and discourages different activities in different rooms (such as kitchens, bedrooms, and bathrooms), and many of the most essential operations of a building (such as heating and air conditioning) are mostly invisible to us. In the same way, the structure of our *institutions*—a term sociologists use to describe some of the major components of social structure, including economy, family, education, government, and religion—shapes what is expected of us. For example, the choices that are available to us in the context of the modern family, such as to go off and pursue our own education and career, are much different from the obligations we would face in more traditional family contexts. Nested within institutions are the groups, subgroups, and statuses that we occupy. We look at the details of these institutions in coming chapters, but it is helpful to remember that, in order to provide clear pathways for action, we construct culture and inhabit society.

The Consequences of Difference The final part of the definition of sociology involves the consequences of difference. Sociology does more than just describe our structure, culture, and interaction; it also analyzes how economic, social, and cultural resources are allocated and the implications of these patterns in terms of the opportunities and obstacles they create for individuals and groups. Since the founding of sociology, sociologists have been concerned with the impact our social location has on our opportunities or lack thereof. As noted earlier, differential outcomes that result from class, gender, and race have been of particular interest to sociologists.

The analysis of social power deserves particular attention because it shapes how and why we think and act as we do. The simple fact is that those who have access to and control over valued material, social, and cultural resources have different options available to them than do those without such access and control. One of the main tasks of sociology is to investigate and reveal levels of **social inequality**—a condition in which members of society have differing amounts of wealth, prestige, or power. That is why the definition of sociology draws particular

> **Social inequality** A condition in which members of society have different amounts of wealth, prestige, or power.

Source: Library of Congress Prints and Photographs Division [LC-DIG-fsa-8b29516]

attention to the consequences of difference.

In combination, these four aspects of sociology help us understand the things that influence our beliefs and actions. Coming to terms with the reality that our choices are constrained by the positions we occupy can seem depressing, but sociology actually empowers us by providing a more complete picture of the worlds within which we live. French sociologist Pierre Bourdieu (1998a) put it this way: "Sociology teaches how groups function and how to make use of the laws governing the way they function so as to try to circumvent them" (p. 57). In other words, understanding the ways in which our thoughts and actions are determined enhances our freedom to make more effective and informed choices.

>> Sociology's Roots

Sociology, as a discipline, grew up in the midst of significant social upheaval. The advent of the Industrial Revolution and urbanization in the early 19th century led to changes in how we think and act. Aristocracy was on the decline while democracy was spreading; people were moving from a primarily religious view of the world and its phenomena to a more scientific one; and life in the village and on the farm was rapidly giving way to life in the city and factory. The old rules that provided for social order no longer applied. The world seemed to be falling apart. Sociology arose as a means to understand and control the social forces that shaped our lives.

A SCIENCE OF SOCIETY

Science provided the foundation upon which sociology was built. Early scientists, such as Francis Bacon, Robert Boyle, and Isaac Newton, challenged conventional ideas about how the world worked. They didn't accept something as fact simply because others in authority said so, They questioned the authority of politicians, priests, and philosophers, viewing them as insufficient sources of truth. This sometimes got them in trouble, as Galileo learned in the 1600s. He claimed that observations he'd made using his telescope, a recent invention, supported Copernicus's

heliocentric theory that the Earth revolved around the sun. However, because this theory contradicted the Catholic Church's geocentric teaching that the Earth was the center of the universe, he was charged with heresy and kept under house arrest until his death.

Through meticulous observation and experimentation, these and other early scientists uncovered fundamental truths about the natural world. The scientific method they developed follows what we might now call the Missouri principle: Don't just tell me, show me. Missouri's nickname as the "show-me state" reportedly traces its roots back to Missouri Congressman Willard Duncan Vandiver's 1899 speech in which he stated, "Frothy eloquence neither convinces nor satisfies me. I am from Missouri. You have got to show me" (March 1998:167).

Courtesy of Jon Witt

In previous eras, it may have been sufficient to rely on the authority of priests or philosophers who argued that things happen due to other-worldly forces such as God's will or fate. The scientific method insists on this-worldly, empirical investigation that can be measured using our senses. If we can't see it, touch it, smell it, or in some way measure it, we shouldn't accept it as a fact. And even then we should engage in repeated experiments to protect against the possibility that our senses are fooling us. The laws of nature that resulted from these early scientific experiments, such as Newton's $F = ma$, held firm across time and place, thus providing universally true explanations about how nature operates.

The explanatory power of these laws of nature led others to explore the possibility of uncovering equally powerful laws of society. It was in this mid-1800s context that French social philosopher Auguste Comte (1798–1857) made three significant contributions to the founding of sociology. First, in his quest to uncover the laws of society, he identified two important societal forces worthy of in-depth study: social stability and social change. He used the expressions "social statics" to refer to the principles by which societies hold together and order is maintained and "social dynamics" to describe the factors that bring about change and shape the nature and direction of that change. Second, to give this new discipline a name, Comte coined the term *sociology*—which literally means "the study of the processes of companionship" (Abercrombie, Hill, and Turner 2006:367). And third, he argued that sociologists should serve in a leadership role, as something akin to a new priesthood of humanity, using their knowledge of the laws of society to advance policies that would enhance social stability while also working toward positive social change (Gane 2006; A. Wilson 1999).

English-speaking scholars learned of Comte's work largely through translations by another of sociology's founders, the English sociologist Harriet Martineau (1802–1876). We can also single out three significant contributions Martineau made to the founding of sociology. First, seeking to systematize the research essential to conducting a science of society, Martineau ([1838] 1989) wrote the first book on sociological methods. Second, as a path-breaking theorist in her own right, she introduced the significance of inequality and power into the discipline. Martineau's book *Society in America* ([1837] 1962) examined religion, politics, child rearing, and immigration in the young nation. It gave special attention to social class distinctions and to such factors as gender and race. Third, Martineau ([1837] 1962) maintained that intellectuals and scholars should not simply offer observations of social conditions; they should act on their convictions in a manner that would benefit society. Martineau spoke out in favor of the rights of women, the emancipation of slaves, and religious tolerance.

These two themes—social order and social inequality—have shaped the theoretical and research paths sociologists have pursued since sociology's founding as a discipline. In early sociological theory, they find their fullest development in the works of Émile Durkheim and Karl Marx, respectively. As we will see throughout this book, they continue to be primary concerns for sociologists.

THEORY AND RESEARCH

French sociologist Émile Durkheim (1858–1917) was strongly influenced by Comte's dream of establishing sociology as a science. They both envisioned sociology as a conversation between theory and research. Unlike Comte, however, Durkheim gathered data to test basic sociological theories about social order. A **theory** is a set of statements that seeks to explain problems, actions, or behavior. Theories represent our attempts to make the best possible sense of the world around us. They often start out general and vague, but over time and informed by research, theories provide richer, more complete interpretations of the worlds in which we live. Durkheim provided an early model of the interplay between theory and research with his work on the impact our social connectedness has on the choices we make.

Harriet Martineau *(Martineau):* Alonzo Chappel/ Georgios Kollidas/Alamy Stock Photo; *(frame):* kittimages/iStockphoto/Getty Images

Formulating Sociological Theories We can better understand how theories develop in sociology by following the logic Émile Durkheim employed more than a century ago when sociology was just emerging as a social science. At the time, there were no sociology departments in universities and no academic positions for sociologists. Durkheim wanted to establish sociology's legitimacy as a distinct discipline. His theory was that social forces shape individual action. This contradicted the dominant theories of the time that biology, the individual's psyche, or God were the primary causes for our behaviors. In an attempt to create space for sociology as a discipline, he argued that factors above the level of the individual but within the domain of human society shape our actions.

Theory In sociology, a set of statements that seeks to explain problems, actions, or behavior.

Harriet Martineau argued that we could learn a lot about a culture by analyzing the ideas, images, and themes reflected in its popular songs. She wrote, "The Songs of every nation must always be the most familiar and truly popular part of its poetry. . . . They present also the most prevalent feelings on subjects of the highest popular interest. If it were not so, they would not have been popular songs" ([1838] 1989). What might we learn about American culture based on analysis of the lyrics of the current top-10 songs? What themes, ideas, images, and expectations are prevalent? (Lists are available at "The Billboard Hot 100" or www.top10songs.com.)

POPSOC

Photo: Brian Ach/Getty Images

Massimo Valicchia/NurPhoto/Getty Images

Social facts Manners of acting, thinking, and feeling external to the individual with coercive power to shape how we act, think, and feel.

Durkheim set out to prove that social facts exist and affect what we do. He defined **social facts** as manners of acting, thinking, and feeling external to the individual that have coercive power to shape how we act, think, and feel. In other words, how we act, think, and feel is both enabled and constrained by social forces outside of us. But a social fact is kind of like gravity. We can't really see it or measure it directly, but we can observe its effects. Proving the power of social facts depends on demonstrating the impact they have on the choices we make.

To make the strongest case possible, Durkheim chose to study what he saw as the ultimate individual choice: suicide. He theorized that people choose suicide because they lack the social connections and obligations that prevent them from taking their own life. His hypothesis was as follows: "Suicide varies inversely with the degree of integration of the social groups of which the individual forms a part" ([1897] 1951:209). Durkheim chose religious affiliation as an indicator of social integration, arguing that Protestants are less socially integrated than Roman Catholics. He claimed that Catholicism is a traditional faith with a hierarchical system of authority in which variation in belief (on such topics as birth control, abortion, and women priests) is not up to the individual. Protestantism, in contrast, gives individual believers more power to interpret the Bible for themselves. As a result, when disagreement arises, Protestants feel freer to form new churches. Whereas there is only one Roman Catholic Church, Protestantism includes Baptist, Methodist, Reformed, Episcopalian, Presbyterian, and many other denominations. Protestants' increased individual autonomy reflects reduced levels of social integration, leading Durkheim to predict that Protestants would be more likely to die by suicide than Catholics.

Testing Sociological Theories To test his theory, Durkheim gathered data from different countries to see if suicide rates varied. Looking at France, England, and Denmark, he found that England had 67 reported suicides per million inhabitants, France had 135 per million, and Denmark had 277 per million. Durkheim concluded that Denmark's comparatively high suicide rate was due to the fact that Denmark was a more Protestant nation than either France or England. In other words, it was the social makeup of these nations that shaped their suicide rates. More recent research focusing on individual rather than national rates continues to find this same relationship (Torgler and Schaltegger 2014).

In extending his analysis to look at other indicators of social integration, Durkheim continued to obtain results that confirmed his underlying theory: the unmarried had much higher rates of suicide than married people; and people without children were more likely to take their lives than people with children. In addition, there were higher rates in times of economic instability and recession than in times of prosperity. Durkheim concluded that his theory was correct: the suicide rate of a society reflects the extent to which people are or are not integrated into the group life of the society. Durkheim presented his results in his landmark work *Suicide,* published in 1897.

Applying Sociological Theories Built into Durkheim's theory is the presupposition that we find meaning in life through our relationships with others. The more interconnected and interdependent we are, the less likely we are to kill ourselves. Attempting to summarize the significance of our attachment to society, Durkheim put it this way: "The individual alone is not a sufficient end for his activity. He is too little. . . . When, therefore, we have no other object than ourselves we cannot avoid the thought that our efforts will finally end in nothingness. . . . Under these conditions one would lose the courage to live, that

Going GLOBAL

What Makes a Country Happy?

As a flip side to the suicide research, sociologists have also shown that happiness rates vary from country to country. The five nations that score highest according to the "World Happiness Report" are Finland, Norway, Denmark, Iceland, and Switzerland. The bottom five are Yemen, Tanzania, South Sudan, Central African Republic, and Burundi. The United States ranks 18th out of 156 nations (Helliwell, Layard, and Sachs 2018). The index considers indicators of both subjective well-being ("Were you happy yesterday?") and life satisfaction ("Are you happy with your life as a whole?").

Greetings from Denmark, one of the happiest nations on the planet. ©Rafael Elias/Moment Open/Getty Images

is, to act and struggle" ([1897] 1951:210). Human beings are, at their very foundation, social beings. According to Durkheim, we cannot consider what it means to be an individual apart from our position in society. This social dimension of individual behavior is what Durkheim wants sociology to explore, elaborate, and explain.

Durkheim's work on suicide provides a classic case of sociological theory at work. He theorized that social facts shape individual actions. He tested this theory by investigating suicide as one such individual choice—perhaps the most individual of all choices—and demonstrated that the likelihood of dying by suicide varied based on group membership. As the accompanying "Suicide Rates" map and graphs demonstrate, analysis of more recent data shows that suicide rates continue to vary based on social position. Durkheim concluded that if social facts are at work in this most extreme example of individual choice, they similarly shape all other individual choices. He argued that if social facts have such power in our lives, there should be a discipline dedicated to their study. As a result of Durkheim's efforts, the University of Bordeaux established Europe's first department of sociology in 1895.

Suicide has become a significant public health concern in the United States. In 2016, 44,965 people died as a result of suicide, which represents an increase of 30 percent since 1999. The rates of emergency room visits for nonfatal suicide attempts rose even more. People aged 45–64 had the highest rate of increase of any age group. Overall, 48.5 percent of those who died due to suicide, died by firearm (Stone et al. 2018; Xu et al. 2018). Sociologists and others continue to explore the contextual elements that influence likelihood of suicide, including factors such as relative social well-being and relative income (Daly, Oswald, Wilson, and Wu 2011; Daly, Wilson, and Johnson 2013).

Sociologists weren't the only ones who sought to apply the scientific method to social behavior. A number of additional disciplines emerged around the same time giving rise to **social science**—the systematic study of human behavior, interaction, and change—as an umbrella term to distinguish these fields of study from **natural science,** which involves the systematic study of the physical features of nature and the ways in which they interact

Social science The systematic study of human behavior, interaction, and change.

Natural science The systematic study of the physical features of nature and the ways in which they interact and change.

and change. Social sciences include sociology, anthropology, psychology, economics, political science, and history. Each of these disciplines carved out its own subject matter niche and applied its version of the scientific method accordingly. Sociology's boundaries emerged over time as sociologists explored new questions about why we think and act as we do.

Suicide Rates

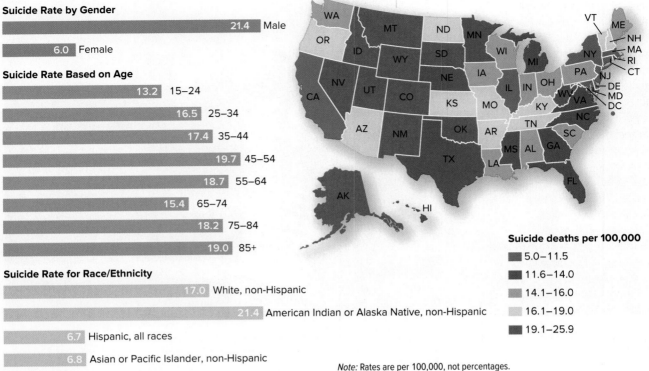

Suicide Rate by Gender

- 21.4 Male
- 6.0 Female

Suicide Rate Based on Age

- 13.2 15–24
- 16.5 25–34
- 17.4 35–44
- 19.7 45–54
- 18.7 55–64
- 15.4 65–74
- 18.2 75–84
- 19.0 85+

Suicide Rate for Race/Ethnicity

- 17.0 White, non-Hispanic
- 21.4 American Indian or Alaska Native, non-Hispanic
- 6.7 Hispanic, all races
- 6.8 Asian or Pacific Islander, non-Hispanic
- 6.3 Black, non-Hispanic

Suicide deaths per 100,000

- 5.0–11.5
- 11.6–14.0
- 14.1–16.0
- 16.1–19.0
- 19.1–25.9

Note: Rates are per 100,000, not percentages.

Source: Xu et al. 2018.

SOCTHINK

If Durkheim is correct and the level of social integration influences the likelihood of suicide, why do rates vary for the groups listed in the "Suicide Rates" figure? Why is the rate for men so much higher than that for women? Why are the rates for non-Hispanic Whites and non-Hispanic American Indian or Alaska Native's higher than that for other racial/ethnic groups? Why is there a midlife suicide peak? Why do rates vary by state and region? What might these patterns suggest about the social integration of people in these categories?

>> Five Big Questions

Given the complexity of human life, sociologists have developed a wide range of theories in which they describe and explain the diversity of social behavior. Sometimes their theories can be grand in scope, seeking to encompass the "big picture"; other times they can be more personal, intimate, and immediate. Although we spend most of the rest of this book investigating the insights sociological theories provide, here we will briefly address five big sociological questions. Each represents a significant door sociologists have opened in their quest to understand why we think and act as we do. The questions are these: How is social order maintained? How do power and inequality shape outcomes? How does interaction shape our worlds? How does group membership (especially class, race, and gender) influence opportunity? How should sociologists respond?

HOW IS SOCIAL ORDER MAINTAINED?

Because of the unsettled times within which they lived, early sociologists in general, and Émile Durkheim in particular, placed a premium on understanding how social order was achieved and maintained. As his concept of social facts demonstrates, Durkheim saw society as a real, external force existing above the level of the individual, exerting its influence over individual behavior. We act, think, and feel the way we do, according to Durkheim, largely due to the structure of society. Understanding those social forces, especially in light of changes brought on by the Industrial Revolution, was sociology's primary mission.

Durkheim theorized that the Industrial Revolution and the resulting rise in the division of labor, in which jobs became more and more specialized, meant that individuals had fewer experiences in common. Lives became increasingly segmented. This was true not only within the workplace, but within the larger community. The worlds of family, work, school, and faith, which had mostly overlapped in traditional societies, became increasingly distinct from each other. Durkheim argued that the resulting decrease in social integration put us at great risk of **anomie,** which he defined as a weak sense of social solidarity due to a lack of agreed-upon rules to guide behavior. Anomie increases the likelihood of loneliness, isolation, and despair, and thus, also, of suicide. Using Durkheim's theory, one sociological response to the problem of suicide is to build up social integration by multiplying our shared experiences across social boundaries.

Émile Durkheim. *(Durkheim):* ©Bettmann/Getty Images; *(frame):* ©Wrangel/iStock/Getty Images

HOW DO POWER AND INEQUALITY SHAPE OUTCOMES?

Karl Marx (1818–1883) took a different approach. He emphasized the role that power and control over resources played in how social order is established and maintained. Marx viewed our creative capacity to transform raw materials into products—for example, to take clay and make a pot, or cut down a tree and make a desk—as the key factor distinguishing humans from other animals (whose behavior is ruled by their instincts). For Marx, human history is the progressive unfolding of human creativity in the form of new technology through which we establish our relationship to the natural world and with each other. Unfortunately, for most of human history, we lacked sufficient technology to provide enough material goods (such as food, clothes, and shelter)

Karl Marx. *(Marx):* Source: Library of Congress Prints and Photographs Division [LC-USZ62-16530]; *(frame):* ©Peter Zelei/iStock/Getty Images

to meet everyone's needs, so not all people had enough.

Social inequality for Marx, then, is determined by ownership, or lack thereof, of key material resources. The ruling class is defined by its ownership and control of the means of production—the tools and resources necessary for that transformation to happen. Members of the working class, in contrast, own only their capacity to transform raw materials into products, which requires access to the means of production controlled by the ruling class. Whereas Durkheim was concerned with anomie, Marx was concerned with **alienation,** by which he meant loss of control over our creative human capacity to produce, separation from the products we make, and isolation from our fellow workers. We consider Marx's work as it relates to capitalism as an economic system in more detail in Chapter 9's "Economic Systems" section. His influence on sociological theory, however, extends beyond social class to an analysis of additional forms of inequality, such as how gender, race, ethnicity, nationality, and age influence individual opportunity.

Seeking to expand sociological theory further, Max Weber (1864–1920; pronounced "VAY-ber") offered a more general theory of power that was less wedded to capitalism and ownership of the means of production. Weber argued that, although social class and its associated control over material resources may determine who has power in most instances, these are not the only possible foundations for power. Other sources he identified include social status, in which people defer to others out of

> **Anomie** A weak sense of social solidarity due to a lack of agreed-upon rules to guide behavior.
>
> **Alienation** Loss of control over our creative human capacity to produce, separation from the products we make, and isolation from our fellow producers.

Max Weber. *(Weber):* ©HultonArchive/Getty Images; *(frame):* ©Visivasnc/iStock/Getty Images respect for their social position or prestige, and organizational resources, in which members of a group gain power through their ability to organize to accomplish some specific goal by maximizing their available resources. Weber argued that these social resources draw their power from people's willingness to obey the authority of another person, which in turn is based on their perception of the legitimacy of that person's right to rule. Marx's and Weber's models of inequality and power are considered in more detail in Chapter 10's "Sociological Perspectives on Stratification."

HOW DOES INTERACTION SHAPE OUR WORLDS?

Much of the work of Durkheim, Marx, and Weber involves **macrosociology,** which concentrates on large-scale phenomena or entire civilizations. This top-down approach focuses on society as a whole and how broad social forces shape our lives. A later school of sociologists turned away from this approach in favor of **microsociology,** which stresses the study of small groups and the analysis of our everyday experiences and interactions. Our interactions with others have a profound effect on us. Parents, siblings, friends, teachers, classmates, coworkers, and even total strangers influence how we talk, act, think, and feel. Through such interactions we learn what is appropriate and inappropriate, responding accordingly. To describe this process, sociologist W. I. Thomas established what has come to be known in sociology as the **Thomas theorem:** "If men define situations as real, they are real in their consequences" (Thomas and Thomas 1928:571–572). Or, more simply, how we see the world shapes what we do. We act on the basis of perception, and our perception is a consequence of the interactions we have had with others.

To better understand the processes at work, sociologist Erving Goffman (1922–1982) recommended studying everyday interactions as if we are all actors on a stage seeking to successfully put on a performance. In every encounter we have, he said, we all play roles, follow scripts, use props, work together, and seek to win over our audiences. The parts of ourselves that we display vary based on the roles that we perform. As a student in a class, we may project a serious image; at a party, we may want to look relaxed and friendly. The immediate context of our everyday interactions shapes who we are, what we think, and how we act. Goffman's work, along with that of other interactionists, is covered in more depth in Chapter 4's "The Self and Socialization."

Macrosociology Sociological investigation that concentrates on large-scale phenomena or entire civilizations.

Microsociology Sociological investigation that stresses the study of small groups and the analysis of our everyday experiences and interactions.

Thomas theorem What we perceive as real is real in its consequences.

HOW DOES GROUP MEMBERSHIP INFLUENCE OPPORTUNITY?

Over time, sociologists came to more fully understand and appreciate the consequences that group membership, especially class, race, and gender, has for opportunity. African American sociologist W. E. B. Du Bois (1868–1963; pronounced "dew BOYS") combined an emphasis on the analysis of the everyday lived experience with a commitment to investigating power and inequality based on race. He was critical of those who relied on common sense or on all-too-brief investigations, arguing that a researcher has to be more than just a "car-window sociologist" because true understanding demands more than "the few leisure hours of a holiday trip to unravel the snarl of centuries" (Du Bois [1903] 1994:154). Du Bois's detailed, exhaustive, and groundbreaking work on the lives of African Americans in 1890s Philadelphia represents one of sociology's first truly empirical studies (Du Bois 1899; Morris 2015). His research revealed the social processes that contributed to the maintenance of racial separation, which extended beyond material differences to include social separation, which he referred to as the "color line" (Du Bois [1903] 1994).

Similarly, feminist scholarship has broadened our understanding of social behavior by extending the analysis beyond the male point of view that dominated classic sociology. An early example of this perspective can be seen in the life and writings of Ida Wells-Barnett (1862–1931). Carrying on a tradition begun with Martineau, Wells-Barnett argued that societies can be judged based on whether the principles they claim to believe in match their actions. Wells-Barnett found that when it came to the principles of equality and opportunity for women and African Americans, America came up short. Part of the task for the sociologist, then, is to bring to light such inconsistencies that may otherwise go largely unnoticed. This is something Wells-Barnett sought to do in her groundbreaking publications in the 1890s on the practice of lynching African Americans, as well as with her advocacy of women's rights, especially the struggle to win the vote for women. Like feminist theorists who succeeded her, Wells-Barnett used her analysis of society

W. E. B. Du Bois. (Du Bois): Source: Library of Congress Prints and Photographs Division [LC-USZ62-16767]; *(frame):* ©Visivasnc/iStock/Getty Images

as a means of resisting oppression. As an African American woman, she brought attention to the overlapping impacts of race, gender, and class (Wells-Barnett [1928] 1970).

HOW SHOULD SOCIOLOGISTS RESPOND?

Throughout sociology's history, a recurring theme has been the idea that sociological theory and research should contribute to positive social change. In the early 1900s many leading sociologists in the United States saw themselves as social reformers dedicated to systematically studying and then improving a corrupt society. They were genuinely concerned about the lives of immigrants in the nation's growing cities, whether those immigrants came from Europe or from the rural American South. Early female sociologists, in particular, often took active roles in poor urban areas as leaders of community centers known as settlement houses. For example, Jane Addams (1860–1935), an early member of the American Sociological Society, cofounded the famous Chicago settlement, Hull House, which provided social, educational, and cultural programs for recent immigrants. Addams and other pioneering female sociologists commonly combined intellectual inquiry, social service work, and political activism—all with the goal of assisting the underprivileged and creating a more egalitarian society. Working with Ida Wells-Barnett, Addams successfully prevented racial segregation in the Chicago public schools, and her efforts to establish a juvenile court system and a women's trade union reflect the practical focus of her work (Addams 1910, 1930; Lengermann and Niebrugge-Brantley 1998).

This commitment to positive social change was not unique to Addams and her colleagues. From the very beginning to

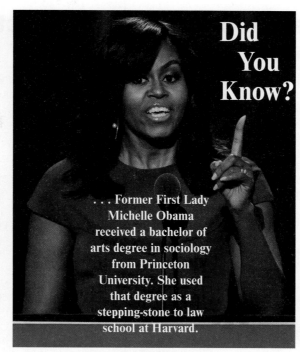

Did You Know?

. . . Former First Lady Michelle Obama received a bachelor of arts degree in sociology from Princeton University. She used that degree as a stepping-stone to law school at Harvard.

Photo: ©David Paul Morris/Bloomberg/Getty Images

Jane Addams. (Addams): ©Hulton Archive/Getty Images; *(frame):* ©Andrea Gingerich/iStock/Getty Images

the present, sociologists have recognized an obligation to go beyond explaining how the world works and become actively engaged in making the world a better place. In the words of French sociologist Pierre Bourdieu, "I have come to believe that those who have the good fortune to be able to devote their lives to the study of the social world cannot stand aside, neutral and indifferent, from the struggles in which the future of that world is at stake" (1998a:11).

For some sociologists, working toward change has meant publishing the results of their work so that it might enhance our understanding and inform our decisions; for others it has meant active engagement in establishing social policy or assisting in the lives of others. For example, Durkheim, who considered an educated citizenry essential to democratic success, used his appointment to the Department of Science of Education and Sociology at the Sorbonne in Paris, along with his political connections and appointments, to shape French educational policy and practice. Du Bois cofounded the National Association for the Advancement of Colored People, better known as the NAACP. In fact, one of the dominant reasons students choose to major in sociology is that they want to make a difference, and sociology provides a pathway to do just that.

>> Three Sociological Perspectives

As we will see throughout this book, the answers sociologists offer to these five questions provide a glimpse of sociology's complexity. Some theorists focus on society as a whole; others concentrate on individual interactions. Some are particularly concerned with inequality; others focus on maintaining social cohesion. Some approaches seem to overlap; others seem at odds with one another. But, regardless of their stance, all theorists share a common commitment to provide us with greater understanding of why we think and act the way we do. Each theory, whether broad or narrow, offers a way of seeing that allows us to perceive things we might have otherwise missed.

To simplify the rich array of sociological theories (especially for someone new to sociology), sociologists have classified various theories into three major theoretical

Three Sociological Perspectives

	Functionalist	Conflict	Interactionist
View of society	Stable, well integrated	Characterized by tension and struggle between groups	Active in influencing and affecting everyday social interaction
Level of analysis emphasized	Macro	Macro	Micro, as a way of understanding the larger macro phenomena
Key concepts	Social integration Institutions Anomie	Inequality Power Alienation	Symbols Self Generalized other
View of the individual	People create and share culture in order to establish a relationship to nature and with each other	People are shaped by power, coercion, and authority	People manipulate symbols and create their social worlds through interaction
View of the social order	Maintained through cooperation and consensus	Maintained through force and coercion	Maintained by shared understanding of everyday behavior
View of social change	Enhances social order over the long run	Challenges to existing system of inequality are resisted by those in power	Occurs as a consequence of people exercising their agency to choose new pathways
Example	Public punishments reinforce the social order	Laws enforce the positions of those in power	People respect laws or disobey them based on their own past experience
Proponents	Émile Durkheim Talcott Parsons Robert Merton	Karl Marx W. E. B. Du Bois Ida Wells-Barnett	George Herbert Mead Charles Horton Cooley Erving Goffman

Functionalist perspective A sociological paradigm that sees society as like a living organism in which its various parts work together for the good of the whole.

Conflict perspective A sociological paradigm that focuses on power and the allocation of valued resources in society.

perspectives or paradigms: functionalist, conflict, and interactionist. Each perspective offers a different set of lenses, focusing our attention in slightly different ways. Or, to put it another way, it is like three people standing on the edge of a circle looking in at the same thing but each seeing it from a different point of view, able to recognize things that others might not even see.

According to the **functionalist perspective,** society is like a living organism with its various parts working together (or functioning) for the good of the whole. Functionalists posit that society and its parts are structured to provide social order and maintain stability. Aspects of society that may appear dysfunctional, such as crime or poverty, either contribute some hidden benefits that researchers have not yet uncovered or will wither away over time. Durkheim's research into social order and its challenges, especially within modern societies, is a classic example of the functionalist perspective. Durkheim assumed that, over time, society would progress toward greater order as it came to terms with apparent threats or challenges.

Whereas the functionalist perspective emphasizes consensus and cooperation, the **conflict perspective** focuses on power and the allocation of valued resources in society. According to conflict theorists, social order cannot be fully understood apart from an analysis of how the status quo is established and maintained by those who control key resources. Such resources include material resources (such as money, land, and property), social resources (such as family connections, social networks, and prestige), and cultural resources (such as education, beliefs, knowledge, and taste). The existing social structure

SOCTHINK

From a functionalist approach, to what extent was your decision to go to college driven by a desire to fit in and contribute to society? From a conflict approach, how might access to resources have shaped your decisions about going to college? From an interactionist approach, what specific individuals influenced your decision and how did they do so?

helps maintain the privileges of some groups and keep others in inferior positions. Marx's work on inequality, social class, and alienation provides a classic example of the conflict perspective.

Finally, whereas functionalist and conflict theorists both analyze large-scale, society-wide patterns of behavior, theorists who take the **interactionist perspective** maintain that society is the product of our everyday encounters (with parents, friends, teachers, or strangers) through which we establish shared meanings and thus construct order. Because it emphasizes the role we play in making sense of our interactions, this approach highlights our agency as humans. Society is dependent on this ongoing construction, making it fluid and subject to change. Goffman's research focusing on life as a performance provides an example of the interactionist perspective.

The three-perspectives model has the advantage of providing us with conceptual hooks that allow us to recall some of the key concerns and issues sociologists have raised. A disadvantage, however, is that it gives the illusion that these three are discrete categories with fundamentally different and incompatible ways of looking at the world. In practice, research rooted in one perspective almost inevitably draws on or addresses insights from the other two.

Personal Sociology

Introducing Sociology

I still remember my first sociology class. At first, I felt overwhelmed. I tried hard to memorize all the terms and concepts, yet I still ended up getting a D on the first exam. It wasn't until later that I realized that the main reason I struggled was that I couldn't see how all the pieces fit together. Once I internalized the sociological imagination as a way of seeing, it became easier to put the various facts, figures, and key terms together into a coherent whole. So my advice to you is this: Look for ways that the ideas of sociology help us better understand the ways in which the positions we occupy, whether as student, daughter, coworker, or soldier, shape how we think, act, and feel.

>> Sociology Is a Verb

One of the questions that students frequently ask about sociology is "What can I do with it?" This query often comes from students who really like sociology, and might want to pursue it further, but are uncertain where it leads. The good news is that there are many ways people can practice sociology.

PERSONAL SOCIOLOGY

We don't have to become professional sociologists to apply what we have learned. The sociological imagination can help all of us better understand our beliefs and actions and make more informed choices. We can all practice **personal sociology** by recognizing the impact the positions we occupy have on who we are and how we think and act. For example, by drawing on insights gained from sociological theory and research, we might watch the news and ask whose interests are being represented. When we walk through the mall, we might observe how people display their social status and how they are treated accordingly. When we go in for a job interview, we might abide by the largely unspoken norms of conduct that shape interaction and influence our likelihood for success. Personal sociology empowers us by allowing us to see things that were previously invisible and to act on those insights.

The sociological imagination provides us with the tools necessary to respond to challenges we face today. Though the expression has become something of a cliché, it truly is a small world after all. Social, cultural, political, and economic events around the world—including, for example, the global financial trends or terrorist attacks—have a profound effect on how we think and what we do. The process of **globalization**—the worldwide integration of government policies, cultures, social movements, and financial markets through trade and the exchange of ideas—shows no signs of stopping. College and university campuses often provide a microcosm of this trend. Students, faculty, staff, and administrators with radically different values, political views, customs, experiences, and expectations assemble together from around the world into a relatively confined space. If the resulting interactions are to be meaningful, positive, and respectful, we must better understand the factors that shape them.

Conflicts with roommates, classmates, and professors are often chalked up to personality clashes and other individual attributes, but we cannot fully understood or deal with them unless we come to terms with the ways our social backgrounds have shaped how we think, act, and feel. For each of us, the social positions we occupy shape the opportunities and obstacles we face. We must learn to see the implications of this reality both for

Interactionist perspective A sociological paradigm that maintains that society is a product of our everyday encounters with others through which we establish shared meanings and thus construct order.

Personal sociology The practice of recognizing the impact the positions we occupy have on who we are and how we think and act.

Globalization The worldwide integration of government policies, cultures, social movements, and financial markets through trade and the exchange of ideas.

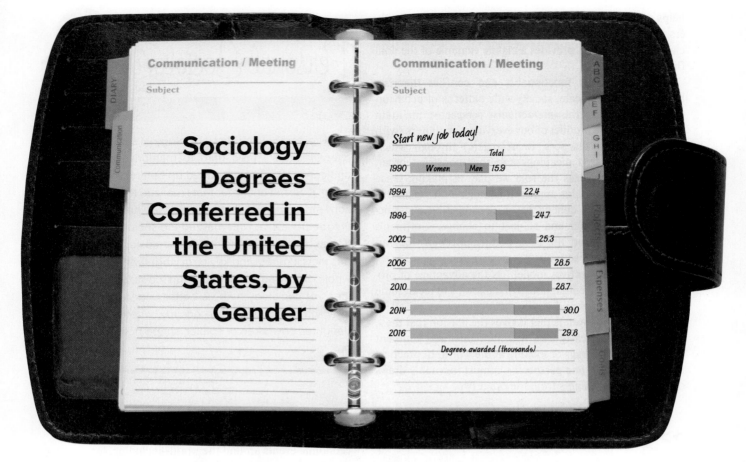

Communication / Meeting

Subject _____

Sociology Degrees Conferred in the United States, by Gender

Communication / Meeting

Subject _____

Start new job today!

	Total
1990	Women Men 15.9
1994	22.4
1998	24.7
2002	25.3
2006	28.5
2010	28.7
2014	30.0
2016	29.8

Degrees awarded (thousands)

Source: National Center for Education Statistics, Digest of Education Statistics—Most Current Digest Tables. Washington, DC: Institute of Education Services, U.S. Department of Education, September 6, 2016. www.nces.ed.gov. *Photo:* ©Maria Suleymenova/Shutterstock

ourselves and for others. This self-knowledge necessitates a more complete appreciation of the intersection of history and biography in all of our lives.

ACADEMIC SOCIOLOGY

Many students opt to take their sociology education further, and the number of U.S. college students who have graduated with a degree in sociology has risen steadily, as the "Sociology Degrees Conferred in the United States, by Gender" graph demonstrates. The American Sociological Association (ASA) conducted research on recent sociology graduates and discovered that the top reasons for choosing sociology as a major are because students found the sociological concepts interesting, sociology helped them understand the impact society has on individuals, they particularly enjoyed their first sociology course, sociology helped them understand themselves better, and they wanted to make a difference in the world (Senter, Spalter-Roth, and Van Vooren 2015). As part of their sociology education, sociology majors cultivate a variety of skills, such as using the sociological imagination, conducting data analysis, working in teams, writing reports, creating

presentations, analyzing social problems, and addressing diversity. Sociology graduates who later use these skills in their jobs express the highest levels of job satisfaction (Senter 2016; Spalter-Roth and Van Vooren 2015).

The jobs that sociology majors find shortly after graduation, according to the ASA study, are in a range of fields. The most common occupational category is social services. Examples of jobs include domestic violence victims advocate, residential crisis counselor, justice and peace liaison, and teen court case manager. Researchers also found that graduates were employed in a variety of other positions, including teacher, librarian, paralegal, immigration specialist, office manager, quality assurance manager, crime scene investigator, police officer, probation officer, social media/marketing analyst, research assistant, program evaluator, statistician, and editor (Senter et al. 2015; Spalter-Roth and Van Vooren 2008).

In another ASA study looking at longer-term outcomes of sociology majors who pursued graduate school degrees, only about one-quarter did so in sociology. Instead, most used their sociology major as a stepping-stone to graduate study in social work, education, law, psychology, engineering, and business management (Spalter-Roth and Van

Where Are They Now?

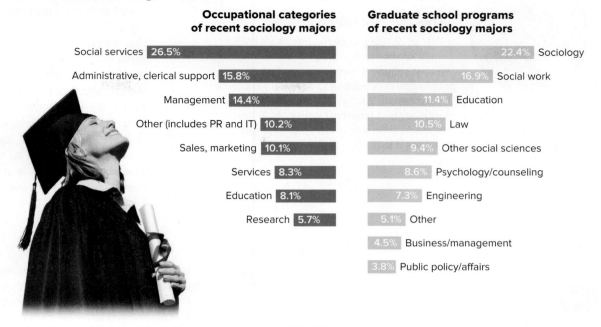

Occupational categories of recent sociology majors

Social services **26.5%**
Administrative, clerical support **15.8%**
Management **14.4%**
Other (includes PR and IT) **10.2%**
Sales, marketing **10.1%**
Services **8.3%**
Education **8.1%**
Research **5.7%**

Graduate school programs of recent sociology majors

22.4% Sociology
16.9% Social work
11.4% Education
10.5% Law
9.4% Other social sciences
8.6% Psychology/counseling
7.3% Engineering
5.1% Other
4.5% Business/management
3.8% Public policy/affairs

Note: Percentage based on sociology majors attending graduate school 18 months after graduation. *Source:* Spalter-Roth, Roberta, and Nicole Van Vooren. 2009. "Idealists vs. Careerists: Graduate School Choices of Sociology Majors." American Sociological Association Department of Research and Development. Washington, DC: American Sociological Association. www.asanet.org. *Photo:* ©Stockbyte/PunchStock

Vooren 2009:9). Overall, 51.9 percent of the majors completed a graduate degree within four years of college graduation. Of those who pursued advanced degrees in sociology, the majority enrolled in some form of an applied sociology program (Spalter-Roth and Van Vooren 2010).

APPLIED AND CLINICAL SOCIOLOGY

Applied sociology is the use of the discipline of sociology with the specific intent of yielding practical applications for human behavior and organizations. Often, the goal of such work is to assist in resolving a social problem. For example, numerous U.S. presidents over the years have established commissions to delve into major societal concerns facing our nation. In the Obama administration, for example, the Social and Behavioral Sciences Team (SBST) conducted numerous experiments to uncover ways to improve how government functions. In one case, they discovered that putting the signature box at the beginning of forms vendors sign when reporting rebates they owed to the federal government significantly increased the vendors' honesty in what they reported. In another case, the SBST used empirical data to create a reentry handbook to increase the odds of successful outcomes for those who leave prison (Applebaum 2015; Shankar 2016). Sociologists are often asked to apply their expertise to studying such issues as violence, pornography, crime, immigration, and population.

The growing popularity of applied sociology has led to the rise of the specialty of clinical sociology. Whereas applied sociology may involve simply evaluating social issues, **clinical sociology** is dedicated to facilitating change by altering organizations (as in family therapy) or restructuring social institutions (as in the reorganization of a medical center). Urban sociologist Louis Wirth (1931) wrote about clinical sociology more than 85 years ago, but the term itself has become popular only in recent years. The Association for Applied and Clinical Sociology was founded in 1978 to promote the application of sociological knowledge in interventions for individual and social change. This professional group has developed a procedure for certifying clinical sociologists—much as physical therapists or psychologists are certified.

Applied sociologists generally leave it to others to act on their evaluations, but clinical sociologists take direct responsibility for implementation and view those with whom they work as their clients. This specialty has become increasingly attractive to graduate students in sociology because it offers an opportunity to apply intellectual learning in practical ways. A competitive job market in the academic world has made such alternative career routes appealing.

Regardless of the level at which it is practiced, sociology is about more than the knowledge gained or career attained. Using the sociological imagination in our everyday lives

> **Applied sociology** The use of the discipline of sociology with the specific intent of yielding practical applications for human behavior and organizations.
>
> **Clinical sociology** The use of the discipline of sociology with the specific intent of altering social relationships or restructuring social institutions.

SOCIOLOGY IS A VERB

The Ties That Bind

Pick an object you own—maybe a pencil, a pair of shoes, or a cell phone—and trace its history. Include a diagram or map of all the people and processes it took for it to come into your possession. What is it made of? Where did all its components come from? Who contributed to its production? After it was made, who was involved in getting it into your hands? What story does it tell?

enables us to understand others from their perspective and even understand ourselves through their eyes. By opening our eyes to patterns and practices that are often invisible to us, we can make more informed decisions about which pathways we choose to follow. We can also take greater responsibility for the impact that our choices have on others. Sociology provides us with tools to better understand, interpret, and respond to the world around us. Sociology is a verb; it's something you do—it's a way of life.

For REVIEW

I. What is sociology?

- Sociology is a way of seeing that joins theory and research to investigate the relationship between the individual and society and the impact unequal distribution of resources has on opportunity.

II. How do sociologists look at the world?

- Sociologists developed theories to provide windows into our lives, including three primary perspectives: functionalist (emphasizing social order), conflict (focusing on inequality), and interactionist (highlighting the significance of our everyday relationships and exchanges).

III. How might someone practice sociology?

- Sociology can provide a pathway to a career in a related applied, clinical, or academic context. But more than that, we can practice sociology in our everyday lives by utilizing the sociological imagination to better understand ourselves and others.

SOCVIEWS on the Sociological Imagination

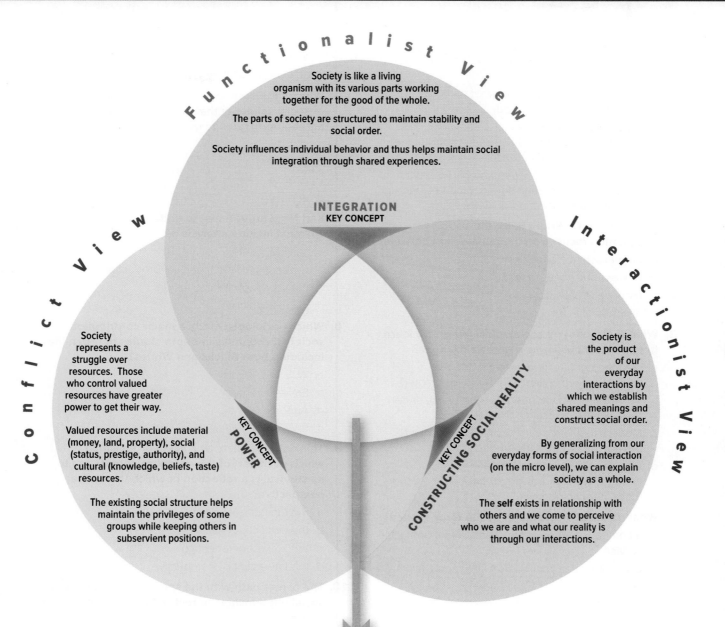

Functionalist View

Society is like a living organism with its various parts working together for the good of the whole.

The parts of society are structured to maintain stability and social order.

Society influences individual behavior and thus helps maintain social integration through shared experiences.

INTEGRATION
KEY CONCEPT

Conflict View

Society represents a struggle over resources. Those who control valued resources have greater power to get their way.

Valued resources include material (money, land, property), social (status, prestige, authority), and cultural (knowledge, beliefs, taste) resources.

The existing social structure helps maintain the privileges of some groups while keeping others in subservient positions.

KEY CONCEPT
POWER

Interactionist View

Society is the product of our everyday interactions by which we establish shared meanings and construct social order.

By generalizing from our everyday forms of social interaction (on the micro level), we can explain society as a whole.

The **self** exists in relationship with others and we come to perceive who we are and what our reality is through our interactions.

KEY CONCEPT
CONSTRUCTING SOCIAL REALITY

MAKE THE CONNECTION
After reviewing the chapter, answer the following questions:

1
Why might having multiple theoretical perspectives help us when we practice the sociological imagination?

2
How might each perspective differ in how it looks at what it takes to produce something (such as a hamburger, a house, a book, and so on)?

3
How might each perspective approach the study of unemployment? Of suicide?

4
How does each perspective enable you to see the way you participate in sports, either as a fan or as an athlete, in a different light?

Pop Quiz

1. **Sociology is**
   a. the analysis of individual motivations and internal struggles.
   b. concerned with predicting what particular individuals do or do not do.
   c. the systematic study of the relationship between the individual and society and of the consequences of difference.
   d. the integration of government policies, cultures, social movements, and financial markets through trade and the exchange of ideas.

2. **According to C. Wright Mills, the sociological imagination focuses on the intersection between**
   a. natural science and social science.
   b. power and access to resources.
   c. theory and research.
   d. history and biography.

3. **What is the primary sociological lesson we learn from the hamburger-as-a-miracle example?**
   a. We take our interdependence and the knowledge we collectively share for granted.
   b. An individual could easily survive on his or her own without assistance from others.
   c. Modern technology makes it difficult for us to provide for our individual needs.
   d. Interdependence is no longer necessary because we can provide for our needs through modern technology.

4. **What do sociologists mean by the term *agency*?**
   a. a company that provides clients with a particular service
   b. our freedom as individuals to think and act as we choose
   c. an organization devoted to collecting and processing information
   d. the constraints we face as a consequence of the positions we occupy in society

5. **Émile Durkheim's research on suicide found that**
   a. Catholics had much higher suicide rates than Protestants.
   b. the more socially integrated someone is the less likely he or she is to die by suicide.
   c. married people are more likely to take their lives than single people.
   d. suicide is a solitary act, unrelated to group life.

6. **What is the sociological term for the weak sense of social solidarity that arises due to a lack of agreed-upon rules to guide behavior?**
   a. suicide
   b. alienation
   c. anomie
   d. agency

7. **Karl Marx argued that to understand social order we must include analysis of**
   a. suicide.
   b. ownership of the means of production.
   c. the sociological imagination.
   d. microsociology.

8. **Which sociologist made a major contribution to society through his in-depth studies of urban life, including both Blacks and Whites?**
   a. W. E. B. Du Bois
   b. Émile Durkheim
   c. Auguste Comte
   d. Erving Goffman

9. **Thinking of society as a living organism in which each part of the organism contributes to its survival is a reflection of which theoretical perspective?**
   a. the functionalist perspective
   b. the conflict perspective
   c. the Marxist perspective
   d. the interactionist perspective

10. **The career path with the specific intent of altering social relationships or restructuring organizations is known as**
    a. dramaturgical sociology.
    b. applied sociology.
    c. academic sociology.
    d. clinical sociology.

1. (c), 2. (d), 3. (a), 4. (b), 5. (b), 6. (c), 7. (b), 8. (a), 9. (a), 10. (d)

Sociological Research

ASKING QUESTIONS AND FINDING ANSWERS

As a first-year college student, Alice Goffman got a job at her college cafeteria that changed her life forever. She needed a research site for her ethnography class, a course in which you embed yourself into a social setting to understand it from within, and the cafeteria seemed perfect. She'd heard her fellow students refer to the cafeteria workers—most of whom were older, African American women—as lazy and rude, and she wondered what the workers thought of her, a young, White, comparatively privileged woman and her similarly privileged peers (Parry 2013).

After a year filling plates and scrubbing dishes, Goffman began tutoring the grandchildren of her cafeteria boss, an African American woman in her 60s who lived in a poor Philadelphia neighborhood. Through those grandchildren, Goffman made contacts with others, and before long, a second research project was born. She moved into the neighborhood during her sophomore year to better observe and understand their

social world. She became so committed to the project and connected to the people that she continued her research work through college and graduate school and ultimately published a book telling their stories.

Goffman gained a much deeper understanding of the challenges faced by young African American males living in the neighborhood. As boys, they get told to run from police because, "even if it's not you [they are looking for], nine times out of ten, they'll probably book you" (Goffman 2014a:24). According to Goffman, these young men get taken away for what they see as petty offenses, contributing to suspicions that police are targeting them. Those with legal entanglements—missed court dates, unpaid court fees, parole curfew violations—face the threat of warrants for their arrest. Their fear of capture and confinement leads them to avoid beneficial social connections—visiting family, getting a job, going to the hospital when sick or injured. Such conventional social connections can be used against them, as happens when girlfriends or moms are pressured by police to inform on them. Goffman describes the resulting social fabric as "one woven in suspicion, distrust, and the paranoiac practices of secrecy, evasion, and unpredictability" (2014a:8).

At the same time, Goffman noticed that her fellow college students, who were often White and from financially secure backgrounds, engaged in similar activities—drinking, doing drugs, getting into fights—but no police raided their parties, and they walked away from their

adolescence with college diplomas and good jobs instead of jail time and permanent police records (Goffman 2014b). As the sociological imagination suggests, if a lot of people in similar positions experience the same result, it likely says more about the position than the person. Through sociological research we can see patterns shaping people's outcomes that might otherwise be invisible to us.

As You READ >>

- **What distinguishes sociology from common sense as a way of knowing?**
- **What steps do sociologists take when seeking to answer why people think and act the way they do?**
- **What techniques do sociologists use to collect data?**
- **What ethical concerns must sociologists consider while conducting research?**

>> Sociology as a Science

By engaging directly in the lives of both cafeteria workers and inner-city African American residents in a deliberate and sustained way, Alice Goffman learned that our taken-for-granted assumptions are frequently flawed. In doing so, she carried on a tradition that goes back to sociology's founding. Early sociologists rejected explanations based on tradition ("it's always been this way"), authority ("the king says so"), or mystical insight ("God revealed it to me in a dream"). Like all scientists, sociologists are suspicious of conventional wisdom, using doubt as a tool for the advancement of knowledge.

SOCIOLOGY AND COMMON SENSE

Most of us, most of the time, think we already know why we think and act as we do. We trust the accuracy of our taken-for-granted knowledge. It turns out, however, that things we

think we know aren't necessarily so. For example, many people believe that drinking eight glasses of water per day has health benefits, that giving kids too much sugar makes them hyper, and that women's periods will synchronize when they live together, such as in a dorm. None of these beliefs hold up under careful scrutiny.

Researchers have explored all three of these claims and found each wanting.

- Investigators have uncovered no medical evidence of significant health benefits from drinking eight glasses of water per day. Consuming that much water doesn't reduce wrinkles, clean out toxins, improve kidney function, decrease constipation, prevent cancer, or have any other notable benefit. The best medical advice? Drink when you are thirsty (Carroll 2015; Carroll and Vreeman 2009; Negoianu and Goldfarb 2008; Valtin 2002; Williams 2013).
- The sugar-high hypothesis about kids has been tested repeatedly, and the results continue to find no causal link. Researchers suggest that parents' strong belief that a relationship exists leads them to notice times when the two go together and ignore times when they don't (Flora and Polenik 2013; Geggel 2016; Wolraich et al. 1994; Wolraich, Wilson, and White 1995).
- And when it comes to "menstrual synchrony," a reanalysis of the data used in the original scientific study to "prove" its existence showed no statistically significant relationship. Since then, additional, more rigorous, studies have found that any apparent menstrual overlap that does occur is more likely due to chance than any biological shifts over time (Fahs et al. 2014; Pettit and Vigor 2015; Strassmann 1999; Yang and Schank 2006; Ziomkiewicz 2006).

When confronted with empirical research demonstrating that each of these claims is false, however, people still tend to trust what they call their own common sense.

Common sense can and does serve a useful function. The knowledge it provides enables us to make it through

©Monkey Business Images/Shutterstock

each day. Sociologist Duncan Watts (2011) defines common sense as "the loosely organized set of facts, observations, experiences, insights, and pieces of received wisdom that each of us accumulates over a lifetime, in the course of encountering, dealing with, and learning from, everyday situations" (p. 8). Watts argues that common sense is practical and concrete. It enables us to navigate our way through our day without having to work so hard, without doubting every thought or anguishing over every action. Its primary appeal is that, on an everyday level, it just works.

As a way of knowing, however, we seldom take the time to consider the four related limitations of such particularistic and improvisational knowledge. First, commonsense claims are not subject to empirical testing. Instead, it is enough for us to know that it works in particular times and places without careful consideration of the times and places it fails us. Second, commonsense claims may be incompatible with each other. For example, when two people who are very different from each other marry, we say something like "opposites attract," yet when two people who are quite similar get married, we say "birds of a feather flock together." But which is more likely? Common sense can't say for sure, and doesn't really try to, but sociology can and does, as we will see in Chapter 7.

Related to this is a third limitation, referred to as hindsight bias, which is our tendency to apply commonsense reasoning after the fact rather than before. Once we know what we are seeking to explain, we pick an appropriate nugget of commonsense wisdom out of our toolkit of possible explanations and apply it. For example, in the case of explaining why couples who are similar marry, as opposed to those who are different, our tendency is to invoke our commonsense explanation after the fact because, at that time, it seems obvious. We typically do so without critically assessing which possible alternative explanations might be refuted had we picked those instead.

Confirmation bias represents the fourth limitation of common sense, which involves our tendency to favor evidence that supports our existing beliefs while minimizing or ignoring contrary evidence. Psychologist Raymond Nickerson describes confirmation bias as "unwitting selectivity in the acquisition and use of evidence" (1998:175). The research on the impact sugar has on children, cited above, provides a classic example. Because parents believe that consuming sugar leads to hyperactivity, they notice when the two seem to occur together and conclude that it proves the theory. But they fail to recognize the disconfirming times—that is, when their children consumed sugar but did not become hyperactive or when they became hyperactive without consuming sugar (Hoover and Millich 1994; Wolraich, Wilson, and White 1995).

The danger of common sense is that we overestimate its ability to know something for sure. Human behavior is complex involving many factors influencing why we think and act as we do. That very complexity ironically makes it more likely that we will reach for simple explanations because the complexity of human behavior makes multiple explanations seem plausible. Years ago, sociologist Paul

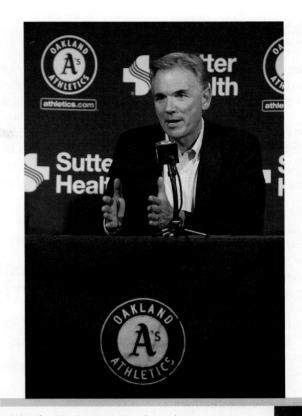

We often make decisions based on common sense, but doing so can result in errors. Analyzing data reveals underlying patterns we might otherwise miss, enabling us to make more effective decisions. In the film *Moneyball*, and in the book it's based on, Michael Lewis (2003) tells the story of general manager Billy Beane, whose Oakland A's team lacked the money to afford big-money free agents. Beane goes against baseball's conventional wisdom and uses statistical analyses to make decisions about how best to produce runs; by bringing the nonobvious patterns to the surface, he turns the team into a winner. Ironically, Beane's statistical analytics has become the norm, as professional teams in all sports now utilize such data to inform their decisions.

POPSOC

Photo: Jane Tyska/Digital First Media/The Mercury News/Getty Images

Lazarsfeld, based on extensive research on U.S. soldiers, presented six straightforward claims that he said could all be explained using common sense. But in each case, the research they conducted concluded the exact opposite. But, had these incompatible claims been initially stated instead, they, too, could be validated using common sense. If contradictory claims can equally be justified as obviously true, in the words of Lazarsfeld, "Obviously something is wrong with the entire argument of 'obviousness'" (1949:380). Sociology provides us with the tools necessary to test the validity of one claim over another.

SOCIOLOGY AND THE SCIENTIFIC METHOD

Sociology puts ideas to the test. To do so, sociologists rely on the **scientific method** which is the systematic observation of empirical, this-worldly evidence to assess and refine ideas about what happens and why. If we want to know why people think and act the way they do, we need to know more about what they actually think and do.

Scientific method The systematic observation of empirical, this-worldly evidence to assess and refine ideas about what happens and why.

We need to observe them, ask them questions, participate in their lives, or in other ways seek to understand their experiences from their perspective. We cannot sit back and guess.

In conducting their research, sociologists face a challenge quite different from that of researchers in the natural sciences. Even though both rely on the scientific method to guide them, the objects each studies differ greatly. Humans have agency in a way that molecules or rocks do not. Humans can choose to act in any number of ways under a variety of circumstances, whereas we can reliably predict that two atoms of hydrogen will always bond with one atom of oxygen to form a molecule of water given the appropriate conditions. To put it simply, explaining human behavior is a far more complex undertaking than deriving the physical laws of nature. And yet, behavioral patterns do exist in which we can identify causal factors influencing how we think and act. By collecting and analyzing data, we can observe such patterns and draw informed conclusions about their significance (as Durkheim's research on suicide demonstrated in the "Theory and Research" subsection in Chapter 1). Throughout this book we will encounter a multitude of sociological insights derived from empirical research.

Sometimes sociology confirms what we all take for granted as true. Other times it clarifies the circumstances under which one thing is true as opposed to another. Yet other times, it reveals new, unanticipated truths about why we think and act as we do. Sometimes it explains what has happened in the past, whereas at other times it predicts what might happen in the future. Sociology does all this through meticulous empirical investigation, with each new investigation seeking to expand, clarify, and refine what we know.

>> Steps in the Research Process

As science developed, general principles emerged for how best to put the scientific method into practice. Because these processes have become widely accepted in both the natural and social sciences, adhering to them helps ensure the legitimacy of the results. These procedures are built on the principle that scientific exploration involves a conversation between theory and research. As such, the scientific method can be represented as an ever-turning wheel, with new ideas leading to new research, which produces new theories, and so on. Presented graphically in the figure "The Wheel of Science," the scientific method includes five primary stages: (1) defining the problem, (2) reviewing the literature, (3) formulating the hypothesis, (4) collecting and analyzing data, and (5) developing the conclusion.

> In science, when human behavior enters the equation, things go nonlinear. That's why Physics is easy and Sociology is hard.
>
> Neil de Grasse Tyson (2016)

DEFINING THE PROBLEM

As we have already seen, sociology, like all sciences, explores theories about how the world works, and the initial step—defining the problem—represents the idea stage of the research process. The primary goals here are to clarify the concepts we want to learn more about and specify the nature of the relationship we suspect might exist between those concepts.

The ideas we explore can come from anywhere, including common sense, but most sociological research draws inspiration from existing sociological theories. Theories represent our most informed explanations about what happens

The Wheel of Science

Define the problem
Investigate existing theories

Review the literature
Explore existing research

Formulate a testable hypothesis
Identify variables and relationships

Collect and analyze data
Select a research design
Survey • Observation • Experiment • Existing sources

Develop the conclusion
Propose ideas for further research

Photo: ©Photodisc/Getty Images

and why. For example, as we saw in Chapter 1, Durkheim theorized that social integration shapes individual action. He set out to test this theory by conducting research on suicide as an example of the most extreme individual action he could imagine. By clarifying possible factors to consider, existing theories help us define the new problem we want to explore, especially when we come up against something we do not yet understand.

As an example of issues we might consider when defining a problem, take the question "Is college worth it?" The implied concepts here include college attendance and possible benefits. In asking that question, perhaps we are mostly curious about the individual benefits that might result from going to college and getting a degree. Or, drawing on the functionalist perspective in sociology, maybe we want to know how a highly educated citizenry helps society operate more effectively. Another possibility, from the conflict perspective, is that we want to know whether education reinforces the existing system of inequality, providing only the illusion of opportunity because children from wealthier families are more likely to afford and complete college. The initial question, "Is college worth it?," does not specify which of those paths was intended. If a research question is unclear or too broad, we will lack the terms and topics necessary to track down existing research in the review of the literature, the next stage in the research process.

> ## Without theory we are blind— we cannot see the world.
>
> Michael Burawoy (2009)

Finding Information

Begin with material you already have, including this text and others.

Beware of using online sources such as Wikipedia; they can be a helpful place to start, but always double-check claims with an authoritative source.

Use books, news sites, and scholarly journals.

Search using the library catalog and databases to find related academic journal articles.

Examine government documents (including the U.S. Census).

Contact people, organizations, and agencies related to your topic.

Consult with your instructor, teaching assistant, or reference librarian.

Photo: ©Hill Street Studios/Blend Images LLC

REVIEWING THE LITERATURE

After we've defined the problem, our next step is to conduct a review of existing literature to see what others have already written about our topic. Rather than starting from scratch, we can build on what they have already uncovered. In the words of Isaac Newton, one of the greatest natural scientists of all time, "If I have seen further, it is by standing on the shoulders of giants," meaning the work of those who came before him was essential to his discoveries. Analyzing how others studied concepts of interest to us enables us to refine our ideas, identify additional items or relationships we want to include, clarify possible techniques for collecting data, and eliminate or reduce avoidable mistakes. Demonstrating how existing work informed and influenced our work also increases the legitimacy of our claims in the eyes of others when we report our results.

Sociological journals provide the most reliable source of existing research. Examples, among many others, include *American Sociological Review, Social Problems, Gender and Society,* and *Sociology of Education.* Most academic libraries have access to such journals in print, via digital access, or through interlibrary loan. Academic books written by recognized sociologists and published by respected presses also serve as valuable resources. Such books provide a more comprehensive account of the author's research, as Alice Goffman's does in *On the Run: Fugitive Life in an American City* (2014a).

Secondary sources, in which others report on existing sociological research, can also be valuable. In fact, they are often the places where we encounter the research to begin with. Stories with a sociological twist frequently appear in newspapers and magazines such as *The New York Times, The Washington Post, The New Yorker, The Atlantic,* and *Contexts.* Such accounts are often more accessible, both easier to find and easier to understand, and because they may mention numerous studies, can connect us to additional research we might not otherwise know about. We can use the information included in these accounts to trace back to the original and related research.

Online sources can present a challenge for academic research because anyone anywhere can post anything without regard for the truth. The most important principle? Consider the source. Online academic databases provide perhaps the best way of tracking down existing research.

Hypothesis A testable statement about the relationship between two or more variables.

Causal logic A relationship exists between variables in which change in one brings about change in the other.

Variable A measurable trait or characteristic that is subject to change under different conditions.

Independent variable The variable in a causal relationship that causes or influences a change in a second variable.

Dependent variable The variable in a causal relationship that is subject to the influence of another variable.

Did You Know?

. . . U.S. government agencies regularly release reports on income, education, poverty, and health care. According to the Department of Education, 89.1 percent of people aged 25 and older have received their high school diploma or equivalent, and 33.7 percent have earned at least a bachelor's degree.

Source: National Center for Education Statistics 2018:Table 104.10. *Photo:* ©Laura Doss/Fancy Photography/Veer

Most academic libraries provide links to databases, such as *Academic Search, JSTOR,* and *SocINDEX.* The U.S. Census Bureau makes available numerous reports along with access to a wealth of data on income, education, gender, race, and so on. Many other sites provide annual reports and access to data, including the U.S. Department of Education, the U.S. Bureau of Labor Statistics, the Organisation for Economic Co-operation and Development (OECD), and the World Bank.

Wikipedia by itself is not considered a sufficiently legitimate academic source, but it can be a useful place to start because entries often include links to recognized academic references. Online search engines, such as Google or Bing, can turn up all kinds of interesting material, including videos of sociologists talking about their research in interviews and conference presentations. When using such search results, however, always assess the quality of the source. Professors and librarians can provide invaluable assistance when it comes to judging sources.

FORMULATING THE HYPOTHESIS

The next step in the research process, formulating the hypothesis, involves specifying exactly what we plan to observe and what outcomes to expect. A hypothesis is more than just an educated guess. In research, a **hypothesis** is a testable statement about the relationship between two or more variables. It represents an explicit attempt to indicate what we think is happening and why. It presupposes that **causal logic** is at work, meaning that a relationship exists between variables in which change in one brings about change in the other.

Variables serve as the building blocks for hypotheses. A **variable** is a measurable trait or characteristic that is subject to change under different conditions. Income, religion, gender, and occupation can all serve as variables in a study. For example, among numerous possible values within each of these variables, you might be rich or poor, Buddhist or Christian, female or male, a music teacher or an astrophysicist.

Within a hypothesis, we distinguish between cause and effect variables. The causal variable that brings about change is called the **independent variable** (often referred to in equations as x). The variable that is affected is known as the **dependent variable,** because change in it depends on the influence of the independent variable (typically represented in equations as y). For example, as we saw in the "Sociology's Roots" section of Chapter 1, Durkheim hypothesized that a cause-and-effect relationship existed between religious affiliation (his independent variable) and suicide rates (his dependent variable).

SOCTHINK

To what extent do you think each of the independent variables listed in the "Causal Logic" figure would help explain variation in college grade point average? Can you think of any additional independent variables that would help explain GPA?

A generic hypothesis statement would look something like this: knowledge of the independent variable (*x*) allows us to better explain or predict the value or position of the dependent variable (*y*). We could then place variables we are interested in studying, such as those in the "Causal Logic" figure, into this statement to clearly present what we expect to find. For example, we could hypothesize that knowledge of a person's education level allows us to better explain or predict his or her level of income.

In sociology, we are frequently interested in abstract concepts and principles, but in order to abide by our commitment to conducting empirical research—in keeping with the Missouri principle of don't just tell me, show me—we need to ensure that we can observe, measure, or otherwise demonstrate cause-and-effect relationships. That means we must create an **operational definition** for each of our variables by transforming abstract concepts into concrete indicators that are observable and measurable. Durkheim did this when he operationalized the abstract concept of social integration into the concrete indicator of religious affiliation (Protestant versus Catholic). If we were interested in studying ability, initiative, and accomplishment, we might operationalize these concepts by using educational attainment, which might concretely be measured by highest degree attained or number of years of school completed. If we wanted to know more about social inequality, we might use annual income as a concrete indicator of differential outcomes. If we wanted to create an operational definition of religiosity, we might use a combination of indicators, including attendance at religious services, time spent studying religious texts, frequency of engaging in prayer or meditation, adherence to religious beliefs, or other possible benchmarks we might combine. The goal in creating operational definitions is to indicate as clearly as possible exactly what the researcher plans to observe.

COLLECTING AND ANALYZING DATA

When we have clearly indicated which hypotheses we seek to explore, we move on to collecting and then analyzing data. Sociologists gather data via surveys, observation, experiments, and existing research. We will explore each

Causal Logic

Independent variable		Dependent variable
x	→	*y*
Level of educational degree	→	Level of income
Degree of integration into society	→	Likelihood of suicide
Availability of affordable housing	→	Level of homelessness
Parents' church attendance	→	Children's church attendance
Time spent preparing for quiz	→	Performance on quiz
Parents' income	→	Likelihood of children's enrolling in college

Photo: ©fStop Images GmbH/Shutterstock

technique in more detail in the "Major Research Designs" section later in this chapter. Here we will focus on more general data collection issues researchers must address regardless of the research design they select.

Selecting the Sample One of the most basic questions sociologists must answer is, "From whom shall I gather data?" For the most part, especially in the case of large-scale research projects, sociologists cannot gather information from everyone in the population they want to study. As a result, they typically include only a subset of people from that population. A **sample** is a selection from a larger population that is representative of that population. To ensure that a sample is representative, sociologists typically use some form of a **random sample,** in which every member of the entire population being studied has an equal chance of being selected. In conducting polls by telephone, for example, polling organizations often use a random digit dialing system to ensure all numbers, including those that are unlisted, have an equal likelihood of being included.

When conducted properly, such sampling allows researchers to statistically estimate how representative their results are likely to be. For example, the U.S. Census produces an annual report, titled "Income and Poverty in the United

©Mike Kemp/Rubberball/Getty Images

> **Operational definition** Transformation of an abstract concept into indicators that are observable and measurable.
>
> **Sample** A selection from a larger population that is statistically representative of that population.
>
> **Random sample** A sample for which every member of an entire population has the same chance of being selected.

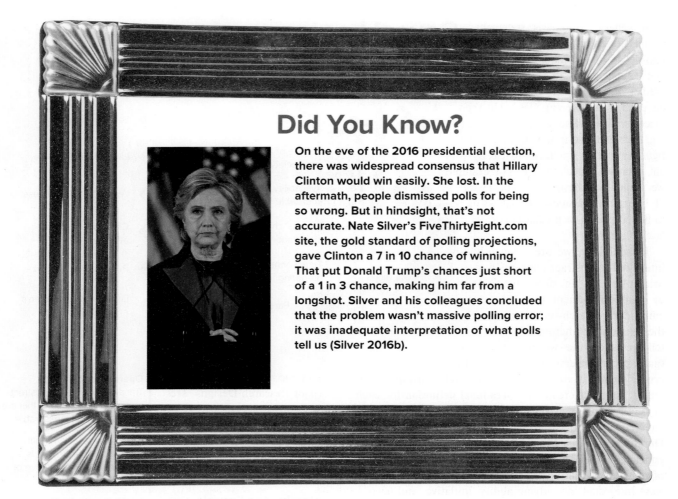

Did You Know?

On the eve of the 2016 presidential election, there was widespread consensus that Hillary Clinton would win easily. She lost. In the aftermath, people dismissed polls for being so wrong. But in hindsight, that's not accurate. Nate Silver's FiveThirtyEight.com site, the gold standard of polling projections, gave Clinton a 7 in 10 chance of winning. That put Donald Trump's chances just short of a 1 in 3 chance, making him far from a longshot. Silver and his colleagues concluded that the problem wasn't massive polling error; it was inadequate interpretation of what polls tell us (Silver 2016b).

(frame): Ingram Publishing; *(Clinton):* Matt McClain/The Washington Post/Getty Images

States," based on a statistically representative sample of the population (Fontenot, Semega, and Kollar 2018). Released each fall, it provides an abundance of data on, for example, types of household, regions of the country, race, ethnicity, and gender, providing statistical estimates of the margin of error for each. The same cannot be said of most online polls, such as those on Twitter, Facebook, or news sites, because they rely solely on whoever logs in and chooses to participate. Although such surveys can be interesting, fun, or provocative, there is no way to tell if they are representative.

Validity The degree to which a measure or scale truly reflects the phenomenon under study.

Reliability The extent to which a measure produces consistent results.

Ensuring Validity and Reliability To have confidence in their findings, and in keeping with the scientific method, sociologists pursue research results that are both valid and reliable. **Validity** refers to the degree to which a measure or scale truly reflects the phenomenon under study. A valid measure of income, for example, would accurately represent how much money a person earned in a given time period, such as per hour or per year. For example, if a survey question about income is not written clearly, some respondents might interpret it as asking about earnings from a job; others might add income from other sources, such as investments; and others might report household income, including earnings from children or a spouse.

Reliability refers to the extent to which a measure produces consistent results. That is, using the same instrument to collect data from the same people in similar circumstances should provide the same results. For example, if you give people the same questionnaire about income and education at two different times, unless something significant has changed between times, the responses should be approximately the same. Together, reliability and validity enable us to move on to the next stage with confidence in our findings.

DEVELOPING THE CONCLUSION

In the final stage of the research process, sociologists draw conclusions about what they have learned. To do so, they must make decisions about the fate of their hypotheses and consider possible alternative explanations for their results.

Supporting Hypotheses The data provide the foundation on which we decide whether we should accept or reject our hypotheses. Whether collected from surveys, observations,

Degree Attainment and Income

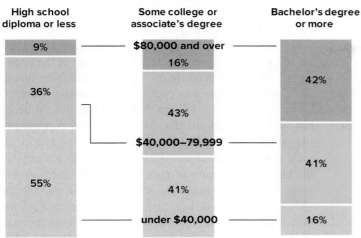

High school diploma or less	Some college or associate's degree	Bachelor's degree or more
9%	**$80,000 and over**	
	16%	42%
36%	43%	
	$40,000–79,999	41%
55%	41%	
	under $40,000	16%

Note: Data include those aged 25–64 working full-time, year-round. High school category includes those with some college but no degree.

Source: U.S. Census Bureau 2018b:Table PINC-03.

experiments, or other sources, we use what we found to draw conclusions about possible causality between our independent and dependent variables. First, we must decide whether our variables are correlated. A **correlation** is a relationship between two variables in which change in one coincides with change in the other. For example, as a person's educational attainment rises, does income also go up? We can use existing data sources to answer that question. According to data from the Census Bureau, a person's odds of having a high income go up significantly if the person has more education. As the "Degree Attainment and Income" graphic demonstrates, those whose highest degree attained is a high school diploma are most likely to fall in the lowest-income group, earning less than $40,000 per year and least likely to find themselves in the high-income category. The reverse is true for those who have earned a bachelor's degree, who are most likely to fall in the high-income group, earning $80,000 per year and up, and least likely to fall in the low-income group. We can also see that the correlation isn't perfect. Some people in the high school diploma category have high incomes, and others with a bachelor's degree or more are in the low-income group.

Assuming we find that our variables are correlated, the second decision we must make is whether that relationship is causal. One fundamental truth when interpreting results is that correlation does not equal causation. It may well be that the apparent relationship is due to chance or to the influence of some other factors. It is the task of the researcher to demonstrate—drawing on time-ordering, logical reasoning, and theory—that variation in the independent variable caused change in the dependent variable. Statistics alone are not enough.

Take, for example, the effect that divorce has on the well-being of children. Studies have shown that the two variables

are correlated—children of divorce exhibit long-term adverse effects—but is that relationship causal? Before reaching a conclusion, we should consider other factors. Perhaps negative outcomes for children are due to levels of parental conflict rather than divorce itself, or to the nature of the relationship between the parents and the children, or to contextual factors such as unemployment or geographic mobility (Bhrolcháin 2001; Sun and Li 2008). In other words, we must consider the possibility that other variables besides divorce may be involved.

Controlling for Other Factors Given the complexity of human behavior, it is seldom sufficient to study only one independent and one dependent variable. Although such analyses can provide us with insight, to consider additional causal factors that might influence the dependent variable, we can introduce **control variables,** which are factors the researcher holds constant to test the relative impact of an independent variable.

In exploring the relationship between education and income, for example, we should consider the possibility that variables such as parents' income or social network connections account for the correlation. In this case, perhaps "who you know" matters more than "what you know." The introduction of the control variables allows us to test how much of the variation in income that was initially assumed to be due to education is actually due to the influence of parents' income or social network connections. In later chapters we consider such additional background factors that help explain income differences, including gender, race, ethnicity, and social class.

> **Correlation** A relationship between two variables in which a change in one coincides with a change in the other.
>
> **Control variable** A factor that is held constant to test the relative impact of an independent variable.

IN SUMMARY: THE RESEARCH PROCESS

When our research is complete, we share our results with sociologists, policy makers, and others, primarily via presentations at professional conferences and articles

SOCTHINK

Although education plays a significant role in explaining income, some people with minimal education earn high incomes, and some with advanced degrees earn relatively little. What additional social factors do you think might explain a person's income? What effects might a person's gender, race, ethnicity, religion, age, and social background have on income?

in academic journals. Presenting our results in such public ways makes our research part of the literature to be reviewed for future studies. Subjecting our research to such scrutiny can uncover mistakes we made or reveal things we might have done differently, such as including additional variables or using alternative techniques for collecting data.

Research is cyclical. Having drawn our conclusions about our hypotheses, we use those results to refine our initial theories about why we think and act as we do. And the process starts again. We generate new ideas that lead to new hypotheses, which in turn lead to more data collection. In the end we find answers, but we also have new questions, and the wheel of science continues to turn.

>> Major Research Designs

Sociologists gather information to tell the stories of our lives in a variety of ways. Sometimes they want to explore a collective story, perhaps to get a sense of the national mood about issues such as education, politics, or religion; other times they want to tell the stories of individuals and groups who are often left out of such large-scale accounts, as we saw Alice Goffman (2014a) do with her research in inner-city Philadelphia. To collect the information necessary to tell these tales, sociologists follow the guidelines set forth in a given **research design,** which is a detailed plan or method for obtaining data scientifically. There are four primary research designs in sociology: surveys, observation, experiments, and use of existing sources.

Research design A detailed plan or method for obtaining data scientifically.

Survey A predefined series of questions designed to collect information about people's particular attributes, beliefs, and actions.

SURVEYS

Surveys represent the most commonly used research design. All of us have likely been surveyed about something: which presidential candidate we intend to vote for, what our favorite television program is, or how much time we spent studying for a course. A **survey** is a predefined series of questions designed to collect information about people's particular attributes, beliefs, and actions. Surveys become particularly commonplace during election seasons in the form of political polls. Major polling organizations include Gallup, Pew Research, SurveyUSA, ABC News/Washington Post, and Quinnipiac University. All these firms use careful techniques to ensure the accuracy of their results.

Issues in Designing Surveys As indicated earlier, a survey must be based on precise, representative sampling if it is to genuinely reflect a broad range of the population. We might be skeptical that feedback from just a few hundred people can provide an accurate picture of how more than 300 million people think, but properly run surveys can do just that. When it comes to presidential polling, for example, we can compare the results of such polls against actual election results. In a study of the historical accuracy of presidential polls, political scientist Costas Panagopoulos reports that the polls from 1956 to 2012 were, on average, within 2 percentage points of accurately predicting the final result (Panagopoulos 2009; Panagopoulos and Farrer 2014). Even in the 2016 presidential election, in which pollsters incorrectly predicted that Hillary Clinton would defeat Donald Trump, their projection of the popular vote was not far off. On the eve of the election, the national polling average showed Clinton 3.1 percentage points ahead of Trump and the final vote tally showed her receiving 2.1 percent more votes nationally than did Trump (Andrews, Katz, and Patel 2016; Wasserman 2016). Although pollsters sometimes fail to "get it right" (for example, mistakenly predicting that Dewey would defeat Truman in the 1948 presidential election), most often they do, and with amazing precision.

In recent years, analysts have taken to aggregating poll results, meaning they produce a single score based on averaging the results of numerous individual polls. The graph "Presidential Approval and Disapproval Ratings for Donald Trump" provides an example. Each individual dot represents a single poll result, and the line represents the average. With graphs such as these, we can see that although any individual

©Bettmann/Getty Images

Presidential Approval and Disapproval Ratings for Donald Trump

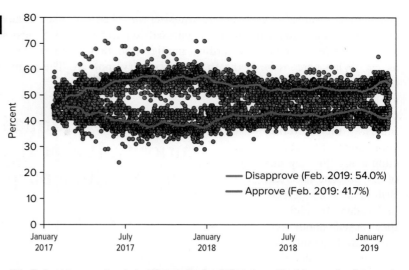

Note: Each point represents a single poll measuring Donald Trump's presidential approval or disapproval ratings throughout his administration. The lines represent the polling averages for approval and disapproval.

Source: Based on data from FiveThirtyEight 2019.

poll can vary significantly from the average, taken together they provide a much better measure of the likely result. Sites regularly producing up-to-date polling results include FiveThirtyEight.com, Pollster.com, and PollingReport.com.

In addition to ensuring samples are representative, sociologists must exercise great care in the wording of questions when conducting surveys. Failure to do so threatens the reliability and validity of their results. An effective survey question must be simple and clear enough for people to understand. It must also be specific enough that researchers have no problems interpreting the results. Open-ended questions ("What do you think of the programming on educational television?") must be carefully phrased to solicit the type of information desired. Surveys can be indispensable sources of information, but only if the sampling is done properly and the questions are worded accurately and without bias.

Another concern involves the possible impact an interviewer's characteristics can have on survey results. For example, female interviewers tend to receive more feminist responses from female subjects than do male researchers, and African American interviewers tend to receive more detailed responses about race-related issues from Black subjects than do White interviewers. The possible impact of gender and race indicates again how much care social research requires (Chun et al. 2011; Davis and Silver 2003).

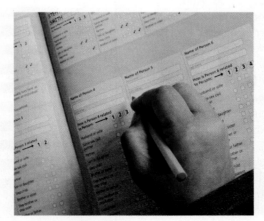

Charles Bowman/Getty Images

Types of Surveys When it comes to administering surveys, there are two primary options: interviews and questionnaires. In an **interview,** a researcher obtains information through face-to-face or telephone questioning. With a **questionnaire,** a respondent completes a printed or computerized form and returns it to the researcher. Each of these has its advantages. An interviewer can obtain a higher response rate because people find it more difficult to turn down a personal request for an interview than to throw away a printed questionnaire. In addition, a skillful interviewer can follow up on questions to clarify a subject's underlying feelings and reasons for responding. For their part, questionnaires have the advantage of being cheaper and easier to distribute to large numbers of people. Either way, what we can learn from surveys can be amazing.

Researchers used surveys, for example, to better understand how perceptions vary between countries. They administered it to a representative sample of 11,527 people in 14 nations, asking questions about a variety of topics (Ipsos MORI 2014). For example, regarding teenage pregnancy they asked, "In your opinion, what percentage of girls aged between 15 and 19 years in [name of country] give birth each

> **Interview** A face-to-face or telephone questioning of a respondent to obtain desired information.
>
> **Questionnaire** A respondent completes a printed or computerized form and returns it to the researcher.

year?" In the United States, the average answer was 24 percent, whereas in Great Britain people guessed 16 percent and in Sweden it was 7. Regarding immigration they asked, "What percentage of the [name of country] population do you think are immigrants to this country?" In the United States, the average guess was 32 percent compared to guesses of 24 percent in Great Britain and 23 percent in Sweden. In addition, they asked about religion, elderly people, voting rates, unemployment rates, homicide rates, and life expectancy. The answers varied significantly from country to country.

Researchers then compared the perceptions to the actual rates for each question asked (Ipsos MORI 2014). They wondered if the degree of difference between the two varied by country. On the question of teenage pregnancy, the actual U.S. rate is 3 percent, a 21-point difference from the perceived rate. People in all 14 countries overestimated their teenage pregnancy rates. The actual percentage of immigrants in the United States is 13 percent, a 19-point difference from the perceived rate. Again, people in all 14 countries overestimated the percentage of their immigrant population. They then ranked each country based on how close their perception was to the actual data. The country that came out on top as the most accurate was Sweden. The country in last place was Italy. The United States finished in 13th place. Understanding perception is important because, as we learned from the Thomas theorem, we act on the basis of what we *think* is true, rather than what *is* true. And if our perceptions are inaccurate, our corresponding actions may prove less effective.

Quantitative research Research that collects and reports data primarily in numerical form.

Mean A number calculated by adding a series of values and then dividing by the number of values.

Median The midpoint, or number that divides a series of values into two groups of equal numbers of values.

Mode The most common value in a series of scores.

Qualitative research Descriptive research that relies on narrative accounts rather than statistical procedures.

Quantitative and Qualitative Research Surveys typically represent an example of **quantitative research,** which collects and reports data primarily in numerical form. Analysis of these data depends on statistics, from the simple to the complex. Statistics can seem intimidating. It helps if we think of statistics as just another way of telling a story. They are tools that provide an additional window into what is happening and why. Though it takes training to understand the complex statistics

> ## Research is formalized curiosity. It is poking and prying with a purpose.
>
> Zora Neale Hurston (1997)

used in advanced sociological research, basic descriptive statistics, such as percentages and measures of central tendency, are more familiar and are still quite helpful. The **mean,** or average, is a number calculated by adding a series of values and then dividing by the number of values. The **median,** or midpoint, is the number that divides a series of values into two groups of equal numbers of values. The median is most often used when there are extreme scores that would distort the mean. The **mode** is the most common value in a series of scores and is seldom used in sociological research. As measures of central tendency, the mean, median, and mode all provide a single score that serves as a simple summary for the whole distribution of scores.

Quantitative research proves particularly useful on familiar, well-defined topics, but when we seek to explore new concepts and contexts, researchers frequently turn to **qualitative research,** which is descriptive research that relies on narrative accounts rather than statistical procedures. Whereas quantitative research focuses on varieties of ways to count things, qualitative research seeks to make sense of the contexts within which people construct meaning through interactions with others. It focuses on small

Immigration Rates: Perception versus Reality

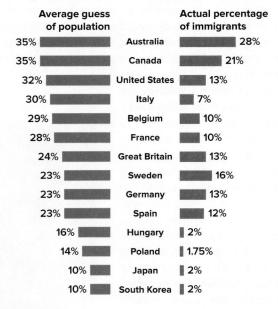

Average guess of population		Actual percentage of immigrants
35%	Australia	28%
35%	Canada	21%
32%	United States	13%
30%	Italy	7%
29%	Belgium	10%
28%	France	10%
24%	Great Britain	13%
23%	Sweden	16%
23%	Germany	13%
23%	Spain	12%
16%	Hungary	2%
14%	Poland	1.75%
10%	Japan	2%
10%	South Korea	2%

Source: Ipsos MORI 2014.

groups and communities rather than on large groups or whole nations. The most common research design for qualitative research is observation.

OBSERVATION

Investigators who collect information by participating directly and/or by closely watching a group or community are engaged in **observation.** This research design allows sociologists to examine behaviors and communities in greater depth than is possible using other methods. Though observation may seem a relatively informal method compared to surveys, researchers are careful to take detailed notes and follow appropriate procedures while observing their subjects.

A popular and useful form of qualitative research in sociology today is **ethnography**—the study of an entire social setting through extended systematic observation. Typically, the emphasis is on how the subjects themselves view their social life in some setting. In some cases, the sociologist actually joins the group for a period to get an accurate sense of how it operates. This approach is called *participant observation.*

This is the approach Alice Goffman (2014a) took in her study in Philadelphia. As a result of embedding herself in the community, she was able to portray a fuller description of the lives of the young African American males who lived there. In addition, she describes the experience of the women in their lives (their wives, sisters, and girlfriends); the underground marketplace that emerges in which local entrepreneurs provide goods and services, such as clean urine for drug tests, faked documents, and prison

Going GLOBAL

Research Abroad

Researchers now regularly gather data from around the world, even under difficult circumstances. Since 2004, for example, researchers have conducted an annual national survey in Afghanistan. In 2017, they sent out 929 Afghani interviewers who conducted 10,012 face-to-face interviews with Afghans throughout the country. They learned people's opinion about the overall direction of the country remains low with 61 percent saying Afghanistan was moving in the wrong direction. If given the opportunity to do so, 39 percent of Afghans would leave the country with fear for their safety a major reason for wanting to emigrate. At the same time, 77 percent of those interviewed said they are generally happy with their lives (Akseer et al. 2017).

─**SOC**THINK─

What social group or setting (such as a religious group, political organization, sorority/fraternity, laboratory, or office) might you want to learn more about through in-depth participant observation? How would you go about making contact? How would you gain members' trust?

guards who provide cell phones to inmates; and the lives of those living in the inner city who keep their distance from illegal activity and those involved in it. Because she used participant observation, her descriptions are deep and rich and she includes many extended quotes from the individuals involved.

Observation research raises questions about the appropriate nature of the relationship between researchers and their subjects. Full participation with study subjects allows for a deeper understanding of life in such social worlds (Adler and Adler 2012), but this depth must be balanced against the need for objectivity. For example, Alice Goffman's decision to become roommates with two of her informants provided her with up-close access to the reality of their everyday experiences, but it also raised questions about her capacity to remain objective. When one of those informants was later murdered, and the other wanted to go out looking for the killer, she volunteered to drive. Critics later raised questions about whether this act constituted conspiracy to commit murder (Volokh 2015).

In addition to the problem of objectivity, a related concern is whether closeness to those in one part of a community may result in insufficient detail in describing another part. It is impossible to be in all places at all times. The depth that results from a narrow focus on a specific community, and on particular members within it, comes at the expense of breadth.

> **Observation** A research technique in which an investigator collects information through direct participation and/or by closely watching a group or community.
>
> **Ethnography** The study of an entire social setting through extended systematic observation.
>
> **Experiment** An artificially created situation that allows a researcher to manipulate variables.

EXPERIMENTS

Experiments represent the third major research design for collecting data. An **experiment** is a controlled procedure in which researchers assess the effect independent variables have on dependent variables. As much as possible, the goal is to isolate the dependent variable from any other influences so that any change in the dependent variable can be attributed only to the independent variable. In a classic experiment, researchers begin by dividing subjects

Employees at a Westinghouse Electric and Manufacturing Company in 1925.   ©Topical Press Agency/Hulton Archive/Getty Images

Experimental group The subjects in an experiment who are exposed to an independent variable introduced by a researcher.

Control group The subjects in an experiment who are not introduced to the independent variable by the researcher.

Hawthorne effect The unintended influence that observers of experiments can have on their subjects.

with similar characteristics into two groups. Those in the **experimental group** are exposed to an independent variable; those in the **control group** are not. Thus, if scientists were testing a new type of antibiotic, they would administer the drug to an experimental group but not to a control group and compare the outcomes for both groups.

Experiments have become more common in sociology, but they do represent a challenge. Sociologists want to understand people's natural responses in everyday contexts. Most human behavior does not happen in isolation from other influences, so specially created experimental conditions are unlikely to exist in the real world. Sociologists also express ethical concerns about the appropriateness of deliberately manipulating people's responses.

An additional challenge with experiments, which also impacts observation research, is that the mere presence of a social scientist or other observer may affect the behavior of the people being studied. The recognition of this

phenomenon grew out of an experiment conducted during the 1920s and 1930s at the Hawthorne plant of the Western Electric Company near Chicago. A group of researchers set out to determine how to improve the productivity of workers at the plant. The investigators manipulated such variables as lighting and working hours to see what impact the changes would have on how much workers produce. To their surprise, they found that every step they took seemed to increase output. Even measures that seemed likely to have the opposite effect, such as reducing the amount of lighting in the plant down to moonlight levels, led to higher productivity (Mayo 1933).

Why did the plant's employees work harder even under less favorable conditions? The researchers initially concluded that the workers modified their behavior because they knew they were being studied. They responded positively to the novelty of being subjects in an experiment and to the fact that researchers were interested in them. Since that time, sociologists have used the term **Hawthorne effect** to describe the unintended influence that observers of experiments can have on their subjects, even though later studies show the situation in the plant was more complex (Brannigan and Zwerman 2001). It highlights the difficulties experiments present in seeking to understand how people behave in their real-world environments.

White Privilege in Job Seeking

Percent chance of getting a call back

White — No criminal record: **34%**

17% Criminal record

Black — No criminal record: **14%**

5% Criminal record

Source: Pager 2003:958. *Photo:* ©Dolas/iStock/Getty Images

SOCTHINK

Imagine you are a researcher interested in the effect playing computer or console games has on a college student's grades. How might you go about setting up an experiment to measure this effect?

Sociologists sometimes conduct what are called natural experiments, which seek to approximate experimental conditions in the field. For example, sociologist Devah Pager (2003, 2007) devised an experiment to assess the impact a job applicant's criminal background might have on an individual's employment opportunities. In addition, she introduced race as a control variable. She sent four polite, well-dressed young men out to look for an entry-level job in Milwaukee, Wisconsin. All four were 23-year-old college students, but they presented themselves as high school graduates with similar job histories. Two of the men were Black and two were White. One Black applicant and one White applicant claimed to have served 18 months in jail for a felony conviction—possession of cocaine with intent to distribute.

The experiences of the four men with 350 potential employers were vastly different. The White applicant with a purported prison record received only half as many callbacks as the other White applicant—17 percent compared to 34 percent. But as dramatic as the effect of his criminal record was, the effect of his race was more significant, as is evident in the "White Privilege in Job Seeking" graphic. Despite his prison record, the White ex-con received

slightly more callbacks than the Black applicant with no criminal record, 17 percent compared to 14 percent. To assess the validity of her findings, Pager and colleagues later conducted a similar experiment in New York City, and the results were the same (Pager and Pedulla 2015; Pager and Western 2012; Pager, Western, and Bonikowski 2009; Pager, Western, and Sugie 2009). This experiment revealed that when it comes to getting a job, race matters.

USE OF EXISTING SOURCES

Sociologists do not necessarily need to collect new data to conduct research. The fourth major research design, **secondary analysis,** refers to a variety of research techniques that make use of existing data for new analysis. The two major categories of secondary analysis are use of existing data sets and analysis of existing documents.

> **Secondary analysis** A variety of research techniques that make use of existing data for the purpose of new analysis.

Existing data sets consist of data collected by researchers, often for other purposes, that other researchers can then use to investigate their own hypotheses. Existing data sets provide a simple record of the responses the original investigators gathered before they conducted their analysis. The U.S. Census Bureau provides a treasure trove of such data. Every 10 years, as required by the U.S. Constitution, the Bureau attempts to collect data from every household in the United States. In 2010, it ultimately gathered information from 99.62 percent of the nation's housing units. In addition to their decennial census, Census researchers also regularly collect data using representative samples of the U.S. population. Gathering data on that scale is very expensive and time-consuming, so the information the Census provides is extremely valuable to researchers.

Another invaluable existing data set comes from NORC (National Opinion Research Center) in the form of its General Social Survey (GSS). First administered in 1972, the GSS is a national survey conducted every other year, administered in both English and Spanish, of a representative sample of the U.S. adult population who are interviewed in depth on a variety

Source: U.S. Census Bureau, Public Information Office (PIO)

of topics, including employment history, education, political preferences, religious beliefs, gun ownership, abortion rights, and more. NORC surveyors frequently ask the same questions over multiple years, allowing for analysis of how responses change over time. The GSS Data Explorer is available online for anyone to use.

Using existing data sets can allow us to see trends or patterns that the original researchers might have never considered. For example, every year the Social Security Administration's Popular Baby Names site updates its data on the thousands of registrations it receives for newborn babies. Using these data, we can recognize shifts in cultural trends. The name John was in the top five for boys from 1900 until 1972 but has since fallen to 27th. The name Mary ranked number one or two from 1900 through 1965 and now ranks 126th. By contrast, the name Juan was ranked 215th in 1900, peaked at 46th in 1999, and now ranks 137th. Maria went from 150th in 1900, peaked at 31st from 1973 to 1975, and now ranks 111th (Social Security Administration 2018). These shifts reflect the growing influence of the Latinx population in the United States.

> **Content analysis** The systematic coding and objective recording of data, guided by some rationale.

Existing data from another source, the U.S. Census Bureau, confirm this shift. Analysis of these data revealed that although Smith remained the most common surname in the United States, Garcia and Rodriguez rose into the top 10 starting in 2007 (Chalabi and Flowers 2014). This marked the first time in the nation's history that a non-Anglo name had been counted among the most common names. Such name changes reflect an overall shift in the U.S. population from a nation composed primarily of European descendants to one that is more globally diverse, a trend sociologists expect will continue (Word et al. 2007). In a statistical analysis seeking to combine first and last names, researchers estimate that James Smith is the most common name in the United States. Maria Garcia comes in at 15th (Chalabi and Flowers 2014).

In addition to using existing data sets, secondary analysis can also involve existing documents. Studying newspapers, periodicals, diaries, songs, radio and television recordings, websites, legal papers, and many other possible types of documents provides insight into how people think and act. Even better is that documents can come not only from the present, but also from the past, making historical sociology possible. We cannot conduct surveys, interviews, participant observation, or experiments with people in the 1860s, for example, but we can still learn valuable sociological lessons about them by analyzing the records they left behind.

One of the most frequently used techniques when conducting such research is **content analysis,** which is the systematic coding and objective recording of data, guided by a given rationale. Erving Goffman (1979) used content analysis when he conducted a pioneering exploration of how advertisements portray women. The ads he studied typically showed women in secondary and dependent roles.

SOCTHINK

"Name Voyager" at www.babynamewizard.com is an application that allows you to type in any name to trace its popularity over time. Go there and enter several names to see how their use has changed. Considering some of the names you tried, what factors might have contributed to their rise and fall? How popular is your first name? How and why has its popularity changed over time?

Ads portrayed women using caressing and touching gestures more than men. Even when presented in leadership roles, women were likely to be shown striking seductive poses or gazing out into space. Jeanne Kilbourne's content analysis of ads in her film *Killing Us Softly 4: Advertising's Image of Women* (2010) demonstrates that women continued to be portrayed as objects. She found that advertisers' primary message is that women should spend their time, energy, and money trying to attain the idealized, airbrushed image of female beauty achievable only with the assistance of Photoshop. She quotes supermodel Cindy Crawford as saying, "I wish I looked like Cindy Crawford" (Kilbourne 2010).

In addition to allowing for historical research, one of the appeals for sociologists of secondary analysis is that it is nonreactive—that is, doing this type of study does not influence how people respond. For example, Émile Durkheim's statistical analysis of existing suicide data had no impact on people's likelihood of dying by suicide. In other words, secondary analysis enables researchers to avoid the problems associated with the Hawthorne effect.

Most Common U.S. Surnames

Surname	Value
Smith	8.0
Johnson	6.3
Williams	5.3
Brown	4.7
Jones	4.7
Garcia	4.1
Rodriguez	3.8
Miller	3.7
Martinez	3.7
Davis	3.6
Hernandez	3.4
Lopez	2.9
Gonzalez	2.8
Wilson	2.7
Anderson	2.6

Note: Numbers are per 1,000 people in the population.
Source: Chalabi and Flowers 2014.

Have you ever asked yourself, "What were they thinking?" Maybe it's the music people like, the clothes they wear, the major they choose, the job they get, the person they date, the religion they practice, or the candidate they support. Although sociology cannot provide specific answers for why particular individuals think and act the way they do, it does offer insight into the social factors that influence our choices. Imagine that you had the chance to answer a specific question such as those above. Which would you choose? What independent and dependent variables might you identify? What would your hypothesis be? What research design might you select? What makes sociology fun is that we get to ask questions we are curious about and then go find answers through research.

Model Cindy Crawford, responding to Photoshop airbrushing in ads, once said, "I wish I looked like Cindy Crawford." ©Chirag Wakaskar/Getty Images

Secondary analysis can also be much cheaper, both in terms of time and money, than the other research designs. But that works only if access to the data exists. The biggest challenge secondary analysis faces is that the researcher relies on data collected by someone else. As a result, researchers using existing sources may not find exactly what they want

or need. For example, sociologists who study family violence use data from police and social service agencies on reported cases of spouse abuse and child abuse, but not all incidents get reported to authorities. As a result, important information from nonreporters gets left out of the analysis.

Each of these research designs provides sociologists with data they need to conduct their analyses and draw their conclusions. Although most studies rely on only one type, others use a combination. By conducting both surveys and participant observation, for example, researchers benefit from the advantages both provide. In all cases, however, availability of resources, in terms of both time and money, constrain what is possible.

Major Research Designs

Method	Examples	Advantages	Limitations
Survey	Questionnaires Interviews	Detail and breadth	Depth, time, and money
Observation	Ethnography	Depth and explanation	Time and access
Experiment	Deliberate manipulation of people's social behavior	Control and specificity of cause/effect	Unnatural settings and ethical concerns
Existing sources/ Secondary analysis	Analysis of census or health data Analysis of films or TV commercials	Historical analysis, nonreactivity, and cost	Data collected for some other purpose

>> Research Ethics

Because sociological research involves studying human beings, sociologists must take special care to treat their subjects with respect and not expose them to undue harm. The American Sociological Association (ASA) (1999), in its **Code of Ethics**, laid out its standards of acceptable behavior developed by and for members of a profession. It sets forth the following general principles:

- *Professional Competence:* Use appropriate research techniques in proper ways.
- *Integrity:* Be honest, respectful, and fair.
- *Professional and Scientific Responsibility:* Adhere to the highest scientific and professional standards.
- *Respect for People's Rights, Dignity, and Diversity:* Be unbiased and nondiscriminatory, respecting the dignity and worth of all people.
- *Social Responsibility:* Contribute to the public good.

Over time, these general principles have given rise to some concrete practices for researchers to follow. For example, researchers should secure informed consent from subjects, meaning that, if at all possible, the people being studied should be aware of any possible risks of participation and explicitly agree to participate. To confirm that the research does not place subjects at an unreasonable level of risk, researchers typically submit their proposals to an institutional review board.

Code of ethics The standards of acceptable behavior developed by and for members of a profession.

CONFIDENTIALITY

One of the most common techniques used to protect subjects is to promise them confidentiality, shielding their identity so that others cannot know who participated. Ensuring the privacy of subjects helps protect them from potential negative effects of participation. Sometimes participation can be totally anonymous, so that not even the researcher knows who provided which responses.

Promising confidentiality may seem clear-cut in the abstract but can be difficult to adhere to in practice. For example, should a sociologist who is engaged in participant observation research protect the confidentiality of subjects who break the law? What if the sociologist is interviewing political activists and is questioned by government authorities about the research?

Like journalists, sociologists occasionally find themselves facing the ethical dilemma of whether to reveal their sources to law enforcement authorities. In May 1993 sociologist Rik Scarce was jailed for

─SOC THINK─

Under what circumstances might researchers need to deceive subjects, even if it might result in their emotional harm, in order to get genuine responses?

contempt of court because he declined to tell a federal grand jury what he knew—or even whether he knew anything—about a 1991 raid on a university research laboratory by animal rights activists. At the time, Scarce was doing research for a book about environmental protesters and knew at least one suspect in the break-in. Although he was chastised by a federal judge, Scarce won respect from fellow prison inmates, who regarded him as a man who "won't snitch" (Monaghan 2012; Scarce 2005b).

The ASA, in defense of the principle of confidentiality, supported Scarce's position when he appealed his sentence. Scarce maintained his silence. Ultimately, the judge ruled that nothing would be gained by further incarceration, and Scarce was released after spending 159 days in jail. The U.S. Supreme Court ultimately declined to hear Scarce's case on appeal. The Court's failure to consider his case led Scarce (1994, 1995, 2005a, 2005b) to argue that federal legislation is needed to clarify the right of scholars and members of the press to preserve the confidentiality of those they interview.

RESEARCH FUNDING

An additional concern of the ASA's Code of Ethics is the possibility that funding sources could influence research findings. Accepting funds from a private organization or

The *Exxon Valdez case raised ethical questions about research funding for social scientists.* Bob Hallinen/Anchorage Daily News/MCT/Tribune News Service/Getty Images

even a government agency that stands to benefit from a study's results can clash with the ASA's first principle of maintaining objectivity and integrity in research. As such, all sources of funding should be disclosed.

As an example, when ExxonMobil was ordered to pay $5.3 billion in damages because its oil tanker, *Exxon Valdez*, hit a reef off the coast of Alaska, spilling more than 11 million gallons of oil into Prince William Sound, it appealed the verdict and approached legal scholars, sociologists, and psychologists who might be willing to study jury deliberations. The corporation's objective was to develop academic support for its lawyers' contention that the punitive judgments in such cases result from faulty deliberations and do not deter future incidents. Some scholars have questioned the propriety of accepting funds under such circumstances, even if the source is disclosed. The scholars who accepted ExxonMobil's support deny that it influenced their work or changed their conclusions. ExxonMobil used results from such studies as part of their appeal, ultimately paying $1.25 billion in fines and penalties (Rosen 2016).

VALUE NEUTRALITY

The ethical considerations of sociologists lie not only in the methods they use and the funding they accept but also in the way they interpret their results. Sociologist Max Weber ([1904] 1949) recognized that personal values would influence the topics that sociologists select for research. In his view, that was perfectly acceptable, but he argued that researchers should not allow their personal feelings to influence the interpretation of data. In Weber's phrase, sociologists must practice **value neutrality** in their research. As part of this neutrality, investigators have an ethical obligation to accept research findings even when the data run counter to their own personal views, to theoretically based explanations, or to widely accepted beliefs. One concern raised about Alice Goffman's research on inner-city Philadelphia was that she got too close to her subjects and lost her objectivity. The presupposition in this critique is that taking sides might undercut a researcher's capacity to accurately describe what is going on.

Some sociologists believe that such neutrality is impossible. They worry that Weber's insistence on value-free sociology may lead the public to accept sociological conclusions without exploring researchers' biases. Others have suggested that sociologists may use objectivity as a justification for remaining uncritical of existing institutions and centers of power (Gouldner 1970). Despite the early work of W. E. B. Du Bois and Jane Addams, for example, sociologists still need to be reminded that the discipline often fails to adequately consider all people's social behavior.

Sociologists should not focus only on those in the majority but must also seek out the stories of those

SOCTHINK

To what extent is it possible to maintain value neutrality when studying a social group with which you might disagree (such as White supremacists or convicted child molesters)? Why might sociologists choose to study such groups?

who are often invisible due to their relative lack of power and resources. In fact, sociologists have learned much about society by listening to the voices of those who are excluded from mainstream sources of power and denied access to valuable resources. In her classic book *The Death of White Sociology* (1973), Joyce Ladner called attention to the tendency of mainstream sociologists to investigate the lives of African Americans only in the context of social problems. Similarly, feminist sociologist Shulamit Reinharz (1992) has argued that sociological research should not only include the research of sociologists who are outside the mainstream but should also be open to drawing on relevant research by nonsociologists who might provide additional depth and understanding of social life. The issue of value neutrality does not mean that sociologists can't have opinions, but it does mean that they must work to overcome any biases, however unintentional, that they may bring to their analysis of research.

> **Value neutrality** Max Weber's term for objectivity of sociologists in the interpretation of data.

Movies on SOCIOLOGICAL RESEARCH

5

Kinsey
The father of modern sexual research employs individual case studies.

Science Fair
An exploration of geek culture at the International Science and Engineering Fair for high schoolers.

Monrovia, Indiana
Up close and personal in small-town America.

56 Up
Documentary following 14 children as their lives progress from age 7 to 56.

Devil's Playground
Amish teens experiment with drinking, drugs, and sex before committing to a lifetime within the Amish community.

FEMINIST METHODOLOGY

Although researchers must be objective, their theoretical orientation necessarily influences the questions they ask—or, just as important, the questions they fail to ask. Because their contributions have opened up so many new lines of inquiry, sociologists using the feminist perspective have had perhaps the greatest impact on the current generation of social researchers. Until the 1960s, for example, researchers frequently studied work and family separately, as if they were two discrete institutions. Feminist theorists, however, reject the notion that these are separate spheres. They were the first sociologists to look at housework as real work and to investigate the struggles people face in balancing the demands of work and family (Hochschild 1989; Lopata 1971).

Feminist theorists have also drawn attention to researchers' tendency to overlook women in sociological studies. For most of the history of sociology, researchers conducted studies of male subjects or male-led groups and organizations, then generalized their findings to all people. For many decades, for example, ethnographic studies of urban life focused on street corners, neighborhood taverns, and bowling alleys—places where men typically congregated. Although researchers gained valuable insights in this way, they did not form a true impression of city life, because they overlooked the areas where women were likely to gather, such as playgrounds, grocery stores, and front stoops. These are the arenas that the feminist perspective focuses on.

Feminist scholars have also contributed to a greater global awareness within sociology. To feminist theorists, the traditional distinction between industrial nations and developing countries overlooks the close relationship between these two supposedly separate worlds. Feminist theorists have called for more research on the special role that immigrant women play in maintaining their households, on the use of domestic workers from less developed nations by households in industrial countries, and on the global trafficking of sex workers (Cheng 2003; K. Cooper et al. 2007).

Finally, feminist researchers tend to involve and consult their subjects more than other researchers, contributing to a significant increase in more qualitative and participatory research. They are also more oriented toward seeking change, raising the public consciousness, and influencing policy, which represents a return to sociology's roots (Harding 2003; Naples 2003; Sprague 2005).

Sociologists must be engaged with the world. Although there are numerous ways in which they accomplish this, first and foremost this involvement comes through research. As we have seen throughout this chapter, it is not enough for sociologists to stand back and theorize or even hypothesize about why we think and act the way we do. We must go out, collect data, and use it to inform our interpretations and explanations of human behavior. Having done so, we bear a responsibility for that knowledge, whether that means simply sharing it with other sociologists through conference presentations and journal articles or actively working for positive social change.

> ## The greatest obstacle to discovery is not ignorance—it is the illusion of knowledge.
>
> Daniel Boorstin (1985)

SOCIOLOGY IS A VERB

People Watching

As a mini-observation project, do some intentional people watching. Pick a public place, such as a mall, where people frequently walk by, and record what you observe. What characteristics stick out? How do people vary by gender, age, race, or ethnicity? To what extent do they travel individually or in groups? Record all your observations and then use your data to write up a summary of what you have learned.

FOR REVIEW

I. What distinguishes sociology from common sense as a way of knowing?
- Sociologists conduct systematic empirical research to better understand why we think and act as we do.

II. What steps do sociologists take when seeking to answer why people think and act the way they do?
- They need to define the problem, review existing literature, formulate a hypothesis, collect and analyze data, and develop a conclusion.

III. What techniques do sociologists use to collect data?
- Research designs used to collect data include surveys, observation, experiments, and use of existing sources.

IV. What ethical concerns must sociologists consider while conducting research?
- They have a responsibility to follow the ASA Code of Ethics, particularly respecting confidentiality, revealing research funding, maintaining value neutrality, and overall, treating their subjects with respect.

Functionalist View

Sociological research seeks to better understand how the various parts of society fit together to create social order and stability.

Researchers focus on consensus and cooperation and on the large-scale (or macro) level, looking at society from the top down.

Research can also help determine whether the facets of our society are functioning as intended. For example, does more education "pay off" in higher income?

STABILITY, CONSENSUS, COOPERATION
KEY CONCEPTS

Conflict View

Sociological research seeks to better understand how power operates and how resources are distributed and controlled.

Focus of research tends to be on the large-scale (or **macro**) level, looking at society from the top down.

Key questions behind research include: Who benefits? How does the status quo maintain privileges for some and denial of opportunity for others? How does access to resources shape outcomes?

KEY CONCEPTS
INEQUALITY, STRATIFICATION, INTERESTS

Interactionist View

Sociological research seeks to better understand how we construct meaning and establish order through everyday interactions with others.

Focus of research is on the small-scale (or micro) level, looking at the construction of society from the bottom up.

Researchers are most likely to use participant observation because it provides a window into people's everyday lived experiences.

KEY CONCEPTS
ROLES, SYMBOLS, LABELING

MAKE THE CONNECTION

After reviewing the chapter, answer the following questions:

1
Which perspective did Alice Goffman use in her research? Why?

2
How might each perspective study the relationship between education and income in a slightly different way?

3
How might a researcher's perspective influence the research design he or she picks? Give an example for each perspective.

4
How might each perspective interpret Devah Pager's findings in her experiment about race and job seeking?

Pop Quiz

1. One limit of common sense as a way of knowing is its tendency to favor evidence that supports our existing beliefs while minimizing or ignoring contrary evidence, which is known as
   a. operationalization.
   b. confirmation bias.
   c. correlation.
   d. value neutrality.

2. An explanation of an abstract concept that is specific enough to allow a researcher to measure the concept is a(n)
   a. hypothesis.
   b. correlation.
   c. operational definition.
   d. variable.

3. In sociological and scientific research, a hypothesis
   a. is an educated guess.
   b. is a testable statement about the relationship between two or more variables.
   c. insists that science can deal only with observable entities known directly to experience.
   d. ensures that the people being studied are representative of the population as a whole.

4. The variable hypothesized to cause or influence another is called the
   a. dependent variable.
   b. hypothetical variable.
   c. correlation variable.
   d. independent variable.

5. The degree to which a measure or scale truly reflects the phenomenon under study is known as
   a. reliability.
   b. sampling.
   c. validity.
   d. control.

6. Which research technique do sociologists use to ensure that data are statistically representative of the population being studied?
   a. sampling
   b. experiment
   c. correlation
   d. control variables

7. Ethnography is an example of which type of research design?
   a. surveys
   b. observation
   c. experiment
   d. use of existing resources

8. When Devah Pager did her studies analyzing the relationship between race, criminal records, and job callbacks, which research technique did she use?
   a. experiment
   b. survey
   c. secondary analysis
   d. participant observation

9. The unintended influence that observers of experiments can have on their subjects is known as
   a. the correlation effect.
   b. confidentiality.
   c. validity.
   d. the Hawthorne effect.

10. According to Max Weber, researchers should not allow their personal feelings to influence the interpretation of data. He referred to this as
    a. the code of ethics.
    b. content analysis.
    c. value neutrality.
    d. secondary analysis.

1. (b), 2. (c), 3. (b), 4. (d), 5. (c), 6. (a), 7. (b), 8. (a), 9. (d), 10. (c)

3

Culture

MAKING A SCENE

On January 13, 2019, Charlie Todd took a train ride on the New York City subway. He wasn't wearing any pants. Charlie was not alone. In fact, he was joined by thousands of other pantsless riders in New York City that day. They gathered in six locations around the city, boarded numerous different subway lines, and headed toward a rendezvous at Union Station. They spaced themselves out across many subway cars, had minimal interaction with one another, and acted as normally as possible. The event was all part of the now-annual No Pants Subway Ride coordinated by Improv Everywhere, a self-described "prank collective that causes scenes of chaos and joy in public places," which Charlie Todd founded in 2001.

Improv Everywhere has sponsored more than 160 missions, some of which may be familiar because its videos have often gone viral. The No

Pants event started in 2002 with just seven participants and grew larger and larger, celebrating its 18th anniversary in 2019 with thousands of participants worldwide in dozens of cities, including Amsterdam, Buenos Aires, and Prague. One of Improv Everywhere's most popular viral videos came from its 2008 mission in New York City's Grand Central Station when more than 200 participants ("agents") converged on Grand Central Station and simultaneously froze in place for five minutes, after which they resumed what they were doing as if nothing had happened. In 2017, Improv Everywhere threw a pretend Sweet 16 surprise birthday party on a subway car, complete with balloons, streamers, and cupcakes, to see if it could get a car full of random strangers to play along. In 2018, it staged a bar trivia contest surprise, complete with a gameshow host, cheering audience, and confetti and cash for the win. (Videos for these and many other missions are available at ImprovEverywhere.com.)

The scenes that Improv Everywhere creates help reveal our taken-for-granted rules for behavior. In our daily lives we follow routines that are largely invisible to us, and we expect others to do likewise. When people do things differently, we tend to get uncomfortable. It disrupts our sense of order. One of the best parts of the Improv Everywhere videos is watching how people respond. Initial confusion and nervousness are often followed by smiles as people realize they are participating in a performance. We want and need the actions of others to be predictable, so we create both formal and informal rules to guide our behaviors. Such rules are an important component of culture.

As You READ >>

- **Why do humans create culture?**
- **What does culture consist of?**
- **How does culture both enable and constrain?**

>> The Social Construction of Reality

The relationship between the individual and society rests at the very heart of sociology. Sometimes we choose to do the unexpected, like not wear pants on the subway, but most of the time we obey normal social conventions, such as only going pantsless on No Pants Subway Ride days. In working out the relationship between our individual selves and our social context, we are engaged in the "**social construction of reality.**" Sociologists Peter Berger and Thomas Luckmann (1966) coined this phrase to describe the ongoing interdependent relationship within which individuals create society through our actions and, at the same time, become products of the society we construct. Their three-step model of world construction includes the following elements.

- *Constructing culture.* Our actions are not strictly determined by biological instincts. To survive, we must establish a relationship to nature and with one another. We do so by creating tools, language, ideas, beliefs, rules for behavior, and so on to establish order and meaning. Culture enables us to make sense of our experiences and to pattern our actions. (See the section "Constructing Culture" for more on this.)
- *Constructing the self.* Through socialization, we become products of the worlds we create. Anytime we enter into a new social world (for example, at birth, going away to college, the first day at a new job, marriage) we do not begin from scratch. We are shaped by the tools, ideas, and rules for action that have been constructed by others who have gone before us. We learn how we should think and act through our interactions with others, sharing ideas and experiences. Through socialization, we are constrained by the very culture we construct. (See Chapter 4 on socialization.)
- *Constructing society.* Between these first two steps is an intervening stage in which we share the culture we create

with others. After it is shared, we lose control over it as individuals. It is no longer something "I" control; it is now in "our" hands. As a result of our shared acceptance, it comes to feel solid, real, or natural, even though we created it in the first place. One way to think of it is as an environment, a social world, or a structure within which we live. We come to take for granted that it simply "is." (See Chapter 5 on society and social structure.)

In short, the social construction of reality involves an ongoing interaction between individuals and society. As we can see in the "World Construction" graphic, in the first stage, as individuals we have the agency to create and reproduce the material, cognitive, and normative culture we need to survive. At the same time, in the second stage we become ourselves as a consequence of

> **Social construction of reality** The ongoing interdependent relationship within which individuals create society through our actions and, at the same time, become products of the society we construct.

World Construction

Source: McGraw-Hill Education. *Photo:* RTimages/Alamy Stock Photo the socialization we receive from those around us. Through socialization we learn to make choices that reinforce the existing relationships and expected behaviors that have been routinized and solidified over time in the form of society, as represented in the third stage. As a result, the world around us becomes ordered and predictable. Through social interaction, we are always creating and being created, producers and products. In this chapter, focusing on the first stage of the model, we explore the ways in which we create culture and why we do so. We will explore the other two stages in Chapters 4 and 5.

>> Constructing Culture

We need culture. As humans, we lack the complex instincts other species are born with that enable them to survive.

Culture Everything humans create in establishing our relationships to nature and with each other.

Society The structure of relationships within which culture is created and shared through regularized patterns of social interaction.

Unlike birds, for example, our genes do not provide us with the knowledge to build nests (or homes) for ourselves, and we can choose whether to seek out warmer climates for the winter or cooler ones in the summer. Because our actions are not narrowly determined by such instincts, we must construct their equivalent in order to provide food, clothes, shelter, and a host of other human needs. **Culture** consists of everything humans create in establishing our relationships to nature and with each other. It includes language, knowledge, material creations, and rules for behavior. In other words, it encompasses all that we say, know, make, and do in our efforts to survive and thrive.

Culture mediates between individuals and the external world. While we experience the natural world through our senses—hearing, sight, touch, smell, and taste—we depend on culture to interpret those sensations. Our retinas may send nerve impulses to our brains, but culture gives our brains the ability to transform those nerve

©McGraw-Hill Education/
Jill Braaten, photographer

signals into meaningful patterns. For example, we might fail to see an image in an optical illusion until someone nudges us to "look at it this way." Nothing about the physical image changed, but our perspective on it, with the help of others, has. We do not perceive nature directly; we perceive the world around us through the lens of culture.

Through interactions with others, we develop and share perceptions of what the world is like and how we should act within it. The shared culture that results provides us with a tool kit of similar habits, skills, and styles (Swidler 1986). For example, when someone says hello, we know how to respond. When we show up for the first day of class, we know where to sit or stand depending on whether we are the student or professor. Culture facilitates social interaction.

Over time, we take shared culture for granted. The ways we think, the rules we follow, the things we have created all seem natural to us. We pass along these expectations to others within the contexts of families, schools, places of worship, and workplaces. As a result, we know what to do, when to do it, and with whom. In so doing, we create society. **Society** consists of the structure of relationships within which culture is created and shared through regularized patterns of social interaction. Society provides the taken-for-granted structure within which we interact. It both enables and constrains the culture we construct. In a given society, some ways of thinking, acting, and making seem inevitable, whereas other ways may not even be conceivable. For example, the way our society organizes government determines our rights and responsibilities, and the way we organize education shapes how and what we learn.

Societies construct cultures in different ways, which results in significant cross-cultural variation. People often confront this reality when they travel abroad and find their taken-for-granted ideas and actions to be out of place and inappropriate. Language, gestures, marriage ceremonies, and religious doctrines vary significantly. In India, parents are accustomed to arranging marriages for their children, but in the United States,

Going GLOBAL

Is Success in Life Determined by Forces Outside Our Control?

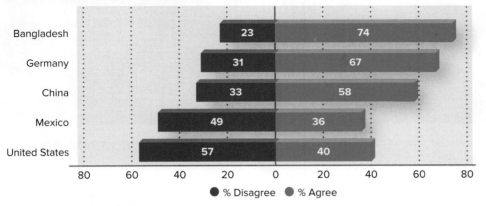

● % Disagree ● % Agree

Source: Pew Research Center 2014a.

As the graph illustrates, perceptions about the degree to which we control our fates vary by country. In a survey of 44 nations, only Venezuelans (62 percent) were more likely than people in the United States to disagree. The global median was 38 percent.

argument, the genes we inherit determine our outcomes, as if our fates were programmed by computer code over which we have limited control. **Sociobiology** is a discipline dedicated to the systematic study of how biology affects human social behavior. On the other side, "nurture" means that our destiny is shaped primarily by the social influences that others, especially parents and early childhood caregivers, have on us. From the nurture perspective, human nature is malleable, and we become who we are in the contexts of the societies we create.

Sociological research reveals significant cross-cultural and cross-time variation in how we think and act, leading sociologists to prioritize the significance of nurture. For example, in the 19th century, experts thought that, biologically speaking, women were not capable of success in college because their brains were too small and their reproductive organs made them too emotional. As a result, they denied women the opportunity to go to college, justifying it as as being in women's best interest not to do so. Over time we learned that such presuppositions are false—women now make up almost 60 percent of college graduates—but at one time these assertions were accepted as "natural" and therefore resistant to change. Similar biologically based claims have been used in the past to justify racial, ethnic, and social class inequality (claims that were later revealed to be scientifically untrue), leading many sociologists to question biological explanations for human behavior (Lucal 2010).

> **Cultural universal** A common belief or practice shared by all societies.
>
> **Sociobiology** The systematic study of how biology affects human social behavior.

Over time, natural scientists have increasingly affirmed that the either-or quality of the nature-nurture argument conceals the fluid nature of the two forces. Within the scientific community, support has grown for gene-culture coevolution, in which each shapes the other through the course of human development. From this perspective, how individuals turn out isn't simply a matter of whether they inherited a set of "bad genes" or "good genes." Instead, researchers argue that an interdependent relationship exists between genes and environment. How genes are expressed (whether or not they are triggered, in other words) can depend on our natural, social, and cultural contexts. Genes are responsive to the social context and do not inevitably trigger predetermined responses at predetermined times (Rutter 2010; Rutter, Moffitt, and Caspi 2006; Shenk 2010).

parents typically leave such choices up to their children. Lifelong residents of Cairo consider it natural to speak Arabic, whereas most Buenos Aires natives feel the same way about Spanish.

CULTURAL UNIVERSALS

Early sociologists explored the possibility that natural or social forces might determine what human culture would look like. Auguste Comte, for example, suggested that fundamental laws of society, equivalent to the laws of nature, might dictate the essential elements of all human cultures. Such patterns were referred to as **cultural universals**—common beliefs and practices shared by all societies. Anthropologist George Murdock (1945) compared results from studies of hundreds of cultures and concluded that, although there are common denominators shared by all cultures, how cultures go about addressing each varies significantly. Included among his list of 70 categories were athletic sports, community organization, dancing, division of labor, folklore, funeral rites, housing, incest taboos, marriage, personal names, property rights, religious ritual, sexual restrictions, and trade. The degree of human variation we see in how we organize such activities suggests that we do not have universal laws strictly determining human behavior.

The debate about the degree to which our behavior is determined harkens back to philosophical questions regarding nature versus nurture. According to the "nature"

In Guatemala, Tanzania, and around the world, material culture varies across time and place. (left): ©Chris Rennie/Robertharding/Getty Images; (right): ©Judy Bellah/Lonely Planet Images/Getty Images

INNOVATION

Because our genes do not narrowly determine our behavior, humans have the freedom and ability to create new things. Whereas a robin's nest in the year 2020 looks very much like one in 1920 or 1020 because robins act on a nest-building instinct, human abodes vary widely. We can live in a cave, a castle, a sod house, a pueblo, a high-rise apartment, a McMansion, or a dorm room. Such variation is possible because we are free to innovate. **Innovation** is the process of introducing a new idea or object to a culture. There are two main forms of innovation: discovery and invention.

A **discovery** occurs when someone reveals a previously unknown aspect of reality. The identification of the DNA molecule and the detection of Proxima b orbiting the nearest star to our Sun, the closest Earth-like planet with the potential capacity to host life ever found, are both acts of discovery. For a claim to count as a discovery, it must be both novel and significant (Woolgar 1988). In other words, it must be something that was previously unknown and something that matters to others. Finding a hole in my sock might be news to everyone, including myself, but it's not particularly important. Attending a Shakespeare play for the first time and being blown away by how amazing it is might matter a lot to me, but it's not exactly a revelation to others. In other words, when deciding whether something counts as a discovery, we should always ask "To whom is this news?" and "How much does it matter to them?" For example, the notion that Columbus was the one who "discovered" America would come as a surprise to the people already living there, not to mention the many generations of their ancestors who preceded them.

Innovation The process of introducing a new idea or object to a culture through discovery or invention.

Discovery The process of revealing a previously unknown aspect of reality.

Comedy often draws inspiration from the sociological imagination. The website College Humor, for example, coined the term *Columbusing* to describe the process of White people taking credit for discovering things others have known about for a long time. In its satirical video, a young, White man claims to have "discovered" a bar, despite the fact that his African American friend has been going there for some time. Debates about what counts as Columbusing can divide people. For instance, some people argue that "color runs," in which participants get their shirts splashed with various colors along the running route, derive their inspiration from Holi, the Hindu spring festival of colors without any recognition of, or respect for, this foundation. Others view such runs as harmless fun (Agrawal 2013; Salinas 2014).

Photo: ©Chelsea Lauren/S. C. Johnson & Son, Inc./Getty Images

POPSOC

The second form of innovation, **invention,** combines existing materials to create something new. We are creative beings. We invent new technologies, new theories, new works of art, new ways of doing things, and so much more. The bow and arrow, the automobile, and the iPhone are all examples of inventions, as are abstract concepts such as Protestantism and democracy. Inventors are often portrayed as solitary geniuses who experience "Eureka!" moments of inspiration, but research on technological innovation, for example, reveals just how social the process is. To invent something, we must take into account existing social networks, available resources, possible sponsors, potential consumers, probable critics, and so much more. A great idea or object alone is not enough (Bijker, Hughes, and Pinch 2012). Neither discovery nor invention should be divorced from the social context within which it arises. Existing culture can both facilitate and impede possible innovation.

Belinda Wong, CEO of Starbucks China, oversees the company's fastest-growing market.
Jason Redmond/AFP/Getty Images

DIFFUSION

For innovation to succeed, others must recognize and accept the new discovery or invention. Sociologists use the term **diffusion** to refer to the process by which some aspect of culture spreads within and between societies. Historically, diffusion between societies occurred primarily through deliberate cross-cultural contact, often in the form of exploration, war, and missionary work. Today, societal boundaries that were once relatively closed have become more permeable, largely as a result of innovations in transportation and communication. Through the mass media, the Internet, immigration, and tourism, we regularly confront the people, beliefs, practices, and artifacts of other cultures.

The global expansion of fast-food chains provides a classic example of cultural diffusion. McDonald's began with a single restaurant in San Bernadino, California, in 1940, and now has 14,036 U.S. locations and 23,205 in other nations around the world (McDonald's Corporation 2018). Similarly, Starbucks, with its familiar green logo, was founded in Seattle, Washington, in 1971 but now has 28,916 stores globally which includes 14,451 in the United States. The first Starbucks in mainland China opened in 1999, and by 2018 China had 3,598 of them. The success of Starbucks in a country where tea has always been the beverage of choice is striking. In fact, for many in China, drinking coffee has now become a status symbol of middle-class success (Christian 2009; Halper 2013; Loxcel Geomatics 2018).

Diffusion often comes at a cost. In practice, globalization has led to the cultural domination of developing nations by more affluent nations. In these encounters, people in developed nations often pick and choose the cultural practices they find intriguing or exotic, whereas people in developing nations often lose their traditional values and begin to identify with the culture of the dominant nations. They may discard or neglect their native language and dress, attempting to imitate the icons of mass-market entertainment and fashion. In this way, Western popular culture represents a threat to native cultures. For example, Walt Disney's critics have called his work "perhaps the primary example of America's cultural imperialism, supplanting the myths of native cultures with his own" (Gabler 2006). So something is gained and something is lost through diffusion, and often it is the poorer societies that sacrifice more of their culture.

Invention The combination of existing materials to create something new.

Diffusion The process by which a cultural item spreads within and between societies.

>> Three Elements of Culture

The culture we create can be grouped into three general categories: material, cognitive, and normative. Each type enables us to interact more effectively with the world around us. We look at each in turn.

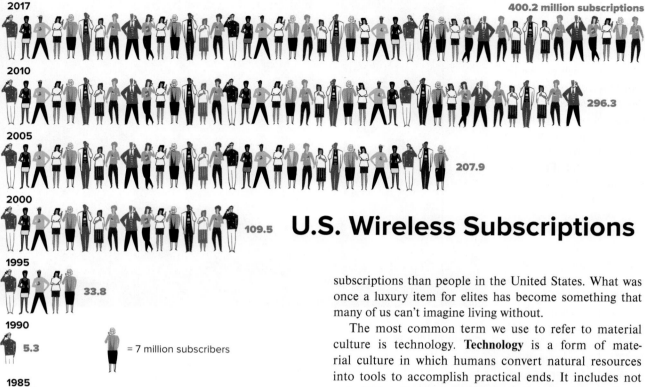

2017   400.2 million subscriptions

2010   296.3

2005   207.9

2000   109.5

U.S. Wireless Subscriptions

1995   33.8

1990   5.3   = 7 million subscribers

1985   0.3

Technology makes it possible for us to keep in touch with almost anyone anywhere, as these numbers showing the explosion in the number of wireless device subscriptions since 1985 demonstrate.

Source: CTIA 2018.

MATERIAL CULTURE

Because we lack complex instincts that determine our behavior, we must establish a relationship to the natural world in order to survive. We do so by creating **material culture,** our physical modification of the natural environment to suit our purposes. Material culture includes the clothes we wear, the books we read, the chairs we sit in, the carpets we walk on, the lights we use, the buildings we live in, the cars we drive, the roads we drive on, and so much more.

Once created, such objects become part of our lives. We lose sight of the fact that we made them, thinking of them as just natural. Take cell phones, for example. As we can see in the "U.S. Wireless Subscriptions" graph, back in 1985 there were only 340,213 total cell phone subscribers in the United States. By the end of 2017, that number rose to 400,205,829 including 273 million smartphones (CTIA 2018). There are now more wireless device

Material culture Our physical modification of the natural environment to suit our purposes.

Technology A form of material culture in which humans convert natural resources into tools to accomplish practical ends.

Cultural lag The general principle that technological innovation occurs more quickly than does our capacity to perceive, interpret, and respond to that change.

subscriptions than people in the United States. What was once a luxury item for elites has become something that many of us can't imagine living without.

The most common term we use to refer to material culture is technology. **Technology** is a form of material culture in which humans convert natural resources into tools to accomplish practical ends. It includes not only high-tech items such as computers, cars, and cell phones, but low-tech items including clubs, wheels, spoons, and chalk.

Technology enhances our human abilities, giving us powers we often associate with superheroes, including X-ray vision, healing powers, flight, and more. A pivotal moment in the development of such power was the invention of the steam engine during the Industrial Revolution. It provided us with historically unprecedented strength and stamina—the ability to lift and move extremely heavy objects and to do so over sustained periods of time. It made modern coal mining practical, provided manufacturing machinery with the power needed for early factories, and powered early tractors and locomotives, setting the stage for modern global mobility (Rosen 2010).

Advances in technology, especially when it comes to the revolutions in communication and transportation, have linked more individuals in a global network than was ever possible in the past. Cell phones enable us to stay in touch with friends and family from almost anywhere. Planes, trains, and automobiles allow us to travel over long distances in almost no time at all, reducing the historic significance of geographic separation and isolation. And laptops and iPads allow us to bring the workplace with us wherever we go.

Our knowledge, beliefs, values, and laws—core elements of cognitive and normative culture described in more detail below—cannot always keep up with the pace at which we invent new things. Sociologist William F. Ogburn (1922) coined the term **cultural lag** to describe the general principle that technological innovation occurs more quickly than does our capacity to perceive, interpret, and respond to that change. For example, the nine-month school calendar was designed with an agricultural economy in mind so that children would be home to help families in the fields during the summer months. Even though only a small percentage of jobs remain agricultural, most schools still adopt it. Another example is that global climate change has become a pressing concern. Scientists overwhelmingly point to the role carbon dioxide plays, yet we find it difficult to make the kinds of lifestyle changes that might be called for, such as driving smaller cars, using more public transportation, or reducing consumption.

COGNITIVE CULTURE

The second component of culture, **cognitive culture,** consists of our mental and symbolic representations of reality. It is the part of culture that includes values, beliefs, knowledge, and all other ideas we construct to make sense of the world around us. Its most basic component, and perhaps the most important human cultural creation of all, is language.

Language The building block of all communication and cooperation, **language** is a system of shared symbols; it includes speech, written characters, numerals, symbols, and nonverbal gestures and expressions. It provides the foundation of a common culture because it facilitates day-to-day exchanges with others, making collective action possible. According to Ethnologue, a database of all known languages around the world, 7,097 living languages exist today. Of these, 1,559 (22 percent) are classified as "in trouble," and 922 (13 percent) are "dying." There are 151 languages with fewer than 10 speakers, and 370 languages have become extinct since 1950 (Simons and Fennig 2018).

> **Cognitive culture** Our mental and symbolic representations of reality.
>
> **Language** A system of shared symbols; it includes speech, written characters, numerals, symbols, and nonverbal gestures and expressions.

Culture, Technology, and Superheroes

Have you ever thought about technology as providing us with superhero powers? Some superheroes (Superman and the X-Men) are born that way, but others gain their powers the old-fashioned way: They invent them. Characters such as Ironman and Batman appeal to us in part because they rely on human innovation for their strength and stamina. Technology makes them faster than a speeding bullet or more powerful than a locomotive. What other superhero-like powers does technology provide us?

POPSOC

Photo: Marvel Enterprises/Album/Alamy Stock Photo

Did You Know?

. . . **James Watt is widely credited as the inventor of the steam engine. But Hero of Alexandria was a mathematician in the 1st century AD who reportedly invented a steam engine device known as an *Aeolipile*. And Thomas Newcomen invented the first practical steam engine in 1712 to pump water from coal mines. It was this invention that Watt modified with the addition of a separate condenser to make it more efficient, for which he received a patent in 1769 (Rosen 2010).**

Photo: Album/Alamy Stock Photo

Did You Know?

. . . Marc Platt, producer of the Broadway play *Wicked* and numerous movies and TV series, including *Legally Blonde*, *La La Land*, *The Girl on the Train*, and *Mary Poppins Returns*, was a sociology major.

Photo: Thomas Kienzle/AP Images

Language is fundamentally social in nature. Together we agree that certain sounds or shapes mean certain things, and then we act based on those shared meanings. What matters most is our shared perception rather than the actual sound or image we use. We could, for example, teach a dog the wrong meanings of commands (*fetch* means stay, *roll over* means shake, and so on). The dog would never know the difference, but we would laugh because its responses would clash with our expectations. When we start to learn a new language, we are at the mercy of those who teach us. We rely on their authority, and the only way to test our fluency is through interactions with other speakers.

Because language is socially constructed, it is open to change. We create new words and modify existing ones to suit our needs—especially in our modern global culture where innovation seems never-ending. Dictionaries are regularly modified in an effort to keep up. In 2018, the *Merriam-Webster Collegiate Dictionary* added more than 800 new words and phrases, including *bougie, hangry, Latinx, bingeable, tl;dr,* and *GOAT* as in greatest of

all time (Debczak 2018). At the other end of the spectrum, words also disappear over time. The six-volume *Dictionary of American Regional English* documents words with meanings that seldom extend beyond their local U.S. context. Among many possible candidates are 50 words and phrases in danger of extinction, including *bonnyclabber, fleech, frog strangler, popskull,* and *winklehawk* (LaFrance 2016).

Some linguists, including amateurs, have seized on the socially constructed nature of language in hopes of creating whole new languages from scratch, with varying motivations (Peterson 2015). Linguist Arika Okrent (2009) has identified three eras of invented languages. In the first, language creators, sought to establish a more logical system of communication. Inspired by the scientific revolution, they were appalled by the inefficiencies and irregularities of existing languages. They invented new languages in the 17th and 18th centuries (such as Francis Lodwick's *Common Writing* or John Wilkins's *Philosophical Language*) in hopes of providing us with a language in which the relationships between concepts were rational and all the pieces fit together into a coherent whole. They didn't want words to be arbitrary sounds we attach to things, hoping instead to map the essence of things through language. Even though they succeeded in creating coherent systems, the languages they created were difficult to use and failed to attract widespread acceptance.

During the 20th century, the second era of language inventors were motivated by the desire to construct a relatively easy-to-learn, universally accepted language that would transcend national and ethnic differences. They believed that lowering language barriers between nations increased the prospects for world peace. Rather than focus on purity of representation, such inventors emphasized pragmatic communication (Okrent 2009; Peterson 2015). The most successful language of this type was Esperanto, which continues to be used today. It was originally created by Ludwik Zamenhof in 1887 and literally means "one who hopes." Esperanto was intended as a second language, something that people across the world would learn in addition to their native language. It combined various aspects of existing languages in a simplified form to make it easier to learn. Free Esperanto lessons are available on the language learning site Duolingo.

More recently, the third era of constructed languages comes mostly from hobbyists, known as "conlangers," who invent languages for fun and profit. Most undertake the construction of a complete, functioning language as a challenge. The inspiration for these attempts often traces back to J. R. R. Tolkien's creation of Elvish for the *Lord of the Rings* book trilogy. Tolkien was a philologist—one who studies the history, structure, and criticism of language—and he used this knowledge to ensure that his constructed languages followed common linguistic

Going GLOBAL

Distribution of the World's Living Languages by Region of Origin

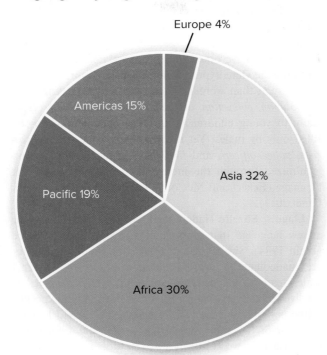

Note: A total of 7,097 languages are represented.
Source: Simons and Fennig 2018.

Of the 7,097 living languages around the world today, 2,143 originated in Africa. Even though 30 percent of current languages come from Africa, only 15 percent of the world's speakers use those languages as their first language. European-based languages claim 26 percent of the world's speakers, despite the fact that only 4 percent of the world's total languages originated there. This difference is due primarily to the global spread of English and Spanish (Simons and Fennig 2018).

patterns and practices. Due to the level of technical detail required, many recent conlangers are often similarly trained, such as Marc Okrand who created Klingon for the *Star Trek* movie franchise (see www.kli.org) and Paul Frommer who created the Na'vi language used in the film *Avatar* (see www.LearnNavi.org). For those who'd like to learn, Duolingo also offers free language instruction in *Star Trek*'s Klingon along with High Valyrian, one of many constructed languages used in the *Game of Thrones* series (Sperling 2016).

Personal Sociology

Inventing New Words

I was reminded of our ability to create new words while on a family hiking trip near Ashland, Oregon. Eleanor, who was four at the time, was riding on my shoulders while on a hike in the mountains. Her sister, Emily, and my wife, Lori, were falling behind. Eleanor turned and yelled to them as loud as she could, "Stop chicken-jagging!" We knew immediately what she meant and have used this word ever since. In order for a sound to become a word, its meaning must be shared by others. For Eleanor's new word to receive formal recognition as a word, in a dictionary, for example, the meaning of *chickenjagging* must be understood and used beyond our immediate family. Have you ever created words and phrases that have meaning only among your friends or family?

In spite of the relative success of Esperanto, none of these invented languages has achieved widespread adoption. Part of what such attempts seem to miss is that language is a community endeavor built up over generations of shared experiences that lead to common understandings of how the world works. Though it is technically possible to create a language from scratch, doing so undercuts the importance that such experiences have in shaping who we are. As linguist Arika Okrent put it in her history of invented languages, "[Languages] are the repositories of our very identities. . . . [Esperanto, along with other invented languages,] asks us to turn away from what makes our languages personal and unique and choose one that is generic and universal. It asks us to give up what distinguishes us from the rest of the world for something that makes everyone in the world the same" (Okrent 2009:112). To the extent that languages such as Esperanto, Klingon, or High Valyrian have succeeded, they do so by creating a community of shared participants who are committed to keeping the language alive.

Once created and shared, the languages we use influence what we see in the world around us. This insight was captured by linguists Edward Sapir and Benjamin Whorf. According to their **Sapir-Whorf hypothesis,** the structure and vocabulary of language shapes our perception of reality and

> **Sapir-Whorf hypothesis** The structure and vocabulary of language shapes our perception of reality and therefore also our actions.

The HBO series *Game of Thrones* utilizes multiple constructed languages. One of them, Dothraki, was created by linguist David J. Peterson, who was a founder of the Language Creation Society. Using just a handful of words and names coined by George R. R. Martin, the author of the book series the show is based on, Peterson built a complete language system (including grammar, syntax, and vocabulary). In 2017, according to the Social Security Administration, 466 parents named their daughters Khaleesi, the Dothraki word for "queen." An introduction to the language is available at www.livinglanguage.com/dothraki. Athchomar chomakaan!

POPSOC

Photo: HBO/Album/Alamy Stock Photo

more recent practice of making a clear distinction between the two colors in Japan has been tied to the importation of crayons into Japan starting in 1917, which distinguished between *midori* (緑) for green and *ao* for blue. The Allied occupation of Japan after World War II reinforced this distinction in educational materials distributed throughout the country (Bhatia 2012). And yet remnants of the earlier linguistic pattern remain in the form not only of "blue" traffic lights, but also of "blue" vegetables, "blue" apples, and "blue" leaves.

Feminists have noted that gender-related language can reinforce the stereotype that some jobs are more appropriate for men than women. Each time we use a term such as *mailman, policeman,* or *fireman,* we are implying (especially to young children) that these occupations can be filled only by males. Yet many women work as *letter carriers, police officers,* and *firefighters*—a fact that has been legitimized through the increased use of such nonsexist language (Eckert and McConnell-Ginet 2003; McConnell-Ginet 2011).

Linguist Suzette Haden Elgin went so far as to invent a new language that gives voice to women's experience (Elgin 1984). She argued that "existing human languages are inadequate to express the perceptions of women," which leads to inadequate perception of critical issues in the lives of women (Elgin 1988). Drawing on her expertise in the Navajo language (*Diné bizaad*), she created Láadan as a test of the Sapir-Whorf hypothesis. She argued that using Láadan would open up new dimensions of reality that are not easily accessible using such languages as English. Láadan lessons for beginners are available at www.LáadanLanguage.org.

therefore also our actions. Also known as the linguistic relativity hypothesis, it suggests that our conception of reality is not strictly determined by nature, but more so by the words, syntax, and semantics available to us in the languages we use. For example, in a literal sense language may color how we see the world. Anthropologist Brent Berlin and linguist Paul Kay (1991) noted that humans possess the physical ability to make millions of color distinctions, yet languages differ in the number of colors they recognize. The English language distinguishes between yellow and orange, but some other languages do not. In the Dugum Dani language of New Guinea's West Highlands, there are only two basic color terms—*modla* for "white" and *mili* for "black" (Roberson, Davies, and Davidoff 2000; Wierzbicka 2008).

In Japan, what people in the United States would call a green light is often called a blue light, even though it is the same color there as it is here. This practice derives from an earlier time in Japan when there was only one word, *ao* (青), to describe both green and blue (Backhaus 2013). The

SOCTHINK

What are some of the slang terms we use to refer to men and to women? Are there more for one gender than the other? What images do such terms convey for what it means to be male or female?

Language can also transmit stereotypes related to race. Look up the meanings of the adjective *black* in dictionaries published in the United States, and you will find "dismal, gloomy or forbidding, destitute of moral light or goodness, atrocious, evil, threatening, clouded with anger." By contrast, dictionaries list "pure" and "innocent" among the meanings of the adjective *white.* Through such patterns of language, our culture reinforces positive associations with the term (and skin color) *white* and negative associations with *black.* Is it surprising, then, that a list meant to prevent people from working in a profession is called a "blacklist," and a fib that we think of as somewhat acceptable is called a "white lie"? Such examples demonstrate that language can shape how we see, taste, smell, feel, and hear (Henderson 2003; Moore 1976; Reitman 2006).

Of course, we communicate using more than just words. If you do not like the way a meeting is going, you might suddenly sit back, fold your arms, and turn down the corners of your mouth. When you see a friend in tears, you may give them a quick hug. After winning a big game, you may high-five your teammates. These are all examples of **nonverbal communication**—the use of gestures, facial expressions, and other visual images to communicate. We are not born with these expressions. We learn them, just as we learn other forms of language, from people who share our culture. We learn how to show—and to recognize—happiness, sadness, pleasure, shame, distress, and other emotional states (Burgoon, Guerrero, and Floyd 2010).

Like other forms of language, nonverbal communication is not the same in all cultures. For example, people from various cultures differ in the degree to which they touch others during the course of normal social interactions. Even experienced travelers are sometimes caught off guard by these differences. In Saudi Arabia a middle-aged man may want to hold hands with a male partner after closing a business deal. The gesture, which would surprise most Americans, is considered a compliment in that culture. The meaning of hand signals is another form of nonverbal communication that can differ from one culture to the next. For instance, in both Australia and Iraq, the thumbs-up sign is considered crude (Koerner 2003; Lefevre 2011).

Values In addition to creating a shared language as part of our cognitive culture, we also jointly agree that some principles are at the core of who we are and what we believe. **Values** are the collective conceptions of what is considered good, desirable, and proper—or bad, undesirable, and improper—in a culture. They are typically expressed as general principles that then shape what we see as appropriate actions. Examples include family, love, opportunity, community, and freedom. Even individualism represents a collective value. As American essayist Richard Rodriguez points out, "American individualism is a communally derived value, not truly an expression of individuality. The teenager persists in rebelling against her parents, against tradition or custom, because she is shielded . . . by American culture from the knowledge that she inherited her rebellion from dead ancestors and living parents" (2002:130). Of course, all members of a society do not uniformly agree on its values. Angry political debates and billboards promoting conflicting causes tell us that much.

> **Nonverbal communication** The use of gestures, facial expressions, and other visual images to communicate.
>
> **Value** A collective conception of what is considered good, desirable, and proper—or bad, undesirable, and improper—in a culture.

The values of a culture may change, but most remain relatively stable during any one person's lifetime. Socially shared, intensely felt values are a fundamental part of our lives in the United States. Sociologist Robin Williams (1970) offered a list of U.S. basic values. These include freedom, equality, democracy, morality, conformity, progress, humanitarianism, and material comfort. Obviously, not all 329 million people in the United States agree on all these values, but such a list serves as a starting point in defining America's national character.

Each year more than 135,000 first-year college students at more than 180 of the nation's four-year colleges fill out a questionnaire asking them which values are most important to them. Because of its coverage, content, and scope, this survey provides a kind of barometer of the nation's values. The top value of the first-year class of 1966, the year the survey was first conducted, was "developing a meaningful philosophy of life," with 80 percent of the new students identifying it as either essential or very important. By contrast, only 44 percent chose "being very well-off financially." Since that time, the relative position of these two values has flipped, as

The classic adolescent eye roll communicates a clear nonverbal message.
©Echo/Cultura/Getty Images

In Arab cultures, men sometimes hold hands as a sign of affection and friendship. ©Dbimages/Alamy Stock Photo

Life Goals of First-Year College Students in the United States

Percentage who identify goal as very important or essential

Develop a meaningful philosophy of life 82.5

Be very well-off financially 49.7
48.1

Help promote racial understanding

Source: Stolzenberg et al. 2019. Photo: ©Carson Ganci/Design Pics

the "Life Goals" graph demonstrates. Among the first-year class of 2017, for example, 82.5 percent identified "being very well-off financially" as a significant value compared to 48.1 percent who selected "developing a meaningful philosophy of life" (Stolzenberg et al. 2019).

SOCTHINK

Consider Williams's list of basic values. Do you think most people value these things? How might some values, such as freedom and conformity, conflict? How do we resolve such conflicts?

Researchers have also studied other family and community values among first-year students. After "being very well-off financially," the second-highest-rated value identified by the 2017 class was "raising a family," at 73.1 percent. "Helping others in difficulty" came in third at 72 percent. The proportion that identified "helping promote racial understanding" rose over the previous year to 49.7 percent (Stolzenberg at al. 2019). As these numbers demonstrate, a nation's values can fluctuate over time.

Because it challenges honesty as a shared value, cheating is a significant concern on college campuses. Professors who take advantage of computerized services that can identify

©Ballyscanion/PhotoDisc/Getty Images

plagiarism, such as the search engine Google or TurnItIn. com, have found that many of the papers their students hand in are plagiarized, in whole or in part. When high school students were asked about academic honesty, 32 percent admitted to copying an Internet document for a classroom assignment, 51 percent said they'd cheated during a test at school, and 74 percent had copied someone's homework, all within the past year. At the same time, 86 percent agreed that "it's not worth it to lie or cheat because it hurts your character" (Josephson Institute of Ethics 2012). Perhaps cheating has become a normal part of student culture even if it is at odds with dominant school values.

NORMATIVE CULTURE

Whereas cognitive culture highlights what we think or believe, normative culture, the third element of culture, focuses on how we act. **Normative culture** consists of the ways we establish, abide by, and enforce principles of conduct. In our everyday lives, we typically abide by **norms**— the established standards of behavior maintained by a society—both big and small, from "Thou shalt not kill" to "Chew with your mouth closed." For a norm to become significant, people must widely recognize and obey it. Most of the time, we follow norms without thinking much about them. Their power derives from our adherence.

Types of Norms Sociologists classify norms into three primary categories: centrality, formality, and adherence. Each represents a continuum along which particular norms fall. First, norms are grouped by their *centrality* to society. **Mores** (pronounced "MOR-ays") are norms deemed highly necessary to the welfare of a society, often because they embody core values. Each society demands strict obedience to its mores; violation can lead to significant penalties. Thus, the United States has strong mores against murder, treason, and child abuse, and punishes each severely. **Folkways** are norms governing everyday behavior. When we are polite—saying please and thank you, not cutting in line, and so on—we are following folkways. Such norms are less rigid in their application, and their violation raises comparatively little concern. Fashion usually represents a folkway. We have some freedom in what we choose to wear. But choosing not to wear clothes, except in clearly defined situations, violates a norm.

Norms are also classified based on levels of *formality.* **Formal norms** generally have been written down and specify strict punishments for violators. In the United States we often formalize norms into **laws,** which are formal norms enforced by the state. But laws are just one example of formal norms. Any systematized set of guidelines, such as the requirements for a college major set forth in a college catalog or the rules of a card game, are also considered formal norms. By contrast, **informal norms** are generally understood but not precisely recorded. We follow largely unspoken rules for all kinds of everyday interactions, such as how to ride on an elevator, how to pass someone on a sidewalk, and how to behave in a college classroom. Knowledge of such norms is often taken for granted.

The third category of norms relates to expected *adherence.* **Ideal norms** are those guidelines for behavior that people agree should be followed. **Real norms** are rules of conduct generated from people's actual behavior. Ideal norms reflect what we collectively say *ought* to be, and real norms reflect what actually *is.* Speeding provides a classic example of the contrast between the two. The posted speed limit reflects the ideal norm, but the truth is that most people exceed that limit regularly, which is a reflection of

> **Normative culture** Consists of the ways we establish, abide by, and enforce principles of conduct.
>
> **Norm** An established standard of behavior maintained by a society.
>
> **Mores** Norms deemed highly necessary to the welfare of a society.
>
> **Folkways** Norms governing everyday behavior, whose violation raises comparatively little concern.
>
> **Formal norm** A norm that generally has been written down and that specifies strict punishments for violators.
>
> **Laws** Formal norms enforced by the state.
>
> **Informal norm** A norm that is generally understood but not precisely recorded.
>
> **Ideal norms** Guidelines for behavior that people agree should be followed.
>
> **Real norms** Rules of conduct generated from people's actual behavior.

5 Movies on U.S. CULTURE

Sorry to Bother You
An African American telemarketer adopts a White accent in pursuit of the American Dream.

En el Séptimo Día (On the Seventh Day)
There's power in community.

If Beale Street Could Talk
A young couple's love runs up against society's injustice.

The Rider
A rodeo champion's riding accident shatters his dreams.

Revolutionary Road
When living the American Dream becomes a nightmare.

the real norm. In a bid to show the difference between the two, students for their film festival entry, *55: A Meditation on the Speed Limit,* stuck to the speed limit while driving side-by-side on the freeway, and blocked traffic for miles with nearly disastrous results. They referred to it as "an extraordinary act of public obedience" (Five Year Plan 2006).

Breaking Norms Although norms provide us with guidelines on how to act, we can choose not to abide by them. Sometimes we violate a norm because we face a choice between conflicting ones. For example, suppose you live in an apartment building and one night hear the screams of the woman next door, who is being beaten by her husband. If you decide to intervene by knocking on your neighbors' door or calling the police, you are violating the norm of minding your own business while at the same time following the norm of assisting a victim of domestic violence.

The speed limit represents one of the most widely violated ideal norms. The posted speed limit makes the law clear, but in practice most people follow the real norm of driving several miles per hour faster.
Rob Byron/Shutterstock

Sometimes we violate a norm because we belong to different societal subgroups that have clashing norms. For example, teenage drinkers may rebel against parental norms by conforming to the standards of their peer group. Similarly, business executives may reject the norms they learned in their graduate school training and choose shady accounting techniques in response to a corporate culture that demands the maximization of profits at any cost, including the deception of investors and government regulatory agencies.

Sanction A penalty or reward for conduct concerning a social norm.

Even if norms do not conflict, there are exceptions to any norm. The same action, under different circumstances, can cause one to be viewed as either a hero or a villain. For instance, secretly taping telephone conversations is normally considered not just intrusive but illegal. However, it can be done with a court order to obtain valid evidence for a criminal trial. We would heap praise on a government agent who used such methods to convict an organized crime figure. In our culture we tolerate killing another human being in self-defense, and

SOCTHINK

Improv Everywhere's No Pants Subway Ride calls people to do something outside their comfort zone. What factors might influence someone's decision to participate? What would it take to get you to participate?

we actually reward killing in warfare, as was evident in the celebrations that followed the death of Osama bin Laden.

Violating norms can also serve as a foundation for social change. Until the 1960s, for example, formal norms throughout much of the United States prohibited the marriage of people from different racial groups. Same-sex marriage wasn't a formally recognized right until a 2014 Supreme Court decision. In most struggles for social change, people who fight against existing norms face ridicule, scorn, and even death threats. It's not until after the fact that such innovations become the new norm. Yet if it wasn't for trailblazing norm-breakers who fought to legitimize an alternative set of norms, change would not occur.

Sanctions When we violate a norm, we can usually expect a response designed to bring our behavior back into line. **Sanctions** are penalties and rewards for conduct concerning a social norm. Sanctions can be applied both externally and internally. Through external policing we use both positive and negative sanctions to influence the behavior of others. Examples of positive sanctions include a pay raise for strong performance, a medal for winning a race, a word of gratitude for a kind deed, or a pat on the back for a job well done. Negative sanctions include fines for overdue library books, imprisonment for a crime, and stares of contempt for texting in a movie theater. Most of the time we do not even need the external enforcement others provide to sanction our acts. Through internal policing, we reward or punish ourselves in ways that encourage or constrain our actions. The anticipation of joy or pride, or the desire to avoid guilt or shame, can serve as powerful motivations for regulating our behavior.

Every moment of our lives we face a decision. We can do what is expected, or we can set out on a different path. As social scientist Gustave Le Bon claimed, in 1895, "Civilization is impossible without traditions, and progress impossible without the destruction of those traditions. The difficulty, and it is an immense difficulty, is to find a proper equilibrium between stability and variability." Following norms provides the order we need, yet also results in a perpetuation of the status quo. Violating norms can lead to positive social change, but it also results in social disruption. And choosing to

The past is never dead.
It's not even past.

William Faulkner (2013)

Break-a-Norm Day

- Wearing formal clothes in an informal setting
- Eating with the wrong utensil or none at all
- Responding to friends or family the same as to a boss or teacher
- Having long gaps in speech when talking with someone
- Standing just a little too close to or far from someone when talking with him or her
- Facing the back of an elevator instead of getting in and turning around

Norms provide us with rules that guide our everyday behavior. All we need to do is step outside the lines even a little bit to see the influence they have over our lives. These are some examples of how people violate norms. How would you feel about violating any of these norms? How might others respond to you? Photos: (dress): ©C Squared Studios/Photodisc/Getty Images; (jeans): ©Gordana Sermek/iStock/Getty Images

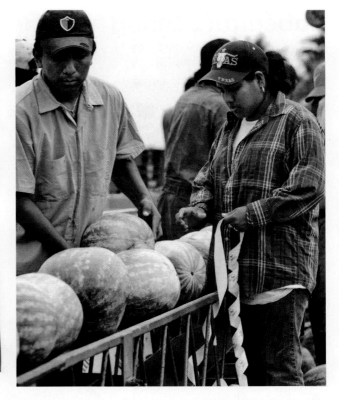

Agricultural strikes and boycotts in the 1960s and 1970s alerted the nation to the harsh economic plight of migrant workers.
©Rob Crandall/The Image Works

5 Movies on CULTURES OUTSIDE THE U.S.

Shoplifters
Sometimes it's better to choose your own family.

Embrace of the Serpent
Worlds collide when an Amazonian shaman, the last of his tribe, encounters two scientists.

Roma
A year in the life of a family living in Mexico City.

Persepolis
An animated coming-of-age film set during the Iranian Revolution.

Departures
An unemployed man violates Japanese norms by becoming an undertaker.

disrupt will likely result in negative sanctions. In a world of norms, we constantly face this tension: to obey or not to obey.

>> Cultural Variation

Together the elements of culture provide us with social coherence and order. But culture also varies across time and place. Individuals' sense of right and wrong works well for them so long as they stay within their usual social confines, but encounters with others beyond that realm can reveal the limits of their conception of reality. Moreover, some people have more power to impose their culture on others, which highlights the importance of understanding the contexts within which culture is created and shared.

ASPECTS OF CULTURAL VARIATION

To more fully understand cultural variation, sociologists pay particular attention to differences that exist both within and between societies. Inuit tribes in northern Canada, clad in furs and dieting on whale blubber, have little in common with farmers in

Subculture Slang

Anime and Manga Fans

chibi eyes: the characteristic, big childlike eyes used in anime

majoko: a girl anime character with magical powers who must save the world

Con Artists & Scammers

grifter: a person who steals through deception

phishing: seeking personal information by sending out emails that appear to be from legitimate companies

Graffiti Writers

bite: to copy another graffiti writer's work

burner: a stylistically impressive, brilliantly colored piece of graffiti, usually written in a complex pattern of interlocking letters and other visual elements

toy: an inexperienced or unskilled graffiti writer

kill: to saturate an area with one's graffiti

Bikers (Motorcyclists)

brain bucket: a helmet

ink slinger: a tattoo artist

pucker factor: the degree of panic felt during a near-accident

yard shark: a dog that races out to attack passing motorcyclists

Skateboarders

deck: a skateboard platform

face plant: a face-first crash

sketchy: in reference to a trick, poorly done

Subcultures often produce their own unique jargon. The words may be appropriate in those subcultures, but they draw a line between insiders and the rest of us.

Source: Reid 2006. Photo: RubberBall Productions/Photodisc/Getty Images

the larger society. Rodeo riders, residents of a retirement community, workers on an offshore oil rig—all are examples of what sociologists refer to as subcultures. The existence of many subcultures is characteristic of complex societies such as the United States.

─SOCTHINK─

What subcultures are common on college and university campuses? What indicators make them recognizable? Why might such subcultures be more likely to form there?

Members of a subculture participate in the dominant culture while engaging in unique and distinctive forms of behavior. Frequently, a subculture will develop its own slang, known as **argot**—specialized language that distinguishes it from the wider society. Such argot allows insiders—the members of the subculture—to understand words with special meanings, which sets them apart from outsiders. In so doing, it clarifies the boundary between "us" and "them" and reinforces a shared identity. We see something like this in the taken-for-granted words and acronyms in the text messaging and social media world. There, abbreviations come fast and furious, from the well known, such as *lol* (laughing out loud), *smh* (shaking my head), *tbt* (throwback Thursday), and *143* (I love you), to the more obscure, such as *1337* (meaning "elite" and referring to symbolic language, or "leet-speak") or *pwned* (leet term meaning "defeated").

In recent years, the growing divide between political subcultures in the United States has led to increased concern about its possible societal consequences. Republicans and Democrats differ on issues such as whether or not immigration is good for America, how commonplace sexual harassment is, whether or not discrimination against Muslims gets taken seriously enough, the degree to which police are mostly fair to people of every race, the likelihood of saying "I'm proud to be an American," and more (Hawkins, Yudkin, Juan-Torres, and Dixon 2018). As everyday encounters between members of the opposite parties decline, as especially evidenced in recent years in social media, misperceptions have grown on both sides of this divide. For example, Republicans think that 38 percent of Democrats are gay, lesbian, or bisexual, when in fact it's 6 percent. On the other hand, Democrats think that 44 percent of Republicans earn over $250,000 per year, when only 2 percent earn that much (Ahler and Sood 2018; Bacon 2018). Such subcultural divisions can reduce trust between the groups which may undercut faith in the common culture presumed to be shared by all (Mason 2018).

Southeast Asia, who dress for the heat and subsist mainly on the rice they grow in their paddies. Cultures adapt to meet specific sets of circumstances, such as climate, level of technology, population, and geography. This adaptation to different conditions shows up in differences in all elements of culture, including language, values, norms, and sanctions.

Subculture A segment of society that shares a distinctive pattern of mores, folkways, and values that differs from the pattern of the larger society.

Argot Specialized language used by members of a group or subculture.

Subcultures Variation can exist within a culture. A **subculture** is a segment of society that shares a distinctive pattern of mores, folkways, and values that differs from the pattern of

©Marvy! Advertising Photography

their repression (Juergensmeyer 2003). Terrorist cells are not necessarily fueled only by outsiders. Frequently, people become disenchanted with the policies of their own country, and a few take very violent steps (Juergensmeyer 2003).

Culture Shock Today we are more and more likely to come into contact with and even immerse ourselves in cultures unlike our own. For example, students increasingly study abroad. Even those who go through predeparture orientation sessions often have a difficult time adjusting once they arrive in-country because so many of the little things that they took for granted, things they barely noticed before, no longer apply. Anyone who feels disoriented, uncertain, out of place, or even fearful when encountering

> **Counterculture** A subculture that deliberately opposes certain aspects of the larger culture.

Countercultures Sometimes a subculture can develop that seeks to set itself up as an alternative to the dominant culture. When a subculture conspicuously and deliberately opposes certain aspects of the larger culture, it is known as a **counterculture.** Countercultures typically thrive among the young, who have the least investment in the existing culture.

The 1960s, now often characterized by the phrase "sex and drugs and rock 'n' roll," provide a classic case of an extensive counterculture. Largely composed of young people, members of this counterculture were turned off by a society they believed was too materialistic and technological. It included many political radicals and "hippies" who had "dropped out" of mainstream social institutions, but its membership was extensive and diverse. The young people expressed in their writings, speeches, and songs their visions, hopes, and dreams for a new society. As was reflected in the 1966 "Life Goals" graph, these young women and men rejected the pressure to accumulate more expensive cars, larger homes, and an endless array of material goods. Instead, they expressed a desire to live in a culture based on more humanistic values, such as sharing, love, and coexistence with the environment. As a political force, they worked for peace—opposing U.S. involvement in the war in Vietnam and encouraging draft resistance—as well as racial and gender equality (Anderson 2007; Gitlin 1993).

In the wake of the attacks of September 11, 2001, people around the United States learned of the existence of terrorist groups operating as a counterculture within their own country. Many nations have had to deal with internal counterculture groups—often rooted in long-standing national, ethnic, or political differences—whose members strongly disagree with the values and norms of the dominant culture. In most cases this does not result in violence, but in some cases, as in Northern Ireland, Israel, and France, groups have used attacks, including suicide bombings, to make a statement, both symbolic and real, seeking to bring attention to their situation and an end to

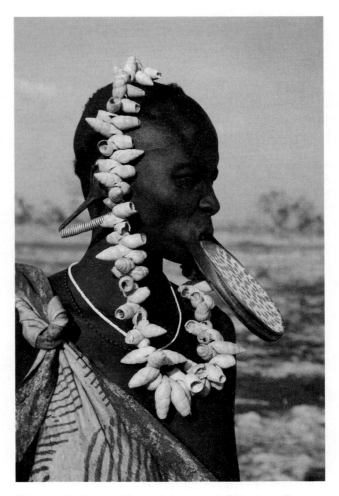

Women in the Suri and Mursi ethnic groups in Ethiopia use lip plates to enhance their beauty. ©Gavin Hellier/Robertharding/Getty Images

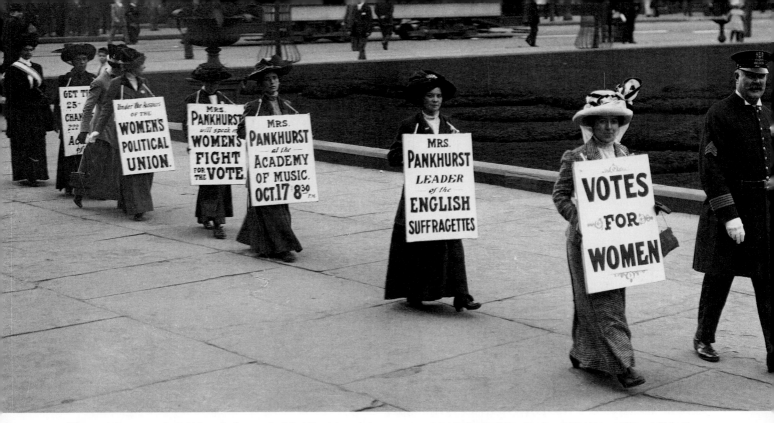

We now take women's right to vote for granted, but it exists only because women challenged the dominant ideology. ©George Rinhart/Corbis Historical/Getty Images

Culture shock The feelings of disorientation, uncertainty, and even fear that people experience when they encounter unfamiliar cultural practices.

Dominant ideology A set of cultural beliefs and practices that legitimates existing powerful social, economic, and political interests.

unfamiliar cultural practices may be experiencing **culture shock.** For example, a resident of the United States who visits certain areas in Cambodia and wants meat for dinner may be stunned to learn that a local specialty is rat meat. Similarly, someone from a strict Islamic culture may be shocked upon first seeing the comparatively provocative dress styles and open displays of affection that are common in the United States and other Western cultures.

Interestingly, after students who study abroad return home, they may experience a kind of reverse culture shock. Their time away has changed them, often in ways they were unaware of, and they find that they cannot so easily slip back into the old routines that those who remained at home expect of them. Culture shock reveals to us both the power and the taken-for-granted nature of culture. The rules we follow are so ingrained that we barely notice that we were following them until they are no longer there to provide the structure and order we assume as a given.

DOMINANT IDEOLOGY

When it comes to gaining cultural acceptance, a group's relative power can determine to what extent it will succeed. One way culture maintains the privileges of certain groups is through the establishment of a **dominant ideology**—the set of cultural beliefs and practices that legitimates existing powerful social, economic, and political interests. The dominant ideology, which is part of cognitive culture, helps explain and justify who gets what and why in a way that justifies and maintains the status quo. Dominant ideas can even squelch alternative expressions of what might be, casting such alternatives as threats to the existing order. Karl Marx argued that the dominant ideas in society maintain the interests of the ruling class. This idea was picked up and developed by sociologists Georg Lukács (1923) and Antonio Gramsci (1929), who argued that the dominant ideology can be used as an instrument of power.

A society's most powerful groups and institutions control wealth and property. They can use their control over these resources to influence religion, education, and the media, thus providing support for the dominant ideology. Feminists argue that if all of society's most important institutions send the message that women should be subservient to men, this dominant ideology helps control and subordinate women (Kleinman 2002). Images of boys and girls in toy ads typically reinforce gender stereotypes, with girls playing with pink and pastel kitchen toys while boys play with pretend power tools and video games. Similarly, women seen in magazine ads reinforce unrealistic (and usually Photoshopped) images of feminine beauty that affect how women see themselves and how men see and treat women.

UNDERSTANDING OTHERS

As sociologists, we have a responsibility to seek to understand others from their perspective. This represents a challenge because our natural inclination is to prefer our own material, cognitive, and normative culture. When we encounter those whose beliefs and practices are significantly different than our own, it is easy to judge their culture as inferior to our own.

Ethnocentrism Sociologist William Graham Sumner (1906) coined the term **ethnocentrism** to refer to the tendency to assume that one's own culture and way of life represent what's normal or is superior to all others. The ethnocentric person sees his or her own group as normal, the standard from which all cultural deviation should be measured. Thus, Westerners who see cattle as a food source might look down on the Hindu religion and culture, which view the cow as sacred. People in one culture may dismiss as unthinkable the mate selection or child-rearing practices of another culture.

Sociologically, we need to understand that some degree of ethnocentrism is normal. If we didn't believe in the values and norms of our community, we would likely change them in favor of something better. The challenge ethnocentrism presents doesn't come from pride in one's community or way of life. It results from the implicit denigration of other nations and cultures when our sense of pride or patriotism comes at the expense of other peoples. Sociologists have a methodological obligation to overcome ethnocentrism in their efforts to better understand why people think and act as they do.

Ethnocentric value judgments complicated U.S. efforts at democratic reform of the Iraqi government. Before the 2003 war in Iraq, U.S. planners had assumed that Iraqis would adapt to a new form of government in the same way the Germans and Japanese did following World War II.

But in the Iraqi culture, unlike the German and Japanese cultures, loyalty to the family and the extended clan comes before patriotism and the common good. In a country in which almost half of all people, even those in the cities, marry a first or second cousin, citizens are predisposed to favor their own kin in government and business dealings. Why trust a stranger from outside the family? What Westerners would criticize as nepotism, then, is actually an acceptable, even admirable, practice to Iraqis (Tierney 2003).

Cultural Relativism Whereas ethnocentrism means evaluating other cultures using the familiar culture of the observer as a standard of correct behavior, **cultural relativism** means viewing other people's behavior from the perspective of those other people's culture. As sociologists we have a responsibility to understand other cultures from their points of view, rather than imposing our own values on them. Unlike ethnocentrists, cultural relativists seek to employ the kind of value neutrality that Max Weber saw as so important.

Cultural relativism stresses that different social contexts give rise to different norms and values. Thus, we must examine practices such as polygamy, bullfighting, and monarchy within the particular contexts of the cultures in which they are found. Cultural relativism is not the same as moral relativism, which implies that no ultimate normative standards exist. Sociologists do not have to abandon their own morals and unquestionably accept every cultural variation. But cultural relativism does require a serious and unbiased effort to evaluate norms, values, and customs in light of their distinctive culture.

Practicing the sociological imagination calls for us to be more fully aware of the culture we as humans have created for ourselves and to be better attuned to the varieties of culture other people have established for themselves. Culture shapes our everyday behaviors all the time, and we select from the tools it provides. For the most part, we are not aware of the degree to which we are immersed in a world of our own making. Whether that includes the capacity to read a book, make a meal, or hug a stranger on the street, it is through culture that we establish our relationship to the external world and with one another.

> **Ethnocentrism** The tendency to assume that one's own culture and way of life represent what's normal or is superior to all others.
>
> **Cultural relativism** The viewing of other people's behavior from the perspective of those other people's culture.

> You never really understand a person until you consider things from his point of view ... until you climb into his skin and walk around in it.
>
> Harper Lee, *To Kill a Mockingbird* (1970)

SOCIOLOGY IS A VERB

Break a Norm

Choose some minor norm of face-to-face interaction (rather than disrupting a group) and violate it. Avoid anything that would harm another person, violate policies, or break the law. Be sure to give the impression that what you are doing is perfectly normal, and record how others respond to you. In what ways do they seek to make sense of your behavior or to restore order? How did breaking the norm affect you? What lessons did you learn about our everyday actions?

For
REVIEW

I. **Why do humans create culture?**

  - Humans lack the complex instincts present in other animals, and as such they must construct a relationship to nature and with each other. We do this through the construction of shared culture.

II. **What does culture consist of?**

  - There are three primary elements of culture. Material culture consists of our modification of the physical environment. Cognitive culture is the thinking part of culture, including language, values, beliefs, and knowledge. Normative culture provides rules for behavior.

III. **How does culture both enable and constrain?**

  - Although culture provides us with the knowledge, rules, and artifacts we need to survive, it also limits our options. Words enable us to see, and tools enable us to make things, but both are designed for particular purposes and shield us from alternative possibilities. Further, with ethnocentrism, we cut ourselves off from new possibilities from different cultures.

PeopleImages/E+/Getty Images

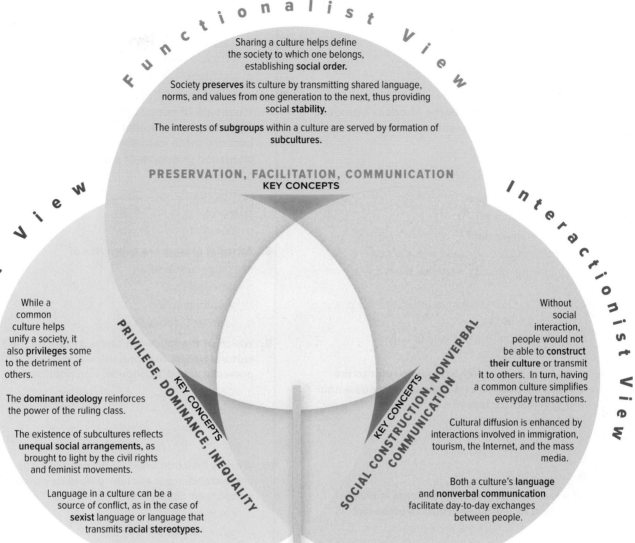

Functionalist View

Sharing a culture helps define the society to which one belongs, establishing **social order.**

Society **preserves** its culture by transmitting shared language, norms, and values from one generation to the next, thus providing social **stability.**

The interests of **subgroups** within a culture are served by formation of **subcultures.**

PRESERVATION, FACILITATION, COMMUNICATION
KEY CONCEPTS

Conflict View

While a common culture helps unify a society, it also **privileges** some to the detriment of others.

The **dominant ideology** reinforces the power of the ruling class.

The existence of subcultures reflects **unequal social arrangements,** as brought to light by the civil rights and feminist movements.

Language in a culture can be a source of conflict, as in the case of **sexist** language or language that transmits **racial stereotypes.**

KEY CONCEPTS
PRIVILEGE, DOMINANCE, INEQUALITY

Interactionist View

Without social interaction, people would not be able to **construct their culture** or transmit it to others. In turn, having a common culture simplifies everyday transactions.

Cultural diffusion is enhanced by interactions involved in immigration, tourism, the Internet, and the mass media.

Both a culture's **language** and **nonverbal communication** facilitate day-to-day exchanges between people.

KEY CONCEPTS
SOCIAL CONSTRUCTION, NONVERBAL COMMUNICATION

MAKE THE CONNECTION
After reviewing the chapter, answer the following questions:

1
How would each of the three perspectives describe the lessons learned from the No Pants Subway Ride?

2
How would each perspective explain the role material, cognitive, and normative culture plays in our lives?

3
How would each perspective approach the role that dominant ideology performs in a culture?

4
How would you use the perspectives to describe one of the subcultures at your school?

Pop Quiz

1. _____ consists of everything humans create in establishing our relationships to nature and with each other.
   a. Innovation
   b. Society
   c. Ethnocentrism
   d. Culture

2. What expression did George Murdock introduce to refer to common practices and beliefs shared by all societies?
   a. norms
   b. folkways
   c. cultural universals
   d. cultural practices

3. What is an invention?
   a. introducing a new idea or object to a culture
   b. combining existing materials to create something new
   c. making known or sharing the existence of an aspect of reality
   d. establishing the legitimacy of a new knowledge claim

4. What term do sociologists use to refer to the process by which a cultural item spreads within and between societies?
   a. diffusion
   b. globalization
   c. innovation
   d. cultural relativism

5. Which of the following statements is true according to the Sapir-Whorf hypothesis?
   a. Language simply describes reality.
   b. Language legitimates existing social, economic, and political interests.
   c. Language shapes our perception of reality.
   d. Language formation is constrained by cultural universals.

6. What do norms provide for us that we need?
   a. shared beliefs that unite us as one
   b. established standards of behavior
   c. a system of shared symbols enabling us to communicate with each other
   d. justification of existing inequality through shared beliefs and practices

7. What type of norms are deemed highly necessary to the welfare of a society, often because these norms embody the most cherished principles of a people?
   a. formal norms
   b. informal norms
   c. mores
   d. folkways

8. Terrorist groups are examples of
   a. cultural universals.
   b. subcultures.
   c. countercultures.
   d. dominant ideologies.

9. Which of the following terms describes the set of cultural beliefs and practices that help maintain powerful social, economic, and political interests?
   a. mores
   b. dominant ideology
   c. consensus
   d. values

10. What is the term used when one seeks to understand another culture from its perspective, rather than dismissing it as "strange" or "exotic"?
    a. ethnocentrism
    b. culture shock
    c. cultural relativism
    d. cultural value

1. (d), 2. (c), 3. (b), 4. (a), 5. (c), 6. (b), 7. (c), 8. (c), 9. (b), 10. (c)

Socialization

SUCCESS AND SOCIAL INFLUENCE

As an unknown author just starting out, J. K. Rowling experienced repeated rejection. Her first book, *Harry Potter and the Philosopher's Stone* (as it's known in England), was turned down by a dozen publishers. Her big break came when Nigel Newton, chair of the board for Bloomsbury Publishing, gave his eight-year-old daughter, Alice, a copy of the first chapter. She loved it. Alice insisted that her father read it and "nagged and nagged" him over the next several months, "wanting to see what came next" (Lawless 2005).

Rowling's story of initial rejection followed by award-winning success and massive sales is hardly unique. Herman Melville's *Moby Dick,* George Orwell's *Animal Farm,* Anne Frank's *The Diary of a Young Girl,* Madeleine L'Engle's *A Wrinkle in Time,* Sylvia Plath's *The Bell Jar,* Ursula K. Le Guin's *The Left Hand of Darkness,* and Meg Cabot's *The Princess Diaries* were all initially rejected by publishers. How is it possible that

the widespread appeal of such works was not obvious to experts in the field who are paid to recognize such things?

Sociologist Duncan Watts, along with two colleagues, conducted an online experiment to measure the power of inherent quality versus social influence in determining artistic success (Salganik, Dodds, and Watts 2006). They presented each of their 14,341 online participants with a list of 48 new songs by unknown artists, asking them to listen to the songs, rate them, and then, if they wanted, download them for free. To test their variables, the researchers divided the participants into nine groups. One of the groups, the control group, was presented only with the name of the artist and title of the song. Participants of the eight other groups, the experimental groups, saw not only the artist and title, but also how many times each song had been downloaded by people within their group. If quality alone mattered, then the same songs should rise to the top or sink to the bottom in all nine groups. But that's not what happened. Knowing how often songs had been downloaded by others affected which songs participants in the experimental groups favored. Songs that were preferred early varied significantly between experimental groups. As a result, the songs that rose to the top also varied (D. Watts 2007, 2011). These results suggest that the popularity of songs, novels, and works of art is not determined by inherent quality alone. Social influence plays a substantial role in determining artistic success. Change that influence, especially early on, and a different outcome is likely.

As You READ >>

- **How do we become ourselves?**
- **Who shapes our socialization?**
- **How does our development change over time?**

>> The Role of Socialization

Babies are extremely vulnerable. They lack even the most basic capacity to care for themselves. Without language to give names to things, without beliefs to give things meaning, without norms to know what to do, without skills to use tools or utensils, how could we possibly survive? The good news is that babies don't have to start from scratch. They benefit from the culture created by those who came before them, learning from them how to talk, think, and act.

In this chapter we will explore the ways in which we become our selves as a consequence of what we learn from

Socialization The lifelong process through which people learn the attitudes, values, and behaviors appropriate for members of a particular culture.

SOCTHINK

What skills that you learned before age two do you now take for granted? From whom did you learn them? In what contexts?

others. This represents the second stage of the "World Construction" graphic introduced in Chapter 3. In the first stage, we construct culture to establish a relationship to nature and with each other. In this second stage, we become products of the worlds we create.

INTERNALIZING CULTURE

Through interactions with others, we learn what we need to know to survive and thrive. Sociologists refer to this practice of internalizing culture as **socialization,** the lifelong process through which people learn the attitudes, values, and behaviors appropriate for members of a particular culture. We absorb culture through interactions with parents, teachers, friends, coworkers, and many others. We are exposed to it in formal contexts, such as schools and workshops, and informal contexts, such as the playground or Instagram. We become who we are through our encounters with others.

Language is perhaps the most basic element of culture we need to learn. We begin teaching it to infants long before they can even understand what we are saying. We start by using baby talk with its higher and more varied pitch, longer vowel sounds, and slower speech. Infants prefer baby talk, also known as infant-directed speech, until they are about eight months old.

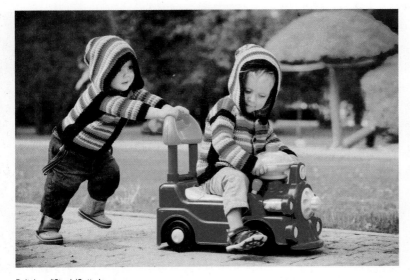

Baltskars/iStock/Getty Images

Such speech provides important building blocks for what will later become a child's native language (Soderstrom 2007).

We can see this process at work when babies begin experimenting with sounds, mimicking what they hear even before they know any words. This was evident when a video of chattering twins went viral. In the video, available on YouTube as "Talking Twin Babies—Part 2," the two 17-month-olds "talked" back and forth, saying little more than "da da da." But they did so with expression, hand gestures, turn taking, and laughter in what seemed like all the right places. They knew what language sounded like—they'd learned that through interactions with family, friends, and others—and it was only a matter of time until they also learned the words that go with it.

Even though baby talk is a near cultural universal, the frequency of sounds, including both vowels and consonants, and the relationships between them vary from culture to culture. An infant in an English-speaking environment hears different combinations than one in a Swedish- or Japanese-speaking context. Such variation provides the foundation for children learning the particulars of their native tongue. For example, English has 10 vowel sounds, whereas Swedish has 16 and Japanese has 5. Baby talk in these different contexts varies accordingly, opening some linguistic pathways while closing others (Kuhl 2004).

THE IMPACT OF ISOLATION

Because socialization at a young age plays a major role in shaping who we become, missing out on such exposure can have a devastating impact on our development. We get a sense for the consequences of such deprivation through studies of children who have experienced extreme childhood isolation and research on primates who are denied care.

Extreme Childhood Isolation
Children who have been isolated or severely neglected (sometimes called *feral children* to suggest that they have reverted to a wild or untamed state) typically have a difficult time

Genie at age 13.   Bettmann/Getty Images

recovering from the lack of early childhood socialization. One famous case was Genie, a 13-year-old girl discovered by California authorities in 1970. Genie had been kept in extreme isolation since she was 20 months old. During the day she was strapped to a potty chair and unable to move about. At night she was bound and placed in a crib. If she made sounds,

Cases of Children Raised in Extreme Isolation

Shamdeo, the Sultanpur Wolf Boy	He was about 4 years old when discovered playing with wolves in 1974.
Memmie LeBlanc, the Wild Girl of Champagne	About 18 to 20 years old when found, she had learned language before having been abandoned.
John Ssebunya, the Ugandan Monkey Boy	Found living with a pack of monkeys in 1991 at age 6, he now gives talks about his experience.
Ng Chhaidy of India	She disappeared in the jungle when she was 4 and, after persistent local rumors about a jungle girl, was found 38 years later in 2012.
Oxana Malaya, the Ukrainian Dog Girl	She was found living in the dog pen in her family's back yard in 1991 at the age of 8.
Vanya Yudin, the Russian Bird Boy	Found in February 2008, he was cared for by his mother but never spoken to and chirps like a bird.
The Leopard Boy of Dihungi	He was found among leopards at age 5 in 1915 after having been in the wild three years.
Kamala and Amala, the Wolf Girls of Midnapore	These two girls were found living among wolves at about the ages of 8 and 2 in 1920.
The Russian Cow Girl	This 5-year-old girl, found living with cows in 2012, communicated using mooing sounds.
Natasha Mikhailova, the Siberian Dog Girl	This 5-year-old Russian girl, discovered in 2009, was raised like a pet in a room full of dogs and cats.

Sources: Keith 2008; Newton 2002; www.feralchildren.com. *Photos: Child:* Denis Gukov/AFP/Getty Images; *Book:* Preto Perola/Shutterstock her father would growl at her, scratch her, and beat her. She was fed baby food instead of solid foods. Family members were prohibited from speaking to her. Because there was no television or radio in her home, she had never heard the sounds of normal human speech. A year after she was rescued, during which she received extensive therapy, Genie's grammar resembled that of a typical 18-month-old. Though she made further advances with continued therapy, she never achieved full language ability. Genie, now in her early 60s, reportedly lives in a foster home for adults with developmental disabilities in California (Carroll 2016; Curtiss 1977; Rymer 1993).

In a similar, more recent case, police were called to investigate a child abuse claim in Plant City, Florida, in 2005. In a trash-filled house overrun with roaches and reeking of urine and feces, they discovered an emaciated girl whose hair was crawling with lice and who had rashes and sores all over her body. She was in a room piled high with her dirty diapers. Her name was Danielle. She was almost seven years old and weighed only 46 pounds. She couldn't eat solid food. She wouldn't make eye contact. She didn't react to pain. She couldn't talk. In terms of her social, psychological, and intellectual development, she was no further along than a six-month-old baby. After running medical tests on Dani, doctors determined that nothing was wrong with her physically that would explain her condition. Instead, they attributed her condition to extreme neglect (DeGregory 2008, 2011; Lierow 2011).

The long-term consequences of extreme isolation can be substantial. Danielle was adopted in 2007 and eventually learned basic self-care skills, including how to go to the bathroom and how to feed herself using a fork and spoon, but she barely speaks and cannot read. For 10 years her family worked with her in hopes that she would learn to dress herself, brush her own teeth, make a sandwich, and recognize classmates. As often happens for couples who face the challenge of raising a child with special needs, Dani's adoptive parents ended up divorcing. When she turned 18, her adoptive father moved Dani into a group home in Tennessee. He continues to visit her monthly (DeGregory 2017; OWN 2015).

Cases of extreme isolation demonstrate the importance of the earliest socialization experiences for children. We now know that it is not enough to attend only to an infant's physical needs; parents must also concern themselves with children's social development. If parents severely limit their children's interaction with family, friends, and others, including strangers—even as infants and toddlers—those children miss out on social interactions with people that are critical for their social, psychological, and emotional development.

Primate Studies Our need for early socialization is reinforced by studies of animals raised in isolation. Because it would violate ethical standards of research to conduct such experiments on human babies, psychologist Harry Harlow (1971) conducted tests with rhesus monkeys so he could better understand the importance of early socialization. By studying monkeys that had been raised away from their mothers and away from contact with other monkeys, he uncovered long-term effects of extreme isolation. As was the case with Genie and Danielle, the rhesus monkeys raised in isolation were fearful and easily frightened. They did not mate, and the females, who were artificially inseminated, became abusive mothers.

A creative aspect of Harlow's experimentation was his use of "artificial mothers." In one such experiment, Harlow presented monkeys raised in isolation with two substitute

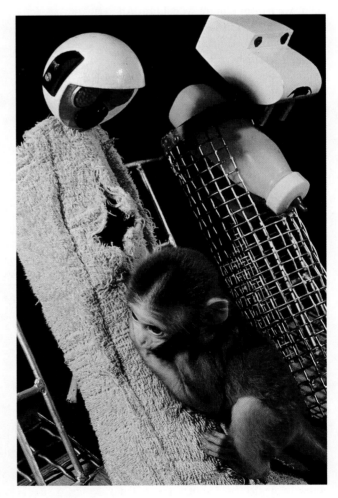

A cloth-covered "artificial mother" of the type used by Harry Harlow. Nina Leen/The Life Picture Collection/Getty Images

mothers—one a cloth-covered replica and one a wire-covered model that had the capacity to offer milk. Monkey after monkey went to the wire mother for the life-giving milk, yet spent much more time clinging to the more motherlike cloth model. Apparently, the infant monkeys developed greater social attachments based on their need for warmth, comfort, and intimacy than their need for food.

What we learn from cases of extreme childhood isolation and research on primates is that we lack complex instincts that will ensure our survival. Instead, we rely on the care and concern provided by others, especially when we are young. Without that early childhood socialization, we would struggle to establish working relationships with the outside world. Biology alone is not enough. The culture we create provides us with the tools we need. And through socialization, we share those tools with others.

>> The Self and Socialization

We learn from others what we need to survive, yet we are not simply robots who are programmed to do what others say, whether they be parents, teachers, bosses, politicians, or religious leaders. As individuals we are engaged in an ongoing dance with the world around us. We choose what to think and how to act, but we do so within the confines of the cultural resources to which we have access.

SOCIOLOGICAL APPROACHES TO THE SELF

We come to be who we are through our relationships with others. The **self** is our sense of who we are, distinct from others and shaped by the unique combination of our social interactions. It is not a static entity; instead, it develops and changes throughout our lives as we seek to make sense of our experiences. The interactionist perspective in sociology developed because early sociologists paid particular attention to the ways in which our every day encounters shape the self we become.

Cooley: The Looking-Glass Self American sociologist Charles Horton Cooley (1864–1929), one of the founders of the interactionist perspective, argued that we become ourselves in response to reactions we receive from others. We use people's responses to the things we say and do as a mirror reflecting back to us how we should think about ourselves, both positively and negatively. Cooley used the expression the **looking-glass self** to describe his theory that we become who we are based on how we think others see us.

> ## Self and others do not exist as mutually exclusive facts.
>
> Charles Horton Cooley (1983)

Our understanding of our self, according to Cooley's theory, involves a complex calculation in which we constantly read and react. This process of self-development has three phases. First, we imagine how others see us—relatives, friends, even strangers on the street. Second, we imagine how others evaluate what we think they see—as intelligent, attractive, shy, or strange. Finally, we define our self as a result of these assumptions—"I am smart" or "I am beautiful" (Cooley 1902). This process is ongoing; it happens during each and every one of our interactions. According to Cooley, we become who we are based not on how others actually see us, and not on how they judge us, but on how we think they will judge us based on what we think they perceive.

In Cooley's model, our sense of self results from our "imagination" of how others view us. Because we never truly know what others think, we can develop self-identities based on often *incorrect* perceptions of how others see us. Imagine you are on a first date or a job interview. All the cues you receive throughout the interaction are positive—your date or interviewer smiles, laughs, and nods at all the right times. You go home feeling happy, confident that things went really well. But your date never returns your call, or the expected job offer never comes. You go from a feeling of elation and confidence to a sense of disappointment, doubt, and recrimination, asking yourself, "What's wrong with me?" without ever really knowing what the date or interviewer truly thought about you. In Cooley's world, who we are is very much dependent on our interpretations of the interactions we have with others.

> **Self** Our sense of who we are, distinct from others, and shaped by the unique combination of our social interactions.
>
> **Looking-glass self** A theory that we become who we are based on how we think others see us.

SOCTHINK

What cues do you rely on to know if things are going well on a first date? How about on a job interview? To what extent do you think people can fake such cues?

Mead: Self and the Generalized Other George Herbert Mead (1863–1931), another American sociologist and advocate of the interactionist perspective, sought to expand on Cooley's theory. Mead (1934, 1964a, 1964b) especially sought to clarify the relationship between our self and our environment. He argued that there are two

Our Me may plan to walk a straight line, but when our I acts, our results may vary. Our Me then uses knowledge gained from that experience to guide future action. Eugene Sergeev/123RF

core components of the self: "I" and "Me." The **I** is our acting self. It is the part of us that walks, reads, sings, smiles, speaks, and performs any other action we might undertake. The **Me** is our socialized self. It draws on all our previous training and experience to plan our actions and then uses these standards to judge our performance afterward.

I The acting self that exists in relation to the Me.

Me The socialized self that plans actions and judges performances based on the standards we have learned from others.

Significant other An individual who is most important in the development of the self, such as a parent, friend, or teacher.

Generalized other The attitudes, viewpoints, and expectations of society as a whole that individuals take into account when interacting with others.

Symbol A gesture, object, or word that forms the basis of human communication.

For Mead our self emerges through the ongoing interaction between the socialized self and the acting self. The Me plans. The I acts. The Me judges. For example, in a classroom discussion, our Me knows, based on past experience, that the professor expects participation and will reward it when it comes to grade time. So, our I gathers up the courage and offers a contribution. After speaking, our Me assesses how it went, using available feedback to guide future participation.

In all our interactions, we rely on a feedback loop in which we gather information, process it, and use it to guide our reaction. In some respects, this relationship is not unlike the technique math teachers turn to when using the "guess and check" problem-solving strategy for certain types of story problems. In this approach, we try a solution to see if it works out, and if it doesn't, we try again. With each successive attempt, we use the information we've gained to make more informed guesses and in so doing find the appropriate pathway to the correct solution. Similarly, in our interactions with others, pathways of appropriate action emerge over time. We become more confident that certain responses are appropriate, making our decisions

about how to act in the future easier and providing us with greater self-confidence.

According to Mead, our Me develops as we generalize from our particular experiences to understand that similar people in similar circumstances act, and expect others to act, in similar ways. Mead used the expression **significant others** to describe the particular individuals we interact with who are most important in the development of our self. This includes encounters with *our* parents, *our* friends, *our* coworkers, *our* coaches, and others. Over time, however, we begin to see that the position these significant others occupy are part of a larger social network.

Through shared experiences, individuals develop a shared map of society in our collective minds. Mead uses the term **generalized other** to refer to the attitudes, viewpoints, and expectations of society as a whole that individuals take into account when interacting with others. Simply put, this concept suggests that when an individual acts, he or she takes into account the relative positions, contributions, and expectations for an entire group of people. For example, a child comes to see that acting courteously is important not just because his or her parent says so; rather, it is a widespread norm expected in a variety of contexts, whether at home, school, religious services, or the grocery store. Children learn to internalize these shared understandings as they grow up, and Mead identifies three stages through which children pass in developing this capacity.

Preparatory Stage When they are young, during what Mead refers to as the *preparatory stage,* children merely imitate the people around them, especially family members with whom they continually interact. That can take the form of babbling babies, who internalize language before they even know the words, or a small child who bangs on a piece of wood while a parent is engaged in carpentry work or tries to throw a ball if an older sibling is doing so nearby. This imitation is largely mindless—simple parroting of the actions of others.

As they grow older, children begin to realize that we attach meanings to our actions, and they become more adept at using symbols to communicate with others. **Symbols** are the gestures, objects, and words that form the basis of human communication. By interacting with family and friends, as well as by watching cartoons on television and looking at picture books, children in the preparatory stage begin to develop interaction skills they will use throughout their lives. They learn that they can use symbols to get their way, such as saying please and thank you, or perhaps throwing a tantrum in the candy aisle of the local supermarket.

Play Stage As children develop skill in communicating through symbols, they gradually become more aware of social relationships out of which those symbols grow. During the *play stage,* from about ages three through five, they begin to pretend to be other people: a doctor, parent, superhero, or teacher. Such play need not make a lot of sense

Young children learn through imitation.   Aurora Photos/Alamy Stock Photo

or be particularly coherent to adults; children, especially when they are young, are able to move in and out of various characters with ease. For Mead, playing make-believe is more than just fun; it is a critical part of our self-development.

Mead, in fact, noted that an important aspect of the play stage is role playing. He used the expression **role taking** to describe the the process of mentally assuming the perspective of another and responding from that imagined viewpoint. Through this process a young child imagines how others might respond in particular situations and gradually learns, for example, when it is best to ask a parent for favors. If the parent usually comes home from work in a bad mood, the child might wait until after dinner, when the parent is more relaxed and approachable.

Game Stage In Mead's third stage, the *game stage,* the child of about six to nine years of age learns to more fully appreciate that he or she is involved in interconnected and interdependent relationships. Success depends on each person playing his or her appropriate part, and each individual must often submit to the expectations of the group. The transition from play to game is evident when teaching kids to play team sports such as T-ball or soccer. When they are little, you will often see a clump of kids chasing after a ball or moving up the field together. They have yet to learn that different people play different positions and that they will be more successful as a team if everyone plays the position to which they are assigned. When they do, they can take for granted that someone will be covering a base so they can throw a runner out or that a goalie will be there to make a save if the ball gets behind them. Visualizing the map of who should be where and who should do what enables us

> It is our choices . . . that show what we truly are, far more than our abilities.
>
> J. K. Rowling (2014)

to see a kind of blueprint for society, and internalizing it represents the final stage of development in Mead's model.

At this stage, children begin to see that there really is something like a game going on with an underlying logic and shared rules and expectations for its various players. They may know their principal, Ms. Sanchez, as a significant other, but also see that the position of principal exists independent of Ms. Sanchez and that it carries with it certain expectations that make sense in the context of a school in which other positions include teacher, custodian, aide, and student. And if the individuals who come to occupy the various positions in the game fail to act accordingly, the whole thing falls apart.

Thomas: Perception and Action American sociologist W. I. Thomas (1863–1947) highlighted the role perception plays in shaping our sense of who we are. According to the Thomas theorem, which we encountered in Chapter 1, "If men define situations as real, they are real in their consequences" (Thomas and Thomas 1928:571–572). In other words, it is perception, more than reality itself, that shapes how we act. For example, if we are taught to see outsiders as threats, we may limit our contacts with them or their contacts with us, even if they aren't really threats. We might even go to war with them.

If perception shapes action, then an important corollary to the Thomas theorem is that position shapes perception. We create culture in order to establish a relationship to nature and with each other, as we saw in Chapter 3. Through socialization, we internalize perceptions of nature and of other people based on that culture. What we learn depends on the positions we occupy relative to others. A person socialized in 21st-century U.S. culture will think and act quite differently than someone raised in 14th-century Japan. Their sense of self will be shaped by the social context within which they develop. Change the context, change the self.

> **Role taking** The process of mentally assuming the perspective of another and responding from that imagined viewpoint.
>
> **Dramaturgical approach** A view of social interaction in which people are seen as actors on a stage attempting to put on a successful performance.

Goffman: Presentation of Self The idea that we must all play our roles based on the context within which we find ourselves led Canadian sociologist Erving Goffman (1922–1982) to establish what he called the **dramaturgical approach,** which studies interaction as if we were all actors on a stage seeking to put on a successful performance. He was inspired, in part, by William Shakespeare's lines from his play *As You Like It,* "All the world's a stage, And all the men and women

According to Erving Goffman, we can analyze all interaction as if we were actors staging a performance. Robbie Jack/Corbis Entertainment/Getty Images

SOCTHINK

Imagine that going to class is like performing in a play. Who are the key players? What are some of their most-used lines? What props do people use to be convincing? How might the performance break down, and what steps might be taken to save the show?

merely players: They have their exits and their entrances; And one man in his time plays many parts" (act 2, scene 7). As we perform our roles, according to Goffman, each of us seeks to convey impressions of who we are to others, even as those others are doing the same with us.

Building on this analogy, Goffman draws our attention to various *aspects of performance,* analysis of which allows us to better understand what makes a show a success. Performances take place on a stage. *Front stage* is where we perform for our audience and includes appropriate sets and may involve other cast members with whom we work as a *team.* We largely follow *scripts* and, although some improvisation is permissible, too much may threaten the credibility of the character we are trying to portray. *Backstage* is where we prepare, including getting into costumes and gathering together appropriate *props* which help make our performance more believable. Ultimately,

Impression management The altering of the presentation of the self in order to create distinctive appearances and satisfy particular audiences.

Face-work Altering our presentation of self in order to maintain a proper image and avoid public embarrassment.

the *audience* judges how well we did. Whether in our role as students, restaurant servers, or even lovers, we all know that we have a part to play and that if we don't say the right lines or use the correct props at the appropriate times, the show will collapse, undermining our sense of self.

Early in life, we learn to slant our presentation of self in order to create distinctive appearances and satisfy particular audiences. Goffman (1959) referred to this modifying of the presentation of the self as **impression management.** When things don't go as well as we might have hoped, we try to "save face." Goffman refers to this process as **face-work** meaning we alter our presentation of self in order to maintain a proper image and avoid public embarrassment. We often initiate some kind of face-saving behavior when we are feeling flustered or rejected. In response to a rejection at a bar, a person may engage in face-work by saying, "This place is full of losers. I'm out of here." Or, if we do poorly on an exam, we may say to a friend who did likewise, "This professor sucks." We feel the need to maintain a positive self-image if we are to continue social interaction.

For Cooley, Mead, Thomas, and Goffman, our self is fundamentally social. Each encounter we have provides opportunities for self-assessment. Even though our sense of self may seem relatively fixed over time, it is always subject to revision as we move into and out of relationships with others. A novel interaction or experience is often all it takes to get us to question things we have taken for granted, leading to new understandings of who we really are.

US VERSUS THEM

Through socialization, we internalize the culture of the groups to which we belong. We learn to think of our groups' norms, values, beliefs, and technology as not only

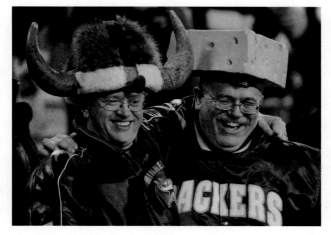

ZUMA Press, Inc./Alamy Stock Photo

normal for us but somewhat superior to those of others. Such ethnocentrism is a natural response, as we saw in the "Understanding Others" section in Chapter 3. We draw lines between ourselves and others and then use those lines to define who we are in opposition to those we are not. We see such divisions in sports (Green Bay Packers fans versus Minnesota Viking fans versus New England Patriot fans), politics (Democrats versus Republicans), high school (jocks versus brains versus populars versus burnouts), the workplace (sales staff versus marketing division), religion (Christians versus Muslims versus Buddhists), and more. Such divisions solidify our identities, but they frequently do so at the expense of how we view others.

Group membership itself shapes how we think and act. Social psychologist Henri Tajfel conducted a series of experiments in which he randomly distributed people into groups. He found that even when people have no group history or common group culture, just being a member leads them to identify with each other, privilege each other, and seek to deny benefits to people in other groups (Tajfel 1981).

Tajfel identified three core elements at work in creating us versus them mentalities (Tajfel and Turner 1979). First, *social categorization* involves the simple recognition of differences between groups. Any marker can serve as the foundation for such difference, such as taste, occupation, or age. Sociologists pay particular attention to categorization based on gender, race, ethnicity, and class. Second, *social identification* occurs when we tie our sense of self with a particular group as opposed to others. We adopt the group's expected cultural practices by following its norms, embracing its beliefs, using appropriate language, and otherwise seeking to fit in. By absorbing the culture of the group, membership becomes part of our identity. And, third, *social comparison* involves ranking groups in relation to each other, drawing a contrast between "us" and "them" in a way favorable to our group. In other words, we build ourselves up or show favoritism toward our group while putting down or denigrating other groups. Enhancing the status of the groups to which we belong elevates both

our identity and our self-esteem by answering the questions "Who am I?" and "What am I worth?" Patriotism, which calls forth pride in flag and country, finds its roots here.

On the flip side, privileging the culture of the groups to which we belong creates a foundation for **prejudice,** which is a preconceived and unjustified judgment of individuals, whether positive or negative, based on their membership in a particular group. We elevate ourselves by viewing those who do not think or act like us as somehow lesser. Our tendency is to think of prejudice as explicit bias, in which individuals voice their opinions about "them," making the bias easy to spot. But because we are socialized to make positive and negative distinctions between groups, we become largely unaware of the degree to which we do so. Theorists refer to such judgments as **implicit bias,** the automatic and unconscious association of value, whether positive or negative, with particular groups, subgroups, or characteristics of people. Researchers have uncovered ways to measure implicit bias using a variety of assessment tools including

> **Prejudice** A preconceived and unjustified judgment of individuals, whether positive or negative, based on their membership in a particular group.
>
> **Implicit bias** The automatic and unconscious association of value, whether positive or negative, with particular groups, subgroups, or characteristics of people.

SOCTHINK

Go to the Project Implicit site and take one of the tests. To what extent do your results match your self-assessment? What factors might influence someone's score? What steps might we take to alter our implicit biases?

Patriotism represents a call to unity, but can also be used as a form of exclusion. Michael B. Thomas/Getty Images implicit association tests (Banaji and Greenwald 2013; Staats, Capatosto, Wright, and Jackson 2016).

Implicit association tests measure participants' reaction time when presented with images, in an attempt to detect positive and negative associations. Researchers have constructed tests to assess implicit bias with regard to race, gender, age, weight, sexuality, disability, and more. Researchers can then compare results based on the test-takers' race, gender, age, region, or any other variable researchers have collected information about. A variety of these tests are available online—for example, Harvard's Project Implicit has several—for anyone to take.

When considering socialization, it is easy to focus on its more positive dimensions—learning how to speak, act, and create. But through our interactions with others, we also learn how to hate and discriminate. Developing an appreciation for where such attitudes come from and why we have them, including the degree to which we may be unaware of them, enables us to take steps to change them.

>> Agents of Socialization

Sociologists refer to the various contexts within which individuals and groups shape our social identity as agents of socialization. Primary examples include family, school, peer groups, the mass media, the workplace, religion, and the state.

FAMILY

Our families are our most important agent of socialization. Research shows that the role of the family in socializing a child cannot be overestimated (McDowell and Parke 2009). Babies are born with certain innate abilities—most can hear,

see, smell, and taste, and can feel heat, cold, and pain—but they would not survive without assistance from others. Responsibility for feeding, cleaning, carrying, and comforting babies falls primarily to family members. In the context of families, we learn to talk, walk, feed ourselves, go to the bathroom, and so on—basic skills that we take for granted as natural but that we learn within families. As children grow up, they observe parents expressing affection, taking care of finances, quarreling, dealing with work stress, and so forth, which prepares them for what family life might be like in their future. We explore definitions and functions of families more fully in Chapter 7.

Children do not play a passive role in their socialization. As Mead's I implies, they choose, sometimes to the disappointment of their parents. In so doing, they are active participants in their self-creation. We can see the power of family socialization among the Amish. Children in Amish communities are raised in a highly structured and disciplined manner, but they are not immune to the temptations posed by their peers in the non-Amish world. Around the time they turn 16, Amish teens begin dating, or courtship. They refer to this phase of their lives as *rumspringa,* a word roughly translated as "running around," which lasts until they get married, usually by their early 20s. During this transitional time between childhood and adulthood, they have greater freedom and can experiment with activities that would otherwise be forbidden, ranging from wearing non-Amish clothes, owning a cell phone, buying a TV and DVD player, driving cars, smoking, drinking, even doing drugs (though most don't go that far). During this time, they must also decide whether to commit to being Amish for the rest of their lives by taking a vow and getting baptized or to pursue life outside the Amish community. Parents often react by looking the other way, sometimes literally, pretending not to notice. They remain secure in the knowledge that, after a lifetime of Amish socialization, their children almost always return to the traditional Amish lifestyle. Research shows that only about 20 percent of Amish youths leave the fold, and most of them join one of the only somewhat more modern Mennonite groups. Rarely does a baptized adult leave (Kraybill, Johnson-Weiner, and Nolt 2013; Schachtman 2006).

Cross-Cultural Variation How children are socialized within families varies significantly around the world. In Vietnam, potty training starts by the time babies are six months old. Mothers whistle to remind their children to go and children are effectively potty trained by the time they are nine months old (Duong, Jansson, and Hellström 2013). In Sweden, parents routinely leave babies asleep in strollers outside shops, even on the coldest days, while the parents go in to buy something or get something to eat, to expose their children to more fresh air. They believe that doing so makes the babies healthier and less likely to get sick (Lee 2013). In Japan, children travel to school on their own from an early age. In cities like Tokyo, first-graders must learn to negotiate buses, subways, and long walks. To ensure their safety, parents carefully lay out rules: never talk to strangers; check with a station attendant if you get off at the wrong stop; stay on to the end of the line, then call if you miss your stop; take stairs, not escalators; don't fall asleep. One parent acknowledges that she worries, "but after they are 6, children are supposed to start being independent from the mother. If you're still taking your child to school after the first month, everyone looks at you funny" (Tolbert 2000:17).

In the United States, whether out of fear for their child's safety or concern about being charged with child endangerment, few parents would consider giving their young child this much independence. Parenting norms in the United States have shifted in recent decades, resulting in greater oversight and involvement in children's lives. Reflecting on the question of whether or not parents have become overprotective, journalist Hanna Rosin (2014) points out, "Actions that would have been considered paranoid in the 70s—walking third-graders to school, forbidding your kid to play ball in the street, going down the slide with your child in your lap—are now routine." The variety of parenting practices across cultures and across time provides additional evidence that our actions are not narrowly determined by our genes.

In many Scandinavian countries, it is not uncommon to leave babies in strollers outside shops and restaurants. Bjoern Kaehler/AP Images

The Influence of Race and Gender In the United States, social development within families includes exposure to cultural assumptions regarding gender and race. African American parents, for example, have learned that children as young as two years old can absorb negative messages about African Americans in children's books, toys, and television shows—the vast majority of which are designed primarily for White consumers. At the same time, as we will see in Chapter 13, African American families own less wealth and are more likely to experience poverty, which limits their children's access to resources such as extracurricular programs, summer camps, and specialized tutors and coaches. Because most U.S. neighborhoods are racially segregated, African American families often live in or near poor neighborhoods. As a result, their children are susceptible to exposure to gangs and drugs, despite their parents' strong family values (Benhorin and McMahon 2008; Friend, Hunter, and Fletcher 2011; Kliewer and Sullivan 2009).

Socialization within families also plays a significant role in whether we conform to conventional **gender roles,** meaning the

Blue jean images/Getty Images

normative expectations regarding proper behavior, attitudes, and activities associated with maleness and femaleness. In mainstream U.S. culture, for example, people traditionally identified "toughness" as masculine—and desirable only in men—while associating "tenderness" as feminine. As we will see in Chapter 12, not all societies share this model, allowing for a wider range of roles. Some societies have three or more gender categories. In the United States, people have increasingly come to see gender as a fluid concept allowing for a variety of expressions. Socialization experiences within the families play a major role in both our personal and societal acceptance of such variety.

> **Gender roles** The normative expectations regarding proper behavior, attitudes, and activities associated with maleness and femaleness.

SCHOOL

In school we typically move beyond the more sheltered confines of our family and learn to become members of the larger social groups to which we belong. Schools in the United States, for example, teach students the taken-for-granted knowledge of the broader society—not only basic skills such as reading, writing, and 'rithmatic but also shared cultural knowledge, such as the national anthem, the heroes of the American Revolution, and the pillars of good character. Like the family, schools have an explicit mandate to socialize people—and especially children—into the norms and values of the society to which they belong.

Schools teach children the values and customs of the larger society because

Robert Daly/Caia Image/Glow Images

High School Behavior: Perception versus Reality

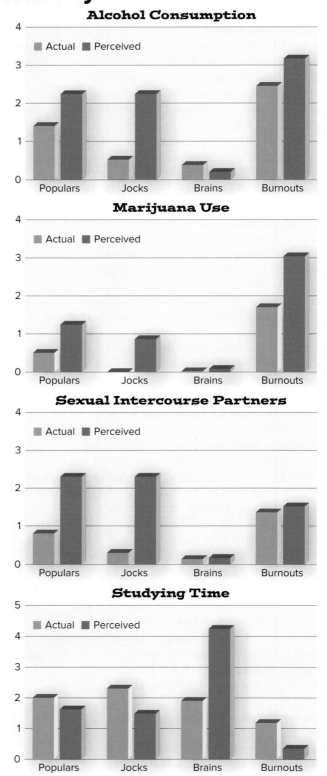

Alcohol Consumption

■ Actual ■ Perceived

Populars Jocks Brains Burnouts

Marijuana Use

■ Actual ■ Perceived

Populars Jocks Brains Burnouts

Sexual Intercourse Partners

■ Actual ■ Perceived

Populars Jocks Brains Burnouts

Studying Time

■ Actual ■ Perceived

Populars Jocks Brains Burnouts

Note: Actual represents the average of self-reported practices for students within that peer group; Perceived represents responses from students outside the group. *Source:* Helms et al. 2014.

that shared culture provides the glue that holds us together as a society. If we did not transmit our knowledge and skills from one generation to the next, society would collapse. The knowledge we gain at school, however, goes beyond the official curriculum to include the more informal lessons we learn on the playground. We do learn the facts and figures of history, science, reading, math, and more, but we also learn how to stand up for ourselves when our parents or teachers are not there to hover over us or to bail us out.

Although schools provide both social order and individual opportunity, they can also reinforce existing inequality through the ways students are socialized. As economists Samuel Bowles and Herbert Gintis (1976) have observed, schools produce teachable students who become manageable workers. They argue that schools' primary function has less to do with transmitting academic content and more to do with socializing students to conform to, and accept, workplace authority. Schools teach students how to work for rewards, how to work in teams, how to meet deadlines, how to comply with instructions, and so on. The students who internalize these skills best are rewarded with opportunities in the workplace, whereas those who challenge authority and call for change are punished. We more fully explore various elements of education in Chapter 8.

PEER GROUPS

As we grow older, and especially in our adolescent years, our friends, schoolmates, and other peers become increasingly important in shaping how we think and act. To understand the role peers play at a relatively young age, sociologists Patricia and Peter Adler conducted observation research at elementary schools with fourth- through sixth-grade students. They found that, even this early, a pecking order is established, ranging from the "popular clique" at the top that includes the "cool kids" on down to what they call the "social isolates" at the bottom, whom other kids sometimes call "dweebs" or "nerds" (Adler and Adler 1996). Children get the message about where they fit and how they should behave. In another study of elementary schoolchildren, the Adlers found that popularity reinforces gender stereotypes. To be popular as a boy is to be athletic, tough, and not too academic. To be popular as a girl is to be attractive, to be able to manipulate others using social skills, and to come from a family wealthy enough to permit shopping for the latest cool stuff (Adler, Kless, and Adler 1992).

The impact of peer groups among high schoolers has become a pop culture staple, perhaps best captured in the classic film *The Breakfast Club,* in which "a brain, an athlete, a basket case, a princess, and a criminal" were forced together during Saturday morning detention. In the end, the five students got past their stereotypical perceptions of each other to find common ground.

To better understand peer group culture in the real world, researchers from the University of North Carolina explored how high school peer groups were perceived by nonmembers and contrasted those perceptions with the actual, self-reported behaviors of members within each group. Based on interviews with high school students, they focused on four groups: populars, jocks, brains, and burnouts. They found a whole series of misperceptions, such as:

- Non-populars overestimated populars' number of sexual partners.
- Non-jocks overestimated jocks' amount of alcohol consumption.
- Non-brains overestimated brains' time spent studying.
- Non-burnouts overestimated burnouts' frequency of property damage.

Overall, researchers concluded that students especially tend to overestimate the degree to which students in the two most popular groups engage in sex, drugs, and property damage. In a follow-up study, the researchers found that, when analyzed over time, those students who perceived the popular kids as being more likely to engage in risky behaviors were themselves more likely to engage in those behaviors, which is consistent with what we have learned already from the Thomas theorem that perception shapes action.

MASS MEDIA

For most of human history, socialization came primarily in the form of person-to-person contact, and we had limited exposure to what was going on in the wider world. We now receive immediate accounts of incidents around the globe as they are happening. Technological innovations leading to the rise of the mass media made that possible. The word *media* is plural for *medium,* and a medium is something or someone capable of conveying or transmitting ideas or objects. For example, language, as a system of shared symbols, provides the medium through which we communicate. The term *mass media* refers to the variety of technologies that provide the capacity to easily transmit large quantities of information to large groups of people.

If we think of a mass medium as the vessel through which information passes, we can identify seven types of

major media (Ahonen 2008). *Print,* the first type, took off as a mass medium with Johannes Gutenberg's invention of a printing press using movable type in 1439. His press made printing many copies of materials possible, facilitating a publication explosion that continues to this day in the form of books, pamphlets, billboards, newspapers, and magazines. Access to books and pamphlets has played a significant role in historic events ever since, including the Protestant Reformation, which started in 1517, and the American Revolution, which began in 1776 (Edwards 1994; Humphrey 2013).

The second mass media type, *recordings,* got their start in the late 1800s. Since then, recordings have provided mass access to musical performances from classical music to rock and roll and beyond. In time, as a result of technological innovation, video recordings became possible. At various points, recording technology included wax cylinder recordings, vinyl records, magnetic recordings (such as reel-to-reel tape, 8-track cartridges, audio cassettes, and VHS tapes), CDs, and DVDs. Magnetic recordings were particularly transformative due to the inclusion of the "record" button, which opened the door for almost anyone to produce their own recordings, an ability we take for granted today (Marlow and Secunda 1991; Millard 2005; Milner 2009).

Cinema represents the third type of mass media. Starting in the early 1900s, movie theaters were established all over the United States. Pittsburgh's "Nickelodeon," one of the earliest, opened in 1905 with a 5 cent admission fee. Movie theaters became a shared space where people in local communities gained more immediate visual access to popular stories, news accounts, fads, and fashion from the wider world (Charney and Schartz 1995; Sklar 1994).

The fourth type, *radio,* brought mass media broadcasts directly into the home. Pittsburgh's KDKA became the first licensed commercial broadcasting station in the United States in 1920, and stations quickly spread across the country. Programming included music, news, sports, and episodic stories (soap operas, with their open and ongoing storylines originated here). Radio enabled the rapid and widespread dissemination of breaking news to entire populations, including the possibility of direct communication by political leaders. Herbert Hoover was the first presidential candidate to reach a mass audience via radio in 1928, and President Franklin Delano Roosevelt used radio to great effect with his "fireside chat" broadcasts to the nation during the Great Depression and World War II (Brands 2008; Marquis 1984).

Television, the fifth type of mass media, combined the immediacy and reach of radio with the video element of cinema. The world became a smaller place because now it was possible to bring breaking news, sporting events, variety shows, musical concerts, and more into people's living rooms. Television stations began popping up around the United States during the 1940s, and people widely adopted television as a medium in the 1950s (Edgerton 2007). The first broadcast of a presidential debate occurred in 1960

Average Time Spent Using Media per Week by Age Group

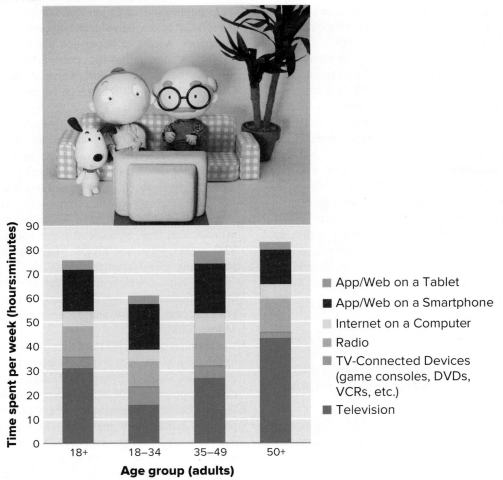

Source: Nielsen 2017. *Photo:* Datacraft Co Ltd/Getty Images

between John F. Kennedy and Richard M. Nixon. Kennedy, with a bronzed tan from campaigning in California, came across as more telegenic, and Nixon, with a pale complexion and visible sweat, appeared uncomfortable on the screen, a difference that might have swayed the election (Druckman 2003; Kraus 1996). Ever since then, candidates and campaigns have been keenly aware of the importance of optics in shaping potential outcomes. With the expansion of cable and satellite television came an explosion of available channels, though the major television networks (including ABC, CBS, FOX, and NBC), along with a select number of major cable channel corporations (especially ESPN), wield significant influence over what gets covered and how, and perhaps just as important, what gets left out.

The sixth type of mass media is referred to generally as *the Internet,* access to which expanded significantly throughout the 1990s. By linking computers through a series of networks, the World Wide Web facilitated connections between computers via web browsers (Isaacson 2014).

Two core elements distinguish the Internet as a mass medium. The first is information retrieval, which provides us with access to untold amounts of data. Whether searching for sources when writing a college paper or looking for pictures of rainbows and unicorns, individuals now have more power to find information than ever before. The second core element is social networking, which provides us with

SOCTHINK

The average 18- to 34-year-old in the United States spends 2 hours and 42 minutes each day using apps or surfing the web on a smartphone (Nielsen 2017). Does that total seem high or low to you? What are possible effects, both positive and negative, of such use?

Video game designer Mike Mika's three-year-old daughter enjoyed playing the classic arcade game *Donkey Kong*. In it, a King Kong–like ape kidnaps Pauline, and Mario's task is to save her. One day Mika's daughter asked, "How can I play as the girl? I want to save Mario!" After days spent hacking the *Donkey Kong* ROM, Mika (2013) fulfilled his daughter's wish to make the princess the hero.

According to Anita Sarkeesian (2013), "Damsel in Distress" plot devices are exceedingly common in video games. She concludes, "Distilled down to its essence, the plot device works by trading the disempowerment of female characters for the empowerment of male characters." With the help of more than 6,000 Kickstarter backers, she has produced a series of videos investigating the portrayal of women in video games, which are available at her website, Feminist Frequency.

Photo: Mike Mika

historically unprecedented access to people. Sites such as Facebook, Twitter, Instagram, and Snapchat provide almost constant access to close friends, continued connections to old friends, and even connections with the rich, powerful, and famous. Getting a "like" or retweet from a celebrity can be cause for significant celebration because the distance between you and them suddenly seems so small.

Mobile phones represent the final mass media type. Although mobile phones were originally invented solely for the purpose of making calls, we now use them to send texts, take photos, access the Internet, record videos, play games, read books, get directions, listen to radio, watch movies, access our music collection, and a whole host of

other actions. Smartphones can take the place of numerous devices, including watches, fitness trackers, calculators, voice recorders, compasses, flashlights, levels, alarm clocks, calendars, portable gaming devices, and more (Agar 2013; Klemens 2010). The intersection of all these elements into a single device provides the possibility to draw on various elements of each to create something new. The game *Pokémon Go,* for example, utilized elements of the smartphone's camera, GPS, fitness tracker, gyroscope, and social networking software to create a whole new augmented reality gaming universe. Exploring the possible health benefits of such augmented reality games, researchers at Microsoft found that *Pokémon Go* increased physical

Telephones and Cell Phones by Country (rates per 100 people)

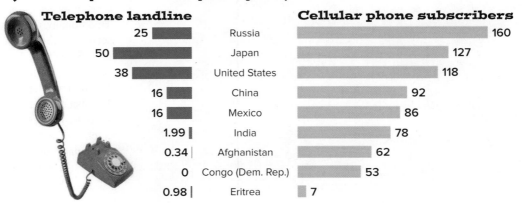

	Telephone landline		Cellular phone subscribers
Russia	25		160
Japan	50		127
United States	38		118
China	16		92
Mexico	16		86
India	1.99		78
Afghanistan	0.34		62
Congo (Dem. Rep.)	0		53
Eritrea	0.98		7

Source: International Telecommunications Union 2017. *Photo:* EyeWire/Getty Images activity among users by almost 1,500 steps per day, with a particular impact among low-activity populations (Althoff, White, and Horvitz 2016).

Many developing nations have essentially skipped over the use of landlines and have gone directly to mobile technology. This process is referred to as leapfrogging because it bypasses an entire generation of technology. In doing so, it saves all the infrastructure costs that the installation of land lines entails (Bauer 2015). In Kenya, Ghana, and Nigeria, for example, 80 percent of the adult population now own a cell phone (Silver and Johnson 2018). Mobile phone access enables people to maintain contact with family, provides access to jobs, and expands social networks. Having a phone can be especially important to families, for example, when children leave the local village to pursue opportunities in urban areas or abroad (Sullivan 2006).

The key element with agents of socialization, including mass media, is that they change how we think and act. With the exposure to new cultural beliefs and practices that media have brought, we may become more accepting of others and gain a deeper understanding of ourselves. Of course, such exposure can also challenge the culture we hold dear, and the kinds of filters that might have been provided by time and distance are a thing of the past. We can see such effects in the hostility sometimes expressed in online forums and Twitter feeds. Given that these outlets for expression are relatively recent mass media creations, perhaps we will develop more effective norms for constructive exchanges in the future.

Did You Know?

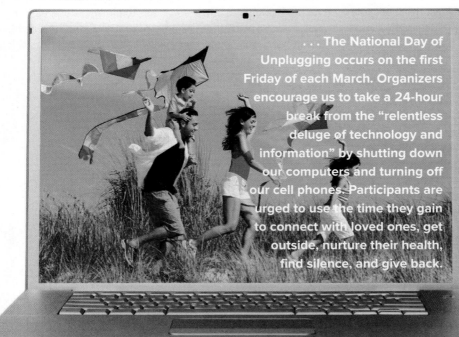

. . . The National Day of Unplugging occurs on the first Friday of each March. Organizers encourage us to take a 24-hour break from the "relentless deluge of technology and information" by shutting down our computers and turning off our cell phones. Participants are urged to use the time they gain to connect with loved ones, get outside, nurture their health, find silence, and give back.

Photos: family: Ariel Skelley/Blend Images/Getty Images; *laptop:* D. Hurst/Alamy Stock Photo

THE WORKPLACE

Learning to behave appropriately in an occupation is a fundamental aspect of human socialization. Employers and coworkers want to be confident that you know what to do and when to do it. As we saw with Mead's concept of the generalized other, the teamwork necessary for successful completion of tasks depends on everyone playing his or her part, and the workplace functions as an agent of socialization to make sure that happens.

It used to be that workplace socialization started young. Generations ago, most children began working at a young age, primarily to provide assistance with farm labor. That practice carried over past the Industrial Revolution, though laws were eventually enacted to limit child labor. Now, rates of employment for high school age students hover around 25 percent, with a peak during summer months of about 33 percent (DeSilver 2015). Adolescents generally seek jobs to earn spending money; 80 percent of high school seniors say that little or none of what they earn goes to family expenses. Moreover, these teens rarely look on their employment as a means of exploring vocational interests or getting on-the-job training (Hirschman and Voloshin 2007).

Socialization in the workplace changes when it involves a more permanent shift to full-time employment. Occupational socialization can be most intense during the transition from school to job, but it continues throughout one's work history. Technological advances and corporate reorganization may alter the requirements of the position and necessitate new training. According to the Bureau of Labor Statistics (2017d), between the ages of 18 and 50, the typical person held 11.9 different jobs. We can no longer assume that we will have a job-for-life, so whether by choice or by necessity, we must be open to ongoing occupational socialization.

RELIGION AND THE STATE

Increasingly, social scientists are recognizing the growing importance of government ("the state") and the continued significance of religion as agents of socialization. Traditionally, family members served as the primary caregivers in U.S. culture, but in the 20th century, the family's protective function was steadily transferred to outside agencies, such as public schools, hospitals, mental health clinics, and child care centers, many of which are run by the state. Increasingly, for example, preschool children are cared for by someone other than a parent,

Leh Village, India, schoolchildren. Nevada Wier/Iconica/Getty Images

symbolic transition from one social position to another, dramatizing and validating changes in a person's status.

In the Kota rite the color blue—the color of death—symbolizes the death of childhood and the passage to adulthood. For adolescent girls in Miami's Cuban American community, the *quinceañera* ceremony celebrating the attainment of womanhood at age 15 supports a network of party planners, caterers, dress designers, and the Miss Quinceañera Latina pageant. For thousands of years, Egyptian mothers have welcomed their newborns to the world in the Soboa ceremony by stepping over the seven-day-old infant seven times. And Naval Academy seniors celebrate their graduation from college by hurling their hats skyward.

including government sponsored or operated programs such as Head Start and public school pre-Kindergarten programs. Historically, religious groups also provided such care and protection. Despite early sociological predictions that religion would cease to play a substantial role in modern society, these groups continue to play a significant role in identity formation and collective life (Warner 2005).

Both government and organized religion act to provide markers representing significant life course transitions. For example, religious organizations continue to celebrate meaningful ritual events—such as baptism, bismillah, or bar/bat mitzvah—that often bring together all the members of an extended family, even if they never meet for any other reason. Government regulations stipulate the ages at which a person may drive a car, drink alcohol, vote in elections, marry without parental permission, work overtime, and retire. Although these regulations do not constitute strict rites of passage—most 18-year-olds choose not to vote, and most people choose their age of retirement without reference to government dictates—they do symbolize the fact that we have moved on to a different stage of our life, with different expectations regarding our behavior.

>> Socialization Throughout the Life Course

Adolescents among the Kota people of the Congo in Africa paint themselves blue. Cuban American girls go on a day-long religious retreat before dancing the night away. These are both **rites of passage**—rituals that mark the

THE LIFE COURSE

Such specific ceremonies mark stages of development in the life course. They indicate that the process of socialization continues through all stages of the life cycle. In fact, some researchers have chosen to concentrate on socialization as a lifelong process. Sociologists and other social scientists who

> **Rite of passage** A ritual marking the symbolic transition from one social position to another, dramatizing and validating changes in a person's status.

Although participation rates vary from year to year, election turnout for the 2018 midterms was higher than for any midterm election dating all the way back to 1912 (McDonald 2018). Autumn Payne/Sacramento Bee/Tribune News Service/MCT/Getty Images take such a **life course approach** look closely at the social factors, including gender and income, that influence people throughout their lives, from birth to death. They recognize that biological changes help mold but do not dictate human behavior.

In the transition from childhood to adulthood, we can identify certain markers that signify the passage from one life stage to the next. These milestones vary from one society, and even one generation, to the next. In the United States, according to one national survey, completion of formal schooling has risen to the top, with 90 percent of people identifying it as an important rite of passage. On average, Americans expect this milestone to be attained by a person's 23rd birthday. Other major events in the life course, such as getting married or becoming a parent, are expected to follow three or four years later. Interestingly, the significance of these markers has declined, with only about one-third of

Life course approach A research orientation in which sociologists and other social scientists look closely at the social factors that influence people throughout their lives, from birth to death.

Milestones in the Transition to Adulthood

Expected age	Life event	Percentage who view event as extremely/quite important
20.9	Financial independence from parents/guardians	80.9%
21.1	Separate residence from parents	57.2%
21.2	Full-time employment	83.8%
22.3	Completion of formal schooling	90.2%
24.5	Capability of supporting family	82.3%
25.7	Marriage	33.2%
26.2	Parenthood	29.0%

Source: Smith 2004.

survey respondents identifying marriage and less than one-third identifying parenthood as important milestones representing adulthood (Furstenberg 2010; Smith 2004).

One result of these staggered steps to independence is that in the United States, unlike some other societies, no clear dividing line exists between adolescence and adulthood. Nowadays, the number of years between childhood and adulthood has grown, and few young people finish school, get married, and leave home at about the same

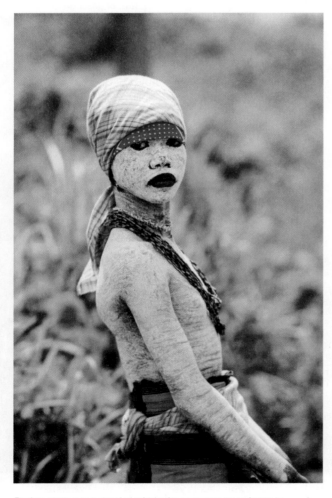

Body painting is a ritual marking the passage to puberty in some cultures. Thomas S. England/Science Source

SOCTHINK

To what extent do you feel like an adult (regardless of your age)? What markers or moments would you identify as significant in your transition to adulthood? What characteristics of our society contribute to ambiguity in our passage into adulthood?

age, clearly establishing their transition to adulthood. The term *youthhood* has been coined to describe the prolonged ambiguous status that young people in their 20s experience (Côté 2000; Roberts and Côté 2014).

ANTICIPATORY SOCIALIZATION AND RESOCIALIZATION

In our journey through our lives, we seek to prepare ourselves for what is coming and to adapt to change as necessary. To prepare, we undergo **anticipatory socialization,** which refers to processes of socialization in which a person "rehearses" for future positions, occupations, and social relationships. A culture can function more efficiently and smoothly if members become acquainted with the norms, values, and behavior associated with a social position before actually assuming that status. Preparation for many aspects of adult life begins with anticipatory socialization during childhood and adolescence and continues throughout our lives as we prepare for new responsibilities (Levine and Hoffner 2006).

High school students experience a bit of anticipatory socialization when they prepare for college. They begin to imagine what college life will be like and what kind of person they will be when they get there. They may seek out information from friends and family to get a better sense of what to expect, but increasingly, they also rely on campus websites and Facebook entries. To assist in this process and to attract more students, colleges are investing more time and money in websites through which students can take "virtual" campus tours, listen to podcasts, and stream videos of everything from the school song to a sample zoology lecture.

Occasionally, assuming a new social or occupational position requires that we *unlearn* an established orientation. **Resocialization** refers to the process of discarding old behavior patterns and accepting new ones as part of a life transition. Often, resocialization results from explicit efforts to transform an individual, as happens in reform schools, therapy groups, prisons, religious conversion settings, and political indoctrination camps. The process of resocialization typically involves considerable stress for the individual—much more so than socialization in general, or even anticipatory socialization (Hart, Miller, and Johnson 2003).

Resocialization is particularly effective when it occurs within a total institution. Erving Goffman (1961) coined the term **total institution** to refer to an institution that

> **Anticipatory socialization** Processes of socialization in which a person "rehearses" for future positions, occupations, and social relationships.
>
> **Resocialization** The process of discarding former behavior patterns and accepting new ones as part of a transition in one's life.
>
> **Total institution** An institution that regulates all aspects of a person's life under a single authority, such as a prison, the military, a mental hospital, or a convent.

Life in prison is highly regulated—even recreation time. Justin Sullivan/Getty Images regulates all aspects of a person's life under a single authority. Examples can be more or less extreme depending on how long it lasts and how easy it is to opt out of it, from summer camp or boarding school to prison, the military, a psychiatric hospital, or a convent. Because the total institution is generally cut off from the rest of society, it provides for all the needs of its members. In its extreme form, so elaborate are its requirements, and so all-encompassing its activities, that the total institution represents a miniature society.

Goffman (1961) identified several common traits of total institutions:

- All aspects of life are conducted in the same place under the control of a single authority.
- Any activities within the institution are conducted in the company of others in the same circumstances—for example, army recruits or novices in a convent.
- The authorities devise rules and schedule activities without consulting the participants.
- All aspects of life within a total institution are designed to fulfill the purpose of the organization. Thus, all activities in a monastery might be centered on prayer and communion with God (Malacrida 2005; Mapel 2007; Williams and Warren 2009).

People often lose their individuality within total institutions. For example, a person entering prison may experience the humiliation of a **degradation ceremony** as he or she is stripped of clothing, jewelry, and other personal possessions. From that point on, scheduled daily routines allow for little or no personal initiative. The individual becomes secondary and rather invisible in the overbearing social environment (Garfinkel 1956).

5 Movies on SOCIALIZATION

Eighth Grade
Being yourself can be hard.

Welcome to Marwen
A man retreats from reality after a violent assault.

The Jungle Book
The live-action remake tells the fictional story of a boy raised by animals.

Don't Think Twice
Friends in an improv group learn to adjust when one of them makes it big.

Three Identical Strangers
Identical triples who never knew each other existed learn a surprising secret about why.

SOCTHINK

To what extent is summer camp, a cruise, or even life at a residential college similar to a total institution? In what ways is it different?

Degradation ceremony An aspect of the socialization process within some total institutions, in which people are subjected to humiliating rituals.

Midlife crisis A stressful period of self-evaluation that begins at about age 40.

Sandwich generation The generation of adults who simultaneously try to meet the competing needs of their parents and their children.

ROLE TRANSITIONS DURING THE LIFE COURSE

As we have seen, one of the key transitional stages we pass through occurs as we enter the adult world, perhaps by moving out of the parental home, beginning a career, or entering a marriage. As we age we move into the midlife transition, which typically begins at about age 40. Men and women often experience a stressful period of self-evaluation, commonly known as the **midlife crisis,** in which they realize that they have not achieved basic goals and ambitions and may feel they have little time left to do so. This conflict between their hopes and their outcomes causes strain. Compounding such stresses that are often associated with one's career or partner is the growing responsibility for caring for two generations at once (Mortimer and Shanahan 2006; Wethington 2000).

An increasingly common midlife challenge involves becoming part of the **sandwich generation** which describes adults who simultaneously try to meet the competing needs of their parents and their children. Their caregiving goes in two directions: to children, who even as young adults may still require significant support and direction; and to aging parents, whose health and economic problems may demand intervention by their adult children. Among adults aged 40–59, 47 percent report having both a parent 65 years old or older and a minor child or are supporting a grown child (Parker and Patten 2013).

Like the role of caring for children, that of caring for aging parents falls disproportionately on women. Overall, women provide 60 percent of the care their parents receive, and even more as the demands of the role grow more intense and time-consuming. Increasingly, middle-aged women and younger are finding themselves on the "daughter track," as their time and attention are diverted by the needs of their aging mothers and fathers (Dotinga 2014; Gross 2005; Taylor et al. 2009).

>> Aging and Society

Due to advances in areas such as health care, nutrition, and working conditions, life expectancy has risen significantly both in the United States and around the world. Someone born in 1900 in the United States had an average life expectancy of 47 years, but babies born in the United States in 2016 can anticipate living to 76.1 if they're boys and 81.1 if they're girls (National Center for Health Statistics 2018a:Table 15). The proportion of the U.S. population that was 65 and older grew from 4.1 percent in 1900 to 15 percent in 2014; it is expected to rise to 24 percent by 2060 (Mather, Jacobsen, and Pollard 2015; Ortman, Velkoff, and Hogan 2014). Globally, life expectancy is 80 years in "high-income nations," such as the United States, France, and Japan, but only 63 years in "low-income nations," such as Afghanistan, Rwanda, and Somalia (World Bank 2018b).

How societies deal with their elderly population varies significantly across cultures. One society may treat older people with reverence, whereas another sees them as unproductive and "difficult." The Sherpas—a Tibetan-speaking Buddhist people in Nepal—live in a culture that idealizes old age. Almost all elderly members of the Sherpa culture own their homes, and most are in relatively good physical condition. Typically, older Sherpas value their independence and prefer not to live with their children. Among the Fulani of Africa, however, older men and women move to the edge of the family homestead. Because that is where people are buried, elderly members sleep over their own graves, for they are viewed socially as already dead (Goldstein and Beall 1981; Stenning 1958; Tonkinson 1978).

Understandably, all societies have some system of age stratification that associates certain social roles with distinct periods in life. In the United States, children are denied certain rights, such as voting or alcohol consumption, until they reach an age when they are deemed sufficiently mature. Some of this age differentiation seems inevitable; it would make little sense to send young children off to war or to expect older citizens to handle physically demanding tasks, such as loading freight at shipyards.

ADJUSTING TO RETIREMENT

Making the role transition into retirement can be a difficult process. Retirement is a rite of passage that typically marks a transition out of active participation in

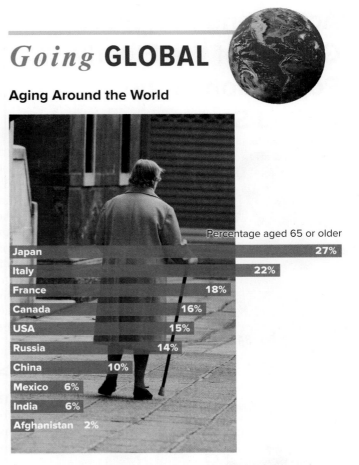

Going **GLOBAL**

Aging Around the World

Percentage aged 65 or older

Country	Percentage
Japan	27%
Italy	22%
France	18%
Canada	16%
USA	15%
Russia	14%
China	10%
Mexico	6%
India	6%
Afghanistan	2%

Source: Population Reference Bureau 2016. *Photo:* Ingram Publishing/age fotostock

the full-time labor market. Symbolic events are associated with this rite of passage, such as retirement gifts, a retirement party, and special moments on the last day on the job. The preretirement period itself can be emotionally

The Sherpas in Nepal show significant respect for their elderly members.
Paula Bronstein/Getty Images

Actual and Projected Growth of the Elderly Population of the United States

65–84 years

85 years and older

Year	65–84 years	85 years and older
1900	3.9%	0.2%
1930	5.1%	0.2%
1980	10.3%	1.0%
2010	11.2%	1.7%
2050 (projection)	16.4%	4.5%

Sources: He et al. 2005:9; Ortman et al. 2014; Werner 2011. *Photo:* Monkey Business Images/Shutterstock

---

• *The reorientation phase,* which involves the development of a more realistic view of retirement alternatives.
• *The stability phase,* in which the person has learned to deal with life after retirement in a reasonable and comfortable fashion.
• *The termination phase,* which begins when the person can no longer engage in basic, day-to-day activities such as self-care and housework.

Retirement is not a single transition, then, but a series of adjustments that varies from one person to another. The length and timing of each phase will differ for each individual, depending on such factors as financial and health status. In fact, a person will not necessarily go through all the phases identified by Atchley. For example, people who are forced to retire or who face financial difficulties may never experience a honeymoon phase. And many retirees continue to be part of the paid labor force of the United States, often taking part-time jobs to supplement their pensions, either because they want to or because they need to.

>> Perspectives on Aging

The particular problems of older adults have become the focus of a specialized field of research and inquiry known as **gerontology**—the study of the sociological and psychological aspects of aging and the problems of aging adults. It originated in the 1930s as an increasing number of social scientists became aware of the plight of this population. Gerontologists rely heavily on sociological principles and theories to explain the effects of aging on the individual and society. They also draw on psychology, anthropology, physical education, counseling, and medicine in their study of the aging process. Three perspectives on aging—disengagement theory, activity theory, and age discrimination—arise out of these studies.

Gerontology The study of the sociological and psychological aspects of aging and the problems of aging adults.

Disengagement theory A theory of aging that suggests that society and the aging individual mutually sever many of their relationships.

charged, especially if the retiree is expected to train his or her successor (Reitzes and Mutran 2004).

Gerontologist Robert Atchley (1976) has identified several phases of the retirement experience:

• *Preretirement,* a period of anticipatory socialization as the person prepares for retirement.
• *The near phase,* when the person establishes a specific departure date from his or her job.
• *The honeymoon phase,* an often euphoric period in which the person pursues activities that he or she never had time for before.
• *The disenchantment phase,* in which retirees feel a sense of letdown or even depression as they cope with their new lives, which may include illness or poverty.

SOC THINK

What age do you think counts as getting "old"? What factors influence our conception of what counts as old?

DISENGAGEMENT THEORY

After studying elderly people in good health and relatively comfortable economic circumstances, Elaine Cumming and William Henry (1961) introduced their **disengagement theory,** which implicitly suggests that society and the aging individual mutually sever many of their relationships. Highlighting the significance of social order in society, disengagement theory emphasizes that passing social roles on from one generation to another ensures social stability.

Living Arrangements by Age

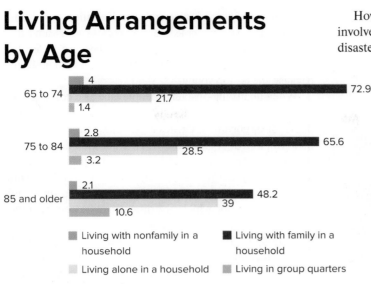

Age		
65 to 74	4	
	72.9	
	21.7	
	1.4	
75 to 84	2.8	
	65.6	
	28.5	
	3.2	
85 and older	2.1	
	48.2	
	39	
	10.6	

■ Living with nonfamily in a household　　■ Living with family in a household

■ Living alone in a household　　■ Living in group quarters

Source: Roberts et al. 2018.

According to this theory, the approach of death forces people to drop most of their social roles—including those of worker, volunteer, spouse, hobby enthusiast, and even reader. Younger members of society then take on these functions. The aging person, it is held, withdraws into an increasing state of inactivity while preparing for death. At the same time, society withdraws from aging adults by segregating them residentially (in retirement homes and communities), educationally (in programs designed solely for senior citizens), and recreationally (in senior citizens' centers). Implicit in disengagement theory is the view that society should help older people withdraw from their accustomed social roles.

Disengagement theory has generated considerable controversy. Some gerontologists have objected to the implication that older people want to be ignored and put away—and even more to the idea that they should be encouraged to withdraw from meaningful social roles. Critics of disengagement theory insist that society forces elderly people into an involuntary and painful withdrawal from the paid labor force and from meaningful social relationships. Rather than voluntarily seeking to disengage, older employees find themselves pushed out of their jobs—in many instances, even before they are entitled to maximum retirement benefits (Boaz 1987).

ACTIVITY THEORY

Often seen as the opposite of disengagement theory, **activity theory** suggests that those elderly people who remain active and socially involved will have an improved quality of life. Proponents of this perspective acknowledge that a 70-year-old person may not have the ability or desire to perform various social roles that he or she had at age 40. Yet they contend that older people have essentially the same need for social interaction as any other group.

How important is it for older people to stay actively involved, whether at a job or in other pursuits? A tragic disaster in Chicago in 1995 showed that it can be a matter of life and death. An intense heat wave lasting more than a week—with a heat index exceeding 115 degrees on two consecutive days—resulted in 733 heat-related deaths. About three-fourths of the deceased were 65 or older. Subsequent analysis showed that older people who lived alone had the highest risk of dying, suggesting that support networks for older adults literally help save lives. Older Hispanics and Asian Americans had lower death rates from the heat wave than other racial and ethnic groups. Their stronger social networks probably resulted in more regular contact with family members and friends (Klinenberg 2002; Schaefer 1998a).

The improved health of older people—sometimes overlooked by social scientists—has strengthened the arguments of activity theorists. Illness and chronic disease are no longer quite the scourge of aging adults that they once were. The recent emphasis on fitness, the availability of better medical care, greater control of infectious diseases, and the reduction in the number of fatal strokes and heart attacks have combined to reduce the traumas of growing older.

Accumulating medical research also points to the importance of remaining socially involved. Among those who decline in their mental capacities later in life, deterioration is most rapid in those who withdraw from social relationships and activities. Fortunately, aging adults are finding new ways to remain socially engaged, as evidenced by their increasing use of the Internet, especially to keep in touch with family and friends (Taylor et al. 2009; Williams et al. 2010).

> **Activity theory** A theory of aging that suggests that those elderly people who remain active and socially involved will have an improved quality of life.

Older individuals continue to be involved both as volunteers and in the workforce. Many activities involve unpaid labor, for which younger adults may receive salaries. Unpaid

Donna Day/Big Cheese Photo/SuperStock

Rising Labor Force Participation Rates among Older Adults

Chart: Labor force participation rates by age group

Age group	1994	2004	2014	2024
65–69 years	21.9%	27.7%	31.6%	36.2%
70–74 years	11.8%	15.3%	18.9%	22.8%
75–79 years	6.6%	8.8%	11.3%	14.4%
75 years and older	5.4%	6.1%	8.0%	10.6%

Note: Data for 2024 are projections.

Source: Toossi 2015:Table 3. *Photo:* Iaflor/Getty Images

ageism to refer to prejudice and discrimination based on a person's age. For example, we may choose to assume that someone cannot handle a rigorous job because he is "too old," or we may refuse to give someone a job with authority because she is "too young."

When analyzing obstacles people face as a consequence of age, we must consider the impact of perception and denial of opportunity. Critics argue that neither disengagement nor activity theory answers the question of *why* social interaction must change or decrease for aging adults. The low status of older people is seen in prejudice and discrimination against them, in age segregation, and in unfair job practices—none of which are directly addressed by either disengagement or activity theory.

Although firing people simply because they are old violates federal law, courts have upheld the right to lay off older workers for economic reasons. Critics contend that, later, the same firms hire young, cheaper workers to replace experienced older workers. When economic growth slows and companies cut back on their workforces, the number of complaints of age bias rises sharply as older workers begin to suspect they were bearing a disproportionate share of the layoffs. For example, between 2006 and 2008, during which the U.S. economy entered into a deep economic recession, complaints of age discrimination filed with the Equal Employment Opportunity Commission rose by 49 percent (EEOC 2014).

As a whole, elderly people in the United States enjoy a standard of living that is much higher now than at any point in the nation's past. To some extent, older people owe their overall improved standard of living to a greater

elderly workers include hospital volunteers (versus aides and orderlies), drivers for charities such as the Red Cross (versus chauffeurs), tutors (in contrast to teachers), and craftspeople for charity bazaars (in contrast to carpenters and dressmakers). Continued engagement in the workforce has been a growing trend. In 2014, for example, 18.6 percent of those aged 65 and older worked full- or part-time (Toossi 2015:Table 3). Though many continue to work because they enjoy the social engagement work provides, others do so out of financial necessity.

AGEISM AND DISCRIMINATION

Physician Robert Butler (1990), through his research as a gerontologist in the 1970s, became concerned when he learned that a housing development near his home in metropolitan Washington, D.C., barred elderly people. Butler coined the term

Ageism Prejudice and discrimination based on a person's age.

5 Movies on AGING

Up
A cranky old man and a young boy embark on an unusual adventure.

Our Souls at Night
Two elderly neighbors find comfort, companionship, and love.

45 Years
On the brink of their 45th wedding anniversary, a couple confronts the past.

Beginners
Love lessons learned from an elderly father.

The Bucket List
Two men confront death by ticking off items on their to-do list.

accumulation of wealth—in the form of home owner-ship, private pensions, and other financial assets. But much of the improvement is due to more generous Social Security benefits. Although modest when compared with other countries' pension programs, Social Security nevertheless provides 33 percent of all income received by older people in the United States. Still, in 2017, 9.2 percent of people aged 65 or older lived below the poverty line (Fontenot, Semega, and Kollar 2018; Social Security Administration 2017).

Members of groups who face a greater likelihood of income inequality earlier in their lives, including women and members of racial and ethnic minorities, continue to do so when they are older. For women aged 65 or older, the poverty rate is 10.5 percent compared to the rate for elderly men of 7.5 percent. Considering race and ethnicity, the 19.3 percent poverty rates for African Americans and 17 percent for Hispanics aged 65 or older was more than twice the 7 percent rate for non-Hispanic Whites of the same age (U.S. Census Bureau 2018c:Table 3 & Table 7).

DEATH AND DYING

In the film *The Bucket List,* Morgan Freeman and Jack Nicholson play the two main characters who are diagnosed with terminal cancer and have less than one year to live. They make a list of all the things they would like to do before they "kick the bucket." On the list are things they had never dared to do, such as traveling the world and sky-diving, but it also includes reconciling broken relationships.

Until recently, death was a taboo topic in the United States. Death represents a fundamental disruption that cannot be undone, so we often find it easier to live with a sense of denial about our mortality. In the words of sociologist Peter Berger, "Death presents society with a formidable problem . . . because it threatens the basic assumptions of order on which society rests" (1969:23). However, psychologist Elisabeth Kübler-Ross (1969), through her pioneering book *On Death and Dying,* greatly encouraged open discussion of the process of dying. Drawing on her work with 200 cancer patients, Kübler-Ross identified five stages of the experience: denial, anger, bargaining, depression, and finally acceptance.

Although we may still be uncomfortable with the topic, *The Bucket List*'s portrayal of a "good death" represents one of the ways we have become more open about it. Gerontologist Richard Kalish (1985) laid out some of the issues people must face to prepare for a "good death." These included completing unfinished business, such as settling insurance and inheritance matters; restoring harmony to social relationships and saying farewell to friends and family; dealing with medical needs; and making funeral plans and other arrangements for survivors. In accomplishing these tasks, the dying person actively contributes to smooth intergenerational transitions, role continuity, compliance with medical procedures, and minimal disruption of the social system, despite the loss of a loved one.

We have also begun to create institutions to facilitate our wishes for a good death. The practice of **hospice care,** introduced in England in the 1960s, is devoted to easing this final transition. Hospice workers seek to improve the quality of a dying person's last days by offering comfort and by helping the person remain at home, or in a home-like setting at a hospital or other special facility, until the end. In 2016, there were 4,382 Medicare-certified hospice programs in operation serving 1.43 million Medicare beneficiaries (NHPCO 2018).

Recent changes in the United States suggest additional ways in which people have broken through the historical taboos about death. For example, bereavement practices—once highly structured—are becoming increasingly varied and therapeutic. More and more people are actively addressing the inevitability of death by making wills, establishing "living wills" (health care proxies that explain their feelings about the use of life support equipment), donating organs, and providing instructions for family members about funerals, cremations, and burials. Given medical and technological advances and increasingly open discussion and negotiation regarding death and dying, it is possible that good deaths may become a social norm in the United States (Meier et al. 2016; Solomon 2016).

> **Hospice care** Treatment of terminally ill individuals in their own homes, or in special hospital units or other facilities, with the goal of helping them die comfortably, without pain.

We encounter some of the most difficult socialization challenges (and rites of passage) in these later years of life. Retirement undermines the sense of self we had that was based in our occupation, a particularly significant source of identity in the United States. Similarly, taking stock of our accomplishments and disappointments, coping with declining physical abilities, and recognizing the inevitability of death may lead to painful adjustments. Part of the difficulty is that potential answers to the "Now what?" question that we might have asked in previous life stages are dwindling, and we begin to face the end of our days.

> Old age has its pleasures, which though different, are not less than the pleasures of youth.
>
> W. Somerset Maugham (2010)

And yet, as we reflect on the story of our lives, we can look back to see all the people who shaped us into becoming who we are. Such relationships play a crucial role in our overall self-concept and self-satisfaction. As we have already seen, we are interdependent. And, though the influences of others on our life can be both a blessing and a curse, we wouldn't be who we are without them.

SOCIOLOGY IS A VERB

Technology Fast

To learn more about how much we take technology and its impact for granted, go on a "technology fast." In other words, give up your cell phone, computer, television, Internet access, and so on for some preset period of time, such as a day, several days, or a week. Keep a journal. What did you miss most? What did you find yourself doing instead? How difficult was it? Did it get any easier over time? What lessons did you learn?

For REVIEW

I. **How do we become ourselves?**
    - We are vulnerable at birth and depend on the socializing influences of others with whom we interact to provide us with the cultural tools necessary for our survival.

II. **Who shapes our socialization?**
    - Although almost anyone with whom we interact can have a significant influence on us, particularly important to our development are family, school, peer group, mass media, religion, and the state.

III. **How does our development change over time?**
    - We learn new things at various stages of our life course, experiencing significant transitions as we pass from childhood to adulthood and again from adulthood into old age. At each stage, the kinds of things expected of us by others shift significantly.

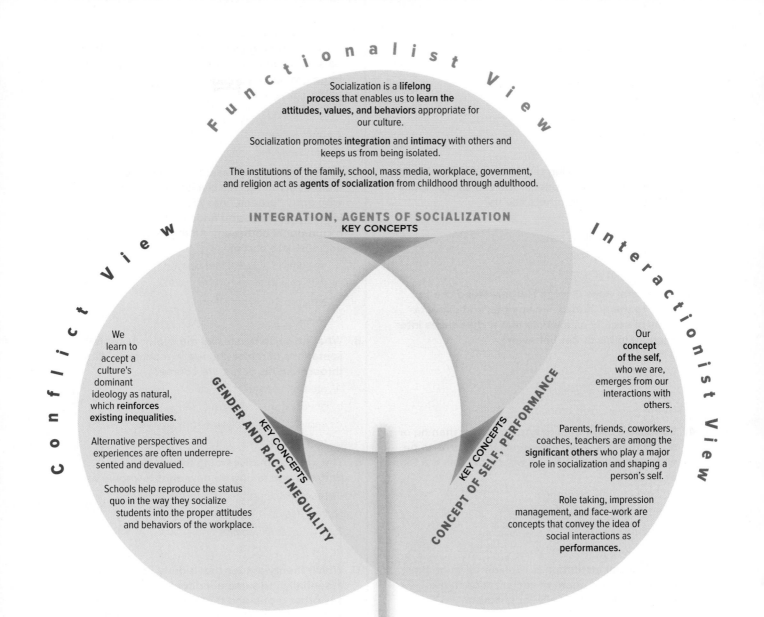

Functionalist View

Socialization is a **lifelong process** that enables us to **learn the attitudes, values, and behaviors** appropriate for our culture.

Socialization promotes **integration** and **intimacy** with others and keeps us from being isolated.

The institutions of the family, school, mass media, workplace, government, and religion act as **agents of socialization** from childhood through adulthood.

INTEGRATION, AGENTS OF SOCIALIZATION
KEY CONCEPTS

Conflict View

We learn to accept a culture's dominant ideology as natural, which **reinforces existing inequalities.**

Alternative perspectives and experiences are often underrepresented and devalued.

Schools help reproduce the status quo in the way they socialize students into the proper attitudes and behaviors of the workplace.

KEY CONCEPTS
GENDER AND RACE, INEQUALITY

Interactionist View

Our **concept of the self,** who we are, emerges from our interactions with others.

Parents, friends, coworkers, coaches, teachers are among the **significant others** who play a major role in socialization and shaping a person's self.

Role taking, impression management, and face-work are concepts that convey the idea of social interactions as **performances.**

KEY CONCEPTS
CONCEPT OF SELF, PERFORMANCE

MAKE THE CONNECTION

After reviewing the chapter, answer the following questions:

1

How would each perspective describe the impact that extreme isolation has on people?

2

How would each perspective explain the role socialization performs among children?

3

How would a functionalist look at anticipatory socialization? How might this view differ from a conflict approach?

4

Which agents of socialization have been most influential in your life? How does each perspective help shed light on those influences?

Pop Quiz

1. **Babies learn to imitate the sounds of the language they hear even before they know the words. What term do sociologists use to describe the process of internalizing culture?**
   a. socialization
   b. culturalization
   c. symbolization
   d. degradation

2. **Which of the following terms does Charles Horton Cooley use for his model of the self as a product of how we imagine others see us?**
   a. socialization
   b. the looking-glass self
   c. the I and the Me
   d. internalization

3. **What term does George Herbert Mead use to refer to the attitudes, viewpoints, and expectations of society as a whole that a child takes into account in his or her behavior?**
   a. play
   b. role taking
   c. dramaturgical analysis
   d. the generalized other

4. **Suppose a clerk tries to appear busier than he or she actually is when a supervisor happens to be watching. Erving Goffman would say this is a form of what?**
   a. degradation ceremony
   b. impression management
   c. resocialization
   d. looking-glass self

5. **Which social institution is considered to be the most important agent of socialization in the United States, especially for children?**
   a. family
   b. school
   c. peer group
   d. mass media

6. **Which of the following terms describes the variety of technologies that provide the capacity to easily transmit large quantities of information to large groups of people?**
   a. the Internet
   b. material culture
   c. print
   d. mass media

7. **On the first day of basic training in the army, a male recruit has his civilian clothes replaced with army "greens," has his hair shaved off, loses his privacy, and finds that he must use a communal bathroom. All these humiliating activities are part of**
   a. becoming a significant other.
   b. impression management.
   c. a degradation ceremony.
   d. face-work.

8. **What do sociologists call the symbolic representations of major change in a person's status throughout his or her life course?**
   a. rites of passage
   b. anticipatory socialization
   c. impression management
   d. role taking

9. **The process of discarding former behavior patterns and taking on new ones is known as**
   a. resocialization.
   b. impression management.
   c. anticipatory socialization.
   d. the I.

10. **Which theory argues that elderly people have essentially the same need for social interaction as any other group and that those who remain active and socially involved will be best adjusted?**
    a. disengagement theory
    b. institutional discrimination theory
    c. activity theory
    d. ageism theory

1. (a), 2. (b), 3. (d), 4. (b), 5. (a), 6. (d), 7. (c), 8. (a), 9. (a), 10. (c)

WINNING AND LOSING

Life is like a game. Saying so has become something of a cliché, the kind of thing that appears on greeting cards and motivational posters, usually followed by some inspirational comments about how one should play. And yet, sociologically speaking, paying attention to how games operate can help us better understand what happens in our lives and why.

In the United States, players in most games start with the same basic chances—equal numbers of cards, identical amounts of cash, or the same space on the board. Card shuffling and dice throwing introduce randomness that could tilt the odds, but the presupposition is that winners and losers are determined more by skill than by anything else. In some games, however, the structure of the game itself shapes likely outcomes. One example is the traditional Chinese card game Zheng Shangyou (争上游), meaning "struggling upstream." Many variations of this game exist, including Dai Hin Min (大貧民), in Japan and Tiên Lên in Vietnam. In the United States, adaptations include Kings and Servants, the Great Dalmuti, President, and Scum.

What makes such games distinctive is that the position each player occupies conveys advantages or disadvantages. In one six-player version, positions include king, queen, jack, merchant, peasant, and servant. After all the cards have been dealt, the servant gives the king his or her best three cards, receiving the king's three worst cards in return. The peasant and queen similarly exchange two cards and the merchant and jack exchange one. Play then commences with people seeking to get rid of their cards by playing higher cards than those played by the person with the lead. At the end of each hand, after all the cards have been played, players change seats: The first person to go out, having played all his or her cards, becomes the new king, continuing until the last one out becomes the new servant. Because of the card exchanges, people at the top tend to stay at the top and those at the bottom stay at the bottom.

As a player at the top, you can easily feel good about yourself and chalk up your success to skill. As a player at the bottom, you can get discouraged, doubt your skill, and resent the unfair advantages of those at the top. There's nothing like having to give up two aces and a king only to receive worthless cards in return to make transparent the consequences of the game's unequal structure.

The choices we make do not occur in a vacuum. What these games suggest for those at the bottom is that, even if you play your cards right, you can still lose. In these games, as in life, our structural positions shape the options and opportunities available to us.

As You READ >>

- **What does society provide that we need?**
- **How do sociologists describe traditional versus modern societies?**
- **How does social structure shape individual action?**

>> Social Interaction

We like to believe we are masters of our own fates, yet the contexts within which we can make choices, such as at home, school, or the workplace, shape the choices we make. In this chapter we address how we construct society, the third stage of the three-step model of "World Construction." In the first stage of that model, we construct culture in order to establish a relationship to nature and with each other, as we saw in Chapter 3. During the second stage, through socialization, our selves become products of culture we've created, as explored in Chapter 4. Turning now to the third stage, we focus on **social structure,** which provides the underlying framework of society, consisting of the positions people occupy and the relationships between them. We can think of structure as a kind of social geography or environment. When sociologists ask questions about the significance of place, they look at the ways in which the positions we occupy shape how we think and act.

In this chapter we explore the core elements that make up society. Elements include statuses, groups, and networks, along with institutions such as family, education, and religion. We will go on to explore those institutions and others in greater depth in the chapters that follow.

Social structure The underlying framework of society consisting of the positions people occupy and the relationships between them.

Social interaction A reciprocal exchange in which two or more people read, react, and respond to each other.

SELF AND SOCIETY

To better understand the social positions we occupy, such as daughter, student, or employee, we can begin by taking a look at our everyday exchanges with others. Whether we are working together to construct culture or learning from each other through socialization, we do so via **social interaction,** a reciprocal exchange in which two or more people read, react, and respond to each other. Through this process we come to know what is expected of us. When parents discipline us or teachers praise us, we use those punishments and rewards to better inform how we might act in the future. The choices we make create patterns of behavior over time; thus our everyday interactions form the building blocks of society.

Our daily encounters with others—whether going to class, working on the job, or driving in traffic—shape who we become. Our self, as we saw in Chapter 4, must be understood as an ongoing project, constantly created and revised through our exchanges with others. Society provides the context within which that dynamic process of self-creation occurs. In the words of George Herbert Mead, "Selves can only exist in definite relationships to other selves. No hard-and-fast line can be drawn between our own selves and the selves of others" (1934:164). This social or relational conception of the self runs counter to the dominant sense of the self in the United States expressed in phrases such as "rugged individualism" or "I did it my way."

Over time, through interactions with others, we develop routine patterns of behavior that we take for granted—sitting at the same desk, having lunch with the same coworkers, traveling the same route. We do the same things and think many of the same thoughts, day after day. And so do others. Eventually such repeated practices can solidify into formal and informal norms, or become institutionalized in the form of laws. The resulting predictability allows us to know what to do most of the time.

In time, the positions we occupy relative to others (such as student, boss, or traffic cop) also solidify, and we develop mutual expectations of how people in such positions should act. As these perceptions are shared with others beyond our immediate sphere of experience, it becomes possible to talk about the positions themselves—and the various relationships between them—apart from the individuals who occupy them. The end result is society—the structure of relationships within which culture is created and shared through regularized patterns of social interaction.

POSITIONS AND POWER

As the patterns of relationships between us become routine, alternative ways of organizing society seem less possible. According to the conflict perspective, those taken-for-granted patterns create a power differential in which some people's values and voices are privileged over others. And, as we saw in the "Us versus Them" section in Chapter 4, we can become largely unaware that such differences exist.

When members of less powerful groups challenge existing social norms, they can raise society's collective awareness about the consequences of group membership or social position and help us perceive reality in a new way. For example, when Olympic gold medalist Muhammad Ali began his professional boxing career in the early 1960s, he was much like any other young African American fighter. He was managed and sponsored by a White boxing syndicate and went by his given name, Cassius Clay. Soon, however, the young boxer rebelled against the stereotypes of the self-effacing Black athlete and began to define his own social role. He converted to Islam, becoming a member of the U.S.-based Nation of Islam, and abandoned his "slave name" to take the name Muhammad Ali. He insisted on expressing his own political views, including refusing to fight in the Vietnam War. Ali changed the terms of social interaction for African American athletes by rebelling against racist thinking and terminology. In redefining culture, he helped open up new opportunities for himself and for other African Americans in the world of sports and beyond.

>> Elements of Social Structure

When it comes to games, as we saw earlier, the rules we invent provide us with a coherent structure. Rules specify whether to use a board, cards, dice, or tokens. They tell us what actions players can take and when they can take them. When rules change, whether in a game or in society, we must alter our actions accordingly. Game designer Zach Gage decided to mess with the rules of a classic game in his smartphone app *Really Bad Chess*. His game randomly distributes which chess pieces you receive and where they are placed. You might have five queens while your opponent has only one. As a result, the tried-and-true chess strategies and tactics that have worked for hundreds of years no longer apply. Players must adapt to the changing circumstances each time they play (Suellentrop 2016). Imagine if society was like that, if each morning we learned that the rules of the game—our material, cognitive, and normative culture—had changed and we had to adapt on the fly.

Every game has its own internal logic, the parameters within which we play. Society, though vastly more complex, functions in a similar manner. Social structure provides the underlying framework of society by linking together the positions people occupy and defining the relationships between them. A building under construction provides a helpful analogy. Only early on can we see the framework—the girders, joists, studs, trusses, and the like—that composes the internal skeleton on which the building depends. In the same way, sociologists seek to identify and reveal society's four elemental building blocks, which include statuses and roles, groups, social networks, and social institutions. We look at each of these below.

STATUSES AND ROLES

Though the interaction between individuals provides the foundation upon which society exists, social structure transcends the particular people who populate it. In a college classroom, for example, from a structural perspective, the specific individuals who play the parts of student and professor matter less than the parts they play. To better understand how this works, we can begin by looking at both statuses and roles.

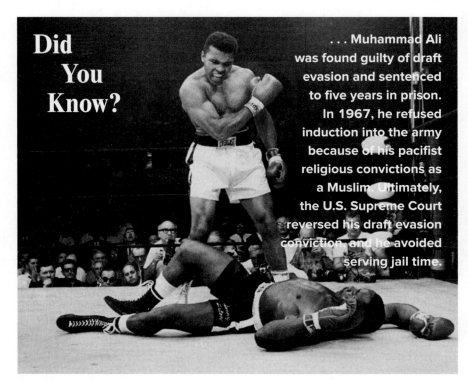

Did You Know?

. . . Muhammad Ali was found guilty of draft evasion and sentenced to five years in prison. In 1967, he refused induction into the army because of his pacifist religious convictions as a Muslim. Ultimately, the U.S. Supreme Court reversed his draft evasion conviction, and he avoided serving jail time.

Photo: John Rooney/AP Images

Achieved and Ascribed Status In sociology, **status,** which refers to the social positions we occupy relative to others, is the most basic component of social structure. In the context of families we might occupy the status of daughter, grandmother, or nephew; within the workplace, we might be an assistant manager, CEO, or salesperson. Because they emphasize the position rather than the person, statuses exist independent of the individuals who occupy them. We can occupy multiple statuses at the same time and move between a variety of statuses over the course of our lives.

> **Status** The social positions we occupy relative to others.
>
> **Achieved status** A social position that is within our power to change.
>
> **Ascribed status** A social position assigned to a person by society without regard for the person's unique talents or characteristics.
>
> **Master status** A status that dominates others and thereby determines a person's general position in society.

Sociologists categorize statuses based on how we come to occupy them. An **achieved status** is a social position we have earned as a consequence of something we have done. Those accomplishments can be either positive or negative. For example, pianist, college graduate, sorority member, and parent are all achieved statuses. Each is realized by taking actions necessary for their attainment—practicing, studying, pledging, and having a baby. These are the kinds of accomplishments we generally celebrate. But becoming a prisoner is also an achieved status, a consequence of committing a crime. As we explore in the section "The American Dream" in Chapter 10, the rags-to-riches stories that are part of the American Dream presuppose the possibility of achieving a higher social status.

By contrast, an **ascribed status** is assigned to a person by society without regard for the person's unique talents or characteristics. Whereas achieved statuses are earned, ascribed statuses are imposed. The assignment frequently takes place at birth—age, race/ethnicity, and sex are all considered ascribed statuses—but any characteristic can become an ascribed status so long as a sufficient number of people in society with the power to do so assign it significance and impose it on others. As we will see in Chapter 13, for example, conceptions of race in the United States have changed over time, which suggests that biology alone does not justify the significance attached to these statuses. Ascribed statuses are often used to justify privileges or to assign a person membership in a subordinate group.

Because statuses are social constructions we create, they are subject to change, and the line between them can become fuzzy. We see that happening now with regard to definitions of sex, gender, and sexuality. For a long time in the United States, people assumed that our sex was determined at conception, that there are only two distinct sexes, and that the one you belong to is patently obvious, a topic we will explore in more detail in Chapter 12. Furthermore, they assumed that how you think and act was largely determined by which category you were in, and that there was nothing you could do about it.

Americans have increasingly come to believe that biology is not destiny. People can make choices about what career they pursue, whether they want to have and raise children, what emotions they exhibit, what they wear, or how they express their sexuality. For example, until very recently, most Americans assumed that people's ascribed status as "male" or "female" limited their choice in marriage partners to members of the opposite sex. In 1996, 27 percent of U.S. adults thought same-sex marriage should be legal, but by 2018 that number rose to 67 percent. Perceptions vary based on political party affiliation, with 83 percent of Democrats supporting the right of same-sex couples to marry compared to 44 percent of Republicans (McCarthy 2018). The 2015 Supreme Court decision to recognize the legal right of same-sex couples to marry reflected changing public sentiment on the matter.

Master Status Not all statuses are created equal. Whether achieved or ascribed, some statuses are seen as having greater significance in defining who we are than are others (Hughes 1945). Sociologists use the term **master status** to describe a status that dominates others and thereby determines a person's general position in society. This status serves as the primary lens through

Social Statuses

Photo: Amos Morgan/Photodisc/Getty Images

In a 2015 decision, the Supreme Court opened up a new status for same-sex couples: married.   Rob Melnychuk/DigitalVision/Getty Images

possible, which can lead to systematic denial of opportunities for those in the negatively stigmatized status.

Roles Each status you occupy, whether it be parent, college student, social worker, or Muslim, comes with a set of actions expected of people in that status. If you are a parent, you are expected to provide food, clothes, and shelter for your child. If you are a student, you should go to class, study, and more. Sociologists use the term **social role** to describe the set of expected behaviors for people who occupy a given social status. To distinguish between the two, a status is something you are, and a role is something you do. You occupy a status and play a role.

In some roles, our performance feels perfectly natural. We feel comfortable just being ourselves. This occurs most frequently when the status we occupy provides a clear sense of what others expect of us and what we can expect of them. For example, we might feel this way while hanging out with close friends who can even fin-

> **Social role** A set of expected behaviors for people who occupy a given social status.

which people view other characteristics someone might have. Persons with disabilities frequently observe that nondisabled individuals see them only as blind, or only as wheelchair users, and so on, rather than as complex human beings with individual strengths and weaknesses whose disability is merely one aspect of their lives. In other words, their status as "disabled" receives undue weight, overshadowing their ability to hold meaningful employment and contributing to widespread discrimination (Banks and Lawrence 2006). In the United States, race, sex, and class often serve as master statuses.

Master status has consequences for opportunity. The African American activist Malcolm X (1925–1965), an eloquent and controversial advocate of Black power and Black pride in the 1960s, recalled that his feelings and perspectives changed dramatically in eighth grade. At that time, his English teacher, a White man, advised him that his goal of becoming a lawyer was ridiculous and suggested he become a carpenter instead. As a result, Malcolm X (1964) realized that, in America, being Black represented a master status that created an obstacle to his dream of achieving the status of lawyer. He spent the rest of his life challenging that assumption. Taken-for-granted conceptions of master status shape perceptions of what's

ish our sentences. Other times, especially when we move into a new status, our actions can seem forced. The first semester at college, a first date, or the first week at a new job are all awkward times when people often fear they are going to be unmasked as frauds.

As we learned with Erving Goffman's dramaturgical approach, we are, all of us, always performing roles regardless of how we feel. Bruce Springsteen, reflecting back on his career as a rock and roll superstar, addressed the seeming conflict between his onstage persona as a hard-rocking hero who's having nothing but a good time and the bouts of depression he experienced throughout his adult life. "I had plenty of days," he said, "where I'd go, 'Man, I wish I could be *that* guy.' And there's a big difference between what you see on stage and then my general daily, my daily existence" (Springsteen 2016). The same might be said for most of us, most of the time.

What we see when we interact with others represents the external presentation of self as dictated by the statuses we occupy.

Throughout his life, Malcolm X worked to redefine the significance of race as master status.   Burt Shavitz/Pic Inc/The LIFE Images Collection/Getty Images

Our status as teacher or child shapes what we do.   ImageDJ/Alamy Stock Photo

a paper for a literature class, going to a work-study job washing dishes in the cafeteria, practicing clarinet for the college band, attending the big game, and managing room-mate drama. **Role conflict** occurs when incompatible expectations arise from two or more social statuses held by the same person. For example, a working mom with kids at home who has returned to school to get her degree might struggle to balance the expectations tied to her multiple statuses as employee, parent, and college student. To keep the difference between strain and conflict clear, remember that role strain addresses tension within a single status, and role conflict deals with tension between statuses.

Role strain and role conflict both produce stress. They challenge our capacity to efficiently allocate our time, attention, and resources. We find ourselves forced to calculate the relative costs and benefits of fulfilling one role obligation while neglecting another. In doing so, we weigh how important each role is to us along with the possible rewards or punishments we might receive from others (Goode 1960).

Changing our status changes how we act, think, and feel. All of us encounter times when we feel awkward and uncomfortable. In Goffman's words, "Behind many masks and many characters, each performer tends to wear a single look, a naked unsocialized look, a look of concentration, a look of one who is privately engaged in a difficult, treacherous task" (Goffman 1959:235). The task of effectively carrying out a successful performance is compounded by the fact that we must perform for multiple, sometimes conflicting, audiences.

─SOCTHINK─

List several social statuses you occupy. Which ones are ascribed, and which are achieved? What roles are you expected to play as a consequence of the positions you occupy?

─SOCTHINK─

Provide an example of both role strain and role conflict from your experience. What changes in the social structure might you propose to help alleviate each?

One way to alleviate role strain and role conflict is modify existing status relationships and role expectations. Doing so is difficult. Lack of power to alter expectations, relationships, and access to valued resources limits an individual's opportunity to bargain with others. As we will see in Chapter 12, for example, women fought hard to alter the social structure that denied them equal access to education, jobs, promotions, and more. Any group working for change but lacking access to power in society faces an uphill challenge to revise the structure because the status quo seeks to reproduce itself.

Role Strain and Role Conflict Given that roles involve expected behaviors, tension can develop when we encounter role expectations that seem at odds with each other. Sociologists explore two types of such tensions: role strain and role conflict. **Role strain** occurs when role expectations within the same social status clash. For example, as a college student, it can be a challenge to balance the time you must spend studying for a sociology exam, writing

Role strain The difficulty that arises when role expectations within the same social status clash.

Role conflict The situation that occurs when incompatible expectations arise from two or more social statuses held by the same person.

Role exit The process of disengagement from a role that is central to one's self-identity in order to establish a new role and identity.

Role Exit In addition to having to learn the social roles expected of us as we enter into new statuses, there are also steps we go through when we are leaving a status. Sociologist Helen Rose Fuchs Ebaugh (1988) used the term **role exit** to describe the process of disengagement

Personal Sociology

Structure Matters

Although I love teaching, I hate grading. When I mention that to students, they say I have no one to blame but myself; if I didn't assign things, I wouldn't have to grade them. But I don't teach in a vacuum. If I didn't assign papers and tests, students would focus their time and energy on their looming chemistry test or their literature paper instead of reading for, participating in, or even attending my course. It is not that students aren't interested or sincere; it's that they are forced to budget their time for which professors compete using assignments. Because we exist in social systems, the expectations of those systems limit the amount of innovation we might desire. In what ways might the structures we are embedded within—school, work, recreation—inhibit us from making changes even if we would like to do so?

from a role that is central to one's self-identity in order to establish a new role and identity. Drawing on interviews—with, among others, ex-convicts, divorced men and women, recovering alcoholics, ex-nuns, former doctors, retirees, and transgender individuals—Ebaugh (herself a former nun) studied the process of voluntarily exiting from significant social roles.

Ebaugh has offered a four-stage model of role exit. The first stage begins with doubt. The person experiences frustration, burnout, or simply unhappiness with an accustomed status and the roles associated with that social position. The second stage involves a search for alternatives. A person who is unhappy with their career may take a leave of absence; an unhappily married couple may begin what they see as a trial separation. The third stage is the action stage: leaving. Ebaugh found that the vast majority of her respondents could identify a clear turning point when it became essential to take final action and quit their jobs, end their marriages, or engage in some other type of role exit. Only 20 percent of respondents saw their role exit as a gradual, evolutionary process that had no definitive turning point.

The last stage of role exit involves the creation of a new identity. College students, for example, may experience role exit as they transition from their high school identity, going from a mostly dependent child living at home to a somewhat independent college student living with peers in a dorm. In doing so, they may leave behind the objects associated with their prior identities, such as trophies, letter jackets, or stuffed animals (Silver 1996). In their place they

Transgender individuals, such as Jenna Talackova (pictured here), often have to negotiate the four stages of role exit. Photo by Kevork Djansezian/Getty Images

may fill their dorm room with objects symbolizing how they wish to be perceived. Clothes, posters, and room decorations, for example, are calculated to say, "This is me."

SOCTHINK

Whether from a sports team, a religious group, the military, or some other close-knit group, what experience, if any, have you had with role exiting? To what extent does your experience match the four stages Ebaugh describes?

GROUPS

The statuses we occupy, along with their corresponding social role expectations, are linked with other statuses to form groups, the second element of social structure. In sociological terms, a **group** consists of two or more people, united by a shared sense of identity or purpose, who interact with each other over time in ways that distinguish them from outsiders. The members of a women's softball team,

> **Group** Two or more people, united by a shared sense of identity or purpose, who interact with each other over time in ways that distinguish them from outsiders.

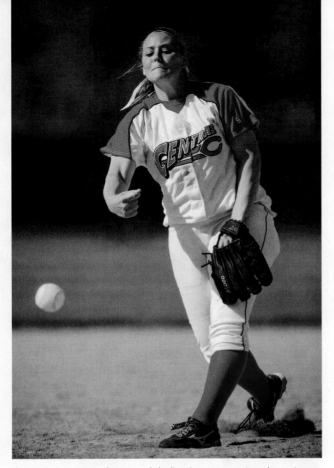

Given the amount of time and dedication teammates share, teams can serve as primary groups. Courtesy of Central College, photographer Dan Vander Beek

a hospital's business office, a synagogue, or a symphony orchestra constitute a group. A group can be distinguished from an aggregate, which consists of a collection of people who happen to be in the same place at the same time but who do not interact regularly or have a shared sense of purpose or common practices. Examples of aggregates include people waiting to cross the street at a busy intersection or riding together in an elevator.

We spend much of our time interacting in group settings. The type of group we are in influences our level of commitment and participation. Some groups demand our almost undivided attention and shape our core identity; others allow us to more easily accomplish specific goals.

Primary and Secondary Groups Charles Horton Cooley (1902), whose theory of the looking-glass self we encountered in Chapter 4, coined the term **primary groups** to refer to small groups characterized by intimate, face-to-face association and cooperation. Such groups often entail long-term commitment and involve more of what we think of as our whole self. Families constitute primary groups for many, although people also build

Primary groups Small group characterized by intimate, face-to-face association and cooperation.

Secondary groups Formal, impersonal groups created to accomplish specific, shared goals.

close-knit, in-depth relationships with teammates, like-minded religious believers, coworkers, and fellow street gang members. In sports, for example, commitment to the cliché that there is "no 'I' in 'team'" often leads to a sense that teammates are "like family." As they work together, their level of trust and interdependence grows. Teammates come to know that the pitcher, outfielder, or catcher on the team not only will be there for them on the field, but will also have their backs when they need it off the field as well.

Historically, primary groups dominated in traditional societies which were smaller in scale and more intimate, but in modern society we spend much of our time interacting with others in **secondary groups** which are formal, impersonal groups created to accomplish specific, shared goals. Relationships between members of these groups may involve relatively little social intimacy. Participation in such groups is typically more instrumental, meaning that these groups exist to accomplish defined objectives. Our involvement is often segmental, meaning that we don't think of our whole self as being part of these groups, just that piece of our self that is relevant for successful accomplishment of our goals. For example, in a primary group, we may feel fully at home in the context of friends and family. But in secondary groups, such as a college class, we may be less willing to lower our emotional shields or bring up topics not appropriate to that context. Instead we may focus on the specific objective of doing what is necessary to pass the class, earn the credit, and ultimately graduate so that we might accomplish other life goals. The same approach may hold true for the workplace.

Comparison of Primary and Secondary Groups

Primary group	Secondary group
Generally small	Usually large
Relatively long period of interaction	Relatively short duration, often temporary
Intimate, face-to-face association	Little social intimacy or mutual understanding
Some emotional depth to relationships	Relationships generally superficial
Cooperative, friendly	More formal and impersonal

In-Groups and Out-Groups The shared norms, values, and goals of group members, along with their common experiences, create a boundary distinguishing insiders and outsiders. The resulting us–them divide can lead to a strong sense of group identity, but it often does so at the expense of others, frequently serving as a basis for exclusion, especially if "they" are perceived as different either culturally or racially. Sociologists use the terms in-group and out-group to identify these two classifications.

An **in-group** consists of a category of people who share a common identity and sense of belonging. Members differentiate between themselves and everybody else (Sumner 1906). The in-group may be as narrow as a teenage clique or as broad as an entire nation. An **out-group** is defined, relative to the in-group, as a category of people who do not belong or do not fit in. Among an in-group of high school "populars" or "jocks," for example, a science "brain" might be considered an out-group member, and vice versa.

Group membership shapes our perceptions. What we see as acceptable behavior for the in-group can be simultaneously viewed as inappropriate behavior for the out-group. Sociologist Robert Merton (1968) described this process as the conversion of "in-group virtues" into "out-group vices." We can see this differential standard operating in the context of terrorism. When a group or a nation takes aggressive actions, it usually justifies them as necessary even if civilians are hurt or killed. Opponents are quick to assign the emotion-laden label of *terrorist* to such actions and to appeal to the world community for condemnation. Yet these same people may themselves retaliate with actions that hurt civilians, which the first group will then condemn as terrorist acts (Juergensmeyer 2003).

College clubs provide many options for students to find others who share common interests.   Rawpixel.com/Shutterstock

Keith Srakocic/AP Images

SOCTHINK

How do in-groups and out-groups function in a typical U.S. high school? What groups are common? How are boundaries separating insiders and outsiders maintained?

Reference Groups Both in-groups and primary groups can dramatically influence the way an individual thinks and behaves. Sociologists call any group that individuals use as a standard for evaluating themselves and their own behavior a **reference group.** Such groups can have a significant impact on a members identity or sense of self. For example, a college student who joins a sorority or fraternity may pattern their behavior after their fellow Greeks. They may begin dressing like members, listening to the same music, sharing "tags" on Instagram, and hanging out at the same stores and clubs.

Reference groups have two basic purposes. First, they serve a normative function by setting and enforcing standards of conduct and belief. The new sorority or fraternity member will have to follow the group's dictates, at least to some extent, if they want to fit in. Second, reference groups perform a comparison function by serving as a standard against which people can measure themselves and others. A fraternity or sorority member will evaluate themself against a reference group composed of members of their "Greek" organizations (Merton and Kitt 1950).

In-group A category of people who share a common identity and sense of belonging.

Out-group A category of people who do not belong or do not fit in.

Reference group Any group that individuals use as a standard for evaluating themselves and their own behavior.

Coalitions As groups grow larger, coalitions begin to develop. A **coalition** is an alliance, whether temporary or permanent, geared toward a common goal. Coalitions form when people with diverse backgrounds or interests come together toward some shared objective that unites them. Coalition building occurs frequently in political movements. William Julius Wilson (1999) has reported on community-based organizations in Texas that include Whites and Latinxs, working-class and affluent, who banded together to work for improved sidewalks, better drainage systems, and comprehensive street paving. Out of this type of coalition building, Wilson hopes, will emerge better interracial understanding.

SOCIAL NETWORKS

These days, the term *social network* is primarily associated with our online connections through Instagram, Twitter, and the like, but it has always been possible to map the links that connect us with others. Networks represent the third element of social structure. A **social network** is a web of relationships through which people interact both directly and indirectly to accomplish formal and informal goals. Networks consist of two principal elements: nodes and relationships. In a social network, nodes consist of individuals, and relationships are the connections between them. The most basic building block of a social network is a **dyad** which consists of two connected nodes—for example, a tutor and a student or a boss and a worker. A **triad** consists of the relationships among three nodes, including both direct relationships (relationships between each of the possible pairs in the group) and indirect relationships (relationships connecting two people through the link provided by the third person).

For example, a friend of a friend would constitute an indirect relationship. Beyond triads, each additional node to the network compounds the complexity of the network's interrelationships, multiplying the number of possible indirect relationships and increasing the possible distance between any two individuals to friend of a friend of a friend status and beyond. Centrality measures the degree to which any particular individual has more direct and indirect relationships than do others (Fowler and Christakis 2009). As networks become larger, centrality becomes an important additional dimension.

Although an almost infinite combination of direct and indirect network links is possible, recurring patterns do occur. Among college students, sociologist Janice McCabe (2016a, 2016b) identified three distinctive types of friendship networks. The first type, *tight-knitters,* consists of one dense network in which nearly all friends are friends with each other. This looks something like a ball of yarn in which the various links intersect and overlap. The group can function like family with members providing social support and encouragement. In cases where these close-knit friends are high academic achievers, members may study together, bounce ideas off each other, proofread each other's papers, and in other ways increase prospects for academic success. If the group consists primarily of low academic achievers, it may reduce motivation and decrease likelihoods for academic success.

The second type, *compartmentalizers,* typically consists of two distinct clusters in which friends within each cluster know and interact with each other, but very few links exist between clusters. This model looks something like a bowtie with the person in the middle providing the primary link between the two groups. Frequently, one group is academically focused, with whom you might study or exchange ideas, while the other is socially focused, consisting of friends with whom you'd catch a cup of coffee or go to parties. This divide might also take the form of college friends versus friends from back home. The main challenge for this type is that the person in the middle can feel torn between the two groups. More than two clusters are possible, but more clusters place even greater stress on the person in the middle both in terms of time and identity.

> ## I belong, therefore I am.
>
> **An old Māori proverb**

Coalition A temporary or permanent alliance geared toward a common goal.

Social network A web of relationships through which people interact both directly and indirectly to accomplish formal and informal goals.

Dyad The most basic building block of a social network, it consists of two nodes and the relationship between them.

Triad Within a social network, it consists of three nodes and the direct and indirect relationships among them.

College Student Friendship Networks

- Tight-knitters: One dense network in which nearly all friends are friends with each other

- Compartmentalizers: Two (or more) separate clusters in which friends on one side do not know or interact with friends on the other

- Samplers: A diverse array of individual friendships with people who, for the most part, don't really know or connect with each other

Adolescent Sexual Networks

Each dot represents a boy or a girl at "Jefferson High." The lines that link them represent romantic and sexual relationships that occurred over an 18-month period. Though most of the teenagers had had just one or two partners, 288 of the 832 students interviewed were linked in a giant sexual network. Another 90 students were involved in relationships outside the school (not shown on this chart).

● Boys
○ Girls

Other relationships. (If a pattern was observed more than once, numeral indicates frequency.)

2   2   9   12   63

Source: Bearman, Moody, and Stovel 2004:58. *Photo:* Stockbyte/Getty Images

The third friendship network type, *samplers,* includes a diverse array of friends, who, for the most part, do not socialize with each other. In this case, the person in the middle is the only link, so it looks something like a daisy, with individual petals radiating away from the center. Individuals here tend to be academically more self-reliant, seeking out assistance as needed. Though more independent, those with this type of friendship network report feeling lonelier and more socially isolated.

Variation in network shapes and sizes became apparent when a group of sociologists set out to explore what the web of romantic relationships at a typical American high school might look like (Bearman, Moody, and Stovel 2004). Using careful data-collection techniques to enhance the validity of their findings, they found that 573 of the 832 students they surveyed had been either romantically or sexually involved in the previous 18 months. Of these, 63 couples represented dyads, connected only with each other as pairs with no other partners. Other students connected directly or indirectly with a handful of partners. As we can see in the "Adolescent Sexual Networks" graphic, one larger group connected 288 students directly or indirectly into a single extended network. Their results reinforce the sociological principle that the people with whom we connect link us together with others who may well be unknown or invisible to us.

Research on how social networks function has produced some surprising results. For example, sociologist Scott Feld (1991) discovered that, on average, "most people have fewer friends than their friends have." This claim, which has come to be known as the friendship paradox, is somewhat counterintuitive; most people believe that the opposite is the case (Zuckerman and Jost 2001). When taking an objective look at the composition of social networks, however, it turns out that the average number of friends our friends have is elevated by the fact that, even though the number of people with many friends is relatively small, those individuals appear repeatedly in our friend's networks, driving up their averages. In other words, popular friends have a disproportionate effect because they are named as friends over and over again. Researchers at Facebook decided to put the friendship paradox to the test. They found that 93 percent of active Facebook users had fewer friends than their friends had. On average, users had 190 friends while their friends averaged 635 friends (Strogatz 2012). Overall, as mathematician Steven Strogatz (2012) put it, "Our friends are typically more popular than we are."

Social network researchers, inspired by the friendship paradox, have explored a number of related phenomena. For example, in an analysis of Twitter users, and in an effort to control for the effect that outliers with high numbers of friends can have on the average, it turns out that, when analyzing the median instead of the mean, it's not just that the average number of our friend's friends is higher, it's also true that the majority of our friends have more friends than we do. This holds true for 98 percent of Twitter users (Kooti, Hodas, and Lerman 2014). Another study found that, if you are a scientist who has published a journal article, your coauthors will have more coauthors, more publications, and more citations than you (Eom and Jo 2014). It is hypothesized that the paradox is likely also true when it comes to wealth and number of sexual partners (Mullins 2014).

It turns out that the networks we participate in can play a major role in our lives. In fact, though our closest ties to family and friends represent our strongest relationships, some of the most valuable connections can come through weaker links we have with others. Sociologist Mark Granovetter (1973) argued that we can categorize our network relationships as more or less strong using measures such as time spent together, emotional intensity, mutual confidences, and a shared sense of reciprocal obligation. In denser parts of a network, clusters of people are drawn together by strong ties that exist between them. The connections between such individuals are typically characterized by **homophily,** which literally means love of the same, a term sociologists use to describe our tendency to establish close social network relationships with others who share our same knowledge, beliefs, practices, and characteristics (McPherson, Smith-Lovin, and Cook 2001). For example, people tend to associate with others who have the same jobs, interests, education, race, ethnicity, and more. These dense clusters within a social network can be linked together through ties between individuals within two different clusters who have direct ties between each other.

In an argument that came to be known as "the strength of weak ties," Granovetter (1973) maintained that weaker ties can be extremely important because they can connect us with whole new networks of people with whom we have no direct relationships. For example, when it comes to getting a job, he reported that most jobs were found not through contacts with close friends, but through people who job seekers saw occasionally or rarely. Such people, with whom we have weak ties, serve as a bridge between social networks, providing us access to valuable resources and information.

Further support for the strength of weak ties principle emerged when Facebook researchers explored how relationships formed. They discovered that the most effective way to meet someone and start a relationship was through friends of friends. Mutual friends, in effect, serve as matchmakers. Those who played this matchmaking role have 73 percent more friends than do the people they set up. Their friendship networks are also less dense, meaning the matchmaker's friends are less likely to know each other, presenting people a potential pool of possible partners. The matchmakers serve as bridges between people who might otherwise never connect (Burke, Diuk, and Friggeri 2015).

Social media theorist Clay Shirky (2008) maintains that the social networking potential of the Internet has radically transformed possibilities for collective action. In a survey of 40 nations, some of which are represented in the "Going Global: Social Networking" graphic, researchers found that 76 percent of Internet users claim to use social networking sites (Poushter 2016). Such connectedness opens up greater possibilities for widespread communication and action. Shirky argues that previous technologies inhibited collective behavior because those that allowed two-way communication (for example, the telephone) were largely limited to one-to-one conversations, and those that facilitated large-scale group formation through broadcasting were mostly limited to one-way communication (for example, television news viewers). With the Internet, he suggests, "group action just got easier" because it supports interactive, large-scale group formation. People can talk back and forth with each other and coordinate action, as occurred with the Women's March on January 21, 2017, in which 3 to 5 million people across the United States participated in marches to make a statement about Donald Trump's inauguration as president that occurred the day before (Chenoweth 2017).

Homophily Our tendency to establish close social network relationships with others who share our same knowledge, beliefs, practices, and characteristics.

Going GLOBAL

Social Networking

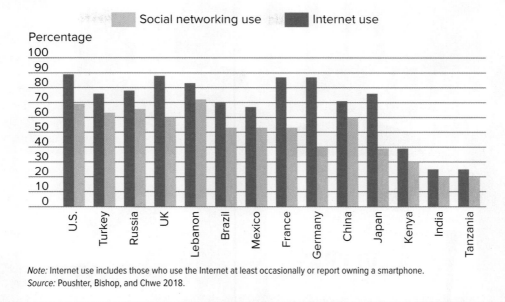

Note: Internet use includes those who use the Internet at least occasionally or report owning a smartphone.
Source: Poushter, Bishop, and Chwe 2018.

SOCIAL INSTITUTIONS

Combinations of statuses, groups, and networks can coalesce to address the needs of a particular sector of society, forming what sociologists refer to as institutions, the fourth element of social structure. **Social institutions** are integrated and persistent social networks dedicated to ensuring that society's core needs are met. Sociologists have tended to focus on five major institutions that serve as key elements of the larger social structure: family, education, religion, economy, and government. Although these institutions frequently overlap and interact, taking each individually enables us to see what functions each serves within the larger social structure. We look in depth at all five in future chapters, but we begin here by considering the functions each serve to society.

If a society is to survive, certain functions must be performed (Aberle et al. 1950). Focusing on institutions enables us to see the different ways in which societies fulfill these needs. It is within the context of *families,* for example, that we ensure the society's continued existence by producing the next generation. Families carry out both biological reproduction (having children) and social reproduction (teaching them the culture they need for survival). Families also provide care and protection for members. Through *education* we teach the more formal and public culture necessary to be members of the larger society. This includes the formal curriculum (history, math, science, and so on) but also includes learning to interact with others outside our immediate families. We rely on *religion* to be the glue that holds society together by establishing a clear identity with shared beliefs and practices, answering basic questions

about meaning, and enforcing both individual and collective discipline. *Government* helps maintain internal order through laws, policing, and punishment and seeks to establish stable relations with other societies through diplomacy. Finally, the *economy* regulates the production, distribution, and consumption of goods and services.

How societies choose to fulfill these functions can vary significantly, as can the degree to which these institutions overlap. When it comes to family, for example, at one point in U.S. history, having large, extended families was the norm, but after the Industrial Revolution, smaller and more diverse families became more common. In politics, one society may protect itself from external attack by amassing a large arsenal of weaponry; another may make determined efforts to remain neutral in world politics and to promote cooperative relationships with its neighbors. According to the functionalist perspective, no matter what its particular strategy, any society or relatively permanent group must address all these functional prerequisites for survival.

Focusing on the functions institutions fulfill can help us better understand social order, but it often implies that the way things are is the way things should be. Sociologists using the conflict perspective focus more on power, the consequences of difference, and resource distribution. They suggest that we must also look at the ways our construction of these institutions reinforces inequality. We can meet these functional needs in a variety of ways, so we should consider why some groups might seek to maintain the status quo.

> **Social institution** An integrated and persistent social network dedicated to ensuring that society's core needs are met.

Institutions, including government, provide the social order societies need.   Amble Design/Shutterstock

Major institutions, such as education, help perpetuate the privileges of the most powerful individuals and groups within a society while contributing to the powerlessness of others. To give one example, public schools in the United States are financed largely through property taxes.

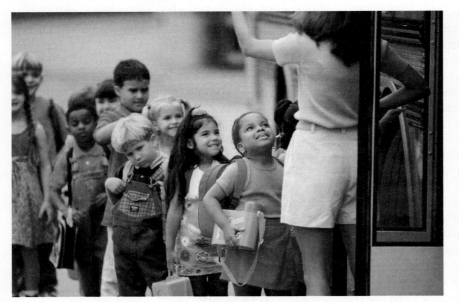

As an institution, education both provides for opportunity and reproduces inequality.
Purestock/SuperStock

This arrangement allows more-affluent areas to provide their children with better-equipped schools and better-paid teachers than low-income areas can afford. As a result, children from prosperous communities are better prepared to compete academically than children from impoverished communities. The structure of the nation's educational system permits and even promotes such unequal treatment of schoolchildren (Khan 2011; Kozol 2005).

By focusing on these four major elements of social structure—statuses and roles, groups, social networks, and social institutions—we gain an understanding of the building blocks of society. They clarify the factors we should consider when sociologists talk about the significance of place. We must look beyond our personal relationships with the significant others in our lives to also consider that those relationships exist as a consequence of a structure created by those who have come before us. We have the potential power to revise that structure. However, we also must recognize that we tend to reproduce the structure we have been socialized to accept as natural. Moreover, those already in power have an interest in maintaining that structure.

>> Traditional, Modern, and Postmodern Social Structures

Sociology arose as a discipline intended to illuminate and direct the transition from traditional to modern society. In the late 1800s, the taken-for-granted patterns and practices that had provided a sense of social order for hundreds of years seemed to be falling apart. Early sociologists believed that constructing a clear picture of the social structure that undergirded traditional societies would enable them to better understand the challenges faced with the rise of modern society.

GEMEINSCHAFT AND GESELLSCHAFT

Sociologist Ferdinand Tönnies (1855–1936) was appalled by the rise of industrial cities in his native Germany during the late 1800s. In his view, urban life was inferior to the close-knit community typical of rural villages. Tönnies ([1887] 1988) used the terms *Gemeinschaft* and *Gesellschaft,* typically translated as community and society, to distinguish the two.

A *Gemeinschaft* (pronounced "guh-MINE-shahft") consists of a close-knit community, often found in rural areas, in which strong personal bonds unite members. Virtually everyone knows one another, and social interactions are intimate and familiar, almost like in an extended family. Members feel a strong sense of loyalty to the group and willingly sacrifice their individual interests for the good of the whole. Social control in *gemeinschaft*-dominated societies occurs primarily through informal means, such as moral persuasion, gossip, and even gestures. These techniques work effectively because people genuinely care how others feel about them. However, with such interpersonal intensity comes minimal privacy and a presumption of individual sacrifice. Social change is relatively limited in societies characterized by *gemeinschaft,* with very few differences in the lifestyles from one generation to the next.

In contrast, a *Gesellschaft* (pronounced "guh-ZELL-shahft") consists of a large, impersonal, task-oriented society, typically urban, in which individuals have a limited commitment to the group. Relationships here, as we saw with secondary groups, emphasize instrumental or transactional exchanges. Interactions are governed by social roles that grow out of immediate tasks, such as purchasing a product or arranging a business meeting. In such societies, most people are strangers who feel little in common with other residents. Individuals can perceive themselves as superior to other members of the society, placing their interests above those of the group. There is minimal consensus concerning shared values beyond those of maximizing self-interest. As a result, social control must rest on formal techniques, such as laws and legally defined sanctions. Social change is a normal part of life in societies characterized by *Gesellschaft,* with substantial shifts evident even within a single generation.

Sociologists use these two terms to compare social structures that stress close relationships with those that feature less personal ties. It is easy to view the *Gemeinschaft* with nostalgia, as far better than the rat race of modern life. However, the more intimate relationships of the *Gemeinschaft* come at a price. The prejudice and discrimination found there can be quite confining; ascribed statuses such as family background often outweigh a person's unique talents and achievements. In addition, the *Gemeinschaft* tends to distrust individuals who are creative or simply different (Garrett 2003).

MECHANICAL AND ORGANIC SOLIDARITY

Whereas Tönnies looked back nostalgically on the *Gemeinschaft,* Émile Durkheim was more interested in the transition to modern society, which he felt represented the birth of a new form of social order. Durkheim hoped to use sociology as a science to better understand this transition. In his book *The Division of Labor in Society* ([1893] 1933), Durkheim highlighted the seemingly inverse relationship between the division of labor and the collective conscience. As jobs became more specialized, the shared sentiments that united communities grew weaker.

In societies in which there is minimal division of labor, a sense of group solidarity develops because people do the same things together over time. Such societies are characterized by what Durkheim calls **mechanical solidarity,** a type of social cohesion based on shared experiences, knowledge, and skill in which social

Gemeinschaft A close-knit community, often found in rural areas, in which strong personal bonds unite members.

Gesellschaft Consists of a large, impersonal, task-oriented society, typically urban, in which individuals have a limited commitment to the group.

Mechanical solidarity Social cohesion based on shared experiences, knowledge, and skills in which things function more or less the way they always have, with minimal change.

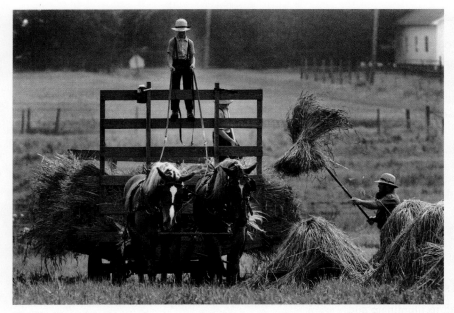

The lifestyles of the Amish change very little from generation to generation. Amy Sancetta/ AP Images

relations function more or less the way they always have. Societies with strong mechanical solidarity operate like a machine with limited change over time, which is why Durkheim chose the term *mechanical*. Most individuals perform the same basic tasks—as did their parents and grandparents before them—and they do so together. These shared experiences—whether hunting, farming, preparing meals, making clothes, or building homes—result in shared perspectives and common values. Each individual acts, thinks, and believes very much like the next. Among the Amish, for example, what you will be when you grow up is virtually set at birth. There is limited opportunity for individual variation, because deviation from expected pathways represents a threat to social solidarity (Kraybill 2001; Kraybill, Johnson-Weiner, and Nolt 2013).

As societies become more advanced technologically, their division of labor expands, and jobs become increasingly specialized. As a result, a new foundation for social order emerges which Durkheim calls organic solidarity. Durkheim defines **organic solidarity** as a type of social cohesion based on our mutual interdependence in the context of extreme division of labor. In these societies, the person who cuts down timber is no longer the same person who builds your house. In most cases, it now takes many people with diverse sets of skills to produce even a single item, such as a chair or a cell phone. As a result, the mechanical solidarity that arose through common experience breaks down as

Organic solidarity Social cohesion based on mutual interdependence in the context of extreme division of labor.

Hunting-and-gathering society A preindustrial society in which people rely on whatever foods and fibers are readily available in order to survive.

Horticultural society A preindustrial society in which people plant seeds and crops rather than merely subsist on available foods.

differences emerge in how the members of the society view the world and their place in it. Whereas Tönnies saw this and despaired, Durkheim suggested that organic solidarity would provide us with a new sense of unity and possibility.

In modern societies, specialization breeds interdependence, as we saw in the "A Hamburger Is a Miracle" section in Chapter 1. The irony of modern society is that we combine extreme interdependence with a strong sense of individualism. We couldn't be self-sufficient because of our extreme division of labor, but we have a strong desire to be independent. We need one another more than ever, but we realize it less. Durkheim argued that society would evolve to address this tension and ensure social order. The various components of society would recognize how much they need one another and work together in the same way as the interdependent organs of the human body do, which is why Durkheim chose the term *organic,* each performing a vital function, but none capable of surviving alone.

TECHNOLOGY AND SOCIETY

Some sociologists focus more explicitly on technology than on social organization, expressed as division of labor, to understand distinctions between traditional and modern societies. In sociologist Gerhard Lenski's view, a society's level of technology is critical to the way it is organized (Nolan and Lenski 2006). As technology changes, new social forms arise, from preindustrial, to industrial, to postindustrial. Available technology does not narrowly determine the form that a particular society takes, but a low level of technology limits the degree to which a society can take advantage of the possibilities technology provides.

Preindustrial Societies Perhaps the earliest form of preindustrial society to emerge in human history was the **hunting-and-gathering society,** in which people simply rely on whatever foods and fibers are readily available. Such groups are typically small and widely dispersed, and technology in such societies is minimal. Organized into groups, people move constantly in search of food. There is minimal division of labor because everyone is engaged in the same basic activities. Because resources are scarce, there is relatively little inequality in terms of material goods.

In **horticultural societies,** people plant seeds and crops rather than merely subsist on available foods. Members of horticultural societies are much less nomadic than hunter-gatherers. They place greater emphasis on the production of tools and household objects. Yet technology remains rather limited in these societies, whose members cultivate crops with the aid of simple tools such as digging sticks or hoes (Wilford 1997).

The third type of preindustrial development is the **agrarian society.** As in horticultural societies, members of agrarian societies are engaged primarily in the production of food, but technological innovations such as the plow allow farmers to dramatically increase their crop yields and cultivate the same fields over generations. As a result, it becomes possible for larger, more permanent settlements to develop.

Agrarian societies continue to rely on the physical power of humans and animals (in contrast to mechanical power). Division of labor increases because technological advances free up some people from food production to focus on specialized tasks, such as the repair of fishing nets or blacksmithing. As human settlements become stabler and more established, social institutions become more elaborate and property rights more important. The comparative permanence and greater surpluses of an agrarian society allow members to specialize in creating artifacts such as statues, public monuments, and art objects and to pass them on from one generation to the next.

Industrial Societies
The Industrial Revolution transformed social life in England beginning in the late 1700s, and within a century its impact on society had extended around the world. An **industrial society** is one that depends on mechanization to produce its goods and services. The strength and stamina humans gained from new inventions such as the steam engine opened up a new world of possibilities by applying nonanimal (mechanical) sources of power to most labor tasks. As such, industrialization significantly altered the way people lived and worked, and it undercut taken-for-granted norms and values. The disruption that occurred during this transition from traditional to modern society led early sociologists,

such as Tönnies, Durkheim, and Marx, to propose their theories of social order and change.

During the Industrial Revolution, many societies underwent an irrevocable shift from an agrarian-oriented economy to an industrial base. Specialization of tasks and manufacture of goods increasingly replaced the practice of individuals or families making an entire product in a home workshop. Workers, generally men but also women and even children, left their family homesteads to work in central locations such as urban factories (Allen 2017; Hobsbawm 1999).

The process of industrialization had distinctive social consequences. Families and communities could not continue to function as self-sufficient units. Individuals, villages, and regions began to exchange goods and services and to become interdependent. As people came to rely on the labor of members of other communities, the family lost its unique position as the main source of power and authority. The need for specialized knowledge led to formalized schooling, and education emerged as a social institution distinct from the family. And bureaucracies were established to manage the complex undertakings of large organizations, which we explore in more detail in the "Bureaucracy" section.

> **Agrarian society** The most technologically advanced form of preindustrial society. Members are engaged primarily in the production of food, but they increase their crop yields through technological innovations such as the plow.
>
> **Industrial society** A society that depends on mechanization to produce its goods and services.

Innovations in agricultural technology meant fewer people were needed to work the land. PhotoDisc/Getty Images

Postindustrial Societies Mechanized production continues to play a substantial role in shaping social order, relationships, and opportunities, but technological innovation again has reshaped social structure by freeing up some people from the demands of material production. This has led to the rise of the service sector of the economy in many technologically advanced countries. In the 1970s, sociologist Daniel Bell wrote about the technologically advanced **postindustrial society,** whose economic system is engaged primarily in the processing and control of information. The main output of a postindustrial society is services rather than manufactured goods. Large numbers of people become involved in occupations devoted to the teaching, generation, or dissemination of ideas. Jobs in fields such as advertising, public relations, human resources, and computer information systems are typical of a postindustrial society (Bell 1999).

> **Postindustrial society** A society whose economic system is engaged primarily in the processing and control of information.
>
> **Postmodern society** A technologically sophisticated, pluralistic, interconnected, globalized society.

Some sociologists, including Bell, view this transition from industrial to postindustrial society as largely a positive development. Others, however, point to the often hidden consequences that result from differential access to resources in postindustrial society. For example, Michael Harrington (1962, 1980), who alerted the nation to the problems of the poor in his book *The Other America,* questions the significance that Bell attaches to the growing class of white-collar workers. Harrington concedes that scientists, engineers, and economists are involved in important political and economic decisions, but he disagrees with Bell's claim that they have a free hand in decision making, independent of the interests of the rich. Harrington follows in the tradition of Marx by arguing that conflict between social classes will continue in the postindustrial society.

POSTMODERN LIFE

Some sociologists have gone beyond discussion of the postindustrial society to contemplate the emergence of postmodern society (Best and Kellner 2001; Susen 2015). A **postmodern society** is a technologically sophisticated, pluralistic, interconnected, globalized society. Although it is difficult to summarize what a whole range of thinkers have said about postmodern life, four elements provide a sense of the key characteristics of such societies today: stories, images, choices, and networks.

Stories Because postmodern societies are pluralistic and individualistic, people hold many different, often competing, sets of norms and values. Fewer people assume that a single, all-inclusive story—whether a particular religious tradition, or an all-encompassing scientific theory of everything, or even the faith many early sociologists had in the inevitability of modern progress—can unite us all under a common umbrella. Instead, we embrace the various individual and group stories that help us make sense of the world and our place in it. We do so in the full knowledge that others out there are doing exactly the same thing and often coming to dramatically different conclusions. This multiplicity of stories undercuts the authority that singular accounts of reality, whether religious or scientific, have had in the past.

Images Postmodern society is also characterized by the explosion of the mass media, which emphasizes the importance of images. The average adult in the United States watches 4 hours and 27 minutes of television per day (Nielsen 2017). This works out to the equivalent of watching television 24 hours a day for almost 68 days per year. We are bombarded by images everywhere we turn.

In postmodern theory, the significance of the image goes much deeper than television and advertisements.

Did You Know?

. . . One of the effects of the Industrial Revolution was that the U.S. population became increasingly urban, with more people living together in closer proximity than ever before.

144
largest counties
population: 159,524,138
50.3% of total population

2,998
smallest counties
population: 159,332,918
49% of total population

Source: Adapted from http://dadaviz.com/s/population-extremes/#4568.

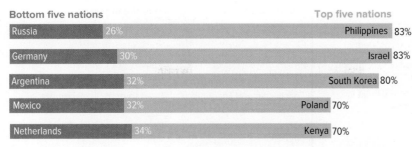

Going GLOBAL

International Favorability Ratings for the United States

Bottom five nations		Top five nations	
Russia	26%	Philippines	83%
Germany	30%	Israel	83%
Argentina	32%	South Korea	80%
Mexico	32%	Poland	70%
Netherlands	34%	Kenya	70%

Note: The numbers represent the percentage of people in each country who responded with a favorable or unfavorable opinion of the United States.
Source: Wike et al. 2018.

Because we exist in an interdependent global network, the consequences of our actions, both large and small, reverberate throughout the world. Views of America changed from the Obama to the Trump administrations, for example. Under Obama, favorability in Mexico was nearly 70% but has since fallen 34 percent to now place it in the bottom 5. Conversely, favorability in Russia was 15% under Obama but has risen to 26% under Trump.

Postmodern theorists argue that we do not confront or interact with the material world directly. Instead, our images or models of reality come first. Postmodern theorist Jean Baudrillard used a geography metaphor to illuminate this concept, writing, "The map precedes the territory" ([1981] 1994). In other words, the images we construct draw our attention to certain features that we might not otherwise notice. A road map, for example, highlights different features, and for different purposes, than does a topographical map or political map. In so doing, it shapes what we see. We cannot step around or look through such cultural constructs to approach the thing itself, and so our knowledge of what is real is always constrained by the images we construct.

Choices In a postmodern world, reality is not simply given; it is negotiated. We pick and choose our reality from the buffet of images and experiences presented to us. In fact, we *must* choose. In contrast to societies characterized by mechanical solidarity, where one's life path is virtually set at birth, members of postmodern societies must make life choices all the time. Assuming we have access to sufficient resources, we choose what to eat, what to wear, and what to drive. Shopping, which in the past would have been viewed primarily as an instrumental necessity to provide for our basic needs, becomes an act of self-creation. As advertising professor James B. Twitchell (2000) put it,

"We don't buy things, we buy meanings" (p. 47). An iPhone, a Coach purse, and a MINI Cooper are more than just a phone, a handbag, and a car. They are statements about the kind of person we are or want to be. The significance of choice goes much deeper than just consumer products. We also choose our partners, our schools, our jobs, our faith, and even our identities. As individuals, we may choose to affirm traditions, language, diet, and values we inherited from our family through socialization, but we can also choose to pursue our own path.

Networks Members of postmodern societies live in a globally interconnected world. The food we eat, the clothes we wear, the books we read, and the products we choose often come to us from the other side of the world. The computer technician we talk to for assistance in the United States may be located in India. McDonald's has experimented with centralized drive-through attendants—who might even be located in another state—who take your order and transmit it to the restaurant you are ordering from (Richtel 2006). Increasingly, all corners of the globe are linked into a vast, interrelated social, cultural, political, and economic system. A rural Iowa farmer, for example, must be concerned with more than just the local weather and community concerns; he or she must know about international innovations in farming technology, including biotech, as well as the current and future state of international markets.

>> Bureaucracy

In their efforts to understand and explain the underlying structure of industrial and postindustrial societies, early sociologists anticipated the rise of bureaucracy, as evidenced by Tönnies's description of *Gesellschaft* and Durkheim's analysis of organic solidarity. A **bureaucracy** is a formal organization built on the principle of maximum efficiency. As globalization expanded and modern life became increasingly complex, the principles used to manage social order in pre–Industrial Revolution societies no longer seemed adequate. Modern society required the more systematic approaches to governance that bureaucracy provides. According to Max Weber ([1913–1922] 1947), bureaucracy represents the most rational form of management ever devised.

> **Bureaucracy** A formal organization built on the principle of maximum efficiency.

CHARACTERISTICS OF A BUREAUCRACY

Bureaucratic success depends on the establishment of rational principles of organization throughout an organization. As indicated in the "Characteristics of a Bureaucracy"

Characteristics of a Bureaucracy

	Positive consequences	Negative consequences	
		For the individual	For the organization
Division of labor	Produces efficiency in a large-scale corporation	Limits knowledge	Creates communication barriers
Hierarchy of authority	Clarifies who is in command	Deprives employees of a voice in decision making	Permits concealment of mistakes
Written rules and regulations	Let workers know what is expected of them	Stifle initiative and imagination	Lead to goal displacement
Impersonality	Reduces bias	Contributes to feelings of alienation	Discourages loyalty to company
Employment based on technical qualifications	Discourages favoritism and reduces petty rivalries	Discourages ambition to improve oneself elsewhere	Inhibits innovative thinking

Photo: Mark Evans/E+/Getty Images

table, Weber identified five core characteristics of bureaucracies. He did so by constructing what he called an **ideal type,** an abstract model of the essential characteristics of a phenomenon. In actuality, perfect bureaucracies do not exist. Nonetheless, Weber's model provided a useful tool for comparing and contrasting functioning bureaucracies.

Ideal type An abstract model of the essential characteristics of a phenomenon.

Division of Labor The objective of a bureaucracy is to accomplish some specific goal in the most efficient manner possible. The most effective way to do so is to identify all the tasks necessary for success and assign specialists in each area to carry out those tasks. In traditional societies, a furniture maker might carry out every step of the production process, from cutting down the tree to finishing the table, herself. On top of that, she might have to do everything else that running a small business entails, including bookkeeping, marketing, and sales. In a modern bureaucracy, that

table will likely be produced on an assembly line where each worker has responsibility for only one part of the process. In addition, workers in other parts of the company would make their contributions, including the engineers who design the product line, marketing experts who create advertising campaigns, salespersons who entice customers to buy, accountants who do the bookkeeping, mechanics who maintain the machines, custodians who clean up afterward, and a whole host of others. The justification for such complexity is that, in the context of a large firm, it would be impossible for one individual to have sufficient expertise to carry out all those tasks well. The combined expertise that each specialized worker contributes produces greater efficiency than would exist if all workers were trained in every skill.

Dividing up labor in this way does have potential disadvantages. Workers who do routine tasks over and over again can feel like little more than a cog in the machine. This can produce a sense of alienation in which we experience loss of control over our creative human capacity to produce, separation from the products we make, and isolation from our

(doctor): ©Creatas/PunchStock; *(butcher):* Adam Crowley/Photodisc/Getty Images;
(man mopping): Muntz/Taxi/Getty Images; *(clothesline):* Ingram Publishing/SuperStock

fellow workers. It also can subject workers to greater job insecurity when jobs are deskilled through simplification and mechanization, making it easier to find and train a replacement worker. In addition, bureaucracy can produce what business executives refer to as "silos" in which there are limited connections between the various parts of a firm, inhibiting possible information exchange and collaboration between departments, thus resulting in greater inefficiencies (Lencioni 2006). Further, the frustration we can experience when dealing with bureaucratic red tape—whether in the workplace, at a university, or with the government—frequently results from having to deal with different segments of a bureaucratic machine.

A chief executive officer (CEO) typically rests atop the pyramid structure of bureaucratic hierarchy. Mary Barra, pictured here, has served as the CEO for General Motors since 2014.
Bill Pugliano/Getty Images

Did You Know?

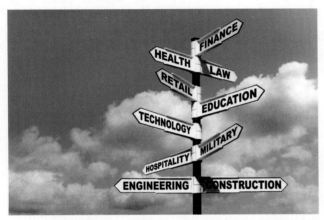

. . . The U.S. Census Bureau (2017c) identifies 539 distinct occupational categories, including Chief Executive, Aerospace Engineer, Music Teacher, Crossing Guard, and Sociologist. They organize these occupations into 23 major categories.

Photo: Rtimages/Alamy Stock Photo

Hierarchy of Authority Bureaucracies follow the principle of hierarchy; that is, each position is under the supervision of a higher authority. A president heads a college bureaucracy; he or she selects members of the administration, who in turn hire their own staff. In the Roman Catholic Church, the pope is the supreme authority; under him are cardinals, bishops, and so forth. In businesses, the most basic relation is between boss and worker, but in large corporations there are multiple levels of authority. To track relationships, such companies map those connections using hierarchical organizational charts that identify all the links of who answers to whom, ultimately leading up to the president or CEO at the top.

Written Rules and Regulations Through written rules and regulations, bureaucracies generally offer employees clear statements of their rights and responsibilities in the form of detailed job descriptions and comprehensive employee handbooks. If situations arise that are not covered by the rules, bureaucracies are self-correcting. They have rules in place to ensure that new rules are established that make work expectations as clear and as exhaustive as possible. Because bureaucracies are hierarchical systems of interrelated positions, such procedures provide a valuable sense of continuity for the organization. Individual workers may come and go, but the structure and past records of the organization give it a life of its own that outlives the services of any one particular person.

Of course, rules and regulations can overshadow the larger goals of an organization to the point that they become dysfunctional. What if a hospital emergency room physician failed to treat a seriously injured person because he or she had no valid proof of U.S. citizenship? If blindly applied, rules no longer serve as a means to achieving an objective but instead become important (perhaps too important) in their own right. Robert Merton (1968) used the term **goal displacement** to refer to overzealous conformity to official regulations of a bureaucracy in which we lose sight of the larger principle from which the rule was created.

> **Goal displacement** Overzealous conformity to official regulations of a bureaucracy.

┌─ **SOC**THINK ─────────────
Why do we tend to associate bureaucracies with red tape and inefficiency when they are explicitly organized to be the opposite? To what extent is our desire to be treated as an individual at odds with the principles of bureaucracies?
└──────────────────────────

Impersonality Bureaucratic norms dictate that officials judge people based on performance rather than personality. So long as everyone follows the rules as written, without regard for emotion or personal preference, the greatest good will result. The intent is to ensure equal treatment for each person. But it can also contribute to the cold, uncaring feeling often associated with modern organizations. Whether registering for college classes or getting tech support for a malfunctioning computer, most of us have had some experience of feeling like a number and longing for some personal attention. The larger the organization or society, however, the less possible such personal care becomes because attending to individual wants and needs is inefficient.

Employment Based on Technical Qualifications Within the ideal bureaucracy, hiring is based on technical qualifications rather than on favoritism, and performance is measured against specific standards. Written personnel policies dictate who gets promoted, and people often have a right to appeal if they believe that particular rules have been violated. In combination with the principle of impersonality, the driving personnel principle is supposed to be that it is "what you know, not who you know" that counts. Such procedures protect workers against arbitrary dismissal, provide a measure of security, and encourage loyalty to the organization.

Weber developed these five indicators of bureaucracy 100 years ago, and they continue to describe the ideal type. Not every formal organization will fully realize all of Weber's characteristics. The underlying logic they represent, however, points toward a way of doing things that is typical of life in modern societies.

BUREAUCRATIZATION AS A WAY OF LIFE

Bureaucracy for Weber was an indicator of a larger trend in modern society toward rational calculation of all decision making, using efficiency and productivity as the primary standards of success. We recognize this pattern first at the level of businesses and organizations. More companies seek greater efficiency through **bureaucratization**—the process by which a group, organization, or social movement increasingly relies on technical-rational decision making in the pursuit of efficiency. Over time,

Bureaucratization The process by which a group, organization, or social movement increasingly relies on technical-rational decision making in the pursuit of efficiency.

McDonaldization The process by which the principles of efficiency, calculability, predictability, and control shape organization and decision making, in the United States and around the world.

however, the technical-rationality approach pervades more and more areas of our lives.

The Spread of Bureaucratization One example of the expansion of bureaucratization is found in the spread of what sociologist George Ritzer (2019) calls **McDonaldization**—the process by which the principles of efficiency, calculability, predictability, and control shape organization and decision making, in the United States and around the world. Ritzer argues that these principles, which are at the heart of the McDonald's fast-food chain's success, have been emulated by many organizations, ranging from medical care to wedding planning to education. Even sporting events reflect the influence of McDonaldization. Around the world, stadiums are becoming increasingly similar, both physically and in the way they present the sport to spectators. Swipe cards, "sports city" garages and parking lots, and automated ticket sales maximize efficiency. All seats offer spectators an unrestricted view, and a big screen guarantees them access to instant replays. Scores, player statistics, and attendance figures are updated by computers and displayed on an automated scoreboard. Spectator enthusiasm is manufactured through video displays urging applause or rhythmic chanting. At food counters, refreshments include well-known brands whose customer loyalty has been nourished by advertisers for decades. And, of course, the merchandising of teams' and even players' names and images is highly controlled.

Weber predicted that eventually even the private sphere would become rationalized. That is, we would turn to rational techniques in an effort to manage our self in order to handle the many challenges of modern life. A trip to any bookstore would seem to prove his point: We find countless self-help books, each with its own system of steps to help us solve life's problems and reach our goals. One of the possible side effects of this approach to self-development might be our fear that whatever we do, or whoever we become, is not good enough, that we could always do more or be better.

Weber was concerned about the depersonalizing consequences of such rationalization, but he saw no way out. Because it is guided by the principle of maximum efficiency, the only way to beat bureaucratization, he thought, was to be more bureaucratic. He argued that, unfortunately, something human gets lost in the process. Culture critic Mike Daisey describes something like this through his experience working at Amazon.com. His job performance was measured based on five factors: time spent on each call, number of phone contacts per hour, time spent on

> Bureaucracy is . . . the most rational known means of exercising authority over human beings.
>
> Max Weber ([1922] 1978)

Source: www.buttersafe.com. 2011 Alex Culang and Raynato Castro Buttersafe.

each customer email, number of email contacts per hour, and the sum total of phone and email contacts per hour. Of these calculations, he writes, "Those five numbers are who you are. They are, in fact, all you are. . . . Metrics will do exactly what it claims to do: It will track everything your employees do, say, and breathe, and consequently create a measurable increase in their productivity" (Daisey 2002:114). Metrics do work, but they do so by dehumanizing the worker. "The sad thing," Daisey continues, "is that metrics work so well precisely because it strips away dignity—it's that absence that makes it possible to see precisely who is pulling his weight and who is not" (p. 114). When workers' performance is measured only in numbers, the only part of the self that counts is that part that produces those numbers. Weber predicted that those parts of the self deemed not necessary to the job, such as emotional needs and family responsibilities, would be dismissed as irrelevant.

From Bureaucracy to Oligarchy One of the dangers, then, is that bureaucratization overwhelms other values and principles, including the goal of greater efficiency. Sociologist Robert Michels ([1915] 1949) studied socialist parties and labor unions in Europe prior to World War I and found that such organizations were becoming increasingly bureaucratic. The emerging leaders of the organizations—even some of the most egalitarian—had a vested interest in clinging to power. If they lost their leadership posts, they would have to return to full-time work as manual laborers.

Through his research, Michels originated the idea of the **iron law of oligarchy,** the principle that all organizations, even democratic ones, tend to develop into a bureaucracy ruled by an elite few (called an oligarchy). Why do oligarchies emerge? People who achieve leadership roles usually have the skills, knowledge, or charisma to direct, if not control, others. Michels argued that the rank and file of a movement or organization look to leaders for direction and thereby reinforce the process of rule by a few. In addition, members of an oligarchy are strongly motivated to maintain their leadership roles, privileges, and power and use their control over resources to do so.

Concerns about oligarchy are often raised when ideologically driven social and political movements become institutionalized. In U.S. politics, ideologically committed followers, who often represent their party's base, frequently complain that elected leaders become "Washington insiders" who look out only for their self-interests. For example, during the 2016 presidential race, conservatives on the right criticized elected Republican leaders for compromising their ideals, which contributed to the selection of outsider Donald Trump as the Republican presidential nominee. Similarly, progressive Democrats, ideologically committed to equality and opportunity, supported Bernie Sanders for president, dismissing the eventual nominee Hillary Clinton as a Wall Street-friendly, overly militaristic enemy of the progressive cause. On both sides, questions were raised about whether the craving to stay in office overshadowed politicians' willingness to do the right thing.

> ## The chains of tormented mankind are made out of red tape.
>
> Franz Kafka (Janouch 1953)

BUREAUCRACY AND ORGANIZATIONAL CULTURE

One of the impressions Weber's model can leave is that there is only one right, most efficient way to organize a firm. Over time, however, managers have adopted a variety of strategies in their efforts to maximize productivity. For example, according to **scientific management,** established by Frederick Winslow Taylor in the late 1800s, managers should seek to measure all aspects of the work process

Iron law of oligarchy The principle that all organizations, even democratic ones, tend to develop into bureaucracies ruled by an elite few.

Scientific management Theory of management that measures all aspects of the work process to eliminate any inefficiencies.

5 Movies on SOCIAL STRUCTURE AND INTERACTION

Office Space
The insanity of life in a modern bureaucracy.

The Truman Show
In this postmodern tale, a man unknowingly lives his life on television.

District 9
The power to define who belongs and who does not.

The Greatest Showman
This is me.

Green Book
An African American pianist hires an Italian bouncer to tour the segregated South.

cares and concerns were of any relevance to the manager (Taylor 1911).

Not until workers organized unions—and forced management to recognize that they were not objects—did theorists of formal organizations begin to revise the scientific management model. Management and administrators, based in part on social scientific research, became aware that the social dimension of work has an important impact on organizations (Perrow 1986). An alternative management philosophy arose known as the **human relations** approach, which emphasizes the role of people, communication, and participation in a bureaucracy. In this model, bosses learned that paying attention to workers' feelings, frustrations, and emotional need for job satisfaction mattered (Mayo 1933). Today, many workplaces—primarily for those in higher-status occupations—have been transformed to family-friendly environments (Hochschild 1997). To the extent that managers are convinced that helping workers meet all their needs increases productivity, care and concern are instituted as a result of rational calculation.

Whether in the form of traditional, modern, or postmodern society, social structure provides order, shaping the options that are available to us. It provides the context within which we interact with others. The statuses we occupy shape the roles we perform. Moreover, what we think and do is influenced by the relationships we have with others in the contexts of groups, networks, and institutions. Sociology as a discipline is committed to making sense of our structural context and the impact it has on our lives.

Still, society and social structure are not singular things. Though we are, in many respects, products of society, socialized to think and act in appropriate ways, we always have the option to think and act in new ways and to construct new culture. The possibility for such change may be more apparent today because our world is so pluralistic. Ours is a world not of "the" structure, "the" family, and "the" religion, but of structures, families, and religions. We have the possibility for more contact with more people who think and act in a greater diversity of ways than at any time in the past. As we become more aware of alternatives ways to think and act, we can use that knowledge to change our worlds for the better.

in an effort to eliminate any inefficiencies. One of the primary tools they used was time-motion studies, in which they used a stopwatch to measure each movement a worker would make. They then sought ways to minimize the amount of time each task took. In this system, workers were treated as objects to be managed rather than as subjects whose

Human relations An approach to the study of formal organizations that emphasizes the role of people, communication, and participation in a bureaucracy and tends to focus on the informal structure of the organization.

SOCIOLOGY IS A VERB

The Significance of Place

We occupy many statuses over the course of our lives, and they can both open and close doors for us. Ask five people in various positions—whether as parents, professors, child care providers, custodians, managers, religious leaders, and so on—how they came to be in those positions. How have the positions they occupy enabled them to accomplish their personal and collective goals? How have they been constrained by those positions?

For REVIEW

I. What does society provide that we need?
- Society provides a structure that is built from the statuses we occupy; the roles we perform; and the groups, networks, and institutions that connect us.

II. How do sociologists describe traditional versus modern societies?
- Sociologists highlight the impact that division of labor and technological development have on the organization of community, work, and social interaction in traditional and modern societies.

III. How does social structure shape individual action?
- The positions we occupy shape our perceptions, the resources to which we have access, and the options that are available. For example, in the context of bureaucracies, our social position, connections, and performance expectations are clearly defined.

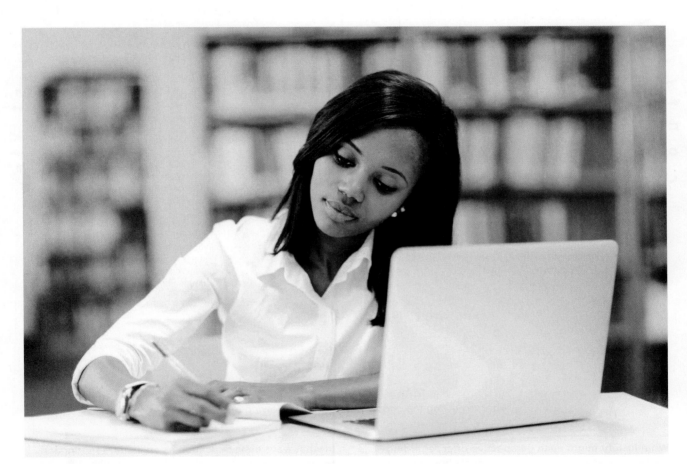

Michaeljung/Shutterstock

Functionalist View

The **elements of social structure**—statuses, groups, social networks, and social institutions—provide order, shape our options, and give context to our lives.

Social roles create a **stable society** by allowing people to anticipate the behavior of others and to act accordingly.

Institutions contribute to **social order** by performing **vital functions,** whether it is producing children (family), teaching them (schools), establishing order (government), or distributing goods and services (economy).

STRUCTURE, ORDER
KEY CONCEPTS

Conflict View

The elements of the social structure justify and reinforce existing systems of inequality and unequal distributions of resources.

Ascribed statuses, often conferred at birth, can be used to justify **privileges** for some while limiting opportunities for others by consigning them to a **subordinate group.**

In-groups and out-groups serve to highlight **differences** between people and can foster antagonism.

KEY CONCEPTS
SUBORDINATION, INEQUALITY, PRIVILEGE

Interactionist View

It is through social interaction—the **shared experiences** through which we relate to others—that the elements of social structure are constructed.

Our social roles are governed by a set of expectations, but how we actually **perform** those roles can vary from individual to individual.

A **micro, bottom-up perspective** of social structure reinforces the significance of our actions, and helps us appreciate how we can think and act in new ways to bring about social change.

KEY CONCEPTS
SHARED EXPERIENCES, MICRO PERSPECTIVE

MAKE THE CONNECTION

After reviewing the chapter, answer the following questions:

1

What insight might each perspective offer regarding the way the structure of games impacts how we play?

2

Briefly describe how a functionalist, a conflict theorist, and an interactionist would view ascribed versus achieved status.

3

In what ways does education as an institution function to provide for greater social order and stability?

4

Have you ever been part of an in- or out-group? If so, how might each perspective shed light on your experience?

Pop Quiz

1. **What type of status does being a college student represent?**
   a. an ascribed status
   b. a developmental status
   c. an achieved status
   d. a conflicted status

2. **In the United States, we expect that cab drivers know how to get around a city. This expectation is an example of which of the following?**
   a. in-group
   b. role strain
   c. social role
   d. status

3. **What occurs when incompatible expectations arise from two or more social statuses held by the same person?**
   a. role conflict
   b. role strain
   c. role exit
   d. role playing

4. **In sociological terms, what do we call any two or more people, united by a shared sense of identity or purpose, who interact with each other over time in ways that distinguish them from outsiders?**
   a. a category
   b. a group
   c. an aggregate
   d. a society

5. **Primary groups are characterized by**
   a. a series of relationships that link individuals directly to others and, through them, indirectly to still more people.
   b. formal, impersonal relationships with minimal social intimacy or mutual understanding.
   c. social positions that are within our power to change.
   d. intimate, face-to-face association and cooperation.

6. **What is the definition of a social institution?**
   a. a series of social relationships that link individuals directly to others, and through them indirectly to still more people
   b. an alliance, whether temporary or permanent, geared toward a common goal
   c. an integrated and persistent social network dedicated to ensuring that society's core needs are met
   d. a component of a formal organization that uses rules and hierarchical ranking to achieve efficiency

7. **What type of society did Ferdinand Tönnies describe as a close-knit community in which members have strong personal bonds?**
   a. *Gesellschaft*
   b. mechanical
   c. *Gemeinschaft*
   d. organic

8. **According to Émile Durkheim, which type of solidarity is characterized by extensive division of labor?**
   a. postindustrial
   b. mechanical
   c. horticultural
   d. organic

9. **What characteristic of postmodern life emphasizes the importance of consumption on identity creation?**
   a. stories
   b. images
   c. choices
   d. networks

10. **Which characteristic of bureaucracy is carried out on the basis of performance rather than personality?**
    a. impersonality
    b. hierarchy of authority
    c. written rules and regulations
    d. division of labor

1. (c), 2. (c), 3. (a), 4. (b), 5. (d), 6. (c), 7. (c), 8. (d), 9. (c), 10. (a)

Jim Watson/AFP/Getty Images

#NEVERAGAIN

On October 1, 2017, during country singer Jason Aldean's performance at an outdoor country music festival on the Las Vegas Strip, bullets rained down from above. The shots came from a 32nd floor hotel room in the Mandalay Bay Resort and Casino across the street. People scattered, seeking protection, but in the end, 58 were shot and killed and another 422 suffered bullet wounds. From start to finish, the gunfire lasted about 10 minutes. It was the deadliest mass shooting in modern U.S. history. Authorities found 24 weapons inside the gunman's hotel suite and calculated that more than 1,100 shots had been fired (Medina 2018).

Just a few months later, near the end of the school day on February 14, 2018, a fire alarm went off at Marjory Stoneman Douglas High School in Parkland, Florida. As students streamed into the hallway, a former student, armed with an assault rifle, started shooting. The whole attack lasted 6 minutes and 20 seconds. When it was over, 17 people were dead, including 14 students and 3 school staff members, and 17 others were injured (Fausset, Kovaleski, and Mazzei 2018). In the aftermath, students expressed outrage at what seemed like the all-too-common occurrence of mass shootings in America.

Their outrage is warranted. Tragic mass shootings in the United States occur with alarming frequency. There were a number of mass shootings that grabbed national headlines after Parkland. On May 18, 2018, at Santa Fe High School in Texas, 8 students and 2 teachers were shot and killed by a student from the school who used a shotgun and a revolver. On October 27, 2018, at the Tree of Life synagogue in Pittsburgh, Pennsylvania, a man armed with an AR-15 semiautomatic rifle and three Glock pistols killed 11 people. On November 8, 2018, at the Borderline Bar & Grill in Thousand Oaks, California, a gunman armed with a Glock semiautomatic pistol killed 12 people. In each case, political officials offered their thoughts and prayers.

Student survivors from the Stoneman Douglas shooting, however, decided to act. Within hours of the attack, they began organizing to fight for change. Their goal: gun-law reform that might reduce the likelihood of similar attacks. They established Never Again as an organization committed to legislative action. They organized the March for Our Lives parades held around the country on March 24, 2018, including a rally in Washington, D.C. Their social action is beginning to make a difference. Florida, for example, raised the age required to purchase guns from 18 to 21 and established a three-day waiting period to purchase guns while background checks could be carried out (Pazzanese 2018; Witt 2018).

To ensure that such actions are effective, we need to understand why mass shootings occur. Do they result from unchecked mental illness? A proliferation of guns? A culture of violence? Through research, sociologists help us better understand deviance by asking such questions so that we, in turn, can better understand how to prevent it.

As You READ >>

- **How do groups maintain social control?**
- **What is the difference between deviance and crime?**
- **How do sociologists explain deviance and crime?**

>> Social Control

As individuals, we all face times when we want to rebel against what is expected of us. We may know better, having been socialized to accept the norms and values of those who surround us, yet when it comes to obedience, sometimes we would prefer not to. Or the urge to disobey may come in the form of friends and colleagues who prod us. If we give in, we are likely to encounter pushback from others in the form of **social control,** which refers to society's power to limit deviance, behavior that violates socially accepted norms, by enforcing conformity to expected norms and values. As we saw in the "Normative Culture" section in Chapter 3, those around us use positive and negative sanctions to encourage and discourage particular behaviors. The scary part about social control is the amount of power that potentially rests in the hands of those with authority over us.

CONFORMITY AND OBEDIENCE

We experience social control in a variety of forms. **Conformity** is a more horizontal form of social control that involves abiding by the norms of our peers even though they have no direct authority over us. Going along with the crowd, whether that means attending a basketball game, studying abroad, or going to a party because your friends do, is a form of conformity. **Obedience,** on the other hand, is a vertical form of social control that involves doing what a person in a position of authority over you says you should. In this form of social control, the social status of a person whose authority we respect, whether as a teacher, religious leader, or coach, gives them power over us. We are inclined to do what they ask because we trust them and defer to their presumed knowledge and wisdom.

Curious about obedience, social psychologist Stanley Milgram (1963, 1974a) wondered how far people would go if a trusted authority figure asked them to do something harmful. He was motivated, in part, because he wanted to better understand the involvement of the German people

Social control Society's power to limit deviance by enforcing conformity to expected norms and values.

Conformity Abiding by the norms of our peers even though they have no direct authority over us.

Obedience Doing what a person in a position of authority over you says you should.

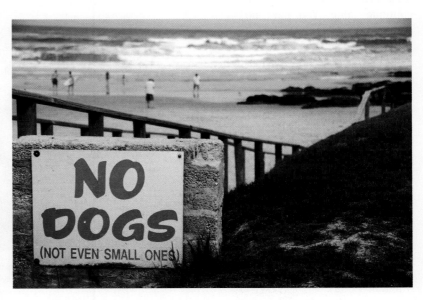
James Harrison/Alamy Stock Photo

in the murder of 6 million Jews and millions of others during World War II. One rationalization people gave after the war was that they were "just following orders." Milgram conceived of a test to assess people's willingness to obey.

He set up a scenario in which a volunteer, recruited from the local community, was told that researchers were investigating the effects of punishment on learning. The volunteer was then brought into a lab setting and asked to serve as a "teacher" who would ask questions of a "learner." If the learner got the question wrong, the teacher was instructed by a scientist, dressed in a lab coat, to administer an electric shock to the learner. For each additional question the learner got wrong, the teacher was instructed to increase the shock's voltage. Unbeknownst to the volunteer, however, no actual shock was administered. The real purpose of the study was to see how far the teacher/volunteer would go before refusing to obey the scientist.

In a prearranged script, the learner deliberately gave incorrect answers and pretended to be in pain when "shocked." For example, at 150 volts the learner would cry out, "Get me out of here!" At 270 volts the learner would scream in agony. When the shock reached 350 volts, the learner would fall silent. If the teacher wanted to stop the experiment, the experimenter would insist that the teacher/volunteer continue, using such statements as "The experiment requires that you continue" and "You have no other choice; you must go on." Milgram repeated this experiment numerous times, altering 23 different experimental conditions, such as the gender of the scientist, the number of scientists, and the presence of the scientist in the room, to see what effects they might have. In Experiment 5, the variation for which Milgram is best known, 65 percent of the volunteers continued all the way up to the 450-volt maximum (Blass 1999; Haslam, Loughnan, and Perry 2014; Milgram 1974a).

The zombie apocalypse has become a pop culture staple. Examples include George Romero's *Living Dead* films, Max Brooks's *World War Z* book and film, and *The Walking Dead* graphic novel and TV series. Such accounts often say more about humans and the breakdown of social order than they do about zombies. In the event of a zombie apocalypse, how quickly do you think social order would break down? What factors might minimize social chaos? What steps should people take to enforce social order?

POPSOC

Photo: Gene Page/AMC/PictureLux/The Hollywood Archive/Alamy Stock Photo

A participant in the Milgram experiment. From the film OBEDIENCE ©1968 by Alexandra Milgram, ©renewed 1993 by Alexandra Milgram. Reprinted by permission of Alexandra Milgram.

Researchers since Milgram have conducted similar demonstrations seeking to replicate his findings and have produced comparable results. The average obedience rate for 17 similar studies was 65 percent, though rates for these studies varied significantly from 28 to 91 percent (Blass 1999). Due to the potentially harmful psychological side effects on the volunteers, studies such as these ceased. In a more recent attempt, social psychologist Jerry Burger (2009) attempted to minimize the ethical concerns by, among other things, assuring volunteers they could stop at any time, guaranteeing they could keep the money they were paid for volunteering even if they stopped, and ending the experiment immediately after the 150-volt level when the "learner" asked for the experiment to stop, at which point the true nature of the experiment was revealed and the learner was shown to be unharmed. Burger found that 65 percent of his subjects continued to administer what they thought were shocks until the end.

─SOCTHINK─

According to the American Sociological Association Code of Ethics, researchers must "protect subjects from personal harm." To what extent might Milgram's subjects have experienced emotional harm? How and why might a researcher seek to justify such a risk?

Milgram concluded that we are willing to do things we would otherwise not do, including inflicting pain, when a person in a position of authority tells us to do so. He pointed out that, in modern society, we are accustomed to submitting to impersonal authority figures whose status is indicated by a title (professor, president, doctor) or by a uniform (police officer, army lieutenant, scientist). Because we defer to authority, we shift responsibility for our behavior to the authority figure without fully appreciating what we are doing. Under similar circumstances, otherwise normal people can and do treat one another inhumanely, as demonstrated by the revealing photos taken at Iraq's Abu Ghraib prison in 2004 which showed U.S. military guards humiliating, if not torturing, Iraqi prisoners (Hayden 2004; Zimbardo 2007).

Reflecting on his research, Milgram wrote, "It may be that we are puppets—puppets controlled by the strings of society. But at least we are puppets with perception, with awareness. And perhaps our awareness is the first step to our liberation" (1974b:568). We do not make choices in a vacuum. Sociology enables us to better recognize the social forces that shape our actions so that we might choose more wisely.

─SOCTHINK─

Do you think a person's background factors would influence how far he or she would go in Milgram's experiment? How might age, gender, religion, or education make a difference?

INFORMAL AND FORMAL SOCIAL CONTROL

In addition to being horizontal and vertical, social control can be informal and formal. **Informal social control** involves the use of interpersonal cues, either positive or negative, through everyday interaction to enforce norms. It's the kind of casual sanction parents might use when they give their child "the look" indicating they've said or done something wrong and had better stop it immediately. Other examples include smiles, laughter, crossed arms, frowns, and ridicule. We seek to read such cues in new situations, such as a first date or a job interview, so we might adjust our behavior accordingly.

Formal social control involves the imposition of sanctions, whether positive or negative, by officially recognized authorities in order to enforce norms. Examples of authorized agents are police officers, judges, school administrators, managers, and military officers. Their task is to ensure that people adhere to the official policies of the organizations to which they belong. Formal social control can serve as a last resort when socialization and informal sanctions do not bring about desired behavior.

The interplay between formal and informal social control can be complicated, because we sometimes have to balance one source of control against another. College students, for example, receive conflicting messages about the acceptability of binge drinking. On the one hand, for most college students, drinking alcohol of any kind is illegal because they are under age, and for all, binge drinking violates student codes-of-conduct policies. On the other hand, as the "Binge Drinking on Campus" graphs demonstrate, those who indulge in binge drinking are conforming with student norms, which vary based on age, gender, and race/ethnicity (SAMHSA 2018). In response, colleges and universities are taking steps to exert greater social control by instituting rules banning kegs, closing fraternities and sororities that violate standards of conduct, expelling students after multiple alcohol-related violations, and working with local liquor retailers to discourage high-volume sales to students (Carey et al. 2012).

Informal social control The use of interpersonal cues through everyday interaction to enforce norms.

Formal social control The imposition of sanctions, whether positive or negative, by officially recognized authorities in order to to enforce norms.

Binge Drinking on Campus

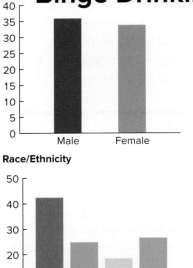

Sex

(bar chart: Male ~36, Female ~34; y-axis 0–40)

Race/Ethnicity

(bar chart: White ~42, Black ~25, Asian ~18, Hispanic ~27; y-axis 0–50)

Full-Time College Students

Age groups

Age 21 **47.4%**
Age 22 **46.1%**

Age 20 **31.2%**
Age 19 **29.9%**

Age 18 **23.0%**

Note: Binge drinking was defined as drinking five drinks or more for men, or four drinks or more for women, on the same occasion at least once in the past 30 days. White, Black, and Asian categories do not include Hispanics.

Source: SAMHSA 2018. *Photo:* ©Comstock/Jupiter Images

dramatic rise included a government crackdown on illegal drug use and the establishment of mandatory sentences. In the early 1970s, for example, President Richard Nixon declared a "war on drugs," a policy President Ronald Reagan expanded in the 1980s and that continues to shape policy today. As a result, efforts to deal with drug abuse shifted from prevention and treatment to law enforcement and punishment. The Anti-Drug Abuse Act of 1986, for example, put mandatory minimum sentences in place for a variety of drugs, including marijuana and cocaine.

In an effort to get tough on crime, this mandatory minimum approach was extended to other crimes. The Sentencing Reform Act of 1984, for example, created the United States Sentencing Commission, which establishes sentencing guidelines, including minimums, for defendants found guilty of any federal statute. Critics of the mass incarceration that resulted from these policies point out that punishment fell, and continues to fall, disproportionately on African Americans and other minority groups (Alexander 2012; Davis 1998; Dufton 2012; United States Sentencing Commission 2016).

LAW AND SOCIETY

Some norms are so important to a society that they are formalized into laws limiting people's behavior. **Laws**—formal norms enforced by the state—are a form of governmental social control. Some laws, such as the prohibition against murder, are directed at all members of society. Others, such as fishing and hunting regulations, primarily affect particular categories of people. Still others govern the behavior of social institutions (for instance, corporate law and laws regarding the taxing of nonprofit organizations).

Laws Formal norms enforced by the state.

Arresting, prosecuting, and convicting a person who breaks the law represents one of the most powerful means of formal social control available. In the United States, in 2016, 6.6 million adults underwent some form of correctional supervision—jail, prison, probation, or parole. Put another way, 2.6 percent, or 1 out of every 38 adult Americans, was subject to this very formal type of social control (Kaeble and Cowhig 2018). As is evident from the "U.S. Incarceration Rates, 1910–2017" graph, rates of imprisonment rose rapidly in the United States during the 1980s and remain high. Factors influencing this

U.S. Incarceration Rates, 1910–2017

(line graph. y-axis: Incarceration Rate, per 100,000 (0–800); x-axis: Year 1910–2017)

Data points: 1910: 121.8; 1920: 103.8; 1930: 146; 1940: 206; 1950: 166.9; 1960: 185.6; 1970: 166.3; 1980: 209.4; 1990: 461; 2000: 691; 2010: 730; 2017: 670

Note: Incarceration rates represent the number of persons in prison or jail per 100,000 people in the U.S. population.

Source: Kaeble and Cowhig 2018. *Photo:* AZemdega/E+/Getty Images

In diverse societies, the establishment of laws inevitably generates conflicts over whose values should prevail or whose interests should be protected. For example, should it be against the law to employ illegal immigrants? To have an abortion? To allow prayer in public schools? To smoke on an airplane? Such issues have been bitterly debated because they require a choice among competing interests. Not surprisingly, unpopular laws—such as the 18th Amendment, which prohibited the manufacture and sale of alcohol (ratified in 1919), or the nationwide 55-mile-per-hour speed limit that was imposed in 1974—become difficult to enforce when there is no consensus supporting the norms. In both cases the public

Each year, millions of people stream or download illegal copies of shows such as HBO's "Game of Thrones."   PictureLux/The Hollywood Archive/Alamy Stock Photo

commonly violated the stated government policy, and the laws proved unenforceable; the states repealed Prohibition in 1933, and Congress overturned the national speed-limit policy in 1987.

As individuals, each and every moment of our lives we face a choice about whether to obey or rebel. That choice gets complicated by the fact that we confront competing and oftentimes incompatible options. Choosing one path may delight some of the people in our lives and enable us to pursue our own self-interests, but doing so might disappoint others and cause us to sacrifice benefits we also desire. Obedience to one group may look like deviance to another.

>> Deviance

The flip side of social control is deviance. **Deviance** is behavior that violates the standards of conduct or expectations of a group or society (Wickman 1991:85). Being late for class is categorized as a deviant act, as is wearing jeans to a formal wedding. On the basis of the sociological definition, we are all deviant from time to time. Each of us violates common social norms in certain situations. As a society, we decide how deviant is *too* deviant, and sociologists provide us with tools to better understand how and why we do so.

WHAT BEHAVIOR IS DEVIANT?

Because deviance involves violation of some group's norms, defining an act as deviant depends on the context. File sharing and streaming on the Internet—including songs, movies, computer games, books, and almost anything else

that can be digitized—provides an example of how deviance can be in the eye of the beholder. Whenever a new film or show is released, online piracy groups compete with each other to see who can be the first to upload a high-definition copy. Competition to upload films nominated for an Academy Award is even more intense. In 2018, 94 percent of Academy Award–nominated films were leaked in a high-quality format by Oscar night (Baio 2015, 2016, 2018; Van der Sar 2017).

HBO's *Game of Thrones* represents one of the most popular illegally available shows online. Season seven alone has been illegally streamed or downloaded more than 1 billion times, and its final episode was pirated more than 120 million times within its first 72 hours of release. Pirated copies of episodes frequently appear for illegal streaming before they even premier on the cable network as a result of preview copies made available to TV critics and reporters getting leaked and uploaded to the Internet (Holloway 2017a). Film and television studios have responded to such practices by limiting preview copies of films and television series' to secure video distribution sites, such as Screeners.com. And yet, online piracy continues to rise. In 2017, more than 10 billion films or TV shows were downloaded globally (Holloway 2017b; Irdeto 2018; Spangler 2018).

> **Deviance** Behavior that violates the standards of conduct or expectations of a group or society.

Because the "property" these movie, music, and game files represent is not physical, it can be copied over and over again for virtually no cost. Anyone with a computer and an Internet connection can grab the files from people willing to share and pass them along to others who want them. People find it easy to justify doing so, thinking it does little harm to anyone. The entertainment companies

Leonard McLane/Digital Vision/Getty Images

that produce these products take a different view. Research projects that $52 billion in revenues were lost to piracy in 2018 (Bevir 2017). However, the widespread availability of these files suggests that many people do not view downloading them as particularly deviant. Some even view it as an act of protest against what they consider unfair prices charged by big corporations.

An important dimension of deviance to remember is that social change occurs when people choose to act differently. Our tendency is to go with the flow, thus reproducing the status quo. As a result, we frequently fail to see the ways in which our existing practices may violate our core principles. When such violations occur, people who stand up for what they believe is right are often punished. The civil rights movement provided numerous examples of this, such as when nonviolent protestors at sit-ins and marches were met with attack dogs, fire hoses, beatings, and jail time. In the end, however, these protests led to greater political, legal, and economic opportunity for African Americans and others. Part of what makes such change difficult is that those with the greatest status have the capacity to define what is acceptable and what is deviant. It often takes a concerted effort, and the mobilization of substantial resources, to counteract such power.

> **Stigma** Labeling individuals or members of a group as less than whole persons due to some attribute that marks them as different in the eyes of others.

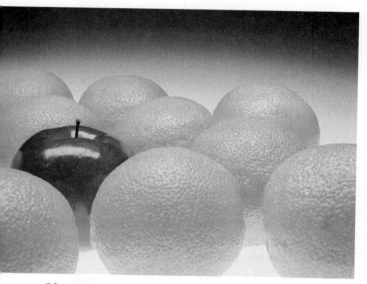

©Comstock/Jupiter Images

DEVIANCE AND SOCIAL STIGMA

People who deviate from the norm in terms of how they think, believe, act, or look are frequently categorized as different, strange, unusual, or abnormal by people in social positions of power. Whole groups of people—whether on the basis of hair color, skin color, height, weight, clothing, nationality, physical ability, or other attributes—can be denied respect due to their presumed shortcomings. Sociologist Erving Goffman (1963) coined the term **stigma** to describe the process of labeling individuals or members of a group as less than whole persons due to some attribute that marks them as different in the eyes of others. Because our perception of others shapes how we treat them, such labels have consequences, as we learned from the Thomas theorem. As a result, stigmatizing represents a form of social control. First we label people as different using stereotypes to characterize them as "other." Then the distinction between "us" versus "them" is used to justify discrimination against those in the stigmatized group, denying them access to valued material, social, and cultural resources (Link and Phelan 2001).

The pressure to conform to the norm, and thus avoid stigma, can have powerful effects. People try not to deviate too far from cultural expectations. Women, for example, can feel pressured to approximate what Naomi Wolf (1992) refers to as the "beauty myth," an exaggerated ideal of beauty, beyond the reach of all but a few females. In an effort to attain this ideal, many women undergo plastic surgery. In 2017, 300,378 women underwent breast augmentation, 218,174 chose liposuction, 177,290 had eyelid surgery, 166,531 opted for nose reshaping, and 124,869 received a tummy tuck. When it comes to less invasive procedures, 6.8 million opted for Botox, and 1.3 million received chemical peels. Overall, women received 13 million cosmetic procedures in 2017 alone. But it wasn't only women. Men, too, are opting for plastic surgery and accounted for 13 percent of all cosmetic surgical procedures. Among men, 52,393 opted for nose reshaping, making it their most common surgical procedure. The estimated total cost of all U.S. cosmetic procedures in 2017 was $16.7 billion (American Society of Plastic Surgeons 2018). The desire to avoid stigma reinforces the standards of the status quo.

Often people are stigmatized for deviant behaviors that they may no longer practice. The labels "ex-convict," "formerly homeless," and "recovering alcoholic" can function like a master status, sticking to a person for life. Goffman

5 Movies on DEVIANCE

The Purge
Once a year, for 12 hours, all crime is legal.

Liar, Liar
What if honesty was your only option?

Compliance
When it comes to obedience, how far would you go?

I Am Not a Witch
An eight-year-old girl is accused of being a witch.

Ghost World
A prank by two outcast teenagers takes an unexpected turn.

always be obvious, they can become a matter of public knowledge. Starting in 1994, many states required convicted sex offenders to register with local police departments. Some communities publish the names and addresses and, in some instances, even the pictures, of convicted sex offenders on the web.

Being stigmatized can limit a person's opportunities. For example, even though they may be fully qualified for a job, people who are homeless often have trouble getting hired because employers are wary of applicants who cannot provide a home address. Though many hiring agencies use a telephone for contacts, cell phones are expensive, and owning one while homeless is often looked at with suspicion by others. If a homeless person has access to a telephone at a shelter, the staff generally answers by announcing the name of the institution, which discourages prospective employers from hiring the applicant. And, even if the person is hired, the stigma attached to homelessness, should the employee's past or present situation become known, can negatively impact opportunities, even in the face of positive work performance.

draws a useful distinction between a prestige symbol that calls attention to a positive aspect of one's identity, such as a wedding band or a police badge, and a stigma symbol that discredits or debases one's identity, such as a conviction for child molestation. Although stigma symbols may not

POPSOC

R. J. Palacio's novel, *Wonder,* tells the story of Auggie Pullman, a homeschooled fifth-grader whose parents decide that he should enroll in public school so he can make more friends. But Auggie has a medical condition that left his face disfigured. On his first day of school, he tries not to stick out, but it doesn't take long for the stigma attached to his physical appearance to take its toll. The book, and the film based on it, provide insight into the challenges stigma presents not only for targeted individuals, but for those around them as well.

Photo: Lionsgate/Entertainment Pictures/ZUMAPREss.com/Alamy Stock Photo

>> Crime

Crime represents a particular form of deviance in which offenders violate formal norms. Sociologists define **crime** as a violation of criminal law for which some governmental authority applies formal penalties. Crimes that violate the central mores of society, such as murder, often result in harsh punishments because they constitute attacks on core social values, such as life, liberty and the pursuit of happiness. The consequences of other crimes, such as burglary, may seem less serious, and, as a result, violators of such crimes typically receive less severe punishments.

> **Crime** A violation of criminal law for which some governmental authority applies formal penalties.

OFFICIAL CRIME REPORTS

Crime is a major concern in any society. It represents a breakdown in social order and a potential threat to the health and safety of individuals and communities. The FBI tracks the frequency of crime in the United States using what it calls its "Crime Clock." For example, a property crime occurs on average every 4.1 seconds and the most frequent category of property crime is larceny-theft, which includes incidents such as shoplifting and stealing items from cars. Violent crimes occur every 24.6 seconds, with perhaps the most serious being murder, which occurs every every 30.5 minutes in the United States (U.S. Department of Justice 2018b).

Trends in Crime The FBI provides a more detailed account of the frequency of crimes in its annual *Uniform Crime Reports (UCR).* These reports focus particular attention

FBI *Uniform Crime Reports* Data

Offenses in 2017	Number reported	Rate per 100,000 inhabitants	Percentage change in rate since 2008 decrease ⟵ ⟶ increase	Clearance Rate
Violent crimes Murder	17,284	5.3	−2.0	62%
Forcible rape	99,856	30.7	2.7	35%
Robbery	319,356	98.0	−32.8	30%
Aggravated assault	810,825	248.9	−10.3	53%
Total	1,247,321	382.9	−10.6	46%
Property crimes Burglary	1,401,840	430.4	−41.3	14%
Larceny-theft	5,519,107	1,694.4	−21.8	19%
Motor vehicle theft	773,139	237.3	7.3	14%
Total	7,694,086	2,362.2	−26.5	18%

0

Note: Insufficient data are available on arson to estimate accurate totals. The official definition for rape changed in 2013. The percentage change data for rape uses the legacy definition to provide an appropriate comparison over time. Clearance rate refers to the percentage of crimes reported to police that were cleared by arrest or exceptional means.

Source: U.S. Department of Justice 2018a:Tables 1, 1A, & 25. *Photo:* D. Hurst/Alamy

on what have come to be known as **index crimes** which include eight types of crime reported on annually: murder, forcible rape, robbery, aggravated assault, burglary, larceny-theft, motor vehicle theft, and arson. The first four are categorized as violent crime, and the second four as property crimes. As evidenced in the "FBI *Uniform Crime Reports* Data" figure, both the numbers and rates of these crimes vary significantly.

Crime rates vary over time, and sociologists seek to explain factors that contribute to these changes. In the past 10 years, as indicated by the percentage change in rate column in the "FBI *Uniform Crime Reports* Data" figure, crime rates have fallen in most major categories. Violent crimes, for example, have declined 10.6 percent since 2008 (U.S. Department of Justice 2018a:Table 1a). To explain these trends, sociologists seek to identify possible causal factors, including the potential effects of

Index crimes The eight types of crime reported annually by the FBI in the *Uniform Crime Reports:* murder, forcible rape, robbery, aggravated assault, burglary, larceny-theft, motor vehicle theft, and arson.

Victimization surveys Questionnaires or interviews that ask representative samples of the population whether or not they have been victims of crime.

- The overall aging of the population, because people are more likely to commit crimes when they are young.
- Changes in the economy, including the economic downturn starting in 2008 and the recovery that followed.
- The expansion of community-oriented policing and crime prevention programs.

- Increased incarceration rates, removing potential offenders from the streets.
- New prison education programs designed to reduce the number of repeat offenders.

Knowledge of the impact of these and other possible factors would help us establish more effective policies designed to further reduce the crime rate in the future (Chettiar 2015; Roeder, Eisen, and Bowling 2015).

The likelihood that a crime will be "solved" varies by the type of offense. According to the FBI, an offense can be "cleared" either though arrest or exceptional means. To be cleared by arrest, at least one person must be arrested, charged with a crime, and turned over to the court for prosecution. Clearance by exceptional means includes examples such as the death of the offender or refusal of the victim to cooperate with prosecution. As the "FBI *Uniform Crime Reports* Data" figure shows, violent crimes, at 46 percent, are more likely to be cleared than property crimes, at 18 percent (U.S. Department of Justice 2018a:Table 25).

Victimization Surveys Because not all crimes that are committed are reported to the police, the *UCR* underestimates the frequency of crime. To get a more accurate count of the actual number of crimes, researchers conduct **victimization surveys** that ask representative samples of the population whether or not they have been victims of crime. The National Crime Victimization Survey, conducted

Crimes Reported to Police

Percentage reported to police

44%	Total violent crime
60%	Aggravated assault
57%	Robbery
23%	Rape/sexual assault
39%	Simple assault
35%	Total property crime
73%	Motor vehicle theft
49%	Burglary
30%	Larceny-theft

Note: Percentages based on the National Crime Victimization Survey for 2016.

Source: Morgan and Kena 2018:Table 4.

annually by the U.S. Department of Justice, reveals that some crimes are more likely to be reported than others. As shown in the "Crimes Reported to Police" graph, motor vehicle theft is the most likely property crime to be reported, with 73 percent of victims contacting the authorities. Larceny-theft is the least likely at 30 percent. When it comes to violent crimes, less than half of victims overall contact the police (Morgan and Kena 2018:Table 4). Because not all crimes get reported, justice does not get served within the U.S. legal system for many offenses.

People choose not to report crimes for a variety of reasons. In the case of larceny-theft, for example, people may conclude that, because there is little chance of getting stolen items back, it simply isn't worth the hassle. More significantly, members of racial and ethnic minority groups often distrust law enforcement agencies and may not contact the police when they are victimized. Further, many women do not report rape or spousal abuse out of fear they will be blamed for the crime.

—SOCTHINK—

The Clery Act, passed in 1990, requires colleges and universities to provide students with timely reports of campus crimes. How much do you trust official campus crime reports? Why might reports of crime on college campuses underestimate the actual number of incidents?

WHITE-COLLAR CRIME

People generally agree that crimes such as theft, assault, or murder call for serious punishment, but research shows that crimes committed by well-respected people are perceived differently. Sociologists define **white-collar crime** as illegal acts committed by high-status individuals who use their positions of power and influence for their own benefit. Examples include tax evasion, embezzlement, stock manipulation, and fraud (Sutherland 1940, 1949, 1983). Frequently, convicted offenders for these kinds of crimes receive less harsh punishments than do those for more common street crimes, even when the dollar values involved in these white-collar crimes is substantially greater.

> **White-collar crime** Illegal acts committed by high-status individuals who use their positions of power and influence for their own benefit.

Over time, the definition of white-collar crimes has expanded to include offenses by businesses and corporations. Corporate crime, or any act by a corporation that is punishable by the government, takes many forms and includes individuals, organizations, and institutions among its victims. Corporations may engage in anticompetitive behavior, environmental pollution, medical fraud, tax fraud, stock fraud and manipulation, accounting fraud, the production of unsafe goods, bribery and corruption, and health and safety violations (Coleman 2006).

The downfall of Bernie Madoff represented the largest case of white-collar crime of its type in history. Madoff, an American businessman who managed people's financial investments, promised investors annual returns of 15 to 20 percent and delivered on that promise for years. This enabled him to attract extremely wealthy clients from around the world, even charitable organizations. In the end, he was just running a scam. Madoff had provided investors with false statements showing nonexistent trades and profits. Estimates are that he defrauded his clients out of $65 billion in purported assets. Life savings and family fortunes were gone in an instant. Madoff ultimately pleaded guilty to 11 felony counts, including securities fraud, mail fraud, money laundering, and perjury (Gaviria and Smith 2009; Henriques and Healy 2009).

What is particularly interesting about the Madoff case is that officials at the Securities and Exchange Commission (SEC) were tipped off numerous times to the possibility that Madoff's investments were a scam. Finally, after receiving documented accusations that he was running a Ponzi scheme, the SEC launched an official investigation in 2006. Two years later it concluded that there was "no evidence of fraud." The SEC failed to see what analysts now say should have been obvious. Red flags were ignored, but why? Sociologists suggest that white-collar criminals are often given the benefit of the doubt. In fact, during each previous investigation, Madoff deliberately and successfully used his status as a respected businessman as evidence of his innocence. He might have avoided detection had it not been for his own confession (Berenson and Henriques 2008).

The 1980s classic film *Wall Street* tells the story of Gordon Gekko, a high-flying stockbroker, who became a role model to many real-life brokers. In perhaps its most famous scene, Gekko gives a speech about what's good about America, reaching its pinnacle with the era-defining line "Greed is good." More recently, the film *The Wolf of Wall Street* presents a very different image, lampooning the world of high finance as one of extreme excess and corruption, as characterized by its takeaway line, "Was all this legal? Absolutely not."

POPSOC

VICTIMLESS CRIMES

Some crimes seem less severe because any negative effects only harm consenting participants. Sociologists refer to **victimless crimes** as the willing exchange among adults of widely desired, but illegal, goods and services. Examples include gambling, drug use, and prostitution (Schur 1965, 1985). The fact that the parties involved are willing participants has led some people to suggest that such transactions should not constitute crimes.

> **Victimless crime** A term used by sociologists to describe the willing exchange among adults of widely desired, but illegal, goods and services.

Some activists are working to decriminalize many of these illegal practices. For example, supporters of decriminalization are troubled by the attempt to legislate a moral code for adults. In their view, prostitution, drug use, gambling, and other victimless crimes are expensive to enforce and impossible to prevent. The already overburdened criminal justice system should instead devote its resources to "street crimes" and other offenses with obvious victims.

The current debate over the legalization of marijuana illustrates the difficulty of enforcing laws involving willing participants engaged in private behavior. Even though marijuana use remains illegal at the federal level, 52 percent of U.S. adults admit to having tried it and 14 percent use it at least once a month (Marist 2017). Over time, attitudes regarding marijuana legalization have shifted dramatically. As the "Marijuana Legalization, 1969–2018" graph illustrates, the percentage of people in the United States favoring legalization rose from 12 percent in 1969 to 62 percent in 2018 (Hartig and Geiger 2018).

Laws at the state level have also changed dramatically. As the "Marijuana Laws by State" map shows, the move to legalize marijuana use has expanded nationally. Thirty-three states have legalized the use of marijuana for medical purposes. Ten states—Washington, Colorado, Oregon, Alaska, Maine, Massachusetts, Nevada, California, Michigan, and Vermont—took the additional step of legalizing marijuana for personal recreational use (National Conference of State Legislatures 2018a, 2018b).

Critics of the term *victimless crime* object to the notion that there is no victim other than the offender in such crimes. Excessive drinking, compulsive gambling, and illegal drug use contribute to an enormous amount of personal and property damage. A person with a drinking problem can become abusive to a spouse or children; a compulsive gambler or drug user may steal to pursue his or her obsession. Feminist sociologists contend that prostitution, as well as the more disturbing aspects of pornography, reinforce the misconception that women are "toys" who can be treated as objects rather than people. According to critics of decriminalization, society must not give tacit approval to conduct that has such harmful consequences (Farley and Malarek 2008; Meier and Geis 1997).

Marijuana Legalization, 1969–2018

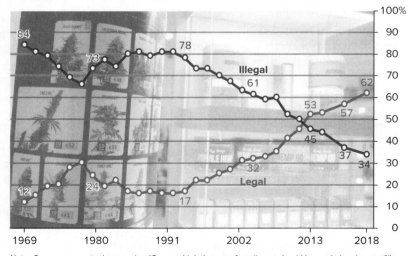

Note: Responses are to the question "Do you think the use of marijuana should be made legal, or not?"
Source: Hartig and Geiger 2018. *Photo:* Beata Zawrzel/NurPhoto/Getty Images

Marijuana Laws by State

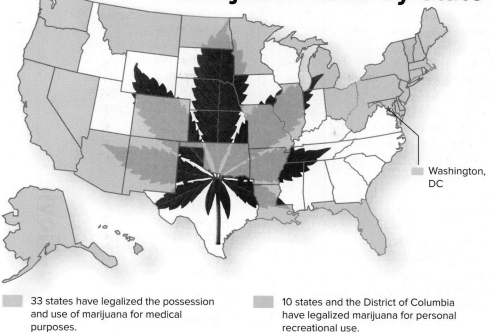

■ Washington, DC

■ 33 states have legalized the possession and use of marijuana for medical purposes.

■ 10 states and the District of Columbia have legalized marijuana for personal recreational use.

Source: National Conference of State Legislatures 2018a. *Photo:* Brand X Pictures/Getty Images

SOCTHINK

Should gambling, prostitution, and recreational drugs be legalized? What are the potential consequences, both positive and negative, of doing so?

ORGANIZED CRIME

When it comes to organized crime, images of pop culture gangsters, such as Tony Soprano from HBO's classic series *The Sopranos,* often come to mind. In real life, examples of organized crime groups go beyond the Mafia to include the Japanese Yakuza, the Russian Organization, Colombian drug cartels, and many other international crime syndicates. **Organized crime** is the work of a group that regulates relations among criminal enterprises involved in illegal activities, including prostitution, gambling, and the smuggling and sale of illegal drugs (National Institute of Justice 2007).

Organized crime dominates the world of illegal business, just as large corporations dominate the conventional business world. It allocates territory, sets prices for goods and services, and acts as an arbiter in internal disputes. A secret, conspiratorial activity, organized crime generally evades law enforcement.

> You come at the king, you best not miss.
>
> Omar Little, *The Wire* (2002)

It takes over legitimate businesses, gains influence over labor unions, corrupts public officials, intimidates witnesses in criminal trials, and even "taxes" merchants in exchange for "protection" (Federal Bureau of Investigation 2016).

Historically, organized crime has provided a means of upward mobility for groups of people struggling to escape poverty. Sociologist Daniel Bell (1953) used the term *ethnic succession* to describe the sequential passage of leadership from Irish Americans in the early 1900s to Jewish Americans in the 1920s and then to Italian Americans in the early 1930s. Recently, ethnic succession has become more complex, reflecting the diversity of the nation's latest immigrants. Colombian, Mexican, Russian, Chinese, Pakistani, and Nigerian immigrants are among those who have begun to play a significant role in organized crime activities (Friman 2004; Kleinknecht 1996).

There has always been a global element in organized crime. However, law enforcement officials and policy makers now acknowledge the emergence of a new form of organized crime that takes advantage of advances in electronic communications. International organized crime includes drug and arms smuggling, money laundering, and trafficking in illegal immigrants and stolen goods (Lumpe 2003; National Institute of Justice 2007).

> **Organized crime** The work of a group that regulates relations among criminal enterprises involved in illegal activities, including prostitution, gambling, and the smuggling and sale of illegal drugs.

INTERNATIONAL CRIME

In the past, international crime was often limited to the clandestine shipment of goods across the border between two countries. Increasingly, however, crime is no more restricted by such borders than is legal commerce. Rather than concentrating on specific countries, international crime now spans the globe.

Transnational Crime More and more, scholars and law enforcement officials are turning their attention to **transnational crime,** or crime that occurs across multiple national borders. Historically, probably the most dreaded example of transnational crime has been slavery. At first, governments did not regard slavery as a crime but merely regulated it as they would trade in any other good. Examples of transnational crime now include human trafficking, illicit trade in firearms, sale of fraudulent medicines, counterfeiting goods, wildlife trafficking, and migrant smuggling (Kelly and Levy 2012; Ruetschlin and Bangura 2012; UNODC 2018a).

One way to fight such crime has been through multilateral cooperation in which countries work together to pursue border-crossing crime. The first global effort to control international crime was the International Criminal Police Organization (Interpol), a cooperative network of European police forces founded to stem the movement of political revolutionaries across borders. Although such efforts to fight transnational crime may seem lofty—an activity with which any government would want to cooperate—they are complicated by sensitive legal and security issues. Most nations that have signed protocols issued by the United Nations, including the United States, have expressed concern over potential encroachments on their national judicial systems, as well as concern over their national security. Thus, they have been reluctant to share certain types of intelligence data. The terrorist attacks of September 11, 2001, increased both the interest in combating transnational crime and sensitivity to the risks of sharing intelligence data (Deflem 2005; Felson and Kalaitzidis 2005).

Transnational crime Crime that occurs across multiple national borders.

Going GLOBAL

International Incarceration Rates

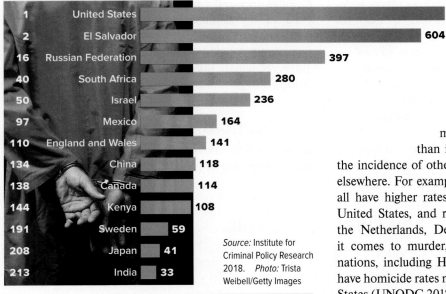

Rank
out of 222 nations

International incarceration rates
(prison population rates per 100,000 of the national population)

Rank	Nation	Rate
1	United States	655
2	El Salvador	604
16	Russian Federation	397
40	South Africa	280
50	Israel	236
97	Mexico	164
110	England and Wales	141
134	China	118
138	Canada	114
144	Kenya	108
191	Sweden	59
208	Japan	41
213	India	33

Source: Institute for Criminal Policy Research 2018. *Photo:* Trista Weibell/Getty Images

International Crime Rates

Taking an international perspective on crime reinforces one of the key sociological lessons about crime and deviance: place matters. Although cross-national data comparison can be difficult, we can offer insight about how crime rates differ around the world.

Violent crimes tend to be much more common in the United States than in the nations of western Europe. Yet the incidence of other types of crime appears to be higher elsewhere. For example, France, Italy, Sweden, and Greece all have higher rates of reported car theft than does the United States, and rates for reported thefts are higher in the Netherlands, Denmark, Sweden, and France. When it comes to murder, most South and Central American nations, including Honduras, El Salvador, and Venezuela, have homicide rates many times higher than does the United States (UNODC 2018b). But when comparing incarceration rates, the United States has the highest rate of putting people behind bars of any nation in the world. On a typical day, the United States imprisons 655 of every 100,000 adults, compared to 397 in Russia, 164 in Mexico, and 114 in Canada (Institute for Criminal Policy Research 2016).

Why are rates of violent crime so much higher in the United States than in western Europe? Sociologist Elliot Currie (1985, 1998) has suggested that U.S. society places greater emphasis on individual economic achievement than other societies. At the same time, many observers have noted that the culture of the United States has long tolerated, if not condoned, many forms of violence. Coupled with sharp disparities between poor and affluent citizens, significant unemployment, and substantial alcohol and drug abuse, these factors combine to produce a climate conducive to crime.

Violent crime remains a serious problem in nations around the world. In Mexico, for example, approximately 44 percent of the 27,734 homicides in 2017 were categorized as organized crime-style killings, involving elements such as group execution, torture, beheadings, and dismemberment. Attacks have been especially concentrated in the Mexican states of Guerrero, Chihuahua, Veracruz, and Guanajuato (Calderón, Ferreira, and Shirk 2018). The violence is a consequence, in part, of governmental attempts to crack down on the illegal drug trade. After his election in 2006, President Felipe Calderón sent in tens of thousands of troops to enforce the law. Since then, drug cartels fought both the authorities and one another in a struggle to maintain their local power (Camp 2010a, 2010b).

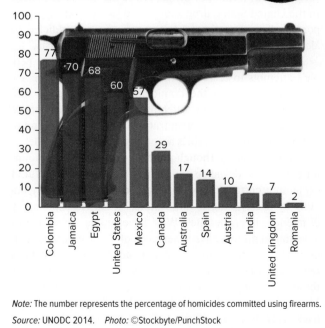

Going GLOBAL

International Gun Homicide Rates

Note: The number represents the percentage of homicides committed using firearms.

Source: UNODC 2014.   *Photo:* ©Stockbyte/PunchStock

>> Sociological Perspectives on Crime and Deviance

Sociologists have always been interested in how and why society holds together. As a result, they have also always explored reasons why people violate accepted social norms. Though we might wish otherwise, there is no one, simple, universal theory that explains all such acts. Here we look to just a few of the theories that sociologists have offered in order to identify significant factors that we must consider in our attempt to understand deviance and crime more fully.

FUNCTIONS OF CRIME AND DEVIANCE

Sociologists drawing on the functionalist perspective explore the ways deviance both challenges and reinforces social order. Émile Durkheim ([1895] 1964), for example, wondered why deviance, which seems to undermine order, is found in all societies. For Durkheim the answer rested with how such actions actually reinforce social order.

Durkheim's Functions of Deviance Durkheim argued that no act is inherently criminal. He put it this way: "We must not say that an action shocks the common consciousness because it is criminal, but rather that it is criminal because it shocks that consciousness" ([1895] 1964:123–24). In other words, the context of the action impacts our perception of whether or not it is right or wrong more than something inherent in the act itself. For example, killing another person isn't always murder. We justify killing in self-defense or in combat as legitimate but condemn killing in cold blood.

Durkheim argued that, because some form of deviance exists in all societies, it must serve a positive social function. One positive effect comes from collectively labeling acts as deviant which clarifies our shared beliefs and values and thus brings us closer together. We say, in effect, "This is who we are, and if you want to be one of us, you cannot cross this line." Another positive function occurs through punishment, which creates solidarity by drawing a group together in opposition to the offender. Punishment also functions as a deterrent. Seeing violators pay the price for their deviance discourages others from similar transgressions. When we see a driver receiving a speeding ticket, a department store cashier being fired for yelling at a customer, or a college student getting a failing grade for plagiarizing a term paper, we are reminded of our collective norms and values and of the consequences of their violation. Finally, Durkheim did recognize that deviant acts might also lead us to recognize the limits of our existing beliefs and practices, resulting in positive social change in which we revise existing norms and values.

Durkheim also recognized that, during times of significant social upheaval, as occurred during the Industrial Revolution, society's capacity to provide direction can breakdown. Durkheim used the term *anomie* to describe the state of normlessness that occurs during times of profound social change and disorder. The power of society to constrain deviant action at such times is limited because there is no clear consensus on shared norms and values. Just as we saw with Durkheim's analysis of suicide, at times when social integration is weak, people are freer to pursue their own deviant paths.

─SOCTHINK─

Durkheim argues that increased division of labor results in fewer shared experiences and thus a weakened sense of community. What impact might a strong commitment to individualism have on our likelihood of committing crime?

Merton's Strain Theory Sociologist Robert Merton (1968) took Durkheim's theory a step further. He suggested that a disconnect can exist between a society's goals and the means people have to attain them. By *goals* he meant the dominant values that most members of a society share, and by *means* he meant the material, social, and cultural resources necessary for success. He did not assume that all people in a society would be equally committed to those values. He also did not assume that everyone would have the same opportunity to attain those goals. Putting these together, he developed the **strain theory of deviance,** which

Strain theory of deviance Robert Merton's theory of deviance as an adaptation of socially prescribed goals or of the means governing their attainment, or both.

views deviance as an adaptation of socially prescribed goals or of the means governing their attainment, or both.

We can better understand Merton's model by looking at economic success as an important goal in the United States. Socially agreed upon pathways exist in order to attain that goal—go to school, work hard, do not quit, take advantage of opportunities, and so forth. Merton wondered what happened when someone who shared the goal of economic success lacked the means to attain that end. For example, a burgler and a small-business owner may share a common goal of making money, but their means of attaining it are radically different. Merton combined acceptance and rejection of goals and means to create a model with five possible adaptations.

Conformity to social norms, the most common adaptation in Merton's typology, is the opposite of deviance. The "conformist" accepts both the overall societal goal (for example, to become wealthy) and the approved means (hard work). In Merton's view, there must be some consensus regarding accepted cultural goals and the legitimate means for attaining them. Without such a consensus, societies could exist only as collectives of people rather than as unified cultures, and they might experience continual chaos.

The other four types of behavior all involve some departure from conformity. The "innovator" accepts the goals of society but pursues them with means that are regarded as improper. For instance, a safecracker may steal money to buy consumer goods and take expensive vacations. The "ritualist" has abandoned the goal of material success and become compulsively committed to the institutional means. Work becomes simply a way of life rather than a means to the goal of success. An example would be the bureaucratic official who blindly applies rules and regulations without remembering the larger goals of the organization. The "retreatist," as described by Merton, has basically withdrawn (or retreated) from both the goals and the means of society. In the United States, drug addicts and vagrants are typically portrayed as retreatists. Adolescents who are addicted to alcohol or drugs at an early age may become retreatists.

The final adaptation identified by Merton reflects people's attempts to create a *new* social structure. The "rebel" feels alienated from the dominant means and goals and may seek a dramatically different social order. Members of a revolutionary political organization, such as a militia group, can be categorized as rebels according to Merton's model.

Merton's theory, though popular, does not fully account for patterns of deviance and crime. Although it is useful in explaining certain types of behavior, such as illegal gambling by disadvantaged "innovators," it fails to explain key differences in crime rates. Why, for example, do some disadvantaged groups have lower rates of reported crime than others? Why do many people in adverse circumstances reject criminal activity as a viable alternative? Merton's theory does not easily answer such questions (Clinard and Miller 1998). Exploring additional sociological perspectives on crime and deviance helps us to more fully appreciate such nuances.

Merton's Typology of Deviance

Source: Merton 1968.

Did You Know?

. . . More people are arrested for drug use in the United States than for any other crime. The FBI reported 1,275,812 arrests for drug abuse violations in 2017, which constitutes 15.5 percent of all arrests. Regionally, the South had the highest rate. The three highest states were South Dakota, Wyoming, and South Carolina, and the three lowest were Alaska, Massachusetts, and Washington.

Source: U.S. Department of Justice 2018c:Tables 30 and 69.
Photo: ESB Professional/Shutterstock

Hirschi's Social Control Theory Rather than asking why people *do* commit crimes, American sociologist Travis Hirschi (1969) asked why they *don't*. He assumed that, left to their own devices, people would naturally seek their own gratification, including lying, cheating, and stealing to get their way, even at the expense of others. Growing out of the functionalist perspective, the theory presupposes that society would be unable to function if people couldn't trust others to work toward common goals. As an answer, he proposed **social control theory,** which posits that the social bonds we share with other members of society lead us to conform to society's norms. According to Hirschi, deviance occurs due to lack of self-control, and self-control develops as a consequence of socialization into society's norms and values through the relationships we have with others. Even if we are tempted at times, we take into account what family, friends, and significant others might think should they find out what we did. As a result, we typically refuse to give in to temptation because we do not want to damage those relationships.

Hirschi identified four key elements involved in strengthening those social bonds. First, *attachment* refers to the emotional ties and sense of connection individuals feel toward significant others in their lives. Second, *commitment* involves the extent to which individuals view their long-term success as tied to the ongoing success of their society. In other words, investing one's time, energy, and resources

in the existing system reduces the likelihood of deviance, which would jeopardize that investment. Third, *involvement* means spending time doing what is expected—for a student, that might include studying for exams, rehearsing lines, going to volleyball practice—which reduces a person's availability for deviance. If, as the old proverb goes, "Idle hands are the devil's workshop," involvement prevents deviance by keeping people busy. And fourth, *belief* involves buying into the society's core values by making them one's own. Those least integrated into society along these four dimensions are the ones most likely to commit deviant acts. According to Hirschi's theory, society can reduce levels of crime and deviance by socializing children effectively at a young age and building strong social ties as children develop (Brown and Jennings 2014; Hirschi 1969, 2004).

INTERPERSONAL INTERACTION AND DEFINING DEVIANCE

Another approach to explaining crime and deviance grows out of insights drawn from the interactionist perspective. Rather than concentrating on the societal level and its presumed needs for social order, these theories emphasize the interpersonal level and highlight the importance of interaction in shaping how deviance occurs. Deviance here is something we learn or something attributed to us by others.

Sutherland's Cultural Transmission Theory As humans, we learn how to behave in social situations, whether properly or improperly. Sociologist Edwin Sutherland (1883–1950) proposed that, just as individuals are socialized to conform to society's basic norms and values, so also are they socialized to learn deviant acts. It's not that we are born to be wild; we learn to be wild.

Sutherland drew on the **cultural transmission** school, which emphasizes that individuals learn criminal behavior by interacting with others. Such learning includes not only the techniques of lawbreaking (for example, how to break into a car quickly and quietly), but also the motives, drives, and rationalizations of the criminal. The cultural transmission approach can also be used to explain the behavior of those who habitually abuse alcohol or drugs.

Sutherland maintained that through interactions with a primary group and significant others, people acquire definitions of proper and improper behavior. He used the term **differential association** to describe the process through which exposure to attitudes favorable to criminal acts leads to the violation of rules. For example, people are more likely to engage in norm-defying behavior if they are part of a group or subculture

> **Social control theory** A theory of deviance that posits that the social bonds we share with other members of society lead us to conform to society's norms
>
> **Cultural transmission** A school of criminology that argues that criminal behavior is learned through social interactions.
>
> **Differential association** A theory of deviance that holds that violation of rules results from exposure to attitudes favorable to criminal acts.

The cafeteria at the school where I teach has an all-you-can-eat policy, but you cannot take food with you when you leave. Most of my students admit they violate this rule. When I suggest that what they are doing might be criminal, they are offended. They justify their theft in any number of ways: they pay a lot for their meal plan, they sometimes miss meals, it wouldn't make sense to throw the food away, etc. Yet there are people who are in prison for having taken things costing less than the total value of food taken by the average student. Why is it that those of us, like me, who are guilty of having taken food do not view ourselves as criminal?

---

that stresses supports and encourages such actions, such as a street gang. Research suggests that this view of differential association also applies to noncriminal deviant acts, such as smoking, binge drinking, and cheating (Higgins, Tewksbury, and Mustaine 2007; Nofziger and Hye-Ryeon 2006; Vowell and Chen 2004).

Sutherland offers the example of a child who is sociable, outgoing, and athletic and who lives in an area with a high rate of delinquency. The youth is very likely to come into contact with peers who commit acts of vandalism, fail to attend school, and so forth, and they may come to adopt such behavior. However, an introverted child who lives in the same neighborhood may stay away from their peers and avoid delinquency. In another community, an outgoing and athletic child may join a Little League baseball team or a scout troop because of their interactions with peers. Thus, Sutherland views improper behavior as the result of the types of groups to which one belongs and the kinds of friendships one has (Sutherland, Cressey, and Luckenbill 1992).

Although the cultural transmission approach may not explain the conduct of the first-time, impulsive shoplifter or the impoverished person who steals out of necessity, it does help explain the deviant behavior of juvenile delinquents or graffiti artists. It directs our attention to the paramount role of social interaction and context in increasing a person's motivation to engage in

Social disorganization theory
The theory that attributes increases in crime and deviance to the absence or breakdown of communal relationships and social institutions, such as the family, school, church, and local government.

Broken windows hypothesis
The theory that physical signs of decline in a community or neighborhood indicate a corresponding breakdown of social order within which crime and deviance are likely to thrive

deviant behavior (Morselli, Tremblay, and McCarthy 2006; Sutherland, Cressey, and Luckenbill 1992).

Social Disorganization Theory The relative strength of social relationships in a community or neighborhood influences the behavior of its members. Social psychologist Philip Zimbardo (2007) studied the effect of these communal relationships by conducting the following experiment. He abandoned a car in each of two different neighborhoods, leaving its hood up and removing its hubcaps. In one neighborhood, people started to strip the car for parts even before Zimbardo had finished setting up a remote video camera to record their behavior. In the other neighborhood, weeks passed without the car being touched, except for a pedestrian who stopped to close the hood during a rainstorm.

Rather than focusing on the positive ways in which communal bonds hold us together, **social disorganization theory** attributes increases in crime and deviance to the absence or breakdown of communal relationships and social institutions, such as the family, school, church, and local government. The lack of such local community connections, with their associated cross-age relationships, makes it difficult to exert informal control within the community, especially of children. Without community supervision and controls, playing outside becomes an opportunity for deviance and for older violators to socialize children into inappropriate paths. Crime becomes a normal response to a local context (Shaw and McKay 1969).

The social disorganization theory gave rise to what is known as the **broken windows hypothesis,** which holds that physical signs of decline in a community or neighborhood indicate a corresponding breakdown of social order within which crime and deviance are likely to thrive (Wilson and Kelling 1982). Indicators of physical decline include abandoned cars, litter, graffiti, and drug paraphernalia, The analogy goes something like this, "If a window in a building is broken and is left unrepaired, all the rest of the windows will soon be broken" (Wilson and Kelling 1982). The broken window gets taken as a sign that no one cares, meaning there will be no consequences for breaking more.

Janine Wiedel Photolibrary/Alamy Stock Photo

As that happens, a perception develops that the community is unsafe, leading people to action. Many community members who can do so will move out. As informal social controls break down, others will be more willing to display deviance publicly, including panhandling, prostitution, public intoxication, drug use, and mugging (Kelling 2015; Kelling and Coles 1996; Wilson and Kelling 1982).

The broken windows model resulted in a theory of policing premised on the idea that the metaphorical broken windows must be addressed early on before the domino effect kicked in and the neighborhood was engulfed in crime. In practice, to prevent this from happening, police focused less on physical indicators of decline and instead targeted individuals who might represent early signs of social disorganization. That included moving homeless people out of areas in an effort to stop the first domino. The challenge arises, however, when undesirability is linked to race, ethnicity, age, and sex.

A particularly controversial implementation of the broken windows hypothesis came in the form of "stop and frisk" policing programs. Such policies encourage police to stop and search individuals for drugs, weapons, or other illegal items, even without probable cause. This technique has been criticized for unfairly targeting and denying the constitutional rights of young African American and Latino males (Gelman, Fagan, and Kiss 2007; Kochel, Wilson, and Mastrofski 2011; Sampson and Raudenbush 2004; Torres 2015), and its effectiveness in reducing crime has been questioned (Rosenfeld and Fornago 2014). In spite of the controversy surrounding this approach, Donald Trump advocated its implementation in Chicago as a way to address the violence in that city (Gonzales and Holland 2018).

Labeling Theory Sometimes when it comes to deviance, perception dominates over reality. In the early 1970s, sociologist William Chambliss (1973) conducted what has become a classic sociological study of deviance. Using observation research at a moderate-sized suburban high school, he followed two groups of male students, which he called the Saints and Roughnecks. Those designated the Saints came from "good families," were active in school organizations, planned on attending college, and received good grades. Those designated the Roughnecks had no such aura of respectability. They drove around town in beat-up cars, were generally unsuccessful in school, and aroused suspicion no matter what they did (Chambliss 1973).

Chambliss learned that boys from both groups repeatedly engaged in excessive drinking, reckless driving, truancy, petty theft, and vandalism. However, students he identified as Saints were never arrested, whereas Roughnecks were frequently in trouble with police and townspeople. Even though their acts of deviance were largely the same, the two groups were not treated equally. The Saints hid behind a facade of respectability, and people generally viewed their delinquent acts as a few isolated cases of sowing wild oats. Consistent with the Thomas theorem, Chambliss concluded that people's perception of the students, as rooted in their social class positions, played an important role in the varying fortunes of the two groups.

We can understand such discrepancies by using an approach to deviance known as **labeling theory,** which emphasizes how a person comes to be labeled as deviant or to accept that label. Unlike Sutherland's work, labeling theory does not focus on why some individuals come to commit deviant acts. Instead, it attempts to explain why society views certain people (such as the Roughnecks) as deviants, delinquents, bad kids, losers, and criminals, while it sees others whose behavior is similar (such as the Saints) in less harsh terms. Sociologist Howard Becker (1963:9; 1964), who popularized this approach, summed up labeling theory with this statement: "Deviant behavior is behavior that people so label."

Labeling theory An approach to deviance that attempts to explain why certain people are viewed as deviants while others engaged in the same behavior are not.

Societal-reaction approach Another name for *labeling theory.*

Labeling theory is also called the **societal-reaction approach,** reminding us that it is the response to an act, not the act itself, that determines deviance. Traditionally, research on deviance has focused on people who violate social norms. In contrast, labeling theory focuses on police, probation officers, psychiatrists, judges, teachers, employers, school officials, and other regulators of social control. These agents, it is argued, play a significant role in creating the deviant identity by designating certain people (and not others) as deviant (Bernburg, Krohn, and Rivera 2006). An important aspect of labeling theory is the recognition that some individuals or groups have the power to define labels and apply them to others. This view ties into the conflict perspective's emphasis on the social significance of power.

The practice of racial profiling, in which people are identified as criminal suspects purely on the basis of their race, frequently occurs in stop-and-frisk policing and has come under public scrutiny. Studies confirm the public's suspicion that in some jurisdictions, police officers are much more likely to stop African American males than White males for routine traffic violations, in the expectation of finding drugs or guns in their cars. Civil rights activists refer to these cases sarcastically as DWB (Driving While Black) violations (Warren et al. 2006). The deaths of numerous young African American men, including Trayvon Martin in Sanford, Florida; Michael Brown in Ferguson, Missouri;

> The degree of civilization in a society can be judged by entering its prisons.
>
> Fyodor Dostoevsky ([1879] 1985)

Eric Garner in New York City; Tamir Rice in Cleveland, Ohio; Philando Castile in Falcon Heights, Minnesota; and, Stephon Clark in Sacramento, California, raised substantial concerns about the life-and-death consequences of labeling young African American males as threats.

Although the labeling approach does not fully explain why certain people accept a label and others manage to reject it, labeling theorists do suggest that the power an individual has relative to others is important in determining his or her ability to resist an undesirable label. It opens the door to additional emphasis on the undeniably important actions of people with power who can shape what counts as deviance.

Before letting them drive, many African American parents have "the talk" with their kids about what to do if they get pulled over by police. EMPPhotography/E+/Getty Images

CONFLICT, POWER, AND CRIMINALITY

In addition to its significance for labeling theory, the story of the Saints and Roughnecks points toward the role that having power and control over valued resources can play in defining deviance. Sociologist Richard Quinney (1974, 1979, 1980) is a leading proponent of the view that the criminal justice system serves the interests of the powerful. Consistent with the conflict perspective, this approach maintains that people with power protect their own interests and define deviance to suit their own needs. Crime, according to Quinney (1970), is defined as such by legislators who may be influenced by the economic elites to advance their interests.

Differential justice Variations in the way social control is exercised over different groups.

Race and Class Looking at crime from this perspective draws our attention to the effects that power and position might have throughout the criminal justice system in the United States. Researchers have found that the system treats suspects differently based on their racial, ethnic, or social class background. In many cases, officials using their own discretion make biased decisions about whether to press charges or drop them, whether to set bail and how much, and whether to offer parole or deny it. Researchers have found that this kind of **differential justice,** which refers to variations in the way social control is exercised over different groups, puts African Americans and Latinxs at a disadvantage in the justice system, both as juveniles and as adults. On average, White offenders receive shorter sentences than comparable Latinx and African American offenders, even when prior arrest records

and the relative severity of the crime are taken into consideration (Brewer and Heitzeg 2008; Quinney 1974; Wakefield and Uggen 2010).

We see this pattern of differential justice at work with death penalty cases. Simply put, poor people cannot afford to hire the best lawyer and often must rely on court-appointed attorneys, who typically are overworked and underpaid. With capital punishment in place, these unequal resources may mean the difference between life and death for poor defendants (Kutateladze et al. 2014; National Center for Access to Justice 2016; National Center for State Courts 2015). Indeed, the American Bar Association has repeatedly expressed concern about the limited defense most defendants facing the death penalty receive. Through the end of 2018, DNA analysis and other new technologies had exonerated 362 inmates, 20 of whom had served time on death row, with an average of 14 years served in prison. Forty of the exonerees pleaded guilty to crimes they did not commit. Overall, 61 percent of those found innocent were African American (Innocence Project 2018).

Various studies show that defendants are more likely to be sentenced to death if their victims were White rather than Black. Even though about half of all murder victims are White, 75 percent of death penalty case victims are White. Some evidence indicates that Black defendants, who constituted 42 percent of all death row inmates, are more likely to face execution than Whites in the same legal circumstances. Overall, 70 percent of those who have been exonerated by DNA testing were African American, Latinx, Native

> # Whenever you find yourself on the side of the majority, it is time to pause and reflect.
>
> **Mark Twain (1909)**

Executions by State since 1976

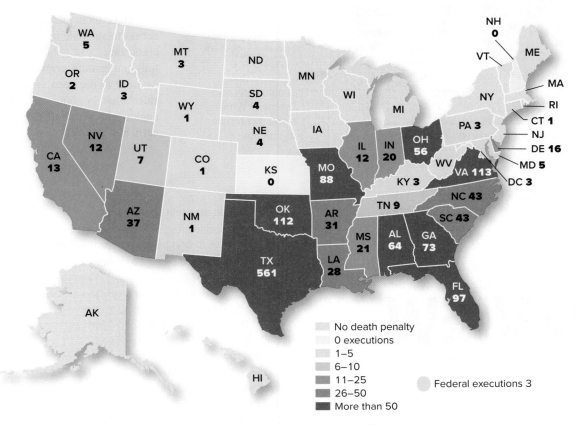

Note: The death penalty was reinstated by the U.S. Supreme Court in 1976. Data current as of May 2019. New Mexico abolished the death penalty in 2009. California established a moratorium on the use of the death penalty in March 2019.

Source: Death Penalty Information Center 2019.

American, or Asian American. Evidence exists, too, that capital defendants receive poor legal services because of the racist attitudes of their own defense counsel. Apparently, discrimination and racism do not end even when the stakes are life and death (Death Penalty Information Center 2018; Innocence Project 2018; Jacobs et al. 2007).

Gender Feminist criminologists such as Meda Chesney-Lind (with Lisa Pasko 2004) and Gillian Balfour (2006) have suggested that many of the existing approaches to deviance and crime were developed with only men in mind. For example, in the United States, for many years any husband who forced his wife to have sexual intercourse—without her consent and against her will—was not legally considered to have committed rape. The law defined rape as pertaining only to sexual relations between people who were not married to each other, reflecting the overwhelmingly male composition of state legislatures at the time. It took repeated protests by feminist organizations to get changes in the criminal law defining rape. It was not until 1993 that husbands in all 50 states could be prosecuted under most circumstances for the rape of their wives; however, significant exceptions remain in no fewer than 30 states (Bergen 2006).

In some parts of the world, laws regarding rape and marriage continue to point toward inequality for women in the eyes of the law. In various countries in the Middle East, for example, rapists can avoid prosecution by marrying their victims. Women's rights groups have protested by displaying bloodied wedding gowns in public places to bring attention to the practice. As a result, some countries, including Morocco, Lebanon, Jordan, and Tunisia, have abolished the marry-your-rapist loophole in recent years (Raphelson 2017; Sengupta 2017).

From the feminist perspective, we also learn that men's greater average earning power disadvantages women. For example, wives may be reluctant to report acts of abuse to the authorities and thereby lose what may be their primary or even sole source of income. But as women have taken more active and powerful roles both in the household and in business, these gender differences in deviance and crime have narrowed (Chesney-Lind 1989; Kruttschnitt 2013).

Together, sociological perspectives on crime and deviance help us better understand and explain such acts. No single explanation is sufficient. We must consider multiple factors from a variety of perspectives, including the extent to which deviance exists for the sake of social order; the degree of opportunity to attain both means and ends; the

SOCIOLOGY IS A VERB

Observing Justice

Visit a local courthouse to observe a trial in action. If possible, stay for several cases in different courts. What do you observe about the key players, including the defendants, attorneys, judge, and witnesses? Drawing on Goffman's dramaturgical analysis, in what ways are the performances staged? What scripts and props are used? How does the trial you observed compare to trials portrayed in television dramas or on cable news channels?

role of socialization in deviance; the strength of local community networks; the power to administer labels and make them stick; and differential access to valuable resources based on class, race, and gender. If we are to fully understand crime and deviance, we need to dig deep enough and consider what is going on from enough angles and with sufficient care, concern, and curiosity.

For REVIEW

I. How do groups maintain social control?
- They use positive and negative sanctions in both formal and informal ways to bring about conformity and obedience.

II. What is the difference between deviance and crime?
- Deviance involves violating a group's expected norms, which may lead the offender to be stigmatized. Crime is a form of deviance that involves violating the formal norms administered by the state for which the offender may receive formal sanctions.

III. How do sociologists explain deviance and crime?
- Sociologists offer a number of theories of crime, each of which provides additional factors to be considered—such as the need for social order, the significance of interpersonal relationships and local context, and the importance of power and access to resources—that help us better understand why deviance and crime occur.

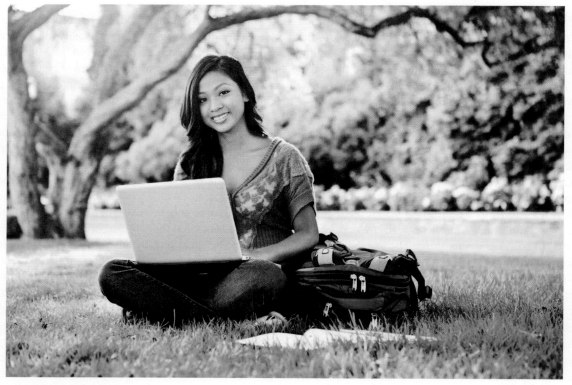

Arek Malang/Shutterstock

SOCVIEWS on Deviance

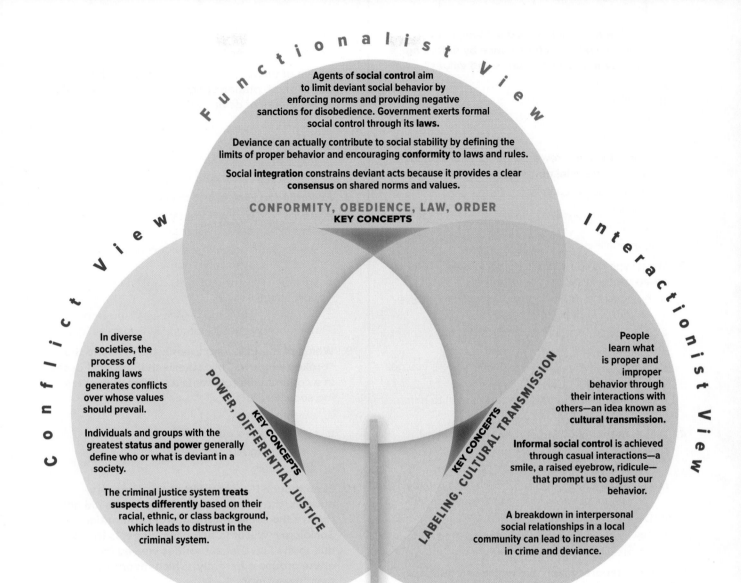

Functionalist View

Agents of **social control** aim to limit deviant social behavior by enforcing norms and providing negative sanctions for disobedience. Government exerts formal social control through its **laws**.

Deviance can actually contribute to social stability by defining the limits of proper behavior and encouraging **conformity** to laws and rules.

Social **integration** constrains deviant acts because it provides a clear **consensus** on shared norms and values.

CONFORMITY, OBEDIENCE, LAW, ORDER
KEY CONCEPTS

Conflict View

In diverse societies, the process of making laws generates conflicts over whose values should prevail.

Individuals and groups with the greatest **status and power** generally define who or what is deviant in a society.

The criminal justice system **treats suspects differently** based on their racial, ethnic, or class background, which leads to distrust in the criminal system.

KEY CONCEPTS
POWER, DIFFERENTIAL JUSTICE

Interactionist View

People learn what is proper and improper behavior through their interactions with others—an idea known as **cultural transmission**.

Informal social control is achieved through casual interactions—a smile, a raised eyebrow, ridicule—that prompt us to adjust our behavior.

A breakdown in interpersonal social relationships in a local community can lead to increases in crime and deviance.

KEY CONCEPTS
LABELING, CULTURAL TRANSMISSION

MAKE THE CONNECTION

After reviewing the chapter, answer the following questions:

1

How would each perspective approach, explore, and explain mass public shootings in the United States?

2

What perspective do you think provides the best explanation for the results of Milgram's experiment on obedience? Why?

3

Describe victimless crime from the point of view of each of the three perspectives, using one of the following examples in your response: drug use, gambling, or prostitution.

4

Which perspective best describes the way you learned proper social behavior? Were social norms socialized and internalized (functionalist), imposed by powerful authority figures (conflict), or learned from observing others (interactionist)? Provide examples.

Pop Quiz

1. What term do sociologists use to describe society's power to limit deviance by enforcing conformity to expected norms and values?
   a. stigmatization
   b. labeling
   c. law
   d. social control

2. The penalties and rewards we face for conduct concerning a social norm are known as
   a. informal social controls.
   b. stigmas.
   c. sanctions.
   d. conformities.

3. What type of compliance do sociologists refer to when using the word *conformity?*
   a. going along with peers even though they have no formal authority over us
   b. obedience to higher authorities in a hierarchical structure
   c. listening to your conscience when it tells you not to do something wrong
   d. acceptance of the court system's right to enforce formal sanctions

4. Which of the following statements is true of deviance?
   a. Deviance is always criminal behavior.
   b. Deviance is behavior that violates the standards of conduct or expectations of a group or society.
   c. Deviance is perverse behavior.
   d. Deviance is inappropriate behavior that cuts across all cultures and social orders.

5. The FBI reports which two major categories of crime in its annual *Uniform Crime Reports?*
   a. violent crime and property crime
   b. organized crime and white-collar crime
   c. victimless crime and transnational crime
   d. transnational crime and victimization crime

6. Which type of crime involves the willing exchange among adults of widely desired, but illegal, goods and services?
   a. index crimes
   b. white-collar crime
   c. victimless crime
   d. organized crime

7. Which of the following is *not* one of the basic forms of adaptation specified in Robert Merton's strain theory of deviance?
   a. conformity
   b. innovation
   c. ritualism
   d. hostility

8. According to Hirschi's social control theory,
   a. deviance involves acceptance and/or rejection of society's goals and means.
   b. our social bonds with members of society lead us to conform to society's norms.
   c. we come to view ourselves as deviant based on how others view us.
   d. power and access to resources shape whose norms and values determine individual action.

9. Which of the following theories gave rise to the "broken windows" hypothesis that physical decay in a community represents a symbol of decreasing social order?
   a. labeling theory
   b. cultural transmission theory
   c. social disorganization theory
   d. strain theory

10. Even though they committed the same deviant acts, the Saints and the Roughnecks did not receive the same treatment from authorities. Sociologist William Chambliss suggests this was due to the fact that authorities viewed members of the groups differently. Which theory supports that conclusion?
    a. Merton's strain theory
    b. culture transmission theory
    c. differential association theory
    d. labeling theory

Families

Yu Chun Christopher Wong/S3studio/Getty Images

LOOKING FOR LOVE

Swipe right or swipe left? It's a question millions of Tinder users ask and answer every day. Finding a love connection can be a tricky thing. Norms for doing so vary over time and across cultures. From arranged marriages to one-night stands, the society we live in shapes the options available to us. Smartphone technology made an app like Tinder possible, opening up a new world of possibilities for people looking for love. Tinder works by connecting people who want to find others who are also looking. When two users "swipe right," signaling that they are both interested in each other, a match occurs. They can then exchange messages within the app to see if anything more might develop.

Tinder realized early on that it might benefit from the insight sociology can provide. As a result, it hired Jessica Carbino, who earned her PhD in sociology from UCLA. Carbino gathered data through surveys, focus groups, and content analysis for Tinder for almost four years before moving on to Bumble, another online dating app. Bumble's claim

to fame is that, for heterosexual relationships, women must make the first move, initiating the contact by swiping right, before a match can be made.

Carbino argues that online dating apps developed as a consequence of society's changing structure. These tools, she claims, have "replaced or supplemented a very fragmented market by which people meet. Historically, people have met through family and friends. But now given delays in marriage and childbearing generally . . . it's becoming far harder to find someone to ultimately mate with" (Titlow 2016). Tinder, Bumble, and other online dating options fulfill the function that those social contacts used to serve.

In her research, Carbino found that 80 percent of Tinder users, and 85 percent of Bumble users, are looking for steady relationships or marriage rather than a hookup (Gay 2018; Titlow 2016). By analyzing profiles, she learned that people who smile in their profile photo are 14 percent more likely to get people to swipe right. Having a front-facing photo increases the odds by 20 percent, but wearing glasses or a hat decreases positive responses by 15 percent and 12 percent, respectively (Lebowitz 2016; Vitto 2017; Yang 2018).

Men and women approach Tinder differently. Men are more likely to swipe right but not follow up with a message. Women are less likely to swipe right but more likely to send a message. After a match occurs, meaning both parties "liked" each other, the median amount of time it took for a man to send a message was 2 minutes compared to

38 minutes for women. The median message length for men was 12 characters compared to 122 for women (Tyson et al. 2016).

When it comes to love, marriage, sex, kids, and all that, the choices people make at one time and place differ from those at another. In this chapter we explore the ways sociology enables us to understand how and why such variations occur.

As You READ >>

- What do we mean by family?
- How do people pick partners?
- How do families vary?

>> Defining Family

Families around the world come in many shapes and sizes. Among Tibetans, a woman may be married simultaneously to more than one man, usually brothers. This system allows sons to share the limited amount of good land. Among the Betsileo of Madagascar, a man has multiple wives, each one living in a different village where he cultivates rice. Wherever he has the best rice field, that woman is considered his first or senior wife. Among the Yanomami of Brazil and Venezuela, it is considered proper to have sexual relations with one's opposite-sex cousins if they are the children of one's mother's brother or father's sister. But if one's opposite-sex cousins are the children of one's mother's sister or father's brother, the same practice is considered to be incest (Haviland et al. 2005; Kottak 2004).

Such cross-cultural variation in family structure supports the sociological principle that culture, including our beliefs and practices about families, is socially constructed. There is no singular, universal model determining what families must look like. To deal with such variation, sociologists have developed two approaches to defining families. The first is a substantive definition that focuses on what a family *is,* and the second is a functional definition that focuses on what families *do.*

Substantive definition of families A definition of families in terms of blood, connecting people biologically, and law, connecting people through formal social recognition.

SUBSTANCE: WHAT A FAMILY IS

Perhaps the most conventional approach to defining family is the **substantive definition,** which defines families in terms of blood, connecting people biologically, and law, connecting people through formal social recognition. When it comes to blood, this approach focuses on people's shared biological heritage, the genes that get passed on directly from parent to child, which also link people indirectly to grandparents,

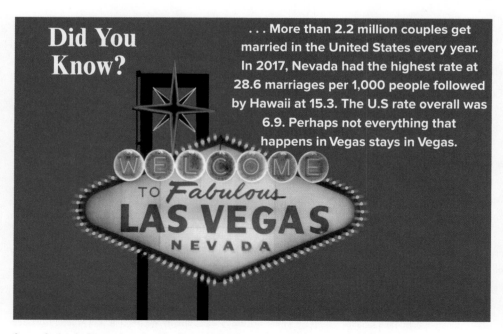

Did You Know?

. . . More than 2.2 million couples get married in the United States every year. In 2017, Nevada had the highest rate at 28.6 marriages per 1,000 people followed by Hawaii at 15.3. The U.S rate overall was 6.9. Perhaps not everything that happens in Vegas stays in Vegas.

Source: Centers for Disease Control and Prevention 2018a. *Photo:* ©Brand X Pictures/Jupiter Images

TV families in the 1950s showed very little diversity in terms of family structure, race, and ethnicity. Hulton Archive/NBC Television/Getty Images

aunts and uncles, and other biological relatives. Law means the socially acknowledged and normatively accepted affirmation of a bond as family, particularly in the forms of marriage and adoption.

The primary advantage of this definitional approach is that boundaries are clear; we can tell who is in and who is out. This makes it easier to count such families, so perhaps it is no surprise that the U.S. Census, whose definition of family remains largely unchanged since 1930, relies on a substantive approach: "A family consists of a householder and one or more other people living in the same household who are related to the householder by birth, marriage or adoption" (Pemberton 2015). It also allows us to track who is related to whom over time.

Kinship Patterns

When considering substantive definition of families, sociologists emphasize the importance of **kinship** to describe the state of being related to others. Our kin groups extend beyond our immediate families to include include aunts, uncles, cousins, in-laws, and so on, and also include relationships across generations. Throughout human history, kinship ties frequently involved obligations and responsibilities. We may feel compelled to assist our kin, and we feel free to call on them for many types of aid, including loans and babysitting (O'Brien 2012; Rossi Del Corso and Lanz 2013).

When tracing kinship across generations, thus emphasizing the "blood" portion of the substantive definition,

sociologists have identified three patterns of descent. Families in the United States typically follow the system of **bilateral descent,** which means that both sides of a person's family are regarded as equally important. For example, no higher value is typically given to family relations on one's father's side compared to one's mother's. Historically, most societies give preference to one side of the family or the other in tracing descent (Murdock 1957). In **patrilineal descent** (from the Latin *pater,* "father"), only the father's relatives are significant in terms of property, inheritance, and emotional ties. Conversely, in societies that favor **matrilineal descent** (from the Latin *mater,* "mother"), only the mother's relatives are significant.

Marriage Types When it comes to the "law" part of the substantive definition of families, historically, in the United States, the vast majority of marriages are monogamous. The term **monogamy** describes a form of marriage in which two people are married only to each other. That does not necessarily mean a person will ever have only one marriage partner. Many people in the United States move into and out of a number of serious romantic relationships over time, what sociologist Andrew Cherlin (2009) refers to as the "marriage-go-round." Termed **serial monogamy,** a person may have several spouses in his or her lifetime, but only one spouse at a time.

Some cultures allow an individual to have several husbands or wives simultaneously. This form of marriage is known as **polygamy.** There are two basic types of polygamy. The more common is **polygyny,** which refers to the marriage of a man to more than one woman at the same time. Less common is **polyandry,** in which a woman may have more than one husband at the same time. Although polygamy declined steadily through most of the 20th century, in 28 sub-Saharan African countries, at least 10 percent of men still have polygamous marriages (Fenske 2013; Tertilt 2005). In a U.S. national survey, researchers found that 19 percent of adults find polygamy to be morally acceptable, up from 7 percent in 2001 (Jones 2018; Newport 2015).

Kinship The state of being related to others.

Bilateral descent A kinship system in which both sides of a person's family are regarded as equally important.

Patrilineal descent A kinship system in which only the father's relatives are significant.

Matrilineal descent A kinship system in which only the mother's relatives are significant.

Monogamy A form of marriage in which two people are married only to each other.

Serial monogamy A form of marriage in which a person may have several spouses in his or her lifetime, but only one spouse at a time.

Polygamy A form of marriage in which an individual may have several husbands or wives simultaneously.

Polygyny A form of polygamy in which a man may have more than one wife at the same time.

Polyandry A form of polygamy in which a woman may have more than one husband at the same time.

SOCTHINK

How important are intergenerational kinship networks and extended family members in your family? How has this changed since your parents' and grandparents' generations?

Family Networks The substantive approach also calls attention to who we count as close family members. Historically, family connections served as a valuable resource, providing us with access to material, social, and cultural resources. As a result, the **extended family,** a family in which relatives—such as grandparents, aunts, or uncles—live in the same or adjacent households as parents and their children was more common. We depended on relatives for food, shelter, opportunities, and knowledge. In fact, historian Stephanie Coontz (2005) argues that, historically, the primary reason to get married was to obtain not a partner but in-laws, thus extending one's network of cooperative relationships. This was the logic of the matchmaker tradition in which resource distribution mattered more than romantic love. The matchmaker, as a member of the community, sought to maximize social network connections for the good of the whole.

> **Extended family** A family in which relatives—such as grandparents, aunts, or uncles—live in the same or adjacent households as parents and their children.
>
> **Nuclear family** A married couple and their unmarried children living together.

With the advent of the Industrial Revolution, a large family went from being an asset to something of a liability. Rather than serving as workers who assisted parents on farms in agricultural communities, children primarily became consumers in cities whom parents had to feed, clothe, and shelter, which represented a significant expense. In addition, jobs were less place specific, so having fewer children made it easier for workers to be mobile, an advantage if the company wanted to transfer them to another location. As a result, families became smaller. The dominant family form transitioned from the extended family to the **nuclear family** which includes a married couple and their unmarried children living together. The concept of nuclear family builds on the essence or nucleus of the substantive definition of blood and law, including as it does both the parent-to-child and the marriage relationship.

The primary advantage of the substantive approach to defining families is that it provides clear boundaries separating who counts as family and who does not. It makes it easy, in theory at least, to trace a family tree by mapping parent-to-child relationships between generations as well as socially sanctioned relationships (such as marriage) within generations. In practice, however, we encounter limits to this substantive approach. In the case of adoption, for example, do you count the child's biological ancestors as part of the family tree? What about the ancestors of a stepfather or stepmother? And what happens when a parent and stepparent divorce? Is that stepparent, who might have played a vital role in child rearing, no longer related? What about close friends who are very much part of the family? Does Dad's college friend "Uncle" Bob count? New forms of reproductive technology, involving donated sperm and eggs and surrogate parents, also challenge the biological preconditions of this approach. Any substantive definition we might come up with runs the risk of excluding those whom we think of as family members. In response, sociologists turn toward the more inclusive functionalist definition of families to address these limitations.

FUNCTIONS: WHAT FAMILIES DO

People in the United States seem to agree that traditional definitions of family are too restrictive. When they are asked how they would define family, their conception is much more inclusive than the substantive definition implies. In one survey, only 22 percent of

Definitions of families have become more inclusive over time to encompass relationships that are heterosexual, same-sex, married, cohabiting, single-parent, stepfamilies, child-free, and more. ©Creatas Images/Jupiter Images

the respondents defined family in the same way as the U.S. Census Bureau. Instead, 74 percent considered a family to be "any group whose members love and care for one another" (Coontz 1992:21).

We need a definition of family that is inclusive enough to encompass the broad range of intimate groups that people form, such as extended families, nuclear families, single-parent families, blended or reconstituted or step-families, gay and lesbian families, child-free families, racially and ethnically mixed families, commuter marriage families, surrogate or chosen families, and more. One way to avoid getting trapped into overly narrow conceptions of families and to embrace their diversity is to shift the emphasis away from what families *are,* which a substantive approach highlights, toward what families *do.* **A functionalist definition of families** focuses on how families provide for the physical, social, and emotional needs of individuals and of society as a whole.

Consistent with the functionalist perspective, sociologist William F. Ogburn (Ogburn and Tibbits 1934) identified six primary functions that families perform for us:

- *Reproduction.* For a society to maintain itself, it must replace dying members. Families provide the context within which biological reproduction takes place.
- *Socialization.* Parents and other family members monitor a child's behavior and transmit the norms, values, and language of their culture to the child.
- *Protection.* Unlike the young of other animal species, human infants need constant care and economic security. In all cultures, the family assumes the ultimate responsibility for the protection and upbringing of children.

U.S. Households by Family Type, 1940–2018

Married couple families — **Male householders**
Female-headed families — **Male-headed families**
Female householders

Note: Male and female householders include men and women living alone or exclusively with people to whom they are not related, including those in a college dormitory, homeless shelter, or military base.

Source: U.S. Census Bureau 2018d:Table HH-1. *Photo:* S. Greg Panosian/Getty Images

SOCstudies

- *Regulation of sexual behavior.* Sexual norms are subject to change both over time (for instance, in the customs for dating) and across cultures (compare strict Saudi Arabia to the more permissive Denmark). However, whatever the time period or cultural values of a society, standards

> **Functionalist definition of families** A definition of families that focuses on how families provide for the physical, social, and emotional needs of individuals and of society as a whole.

Ariel Skelley/Blend Images

of sexual behavior are most clearly defined within the family circle.

- *Affection and companionship.* Ideally, families provide members with warm and intimate relationships, helping them to feel satisfied and secure. Of course, a family member may find such rewards outside the family—from peers, in school, at work—and may even perceive the home as an unpleasant or abusive setting. Nevertheless, we expect our relatives to understand us, to care for us, and to be there for us when we need them.

- *Provision of social status.* We inherit a social position because of the family background and reputation of our parents and siblings. For example, the race, ethnicity, social class, education level, occupation, and religion of our parents all shape the material, social, and cultural resources to which we have access and therefore the options we might have.

From this functionalist approach, no matter how it is composed, any group that fulfills these functions is family to us. For example, members of a sports team can be family to us, as can a group of college friends who remain close for life. They are people we can count on in times of trouble, people who will have our backs. We turn to them for all kinds of support, including care and affection, guidance in how to think and act or who to date, and sometimes even for material support, whether borrowing a car or money for pizza.

Increasingly, people even pets count as family. In the United States, 95 percent of pet owners think of their pets as family members, and 64 percent buy them Christmas or holiday presents. Some couples go so far as to include dogs as participants in their wedding ceremonies (Shannon-Missal 2015; Stoeckel et al. 2014; Walsh 2009a, 2009b). Pets can be especially important to people who might otherwise live alone, providing them with mutual care and affection.

We may find ourselves saying that friends, teammates, "Uncle" Bob, and pets are "like family" to convey the close bond that we have with them. We may even refer to the significant people in our lives as sister, brother, mom, or dad. We do so because, to us, they function like family. For many people, a family *is* what a family *does*.

CONFLICT: WHO RULES?

Regardless of which definition we choose, it is inevitably the case that people living in relationship with each other will have to address the issue of power. Couples, for example, must decide where to live; how to furnish their home; who will shop, cook, and clean; which side of the family to visit on holidays; and a whole host of other decisions both big and small. Siblings may have to decide difficult end-of-life care questions regarding their parents. A society's social norms inform which family members have more or less power over such decisions, and these norms vary cross-culturally and across time.

PETS AS FAMILY

When we discuss families in terms of what they do instead of what they are, my students inevitably ask, "Do pets count as family?" Some strongly agree, while others think it is the most ridiculous thing they have ever heard. Over time, more and more students have begun coming down on the side of pets as family. When Lori and I "adopted" Jessie, our Pembroke Welsh corgi, I better understood why. People develop strong emotional bonds with their pets and some refer to them as their "fur kids." Pets provide a source of comfort and companionship. When Jessie began to show symptoms of degenerative myelopathy, an inherited genetic disorder, we didn't hesitate to provide her with medical care and a set of wheels to help her get around. Pets give us someone to care about, and they care for us in their own ways. Isn't that what family is all about?

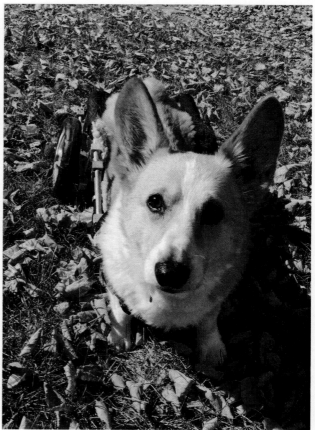

Courtesy of Jon Witt

Historically, decision-making power has largely been shaped by gender. A society that expects males to dominate in all family decision making is termed a **patriarchy.** In patriarchal societies, such as Iran, the eldest male often wields the greatest power, although wives are expected to be treated with respect and kindness. An Iranian woman's status is typically defined by her relationship to a male relative, usually as a wife or daughter. In many patriarchal societies, women find it more difficult to obtain a divorce than a man does (Estin 2017; Farr 1999). In contrast, in a **matriarchy,** women have greater authority than men. Formal matriarchies, which are uncommon, emerged among Native American tribal societies and in nations in which men were absent for long periods because of warfare or food-gathering expeditions.

More than a century ago, Friedrich Engels ([1884] 1959), a colleague of Karl Marx and advocate for the conflict perspective, went so far as to say that the family is the ultimate source of social inequality because of its role in the transfer of power, property, and privilege. Historically, he argues, the family has legitimized and perpetuated male dominance. It has contributed to societal injustice, denied women opportunities that are extended to men, and limited freedom in sexual expression and mate selection. In the United States, it was not until the first wave of contemporary feminism, in the mid-1800s, that there was a substantial challenge to the historical status of wives and children as the legal property of husbands and fathers.

In the United States, the responsibility for raising children and maintaining the home continues to fall largely on women. Sociologists have found that, in heterosexual relationships, fathers have increased their involvement in child care, however, moms still spend more than twice as much time per week on child care and housework than do dads (Parker and Livingston 2018). Furthermore, with 5.1 million married stay-at-home moms versus 190,000 married stay-at-home dads, a ratio of 27 to 1, the dominant practice reinforces normative expectations (U.S. Census Bureau 2018e:Table SHP-1).

Partly because of the efforts of women and men in similar movements over the years, we have seen the rise of a third type of authority pattern, in addition to patriarchy and matriarchy. In the **egalitarian family,** spouses are regarded as equals. This shift has been driven at least in part by occupational and financial opportunities for women that previously had been denied them (Wills and Risman 2006). In practice, this does not mean that all decisions

Patriarchy A society in which men dominate in family decision making.

Matriarchy A society in which women dominate in family decision making

Egalitarian family An authority pattern in which spouses are regarded as equals.

Ben STANSALL - WPA Pool/Getty Images

and duties in all spheres are equally shared in such families. Wives may hold authority in some spheres, and husbands in others. For example, sociologists have found that, in terms of both paid and unpaid labor in two-parent families, the total hours worked by mothers and fathers is roughly equal at about 65 hours per week, though the distribution of tasks varies (Bianchi, Robinson, and Milkie 2006).

Another issue raised by conflict theorists involves the role families play in maintaining the existing system of inequality. Although the United States is widely viewed as a land of opportunity, access to valued resources is not evenly distributed to all. Family serves as the basis for transferring material, social, and cultural resources from one generation to the next. Children inherit the privileged or less-than-privileged social and economic status of their parents (and in some cases, of earlier generations as well). The socioeconomic status of a child's family has a substantial influence on their chances as an adult because it influences access to nutrition, health care, housing, educational opportunities, and more (Lareau 2011; Pew Research Center 2015d; Putnam 2015; Shipler 2004).

>> Marriage, Mating, and Parenting

Historian Stephanie Coontz (2008) suggests that, when it works, marriage today is better than ever. She writes that it "delivers more benefits to its members—adults and children—than ever before. A good marriage is fairer and more fulfilling for both men and women than couples of the past could ever have imagined." She points to shared decision making and housework, increases in time spent with children, and declines in violence and sexual coercion and in the likelihood of adultery.

MARRIAGE TRENDS

People continue to say "yes" to marriage. Currently, almost 80 percent of adults aged 25 and older are, or have been, married. Among never-married adults, 58 percent say they want to get married someday. At the same time, it is also true that the marriage rate in the United States is actually at or near a record low (Parker and Stepler 2017; Wang and Parker 2014).

Marriage rates are so low in part because people are waiting longer to get married. In the United States, the median age of first marriage in 2018 was 27.8 for women and 29.8 for men. Contrast that with the medians in 1960, which were 20.3 for women and 22.8 for men (U.S. Census Bureau 2018f:Table MS-2). Rates also vary based on a variety of factors, including income, education, race, ethnicity, and nationality.

The increased likelihood of delaying marriage is shaped by one's perception of marriage, as the "Milestones in the Transition to Adulthood" feature in Chapter 4 demonstrated. Sociologist Andrew Cherlin (2009) argues that the symbolic significance of marriage shifted as a result. Historically, in the United States, especially in the 1950s, many saw marriage as a *cornerstone,* something that happens relatively early in adulthood, providing the foundation on which other adult relationships and responsibilities are built. Today, people are more likely to view marriage as a *capstone,* something that happens later as a sign we have our act together. From this perspective, people want to complete their educational degrees and establish themselves in a career before settling into marriage and adulthood.

COURTSHIP AND MATE SELECTION

There are many ways that we might go about finding someone to settle down with. Historically, it was not uncommon for marriages to be arranged by families or matchmakers. This is a practice that continues in many cultures today. In the Asian nation of Uzbekistan, for example, courtship is largely orchestrated by the couple's parents. A young Uzbekistani woman is socialized to eagerly anticipate her marriage to a man whom she has met only once, at the final inspection of her dowry (Kamp 2008; Rand 2006).

When it comes to marriage in the United States, most of us assume that true love will guide the way. We can't imagine allowing others, including parents and matchmakers, to select partners for us through arranged marriages. Many are surprised to hear that this practice continues today in some subcultures within the United States. We tend to take for granted that we are best suited to make this personal and intimate selection.

Median Age at First Marriage, United States

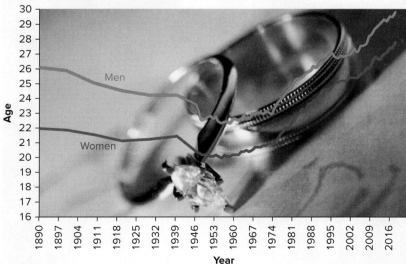

Source: U.S. Census Bureau 2018f:Table MS-2. *Photo:* Janis Christie/Photodisc/Getty Images

Marriage practices, including ceremonial customs, vary significantly across cultures. (hands): ©Erica Simone Leeds; (carriage): Don Tremain/Photodisc/Getty Images

—SOCTHINK**—**

Some well-off professionals in the United States pay huge fees to enlist the help of matchmakers. Why might people choose to do so? What are the disadvantages of relying on one's own contacts and judgment when it comes to finding a romantic partner?

The use of online dating apps represents the latest in our individualistic quest to pick just the right person for ourselves. We swipe right or left based on how people represent themselves on the screen, hoping that others will pick us based on our presentation of self. Yet research reveals that we aren't always honest in how we present ourselves in these online interactions. We seek to make ourselves seem more appealing by exaggerating our interests, experiences, and abilities. We also avoid interactions by claiming to be busy when we are not, we put people off by suggesting we will contact them later, and we justify a lack of communication by suggesting that we forgot even though we didn't. Oftentimes we use such techniques in order to let people down gently, and others do the same with us (Markowitz and Hancock 2018).

Though online dating opens up new possibilities, in practice, our pool of potential partners is substantially reduced by our social location. Sociology enables us to better recognize three basic partner selection principles that inevitably narrow our choices (Kalmijn 1998):

- We are limited to those who are available and with whom we have contact.
- We are heavily influenced by opinions of family, friends, and the organizations to which we belong (including schools, religious groups, and the workplace).
- We are most attracted to people like ourselves.

In the first case, our geographic location and our position in the social structure influences the degree to which we have the opportunity to establish a relationship with someone. Second, our friends, family, fellow believers, coworkers, and more can play a significant role in shaping our dating and mating choices, sometimes even exercising effective veto power, whether formal or informal, about whether a relationship should continue or not. Finally, as the saying goes, like attracts like (or at least it tends to).

Romantic comedies are a dime a dozen, and it's easy to see why. There's the thrill of the chase and the hoped-for, and almost inevitable, happy ending. But how will the contented couple come to terms with the mundane reality of everyday life together? Film historian Jeanine Basinger (2012) argues that films about marriage are a tougher sell because marriage is more like a merry-go-round than a roller-coaster ride. To make films about marriage viable, filmmakers use a predictable plot: They begin by showing the happy couple facing the promise of eternal bliss, disrupt the relationship using one of seven common threats (money, infidelity, in-laws/children, incompatibility, class, addiction, and murder), and finally, restore order by overcoming the threat and recommitting to living happily ever after.

POPSOC

Photo: Collection Christophel/Color Force/SK Global/Warner Bros/Alamy Stock Photo

When sociologists analyze social factors that shape our selection of partners, they pay particular attention to the balance between endogamy and exogamy. **Endogamy** (from the Greek *endon,* "within") specifies the groups within which a spouse must be found and prohibits marriage with outsiders. For example, in the United States, many people are expected to marry within their own racial, ethnic, or religious group and are strongly discouraged or even prohibited from marrying outside the group. Endogamy is intended to reinforce the cohesiveness of the group by suggesting that we should marry someone "of our own kind."

In contrast, **exogamy** (from the Greek *exo,* "outside") requires mate selection outside certain groups, usually one's own family or certain kinfolk. Rules for how close is too close vary across cultures and over time. The **incest taboo,** a social norm common to virtually all societies, prohibits sexual relationships between certain culturally specified relatives. In the United States, this taboo means that we must marry outside the nuclear family. We cannot marry our siblings, and in most states, we cannot marry our first cousins.

Endogamy The restriction of mate selection to people within the same group.

Exogamy The requirement that people select a mate outside certain groups.

Incest taboo The prohibition of sexual relationships between certain culturally specified relatives.

Endogamy influences a number of social location variables. We tend to pick partners who are the same age, race, ethnicity, education, and religion. Although the degree of influence of these variables has shifted over time, each continues to play a significant role. When it comes to age, for example, 34 percent of all married couples in the United States are within one year of each other and 77 percent are within five years. Only 9 percent of U.S. couples have an age difference of 10 or more years, and just 1.3 percent have an age difference of 20 or more (U.S. Census Bureau 2018g:Table FG3). Age is one factor for which third-party pressure can exert significant influence; people tend to look suspiciously at relationships in which the age difference is perceived to be too large.

The role of race in selecting partners demonstrates how social norms can both change and remain the same. For a long time, interracial marriage was illegal in the United States. This remained true in 16 southern states until 1967 when a court case brought by Mildred and Richard Loving, an African American woman with Native American ancestry and a White man, changed the law of the land. The Lovings' home state, Virginia, banned interracial marriages, so they traveled to Washington, D.C., to marry. But a month after they returned home to Virginia, in a nighttime raid on their bedroom while they were sleeping, they were arrested and taken to jail. After pleading guilty to violating Virginia's Racial Integrity Act of 1924, the Lovings avoided prison by agreeing to leave the state and not return together for 25 years. In arguing their case before the Supreme Court, their attorney relayed Richard

Ten Questions Couples Should Ask (or Wish They Had) before Marrying

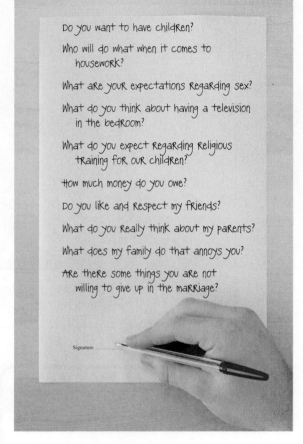

Do you want to have children?

Who will do what when it comes to housework?

What are your expectations regarding sex?

What do you think about having a television in the bedroom?

What do you expect regarding religious training for our children?

How much money do you owe?

Do you like and respect my friends?

What do you really think about my parents?

What does my family do that annoys you?

Are there some things you are not willing to give up in the marriage?

Signature

Source: The New York Times 2006. Photo: ©Jasper White/Image Source

Loving's words to the Court: "Mr. Cohen, tell the Court I love my wife, and it is just unfair that I can't live with her in Virginia." As a result of their case, the Supreme Court overturned laws banning interracial marriage in the United States (Wallenstein 2014). Since then, interracial marriages in the United States have become more common. Now, 3.2 million married couples, or 5.1 percent of the total, include partners from different racial groups (U.S. Census Bureau 2018g:Table FG3). Among newlyweds in the United States, 17 percent had a spouse of a different racial or ethnic background, suggesting that the overall rate will continue to climb in the future (Livingston and Brown 2017).

Despite the overall increase in the acceptance and practice of interracial marriage, most married people continue to select a partner of the same race. As we can see from the accompanying "Patterns of Interracial Marriage" table, however, there is some variation both by race and by gender. Those who are White are the most likely to practice racial endogamy; approximately 97 percent of both men and women select a marital partner of the same race. Among African Americans, men are more likely than women to be involved in interracial marriages. For those who are Asian, however, there is an even larger gender difference; women are much more likely to be in an interracial marriage than men. Still, more than 80 percent of Asian women select a partner of the same race. Such patterns demonstrate the continued significance endogamy plays in partner selection (U.S. Census Bureau 2018g:Table FG3; Wang 2012).

Even within these broader endogamous social categories, we tend to pick people like ourselves. This is known as **homogamy**—the conscious or unconscious tendency to select a mate with personal and social characteristics similar to one's own. We tend, for example, to partner with people who have similar educational, occupational, and income characteristics to ourselves (Mare 2016; Qian 2018).

Most online dating services use the homogamy principle to help couples make matches. Long before Tinder enlisted the help of sociologist Jessica Carbino, an early online dating service hired sociologist Pepper Schwartz (2006) as a consultant to develop a 48-question survey that covered everything from background characteristics to decision-making style to degree of impulsivity. Based on that kind of matching, Internet dating site eHarmony claims that its site is responsible for more than 2 million marriages. Overall, researchers estimate that between a quarter and a third of couples meet online. The rate is even higher for those whose immediate pool of potential partners is smaller, including gays, lesbians, and middle-aged heterosexuals. And some evidence indicates that couples who meet online experience greater marital satisfaction and are slightly less likely to divorce (Cacioppo et al. 2013; eHarmony 2014; Rosenfeld and Thomas 2012).

In theory, Cupid's arrow could strike anyone on our behalf. But love is not blind. Love is a product of the social and cultural forces that shape the choices we make. Of course, in keeping with the sociological imagination, knowing the ways our choices are patterned frees us to decide whether to continue in those ways or decide to follow different paths.

Patterns of Interracial Marriage

	White wife	Black wife	Asian wife
White husband	51,164	254	763
Black husband	411	4,462	83
Asian husband	273	11	4,052

Number in thousands

Percentage of husbands with same-race wife

96.7%	White
88.0%	Black
92.7%	Asian

Percentage of wives with same-race husband

97.8%	White
93.6%	Black
81.9%	Asian

Note: Numbers in thousands. Table does not show data for "Other" race husbands and wives.
Source: U.S. Census Bureau 2018g:Table FG3. Photo: Alexandre Zveiger/Shutterstock

SOCTHINK

How important are factors such as age, education, race, ethnicity, social class, gender, and religion in your choice of someone for a serious relationship? To what extent are (were) you conscious of such influences when you pick (picked) someone to date?

PARENTHOOD PATTERNS AND PRACTICES

Caring for children is a universal function of the family, yet the ways in which different societies assign this function to family members can vary significantly. The Nayars of southern India acknowledge the biological role of fathers, but the mother's eldest brother is responsible for her children (Gough 1959; Lancy 2017). In contrast, uncles play only a peripheral role in child care in the United States. Even within the United States, child-rearing patterns are varied. Just as our conception of families has changed, so also has our practice of child rearing.

> **Homogamy** The conscious or unconscious tendency to select a mate with personal and social characteristics similar to one's own.

Births Overall, in the United States, a mother's average age at first birth was 26.3 in 2016. A woman's education plays an important role in her decision about when to have a baby. Women with at least a college degree have an average age of 30.3 at first birth compared to 23.8 years old for women without a college degree, a difference of six-and-a-half years. Geographic location also has a significant impact. First-time mothers tend to be older in big cities and in both the Northeast and far West. In Manhattan, New York, for example, the average age is 31.1 and in San Francisco it is 31.9. By contrast, average age at first birth is 19.9 in Todd County, South Dakota, and 20.5 in Kimble County, Texas (Bui and Miller 2018).

The average number of babies a woman gives birth to has declined significantly both in the United States and around the world. In 1960, the average number of births a woman had by the end of her childbearing years was 3.65 in the United States. By 2016, the average fell to 1.8 births. Globally, in 1960 the average was 4.98, which fell to 2.44 in 2016 (World Bank 2018c). Many factors account for these declines, including better educational and occupational opportunities for women, improved health care, access to birth control, and delayed age of first marriage.

Adoption The socially recognized and affirmed transfer of the legal rights, responsibilities, and privileges of parenthood.

The relationship between marriage and birth has shifted over time. In the United States, it is now the case that a woman's median age at first birth is younger than her median age at first marriage. This crossover happened around 1988 (Hymowitz et al. 2013). Overall, in 2016, 39.8 percent of births were to unmarried women in the United States, though the birthrate for both unmarried mothers and teens declined (Martin et al. 2018).

Adoption Adoption involves the socially recognized and affirmed transfer of the legal rights, responsibilities, and privileges of parenthood. It fits with the "law" part of the substantive definition of the family. In most cases, parental rights are transferred from the biological or birth parents to the adoptive parents. Approximately 2.3 percent of U.S. children live in a household with at least one adoptive parent (U.S. Census Bureau 2018a:Table B09019).

There are two legal methods of adopting an unrelated person: (1) the adoption may be arranged through a licensed agency, or (2) in some states it may be arranged through a private agreement sanctioned by the courts. Adopted children may come from the United States or from abroad. In 2017, parents in the United States adopted 4,714 children from other countries. The top three nations of origin for U.S. adoptions were China with 1,905, Ethiopia with 313,

Did You Know?

. . . Until **1978** it was legal in the United States to fire a woman for being pregnant. The Supreme Court upheld that principle in key cases in **1974** and **1976**. Two years later, in response to these rulings, Congress passed the Pregnancy Discrimination Act, which prohibited denying benefits to, firing of, or refusing to hire someone for being pregnant.

Photo: Asia Images Group/Shutterstock

Hollywood star Sandra Bullock and her son, the result of a domestic adoption. Marcel Thomas/FilmMagic/Getty Images

and South Korea with 276. The median fee for adopting a child from China was $16,610. Although the number of international adoptions remains substantial, it has declined substantially since it peaked in 2004, when 23,000 such adoptions occurred (U.S. Department of State 2018a).

In the United States, one of the limitations historically was that only married couples could adopt. In 1995 an important court decision in New York held that a couple does not have to be married to adopt a child. Under this ruling, unmarried heterosexual couples, lesbian couples, and gay couples can all legally adopt children in New York. Writing for the majority, Chief Justice Judith Kaye argued that by expanding the boundaries of who can be legally recognized as parents, the state may be able to assist more children in securing "the best possible home." At the time, New York became the third state (after Vermont and Massachusetts) to recognize the right of unmarried couples to adopt children. Now adoption by unmarried persons is legal in all 50 states (Dao 1995; Human Rights Campaign 2009).

For every child who is adopted, many more remain the wards of state-sponsored child protective services. In 2017, 442,995 children in the United States were living in foster care. Of these children, 123,437 were waiting for adoption (U.S. Department of Health and Human Services 2016).

Parenting The family represents the primary agent of socialization in our lives. In the contexts of families we learn the most basic skills and knowledge necessary for survival, including how to walk, talk, feed ourselves, interact with others and much more. And yet, when it comes to parenting, we receive little to no formal training on how to be effective (Rossi 1968, 1984). We mostly rely on the parenting we received during our own childhoods and on our observations of the parenting practices of family and friends around us. In the 20th century, a whole publishing industry developed offering expert advice to help parents know what to expect when expecting (Fass 2016; Hulbert 2003).

Parenting and Social Class Based on an in-depth study of parenting, sociologist Annette Lareau (2003) identified two distinctive approaches to parenting rooted primarily in the social class backgrounds of the parents. She found that middle- and upper-middle-class parents tend to see their children as a project. Using a gardening analogy, she labeled this approach **concerted cultivation,** which refers to a style of parenting that involves active engagement with, and sustained supervision over, children in order to foster their growth and development. From this approach, children are like flowers grown in a greenhouse that receive oversight, care, and protection. These children are encouraged to participate in varieties of activities, including organized sports and summer camps. They are taught to engage with adults, including physicians and teachers, and ask them questions. As a result, they often grow up with a sense of entitlement.

The upper- and middle-class parenting approach differed from that found in working-class and poor families. These parents see their primary responsibility as ensuring that their children's material needs are met and then granting their children greater freedom to navigate the world on their own. Lareau calls this approach **accomplishment of natural growth,** which refers to a style of parenting that provides broad guidelines for behavior, allowing children greater freedom to navigate the world on their own. Parents' instructions to children are more directive—do this, don't do that—rather than viewing encounters as teachable moments. Children in these families are more like seeds that have been thrown to the wind and grow to be wildflowers. Parents relying on accomplishment of natural growth presume that children will spontaneously grow and thrive. They believe that children will learn more responsibility if they face challenges on their own rather than having a hovering helicopter parent there to bail them out. Lareau found that these children, much like their parents, were less likely to engage with authority figures such as teachers or doctors.

Because children are taught interpersonal skills that grow out of their social class positions, the social class of their childhood is a strong predictor of their social class as adults. Lareau (2011) confirmed as much when she checked back with the children and their families 10 years after her initial research. Working-class kids tended to become working-class adults, and children of professional parents tended to become professionals themselves.

> **Concerted cultivation** A style of parenting that involves active engagement with, and sustained supervision over, children in order to foster their growth and development.
>
> **Accomplishment of natural growth** A style of parenting that provides broad guidelines for behavior, allowing children greater freedom to navigate the world on their own.
>
> **Familism** Placing the interests of the family before those of the individual.

Parenting, Race, and Ethnicity Parenting also varies by race and ethnicity. Among Mexican American families, for example, placing the interests of the family before those of the individual, also known as **familism,** is a core value. The importance of the extended family is manifested through the maintenance of close ties and strong obligations to kinfolk outside the immediate family. Research suggests that a commitment to familism increases closeness within families which contributes to better psychological health (Campos et al. 2014). One possible consequence, however, is that this commitment to family may reduce the likelihood that Latinx students apply to, attend, and graduate from college (Desmond and Turley 2009).

Within African American families, too, strong kinship networks matter. Kinship ties, especially through mothers, grandmothers, and aunts, serve as valuable conduits for sharing material, social, and cultural resources (Goffman 2014a; Stack 1974). Researchers found that African American kinship networks provide reciprocal support when it comes to childcare, financial assistance, advice and emotional support, and resolving interfamilial conflict (Cross, Taylor, and Chatters 2018; St. Vil, McDonald, and Cross-Barnet 2018).

Parenting among Asian American families received significant attention with publication of Amy Chua's book *Battle Hymn of the Tiger Mother* (2011). Her strict and extremely demanding parenting style concentrates less on developing a child's self-esteem and focuses more on achievement, especially academic achievement. For Chua, that meant denying her daughters things other children might take for granted, such as attending sleepovers, being in school plays, watching television or playing computer games, playing any instrument other than piano or violin, or getting any grade less than an A. Research among Chinese American families, however, finds significant variation in parenting styles and suggests that the tiger mom approach is neither the most typical nor the most effective. The more common supportive parenting profile found among these families produced children with better GPAs, higher educational attainment, less depressive symptoms, and a stronger sense of family obligation (Kim et al. 2013).

>> Modern Families

As the functionalist definition of family suggests, families today come in many different shapes and sizes. In order to better understand families today, sociologists have identified and investigated a number of specific family variations. In truth, these family types can also overlap and combine to form even more varieties of families.

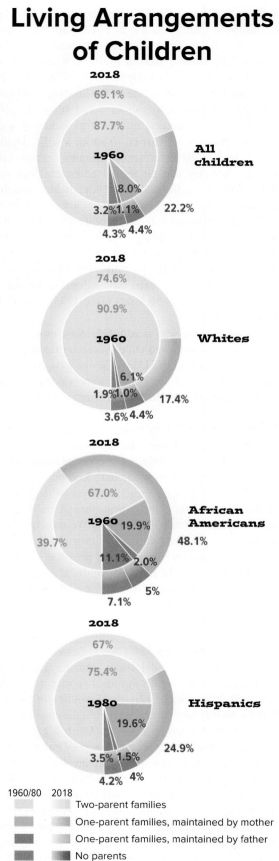

Living Arrangements of Children

2018 — **All children**
69.1% / 87.7% (1960)
8.0%, 3.2%, 1.1%, 4.3%, 4.4%, 22.2%

2018 — **Whites**
74.6% / 90.9% (1960)
6.1%, 1.9%, 1.0%, 3.6%, 4.4%, 17.4%

2018 — **African Americans**
67.0% / 39.7% (1960)
19.9%, 11.1%, 2.0%, 7.1%, 5%, 48.1%

2018 — **Hispanics**
67% / 75.4% (1980)
19.6%, 3.5%, 1.5%, 4.2%, 4%, 24.9%

1960/80 — 2018
- Two-parent families
- One-parent families, maintained by mother
- One-parent families, maintained by father
- No parents

Note: The "No parents" category includes children living with either other relatives or nonrelatives. Persons of Hispanic origin can be of any race.

Source: U.S. Census Bureau 2018h:Tables Ch-1, Ch-2, Ch-3, Ch-4.

Television shows and films now present a much more inclusive portrayal of modern families. Album/20TH CENTURY FOX TV/Alamy Stock Photo

couples. Women now have the chance to pursue opportunities in a way that previously had been closed due to cultural expectations regarding gender. This has resulted in increased education levels for women and increased participation in occupational fields that had been largely closed. At the same time, however, couples find it harder to make it on a single income. Even with more women entering the workforce, average income per household has remained relatively flat since the early 1970s (Fontenot, Semega, and Kollar 2018).

SAME-SEX MARRIAGE

One of the more active political debates about how we define family in recent years involved marriage of same-sex couples. Some argued in favor of a narrow definition that marriage necessarily involves one man and one woman. Others favored a more inclusive definition. Over time, attitudes shifted dramatically. In 1996, 27 percent of Americans favored allowing gays and lesbians to marry. By 2018, support for legalizing

SOCTHINK

What are the advantages and disadvantages of the dual-income model for women, for men, for children, and for society as a whole?

DUAL-INCOME FAMILIES

The mythical image of the 1950s family, idealized in TV shows such as *Father Knows Best* and *Leave It to Beaver,* portrayed a breadwinner father and a homemaker wife. His job was to provide for the family's material needs by earning money, and her job was to nurture and care for her husband and their children. That image was more legend than fact for millions of American families at the time (Coontz 1992; Livingston 2015), and today even fewer families conform to it. For example, among married couples with children under age 6, 57 percent have both a husband and a wife in the labor force and among those with children aged 6–17, it is 65.6 percent. Among all married couples, with or without children, 20 percent of wives make $5,000-plus more than their husbands (Bureau of Labor Statistics 2018d:Table 4; Pew Research Center 2015a; U.S. Census Bureau 2018g:Table FG3).

Both opportunity and need have driven the rise in the number of dual-income

Approval of Same-Sex Marriage by Age

| Silent Generation (1928–1945) | Baby Boomers (1946–1964) |
| Generation X (1965–1980) | Millennials (1981 or later) |

Note: Responses are to the question, "Do you favor allowing gays or lesbians to marry legally?"
Source: Pew Research Center 2019b. *Photo:* Angela Wyant/The Image Bank/Getty Images

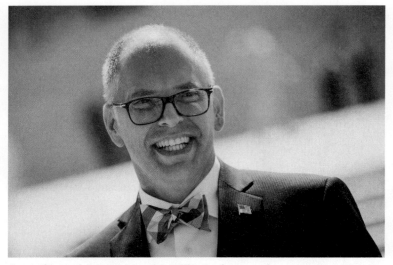

James Obergefell was the lead plaintiff in the Supreme Court case that affirmed same-sex couples' constitutional right to marry. Drew Angerer/Bloomberg/Getty Images

marriage between same-sex couples rose to 67 percent (McCarthy 2018). As the "Approval of Same-Sex Marriage by Age" graph demonstrates, younger people are more supportive. Attitudes also vary by religious affiliation, political party, race, and gender (Pew Research Center 2017a).

The movement to legalize same-sex marriage in the United States crossed its first major legal hurdle in 2003 when the Massachusetts Supreme Judicial Court ruled 4–3 that, under the state's constitution, gay couples have the right to marry. In 2008 the Connecticut Supreme Court reached the same conclusion, as did Iowa's in 2009. Vermont, also in 2009, became the first state to pass a law that legalized same-sex marriage. By June 2015, 37 states

Single-parent family A family in which only one parent is present to care for the children.

Same-sex couples throughout the United States, including Jack Evans and George Harris, took advantage of the opportunity to marry as soon as their legal right to do so was recognized. Tony Gutierrez/AP images

and the District of Columbia provided gay and lesbian couples the same right to marry as guaranteed to heterosexual couples.

On June 26, 2015, same-sex marriage became legal in all 50 states as a result of a decision by the United States Supreme Court. In the ruling, Justice Anthony Kennedy, writing for the majority, declared:

> the right to marry is a fundamental right inherent in the liberty of the person, and under the Due Process and Equal Protection Clauses of the Fourteenth Amendment couples of the same-sex may not be deprived of that right and that liberty. The Court now holds that same-sex couples may exercise the fundamental right to marry. (*Obergefell v. Hodges* 2015)

The decision set off a celebration by same-sex marriage advocates across the land. Many got married that same day, including Jack Evans, 85, and George Harris, 82, of Dallas County, Texas, who tied the knot after having been together for 54 years. Within two years of the Supreme Court decision legalizing same-sex marriage, 61 percent of cohabiting same-sex couples were married (Jones 2017).

SINGLE-PARENT FAMILIES

Over time, **single-parent families,** those in which only one parent is present, have become more common and more accepted in the United States. In 2018, 26.6 percent of all children lived with only one parent. This varied by race and ethnicity with 19.4 percent of White, non-Hispanic children, 53.2 percent of African American children, 10.8 percent of Asian children, and 28.9 percent of Hispanic children living with one parent (U.S. Census Bureau 2018g:Table C3).

The life of single parents and their children is not inevitably more difficult than that of a traditional nuclear family. It is as inaccurate to assume that a single-parent family is necessarily deprived as it is to assume that a two-parent family is always secure and happy. Nevertheless, to the extent that such families have to rely on a single income or a sole caregiver, life in the single-parent family can be stressful. A family headed by a single mother faces particularly difficult problems when the mother is a teenager, especially when she lacks access to significant social and economic resources. Since 2007, however, the birthrate for unmarried mothers has declined for all age groups under 35 while rising for women aged 35 to 44 (Edin and Kefalas 2005; Harris 2015; Miller 2015; Sawhill 2006).

Although 83 percent of single parents in the United States are mothers, the number of households headed by single fathers more than

PictureLux/The Hollywood Archive/Alamy Stock Photo

quadrupled between 1970 and 2018. Single mothers often develop social networks, but single fathers are typically more isolated. In addition, they must deal with schools and social service agencies that are more accustomed to women as custodial parents (U.S. Census Bureau 2018h:Table CH1).

STEPFAMILIES

The most frequent image that comes to mind when thinking about stepfamilies is a stepparent with young stepchildren. Approximately 4.1 percent of children under 18 live with at least one stepparent (U.S. Census Bureau 2018a:Table B09019). But sociologist Susan Stewart (2007) recommends expanding our conception of stepfamilies to include cohabiting couples with children from previous relationships, families whose stepchildren do not live with them full-time, gay or lesbian couples with children from former heterosexual relationships, and stepfamilies with adult children. This expanded approach highlights the fact that stepfamily membership extends throughout the life course.

Family members in stepfamilies often deal with resocialization issues when an adult becomes a stepparent or a child becomes a stepchild and stepsibling. In evaluating these stepfamilies, some observers have assumed that children would benefit from remarriage, because they would be gaining a second custodial parent and would potentially enjoy greater economic security. However, after reviewing many studies of stepfamilies, sociologist Andrew J. Cherlin (2008:800) concluded that "the well-being of children in stepfamilies is no better, on average, than the well-being of children in divorced, single-parent households."

Stepparents can and do play valuable and unique roles in their stepchildren's lives, but their involvement does not guarantee an improvement in family life. In fact, standards may decline. Studies suggest that children raised in families with stepmothers are likely to have less health care, education, and money spent on their food than children raised by biological mothers. The measures are also negative for children raised by stepfathers, but only half as negative as in the case of stepmothers. This may be due to the stepmother holding back out of concern for seeming too intrusive or relying on the biological father to carry out parental duties (Schmeeckle 2007; Schmeeckle et al. 2006).

> What greater thing is there for human souls than to feel that they are joined for life—to be with each other in silent unspeakable memories.
>
> **George Eliot (1859)**

MULTIGENERATIONAL FAMILIES

With the rise of the Industrial Revolution and the corresponding spread of the nuclear family model, the era of multiple generations of families living in the same household seemed largely to be over. Throughout much of the 20th century that appeared correct. The percentage of multigenerational households in the United States dropped from 24.7 percent in 1940 to 12.1 percent in 1980. Since that time, however, the percentage of such households rose to 20 percent. Multigenerational households are defined as including two or more adult generations (if including parents and children, children must be 25 and older), or grandparents with grandchildren younger than 25 (Cohn and Passel 2018; Fry and Passel 2014; Pew Research Center 2010:Table 1).

Much of that change can be attributed to the rise in the percentage of younger adults who either continue to live with, or move back in with, their parents. This represents a change from what had been the much more common multigenerational pattern of elderly parents living with their middle-aged adult children. In 1940, 63 percent of adults aged 85 and older lived in a multigenerational household, which dropped down to 18 percent in 1990, and has since risen to 25 percent. Among young adults aged 25-29, 32 percent lived in multigenerational households in 1940, which fell to 19 percent in 1990, and subsequently rose to 33 percent. As of 2016, 32.3 million people lived in households with two adult generations, 28.4 million lived in households with three or more generations, and 3.2 million lived in households composed of grandparents and grandchildren less than 25 years old (Cohn and Passel 2018).

Cohabitation Two adults living in a committed relationship with an unmarried partner.

Limited job opportunities with low starting salaries, especially after the 2007 economic downturn, along with significant amounts of student loan debt, together have prompted the rise in number of students who are returning home to live with parents, though 18- to 34-year-old college graduates are half as likely to live with parents than are high school grads (DeSilver 2016; Fry 2016; Pew Research Center 2014c). In addition, as we have already seen, the average age of first marriage has gone up, and for some percentage of young adults, opting to live with family represents a rational choice to minimize expenses (Casselman 2016). Focusing on the slightly younger 18–24 age demographic, some percentage of which includes college graduates who return home, 55 percent now live with their parents compared to 43 percent in 1960 (U.S. Census Bureau 2018i:Table AD-1). Just as changes in the economy helped drive the post–Industrial Revolution rise of the isolated nuclear family, these more recent economic events may well be contributing to the emergence of a new form of the extended family whose members leverage the material, social, and cultural resource advantages that such an arrangement provides.

COHABITATION

In the United States, testing the relationship waters by living together without being married is an increasingly common practice. **Cohabitation** is defined as two adults living in a committed relationship with an unmarried partner. Overall, 7 percent of U.S. adults are cohabiting for a total of 18 million, 29 percent more than in 2007. Younger people are more likely to opt for cohabitation, with 14 percent of adults aged 25–34 choosing this option compared to 4 percent for those 50 and older (Stepler 2017a).

About half of all currently married couples in the United States say that they lived together before marriage. And this percentage is likely to increase. The number of unmarried-couple households in the United States rose sixfold in the 1960s and increased another 72 percent between 1990 and 2000. Adults aged 30–44 without a college education are more likely to cohabit than those with a college degree. Cohabitation is more common among African Americans and American Indians than among other racial and ethnic groups; it is least common among Asian Americans. The "Unmarried-Couple Households by State" map shows how cohabitation varies by region (Goodwin et al. 2010; Kreider 2010; Simmons and O'Connell 2003; U.S. Census Bureau 2015b:Table 11009).

Population in Multigenerational Households

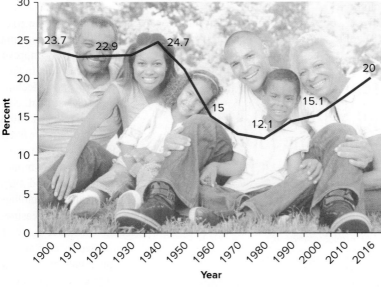

Note: Multigenerational households are defined as including two or more adult generations (if including parents and children, children must be 25 and older), or grandparents with grandchildren younger than 25.

Sources: Cohn and Passel 2018; Fry and Passel 2014; Pew Research Center 2010:Table 1.

Photo: Cathy Yeulet/stockbroker/123RF

Unmarried-Couple Households by State

Percentage of unmarried-partner households

- 0–2.49%
- 2.5–4.99%
- 5.0–7.49%
- 7.5–9.99%
- 10.0%+

Source: U.S. Census Bureau 2015b:Table 11009.

In much of Europe, cohabitation is so common that the general sentiment seems to be "Love, yes; marriage, maybe." In Iceland, 62 percent of all children are born to single mothers; in France, Great Britain, and Norway, the proportion is about 40 percent. Government policies in these countries make few legal distinctions between married and unmarried couples or households. Unlike in the United States, where the best word option to describe cohabitating couple seems to be "partners," in Sweden they use the word *sambo* to refer to someone you live with but aren't married to. It combines elements of the Swedish words *samman,* meaning together, and *boende,* which means accommodation, and implies a level of commitment above that of boyfriend or girlfriend (Lyall 2002; Moore 2006; Thomson and Bernhardt 2010).

REMAINING SINGLE

Increasingly, people are opting to remain single. In 1960, 9 percent of adults aged 25 and older had never married. It has since more than doubled to 20.6 percent (U.S. Census Bureau 2018g:Table A1; Wang and Parker 2014). When looking more generally at the share of adults living without a spouse or partner, 42 percent of adults fall in this category. Of these, 35 percent are living alone and 22 percent are living with others, including children.

When considering age, 61 percent of adults under the age of 25 live without a spouse or partner (Fry 2017).

A variety of factors help explain the trend toward remaining single, including rising cohabitation rates and, as we saw earlier, the fact that those who do marry are waiting longer to do so. Of those who have never married, 14 percent do not want to marry compared to 58 percent who say they hope to get married someday. When taking age into account, 32 percent of never-married adults aged 50 and older say they don't want to get married compared to 11 percent for those younger than 50 (Parker and Stepler 2017; Vespa 2017).

There are many reasons a person may choose not to marry. Many indicate that they have never found the right person. Others point to a lack of financial stability. Some singles do not want to limit their sexual intimacy to one lifetime partner. Some men and women do not want to become highly dependent on any one person—and do not want anyone depending heavily on them. In a society that values individuality and self-fulfillment, the single lifestyle can offer certain freedoms that marriage may not (Klinenberg 2012; Parker and Stepler 2017).

In contrast with the stereotype that single people are lonely, research shows that people who remain single have stronger social connections to parents, siblings, friends, and neighbors than do those who marry. Singles are more likely to stay in touch and to give and receive help from others in their social networks. Other research suggests that single people experience more personal growth than do their married counterparts and have a greater sense of autonomy and self-determination. By culturally privileging marriage, we may underestimate, and under-research, the benefits of singlehood (DePaulo 2014; Marks and Lambert 1998; Sarkisian and Gerstel 2016).

REMAINING CHILD-FREE

In the past, childlessness was often portrayed as a curse. Now, however, thanks in part to the development of modern birth control, an increasing number of people actively choose to remain child-free. More and more couples reject the notion that marriage inevitably leads to a baby carriage. According to census data, 15.9 percent of women aged 40–50 have never had children. Those with at least a college degree are more likely to opt out of parenthood than those who have less education. At 22.3 percent, the childless rate for women aged 40–50 who have graduate or professional degrees is nearly twice the 11.6 percent rate for those who have not completed high school. Looking to the future, nearly one-third of millennials report they do not want to have children (Monte and Ellis 2014; U.S. Census Bureau 2018j:Table 3c).

Economic considerations have contributed to this shift in attitudes; having children has become quite expensive. Estimates are that middle-income parents of children born in 2015 can anticipate spending $284,570 to feed, clothe, and shelter a child from birth to age 18. If the child attends college, that amount could double, depending on the college chosen. Aware of the financial pressures, some couples are having fewer children than they otherwise might, and others are weighing the advantages of a child-free marriage (Lino et al. 2017).

>> Divorce

"Do you promise to love, honor, and cherish . . . until death do you part?" Every year, people of all social classes and racial and ethnic groups make this legally binding agreement. Yet a significant number of these promises shatter, ending in divorce.

STATISTICAL TRENDS IN DIVORCE

Just how common is divorce? Surprisingly, this is not a simple question to answer; divorce statistics are difficult to interpret. The media frequently report that one out of every two marriages ends in divorce. But that figure is misleading in that many marriages last for decades. It is based on a comparison of all divorces that occur in a single year (regardless of when the couples were married) with the number of new marriages in that same year. Sociologist Philip Cohen projects that based on current rates, 52.7 percent of people who marry today will divorce before one of the partners dies. The longer a couple is married, the more that likelihood drops. For example, a couple that makes it to year 15 has a 30 percent chance of divorcing (Cohen 2016; Steverman 2016).

Divorce rates in the United States have fallen steadily since the 1980s. As the "Trends in Marriage and Divorce in the United States" graph represents, there was a significant spike in divorce rates that started in the 1960s, but since then, the trend has been downward

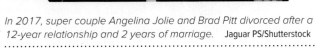

In 2017, super couple Angelina Jolie and Brad Pitt divorced after a 12-year relationship and 2 years of marriage. Jaguar PS/Shutterstock

(Centers for Disease Control and Prevention 2018a). Rates do vary by age. For those over the age of 50, divorce rates have doubled since 1990. But divorce rates among adults aged 25 to 39 fell 21 percent over the same time period (Brown and Lin 2012; Stepler 2017b). Part of the reason for this decline among millennials, according to sociologist Philip Cohen (2018), is that marriage is becoming both rarer and more stable. Young people opt in to marriage more cautiously, but when they do, they are more likely to stay together.

Getting divorced does not necessarily sour people on marriage. About 63 percent of all divorced people in the United States have remarried. The median time between their divorce and second marriage is four years. Women are less likely than men to remarry, because many retain custody of their children after a divorce, which complicates a new adult relationship (Kreider and Ellis 2011; Saad 2004).

FACTORS ASSOCIATED WITH DIVORCE

One of the major factors shaping the increase in divorce compared to 100 years ago has been the greater social acceptance of divorce. It is no longer considered necessary to endure an unhappy marriage. Even major religious groups have relaxed what were often negative attitudes toward divorce, commonly having treated it as a sin in the past.

In the United States, a variety of factors have contributed to the growing social acceptance of divorce. For instance, most states have adopted less restrictive divorce laws in the past three decades. No-fault divorce laws, which allow a couple to end their marriage without assigning blame (by specifying adultery, for instance), accounted for an initial surge in the divorce rate after they were introduced in the 1970s, though these laws appear to have had little effect beyond that. Additionally, a general increase in family incomes, coupled with the availability of free legal aid to some poor people, has meant that more couples can afford costly divorce proceedings. Also, as society provides greater opportunities for women, more and more wives are becoming less dependent on their husbands, both economically and emotionally. They may feel more able to leave a marriage if it seems hopeless (Coontz 2011).

IMPACT OF DIVORCE ON CHILDREN

Divorce is traumatic for all involved, but it has special meaning for the more than 1 million children whose parents divorce each year. There is significant socio-logical debate on the effects divorce has on children. One major study tracked 131 children of divorce over a 25-year period. It concluded that the impacts of divorce are substantial and long-lasting, including higher rates of drug and alcohol abuse, limited resources for college, and fear of intimacy in adulthood (Wallerstein, Lewis, and Blakeslee 2000). These researchers recom-mended that parents should stay together in a "good enough" mar-riage for the sake of the children. One of the limitations of this research is the relatively small sample size, raising questions about the degree to which the results can be generalized.

Other sociologists have concluded that, for many children, divorce signals the welcome end to a highly dysfunctional relationship. A national study conducted by sociologists Paul R. Amato and Alan Booth (1997) showed that in about one-third of divorces, the children actually benefited from parental separation because it lessened their exposure to conflict. Additional researchers, also using larger samples, have concluded that the long-term harmful effects of divorce affect only a minority of chil-dren (Booth and Amato 2001; Cherlin 2009; Hetherington and Kelly 2002; Sun and Li 2008).

The debates surrounding issues such as divorce, cohabitation, and same-sex families highlight many of the issues sociologists seek to address in their investigation of family life. What families are, what they do, how they do it, and what obstacles they face are issues relevant for all families. In our modern, pluralistic world, the singular traditions of the past can no longer be taken for granted. People come from many differ-ent cultures with multiple taken-for-granted assumptions. Sociology investigates such complexity, providing us with tools so that we might better understand how we think and act in the context of families.

Trends in Marriage and Divorce in the United States

Rate per 1,000 total population

Sources: Centers for Disease Control and Prevention 2018a; Tejada-Vera and Sutton 2010; U.S. Census Bureau 1975:64.
Photo: TriggerPhoto/E+/Getty Images

SOCIOLOGY IS A VERB

Family Counts

Interview 5 to 10 people (such as classmates) about families. Ask them questions such as: How do they define family? Does family include only those related by blood and law or does it include others? Do pets count as family? How many siblings do they have? How many siblings did their parents have? What role should parents and friends play in partner selection? Take notes on their responses. Do any patterns emerge? What con-clusions can you draw from such a sample?

FOR REVIEW

I. What do we mean by family?
- Sociologists define the family in terms of both what a family is, with an emphasis on blood and law, and what families do or what functions they perform, including reproduction, socialization, protection, regulation of sexual behavior, affection and companionship, and provision of social status.

II. How do people pick partners?
- Social factors shape the pool of potential partners from which individuals select. People balance selection, favoring someone who is from within their group (endogamy) but not too close (exogamy). People tend to pick partners with similar social characteristics (homogamy), including age, education, class, race, and ethnicity.

III. How do families vary?
- There is significant variation in terms of proximity (extended versus nuclear), authority (patriarchal, matriarchal, and egalitarian), duration (divorce), and structure (dual-income, single-parent, stepfamilies, cohabitation, singlehood, child-free, and same-sex).

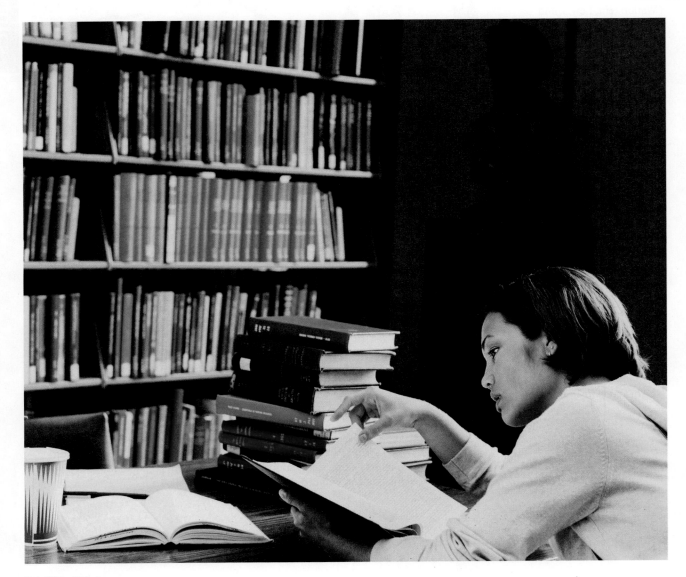

Digital Vision/Getty Images

SOCVIEWS on Families

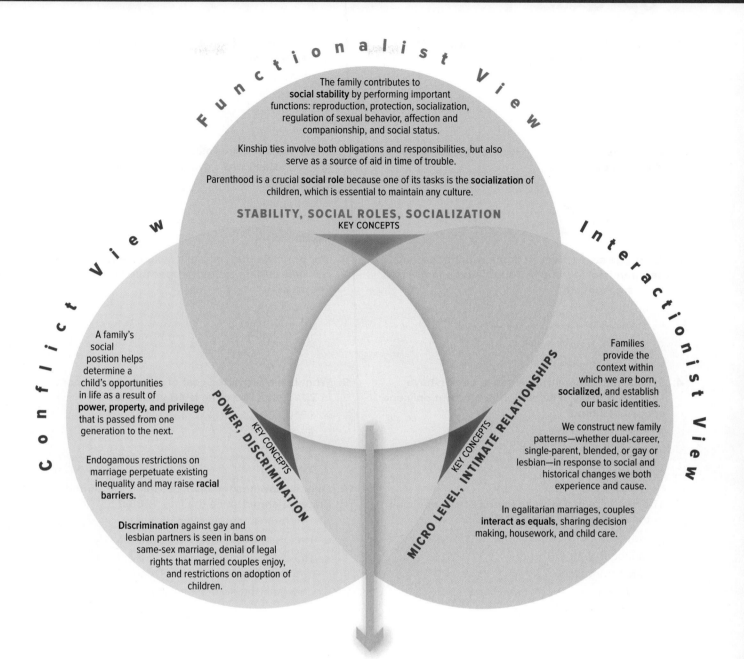

Functionalist View

The family contributes to **social stability** by performing important functions: reproduction, protection, socialization, regulation of sexual behavior, affection and companionship, and social status.

Kinship ties involve both obligations and responsibilities, but also serve as a source of aid in time of trouble.

Parenthood is a crucial **social role** because one of its tasks is the **socialization** of children, which is essential to maintain any culture.

STABILITY, SOCIAL ROLES, SOCIALIZATION
KEY CONCEPTS

Conflict View

A family's social position helps determine a child's opportunities in life as a result of **power, property, and privilege** that is passed from one generation to the next.

Endogamous restrictions on marriage perpetuate existing inequality and may raise **racial barriers.**

Discrimination against gay and lesbian partners is seen in bans on same-sex marriage, denial of legal rights that married couples enjoy, and restrictions on adoption of children.

POWER, DISCRIMINATION
KEY CONCEPTS

Interactionist View

Families provide the context within which we are born, **socialized**, and establish our basic identities.

We construct new family patterns—whether dual-career, single-parent, blended, or gay or lesbian—in response to social and historical changes we both experience and cause.

In egalitarian marriages, couples **interact as equals**, sharing decision making, housework, and child care.

MICRO LEVEL, INTIMATE RELATIONSHIPS
KEY CONCEPTS

MAKE THE CONNECTION
After reviewing the chapter, answer the following questions:

1
How would each perspective shed light on the use of online dating services and apps such as Tinder and Bumble?

2
Take a look at the "U.S. Households by Family Type, 1940–2018" graph. What factors would each perspective focus on to explain the changes over the years?

3
Why does a functionalist definition of what the family does provide more insight into families today than trying to define what it is?

4
Who rules in your family? Would a functionalist, conflict, or interactionist perspective best describe your family dynamics?

Pop Quiz

1. **Which definition of the family focuses on the importance of blood and law?**
   a. functionalist
   b. matrilineal
   c. substantive
   d. extended

2. **Which system of descent is most typical in the United States?**
   a. matrilineal
   b. patrilineal
   c. bilateral
   d. unilateral

3. **Alice, age seven, lives at home with her parents, her grandmother, and her aunt. Alice's family is an example of a(n)**
   a. nuclear family.
   b. patrilineal family.
   c. extended family.
   d. polygynous family.

4. **In which form of marriage may a person have several spouses in his or her lifetime but only one spouse at a time?**
   a. serial monogamy
   b. monogamy
   c. polygamy
   d. polyandry

5. **The marriage of a woman to more than one man at the same time is referred to as**
   a. polygyny.
   b. monogamy.
   c. serial monogamy.
   d. polyandry.

6. **In what type of societies do women dominate in family decision making?**
   a. polygyny
   b. egalitarian
   c. patriarchy
   d. matriarchy

7. **Which norm requires mate selection outside certain groups, usually one's own family or certain kinfolk?**
   a. exogamy
   b. endogamy
   c. matriarchy
   d. patriarchy

8. **The principle that prohibits sexual relationships between certain culturally specified relatives is known as**
   a. monogamy.
   b. the incest taboo.
   c. polygamy.
   d. endogamy.

9. **What is the projected cost of raising a child born in 2015 until she or he is 18 years old?**
   a. $212,300
   b. $284,570
   c. $454,770
   d. $646,465

10. **Overall, how has the divorce rate in the United States changed since the late 1980s?**
    a. The divorce rate rose dramatically.
    b. The divorce rate rose slowly, but steadily.
    c. The divorce rate declined steadily after having risen significantly in the 1960s and 1970s.
    d. Change in the divorce rate shows no clear pattern.

1. (c), 2. (c), 3. (c), 4. (a), 5. (d), 6. (d), 7. (a), 8. (b), 9. (b), 10. (c)

Ilene MacDonald/Alamy Stock Photo

Education and Religion

TRADING PLACES

Melanie was an extremely bright student who lived in an impoverished area of the Bronx, New York. She loved reading and excelled in school. She dreamed of going to college. All her teachers and friends believed she could accomplish whatever she put her mind to. Her first real sense that things might not go as planned occurred on her first day of high school. When Melanie walked through the doors of University Heights, a public school located in her neighborhood, her dreams of what high school would provide were crushed. She was an advanced student, but the school lacked basic resources. It offered no AP courses. It didn't even have a library. She couldn't imagine a pathway forward there (Joffe-Walt 2015; Lovell and Pfluger 2014).

A fieldtrip to a nearby high school provided another turning point in her life. She visited Fieldston School, located only three miles from her school. Fieldston is an elite private school located on an 18-acre campus in an exclusive sector of the Bronx. Tuition at Fieldston in 2018

cost over $50,000 per year. When Melanie got off the bus at Fieldston, she couldn't believe her eyes. She saw the school she always imagined. It wasn't merely a dream. It really did exist. It just wasn't accessible to her. She broke down and cried on the spot (Joffe-Walt 2015; Lovell and Pfluger 2014).

Still, Melanie had a chance. Her University Heights teachers nominated her for the prestigious Posse Foundation scholarship, which identifies high school students with academic and leadership potential who might otherwise be overlooked and provides them with full-tuition scholarships to elite private colleges. After a rigorous winnowing process, Melanie made it to the final round. But she was not selected to receive a scholarship. Again, her dreams were shattered (Joffe-Walt 2015).

Melanie decided to graduate from high school early and, not seeing any way to make it work, largely abandoned her college dreams. She got a job working in a neighborhood supermarket, occasionally taking classes as a part-time student at a local college. Ten years later, she was still there. She's angry at herself for having checked out, wishing that she'd continued to fight for her educational dreams—but it all seemed so impossible at the time (Joffe-Walt 2015).

For Melanie, the issue wasn't ability. Melanie's peers described her as "clearly the smartest person in the room," an assessment echoed by her teachers who described her as "very, very, very smart" (Joffe-Walt 2015). She had more than enough intelligence to excel in college. The challenge she faced was a lack of economic, social, and culture resources to compete effectively with students who did have access to such resources, who could, in fact, simply take those resources for granted.

Melanie's story is unfortunately not an isolated one. It's tragically common. In the United States, education is seen as a pathway to opportunity for all. Yet not all students have equal access to facilities, staffing, programming, and other resources. Sociology explores the consequences of such differences.

As You READ >>

- **How does education maintain social order?**
- **How does education support the existing system of inequality?**
- **How do sociologists define religion?**

>> Education in Society

Sociologically, **education** is a social institution dedicated to the formal process of transmitting culture from teachers to students. With the advent of the Industrial Revolution and the rise of globalization, the responsibility of teaching children the knowledge and skills necessary to operate effectively within society largely transitioned from families to schools. We now invest a substantial amount of time and money in education, believing that the individual and collective benefits of doing so are worth it.

Education A social institution dedicated to the formal process of transmitting culture from teachers to students.

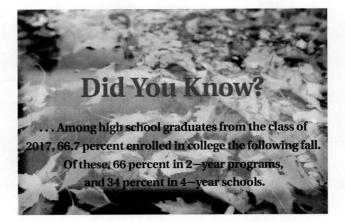

Did You Know?

... Among high school graduates from the class of 2017, 66.7 percent enrolled in college the following fall. Of these, 66 percent in 2—year programs, and 34 percent in 4—year schools.

Source: Bureau of Labor Statistics 2018e. *Photo:* ©Kristy-Anne Glubish/Design Pics/PunchStock

EDUCATION AND OPPORTUNITY

The history of education in the United States involves a cycle of advocating the principle of inclusion, expanding opportunities for participation, and then recognizing the degree to which principle does not match practice in hope that the cycle begins again. The shared principles of democracy and meritocracy shaped the U.S. commitment to education from its very earliest days. The Constitution's opening line, "We the people," highlighted the importance of individual participation in governance. As Thomas Jefferson, an early advocate for public education, wrote in 1816, "If a nation expects to be ignorant and free . . . it expects what never was and never will be" ([1816] 1905:497). Democracy, in other words, requires educated citizens—capable of reading, writing, and arithmetic—so that they might make informed decisions in the voting booth.

Meritocracy represents another important value used to justify public education in the United States. Meritocracy is the principle that our social and economic positions should be based on ability and effort rather than inheritance. Jefferson (1787), for example, maintained that public schools provided a mechanism to identify those with talent and train them. He argued that society would suffer if young geniuses born into poor families never received the opportunity to develop their skills because they lacked the means necessary to afford education. In the same spirit, Horace Mann, sometimes called the "father of American public education," wrote in 1848, "Education, beyond all other devices of human origin, is the *great equalizer* of the conditions of men ([1848]1957). Mann believed that building high-quality, well-staffed public schools would ensure that children without means would share the same classrooms, curriculum, and experiences with children of the well-off, thus providing everyone a chance for success.

EDUCATIONAL ATTAINMENT

The resulting societal commitment to education in the United States led to the expansion of education as a social institution. The degree of expansion is reflected in

Educational Attainment in the United States

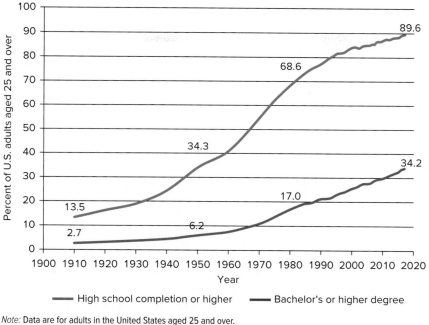

Percent of U.S. adults aged 25 and over

89.6

68.6

34.3

13.5

2.7

17.0

6.2

34.2

High school completion or higher — Bachelor's or higher degree

Note: Data are for adults in the United States aged 25 and over.

Source: National Center for Education Statistics 2018:Table 104.10.

dramatically increased rates of educational attainment over the past 100 years or so. As the "Educational Attainment in the United States" graph shows, from 1910 to 2017, the proportion of people with a high school diploma rose from 13.5 to 89.6 percent, and the number with a college degree increased from 2.7 to 34.2 percent (National Center for Education Statistics 2018:Table 104.10). As education became both more available and more expected, more and more people pursued the pathway it provided.

This growth is due in part to the fact that education in the United States became more inclusive over time. Initially, public schools were open only to White males. In the 19th century, education was for the most part racially segregated, a practice that was affirmed by the 1896 Supreme Court decision in *Plessy v. Ferguson,* which reinforced the principle of "separate, but equal." Through education reform efforts and legal decisions over two centuries, public education eventually opened up to include

everyone regardless of race, ethnicity, sex, or national origin. Examples of education reformers include Emma Hart Willard, who opened the first college-level school for women in 1821, and sociologists such as W. E. B. Du Bois and Jane Addams, both of whom fought for racial and gender equality in the late 19th century. Legal decisions, such as *Brown v. Board of Education* in 1954, found that separate facilities are inherently unequal, and laws such as Title IX in 1972 required equal educational opportunities for both males and females as a requisite for receiving federal funding.

The rise of education as a public institution has not been limited to the United States. As the "Going Global: Educational Attainment of 25- to 34-Year-Olds" graph shows, countries all around the world have made a significant commitment to education, though levels of attainment vary. Increased educational attainment opens doors for individuals and produces a more educated citizenry for societies. Because education has become such a significant social institution in the world, sociologists seek to describe and explain the functions it fulfills.

Going **GLOBAL**

Educational Attainment of 25- to 34-Year-Olds

Note: Educational systems vary around the world, making exact comparison difficult. *Upper Secondary* is roughly equivalent to high school in the United States. *Tertiary* refers to postsecondary education including associate's, bachelor's, master's, and doctoral degrees.

Source: OECD 2018a:Table A1.2. *Photo:* McGraw-Hill Education

COMMUNITY COLLEGES

Community colleges exist as a testament to the ideals put forth by early education advocates. The GI bill in the 1940s and Pell Grants in the 1960s provided significant college financial aid for those with limited means, opening wide the doors to college. But the cost of higher education continues to rise dramatically. Community colleges, however, lower the barriers to student success with their relatively low cost and open enrollment. As the "The Net Price Cost of College" graph shows, community colleges are significantly less expensive than public in-state four-year or private four-year colleges or universities. For the sake of comparison, this graph shows the cost of tuition, fees, and room and board minus any grant aid. Choosing to not live on campus, as many community college students do, can significantly lower the cost of this option.

In 2016, 6.1 million students in the United States attended community college, almost three times as many as in 1970. They constitute 31 percent of all enrolled college students. These students are more likely to be older, female, Black, Hispanic, low-income, and part-time, compared to their peers at four-year schools. In fact, the more income and education a student's parents have, the less likely she or he is to attend a community college. This highlights the role these schools play in providing opportunity for those with limited resources. Enrollment at community colleges raises the aspirations of students. Whether they initially expected to take only a few courses or to finish with a two-year degree, almost one-half of these students later aspired to more education, including a four-year degree or beyond (Ginder, Kelly-Reid, and Mann 2014; National Center for Education Statistics 2018:Table 303.25; Provasnik and Planty 2008).

Community colleges do provide opportunity for many, but the likelihood of completing a degree varies significantly when comparing students at two- and four-year institutions. For students who start at two-year schools, 35.1 percent go on to earn a certificate, an associate's degree, or a bachelor's degree. Contrast that with the 64.2 percent of students who start at four-year schools and earn a degree. The likelihood of giving up also differs. Six years after they started, 46.2 percent of students from two-year schools are no longer enrolled and have no degree. Compare that to 23.6 percent of students who started at four-year schools (U.S. Department of Education 2018:Table 326.40).

Some sociologists have suggested that community colleges serve a "cooling out" function in which students who fail to complete a degree blame themselves for their lack of success. According to this theory, society has fewer good jobs than it has people who want them. Earning a degree increases one's odds of getting one of those jobs. At the level of the individual, community colleges appear to provide opportunity for everyone. Because they had the chance to get a degree, students who give up are more likely to blame themselves for failure than to develop a critique of the social structure that doesn't supply enough good jobs in the first place. In this way, community colleges can help justify the existing system of inequality (Bahr 2008; Clark 1960, 1980).

The Net Price Cost of College

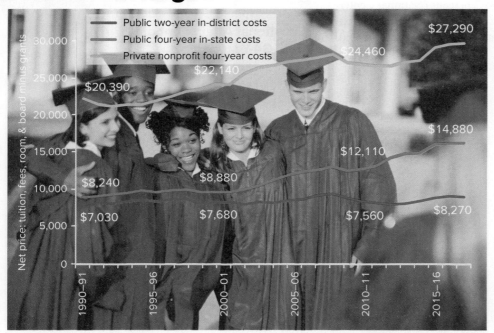

Legend:
- Public two-year in-district costs
- Public four-year in-state costs
- Private nonprofit four-year costs

Y-axis: Net price: tuition, fees, room, & board minus grants

Values shown: $20,390 · $22,140 · $24,460 · $27,290 · $14,880 · $12,110 · $8,240 · $8,880 · $7,030 · $7,680 · $7,560 · $8,270

X-axis: 1990–91, 1995–96, 2000–01, 2005–06, 2010–11, 2015–16

Note: Net price refers to the amount students and/or families must pay for tuition, fees, room, and board after subtracting federal, state, local, and institutional grant aid, along with education tax credits. Costs for all years are reported using 2018 dollars. Values for 2017–2018 represent estimates.

Source: College Board 2018b:Table 7. *Photo:* Purestock/SuperStock

TEACHING AS A PROFESSION

Schools cannot function without teachers. At the primary and elementary level, however, teachers increasingly encounter the conflicts inherent in serving as a professional within the context of a bureaucracy. Teachers must work within the system, submitting to its hierarchical structure and abiding by its established rules. At the same time, teachers want to practice their profession with some degree of autonomy and respect for their judgment. Conflicts arise from having to serve simultaneously as instructor, disciplinarian, administrator, and employee of a school district.

As professionals, teachers feel pressure from a number of directions. First, the level of formal schooling required for teaching remains high, and the public has begun to call for new competency examinations. Second, teachers' salaries are significantly lower than those of many comparably educated professionals and skilled workers. Finally, respect for teachers as competent and responsible professionals has been challenged in the political arena. Many teachers, disappointed and frustrated, have left the educational world for careers in other professions. In fact, between a quarter and a third of new teachers quit within their first three years, and as many as half leave poor urban schools within their first five years. Even within a single year, teacher turnover is significant; in high-poverty areas, more than 20 percent of teachers did not teach in the same school the following year (Goldring et al. 2014; Planty et al. 2008; Wallis 2008).

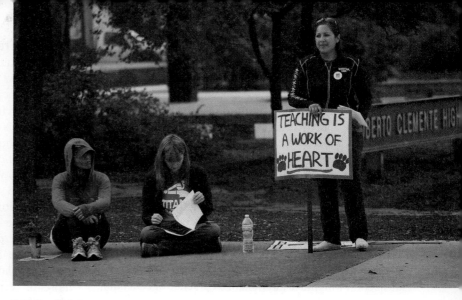

Scott Olson/Getty Images

At the college and university level, having a PhD or similar terminal degree can be a source of pride, and carry with it significant prestige. But the academic job market for professors can prove challenging. Tenure-track jobs, which provide better job security, salaries, and benefits, have become less common. In 2016, 73 percent of instructional positions at colleges and universities consisted of graduate students, part-time teachers, and full-time non-tenure-track professors. At two-year schools, including community colleges, 63 percent of full-time, non-tenure-track faculty are on annual contracts, making them vulnerable from year to year. Pay for part-time adjunct professors who get hired by the course is notoriously low and benefits are typically nonexistent (AAUP 2018).

HOME SCHOOLING

The commitment to public education in the United States opened up the doors for opportunity to a wider array of students. But in recent years, a countertrend developed in which an increasing number of families decided to opt out of both public and private schooling and revert to educating their children at home. Almost 1.7 million students are now being educated at home—about 3.3 percent of the K–12 school population. Home-schooled families are more likely to be White, have two parents in the household with only one in the labor force, have parents with a bachelor's degree, and have three or more children (National Center for Education Statistics 2018:Table 206.10; Redford, Battle, and Bielick 2017).

When asked to identify the most important reason for choosing this path, 25 percent of parents identified "concern about the environment

Average Salaries for Teachers

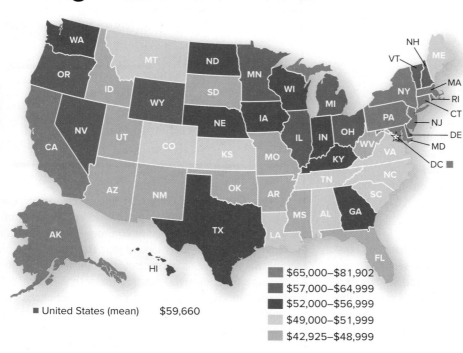

■ United States (mean) $59,660

■ $65,000–$81,902
■ $57,000–$64,999
■ $52,000–$56,999
□ $49,000–$51,999
□ $42,925–$48,999

Note: Data are for 2016–2017.

Source: National Education Association 2018:Table B-6.

of other schools, such as safety, drugs, or negative peer pressure" as the most important factor. Dissatisfaction with the academic instruction at other schools was most important to 19 percent, and 17 percent attributed their decision primarily to a desire to provide religious instruction (Redford, Battle, and Bielick 2017). In addition, some immigrants choose homeschooling as a way to ease their children's transition to a new society. For example, increasing numbers of the nation's growing Arab American population have joined the movement toward homeschooling. Other parents see it as a good alternative for children who suffer from attention deficit hyperactivity disorder (ADHD) and learning disorders (Cooper and Sureau 2007; MacFarquhar 2008).

The rise in homeschooling points toward a growing dissatisfaction with the institutionalized practice of education. Early public school advocates argued for the importance of a common curriculum rooted in a shared sense of values. Homeschooling, however, points toward pluralism and the desire to retain the unique subcultural values of a community. Although new forms of schooling may meet the individual needs of diverse groups in today's society, they also undermine the historical commitment to public education as a means of fostering unity within society.

-SOCTHINK-

What do you think are the advantages and disadvantages of being homeschooled? How might it contribute to a stronger sense of identity? How might it threaten the social order?

>> Sociological Perspectives on Education

Education helps provide for and maintain a sense of social order. But it can also reinforce existing systems of inequality. Sociologists explore ways in which it does both by drawing on the functionalist, conflict, and interactionist perspectives.

FUNCTIONS OF EDUCATION

Society needs to ensure that each generation has the knowledge and skills necessary to ensure that the society continues to evolve and progress in the future. Individuals need this know-how to survive and prosper. Schools provide that knowledge by teaching students how to read, speak foreign languages, repair automobiles, and much more. Consistent with sociology's functionalist perspective, sociologists have identified five functions that education fulfills for both individuals and society.

Culture Transmission Each society has a common stock of cultural knowledge deemed important for its members. As a social institution, education preserves and transmits society's norms, values, beliefs, ideas, and skills, thus reinforcing society's dominant culture. This endorsed knowledge is transmitted through the formal curriculum taught in schools including "the three 'Rs" (reading, 'riting, and 'rithmetic), as well as history, science, and much more. As a result, young people of each generation learn what they need to survive and succeed.

In addition to the formal curriculum, schools create social space for children to transmit unofficial culture among their peers and to establish themselves as individuals separate from their families. Parents aren't hovering over their shoulders to ensure their children say the right things or keep their coats on at recess, and they can't protect children from getting hurt. School is the place where children learn to stand on their own and to establish relationships with their peer group (Adler and Adler 1996). As children get older, peer relationships grow stronger, and the distance from the parental world grows greater.

Social Integration Our shared knowledge also contributes to a sense of common identity or purpose. Students sometimes wonder why they need to know seemingly trivial facts about history or mathematical equations such as $a^2 + b^2 = c^2$. The answer is simple. The culture we share binds us together. Even if no one individual possesses all of it—and even if any single item seems necessary only for contestants on *Jeopardy!*—such knowledge represents who we are and what we believe is important. To put it in Durkheim's terms, it is part of our collective conscience, the social glue that holds us together; or, in Mead's terms, the shared culture we learn in schools contributes to our sense of the generalized other, the map of society we hold in our heads.

-SOCTHINK-

Why do students often feel like schools teach a lot of useless facts? What might this attitude suggest about social integration in modern society?

In an effort to promote social integration, many colleges and universities have established learning communities within which students share common experiences, or they may require first- and second-year students to live on campus. Such programs become more important when students come from diverse backgrounds with different cultural expectations. The goal is to provide experiences that will unify a population composed of diverse racial, ethnic, and religious groups into a community whose members share—to some extent—a common identity. The social integration fostered by education contributes to societal stability and consensus.

Soft Skills and Job Training In addition to the more general knowledge that unites us, schools also teach more particular skills important for individual success, including both behavioral norms and job skills. In the early grades in particular, significant time and effort are spent getting students to do what the teacher wants them to do, when and how the teacher wants them to do it. By exercising formal social control, schools teach students to internalize expected behavioral social norms. As a result, students learn what have come to be called "soft skills," including manners, punctuality, creativity, self-discipline, and responsibility. These characteristics play an important role in educational and employment success (Heckman 2013; Hurrell, Scholarios, and Thompson 2013; Lareau 2015).

Given modern society's complex division of labor, we count on schools to teach students the specific abilities—sometimes called "hard skills"—necessary to become effective workers in specialized jobs. In a classic study from the functionalist perspective, sociologists Kingsley Davis and Wilbert E. Moore (1945) argued that all societies have positions that are more important for society's survival or that require greater skill or knowledge to perform and that not everyone has the ability to fill those jobs. For example, not everyone has what it takes to become a medical doctor, accountant, or lawyer. Because we value workers' knowledge, skills, abilities, and experience, which Davis and Moore referred to as human capital, we collectively pledge that we will reward those who take the time and effort required to develop those skills with high incomes and social esteem. We use grades as an indicator of ability and provide degrees to certify to employers that the graduate has sufficient training to perform the job well. As the "Education Pays" graph demonstrates for 25- to 34-year-olds, we deliver on the promise that making the sacrifice of increasing one's education leads to higher incomes, even relatively early on in careers.

Cultural Innovation Although schools do preserve and transmit existing culture, educational institutions can also stimulate social change. This occurs most frequently at the college and university level where two types of innovation are common. The first involves pursuing new technologies, techniques, and data. This takes place most frequently at larger research universities. Professors at such schools frequently see their primary role as researchers rather than as teachers. Their professional status typically gets measured based on their success at obtaining research grants, securing patents, publishing articles in journals, presenting results at professional conferences, and the like. Research of this type has resulted in cultural innovation in many areas, including space exploration, medical technology, and consumer products.

A second category of cultural innovation involves the exploration of new ideas. Colleges and universities provide a kind of protected environment within which professors and students can challenge existing values and norms and try out new ones. In the 1960s, for example, students and professors explored questions

> Education is our passport to the future, for tomorrow belongs only to the people who prepare for it today.
>
> Malcolm X (1964)

Education Pays

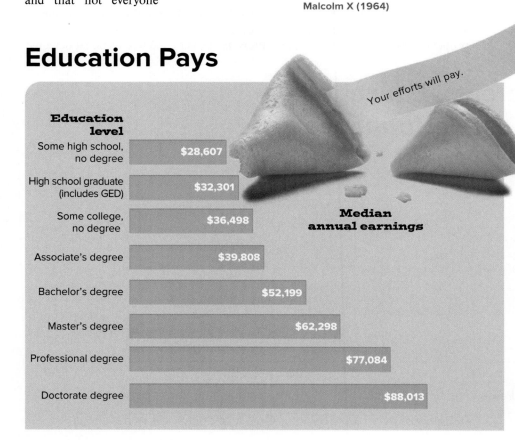

Education level	Median annual earnings
Some high school, no degree	$28,607
High school graduate (includes GED)	$32,301
Some college, no degree	$36,498
Associate's degree	$39,808
Bachelor's degree	$52,199
Master's degree	$62,298
Professional degree	$77,084
Doctorate degree	$88,013

Note: Includes full-time, full-year wage and salary for workers aged 25–34.

Source: U.S. Census Bureau 2018b:Table PINC-03.1.3.2.1. *Photo:* Don Farrall/Photodisc/Getty Images involving war and peace, racial inequality, gender norms, the use of recreational drugs, and more. Professors who engage in such experimentation, especially if it involves innovative or unpopular ideas, may be accused of being out of touch or out of line, but we need people to experiment with new ideas so that our culture does not stagnate.

Child Care Historically, family members had the primary responsibility to teach and care for their children until adulthood. Increasingly, we expect schools and teachers to do more of the job—and at younger and younger ages. From 1970 to 2016, the percentage of 3- to 5-year-olds enrolled in preschool or kindergarten programs rose from 37.5 percent to 64.6 percent, and the number enrolled in full-day programs rose from 6.4 percent to 41.9 percent (National Center for Education Statistics 2018:Table 202.10). The movement toward day care and preschool is driven in part by changes in the economy. Although this shift does provide children with a head start in learning the skills they will need in a globally competitive world, working parents have come to depend on schools to essentially babysit their kids, making sure they are cared for and protected. Because they take responsibility for the children during the school day, schools effectively free up parents to participate in the paid labor force.

EDUCATION AND THE CONFLICT PERSPECTIVE

Education does not provide equal opportunity for all. To the extent that unequal outcomes based on ascribed status are built into the existing system, society operates less like a *meritocracy,* in which our outcomes in life should be determined by ability and effort, and more like an *aristocracy,* a system in which outcomes are determined by inherited position or wealth. Sociologists draw on the conflict perspective to better understand how education can reproduce existing systems of inequality.

Unequal Resource Distribution As we saw at the beginning of this chapter, schools are not all the same. The facilities and programs available to students vary widely. Jonathan Kozol (1991, 2005, 2012), who has studied educational inequality for decades, argues that wealthier districts have the money to offer opportunities that poor districts cannot hope to match, including more AP (Advanced Placement) classes, high-tech labs, athletic facilities, and elective courses in art, music, and languages. This type of disparity occurs because school funding comes primarily through local property taxes. As a result, schools in wealthier areas have access to more funds than do schools in poor communities. In Chicago, for example, the public school district spent $15,412 per student in 2017. Compare that to the $25,520 per student spent by the wealthy northern suburban Highland Park/Deerfield district (Illinois State Board of Education 2018). As a former New York City principal put it, "I'll believe money doesn't count the day the rich stop spending so much on their own children" (quoted in Kozol 2005:59).

Of course, money isn't the only factor shaping outcomes. We must also take into account social and cultural resources. Sociologist Annette Lareau, for example, found that a parent's level of educational attainment is a strong predictor of his or her child's educational outcome

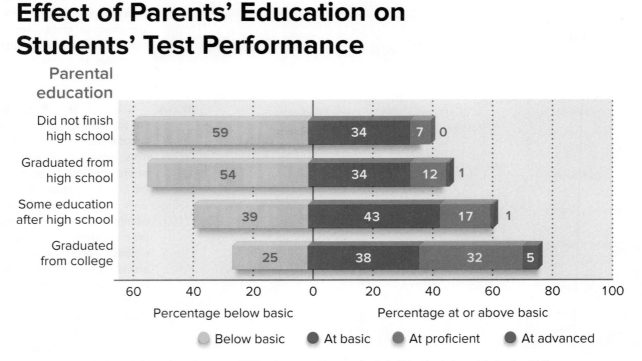

Effect of Parents' Education on Students' Test Performance

Parental education

	Below basic	At basic	At proficient	At advanced
Did not finish high school	59	34	7	0
Graduated from high school	54	34	12	1
Some education after high school	39	43	17	1
Graduated from college	25	38	32	5

Percentage below basic   Percentage at or above basic

● Below basic   ● At basic   ● At proficient   ● At advanced

Note: Percentage distribution of 12th-grade students across NAEP mathematics achievement levels, by highest level of parental education, 2015.

Source: NAEP 2016.

(Lareau 2011). This is due, in part, to a cultural divide created by differing parenting styles that begins at a young age and carries through students' school years. For example, as the "Effect of Parents' Education on Students' Test Performance" graph demonstrates, performance on standardized tests, in this case for math, vary based on the educational attainment of parents. Among high school seniors whose parents have graduated from college, 37 percent score at proficient or advanced levels in math. Compare that to 13 percent for those whose parents have graduated from high school (NAEP 2016). SAT scores are similarly influenced by factors such as race, ethnicity, family income, and school type (National Center for Education Statistics 2018:Tables 226.10, 226.30).

The Correspondence Principle Sociologists Samuel Bowles and Herbert Gintis (1976) claim that the primary function of education is to serve the interests of the ruling elite. Capitalism requires a diverse workforce with varieties of skill levels from the simple to complex. What that means in terms of workers is that a smaller percentage need advanced skills to handle those complex jobs, and a larger percentage needs only the skills necessary to serve as effective workers in jobs requiring less skill. Rather than offering a pathway to opportunity for all, education in the United States follows what Bowles and Gintis call the **correspondence principle,** in which schools reproduce the existing class structure by socializing students to embrace their social class position. Schools effectively operate like factories, producing the right numbers and kinds of work to serve the needs of the capitalist economy. Some students, typically from working-class backgrounds, get taught skills appropriate for subordinate positions, especially emphasizing acceptance of, and obedience to, authority. Other students, more likely from upper-middle class backgrounds, learn skills appropriate to their higher level jobs, which stress leadership, creativity, and decision making.

Did You Know?

. . . The likelihood of going to college directly after high school varies by family income. For example, 83 percent of students from high-income families enroll in college by the following October compared to 65 percent from low-income families who do the same.

Source: National Center for Education Statistics 2018:Table 302.30. *Photo:* Jeremy Baumann/123RF

Bowles and Gintis use the term *hidden curriculum* to distinguish between the formal curriculum schools teach students, which include the primary academic content students learn, and this knowledge associated with the correspondence principle. They define **hidden curriculum** as teaching students to submit to authority and accept society's dominant ideology. Submitting to authority includes learning to obey orders, not speaking until called on, providing appropriate answers, regulating their behavior according to the clock and the like. Accepting the dominant ideology involves taking capitalism's superiority for granted and embracing private property as the only appropriate form of ownership. In ways such as these, schools socialize students to willingly submit to authority figures and uncritically accept society's dominant values.

Credentialism When concerns about inequality arise, education is often presented as a pathway to opportunity. This works as good advice at the individual level, but there is a structural problem with that solution. The more people who get degrees, the less valuable those degrees become. If everyone has a high school diploma, it loses its power as a source of distinction. As the supply of high school graduates exceeds employers' demand, students feel compelled to pursue associate's or bachelor's degrees to stand out from the crowd. This leads to **credentialism,** the increase in the lowest level of education needed to enter a field. Many students today fear that such credential inflation means that even a college degree is not enough to ensure a good job.

> **Correspondence principle** Schools' reproduction of the existing class structure through socializing students to embrace their social class position.
>
> **Hidden curriculum** Teaching students to submit to authority and accept society's dominant ideology.
>
> **Credentialism** An increase in the lowest level of education required to enter a field.

Credentialism can reinforce existing patterns of social inequality. Students from poor, working-class, and middle-class families, including those in minority groups, recognize that getting ahead increasingly requires a college degree, but because they lack sufficient resources, they may have to take on significant levels of debt in the form of student loans to do so (Pew Research Center 2014d). In 2017–2018, students and parents in the United States took out $105.6 billion in student loans. At *public* colleges and universities, 58 percent of graduates who received bachelor's degrees in 2016–2017 took out student loans with an average debt of $26,900. At *private* colleges and universities, the 61 percent who graduated with loans had an average debt of $32,600. As you might expect, students from high-income families were more likely to graduate debt-free than those from lower-income families. Forty-five percent of students from families in the top 25 percent of income earners graduated with no student debt, compared to 21 percent of debt-free students in the lowest-income quartile (College Board 2016a, 2018a).

5 **Movies** on EDUCATION

Dead Poets Society
*Dare to walk
a new path.*

Night School
*Everyone deserves
a second chance.*

Freedom Writers
*Students bond by
giving voice to the
stories of their lives.*

Terri
*An assistant
principal looks out
for an oversized
teen misfit.*

The Perks of Being a Wallflower
*The trials and tribulations of
navigating high school.*

Gender Women and girls in the United States experienced a long history of educational discrimination. But, as noted above, and largely as a consequence of social action on the part of women fighting for change, opportunities opened up for women and girls. Title IX of the Education Amendments of 1972 played a pivotal role in expanding access. It states, "No person in the United States shall, on the basis of sex, be excluded from participation in, be denied the benefits of, or be subjected to discrimination under any education program or activity receiving Federal financial assistance" (U.S. Department of Education 1972). Although Title IX is most commonly associated with equal opportunity for girls and women in athletics, among other things, it also eliminated sex-segregated classes and prohibited sex discrimination in admissions.

Teacher-expectancy effect The impact that a teacher's expectations about a student's performance may have on the student's actual achievements.

Colleges, early on in U.S. history, did not even admit women. Oberlin College was the first in 1833, but other schools denied entry long after that. Yale, Dartmouth, and Harvard, for example, didn't become fully coeducational until the 1960s and 1970s. Over time, however, the percentage of women going to, and graduating from, college rose dramatically. In 1900, women received 19 percent of bachelor's degrees conferred. Since the 1950s, the percentage has risen dramatically so that by 2016, 57 percent of bachelor's degrees went to women. College students are also more likely to be taught by women professors, who now compose 49 percent of total faculty compared to 23 percent in 1970 (National Center for Education Statistics 2018:Table 301.20).

When it comes to educational outcomes at the collegiate level, gender shapes the academic majors college students choose. As the "College Majors by Gender, Percentage Female" graph demonstrates, women are more likely to graduate with bachelor's degrees in elementary education, registered nursing, or psychology than in philosophy, physics, or aerospace engineering (National Center for Education Statistics 2018:Table 318.30). As we will explore in the "Gender and Inequality" section of Chapter 12, the selection of a college major has consequences for income differences between men and women.

EDUCATION AND INTERACTION

To better understand factors shaping outcomes, sociologists using the interactionist perspective have explored what happens at the micro-level. This includes observations of how teachers perceive students, how that perception shapes their treatment of students, and the possible outcomes for students of those actions.

Teacher Expectancy Teacher's perceptions have powerful effects on student outcomes. Psychologist Robert Rosenthal and school principal Lenore Jacobson (1968) documented what they referred to as a **teacher-expectancy effect**—the impact that a teacher's expectations about a student's performance may have on the student's actual achievements. Consistent with sociology's interactionist perspective, including the Thomas theorem's suggestion that perceptions shape actions, their experiments documented this effect.

Rosenthal and Jacobson informed teachers that they were administering a verbal and reasoning pretest to children in a San Francisco elementary school. After administering the tests, the researchers told the teachers that some of the students were "spurters"—children who showed particular academic potential. However, rather than using the actual test scores to make this determination, the

Women's participation in high school rates rose from 294,015 in 1972 to 3,415,306 in 2018 (NFHS 2018). At the college level, the number of women participating in NCAA sports increased from 31,852 in 1972 to 216,378 in 2018. Women now compose 44 percent of NCAA athletes (NCAA 2018). To what extent would we have seen such an increase had it not been for a law that mandated increased opportunity? How might increased opportunity for women in athletics have an impact on increased opportunity in other areas?

College Majors by Gender, Percentage Female

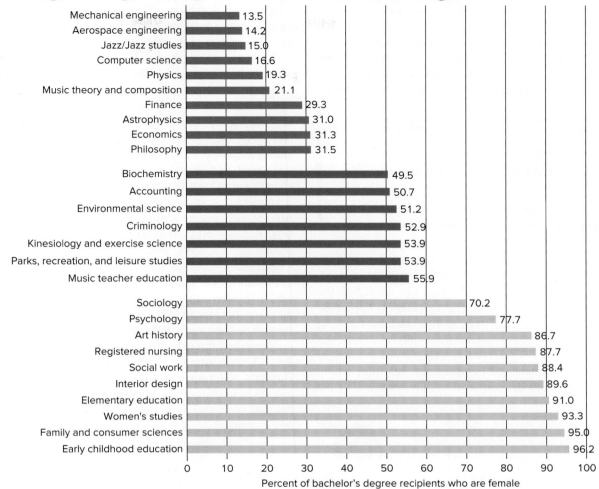

Major	Percent
Mechanical engineering	13.5
Aerospace engineering	14.2
Jazz/Jazz studies	15.0
Computer science	16.6
Physics	19.3
Music theory and composition	21.1
Finance	29.3
Astrophysics	31.0
Economics	31.3
Philosophy	31.5
Biochemistry	49.5
Accounting	50.7
Environmental science	51.2
Criminology	52.9
Kinesiology and exercise science	53.9
Parks, recreation, and leisure studies	53.9
Music teacher education	55.9
Sociology	70.2
Psychology	77.7
Art history	86.7
Registered nursing	87.7
Social work	88.4
Interior design	89.6
Elementary education	91.0
Women's studies	93.3
Family and consumer sciences	95.0
Early childhood education	96.2

Percent of bachelor's degree recipients who are female

Note: Each bar represents the percentage of female bachelor's degree recipients for selected majors.

Source: National Center for Education Statistics 2018:Table 318.30.

researchers randomly selected the 20 percent of the students they identified as spurters. When the students were later retested, the spurters scored not only significantly higher than they had in previous tests but also significantly higher than their peers. Moreover, teachers evaluated the spurters as more interesting, more curious, and better adjusted than their classmates. As the flip-side to labeling theory in criminology, these results provide a classic case of a self-fulfilling prophecy at work. Teachers expected some students to do well, and so they did. Such effects are of particular concern given that factors such as race, ethnicity, class, and gender shape teachers' perceptions (McKown and Weinstein 2008; Rubie-Davies 2010; van den Bergh et al. 2010).

Tracking One way schools reproduce the existing system of social inequality is by categorizing students into ability tracks. The term **tracking** refers to the practice of placing students in specific curriculum groups on the basis of their test

> **Tracking** The practice of placing students in specific curriculum groups on the basis of their test scores and other criteria.

Did You Know?

... **Harvard University accepted a record low 4.59 percent of the 42,749 applicants to its anticipated graduating Class of 2022. Other schools with acceptance rates below 10 percent include Stanford, Yale, Princeton, and the University of Chicago.**

Source: Franklin and Zwickel 2018. *Photo:* C Squared Studios/Photodisc/Getty Images scores and other criteria. In theory, tracking is beneficial because it allows students to be taught at a level and pace most consistent with their abilities. In practice, however, tracking often starts at a young age, and student selection for low- versus high-ability groups is often correlated with their social class, race, or ethnicity. In effect, the differences children bring with them on their first day of kindergarten shape their likely long-term educational outcomes (Oakes 2008).

---SOCTHINK---

What experiences have you had with tracking? To what extent do you believe it was effective for both high-track and low-track students? What are its limitations in terms of equal opportunity?

Religion A social institution dedicated to establishing a shared sense of identity, encouraging social integration, and offering believers a sense of meaning and purpose.

One consequence of such tracking is that it closes doors to students who might have the ability to succeed. For example, at a low-income school in California, all interested students were allowed to enroll in Advanced Placement (AP) courses, not just those whom the administration deemed academically worthy. Half the open-enrollment students scored high enough to qualify for college credit—a much higher proportion than in selective programs, in which only 17 percent of students qualified for college credit. When given the opportunity, otherwise-excluded students were able to succeed (Sacks 2007).

Opening up opportunities for students that have historically been blocked or discouraged from pursuing college degrees has positive outcomes. Even if such students try and fail, they still benefit from the effort by developing "adaptive resilience," allowing them to cope with their lack of college success (Reynolds and Baird 2010). Plus, aiming high significantly increases students' chances of getting ahead. In fact, researchers have found that those with characteristics making them least likely to pursue a college degree—such as coming from low-income families, having parents with less education, or being African American or Latinx—are most likely to benefit from obtaining one (Brand and Xie 2010).

Education does establish social order and provide opportunities for individuals to get ahead. At the same time, in preserving the existing order, it reproduces existing patterns of inequality. Sociology allows us to better understand how these seemingly contradictory outcomes can be accomplished through education. As the experience with Title IX demonstrates, positive social change is possible. Having a better appreciation of how education functions enables us to more effectively work toward realizing the initial goal of education: to provide opportunity and a more open society.

Personal Sociology

Unearned Advantages

My daughters Emily and Eleanor make me proud. Throughout their schooling experience, they got good grades, and their scores on the standardized exams were sky high. But as a sociologist, I know that they benefitted from the fact that their parents are college graduates. As parents, Lori and I provided Em and El with economic, social, and cultural resources in the form of books, activities, and even vacations to historic locations. Kids from such families tend to do better in school than children who lack such opportunities. It's almost as if Emily and Eleanor were cheating because they brought more resources to the table. They did nothing to deserve such advantages, and yet, as a society, we act as if educational outcomes—good or bad—are solely based on merit. Looking back, what opportunities or resources did you have, or wish you had, that helped better prepare you for college success?

>> Defining Religion

Education plays a major role in socializing members of society into shared values and norms, and religion helps cement those beliefs and practices into people's hearts and minds. **Religion** is a social institution dedicated to establishing a shared sense of identity, encouraging social integration, and offering believers a sense of meaning and purpose. Though levels of religious participation vary from place to place, religion continues to be a major force both on the world stage and in the lives of individuals.

SUBSTANCE: WHAT RELIGION IS

Because religion comes in many shapes and sizes, sociologists debate how best to define it. They seek a definition *exclusive* enough to clearly identify the boundaries separating what counts as religion from that which does not. At the same time, a definition should be *inclusive* enough to incorporate the religion's diverse manifestations. As a result, and parallel to the definitions of family in Chapter 7, some prefer a more exclusive substantive approach and others prefer a more inclusive functional approach.

Substantive definitions highlight distinct elements that divide one thing from another. In the case of religion, the a transcendence of our everyday, profane experience into contact with the sacred. Believers enhance their likelihood for such experiences by putting themselves in positions for encounters with the sacred realm through ritual practices, such as prayer, meditation, sacrifice, or service.

Different religious groups define their understanding of the sacred or profane in different ways. For example, who or what constitutes "god" varies among Muslims, Christians, and Hindus. Ordinarily, a piece of bread is profane, but it becomes sacred for Christians during their practice of communion because through it believers enter into connection with God. Similarly, a candelabrum becomes sacred to Jews if it is a menorah. For Confucians and Taoists, incense sticks are not mere decorative items, but highly valued offerings to the gods in religious ceremonies that mark the new and full moons.

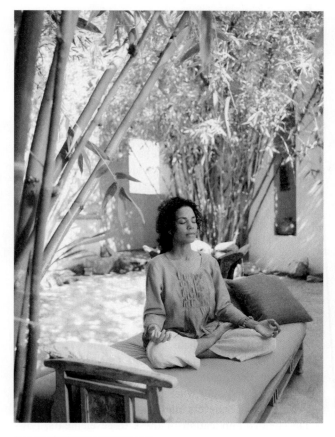

Chris Ryan/OJO Images/Getty Images

unique content or substance that separates it from other forms of knowledge and belief usually involves some form of the supernatural. Sociologist Peter Berger (1969) provided a substantive definition of religion as "the human enterprise by which a sacred cosmos is established" (p. 25). The sacred here refers to that extraordinary realm that becomes the focus of religious faith and practice. It provides believers with meaning, order, and coherence. In describing that sacred realm, people might touch on concepts such as gods and goddesses, angels and demons, heaven and hell, nirvana, or other beings or realms. A society with broad agreement about the nature and importance of this sacred realm is, by this definition, more religious.

According to the substantive perspective, religious believers distinguish between two forms of reality: the sacred and the profane. The **sacred** encompasses elements beyond everyday life that inspire respect, awe, and even fear. The sacred realm exists in contrast to the **profane,** which includes the ordinary and commonplace. Religious experiences often represent

Michael Zak/mischoko/123RF

FUNCTION: WHAT RELIGIONS DO

A functional approach to religion focuses less on the substance of what religion *is* and more on what religion *does.* Functional definitions of religion emphasize religion's unifying dimension. Religion need not have gods or goddesses, an afterlife, or other such conventional elements. In fact, any social practices that strongly unite us can function like religion for the individual and for society.

> **Sacred** Elements beyond everyday life that inspire respect, awe, and even fear.
>
> **Profane** The ordinary and commonplace elements of life, as distinguished from the sacred.

As we saw with family in Chapter 7, sociologists analyzing institutions identify the functions that various institutions fulfill for society. When it comes to religion, we can highlight three core functions. First, religion seeks to *secure greater integration* within society. By linking people together through common beliefs and rituals, religion produces a shared sense of identity. Individuals come to define themselves in terms of their membership in, and participation with, the group. The result is a stronger sense of solidarity. When social integration is strong, believers are more likely to make individual sacrifices for the good of the whole, whether in terms of time, money, or perhaps even their lives.

In order to secure the existing social order, religion's second function is to *enforce existing beliefs and practices,* which form the core around which religious identity comes together. Challenges to those values and norms represent a threat to the group's shared identity. To avoid such hazards, religions put mechanisms in place to limit the likelihood of heresy or deviance. The resulting sanctions can be

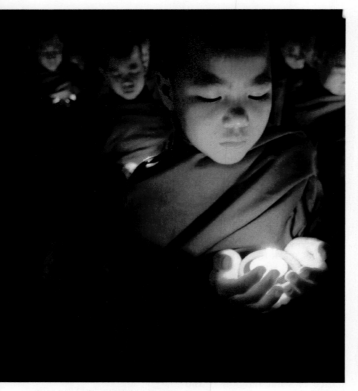

Gavriel Jecan/The Image Bank/Getty Images

FUNCTIONAL EQUIVALENTS OF RELIGION

Emile Durkheim brought together aspects of the substantive and functional approaches to create a definition of religion that both identifies specific elements of religion and remains flexible enough to include varieties of religious experience (Berger 1969). According to Durkheim, religion is "a unified system of beliefs and practices relative to sacred things, that is to say things set apart and forbidden—beliefs and practices which unite into a single moral community, called a 'church,' all those who adhere to them" ([1887] 1972:224). This definition highlights three elements of religion—a unified system of beliefs and practices, sacred things, and community—and sociologists since Durkheim have used them to explore the various forms religion might take.

Based on these three elements, religion as conventionally understood may include beliefs, as recorded in doctrine, dogma, and creeds, and practices, such as attendance at services, prayer, meditation, and fasting. Examples of religious sacred objects include the bread and wine of communion for Roman Catholics or the Qur'an for Mulims. And religious community might take place in a church, mosque, or temple, but what really matters is the unification of a body of believers into a shared community.

Durkheim's application of these three elements, however, need not be limited to conventional conceptions of religion. Functional equivalents to religion include those things that fulfill the functions of religion, even if they don't quite look and act like religion as conventionally understood. Anything that does what Durkheim's three elements do can function as religion. For example, fan-followings in popular culture—of musical groups, television series, film franchises, and more—can be analyzed through the lens of religious devotion. The same might be said in politics, where rallies can take on a religious fervor. But perhaps no place has the religious equivalent argument been made more than in sports (Bain-Selbo 2012; Cusack and Digance 2009; Green 2016; Jindra 1994).

When it comes to beliefs and practices, sports fans—short for *fanatics,* a term that historically had religious connotations—share beliefs about the superiority of their team and regularly practice rituals in hopes that it will help their team win. They may wear the same jersey to watch the game, sit in the same chair, or do a touchdown dance after their team scores, all out of superstitious fear that failure to do so will make their team lose. In terms of sacred things, there are autographs, jerseys, balls; and the stadium where the team plays, often referred to by fans as a shrine, represents a sacred space. Finally, fans are united into a community with other fans of the team. Being a fan of the team becomes part of their identity. It provides them with joy, satisfaction, and even a sense of purpose. In a personal essay recounting his obsession with soccer, journalist Michael Elliott (2005) put it this way: "What does being a fan mean? It means you will never walk alone" (p. 76).

externally enforced by religious authorities. For example, violations might lead to excommunication, shunning, and the like. The sanctions can also be internally enforced. Guilt, or its anticipation, has served various religious traditions well in inhibiting religious deviance.

Religion also *provides believers and communities with a sense of meaning and purpose,* which represents its third function. When questions arise about the meaning of life or why seemingly senseless tragedies occur, religions often provide answers to calm believer's fears. They do so, in part, because religion provides a sense that there is order to the universe, that some larger purpose exists that transcends the here-and-now reality of our mundane existence (Berger 1969).

Goodshoot/Alamy Stock Photo

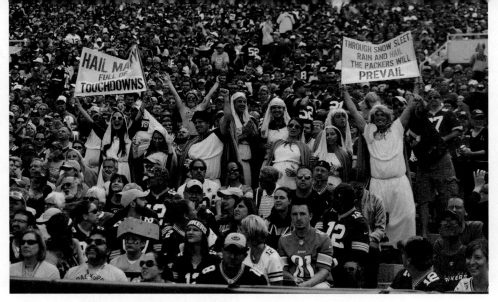

On Sundays each fall, fans gather together to worship at the sacred football shrine of Lambeau Field.
Larry Radloff/Icon Sportswire/Getty Images

Personal Sociology

Victory Dance

I confess to being a Green Bay Packers fan. I follow them religiously. Even though I know better, I practice superstitions in the hope that they will help, including wearing a lucky shirt, not talking on the phone during the game, and although I am embarrassed to admit it, doing a "touchdown dance" around the dining-room table with my wife, Lori, after the Packers score, with high-fives for everyone including our dog Jessie. Lori is an even bigger fan. We own stock in the Packers and have season tickets. We've made many pilgrimages to the "frozen tundra of Lambeau Field." Each time we go to a game, we follow the same rituals: park in the same spot, eat a pre-game meal at the same restaurant, and enter the stadium early so we can soak it all in. Do you, or does anyone you know, have any superstitions when it comes to sports?

SOCTHINK

What other things function like religion for us? How about followers of bands, celebrities, TV shows, or politics? To what extent might consumerism, or even work, function as religion?

>> Components of Religion

Sociologists since Durkheim have elaborated on the three primary elements of religion. They have also added religious experience as a fourth component.

BELIEFS

Some people believe in life after death, in supreme beings with unlimited powers, or in supernatural forces. **Religious beliefs** are statements to which members of a particular religion adhere. They represent the principles believers share through faith. The content of those beliefs can vary dramatically from religion to religion.

One form of belief has become particularly significant in recent times. **Fundamentalism** refers to a rigid adherence to core religious doctrines. In the late 1960s a significant shift occurred in the nature of religious belief in the United States. Denominations that held to relatively liberal interpretations of religious scripture (such as the Presbyterians, Methodists, and Lutherans) declined in membership, while those that held to more conservative interpretations and sought a return to the fundamentals of the faith grew in numbers. Fundamentalism grows out of a sense that the world is falling apart due to a decline in true religious belief and practice. Fundamentalists see themselves as presenting a positive vision for the future through a return to the purity of the original religious message (Aslan 2010; Juergensmeyer 2003).

> **Religious belief** A statement to which members of a particular religion adhere.
>
> **Fundamentalism** Rigid adherence to core religious doctrines, often accompanied by a literal application of scripture or historical beliefs to today's world.

Going GLOBAL

How Often Do You Attend Religious Services?

Percentage attending religious services once a week or more

Country	Percentage
Rwanda	70.6%
Poland	50.4%
Mexico	46.2%
Egypt	45.2%
Iraq	38.4%
United States	33.3%
South Korea	29.9%
India	24.5%
Russia	4.9%
Sweden	4.2%
China	1.9%

Source: World Values Survey 2015:V145.

The phrase "religious fundamentalism" was first applied to Protestants in the United States who took a literal interpretation of the Bible, but fundamentalism is found worldwide among most major religious groups, including Roman Catholicism, Islam, and Judaism. Fundamentalists vary immensely in their beliefs and behavior. Some stress the need to be strict in their own personal faith but take little interest in broad social issues. Others are watchful of societal actions, such as government policies, that they see as conflicting with fundamentalist doctrine (Emerson et al. 2006; Juergensmeyer 2003).

RITUALS

Like any social institution, religion develops distinctive norms to structure people's behavior. **Religious rituals** are practices required or expected of members of a faith. Rituals and beliefs generally reinforce each other. Belief in the importance of loving one's neighbor, for example, impacts how believers acts toward those around them. Moreover, sanctions are attached to religious rituals, in the form of either rewards (such as bar mitzvah gifts) or penalties (such as expulsion from a religious institution for violation of norms).

Religious ritual A practice required or expected of members of a faith.

Religious experience The feeling or perception of being in direct contact with the ultimate reality, such as a divine being, or of being overcome with religious emotion.

Rituals may be very simple, such as saying a prayer at a meal, meditating, or observing a moment of silence to commemorate someone's death. Other rituals, such as the *hajj*—the Muslim pilgrimage to the Grand Mosque in Mecca, Saudi Arabia—are quite elaborate. Most religious rituals in the United States focus on services conducted at houses of worship. Attendance at a service, silent and spoken prayers, communion, and the singing of hymns and chants are common forms of ritual behavior that generally take place in group settings. These rituals serve as important face-to-face encounters in which people reinforce their religious beliefs and their commitment to their faith. Religious participation varies widely from country to country. Part of the effectiveness of rituals is the sense of control they provide (Norton and Gino 2013).

EXPERIENCE

In the sociological study of religion, the term **religious experience** refers to the feeling or perception of being in direct contact with the ultimate reality, such as a divine being, or of being overcome with religious emotion. A religious experience may be rather slight, such as the feeling of exaltation a person might receive from hearing a choir sing Handel's "Hallelujah Chorus." Many religious experiences, however, are more profound, such as a Muslim's experience on a *hajj*. In his autobiography, the late African American activist Malcolm X (1964:338) wrote of his *hajj* and how deeply moved he was by the way that Muslims in Mecca came together across racial and color lines. For Malcolm X, the color blindness of the Muslim world "proved to me the power of the One God."

For evangelical Christians in the United States, becoming "born again" represents a profound religious experience. To do so, an unbeliever asks Jesus Christ into their hearts as their personal Lord and Savior. This emotionally charged experience marks a turning point in their lives when they became a Christian. According to a national

Religious adherents demonstrate commitment to their faiths in various ways, including Muslim women who choose to wear the hijab. Patrick Baz/AFP/Getty Images

survey, 35 percent of adults in the United States self-identify as "born-again or evangelical" Christians. Perhaps not surprisingly, 83 percent of Evangelical Protestants describe themselves in this way, as do 72 percent of those in historically Black Protestant churches. Only 27 percent of mainline Protestants identify as "born-again or evangelical," as do 23 percent of Mormons and 22 percent of Catholics (Pew Research Center 2015f:31). Such statistics demonstrate that what counts as a legitimate and significant religious experience, such as becoming born again, varies from group to group, which highlights the significance of the social context for religious faith.

COMMUNITY

Religious communities organize themselves in varieties of ways. Sociologists find it useful to distinguish between four basic forms of organization: the ecclesia, the denomination, the sect, and the new religious movement, or cult. We can see differences among these four forms of organization in their size, power, degree of commitment expected from members, and historical ties to other faiths (Dawson 2009).

Ecclesiae When studying how groups organize their communities, sociologists have used the term **ecclesia** (plural, *ecclesiae*) to describe a religious organization that claims to include most or all members of a society and is recognized as the national or official religion. Because virtually everyone belongs to the faith, membership is by birth rather than conscious decision. The classic example in sociology was the Roman Catholic Church in medieval Europe. Contemporary examples of ecclesiae include Islam in Saudi Arabia and Buddhism in Thailand. However, significant differences exist within this category. In Saudi Arabia's Islamic regime, leaders of the ecclesia hold vast power over actions of the state. In contrast, the historical state church in Sweden, Lutheranism, holds no such power over the Riksdag (parliament) or the prime minister.

Denominations A **denomination** is a large, organized religion that is not officially linked to the state or government. Like an ecclesia, it tends to have an explicit set of beliefs, a defined system of authority, and a generally respected position in society. Denominations often claim large segments of a population as members. Generally, children accept the denomination of their parents and give little thought to membership in other faiths. Although considered respectable and not viewed as a challenge to the secular government, unlike ecclesia, denominations lack the official recognition and power held by an ecclesia (Doress and Porter 1977).

The United States is home to a large number of denominations, as the "Major Religious Traditions in the United States" graphic shows. This diversity is largely the result of the nation's immigrant heritage. Many settlers brought with them the religious commitments native to their homelands. Some Christian denominations in the United States, such as the Roman Catholics, Episcopalians, and Lutherans, are the outgrowth of ecclesiae established in Europe. New Christian denominations also emerged, including the Mormons and Christian Scientists. Within the last generation, immigrants have increased the number of Muslims, Hindus, and Buddhists living in the United States.

> **Ecclesia** A religious organization that claims to include most or all members of a society and is recognized as the national or official religion.
>
> **Denomination** A large, organized religion that is not officially linked to the state or government.

Individuals who do not identify with any religious tradition fall into the unaffiliated category, which encompasses 22.8 percent of the U.S. adult population. This group includes both self-described atheists and agnostics, but the largest group in this category are those who choose "Nothing in particular" to describe their religious views. Younger people are more likely to select this category. Overall, people in this unaffiliated category may well hold religious beliefs and attend religious services, but they do not associate themselves with any particular religious group. For example, 49 percent of the religiously unaffiliated describe their belief in God as either absolutely certain or fairly certain, 37 percent say they believe in heaven, and

Major Religious Traditions in the United States

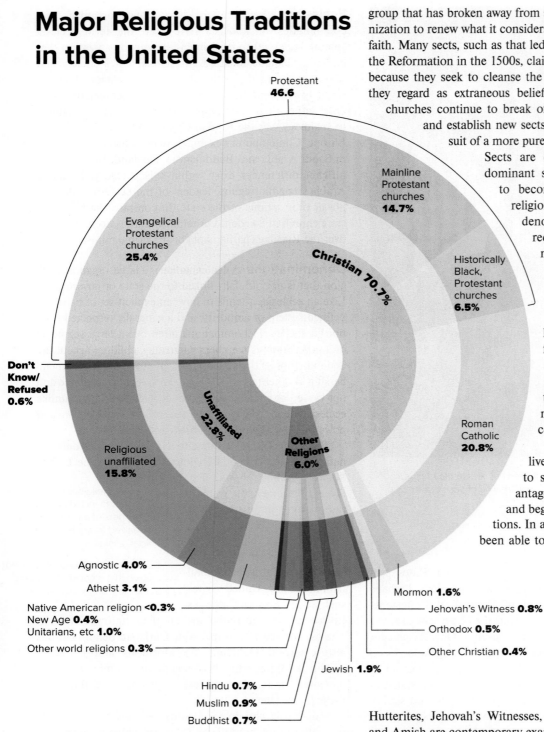

Protestant
46.6

Mainline Protestant churches
14.7%

Evangelical Protestant churches
25.4%

Historically Black, Protestant churches
6.5%

Christian 70.7%

Don't Know/ Refused
0.6%

Unaffiliated 22.8%

Other Religions
6.0%

Roman Catholic
20.8%

Religious unaffiliated
15.8%

Agnostic **4.0%**

Atheist **3.1%**

Native American religion **<0.3%**
New Age **0.4%**
Unitarians, etc **1.0%**
Other world religions **0.3%**

Mormon **1.6%**
Jehovah's Witness **0.8%**
Orthodox **0.5%**
Other Christian **0.4%**

Jewish **1.9%**

Hindu **0.7%**
Muslim **0.9%**
Buddhist **0.7%**

Note: Due to rounding, figures may not add to 100, and nested figures may not add to the subtotal indicated. *Source:* Pew Research Center 2015f:21.

Sect A relatively small religious group that has broken away from some other religious organization to renew what it considers the original vision of the faith.

Established sect A religious group that is the outgrowth of a sect, yet remains isolated from society.

34 percent say religion is either very or somewhat important in their lives (Pew Research Center 2015f).

Sects A sect can be defined as a relatively small religious

group that has broken away from some other religious organization to renew what it considers the original vision of the faith. Many sects, such as that led by Martin Luther during the Reformation in the 1500s, claim to be the "true church" because they seek to cleanse the established faith of what they regard as extraneous beliefs and rituals. Protestant churches continue to break off existing denominations and establish new sects starts today in their pursuit of a more pure faith.

Sects are often at odds with the dominant society and do not seek to become established national religions. Unlike ecclesiae and denominations, they typically require intensive commitments and demonstrations of belief by members. Partly owing to their outsider status, sects frequently exhibit a higher degree of religious fervor and loyalty than more established religious groups. Many seek to recruit adults as new members, and acceptance comes through conversion.

Sects are often short-lived. Those that are able to survive may become less antagonistic to society over time and begin to resemble denominations. In a few instances, sects have been able to endure over several generations while remaining fairly separate from society. Sociologist J. Milton Yinger (1970: 226–73) uses the term **established sect** to describe a religious group that is the outgrowth of a sect, yet remains isolated from society. The Hutterites, Jehovah's Witnesses, Seventh-Day Adventists, and Amish are contemporary examples of established sects in the United States.

New Religious Movements Historically, sociologists used the term *cult* to describe alternative religious groups with unconventional religious beliefs. Over time, however, this term has become problematic. Although sociologists used it to categorize particular kinds of faiths, the term *cult* has taken on a negative connotation. As a result many sociologists have abandoned the use of the term. In its place they have adopted the expression "new religious movement."

A **new religious movement (NRM)** is generally a small, alternative religious group that represents either a new faith community or a major innovation in an existing faith. NRMs are similar to sects in that they tend to be small and are often viewed as less respectable than more established faiths. Unlike sects, however, NRMs normally do not result from schisms or breaks with established ecclesiae or denominations. Some new religious movements, including the Church of Scientology, which was founded in 1954 by science fiction author L. Ron Hubbard, may be totally unrelated to existing faiths. Even when a cult does accept certain fundamental tenets of a dominant faith—such as a belief in Jesus as divine or in Muhammad as a messenger of God—it will offer new revelations or insights to justify its claim to being a more advanced religion (Stark and Bainbridge 1979, 1985).

Most major religions, including Christianity, began as upstart faiths in the context of their larger societies. Over time, as they grew and their beliefs received greater legitimacy, they transitioned into other religious types. Existing NRMs may be in the early stages of developing into a denomination, or they may just as easily fade away through the loss of members or weak leadership (Schaefer and Zellner 2007). The boundaries between the four types are somewhat fluid, and it is helpful to view them as a continuum based on their level of acceptance in the larger society and the expectations they have in terms of faith and practice for their believers.

Pierre-Philippe Marcou/AFP/Getty Images

>> Religions around the World

Early sociologists predicted that modern societies would experience widespread **secularization,** which involves religion's diminishing influence in the public sphere, especially in politics and the economy. In the United States, there has indeed been a dramatic increase in the number of religiously unaffiliated individuals, often referred to by researchers as "nones" because that is how they respond when asked about their religious affiliation. As a portion of the U.S. population, they have increased from 7 percent in 1972 to 16.1 percent in 2007 and 22.8 percent in 2015. That works out to 56 million individuals, an increase of 19 million between 2007 and 2015. In fact, the United States has more "nones" than Catholics (Pew Research Center 2015f; Putnam and Campbell 2012).

Globally, 1.1 billion people, or 16.4 percent of the world's population, identify themselves as religiously unaffiliated. This includes atheists and agnostics along with religious believers who do not identify with a particular religious group. The size of this unaffiliated group might suggest that those early sociologists were correct about secularization and the declining significance of religion in the modern world. Yet projections to 2050 suggest that the proportion of the global population who identify as religiously unaffiliated will actually shrink to 13.2 percent (Pew Research Center 2015g). In the United States and around the world, religion continues to exert a significant influence both individually and collectively.

Christianity is the largest single faith in the world; the second largest is Islam, as the accompanying "Major World Religions" graphic shows. Although global news events often suggest an inherent conflict between Christians and Muslims, the two faiths are similar in many ways. Both are monotheistic, meaning both claim there is only one god, and both include a belief in prophets, an afterlife, and a judgment day. In fact, Islam recognizes Jesus as a prophet, though not as the son of God. Both faiths impose a moral code on believers, which varies from fairly rigid proscriptions for fundamentalists to relatively relaxed guidelines for liberals.

> **New religious movement (NRM)** A small, alternative faith community that represents either a new religion or a major innovation in an existing faith.
>
> **Secularization** Religion's diminishing influence in the public sphere, especially in politics and the economy.

The followers of Islam, called Muslims, believe that the prophet Muhammad received Islam's holy scriptures from Allah (God) nearly 1,400 years ago. They see Muhammad as the last in a long line of prophets, preceded by Adam, Abraham, Moses, and Jesus. Islam is more communal in its expression than Christianity, particularly the more individualistic Protestant denominations. Consequently, in countries that are predominantly Muslim, the separation of religion and the state is not considered necessary or even desirable. In fact, Muslim governments often reinforce Islamic practices through their laws. Muslims do vary sharply in their interpretation of several traditions, some of which—such as the wearing of veils by women—are more cultural than religious in origin.

Like Christianity and Islam, Judaism is monotheistic. Jews believe that God's true nature is revealed in the Torah, which Christians know as the first five books of the Old Testament. According to these scriptures, God formed a

Going GLOBAL

Religions of the World

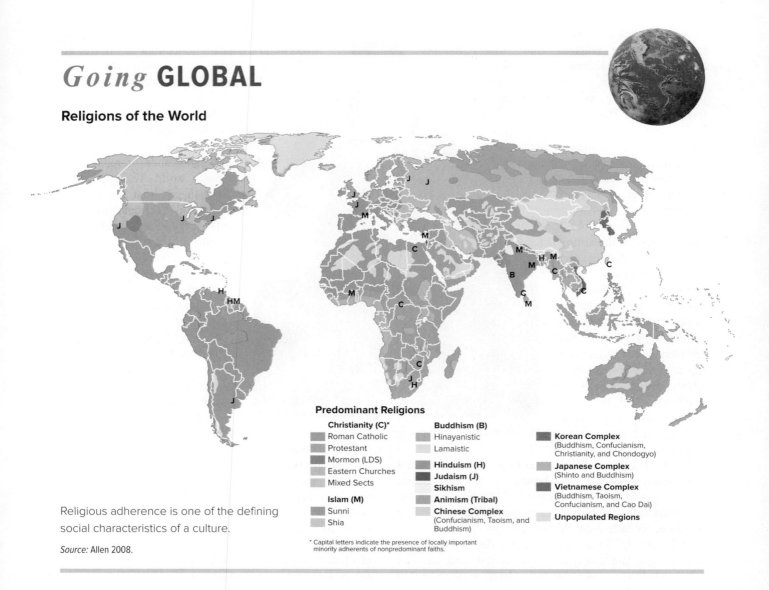

Predominant Religions

Christianity (C)*
- Roman Catholic
- Protestant
- Mormon (LDS)
- Eastern Churches
- Mixed Sects

Islam (M)
- Sunni
- Shia

Buddhism (B)
- Hinayanistic
- Lamaistic

Hinduism (H)
Judaism (J)
Sikhism
Animism (Tribal)
Chinese Complex
(Confucianism, Taoism, and Buddhism)

Korean Complex
(Buddhism, Confucianism, Christianity, and Chondogyo)

Japanese Complex
(Shinto and Buddhism)

Vietnamese Complex
(Buddhism, Taoism, Confucianism, and Cao Dai)

Unpopulated Regions

Religious adherence is one of the defining social characteristics of a culture.

Source: Allen 2008.

* Capital letters indicate the presence of locally important minority adherents of nonpredominant faiths.

---

covenant, or pact, with Abraham and Sarah, the ancestors of the twelve tribes of Israel. Even today, religious Jews believe this covenant holds them accountable to God's will. If they follow both the letter and the spirit of the Torah, a long-awaited Messiah will one day bring paradise to earth. Although Judaism has a relatively small following compared to other major faiths, it forms the historical foundation for both Christianity and Islam. That is why Jews revere many of the same sacred Middle Eastern sites as Christians and Muslims.

Two other major faiths developed in a different part of the world—India. The earliest, Hinduism, originated around 1500 BCE. Hinduism differs from Judaism, Christianity, and Islam in that it embraces a number of gods and minor gods, although most worshipers

George Doyle/Stockbyte/Getty Images

are devoted primarily to a single deity, such as Shiva or Vishnu. Hinduism is also distinguished by a belief in reincarnation, or the perpetual rebirth of the soul after death. Unlike Judaism, Christianity, and Islam, which are based largely on sacred texts, Hindu beliefs have been preserved mostly through oral tradition.

Buddhism developed in the sixth century BCE as a reaction against Hinduism. This faith is founded on the teachings of Siddhartha (later called Buddha, or "The Enlightened One"). Through meditation, followers of Buddhism strive to overcome selfish cravings for physical or material pleasures, with the goal of reaching a state of enlightenment, or nirvana. Buddhists created the first monastic orders, which are thought to be

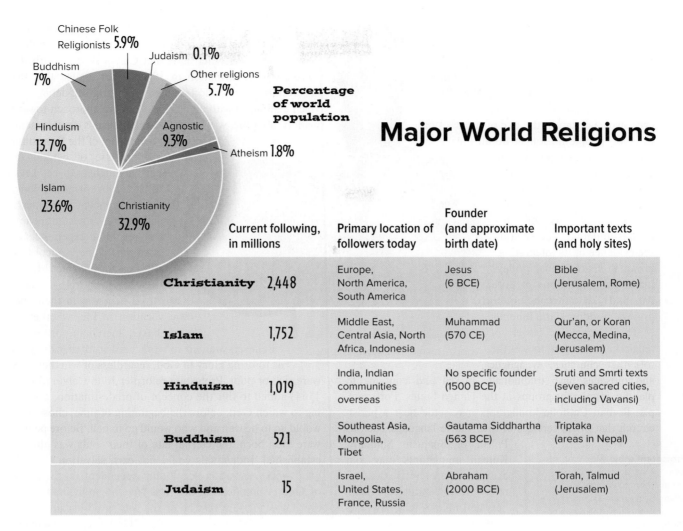

Major World Religions

Percentage of world population

Chinese Folk Religionists 5.9%
Judaism 0.1%
Buddhism 7%
Other religions 5.7%
Hinduism 13.7%
Agnostic 9.3%
Atheism 1.8%
Islam 23.6%
Christianity 32.9%

	Current following, in millions	Primary location of followers today	Founder (and approximate birth date)	Important texts (and holy sites)
Christianity	2,448	Europe, North America, South America	Jesus (6 BCE)	Bible (Jerusalem, Rome)
Islam	1,752	Middle East, Central Asia, North Africa, Indonesia	Muhammad (570 CE)	Qur'an, or Koran (Mecca, Medina, Jerusalem)
Hinduism	1,019	India, Indian communities overseas	No specific founder (1500 BCE)	Sruti and Smrti texts (seven sacred cities, including Vavansi)
Buddhism	521	Southeast Asia, Mongolia, Tibet	Gautama Siddhartha (563 BCE)	Triptaka (areas in Nepal)
Judaism	15	Israel, United States, France, Russia	Abraham (2000 BCE)	Torah, Talmud (Jerusalem)

Sources: Janssen 2019:698; Swatos 2011.

the models for monastic orders in other religions, including Christianity. Though Buddhism emerged in India, its followers were eventually driven out of that country by the Hindus. It is now found primarily in other parts of Asia.

Although the differences among religions are striking, they are exceeded by variations within faiths. Consider the differences within Christianity, from relatively liberal denominations such as Presbyterians or Episcopalians to the more conservative Mormons and Greek Orthodox Catholics. Similar divisions exist within Hinduism, Islam, and other world religions (Swatos 1998, 2011).

>> Sociological Perspectives on Religion

Sociology's interest in religion started at the very beginning of the discipline. Intellectuals at that time felt that the religious teachings that had guided society in times of crisis in the past were failing (Wilson 1999). Auguste Comte and other 19th-century sociologists sought to provide a science of society that would tap the ways of knowing built into the scientific method and apply them to the study of society. They recognized the significant role religion had played in maintaining social order in the past and believed it essential to understand how it had accomplished this.

INTEGRATION AND THE FUNCTIONALIST PERSPECTIVE

As noted previously, Durkheim, in keeping with the functionalist perspective he helped to establish, focused on religion's contribution to social integration. He argued that, in traditional societies, religion served as the social glue holding society together. Religion legitimized society's core values and norms in the form of doctrine, statements of faith, sacraments, and rituals. Violating social norms meant more than just disobeying societal, political, or familial leaders. It meant going against the will of gods, goddesses, supernatural beings, or a whole host of other possible forces throughout human history. In this way, religion helped ensure compliance and minimize deviance.

For Durkheim, religious unity grew out of shared experiences. The Amish still provide an example of how living and working in common gives rise to a unified faith (Kraybill, Johnson-Weiner, and Nolt 2013). With the transition to modern society, however, especially given the rise of the division of labor, people no longer do all the same things together. We no longer possess the same knowledge and skill. As a result, religion's capacity to provide meaning and a shared sense of purpose is undercut. Yet we still see evidence of its integrating power in shared rituals today, including confessions of faith, bar and bat mitzvahs, public prayers, weddings, and funerals.

The integrative power of religion can be seen, too, in the role that churches, synagogues, and mosques have traditionally played and continue to play for immigrant groups in the United States. For example, Roman Catholic immigrants may settle near a parish church that offers services in their native language, such as Polish or Spanish. Similarly, Korean immigrants may join a Presbyterian church that has many Korean American members and follows religious practices similar to those of churches in Korea. Like other religious organizations, these Roman Catholic and Presbyterian churches help integrate immigrants into their new homeland (Peek 2005; Warner 2007).

Pavel Filatov/Alamy Stock Photo

Protestant ethic Max Weber's term for the disciplined commitment to worldly labor driven by a desire to bring glory to God, shared by followers of Martin Luther and John Calvin.

disciplined commitment to worldly labor driven by a desire to bring glory to God that was shared by followers of Martin Luther and John Calvin starting with the Protestant Reformation in 1517. Weber argued that the Protestant combination of hard work and self-denial provided capitalism with an almost obsessive approach toward worldly labor that was essential to capitalism's development.

To explain the impact of the Protestant ethic on the rise of capitalism, Weber highlights three keys: Luther's concept of a calling, Calvin's concept of predestination, and Protestant believers' resulting experience of "salvation panic." According to Protestant reformer Martin Luther (1483–1546), God called all believers to their specific vocation in life, whether as peasant, baker, merchant, or priest. Believers wanted to work hard in their calling so as to bring glory to God, regardless of whether they were rich or poor. Protestant reformer John Calvin (1509–1564) added to this the concept of predestination, according to which God, before the beginning of time, chose who would go to heaven and who would go to hell. Before people were even born, the eternal fate of their souls was already established. Individuals could not earn salvation through good works; salvation was totally dependent on the grace of God. Complicating this was that no individual could ever know for sure that he or she was saved because none could presume to know the mind of God. Weber concluded that this created a sense of salvation panic among believers, who wanted assurance that they were going to heaven.

RELIGION AND SOCIAL CHANGE

Max Weber sought to understand how religion, which so often seems conservative in that it works to maintain order, might also contribute to social change. To do so, he focused on the relationship between religious faith and the rise of capitalism. Weber's findings appeared in his sociology classic, *The Protestant Ethic and the Spirit of Capitalism* ([1904] 2009), one of sociology's most well-known works.

Weber's Protestant Ethic Thesis Weber observed that in the European nations of his time, an overwhelming number of business leaders, owners of capital, and skilled workers were Protestant. He set out to discover why. Through his historical research, Weber concluded that this relationship between religious faith and economic success was a consequence of what he called the **Protestant ethic**—a

5 Movies on RELIGION

The Master
A charismatic religious leader recruits believers into The Cause.

Silence
Two priests face a crisis of faith while searching for their apostate mentor in Japan.

The Apostle
A Pentecostal preacher in the South seeks redemption from his sins.

First Reformed
The dark night of the soul.

Noah
A great flood is coming.

Weber theorized that believers would seek to resolve this uncertainty by leading the kinds of lives they thought God would expect godly people to lead. This meant hard work, humility, and self-denial, not for the sake of salvation or individual gain, but for the sake of God. Although doing so would not earn them salvation, to do otherwise would be an almost certain sign that they were not among the chosen. But they could never fully be sure, so they could never let up in their commitment to do God's will. Thus they worked hard not because they had to (either for subsistence or because they were forced) but because they wanted to in response to the salvation they hoped would come from God. It was precisely this kind of worker, internally motivated to work hard and willing to show up every day even after getting paid, that capitalism needed if it was to engage in rationally planned production. This "spirit of capitalism," to use Weber's phrase, contrasted with the moderate work hours, leisurely work habits, and lack of ambition that Weber saw as typical of traditional labor.

In this way, religion, in the form of the Protestant Reformation, contributed to the rise of capitalism, one of the most significant examples of social change in human history. Weber's argument has been hailed as one of the most important theoretical works in the field and as an excellent example of macrolevel analysis. Like Durkheim, Weber demonstrated that religion is not solely a matter of intimate personal beliefs. He stressed that the collective nature of religion has consequences for society as a whole.

> But the poor person does not exist as an inescapable fact of destiny. . . . The poor are a by-product of the system in which we live and for which we are responsible.
>
> Liberation theologian Gustavo Gutiérrez (1988)

Liberation Theology

A more contemporary example of religion serving as a force for social change came through liberation theology, which has its roots in Latin America in the 1950s and 1960s. Many religious activists, especially Roman Catholic priests, when confronted with the poverty and social injustice of the region, decided the Church had a responsibility to reject the status quo and work actively on behalf of the poor. The term **liberation theology** refers to the use of a church in a political effort to eliminate poverty, discrimination, and other forms of injustice from a secular society. Many felt

> **Liberation theology** Use of a church, primarily Roman Catholic, in a political effort to eliminate poverty, discrimination, and other forms of injustice from a secular society.

Religious Faith and Economic Well-Being

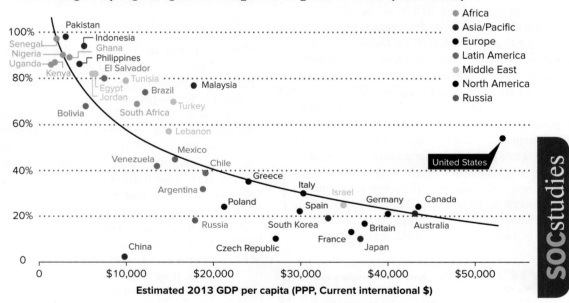

Percentage saying religion an important part of lives (2011–2013)

The curve represents the logarithmic relationship between GDP per capita and the percentage who say that religion plays a very important role in their lives. Notice that the United States is an outlier, falling far from the curve, when it comes to people's continued faith in religion compared to other advanced economies. What factors do you think might contribute to this difference?

Source: Gao 2015.

Mireille Vautier/Alamy Stock Photo

Jesus' teachings about the poor aligned better with the works of Karl Marx than with those of Adam Smith and other European economists and philosophers. They believed that radical social change, rather than economic development in itself, is the only acceptable solution to the desperation of the masses in impoverished developing countries. Activists associated with liberation theology believe that organized religion has a moral responsibility to take a strong public stand against the oppression of the poor, racial and ethnic minorities, and women (Bell 2001; Rowland 2007).

The term *liberation theology* dates back to the publication in 1973 of the English translation of *A Theology of Liberation.* The book was written by a Peruvian priest, Gustavo Gutiérrez, who lived in a slum area of Lima in the early 1960s. After years of exposure to the vast poverty around him, Gutiérrez concluded that "in order to serve the poor, one had to move into political action" (R. M. Brown 1980:23; Gutiérrez 1990). Eventually, politically committed Latin American theologians came under the influence of social scientists who viewed the domination of capitalist multinational corporations as central to the hemisphere's problems. One result was a new approach to theology that built on the cultural and religious traditions of Latin America rather than on models developed in Europe and the United States.

⌐SOCTHINK⌐

To what extent do you think religion can be a force for positive social change? What examples have you seen in your lifetime?

CONFLICT AND SOCIAL CONTROL

Liberation theology is a relatively recent phenomenon that signals a break with the traditional role of Durkheim envisioned for churches—that is, as guarantors of social order and stability. Karl Marx opposed this traditional role of religion, which is in keeping with the conflict perspective he espoused. In his view, religion inhibited positive social change by encouraging oppressed people to focus on otherworldly concerns rather than working in the here-and-now to relieve their immediate poverty or exploitation.

Marx on Religion Marx argued that the study of religion provided an important window into the state of society, calling religion "the sigh of the oppressed creature." Yet, in one of his most famous phrases, he also called religion the "opiate of the masses" ([1843] 1978). He felt that religion often, in essence, drugged the believers into submission by offering a consolation for their harsh lives on earth: the hope of salvation in an ideal afterlife. For example, during the period of slavery in the United States, White masters forbade Blacks to practice native African religions. Instead, they encouraged slaves to adopt Christianity, which taught that obedience would lead to salvation and eternal happiness in the hereafter. Viewed from this perspective, Christianity may have pacified certain slaves and blunted the rage that often fuels rebellion.

For Marx, religion plays an important role in propping up the existing social structure. The values of religion, as already noted, tend to reinforce other social institutions and the social order as a whole. From Marx's perspective, however, religion's promotion of social stability only helps perpetuate patterns of social inequality. According to Marx, the dominant religion reinforces the interests of those in power.

From a Marxist perspective, religion keeps people from seeing their lives and societal conditions in political terms—for example, by obscuring the overriding significance of conflicting economic interests. Marxists suggest that by inducing a "false consciousness" among the disadvantaged, religion lessens the possibility of collective political action that could end capitalist oppression and transform society. Sociological analysis in this tradition seeks to reveal the ways in which religion serves the interests of the powerful at the expense of others.

Gender and Religion Drawing on the feminist approach, researchers and theorists point to the critical role women play in the functioning of religious organizations. Women are more likely than men to say religion is important in their lives, more likely to pray daily, and more likely to attend weekly services. Women also play a vital role as volunteers, staff, and religious educators. Yet when it comes to positions of leadership, women have typically been relegated to a subordinate role. Indeed, most faiths have a long tradition of exclusively male spiritual leadership. Furthermore, because most religions are patriarchal, religious beliefs tend to reinforce men's dominance in secular as well as spiritual matters. Exceptions to this rule, such as the Shakers and Christian Scientists, as well as Hinduism with its long goddess heritage, are relatively rare (Pew Research Center 2009a; Schaefer and Zellner 2007).

In the United States, women compose 17 percent of the clergy, even though they account for 33 percent of students enrolled in theological institutions. Female clerics typically have shorter careers than men and are often relegated to fields that do not involve congregational leadership, such as counseling. In faiths that restrict leadership positions to men, women still serve unofficially. For example, about 4 percent of Roman Catholic congregations are led by women who hold

Photo courtesy of Barb Ashton and Sophie Mathonnet-VanderWell

nonordained pastoral positions—a necessity in a church that faces a shortage of male priests (J. Adams 2007; Association of Theological Schools 2019:Table 2.12B; Bureau of Labor Statistics 2018f:Table 11).

In this chapter we have looked at both education and religion. In both cases we find social institutions that play a powerful role in shaping how we think and act. Each provides opportunity and reinforces the status quo, including its system of inequality. Sociologists believe that by having a better appreciation for both the opportunities and constraints such institutions present, we can better act both individually and collectively to bring about positive social change.

SOCIOLOGY IS A VERB

Exploring Faith

Pick a local religious group that is significantly different from any you may have experienced in the past. Study their history, beliefs, rituals, expectations, and structure. Interview one of their local religious leaders to gain a better understanding of their beliefs and practices from an insider's point of view. If it's okay with them, visit their services at least twice. What were your initial expectations about the group? How, if at all, did your views change?

For REVIEW

I. How does education help maintain social order?
- Education transmits culture, promotes social integration, provides training and social control, stimulates cultural innovation, and provides child care.

II. How does education support the existing system of inequality?
- Education reinforces the status quo, and therefore its existing inequalities, through the hidden curriculum, teacher expectancy, bestowal of status, and credentialism.

III. How do sociologists define religion?
- One approach focuses on the substance of what religion is, defining religion as knowledge and beliefs relating to the sacred realm. The other approach looks at what religions do for society in terms of social order and integration. Both approaches analyze common components including belief, ritual, experience, and community.

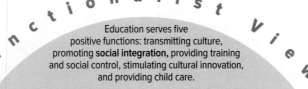

Functionalist View

Education serves five positive functions: transmitting culture, promoting **social integration,** providing training and social control, stimulating cultural innovation, and providing child care.

As societies have become more diverse, education has taken on more of the task of formal **socialization.**

Religion provides **social order,** a sense of **shared identity,** and meaning and purpose in people's lives.

SOCIAL INTEGRATION, SOCIALIZATION, SOCIAL ORDER
KEY CONCEPTS

Conflict View

The education system helps reproduce the existing system of **inequality.**

Unequal funding, **tracking,** the **hidden curriculum,** and **credential-ism** serve to reinforce the status quo.

According to Marx, religion can function like a drug that blinds people to their true interests, prompting them instead to accept **submission to authority,** thereby reinforcing the interests of those in power.

KEY CONCEPTS
INEQUALITY, SUBMISSION TO AUTHORITY

Interactionist View

Students from grade school through graduate school learn formal and informal norms, values, and interpersonal skills through classroom interactions.

A teacher's **expectations** about a student impact on student performance and achievement.

Religious rituals generally involve important **face-to-face interactions** with fellow worshipers at services.

KEY CONCEPTS
EXPECTATIONS, INTERACTIONS

MAKE THE CONNECTION
After reviewing the chapter, answer the following questions:

1
The "Education Pays" graph shows higher income as one benefit of more education. Using each perspective, how else does education pay? Who benefits?

2
How do educational institutions bestow status according to both the functionalist and conflict perspectives?

3
Using the conflict perspective, describe how women experience (or have experienced) discrimination in both the educational and religious spheres.

4
Which perspective do you think best describes the dynamics of a typical classroom setting? Explain, including examples.

Pop Quiz

1. According to Horace Mann, often called the "father of American public education," what role does education play in society?

   a. It is the great equalizer.

   b. It is the opiate of the masses.

   c. It is an instrument for social control.

   d. It is an opportunity engine.

2. Which of the following functions does education fulfill by providing an environment within which we can challenge existing ideas and experiment with new norms and values?

   a. culture transmission

   b. social integration

   c. training and social control

   d. cultural innovation

3. Which of the following terms do conflict theorists Samuel Bowles and Herbert Gintis use in support of their argument that capitalism requires a skilled, disciplined labor force and that the educational system of the United States is structured primarily to provide companies with the number and type of workers they need?

   a. tracking

   b. credentialism

   c. the correspondence principle

   d. the teacher-expectancy effect

4. Fifty years ago, a high school diploma was often enough to get a good job. Today it typically takes a college degree or more. This change reflects the process of

   a. tracking.

   b. credentialism.

   c. the hidden curriculum.

   d. the correspondence principle.

5. Which of the following includes the provision "No person in the United States shall, on the basis of sex, be excluded from participation in, be denied the benefits of, or be subjected to discrimination under any education program or activity receiving Federal financial assistance"?

   a. Title IX of the Education Amendments of 1972

   b. *Brown v. Board of Education of Topeka* (1954)

   c. No Child Left Behind Act of 2001

   d. Higher Education Opportunity Act of 2008

6. The approach to defining religion that emphasizes the significance of the sacred, most often supernatural, realm is known as the

   a. functionalist approach.

   b. conflict approach.

   c. substantive approach.

   d. ecclesia approach.

7. Religious rituals are

   a. statements to which members of a particular religion adhere.

   b. the feelings or perceptions of being in direct contact with the ultimate reality, such as a divine being.

   c. the religious structures through which faith communities organize themselves.

   d. practices required or expected of members of a faith.

8. Which of the following world religions has the most adherents?

   a. Buddhism

   b. Islam

   c. Judaism

   d. Christianity

9. Sociologist Max Weber pointed out that the followers of Martin Luther and John Calvin emphasized a disciplined work ethic, worldly concerns, and a rational orientation to life. Collectively, this point of view has been referred to as

   a. capitalism.

   b. the Protestant ethic.

   c. the sacred.

   d. the profane.

10. The use of a church, primarily Roman Catholic, in a political effort to eliminate poverty, discrimination, and other forms of injustice evident in a secular society is referred to as

    a. creationism.

    b. ritualism.

    c. religious experience.

    d. liberation theology.

1. (a), 2. (d), 3. (c), 4. (b), 5. (a), 6. (c), 7. (d), 8. (d), 9. (b), 10. (d)

Design Elements: *Going Global (Earth):* ©Studio Photogram/Alamy Stock Photo; *Personal Sociology (drawing of author):* McGraw-Hill Education; *5 Movies (popcorn):* ©D. Hurst/Alamy Stock Photo; *Sociology Is a Verb (overlapping hands):* ©Jeff DeWeerd/Imagezoo/Getty Images

Bill Sikes/AP Images

TRUMPED

On November 8, 2016, in an election result that surprised even the winner, Donald Trump defeated Hillary Clinton to become the 45th president of the United States of America. A string of five states—Iowa, Wisconsin, Michigan, Ohio, and Pennsylvania—were decisive in tilting the results in Trump's favor. Democrat Barack Obama won all five in 2012, but in 2016 each flipped its support to the Republican candidate. In seeking an explanation, analysts pointed to the influence of White working-class (WWC) voters (Cohn 2016; Levitz 2016). But what did these voters want? Years before the 2016 election, sociologist Arlie Russell Hochschild (2016) had already been pursuing the answer to that question.

Hochschild had noticed a wide chasm between her sensibilities as a White, politically liberal, upper-middle-class sociology professor living in Berkeley, California, and those of rural, White, politically conservative, working-class Americans. To better understand the world through their eyes, she headed to rural Louisiana, where over the course of five years,

she conducted focus groups, carried out interviews, attended church services, and went to political rallies. She concluded that many attempts at understanding WWC voters, including those focusing narrowly on racism or economic inequality, fall short because they do not address the emotional foundation of WWC political stances.

Most WWC members, according to Hochschild, accept competition as a normal part of life and understand that there will be winners and losers. But they also believe that those who work hard and play by the rules should receive their just reward. In recent years, however, many WWC'ers claimed that their progress toward the American Dream had been blocked by various groups of people they saw as undeserving. Members of such groups broke the rules by cutting in line in front of them. These groups included poor people who receive government assistance, African Americans who benefit from affirmative action, immigrants from Mexico, professionals from India and China, refugees from Syria, and others who the WWC believe receive unearned advantages, often in the form of government help.

To make matters worse, the WWC heard voices from America's cultural elites dismissing them as ignorant, Bible-thumping, White trash rednecks. They felt like strangers in their own land and concluded that the system was rigged. They awaited a champion who would fix things, when along came Donald Trump.

Donald Trump's claim that "We're losing at everything" resonated with their fears about the economy. His pledge to "Make America Great Again" tapped into their hope that things can get better. In Trump, they believed they had found a champion who would restore their honor and ensure their success. And two years into his presidency, they continued to believe. In 2016, 87 percent of Trump voters said they had either "very warm" or "somewhat warm" feelings toward him. By 2018, 82 percent of the same set of voters continued to feel that way (Pew Research Center 2018a).

By drawing on the sociological imagination, Hochschild came to understand her informants' perceptions of reality. Her work represents a classic example of sociology's fundamental commitment to clarifying why people think and act as they do. In this chapter, we explore politics and the economy so that we might know how the positions we occupy within these institutions shape us.

As You READ >>

- **How are economic and political power organized?**
- **How does power operate?**
- **How has the economy changed over time?**

>> Economic Systems

In this chapter we continue to explore the social institutions that form a core part of the social structures we construct. Having already explored family (see Chapter 7), and both education and religion (see Chapter 8), we turn first to economy and then to politics. **Economy** is a social institution dedicated to the production, distribution, and consumption of goods and services. It is in the context of the economy that we provide for our material needs, including food, clothes, and shelter.

Throughout history, people have provided for their needs in varieties of ways, including gift exchange, bartering, and shared ownership of goods. Over time, two economic systems, capitalism and socialism, rose to prominence as dominant ways to organize the supply and distribution of goods and services. Analyzing the characteristics of each allows us to better understand why we think and act as we do.

CAPITALISM

Capitalism is an economic system in which owners of private property compete in the marketplace in pursuit of profit. Value under capitalism is determined based on what people are willing and able to pay for available goods and services. Today, most of us take capitalism for granted. We consider it normal to get a job so that we might earn wages with which we can buy the things we want and need. Yet, relative to the full course of human history, capitalism as we understand it today is a relatively recent invention.

The basic principles of capitalism were laid out in 1776 by Adam Smith in his book *The Wealth of Nations.*

He identified four key concepts: pursuit of profit, competition in the market, the law of supply and demand, and laissez-faire.

- *Pursuit of profit.* One of the basic presuppositions of capitalism is that, in our exchanges with others, human beings naturally seek to get the greatest return on their investments. This extends beyond economic exchanges (i.e., making a financial profit) to include social and cultural exchanges (in which even a conversation represents an exchange of symbolic resources such as status or attention). Under capitalism, humans are seen as naturally competitive, looking out for their own interests above all others. Pursuit of profit is presented as both morally acceptable and socially desirable.

> **Economy** A social institution dedicated to the production, distribution, and consumption of goods and services.
>
> **Capitalism** An economic system in which owners of private property compete in the marketplace in pursuit of profit.

- *Competition in the market.* The marketplace is the context in which we exchange goods and services (such as shoes, cell phones, and college degrees). Producers try to get the most money possible for their products while consumers seek the best deal. Competition keeps prices in check. The marketplace must be open to whoever has the ability to compete so that no individual or firm controls a disproportionate share of the market.

- *Law of supply and demand.* In a competitive marketplace, a natural balance will be reached between production and consumption at the appropriate price. If the demand for a good or service is high and the supply is low, prices will go up, and vice versa. If a producer charges too much, another producer will step in to provide the good or service at a more reasonable price. Adam Smith described this process as the "invisible hand" of the marketplace through which prices reach their natural level. Companies that don't respond to the prompting of the invisible hand—for example, by charging too much or too little—will ultimately go out of business.

- *Laissez-faire.* The expression **laissez-faire** means "let them do [as they please]," and in this context it means that outside entities, especially the government, should not intervene in the marketplace. Instead, the market should be allowed to function free from external influence. Ideally, markets self-correct using the invisible hand. The capitalist model presupposes that, though governments may mean well, they cannot bring about a better result for society as a whole than can individuals who are allowed to compete on their own. In capitalism, the greatest social good is attained through the competition of profit-seeking individuals.

In practice, internal contradictions between these principles inevitably arise. Capitalism needs competition, but capitalists want monopoly. A **monopoly** occurs when a single business firm controls the market. An example might be that only one company produces shoes or jets or aluminum. Establishing a monopoly enables the capitalist to produce more profit because they become the sole supplier of a product. As a result, they can charge whatever they want so long as demand remains. Once a company is large enough, it can use its control over resources to drive smaller companies out of business. This violates the principle of competition in the market.

To ensure that monopolies do not form, governments often respond by intervening in the marketplace to boost competition. Doing so violates the principle of laissez-faire, but is justified as an effort to save capitalism from its own excesses. Examples in U.S. history include the Sherman Anti-Trust Act in 1890, the Federal Reserve System in 1913, New Deal programs in the 1930s to counteract the effects of the Great Depression, and the Troubled Asset Relief Program (TARP) in 2008 in order to save banks and other financial institutions from failing. Governments also intervene in areas deemed important enough for the public good to justify doing so. Examples include police and fire protection, roads, national defense, and public education. The principle behind doing so is that everyone should have a right to these goods and services.

Laissez-faire The principle that people should be able to compete freely, without government interference, in the capitalist marketplace.

Monopoly Control of a market by a single business firm.

Socialism An economic system under which the means of production and distribution are collectively owned.

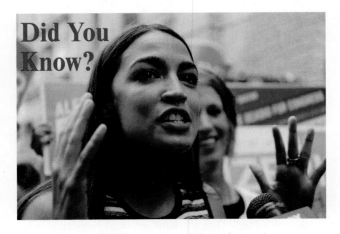

Did You Know?

. . . **Overall, 56 percent of Americans have a positive view of capitalism and 37 percent view socialism positively. Attitudes vary significantly by age. Among 18- to 29-year-olds, 45 percent have a positive view of capitalism compared to 51 percent with positive views toward socialism (Newport 2018).**

Photo: Spencer Platt/Getty Images

SOCIALISM

Socialism is an economic system in which the means of production and distribution in a society are collectively rather than privately owned. Value under socialism is determined by the amount of work it takes to produce products and the use we get out of those products rather than by its value in the market. The basic principles of socialism were laid out by Karl Marx in the middle to late 1800s in a variety of publications, including *The Communist Manifesto,* which he coauthored with Friedrich Engels ([1847] 1955). The following five presuppositions help clarify why he thought socialism would inevitably succeed capitalism.

- *Humans must produce.* Unlike animals, humans lack the complex instincts that determine how we provide for our basic human needs (food, shelter, and clothing) from nature. Therefore, we must meet those basic needs through culture creation and technological innovation. Because humans aren't narrowly constrained by our instincts, how we go about doing so is up to our ingenuity and creativity.
- *Production makes us uniquely human.* Our capacity to produce distinguishes humans from other animals. It is this free and creative productive ability, what Marx referred to as labor power, that must be protected, nourished, and valued because it is at the core of our identity as humans.
- *We pour ourselves into our products.* For Marx, when we make something, we put part of who we are into each product; this is most apparent in craft labor. For example, a handmade bookshelf inspires pride because our labor power is the difference between the original stack of lumber and the finished shelf. To put it in an equation: *Raw materials + Labor power = Products.* According to Marx, we naturally find joy in labor and take pleasure in sharing the process and exchanging the products with others.
- *Economy determines society.* Marx argued that because our capacity and need to produce is at the core of who

we are, it serves as the foundation for society. In essence, how we organize the economy determines all other forms of social relations, such as government, family, education, and religion. In most agrarian societies production is rooted in the land, so ownership and control of land becomes the foundation of power. Social institutions may reinforce the privileged position of landowners, for example, by justifying a king's "divine right" to rule using religious authority. Over time, this material foundation shifts as our capacity to produce evolves through technological innovation. Eventually, the systems of social relations that grew out of that particular set of economic relations no longer match the new economic base, and a revolution to a new set of social relations occurs. Marx contended that this shift brought about the transition from feudalism to capitalism—when the agricultural power base that gave rise to royalty gave way to the industrial power base of capitalists and corporations—and he predicted it will shift again from capitalism to communism.

- *Scarcity and distribution are obstacles to the good of society.* For Marx, the ideal society is one in which we as humans have control over, and reap the full benefits of, our labor power. Until this point in history, however, no large-scale society has fully attained this ideal because we lacked the technological capacity to produce enough for everyone. This has resulted in social systems that divide the haves and have-nots: slavery's separation between masters and slaves, feudalism's separation between lords and peasants, capitalism's separation between owners and workers. Thanks to technological innovation—a consequence of our creative capacity to produce—we can eventually solve the problem of inadequate production. In fact, Marx praised capitalism because it ultimately solves this problem by placing pressure on producers for constant innovation. After we are technically capable of

producing enough for all, any continued poverty, hunger, or extreme inequality is due to how we choose to distribute the products we make, rather than to our inability to produce enough. In other words, it's a social problem, solvable by the establishment of a new set of social relations that ensures equitable distribution. According to Marx, people will eventually decide that it doesn't make sense to maintain such economic extremes in the face of material abundance; thus a revolution in social relations toward socialism is inevitable.

In practice, the socialist ideal of collective ownership has been difficult to attain. The grand experiment in what was known as the Soviet Union—uniting Russia and neighboring countries as one large socialist bloc—ultimately collapsed in 1989. It did so under the weight of bureaucratic inefficiency, political corruption, and insufficient productivity—problems that seem endemic to socialist states. In addition, past crackdowns on dissidents by the totalitarian socialist governments in both the Soviet Union and communist China led to the murders of millions of their own people, purportedly for the good of the state. Surveys in most of the former Soviet-bloc nations showed that people there approved of the transition from socialism toward democracy and free markets (Pew Research Center 2009b).

MIXED ECONOMIES

In practice, no societies conform to the ideal principles of either capitalism or socialism. It might instead be best to think of capitalism and socialism as two ends of a continuum. A **mixed economy** combines elements of both capitalism and socialism. Starting from a socialist ideal and moving toward a mixed economy involves opening up some aspects of the state-controlled economy to competition and the free market. Both Russia and China made this move by incorporating elements of privatization and capitalism into their socialist economic systems. China's reforms began in 1978 under Premier Deng Xiaoping in pursuit of greater economic productivity. Reforms began in agriculture with the division of collectively owned public lands into private plots. This change established a precedent for privatizing other sectors of the economy. As a result, China became one of the world's fastest-growing and most powerful economies.

> **Mixed economy** An economic system that combines elements of both capitalism and socialism.

In the United States, there has long been a debate about the degree to which the government should be involved in the economy, but the economic upheaval of 2008's Great Recession challenged people's commitment to laissez-faire principles. Government officials decided that some companies were "too big to fail," meaning that the domino effect of their failure would be greater than the cost of violating the

Li Keqiang assumed office as premier of the People's Republic of China in 2013. Feng Li - Pool/Getty Images

International Economic Growth, 1980–2017

SOCTHINK

Should the U.S. government let companies fail regardless of apparent economic consequences?

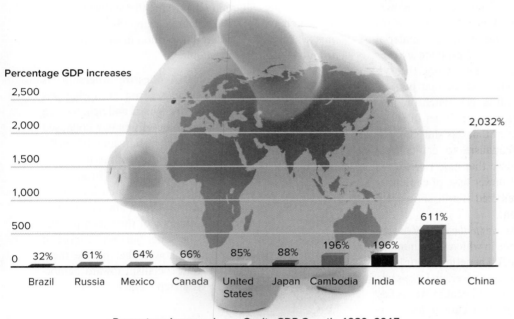

Percentage GDP increases

2,500	
2,000	
1,500	
1,000	
500	
0	

Brazil	Russia	Mexico	Canada	United States	Japan	Cambodia	India	Korea	China
32%	61%	64%	66%	85%	88%	196%	196%	611%	2,032%

Percentage Increase in per Capita GDP Growth, 1980–2017

Source: U.S. Department of Agriculture 2018. *Photo:* Amanda Rhode/E+/Getty Images

nonintervention ideal. The George W. Bush administration, itself a strong proponent of free-market principles, took the first steps toward government intervention in the economy during this crisis. In September 2008 it pushed the Troubled Assets Relief Program (TARP) through Congress to provide up to $700 billion to buy mortgage-backed securities and to prop up the financial sector. The Obama administration continued along the same lines. For example, in an effort to kick-start the U.S. economy, Congress passed the American Recovery and Reinvestment Act in February 2009, providing almost $800 billion for infrastructure projects, education and health care funding, and tax cuts. And in June 2009, General Motors, which for years was the world's largest company, went bankrupt. The U.S. government stepped in and became its majority stockholder, owning 60 percent of its shares. These funds helped many firms survive that otherwise would have failed. Now that they are back on their feet, companies have paid back the loans they received from the government. For example, General Motors paid back its $8.4 billion of government loans in full, with interest, and five years early. In 2013,

the U.S. Department of Treasury sold off the last of its remaining shares of GM stock.

Though critics charged that Presidents Bush and Obama were moving the nation toward socialism, most people hoped that their efforts would minimize the negative effects the economic downturn had on their lives. The majority of citizens ultimately accepted these huge government expenditures as a means to save capitalism from its own excesses. Billionaire investor Warren Buffett later reflected on the government intervention and concluded, "Only one counterforce was available, and that was you, Uncle Sam. . . . Well, Uncle Sam, you delivered" (Buffett 2010).

>> Economic Change

Whether in the form of capitalism or socialism, modern economies arose as a consequence of human economic adaptations over time. From our earliest hunting-and-gathering societies to the global economy of the present, humans have continued to find new ways to provide for our needs. The ripple effects from such innovation fundamentally altered, and continue to alter, our relationship to nature and with each other.

ECONOMIC SECTORS AND TECHNOLOGICAL INNOVATION

Throughout most of human history, labor focused primarily on ensuring that our basic needs get met. Technological innovation, especially tied to the Industrial Revolution, freed people up to focus on other kinds of work. Sociologists highlight three particular sectors of the economy to illustrate this shift: the primary sector focuses on extraction, the secondary sector emphasizes transformation, and the tertiary sector centers on services.

> Nowadays people know the price of everything and the value of nothing.
>
> Oscar Wilde (1890)

As a species, we must provide for our subsistence needs. Without food, clothes, and shelter we will die. Humans have always ensured our survival by taking from nature the things that we need. The **primary sector** of the economy involves activities that extract products directly from the natural environment. The most important manifestation of this sector for us historically was the rise of agriculture, but extraction also includes activities such as fishing, hunting, forestry, and mining. The economies of the hunting-and-gathering, horticultural, and agrarian societies we encountered in the "Technology and Society" section of Chapter 5 were characterized primarily by this economic sector.

The Industrial Revolution fundamentally altered our relationship to nature. Advances in technology, including Eli Whitney's cotton gin, Cyrus McCormick's mechanical reaper, and John Deere's steel plow, all contributed to the mass production of agricultural products. As a result, fewer agricultural workers were needed to produce food, freeing them up for work in the new factories that arose due to technological innovations in industrial production. The **secondary sector** of the economy consists of activities that transform raw or intermediate materials into finished products. Workers in this sector manufacture products. The mechanization of production contributed to revolutions in transportation and communication, which effectively made the world a much smaller place. It became possible to communicate in real time with whomever we wanted, whenever we wanted, or to travel to the other side of the globe in a matter of hours. As a result, companies can now obtain raw materials from almost anywhere, transform them into products, and sell those products to customers around the world.

Technological innovation continued to the point where industrial production also became less labor intensive. The mechanization of production meant that fewer workers were needed in manufacturing, once again freeing them up for new jobs that contributed to the expansion of a third economic sector. The **tertiary sector** of the economy consists of activities that provide services rather than produce tangible goods. Put simply, the service sector involves doing things for others rather than offering them a material product. Service-sector occupations include teacher, physician, social worker, food server, hotel housekeeper, truck driver, data processor, financial adviser, investment counselor, insurance agent, real estate broker, custodian, actor, personal trainer, life coach, and more (U.S. Census Bureau 2013a). Most college students today are pursuing degrees in hopes of obtaining a good job in this sector.

> **Primary sector** The segment of the economy involving activities that extract products directly from the natural environment.
>
> **Secondary sector** The segment of the economy consisting of activities that transform raw or intermediate materials into finished products.
>
> **Tertiary sector** The segment of the economy consisting of activities that provide services rather than produce tangible goods.

ECONOMIC GLOBALIZATION

When a society's economic foundation transitions from one economic sector to another, significant upheaval occurs. Throughout most of human history, economic exchanges happened primarily within a community or between neighboring communities. Technological innovations, such as those in transportation and communication, opened up wide-ranging possibilities for trade. It became possible to sell products to people across the continent or on the other side of the world.

The development of capitalism further encouraged such expansion. Karl Marx, for example, praised capitalism for the impressive technological innovations it helped produce. Of capitalism, he writes, "It has been the first to show what man's activity can bring about. It has accomplished wonders far surpassing Egyptian pyramids, Roman aqueducts, and Gothic cathedrals" (Marx [1848] 1998:38).

As examples of some innovations that arose as a consequence of capitalism, Marx writes, "The bourgeoisie . . . has created more massive and more colossal productive forces than have all preceding generations together. Subjection of nature's forces to man, machinery, application of chemistry to industry and agriculture, steam navigation, railways, electric telegraphs, clearing of whole continents for cultivation of rivers, whole populations conjured out of the ground–what earlier century had even a presentiment that such productive forces slumbered in the lap of social labor?" (Marx [1848] 1998: 40–41). Marx wrote that in 1848. One can only imagine what he might say of the technological accomplishments that have occurred since then.

Such economic change cannot help but have significant effects on our social relations. The economy shifted from being primarily agricultural to industrial. Communities transformed from primarily rural to urban. Politics switched from being mostly local to national and then international. In a word, economic

5 Movies on THE ECONOMY

Les Misérables
A decent man in a time of economic and political crisis.

American Winter
The Great Recession hits home.

Killing Them Softly
A parable about financial crisis and economic collapse.

The Big Short
Investing in failure and winning big.

The Price of Everything
Art as value versus the value of art.

Deindustrialization had a profound impact on communities, such as Detroit, where factories closed, businesses shut down, and whole neighborhoods were abandoned.   Josh Cornish/Shutterstock

globalization altered how people worked, lived, governed, and more. Once this transformation took place, responding to changing economic conditions far beyond the local sphere became the norm. And we continue to live in that world.

The United States, along with other countries, experienced a similar disruption starting in the 1970s when the economy shifted emphasis from the secondary sector, with its emphasis on manufacturing, to the tertiary sector, with its emphasis on services. **Deindustrialization** played a major role in this transition, which refers to the systematic and widespread reduction of investment in domestic manufacturing and material production. This transformation hit the Northeast and Midwest parts of the United States particularly hard. Cities such as Pittsburgh, Pennsylvania, Detroit, Michigan, and Gary, Indiana, along with many others that served as centers for many factories that provided blue-collar workers with good paying jobs in industries such as automobile and steel production, saw jobs disappear as factories shut down (Bluestone and Harrison 1982; Goldstein 2017).

Two principal factors played critical roles in the expansion of deindustrialization. The first involved the mechanization of labor. Through technological innovation, a single machine can do the job of many workers. The coordination of production in the form of the assembly line multiplied that effect, and the advent of robots and computers expanded it even further. Economist John Maynard Keynes (1930a, 1930b) referred to the resulting loss of jobs as "technological unemployment." In such a situation, productivity can remain high

Deindustrialization The systematic and widespread reduction of investment in domestic manufacturing and material production.

Offshoring Outsourcing of work to foreign contractors.

Downsizing Organizational restructuring to reduce the size of a company's workforce.

while the number of secondary-sector manufacturing jobs, along with their level of wages, declines (Carr 2014; Rotman 2013; Smith and Anderson 2014).

The second factor facilitating deindustrialization involves the globalization of labor. In the United States, this began with companies moving their industrial production plants from the nation's central cities to the suburbs, then to the South where labor laws were weaker, and finally out of the country to places such as Mexico and China where wages were lower and health, safety, and environmental regulations were less restrictive. One form this takes is known as **offshoring,** which involves outsourcing work to foreign contractors. This practice hit the manufacturing sector first, as happened when U.S. television companies contracted with Chinese manufacturing firms to produce their TVs. But it is increasingly affecting service-sector jobs as well, due to advanced telecommunications and the growth of skilled, English-speaking workers in developing nations that have relatively inexpensive labor forces. These jobs can require considerable training, such as accounting and financial analysis, computer programming, or radiology. Today, it is increasingly possible that the person reading your CT scan or MRI is located in another country (Clark, Huckman, and Staats 2013; Olofsson et al. 2014).

In addition to the mechanization and globalization of labor, companies also engage in restructuring. They do so in pursuit of greater profitability, even if that comes at the expense of their workforce. One approach to doing so involves **downsizing,** organizational restructuring to reduce the size of a company's workforce. The goal of downsizing is to increase efficiency and reduce costs in the face of worldwide competition. The term *right-sizing* often gets used to justify this move in which job responsibilities get collapsed from two or more workers or divisions into one. Another approach companies use involves outsourcing. For example, companies subcontract, meaning they hire an external firm to cover jobs, such as security or janitorial services, that used to be

SOCTHINK

If you were the CEO of an American manufacturing company that was facing declining profits because of international competition, what would you do? Would you move your production facilities overseas to reduce labor costs? What other options might exist? To what extent does the system within which companies operate shape the choices that are available to them?

performed by employees inside the firm. Companies do so primarily because it saves them money. The people working those jobs typically earn significantly less than was earned by the in-house employees they replaced.

The development of economic globalization carried with it risks. Because the entire economic system involves links between financial institutions, multinational corporations, and national governments around the world, changes in one part of the system can have a domino effect throughout the economic global network. That is precisely what happened starting in 2007 when the global financial crisis that led to what is often referred to as the Great Recession occurred.

The recession hit workers hard. Unemployment became a widespread problem. Rates more than doubled from February 2008 to October 2010 and did not return to their pre-recession levels until late 2016. On top of that, increasing numbers of people experienced long-term unemployment (Pew Charitable Trusts 2012). Among those who were working, wages were flat for most and fell for many. Average family income fell 17.4 percent from 2007 to 2009, the largest two-year decline since the Great Depression (Saez 2016).

For many people, the bad news didn't end there. In the years following the Great Recession, the number of people who were working yet not earning enough to get out of poverty increased (Smiley and West 2012), as did the age at which people could expect to retire (Brandon 2012). Since then, conditions have improved. Average family incomes rose 13 percent from 2009 to 2015. But not everyone shared the benefits of a stronger economy. The number of jobs requiring more education, training, and experience has grown faster than the number requiring less, and wages for jobs requiring higher social and analytical skills have risen faster than for those requiring physical skills. Income for the top 1 percent of the population grew 37.4 percent, while the bottom 99 percent saw only a 7.6 percent increase (Pew Research Center 2016c; Saez 2016). Corporations also did well, earning record profits in part because they reduced their costs by cutting their workforce and expecting more productivity from their remaining employees (Tully 2012).

SOCTHINK

What role have larger economic trends, such as rising and falling unemployment rates, had on you, your friends, and family? How might current economic trends affect your plans for the future?

>> Political Systems

Just as new economic systems developed in response to broader historical changes, political systems also adapted. In all societies, someone or some group—whether it be a tribal chief, a dictator, a council, or a parliament—makes important decisions about how to use resources and allocate goods. Inevitably, the struggle for power and authority involves **politics,** the competition between individuals or groups over the allocation of valued resources. Sociologists use the term **polity** to describe the social institution that establishes and enforces rules within a society and negotiates relationships with other societies. Polity functions to maintain internal order primarily through policing and the courts. It also provides for diplomatic relations, including peace treaties, trade laws, declarations of war, and the like with external entities such as other nations.

Government represents an institutionalized form of authority. Given the responsibilities governments have for establishing and enforcing laws and the scope of international relations and the globalization of national economies, these formal systems of authority make a significant number of critical political decisions. Such systems take a variety of forms, including monarchy, oligarchy, dictatorship, totalitarianism, and democracy.

MONARCHY

A **monarchy** is a form of government headed by a single member of a royal family, usually a king, queen, or some other hereditary ruler. In earlier times, many monarchs claimed that God had granted them a divine right to rule.

Politics The competition between individuals or groups over the allocation of valued resources.

Polity The social institution that establishes and enforces rules within a society and negotiates relationships with other societies.

Monarchy A form of government headed by a single member of a royal family, usually a king, queen, or some other hereditary ruler.

Did You Know?

. . . One of Queen Elizabeth's official duties is to appoint the prime minister. Given that political power rests with Parliament, however, this too has become largely a ceremonial duty.

Photo: Peter Macdiarmid/Getty Images

Typically, they governed on the basis of tradition, sometimes accompanied by the use of force. By the beginning of the 21st century, however, relatively few monarchs held genuine political power. Queen Elizabeth II in England, for example, serves primarily in a ceremonial capacity.

OLIGARCHY

An **oligarchy** is a form of government in which a few individuals rule. A venerable method of governing that flourished in ancient Greece and Egypt, oligarchy now often takes the form of military rule. In developing nations in Africa, Asia, and Latin America, small factions of military officers may forcibly seize power, either from legally elected regimes or from other military cliques (Michels [1915] 1949).

> **Oligarchy** A form of government in which a few individuals rule.
>
> **Dictatorship** A government in which one person has nearly total power to make and enforce laws.
>
> **Totalitarianism** Virtually complete government control and surveillance over all aspects of a society's social and political life.
>
> **Democracy** In a literal sense, government by the people.

Strictly speaking, the term *oligarchy* is reserved for governments that are run by a few selected individuals. However, the People's Republic of China can be classified as an oligarchy if we stretch the meaning of the term. In China, power rests in the hands of a large but exclusive ruling *group,* the Communist Party. In a similar vein, we might argue that many industrialized nations of the West should be considered oligarchies (rather than democracies), because only a powerful few—leaders of big business, government, and the military—actually rule. Later in this chapter, we examine the "elite model" of the U.S. political system in greater detail.

DICTATORSHIP AND TOTALITARIANISM

A **dictatorship** is a government in which one person has nearly total power to make and enforce laws. Dictators rule primarily through the use of force, which often includes imprisonment, torture, and executions. Typically, they seize power rather than being freely elected (as in a democracy) or inheriting power (as in a monarchy). Some dictators rely on their charisma to win people over, although their supporters' enthusiasm is frequently tinged with fear. Dictators who rely primarily on force are often bitterly hated by their people.

Frequently, dictators develop such overwhelming control over people's lives that their governments are called totalitarian. (Monarchies and oligarchies may also achieve this type of dominance.) **Totalitarianism** involves virtually complete government control and surveillance over all aspects of a society's social and political life. Totalitarian regimes typically have an all-encompassing ideology which elevates their version of truth over and

against all others, a strong leader who demands adherence to the party line, and the power to enforce their rule through persuasion, propaganda, and violence if necessary. Germany during Hitler's reign, the Soviet Union under Stalin in the 1930s, and North Korea today are classified as totalitarian states (Arendt 1951; Friedrich and Brzezinski 1956).

Sudan president Omar al-Bashir is widely considered an authoritarian dictator by the international community.
Ashraf Shazly/AFP/Getty Images

DEMOCRACY

In a literal sense, **democracy** means government by the people. The word comes from two Greek roots—*demos,* meaning "the populace" or "the common people," and *kratia,* meaning "rule." In a democracy, power is not vested in a particular person or position. Individual citizens provide the foundation for political authority, and the underlying principle of power is "one person, one vote." This principle implies that, in theory at least, everyone has equal power when it comes to decision making.

Direct democracy, in which all citizens vote on all major decisions and the most votes win, provides democracy's purest form. In large, populous nations such as the

---

SOCTHINK

Early in his presidency, expressing a sentiment shared by some of his predecessors, George W. Bush joked that when it came to working with Congress, "a dictatorship would be a heck of a lot easier." In what ways is the U.S. system of government intentionally inefficient? Why might that be intentional?

United States, direct democracy is impractical at the national level. All Americans cannot vote on every important issue. Consequently, popular rule occurs in the form of **representative democracy,** a system of government in which citizens elect political leaders to make decisions on behalf of the people.

The way representatives are chosen can vary, and the system used to select them influences the kind of politics we get. For example, the two-party system that dominates in the United States is a consequence, in part, of how legislators are selected. To select members to the House of Representatives, the country is divided into 435 geographically distinct congressional districts. Each district has a single seat. Elections are held within each, and the winner becomes the representative for that district. As a result of this winner-take-all system, candidates have an incentive to appeal to a majority of voters, which tends to result in the creation of two parties, each vying to gain that majority. The United States has numerous "third parties." In 2016, for example, Gary Johnson was on the ballot for Libertarian Party, and Jill Stein ran for the Green Party. But the winner-take-all system makes it difficult for a minority party to break through to win a majority of votes, especially against the entrenched power and influence of the two major parties. For example, in 2016, all the third-party candidates together received 7.8 million votes, or 5.7 percent of the total.

An alternative system for selecting legislators involves proportional representation, some form of which exists

Source: National Archives and Records Administration

in Brazil, Israel, the Netherlands, and South Africa. In such cases, a single district can be represented by multiple seats, and winners are determined based on the percentage of votes received in that district. For example, if a party receives 15 percent of the vote, that party would receive approximately 15 percent of the legislative seats. In such a system, parties that might never be able to win a majority of votes can still win seats in the legislature. In addition, the likelihood that a single party secures a majority of seats declines. As a result, parties often need to work together to create a ruling coalition, which has the effect of giving those minority parties more power than they might otherwise have.

If citizens in a democracy are unhappy with the current direction of things, they can vote to establish new policies or elect new leaders. Over time, significant changes in policy can occur in response to the changing will of the people. For example, early on in U.S. history, the "self-evident" truth that everyone was created equal and endowed with unalienable rights applied only to White, property-holding men. Slowly the definition of who counts as a citizen expanded to include others. Debates about who should count as a citizen in the United States continue to this day as evidenced, for example, in arguments regarding the rights of children or immigrants.

> **Representative democracy** A system of government in which citizens elect political leaders to make decisions on behalf of the people.

SOCTHINK

The United States is commonly classified as a representative democracy because the elected members of Congress and state legislatures make our laws. However, critics have questioned how representative our democracy really is. Do Congress and the state legislatures genuinely represent the masses? Are the people of the United States legitimately self-governing, or has our government become a forum for powerful elites?

A record number of women were elected to Congress in the 2018 midterms. Tom Williams/CQ Roll Call/Getty Images

>> Power and Authority

In the domains of both the economy and politics, power matters. And sociologists have always been interested in how power is achieved and maintained. In the midst of major political and economic shifts, early sociologists developed theories of power intended to be sufficiently broad to explain the expansion of market-based capitalism or the rise of democracy yet sufficiently narrow to explain who gets their way within interpersonal relationships.

POWER

According to Max Weber, **power** is the ability to exercise one's will over others, even if they resist. To put it another way, if you can get others to do what you want them to do even if they don't want to—whether that is to go to war, coordinate a business meeting, clean their room, or even take an exam—you have power. Power relations can involve large organizations, small groups, or even people in intimate relationships.

Weber conceived of power as a continuum based on the extent to which it is accepted as legitimate by those over whom it is exercised. On one end is **force,** the actual or threatened use of coercion to impose one's will on others. When leaders imprison or execute political dissidents, they are applying force; so, too, are terrorists when they seize or bomb an embassy or assassinate a political leader. Slave-based economies typically rely on force. Such systems are not terribly efficient because of the policing costs necessary to make people do what they do not want to do.

On the other end of the continuum is what Weber calls **authority,** power that is recognized as legitimate by the people over whom it is exercised. This type of power depends on people's faith in their leader's right to rule. In a democracy, for example, the fact that people continue to obey the laws even if their candidate loses an election demonstrates their underlying faith in the legitimacy of the system. The presidential election in 2016 tested that faith when Hillary Clinton received 2,864,974 more votes nationally than did Donald Trump, yet Trump won the election.

This outcome was possible because in the U.S. system, Trump received more electoral votes, and those are the votes that determine who wins. By edging out Clinton in Wisconsin by 0.7 percent, Michigan by 0.2 percent, and Pennsylvania by 0.7 percent, based on their winner-take-all allocation of electoral votes, Trump received enough electoral votes to win even though more individuals voted for Clinton nationally (Wasserman 2016). People's willingness to accept that result depends completely on their faith in the legitimacy of the electoral system in place. Weber views authority as more efficient than force because the motivation to obey comes from inside the follower rather than having to be externally imposed.

TYPES OF AUTHORITY

In order to better understand the ways in which authority operates in practice, Weber identified three major types: traditional, charismatic, and rational-legal. Often, the legitimacy of leaders depends primarily upon only one, although elements of all three can be present at the same time.

Traditional Authority In a political or economic system based on **traditional authority,** legitimate power is conferred by custom and accepted practice. In other words, past practice justifies our present actions. As Weber put it, such authority rests in the belief that "everyday routine [provides] an inviolable norm of conduct" ([1922] 1958d:296). We do things the way we do because we have always done them that way. The emperor, queen, or tribal leader may be loved or hated, competent or destructive; in terms of legitimacy, that does not matter. For the traditional leader, authority depends on people's faith in custom, not in the leader's personal appeal, technical competence, or even written law. In England, for example, the

---

Power The ability to exercise one's will over others even if they resist.

Force The actual or threatened use of coercion to impose one's will on others.

Authority Power that is recognized as legitimate by the people over whom it is exercised.

Traditional authority Legitimate power conferred by custom and accepted practice.

Personal Sociology
Because I Said So

I am astonished at how often my daughters, Emily and Eleanor, do what I ask. When they were little, if they disobeyed, they had to "sit in the green chair." It wasn't much of a punishment. The chair was located in our living room in full view of the television and not isolated from the rest of the family. In time, just the threat of having to sit there was enough. Eventually they simply accepted the traditional authority of "because I said so" as sufficient justification. Of course, as they grew, they began to question the legitimacy of my authority, seeking reasons for why they should obey. As a result, I often came up with rational justifications for why they should do or not do something. And yet, even now, they are usually willing to do as I say simply because I am their dad.

right of kings and queens to rule, which people believed was ordained by God, went largely unquestioned for hundreds of years. Now, however, the power of royals to make policy has largely passed to Parliament, and the role of the Royal Family is largely ceremonial.

Charismatic Authority According to Weber's second type of authority, power can be legitimized by the charisma of an individual. **Charismatic authority** refers to power made legitimate by a leader's exceptional personal or emotional appeal to his or her followers. For example, Joan of Arc was a simple peasant girl in medieval France. Because people believed in her and the causes she represented, she was able to rally the French people and lead them into major battles against English invaders despite having no formally recognized position of power.

Charisma lets a person such as Joan of Arc lead without relying on set rules or traditions. In fact, charismatic authority is derived more from the beliefs of followers than from the actual qualities of leaders. So long as people perceive a charismatic leader such as Jesus, Joan of Arc, Mahatma Gandhi, Malcolm X, or Martin Luther King, Jr., as having qualities that set them apart from ordinary citizens, that leader's authority will remain secure and often unquestioned (Adair-Toteff 2005; Potts 2009). That unfortunately is also the case with malevolent figures such as Adolf Hitler, whose charismatic appeal turned people toward violent and destructive ends in Nazi Germany.

Religious and political leaders often rely on charismatic authority. For both, the power of persuasion and the ability to charm can be important assets. Religious leaders, for example, often make the bold claim that they speak on behalf of higher spiritual powers, such as gods and goddesses. They frequently call followers to make sacrifices in terms of time and money and, in extreme cases, even death. Political leaders, especially in democratic societies where they must persuade citizens to vote for them, rely on their ability to inspire. As we saw at the beginning of this chapter, a critical dimension of Donald Trump's success with White, working-class voters was his capacity to inspire hope.

Did You Know?

. . . In 2018, for the eleventh consecutive year, Americans identified Barack Obama as the most admired man in America. They chose Michelle Obama as the most admired woman. In second place they selected Donald Trump and Oprah Winfrey.

Source: Jones 2018b. *Photo:* Ron Sachs Pool/Getty Images

Rational-Legal Authority Weber's third type of authority, **rational-legal authority,** involves formally agreed-on and accepted rules, principles, and procedures of conduct that are established to accomplish goals in the most efficient manner possible. Bureaucracies are the purest form of rational-legal authority. As we saw in the "Bureaucracy" section of Chapter 5, in a bureaucracy there's a hierarchy of authority, areas of expertise are clearly defined, rules and regulations guide decision making, people are judged based on their performance, and hiring

People's faith in Mahatma Gandhi as a charismatic leader contributed to India's independence from Britain in 1947. Elliot & Fry/Hulton Archive/Getty Images

Charismatic authority Power made legitimate by a leader's exceptional personal or emotional appeal to his or her followers.

Rational-legal authority Authority based on formally agreed-upon and accepted rules, principles, and procedures of conduct that are established in order to accomplish goals in the most efficient manner possible.

occurs based on competence. Under rational-legal authority, if something occurs for which there are no guidelines indicating how to proceed, new rules will be created to cover how to act should it happen again. As a result, rules and regulations expand, and these systems tend to get bigger and bigger. This leads to concerns about inefficiencies, dehumanization, and dysfunction.

—SOCTHINK—

Which of these three forms of power do parents, bosses, or professors most rely on? Do individuals in these groups sometimes use each of the three types of power?

Analyzing power using Weber's model focuses our attention in a way that allows us to better understand economic and political relationships. The degree to which we accept the legitimacy of the people who rule over us shapes the kind of power they are likely to use. For example, when police confronted civil rights protestors in the 1950s and 1960s, they sometimes used force. Protestors were made to do things that they did not otherwise want to do, and failure to do so resulted in physical injury and jail time for some of those who questioned the legitimacy of the current system. Yet the presupposition that police and political leaders had the legitimate right to act in this way was widespread. As Weber suggested, when the legitimacy to rule is internalized in the form of authority, most people will comply with the wishes of the leader and will expect others to do likewise.

5 Movies on POLITICS

RBG
The notorious Ruth Bader Ginsburg.

The Post
The president, the press, and the people.

Cold War
Finding love in troubled times.

Weiner
A political campaign on a crash course with destruction.

Eye in the Sky
The dilemma of drone warfare in an age of terrorism.

BALANCING ECONOMIC AND POLITICAL POWER

Even though the economy and polity represent two distinct institutions, they overlap and interact in practice. Power in one can influence, both positively or negatively, power in the other. And, in the United States, the values at the heart of each can conflict, resulting in debates about which set of values should take precedence.

Inherent Tensions between Capitalism and Democracy An inherent tension exists between capitalism and democracy in the United States. On the one hand, capitalism presumes the principle of *competition*. In capitalism, individuals compete in the marketplace to sell the most products or get the best deals, always looking out for their own best interests. This competition produces an inevitable economic hierarchy between those who are more or less successful. To put it simply, inequality rests at the heart of capitalism.

On the other hand, at democracy's core we find the principle of *equality*. Democracy presumes the fundamental sameness of individuals. This gets expressed, for example, in the notion of the human dignity of all persons, regardless of their economic position. The democratic commitment to one-person, one-vote highlights the importance of this ideal. A democratic government has the responsibility of ensuring that people's individual rights are secured.

Economist Arthur Okun (1975) explored the tension between capitalism and democracy in detail. He suggested that "capitalist democracy" represents something of an oxymoron. On the one hand capitalism generates "gaping disparities in economic well-being," while on the other hand, democracy presumes "an egalitarian political and social system" (1975:1). Yet he argued that this tension had the potential to produce positive results, so long as a healthy balance was maintained. Capitalism represented an efficient way to distribute goods and services, and democracy provided an egalitarian way to govern society. According to Okun, "Capitalism and democracy are really a most improbable mixture. Maybe that is why they need each other—to put some rationality into equality and some humanity into efficiency" (1975:116). Managing this tension helps explain why the United States can best be described as having a mixed economy.

The simultaneous adherence to these two principles produces social policies that go back and forth over time, sometimes privileging the competition of capitalism and other times the equality of democracy. Leading up to the 2018 midterm elections, for example, conservative Republicans advocated strongly in favor of lower taxes and substantial cuts in federal funding for social welfare programs. They did so based on the presupposition that competition in the marketplace would lead to the greatest social good. Liberal Democrats, on the other hand, advocated in favor of higher taxes on the wealthy and a stronger social support safety net. They did so based on the presupposition that a democratic nation has a responsibility to secure a basic level of equality for its citizens.

Citizenship Rights Another way to explore the inherent tensions between democracy and capitalism looks more closely at the consequences a commitment to rights might have within capitalism. Citizenship rights involve more than just the right to vote. Sociologist T. H. Marshall (1950) identified three categories of such rights, including civil rights, political rights, and social rights:

- *Civil rights.* These citizenship rights protect individual freedoms. We find some of them articulated in the Bill of Rights, the first 10 amendments to the U.S. Constitution. Included are protections such as freedom of speech, freedom of assembly, the right to bear arms, and freedom of religion.
- *Political rights.* These ensure the right to full participation in the political process. In principle, any citizen can be involved in politics by voting or running for office. But universal political participation wasn't always guaranteed. The 15th Amendment to the U.S. Constitution extended political rights to African Americans in 1870 and the 19th Amendment secured those rights for women in 1920.
- *Social rights.* These rights provide for our welfare and security. They are based on the presupposition that a minimum standard of living is necessary to ensure the ability of all to exercise their civil and political rights. To secure these rights, some goods and services—such as public education or police and fire protection—are taken out of the marketplace, ensuring that everyone has at least a minimum amount of access regardless of their ability to pay. Substantial debates exist over the role government should play in ensuring access to basic material and social and cultural resources.

Debates over civil and political rights in the United States are largely settled, though debates about voting rights for convicted felons continue. Political conflict continues, however, over social rights. Whether or not to guarantee health care coverage to all, for example, represents

perhaps the most hotly debated recent example. At its core, this debate is about the relative emphasis on the competitive principles inherent in capitalism versus the egalitarian principles at the heart of democracy.

THE POWER STRUCTURE IN THE UNITED STATES

Over the years, sociologists repeatedly have sought to discover who really holds power in the United States. Do "we the people" genuinely run the country through our elected representatives? Or does a small elite behind the scenes control both the government and the economic system? In exploring these questions, social scientists have developed two basic models of the U.S. power structure: political pluralism versus the power elite.

The Pluralist Model According to the pluralist approach, power is widely dispersed throughout society. Though some groups may have more power in certain areas at particular times, there is no core group at the top that is able to consistently advance its interests at the expense of others. According to this **pluralist model,** many competing groups have access to government so that no single group is dominant.

To support their claims, advocates of the pluralist model point to data gathered from intensive case studies of communities collected using observation research. One of the most famous—an investigation of decision making in New Haven, Connecticut— was reported by Robert Dahl (1961). Dahl found that, although the number of people involved in any important decision was rather small, community power was nonetheless diffuse. Few political actors exercised decision-making power on all issues, and no one group got its way all the time. One individual or group might be influential in a battle over urban renewal but have little effect on educational policy.

> **Pluralist model** A view of society in which many competing groups within the community have access to government so that no single group is dominant.

Historically, pluralists have stressed ways in which large numbers of people can participate in or influence governmental decision making. Communications technologies, such as Facebook and Twitter, have increased the opportunity to be heard, not just in countries such as the United States but in developing countries the world over. The ability to communicate with political leaders via email, for example, increases the opportunity for the average citizen to have a voice in politics.

The pluralist model has its critics. Sociologist G. William Domhoff (1978, 2014) reexamined Dahl's study of decision making in New Haven and argued that Dahl and other pluralists had failed to trace how local elites who were prominent in decision making belonged to a larger national ruling class. In addition, studies of community power, such as Dahl's work in New Haven, can

SOCTHINK

To what extent do you think that the principles of political equality and economic competition are at odds with each other in the United States?

Public Trust in Government

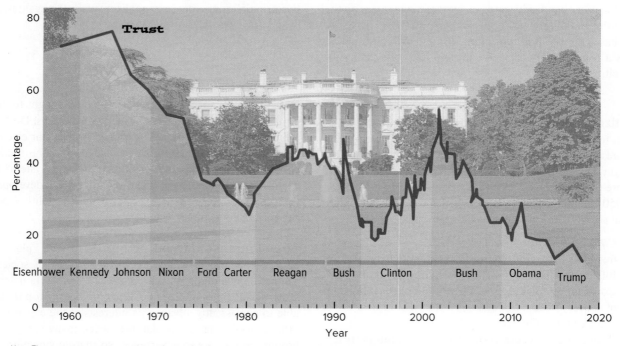

Note: The percentage represents those who say they "can trust the government in Washington to do what is right" either "just about always" or "most of the time."
Source: Pew Research Center 2017b. **Photo:** Digital Vision/PunchStock

---

alternative model of how power functions. Consistent with the conflict perspective, power elite models trace their roots back to Karl Marx, who believed that representative democracy contributed to a shared false consciousness by providing the illusion that power is in the hands of the people. Like others who hold an **elite model** of power relations, Marx believed that society is ruled by a small group of individuals who share political and economic interests. In Marx's view, government officials and military leaders essentially do the bidding of the capitalist class, who own the factories and control natural resources.

examine decision making only on issues that become part of the political agenda. They fail to address the potential power of elites to keep certain matters entirely out of the realm of political debate.

Power Elite Models Such criticisms lend support for an

> Majority rule only works if you're also considering individual rights. Because you can't have five wolves and one sheep voting on what to have for supper.
>
> **Larry Flynt**

Mills's Model Sociologist C. Wright Mills put forth a model similar to Marx's in his pioneering work *The Power Elite* ([1956] 2000). Mills argued that significant decision-making power rested in a handful of people, both inside and outside government. According to Mills, the ruling **power elite** consists of small group of military, industrial, and government leaders who control the fate of the United States. A pyramid illustrates the power structure of the United States in Mills's model, as illustrated in the "Power Elite Models" graphic. The power elite rests at the top and includes the corporate rich, leaders of the executive branch of government, and heads of the military (whom Mills called the "warlords"). Directly below are local opinion leaders, members of the legislative branch of government, and leaders of special-interest groups. Mills contended that these individuals and groups basically follow the wishes of the dominant power elite. At the bottom of the pyramid are the unorganized, exploited masses.

A fundamental element in Mills's thesis is that the power elite not only includes relatively few members but also operates as a self-conscious, cohesive unit. Although not necessarily diabolical or ruthless,

Power Elite Models

C. Wright Mills's model

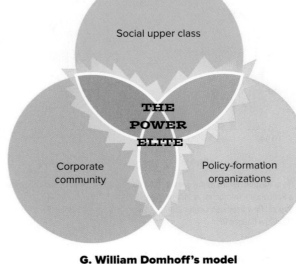

G. William Domhoff's model

Sources: Left, based on C. W. Mills (1956) 2000; right, Domhoff 2009, 2014.

the elite comprises similar types of people who interact regularly with one another and have essentially the same political and economic interests. Mills's power elite represents not a conspiracy but rather a community of interest and sentiment among a small number of influential people (Jenness, Smith, and Stepan-Norris 2006).

Domhoff's Model Sociologist G. William Domhoff (2009, 2014) agrees with Mills that a powerful elite runs the United States. As the "Power Elite Models" graphic shows, Domhoff stresses the role played by elites from three social spheres—the corporate community, the social upper class, and policy-formation organizations such as think tanks, chambers of commerce, and labor unions. Membership in these groups overlaps, and members with connections in more than one of these spheres have more power and influence. Domhoff finds that those in this latter group are still largely White, male, and upper class, but he notes the presence of a small number of women and minority men in key positions—groups that were excluded from Mills's top echelon and are still underrepresented today (Zweigenhaft and Domhoff 2006).

Although the three groups in Domhoff's power elite model do overlap, they do not necessarily agree on specific policies. Domhoff notes that in politics, two different coalitions have exercised influence. A corporate-conservative coalition has played a large role in both political parties, generating support for particular candidates through direct-mail and social media appeals. A liberal-labor coalition is based in unions, local environmental organizations, a segment of the minority group community, liberal churches, and the university and arts communities (Zweigenhaft and Domhoff 2006). The power this coalition wields suggests that the interests of members of the power elite are not

always singular or uniform but that overall they do work together to advance their larger interests.

SOCTHINK

Is it possible for a small and unified group of powerful people in the United States to use their power and influence to, in effect, rule the country? What obstacles exist to prevent that from happening?

>> Political Participation in the United States

To the extent to which power rests in the hands of the people in the United States, they exercise it most clearly at the ballot box. No matter how much money they have, or how famous they might be, candidates must still convince citizens to go out and vote. As a result, campaigns invest considerable resources into developing and mobilizing both paid and volunteer staff to craft messages, make calls, knock on doors, drive voters to polls, and much more because doing so can make all the difference in election outcomes.

VOTER IDENTIFICATION AND PARTICIPATION

From year to year, the political parties voters identify with varies, as is evident in the "What's Your Party" graph.

What's Your Party?

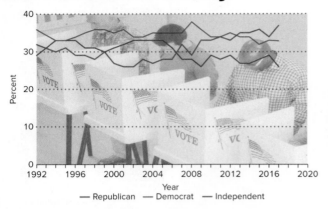

Percent (y-axis: 0, 10, 20, 30, 40)
Year (x-axis: 1992, 1996, 2000, 2004, 2008, 2012, 2016, 2020)

— Republican — Democrat — Independent

Note: Responses are to the question, "In politics today, do you consider yourself a Republican, Democrat, or Independent?"
Source: Pew Research Center 2018b. *Photo:* ©Hill Street Studios/Blend Images LLC/Glow Images RF

In 2017, 33 percent of registered voters in the United States self-identified as Democrats, 26 percent as Republicans, and 37 percent as independents (Pew Research Center 2018b). Because voters tend to support members of their own party, a significant amount of effort goes into persuading those independent voters to swing toward one party versus the other.

Party preferences vary significantly by social factors. In the 2018 midterm elections, for example, 59 percent of women voted for the Democratic candidate for the House of Representatives and 51 percent of men supported the Republican candidate. When it comes to race and ethnicity, 54 percent of non-Hispanic Whites voted for Republicans compared to Democratic support by 90 percent of African Americans and 69 percent of Hispanics. Age also matters, with young people more likely to vote for Democrats (67 percent) and older people more likely to support Republicans (50 percent). Education also influenced party preference, with college-educated women and men more likely to vote for the Democratic congressional candidate and non-college-educated women and men to select the Republican (Tyson 2018).

Political participation makes government accountable to the voters. If participation declines, government operates with less of a sense of accountability to society. Voter participation rates in the United States have varied significantly over time. They reached their highest points from 1848 to 1896, during which an average of about 80 percent of eligible voters participated in presidential elections. At various points during the 20th century they bottomed

Going GLOBAL

Voter Turnout Worldwide

Percentage turnout of registered voters at presidential elections

Rwanda	Brazil	Kenya	France	Namibia	Russian Federation	United States	Mexico	Honduras	Egypt	Afghanistan	Haiti
98.2	79.7	79.5	79.5	71.8	67.5	65.4	63.4	57.5	41.1	38.9	18.1

Note: Results are for the most recent presidential election. U.S. results are from 2016.
Source: International Institute for Democracy and Electoral Assistance 2019a. *Photo:* Evirgen/E+/Getty Images

Young Adults' Reasons for Not Voting

Reason	Percentage
Did not like candidates or campaign issues	24.8
Too busy, conflicting schedule	18.3
Not interested	17.3
Out of town	13.2
Other reason	10.8
Registration problems	5.5
Forgot to vote	4.7
Illness or disability	2.7
Inconvenient polling place	2.3
Transportation problems	1.5

Percentage

Note: Young adults include 18- to 24-year-olds. Results are for the 2016 presidential election.
Source: U.S. Census Bureau 2017d:Table 10. *Photo:* ©Ryan McVay/Getty Images RF

out at about 50 percent. Voter turnout for the past four U.S. presidential elections has hovered around 60 percent. Yet, as the "Going Global: Voter Turnout Worldwide" graph demonstrates, compared to other countries with presidential elections, the United States does not rank very high in turnout. In fact, of 114 countries for which there are data, the United States ranks 56th for voter turnout (International Institute for Democracy and Electoral Assistance 2019a; McDonald 2009, 2016). As the "Young Adults' Reasons for Not Voting" graph portrays, reasons for not voting vary, but the percentage of nonvoting adults in the United States who chose not to vote because they "did not like the candidates or campaign issues" spiked from an average of about 10 percent in recent presidential elections to 24.8 percent in 2016 (File 2018; U.S. Census Bureau 2017d:Table 10).

Voting participation rates vary by social group. Younger voters have significantly lower voter participation rates than do older voters. In the 2016 presidential election, for example, only 46 percent of people aged 18–29 voted compared to 71 percent of those aged 65 and older. That difference is important because voter preferences vary by age. In 2016, 55 percent of 18- to 29-year-olds voted for Clinton and 37 percent supported Trump. Among voters 65 and older, 45 percent supported Clinton and 53 percent voted for Trump. If the turnout rate among young people had been higher, Clinton may have won. In the 2018 midterm elections, however, turnout in this age group rose substantially compared to previous midterm elections (CIRCLE 2016a, 2018; File 2013).

Among African Americans, from 1996 to 2012, participation rates went up each time before falling in 2016. In 1996, 53 percent of African Americans voted. In 2012,

rates jumped to 66.6 percent, overtaking non-Hispanic Whites for the first time. Participation then fell to 59.6 percent in 2016. Among those who did not vote in 2016, 19.6 percent gave their reason as they "Did not like candidates or campaign issues" and 18.6 percent said they were "Not interested" (U.S. Census Bureau 2017b, 2017d:Table 10).

RACE AND GENDER IN POLITICS

Because politics goes hand in hand with power and authority, we should not be surprised that marginalized groups lack political strength. Nationally, women did not get the vote until 1920. Most Chinese Americans were turned away from the polls until 1926. American Indians did not win the right to vote until 1954. And African Americans were, in practice, largely disenfranchised until 1965, when national voting rights legislation was passed.

Denial of political opportunity had long-term consequences when it comes to access to political power. As the "(Under)Representation in Congress" graph portrays, women, African American, Hispanics, and Asian, Hawaiian, and Pacific Islanders all are underrepresented when compared to their percentages in the population as a whole. For example, the percentage of women in both the Senate and the House of Representatives is less than half of their percentage in the U.S. population (Edmondson and Lee 2019; Jin 2019).

As a result of the 2018 midterm elections, however, Congress did become more diverse. Overall, the 116th Congress included a record number of women and people of color. Of the 111 new members elected to Congress, 42 were women and 24 were people of color. Kansas and New Mexico sent the first Native American women to Congress. Michigan and Minnesota elected the first Muslim women to Congress. At age 29, New York's Alexandria Ocasio-Cortez became the youngest woman elected to Congress (Edmondson and Lee 2019; Jin 2019).

Globally, women account for at least half the members of the national legislature in only three countries. The African Republic of Rwanda ranks the highest, with 61.3 percent, Cuba has 53.2 percent, and Bolivia has 53.1 percent, as shown in the "Going Global: Women in National Legislatures" graph. Overall, the United States ranked 103rd among 190 nations in the proportion of women serving as national legislators in 2018 (Inter-Parliamentary Union 2018). To remedy this situation, many countries have adopted quotas for female representatives. In some, the government sets aside a certain

(Under)Representation in Congress

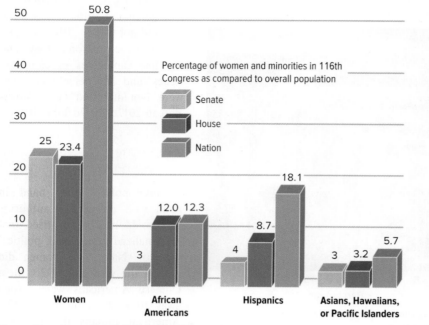

Percentage of women and minorities in 116th Congress as compared to overall population

- Senate
- House
- Nation

	Senate	House	Nation
Women	25	23.4	50.8
African Americans	3	12.0	12.3
Hispanics	4	8.7	18.1
Asians, Hawaiians, or Pacific Islanders	3	3.2	5.7

Sources: Edmondson and Lee 2019; Jin 2019; U.S. Census Bureau 2018a.

Analysis at the global level focuses on macro issues, such as the distribution of resources, struggles over political philosophies, and debates about boundaries. Often it involves nations with competing political and economic systems, as was the case in World War I, World War II, and the Cold War. Some have argued that the conflict in Iraq was about bringing freedom and democracy to the Middle East, and others argue it was motivated by oil and profits.

Sociologists have devoted much effort to studying the internal decision-making process that leads to war. During the Vietnam War, Presidents Johnson and Nixon both misled Congress, painting a falsely optimistic picture of the likely outcome. Based on their intentional distortions, Congress appropriated the military funds the two administrations

percentage of seats for women. In others, political parties have decided that a minimum percentage of their candidates should be women. Worldwide, 120 countries now have some kind of legislated or voluntary quota system in place (International Institute for Democracy and Electoral Assistance 2018b).

>> War and Peace

When it comes to political power, perhaps no decision is as weighty as the decision to go to war. Conflict is a central aspect of social relations. Sociologists Theodore Caplow and Louis Hicks (2002:3) have defined **war** as conflict between organizations that possess trained combat forces equipped with deadly weapons. This meaning is broader than the legal definition, which typically requires a formal declaration of hostilities.

WAR

Sociologists approach war in three ways. Those who take a global view study how and why two or more nations become engaged in military conflict. Those who take a nation-state view stress the interaction of internal political, socioeconomic, and cultural forces. And those who take a micro view focus on the social impact of war on individuals and the groups to which they belong.

War Conflict between organizations that possess trained combat forces equipped with deadly weapons.

Going **GLOBAL**

Women in National Legislatures

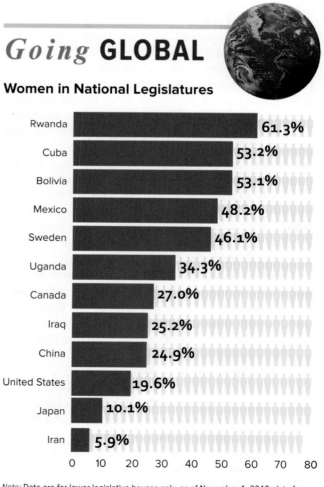

Country	Percentage
Rwanda	61.3%
Cuba	53.2%
Bolivia	53.1%
Mexico	48.2%
Sweden	46.1%
Uganda	34.3%
Canada	27.0%
Iraq	25.2%
China	24.9%
United States	19.6%
Japan	10.1%
Iran	5.9%

Note: Data are for lower legislative houses only, as of November 1, 2018; data for upper houses, such as the U.S. Senate or the UK House of Lords, are not included.
Source: Inter-Parliamentary Union 2018.

U.S. Public Opinion on Defense Spending

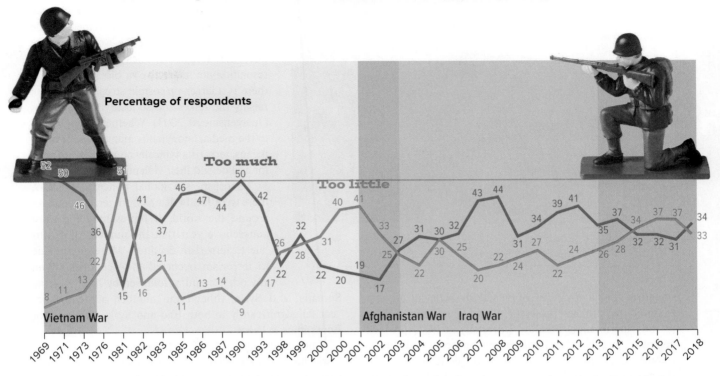

Percentage of respondents

Too much

Too little

52 50 51 50 46 46 47 44 42 41 40 41 37 39 41 43 44 37 37 37 34
46 36 22 13 41 37 21 13 14 11 9 17 22 26 28 32 31 22 20 19 17 25 27 33 31 30 30 32 25 22 24 20 31 27 34 22 24 26 35 28 32 32 34 31 33
8 11 15 16

Vietnam War

Afghanistan War   Iraq War

1969 1971 1973 1976 1981 1982 1983 1985 1986 1987 1990 1993 1998 1999 2000 2000 2001 2002 2003 2004 2005 2006 2007 2008 2009 2010 2011 2012 2013 2014 2015 2016 2017 2018

Note: Respondents replied to the question "There is much discussion as to the amount of money the government in Washington should spend for national defense and military purposes. How do you feel about this? Do you think we are spending too little, about the right amount, or too much?"
Source: Gallup 2018a. *Photos: (left and right):* McGraw-Hill Education

requested. However, in 1971, *The New York Times* published a set of classified documents now known as "The Pentagon Papers," which revealed that many members of both administrations had knowingly distorted the real prospects for the war. Two years later—over Nixon's veto—Congress passed the War Powers Act, which requires the president to notify Congress of the reasons for committing combat troops to a hostile situation (Patterson 2003).

Even though government leaders make the decision to go to war, public opinion plays a significant role in its execution. By 1971 the number of U.S. soldiers killed in

Vietnam had surpassed 50,000, and antiwar sentiment was strong. Wars conducted by the United States since that time have tended to follow a similar pattern. Initial support both for the importance of going to war and for military spending to support it tends to give way the longer it takes to finish the job. This proved true for the conflicts in both Iraq and Afghanistan.

At the level of interpersonal interaction, war can bring out the worst as well as the best in people. In 2004, graphic images of the abuse of Iraqi prisoners by U.S. soldiers at Iraq's Abu Ghraib prison shocked the world. For social

POPSOC

When it first came out, the film *Zero Dark Thirty,* which portrayed the capture and killing of al-Qaeda leader Osama bin Laden, seemed like a lock to win an Oscar for Best Picture. Soon, however, a negative buzz emerged because of its seemingly positive portrayal of the use of torture and questions about whether it was a propaganda film put together with assistance of the U.S. military. It ultimately lost the award to *Argo.* The controversy should not be surprising. Movies with a political agenda have been around since the beginning of Hollywood. Films such as *The Birth of a Nation, This Is the Army, Dr. Strangelove, M*A*S*H, Three Kings,* and *Billy Lynn's Long Halftime Walk* all had political points they sought to make.

Photo: Moviestore collection Ltd/Alamy Stock Photo

Terrorist attacks are designed to disrupt people's daily lives to draw attention to the attacker's cause. Sylvain Lefevre/Getty Images

scientists, the deterioration of the guards' behavior brought to mind psychology professor Philip Zimbardo's mock prison experiment at Stanford University in 1971, in which volunteer guards in a simulated prison acted sadistically toward volunteer prisoners. Zimbardo concluded it was the positions of power the guards occupied relative to the inmates that led to their behavior, rather than the characteristics of the individuals themselves. In July 2004, the U.S. military began using a documentary film about the experiment to train military interrogators to avoid mistreatment of prisoners (Zarembo 2004; Zimbardo 2007).

TERRORISM

The Boston Marathon bombings in April 2013 were yet another reminder of the ability of a small number of people with a political agenda to instill fear in the hearts and minds of millions. Globally, attacks in Brussels, Belgium, where a suicide bombing at an airport killed 32; in Nice, France, where a truck plowed through a Bastille Day crowd killing 84; in Madagali, Nigeria, where a suicide bombing killed 57; and in Berlin, Germany, where a truck tore into a busy Christmas market killing and injuring many, were but a few of the major attacks of 2016. Acts of terror, whether perpetrated by a few or by many people, can be a powerful force. Formally defined, **terrorism** is the use or threat of violence against random or symbolic targets in pursuit of political aims. For terrorists, the end justifies the means. They believe that the status quo is oppressive and that desperate measures are essential to end the suffering of the deprived.

An essential aspect of contemporary terrorism involves use of the media. Terrorists may want to keep secret their individual identities, but they want their political messages and

Terrorism The use or threat of violence against random or symbolic targets in pursuit of political aims.

Peace The absence of war, or, more broadly, a proactive effort to develop cooperative relations among nations.

goals to receive as much publicity as possible. The purpose of many acts of terrorist violence is more symbolic than strategic or tactical. These attacks represent a statement made by people who feel that the world has gone awry, that accepted political paths to problem resolution are ineffective or blocked, and that there is a larger or cosmic struggle going on, raising the stakes and so justifying the means (Juergensmeyer 2003). Whether through calls to the media, anonymous manifestos, or other means, terrorists typically admit responsibility for and defend their violent acts.

Terrorism is a global concern. In 2017, there were 18,814 deaths from terrorist attacks around the world. It represented the third consecutive year that the number of deaths due to terrorism declined. More deaths due to terrorism occurred in Afghanistan than any other country, followed by Iraq, Nigeria, Somalia, and Syria, though the number of deaths per year fell significantly in both Iraq and Syria (Institute for Economics & Peace 2018).

Since September 11, 2001, governments around the world have renewed their efforts to fight terrorism. Even though the public generally regards increased surveillance and social control as a necessary evil, these measures have nonetheless raised governance issues. For example, some citizens in the United States and elsewhere have expressed concern that measures such as the USA PATRIOT Act of 2001 threaten civil liberties. As efforts to combat political violence illustrate, the term *terrorism* is an apt one (Howard and Sawyer 2003).

PEACE

Sociologists have considered **peace** both as the absence of war and as a proactive effort to develop cooperative relations among nations. It is important to note, however, that armed conflict involves more than just warring nations. From 1945 to the end of the 20th century, the 25 major wars that occurred between countries killed a total of 3.3 million people. Although this is significant, the 127 civil wars that occurred in the same time period resulted in 16 million deaths. In other words, five times as many people died as a result of conflicts *within* nations as died in wars *between* nations (Fearon and Laitin 2003).

Sociologists and other social scientists who draw on sociological theory and research have tried to identify conditions that deter war. One of their findings is that international trade may act as a deterrent to armed conflict. As countries exchange goods, people, and then cultures, they become more integrated and less likely to threaten each other's security. Viewed from this perspective, not just trade but also immigration and foreign exchange programs have a beneficial effect on international relations (Acemoglu and Robinson 2012).

Another means of fostering peace is the activity of international charities and activist groups, or nongovernmental organizations (NGOs). The Red Cross and Red Crescent, Doctors Without Borders, and Amnesty International donate their services wherever they are needed, without regard to nationality. Over the past decades, these NGOs have been expanding in number, size, and scope. By sharing news of local conditions and clarifying local issues, they often prevent conflicts from escalating into violence and war. Some NGOs have initiated cease-fires, reached settlements, and even ended warfare between former adversaries.

Finally, many analysts stress that nations cannot maintain their security by threatening violence. Peace, they contend, can best be maintained by developing strong mutual security agreements among potential adversaries (Etzioni 1965; Shostak 2002). Following this path involves active diplomacy and, to the extent that it involves negotiations with countries viewed as enemies, can be controversial.

From surprising election outcomes to peace movements, stories such as these provide hope that people can make a difference. Even though large-scale economic trends can have negative impacts on companies, communities, and individuals, as well as shaping political outcomes, positive social change is possible. Sociological analysis helps us see the underlying processes at work in the economy and politics, and in so doing can assist us in recognizing places in those systems where opportunities for bringing about such change exist.

SOCIOLOGY IS A VERB

Playing Politics

Identify some elected officials—local, state, or federal—and interview them about their life in politics. What motivated them to run? What have they been able to accomplish? What frustrations do they face in getting things done? What would they change if they could? What advice would they give you? Keep notes of what they say, and reflect on the lessons learned about opportunities for, and obstacles to, change.

For REVIEW

I. **How are economic and political power organized?**

- The two major economic systems are capitalism and socialism, though in practice most economies are some mix of the two. Political systems of government include monarchy, oligarchy, dictatorship, totalitarianism, and democracy. A debate exists when looking at formal power in the United States about the degree to which there is a small, cohesive group of power elites who effectively rule or if leadership is more diverse and pluralistic, operating through democratic processes.

II. **How does power operate?**

- Power involves the capacity to get others to do what you want, ranging from use of force to acceptance of authority. In the case of authority, followers accept your power as legitimate, whether based on a traditional, rational-legal, or charismatic foundation.

III. **How has the economy changed over time?**

- From the Industrial Revolution through deindustrialization to the more recent global economic crisis and recovery, the modern economy is more dynamic and the consequences of change more far reaching both for nations and for individuals. Through political engagement people have the potential to influence the direction of that change.

Functionalist View

Power and authority are exercised in society to maintain social order for the good of the whole.

The economic system is a social institution that organizes the production, distribution, and consumption of goods and services.

The political system maintains **order** in society through internal policing and diplomatic relations with outsiders.

ORDER, SYSTEMS, ALLOCATION OF RESOURCES
KEY CONCEPTS

Conflict View

Power and authority are exercised to preserve and extend the integrity of the elites in society.

Capitalism primarily benefits the owners of the means of production; **socialism** allows workers to benefit from their own **labor power.**

The **power elite,** a small group of military, industrial, and government leaders, shapes the direction of society.

KEY CONCEPTS
COERCION, POWER ELITE, LABOR POWER

Interactionist View

Power and authority are **socially constructed** through interactions with others.

Authority depends upon followers accepting the legitimacy of their leader's right to rule.

In the U.S. political system, leaders are selected by those who **vote;** the political parties try to **persuade** the voters to support their positions.

KEY CONCEPTS
AUTHORITY, PERSUASION

MAKE THE CONNECTION

After reviewing the chapter, answer the following questions:

1

How would each perspective explain the political stances of the White working-class workers Hochschild studied?

2

How might each perspective seek to explain charismatic authority?

3

How might theorists from each perspective explain war?

4

Are you an active or an apathetic voter? What factors influence your approach? Which perspective best describes the way you participate in the political world?

Pop Quiz

1. **Within a capitalist economy, what does laissez-faire mean?**

   a. The means of production and distribution in a society are collectively held.

   b. People should compete freely in the marketplace, with minimal government intervention in the economy.

   c. A single business firm controls the market.

   d. Society depends on mechanization to produce its goods and services.

2. **What term does Karl Marx use to describe our creative capacity to transform raw materials into products?**

   a. infrastructure

   b. labor power

   c. proletariat

   d. means of production

3. **The tertiary sector of the economy deals primarily with**

   a. extracting products directly from the natural environment.

   b. providing services to others rather than producing tangible goods.

   c. transforming raw materials into products through manufacturing.

   d. transforming and interpreting data for others to use for decision making.

4. **The systematic and widespread reduction of investment in domestic manufacturing and material production is called**

   a. deindustrialization.

   b. downsizing.

   c. postindustrialization.

   d. gentrification.

5. **What is the term used to describe outsourcing of work to foreign contractors?**

   a. exploitation

   b. offshoring

   c. alienation

   d. downsizing

6. **In which type of government do only a few individuals rule?**

   a. a monarchy

   b. a democracy

   c. a dictatorship

   d. an oligarchy

7. **According to Max Weber, what is the definition of power?**

   a. the recognized set of procedures for implementing and achieving society's goals

   b. the combination of strength and stamina

   c. the mechanical and electrical energy that provided the foundation for the Industrial Revolution

   d. the ability to exercise one's will over others, even if they resist

8. **Which of the following is *not* part of the classification system of authority developed by Max Weber?**

   a. traditional authority

   b. pluralist authority

   c. rational-legal authority

   d. charismatic authority

9. **According to the model proposed by C. Wright Mills, power rests in the hands of**

   a. the people.

   b. the aristocracy.

   c. the power elite.

   d. a representative democracy.

10. **Which of the following terms best describes the threat of violence against random or symbolic targets in pursuit of political aims?**

    a. politics

    b. power

    c. terrorism

    d. authority

1. (b), 2. (b), 3. (b), 4. (a), 5. (b), 6. (d), 7. (d), 8. (b), 9. (c), 10. (c)

JUST GETTING BY

Rae McCormick's father died of a brain aneurysm when she was 11 years old, and her mother abandoned her soon thereafter. Left to fend for herself, Rae lived on her own for a while in her hometown of Cleveland. She then moved in with her older sister for a time before Rae's mom signed custody over to a family friend. When Rae turned 18 and her Social Security survivor benefit checks stopped coming, the woman kicked Rae out, and she was on her own again. At 21, Rae met Donny, and they had a daughter named Azara. Rae and Donny lived together off and on over the next few years, but he hit her and cheated on her multiple times, so she left him. She eventually rented a room from George and Camilla, an older couple who had been friends with her father. The three of them, together with three additional boarders, pooled all their resources to get by. The house they rented lacked pipes for running water, so they hauled water up from the basement in five-gallon buckets to wash dishes, take baths, and flush toilets. Their

kitchen lacked a functioning stove, so they cooked on a charcoal grill outside (Edin and Shaefer 2015).

What Rae wanted more than anything else was a good job and a place of her own to raise Azara. Just when things seemed to be looking up, she lost the job she loved at Walmart, where she'd been named "Cashier of the Month" twice in her first six months working there. She couldn't get to work one day because even though she paid George and Camilla $50 per month for gas and the use of their pickup, the tank was empty, and she'd used the rest of her paycheck for rent, diapers, and groceries. Her store manager told her that if she couldn't find a way to get to work on time, she shouldn't bother coming back. Her many attempts to find another job came up empty (Edin and Shaefer 2015).

Sociologist Kathryn Edin and social work professor Luke Shaefer (2015) told Rae's story, along with those of others like her, in their book *$2.00 a Day: Living on Almost Nothing in America*. They report that 1.5 million households, including about 3 million children, live on cash incomes of less than $2 per person, per day in the United States. Based on their observation research, the interviews they conducted, and the data they analyzed, Edin and Shaefer conclude that like millions of others facing extreme poverty, "Rae, in her current circumstances . . . basically has no shot at achieving [her] dream. . . . Housing is too expensive, the jobs she might get pay far too little, and there's too little help" (2015:91). In this chapter we explore how our position in the social class system affects our life chances.

As You READ >>

- **What is social class?**
- **How does social class operate?**
- **What are the consequences of social class?**

>> Life Chances

One of sociology's core lessons is that place matters. Being born to a wealthy Park Avenue family in New York City confers something quite different than being born into a poor family in Cleveland. To describe the ways in which the positions we occupy shape our outcomes, Max Weber introduced the concept of **life chances** by which he meant that our likelihood for success is shaped by our access to valued material, social, and cultural resources. The college you choose, the job you have, the money you make, the car you drive, the neighborhood you live in, the health care you receive, and many other matters are shaped by the social positions you occupy.

Our definition of sociology highlights the significance of position and power by including the phrase "the consequences of difference." This expression underscores the importance sociologists place on investigating how resources are distributed, and how we justify those distributions. In this chapter and those that follow, we take a closer look at such consequences, with particular attention paid to social class, gender, race, and ethnicity.

SYSTEMS OF STRATIFICATION

To better understand how our economic position shapes our likely outcomes, we need a better appreciation of the structures within which we find ourselves. Not all societies structure themselves in the same way, but difference exists within all societies. Sociologists call the social inequality that is built into the structure of society **stratification,** by which they mean the structured ranking of entire groups of people that perpetuates unequal economic rewards and power in a society. The *strata* in *stratification* refer to different layers or levels of power and influence built into the structure of society. Sociologists focus on four major systems of stratification: slavery, caste, estate, and social class.

Slavery **Slavery** is a system of enforced servitude in which some people are owned by others as property. Enslaved people become objects rather than subjects. Owners are free to treat them in the same way they might their horses or cattle.

The practice of slavery has varied over time. Most of the enslaved people in ancient Greece, for example, were prisoners of war or individuals captured and sold by pirates, and slave status was not necessarily permanent. By contrast, slavery in the United States was an ascribed status, and enslaved people faced racial and legal barriers to freedom. The first enslaved Africans in what later became the United States were brought by Dutch traders to Jamestown in 1619 and worked on the recently established tobacco plantations there (Hashaw 2007). With the founding of the United States as a new nation, the U.S. Constitution established

> **Life chances** The likelihood that our success is shaped by our access to valued material, social, and cultural resources.
>
> **Stratification** A structured ranking of entire groups of people that perpetuates unequal economic rewards and power in a society.
>
> **Slavery** A system of enforced servitude in which some people are owned by others as property.

Edwin J. Morgan/Bettmann/Getty Images

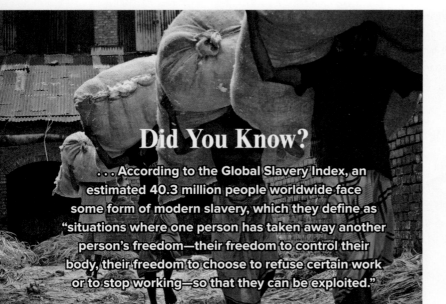

Did You Know?

... According to the Global Slavery Index, an estimated 40.3 million people worldwide face some form of modern slavery, which they define as "situations where one person has taken away another person's freedom—their freedom to control their body, their freedom to choose to refuse certain work or to stop working—so that they can be exploited."

Source: Global Slavery Index 2018. *Photo:* Mahmud Fahm/Moment Open/Getty Images

for crime whereof the party shall have been duly convicted."

Today, the Universal Declaration of Human Rights, which is binding on all members of the United Nations, prohibits slavery in all its forms. According to the United Nations (2018b), contemporary forms of slavery include debt bondage, forced labor, child labor and child servitude, sexual slavery, sale of children, forced marriage, and the sale of wives. In many developing countries, bonded laborers are imprisoned in lifetime employment. Although slavery is outlawed in the United States and Europe, guest workers and illegal immigrants have been forced to labor for years under terrible conditions, either to pay off debts or to avoid being turned over to immigration authorities. In 2018, the National Human Trafficking Resource Center (2018) reported 5,147 incidents in the United States of potential human trafficking, and of these 3,718 involved sex trafficking.

Caste A stratification system in which boundaries between strata are clear, relations between levels are regulated, and social status is ascribed.

slave ownership as a legal right, and numerous founders owned people as slaves, including George Washington and Thomas Jefferson. It wasn't until 1865, with the passage of the 13th Amendment to the U.S. Constitution, that slavery was banned throughout the United States, though the amendment included the clause "except as a punishment

Castes In a stratification system based on **caste,** boundaries between strata are clear, relations between levels are regulated, and social status is ascribed. The caste into which you are born remains the same until you die. It determines your opportunities throughout life, including who your friends are, what occupation you will pursue, and whom you will marry. Caste-based systems are rigid, allowing for limited and formalized interaction between castes.

The most familiar caste-based system is based primarily in India and is associated with Hinduism. This system has four major castes, or *varnas:* priests (*Brahman*), warriors (*Kshatriya*), merchants (*Vaishya*), and artisans/farmers (*Shudra*). Within those four major castes are thousands of sub-caste groupings. A fifth category, the *Dalit,* referred to in the past as untouchables, is considered to be so lowly and unclean as to have no place within this system of stratification. In 1950, after gaining independence from Great Britain, India adopted a new constitution that formally outlawed the caste system. In addition, economic changes tied to urbanization and the impact of technology have undercut its taken-for-granted status. Yet caste continues to play a powerful role in shaping patterns of social interaction throughout India.

Even though individuals can't change their caste, that doesn't mean change over time is impossible. Subcastes within India, for example, have been able to improve their overall standing by adopting the principles and practices of castes above them. This process is known as Sanskritization, after the language of ancient India in which most of the Hindu

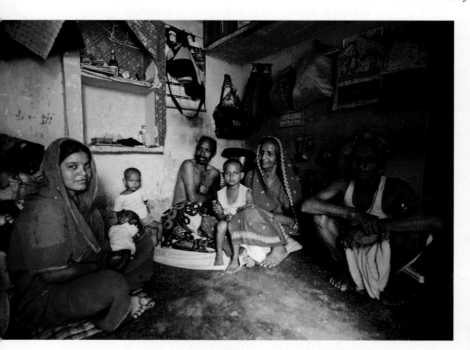

The life chances of families in India continue to be shaped by their caste.
Andrew Aitchison/Alamy Stock Photo

scriptures are written. Because the priestly Brahman caste represents the highest class, adopting that lifestyle, including becoming a vegetarian and giving up alcohol, became a marker of hoped-for higher status for the group, though this is most successful for groups that are already near the top (Bahadur 2008; Srinivas 1956; Staal 1963). Seeking to look and act like members of a higher stratum to gain social status is not unique to caste-based systems.

Estates The **estate system** divides power in society into three primary sectors: the church, the nobility, and the commoners. This stratification system was characteristic of medieval Europe, especially in England and France. French bishop Adalbéron de Laon gave names to these three estates in a poem to French king Robert the Pious around the year 1030. He identified them as *Oratores, Bellatores,* and *Laboratores,* or those who pray, those who fight, and those who work (Le Goff 1990). Members of the first estate included bishops, monks, priests, and nuns. The second estate was composed of knights, lords and ladies, dukes and duchesses, and others of noble birth. Peasants and serfs were part of the third estate, and their labor produced food for all. In this feudal system, the ruling monarch, usually the king, ruled over all, but, over time, representatives from each of these groups were granted some degree of voice in the political system. Vestiges of the estate system remain in England in the form of the Church of England, the House of Lords, and the House of Commons.

The power in this system rested primarily on the nobles' ownership of land, though the church had substantial land holdings as well. Peasants provided the nobles with their income by paying them rents, primarily in the form of produce, in exchange for the opportunity to work the land. The nobles, with help from the knights among them, pledged to maintain order and protect the peasants from bandits and rival nobles. As in the caste system, social status was largely ascribed. The nobles inherited their titles and property, and there was little commoners could do to change their lot in life. One area that did provide some degree of opportunity was the church. By the 12th century, the priesthood emerged as a distinct category in most of Europe. In addition, opportunities for local merchants and artisans began to expand. For the first time, there were groups of people whose wealth did not depend on land ownership or agriculture. Their success ultimately contributed to the demise of feudalism and the rise of capitalism.

Social Class In the final stratification system, **social class,** social position is determined primarily by socioeconomic status, both real and perceived. Social class can be assessed objectively and subjectively. *Objective* indicators primarily include education, occupation, and income. A college graduate who is a mechanical engineer earning $83,000 per year is higher than a high school graduate working as a dental assistant earning $32,000. *Subjective* class identification, the degree to which a person identifies with a particular social class category, also plays a role. It's entirely possible, for example, for a person who makes a lot of money to identify with the lower social class within which she or he was born (Rubin et al. 2014). The perceptions others have also play a significant role because, as we learned with the Thomas theorem, perception shapes action, which, in the case of social class, may well affect the degree to which we are allowed access to valued resources. Because social class can involve multiple, sometimes contradictory, indicators, settling on a universal, all-purpose model of social classes is problematic.

> **Estate system** A system of stratification that divides power in society into three primary sectors: the church, the nobility, and the commoners.
>
> **Social class** A system of stratification primarily based on socioeconomic status, both real and perceived.

Sociologists commonly use a five-class model to describe the class system in the United States, though many other models are available (Beeghley 2007; Kerbo 2011). At the top are the *upper class,* including 1–2 percent of the population who are wealthy, well-respected, and politically powerful. Just beneath them are the *upper-middle class,* which is composed primarily of business executives, doctors, lawyers, architects, and other professionals; they make up about 15 percent of the population. The next 30–35 percent include members of the *middle class,* which is composed of less-affluent professionals, such as school teachers and nurses, along with owners of small businesses, clerical workers, and others who have decent jobs but a minimal amount of autonomy—that is, control over what they do and when they do it. The fourth group is the *working class,* whose jobs typically involve some degree of manual labor, including carpenters, plumbers, and factory workers, who

The British Library/The Image Works

What Class Am I?

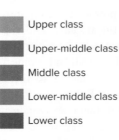

Self-Identified Social Class (vertical axis)

Respondent's Income Level (horizontal axis)

Income categories: <$30,000 | $30,000–49,999 | $50,000–$74,999 | $75,000–99,999 | $100,000+

Class	<$30,000	$30,000–49,999	$50,000–$74,999	$75,000–99,999	$100,000+
Upper class	1%	0%	1%	0%	6%
Upper-middle class	3%	4%	8%	16%	34%
Middle class	34%	36%	61%	68%	51%
Lower-middle class	34%	53%	29%	15%	8%
Lower class	27%	5%	1%	1%	0%

Legend:
- Upper class
- Upper-middle class
- Middle class
- Lower-middle class
- Lower class

Note: Respondents were asked, "Which of the social classes would you say you belong in?" Their answers were then grouped into categories based on family income.
Source: Pew Research Center 2015a.

---

in relationship to others. In particular, people seem averse to categorizing themselves as either rich or poor. As a result, as the "What Class Am I?" graphic demonstrates, 51 percent of people making over $100,000 per year still identify as middle class, rejecting the available Upper-Middle and Upper options (Pew Research Center 2015a). Looked at another way, when asked how much money it takes to consider someone rich, people at different income levels have different perceptions. Among those earning less than $30,000 per year, 54 percent chose an income level of less than $100,000 to be considered rich. Among those making $100,000 or more, only 2 percent indicated a threshold that low. At this much higher income level, 46 percent said it would take $500,000 or more per year to be considered rich (Reeves 2015).

SOCIAL MOBILITY

A society's system of stratification significantly shapes one's life chances. Though the opportunity for changing position is possible in all, the likelihood of doing so varies significantly. In most cases, the story of the peasant girl who marries a prince is nothing more than a fairy tale,

---

make up another 30–35 percent of the population. The final group is the *underclass,* commonly referred to as "the poor," who make up 15–20 percent of the population. People in this class have limited and inconsistent access to resources, and membership includes a disproportionate number of African Americans, Hispanics, immigrants, and single mothers.

When asked to identify their social class, people in the United States struggle with how to respond. One of the difficulties comes from widespread assumption that social classes do not exist in the United States. Another is the difficulty people have in placing themselves

Did You Know?

... Six members of the Walton Family, heirs of Walmart founder Sam Walton, own more wealth than the bottom 40 percent of U.S. families combined.

Source: Bivens 2012. *Photo:* Gilles Mingasson/Getty Images which has its roots in the estate system. To better under-stand opportunities for **social mobility,** meaning movement within or between society's strata, sociologists investigate the degree to which a society is open versus closed.

Open versus Closed Stratification Systems A so-ciety with an **open system** of stratification allows for social mobility between strata. Of the stratification systems discussed earlier, class-based systems have the potential to be more open than others. In principle, capitalism seeks to identify those with the greatest ability and reward them for their efforts regardless of whether their parents were rich or poor. The pos-sibility for mobility becomes an incentive for hard work.

A society with a **closed system** of stratification does not allow for social mobility between strata. Social positions are ascribed, so the position into which you are born is the position within which you remain throughout life. Caste systems are mostly closed with limited opportunity for movement within one's lifetime. Societies with barriers to mobility, whether based on religion, gender, race, ethnic-ity, class, or any other positional variables, are more closed than those without such barriers.

Types of Social Mobility Sociologists also distin-guish between mobility *within* a stratum versus movement *between* strata. For example, a bus driver who becomes a hotel clerk moves from one social position to another of approximately the same rank. Sociologists call this kind of movement **horizontal mobility.** However, if the bus driver were to become a lawyer, they would experience **vertical mobility**—the movement of an individual from one social position to another of a different rank (Sorokin [1927] 1959). Vertical mobility involves moving upward or down-ward in a society's stratification system.

Another contrasting pair of mobility types involves movement that occurs *between* generations versus change that occurs *within* an individual's career as an adult. **Intergenerational mobility** refers to changes in the social position of children relative to their parents. Thus, a college professor whose father was a printer provides an example of vertically upward intergenerational mobility. A plumber whose parents were both physicians illustrates vertically downward intergenerational mobility. Because education contributes significantly to upward mobility, any barrier to the pursuit of advanced degrees limits intergenerational mobility (Isaacs, Sawhill, and Haskins 2008).

Intragenerational mobility, in contrast, involves changes in social position within a person's adult life. Thus, some-one who enters the paid labor force as a teacher's aide and eventually becomes superintendent of the school district experiences vertically upward intragenerational mobility. A person who becomes a cab driver after their accounting firm goes bankrupt undergoes vertically downward intra-generational mobility.

In the United States one way to define the "American Dream" is as vertically upward intragenerational mobility.

In other words, a person would experience a significant shift in social class position over the course of her or his career, from a relatively low-level position to one of sig-nificant wealth and power. Although this does happen, the "American reality" is that we tend to end up in positions relatively close to where we began.

SOCTHINK

What is the story of social mobility in your fam-ily? To what extent have there been shifts both across and within generations? What factors, such as family connections or historical events, contributed to the social mobility that occurred?

>> Social Class in the United States

The stratification system in the United States is predomi-nantly class based. Within it, three categories of resources play a major role in shaping our life chances. *Material* resources refer to economic assets that we own or control, including money, property, and land. *Social* resources include prestige based on the position we occupy and connections based on the social networks we are a part of. It turns out that the old saying "It's not what you know; it's who you know" has some truth to it. Position and con-nections make it possible for us to increase the likelihood of accomplishing our goals. Fi-nally, *cultural* resources include our tastes, language, and way of looking at the world. They represent our knowledge of cognitive, normative, and mate-rial elements of culture that we can draw on when acting to accomplish our goals. A simple but classic example involves knowing which fork to use for the various courses of a formal dinner. But it also includes knowing how to respond when we are put on the spot, whether in a business meeting, at a rock concert, or in class. Viewing so-cial class in terms of material, social, and cultural resources enables us to better understand the degree to which living the American Dream is possible.

Social mobility Movement within or between society's strata.

Open system A society with a system of stratification that allows for social mobility between strata.

Closed system A society with a system of stratification that does not allow for social mobility between strata.

Horizontal mobility The movement of an individual from one social position to another of the same rank.

Vertical mobility The movement of an individual from one social position to another of a different rank.

Intergenerational mobility Changes in the social position of children relative to their parents.

Intragenerational mobility Changes in social position within a person's adult life.

Even though they like to deny that social class exists, Americans have a fascination with class as portrayed in pop culture. This curiosity is especially apparent with the appeal of British programs such as *Downton Abbey, Masterpiece Classic, Sherlock Holmes, Doctor Who,* and *Absolutely Fabulous.* Perhaps it's just the accents, but the social class dimensions of British society are often core elements of these shows. Such programs provide a window into how social stratification is practiced differently in other societies. *Downton Abbey,* for example, portrays the lives of an aristocratic family and their servants in the early 20th century.

Photo: PictureLux/The Hollywood Archive/Alamy Stock Photo

INCOME AND WEALTH

Income and wealth provide social class with its material foundation. **Income** refers to money received over some period of time. It often comes in the form of wages per hour or salary per year, but returns on investments, such as stock dividends or profit from the sale of property, including homes within some time period, also count. **Wealth** consists of the total value of all material assets minus debts at a single point in time. It includes savings, stocks, land, or any other material asset of value. If you were to sell everything you own and pay off all your debts, what you had left would be the value of your wealth. These material resources make our class-based lifestyles possible (Bourdieu 1986). As such, if we are to understand social classes in the United States, we need a clear picture of their distribution.

Income Money received over some period of time.

Wealth The total value of all material assets minus debts at a single point in time.

Income When considering income, it helps to begin by looking at the average income for a population. Doing so provides a simple summary of the typical income for the whole group and establishes a baseline for comparison both within the group and between groups. In 2017, the median household income in the United States was $61,372, which represents a 1.8 percent increase in income over the previous year. Because the median is the middle score in a distribution, half of all households in the United States had incomes higher than $61,372 that year, and half had incomes lower than that amount (Fontenot, Semega, and Kollar 2018).

Sociologists explore the degree to which income inequality exists using a variety of indicators. One way they do so is by highlighting possible differences between the mean and median. For example, in 2017, the mean household income in the United States was $86,220, a substantially higher "average" than the median (Fontenot, Semega, and Kollar 2018). When the mean is significantly higher than the median, it suggests that there are some extremely high incomes that elevate the mean, thus making it a less effective indicator of the typical income of a group. The classic example is that whenever Bill Gates enters a room, the mean income for all individuals in the room usually skyrockets, unless he is in a room of similarly rich multibillionaires. The existence of such extremely high incomes, which sociologists refer to as outliers, points toward significant income inequality.

Another approach sociologists use to explore income inequality involves looking at quintiles, which provides them with a better sense of the distribution of incomes from low to high. Rather than breaking the population in half at the median, the quintile approach creates five groups by lining up all income-earning households, from those who make the least to those who make the most, and then drawing a line at 20, 40, 60, and 80 percent. The United States has approximately 126 million households, so each quintile would include an equal number, or about 25.2 million households. We can then compare what percentage of total income is earned by each quintile and the average income people in each quintile earn.

Looking at the "Percentage Share of Total Income by Quintile" graph allows us to better understand the distribution of income in the United States. If income was equally

Tana Lee Alves/WireImage/Getty Images

Percentage Share of Total Income by Quintile

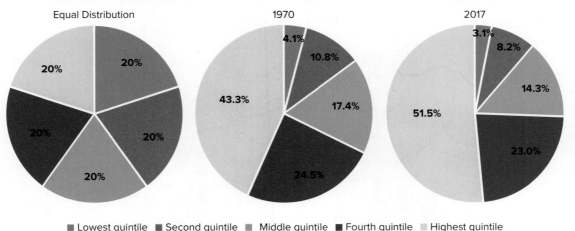

Equal Distribution

20% 20% 20% 20% 20%

1970

4.1% 10.8% 17.4% 24.5% 43.3%

2017

3.1% 8.2% 14.3% 23.0% 51.5%

■ Lowest quintile ■ Second quintile ■ Middle quintile ■ Fourth quintile ■ Highest quintile

Note: Each pie represents the share of total household income earned by quintiles.
Source: Fontenot, Semega, and Kollar 2018:Table A-2.

distributed across all households, each quintile would earn 20 percent of total income. The degree to which each quintile deviates from 20 percent indicates the degree to which income inequality exists. In 2017, for example, the 20 percent of households in the lowest income quintile earned 3.1 percent of all income earned in the United States. Compare that to the 20 percent of households in the highest quintile who earned 51.5 percent of all income. In other words, the top 20 percent of households earned more than that bottom 80 percent of households combined.

Comparing quintile distributions between 1970 and 2017 allows us to see how income inequality has changed over time. The size of the slice earned by the top quintile grew significantly, from 43.3 percent in 1970 to 51.5 percent in 2017. As a result, the other 80 percent of households now split up a much smaller portion of the overall income pie. In fact, each of the other income quintiles takes home a smaller slice of the pie now than in the past. In simple terms, this suggests that perhaps the rich get richer while the poor get poorer (Fontenot, Semega, and Kollar 2018:Table A-2).

In addition to percentages, sociologists also look at the average income each quintile earns in dollars. As the "Average Household Income by Quintile" graph shows, saying that the rich get richer while the poor get poorer needs some refinement. Average incomes earned by those in the top quintile did go up from 1970 to 2017, but incomes went up for all groups. Given that income is measured in constant dollars adjusted for inflation, these increases reflect a real increase. All groups are earning more now than in the past. But the percentage increase for those at the top grew much faster than

for those at the bottom. For those in the lowest quintile, income increased by 17.8 percent to $13,258 in 2017, compared to an 81.1 percent increase to $221,848 in 2017 for those in the top quintile (Fontenot, Semega, and Kollar 2018:Table A-2). Everyone is doing better, but the gap between the top and the bottom is getting larger.

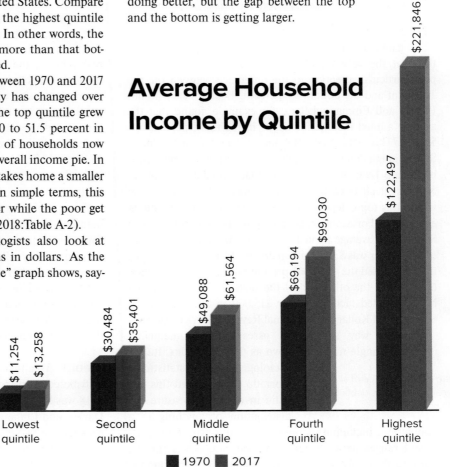

Average Household Income by Quintile

	Lowest quintile	Second quintile	Middle quintile	Fourth quintile	Highest quintile
1970	$11,254	$30,484	$49,088	$69,194	$122,497
2017	$13,258	$35,401	$61,564	$99,030	$221,846

■ 1970 ■ 2017

Note: Income for 1970 shown in 2017 dollars.
Source: Fontenot, Semega, and Kollar 2018:Table A-2.

Income Distribution in the United States

Note: Categories represent percentages of U.S. adults aged 20 and over.
Source: Piketty, Saez, and Zucman 2016. Photo: Mmaxer/Shutterstock

To gain a better understanding of how much more money those at the very top earn, sociologists and others have paid particular attention to the difference between the top 1 percent and the bottom 99 percent. Economists Thomas Piketty and Emmanuel Saez, for example, found that the average annual income for adults in the top 1 percent was $1,304,771 in 2014. As the "Income Distribution in the United States" graph demonstrates, the percentage of income earned by the top 1 percent now exceeds that earned by the bottom 50 percent (Piketty, Saez, and Zucman 2016, 2018). Even within this top category, however, substantial income differences exist. For example, according to the Internal Revenue Service, the average annual income for the top 0.01 percent of tax returns was $32.7 million dollars, and the 1,409 returns that comprised the top 0.001 percent averaged $145.5 million in 2016. On the other end of the scale, 13.7 million households reported incomes under $15,000 in 2017 (Fontenot, Semega, and Kollar 2018; Internal Revenue Service 2018).

A final way sociologists assess income inequality involves a single number known as the Gini index. Italian sociologist and statistician Corrado Gini created this statistic in order to measure the distribution of anything in a population, including income and wealth. The Gini coefficient ranges between zero and one, and the larger the Gini coefficient, the greater the inequality. For example, if everyone in the population earns the same income, the Gini index equals zero. If one person earns everything and

Wealth The total value of all material assets minus debts at a single point in time.

everyone else earns nothing, the Gini index equals one. The real value of the Gini index is as a comparative statistic because it allows us to see whether inequality is increasing or decreasing over time. In the United States, the Gini index for income reached a low of 0.386 in 1968. Since that time it has risen fairly steadily. In 1990 it reached 0.428, and by 2017 it climbed to 0.482 (Fontenot, Semega, and Kollar 2018:Table A-2). This upswing indicates that income inequality in the United States has increased significantly during that time.

Even though income has increased somewhat for all quintiles, income for the average worker has remained relatively flat for a long time. In fact, the typical worker in a nonsupervisory role in a private firm makes roughly the same now as they did in the early 1970s, as portrayed in the "Average Hourly Income, 1964–2018" graph. We cannot fully appreciate our individual outcomes in life without situating them within the context of larger structural forces that shape our access to opportunity.

Wealth Wealth in the United States is even more unevenly distributed than income. The median wealth per adult in 2018 was $61,667, but the mean was $403,974 (Shorrocks, Davies, and Lluberas 2018:Table 2-1). The large difference between the two is a consequence of the extreme amounts of wealth held by the richest households. The top 10 percent of households own 77.2 percent of all wealth in the United States with an average worth of $2.56 million. The bottom 90 percent own the remaining 22.8 percent with a net

Average Hourly Income, 1964–2018

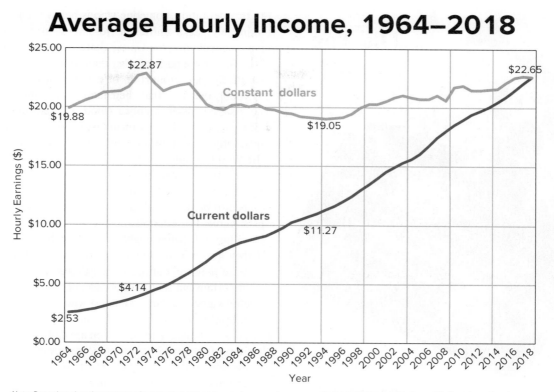

Note: Data show hourly earnings of production and nonsupervisory employees on private nonfarm payrolls. Current dollars shows hourly income at that time. Constant dollars reports income calculated in 2018 dollars to adjust for inflation.
Sources: Bureau of Labor Statistics 2019a, 2019b.

Wealth Distribution in the United States

Note: Categories represent percentages of U.S. households.
Source: Saez and Zucman 2016. *Photo:* C Squared Studios/Photodisc/Getty Images

worth of $84,000 per household (Saez and Zucman 2016). The Gini index value for wealth of 0.852 provides further evidence of significant wealth inequality in the United States (Shorrocks, Davies, and Lluberas 2018).

Breaking down that top 10 percent into smaller pieces reveals significant differences between the wealthy and the very wealthy. As the "Wealth Distribution in the United States" graph shows, the top 1 percent owns 41.8 percent of U.S. household wealth, with an average net worth of $13.8 million. At 22.8 percent, the bottom 90 percent of households collectively own about half as much wealth as that owned by the top 1 percent. Going even higher, households in the top 0.1 percent own 22 percent and are worth $72.8 million. Put another way, the 160,700 households in the top 0.1 percent own about as much wealth as do the 144,600,000 households in the bottom 90 percent. And at the very pinnacle, those in the top 0.01 percent, a total of

Did You Know?

... Consumers in the top quintile spent, on average, $109,743 in 2017 on all items including food, clothes, and housing. To put that in perspective, people in the top quintile spend more than 8 times as much in a year as those in the bottom quintile earn.

Source: Bureau of Labor Statistics 2018i. *Photo:* Brand X Pictures/PunchStock

16,070 households, own 11.2 percent of all U.S. wealth and are worth $371 million (Saez and Zucman 2016:Table 1).

POVERTY

In 2017, 39.7 million people in the United States—12.3 percent of the population—lived in poverty. Based on official calculations, a family consisting of two adults and two children with a combined annual income of $24,858 or less fell below the poverty line. By contrast, a single person under the age of 65 must earn less than $12,752 annually to be officially considered poor (Fontenot, Semega, and Kollar 2018).

Defining Poverty Such figures make it seem like a simple matter to define who is living in poverty: You are either above the threshold or below it. Sociologists have found, however, that our conceptions of poverty vary. For example, we can define poverty in either absolute or relative terms.

Absolute poverty refers to a minimum level of subsistence that no family should be expected to live below. According

Absolute poverty A minimum level of subsistence that no family should be expected to live below.

Relative poverty A floating standard of deprivation by which people at the bottom of a society are judged to be disadvantaged in comparison with the nation as a whole.

Anyone who has ever struggled with poverty knows how extremely expensive it is to be poor.

James A. Baldwin ([1965] 1985)

to this definition, someone who is below the poverty level ultimately lacks sufficient resources to survive. Many nations, including the United States, use some form of this criterion as the basis of their definition of poverty. A comparatively high proportion of children in U.S. households are poor, meaning that their families are unable to afford necessary consumer goods (food, shelter, and clothing). Globally, poverty rates in industrialized nations vary significantly, as portrayed in the "Child Poverty Rates Around the World" graph.

In contrast, **relative poverty** is a floating standard of deprivation by which people at the bottom of a society are judged to be disadvantaged in comparison with the nation as a whole. For example, people who have sufficient food, clothing, and shelter might nonetheless be considered poor if they live in a wealthy nation such as the United States, because they can't afford to buy things the culture defines as important but that are not essential for survival, such as a refrigerator. Similarly, someone who would be considered poor by U.S. standards might be well-off by global standards of poverty; hunger and starvation are daily realities in many regions of the world. In addition, when viewed in historical terms, someone currently defined as poor may be better off in absolute terms than a poor person in the 1930s or 1970s.

Historically, the poverty line in the United States was first calculated based on a formula established in 1964. President Lyndon B. Johnson had declared a War on Poverty, but at the time, no official measure of poverty existed. To enact an official measure, the Johnson administration turned to the work of Mollie Orshansky, a food economist at the research bureau of the Social Security Administration. Orshansky proposed combining two facts to establish a general poverty threshold. The first came from a study that found that families spend approximately one-third of their budget on food. The second was the estimated cost of a minimally nutritious diet established by U.S. Department of Agriculture dieticians. Orshansky combined these two pieces of information to establish the poverty threshold as three times the cost of the USDA diet. She assumed that families facing poverty would cut back on both food and nonfood expenditures at approximately the same rate so that the 3-to-1 ratio would hold (Fisher 1992, 2008; Orshansky 1965).

There has been a long-standing debate about whether this approach to defining poverty in the United States measures the true nature of poverty. For example, critics argue that the measure is too simplistic, or that the multiplier should now be closer to five which would have the effect of raising the poverty line. Recognizing the limits of the official definition, the U.S. government started calculating a supplemental measure of poverty in the fall of 2011.

Robyn Beck/AFP/Getty Images

Going GLOBAL

Child Poverty Rates Around the World

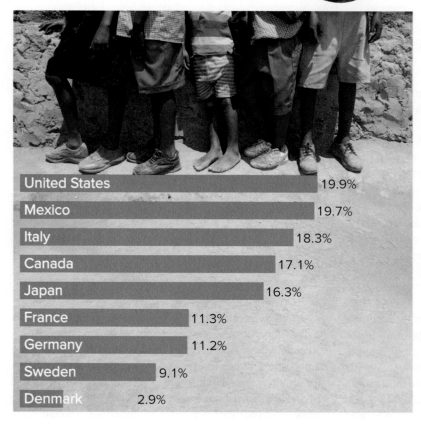

United States	19.9%
Mexico	19.7%
Italy	18.3%
Canada	17.1%
Japan	16.3%
France	11.3%
Germany	11.2%
Sweden	9.1%
Denmark	2.9%

Source: OECD 2018b:Table CO2.2. *Photo:* Jason R Warren/E+/Getty Images

This more complex measure takes into account the actual costs of food, clothing, shelter, utilities, taxes, work expenses, and out-of-pocket medical costs. In addition to income, it counts food stamps and tax credits as available resources, and is adjusted to reflect price differences across geographic regions (Fox 2018).

Who Are the Poor? One of the lessons we learn by analyzing those who fall below the poverty line is that our stereotypes about poverty are flawed. For example, many people in the United States believe that the vast majority of the poor are able to work but will not. Yet, 44.1 percent of people in poverty are either children under age 18 or adults 65 years old or older. Many working-age adults who are poor do work outside the home, although often in part-time positions. In 2017, 2.4 million people who worked full-time, year-round, and 5.7 million of those who worked part-time, were in poverty. Of those poor adults who do not work, many are ill or disabled, or are occupied in maintaining a home (Fontenot, Semega, and Kollar 2018:Table 3).

A person's likelihood of being in poverty varies based on social status. The "Who Are the Poor in the United States?" table demonstrates this by contrasting the percentage of people in a variety of status

Who Are the Poor in the United States?

	Percentage of the total U.S. population	Percentage of the poor population
Age		
Under 18 years old	22.7	32.3
18 to 64 years old	61.4	55.9
65 years and older	15.8	11.8
Race/Ethnicity		
Whites (non-Hispanic)	60.5	42.8
Blacks	13.2	22.7
Hispanics	18.3	27.2
Asians and Pacific Islanders	6.0	4.9
Families		
Married couples	73.7	38.7
Female householder, no husband present	18.6	51.0
Male householder, no wife present	7.7	10.2

Note: Age and race/ethnicity percentages are based on total persons. Families percentages are based on total families.

Source: Fontenot, Semega, and Kollar 2018:Tables 3, 4. *Photos: (top right):* Wild Horse Photography/Getty Images *(bottom right):* David Buffington/Photodisc/Getty Images; *(bottom center):* Con Tanasiuk/Design Pics; *(bottom left):* Jacobs Stock Photography/BananaStock/JupiterImages/PictureQuest; *(top left):* James Pauls/eyecrave LLC/Vetta/iStockphoto

categories in the U.S. population as a whole versus the percentage in those same categories who are officially considered poor. For example, 22.7 percent of people in the United States are under 18, but 32.3 percent of people in poverty are under 18. This suggests that children are overrepresented in the poverty population when compared to the population as a whole. People who are 65 and older are underrepresented in the poverty population because their percentage within the poor population of 11.8 is smaller than their percentage in the population as a whole of 15.8 (Fontenot, Semega, and Kollar 2018:Table 3).

The type of community within which people live also plays a role. In 2017, 41 percent of poor people in the United States lived in big cities within metropolitan areas. But poverty is not an urban problem alone. Overall, 43 percent of people in poverty live outside of metropolitan areas (Fontenot, Semega, and Kollar 2018).

Analyses of people who are poor in general reveal that they are not a static group. The overall composition of the poor changes continually; some individuals and families move above the poverty level after a year or two, while others slip below it. In a study of economic insecurity from ages 25 to 60, sociologist Mark Rank found that 79 percent of the U.S. population experience at least one year in which they are unemployed, receive welfare benefits, or are

officially poor or near poverty. Focusing just on poverty and near poverty, 54.1 percent spend a year with an income less than 150 percent of the poverty line at some point during their prime adult working-age lives. Considering long-term welfare use, only 3.8 percent of that population received such benefits for 10 or more consecutive years (Rank, Hirschl, and Foster 2014:37).

SOCTHINK

Should welfare recipients be required to work? If so, should the government subsidize preschool and afterschool care for their children while they are at work?

In 1996, in a historic shift in federal policy, Congress passed the Personal Responsibility and Work Opportunity Reconciliation Act, ending the long-standing federal guarantee of assistance to every poor family that meets eligibility requirements. The law sets a lifetime limit of five years of welfare benefits and requires all able-bodied adults to work after receiving two years of benefits (although hardship exceptions are allowed). The federal government gives

People Below Poverty Level

Percentage of people below poverty level

- 14.0–21.4
- 12.5–13.9
- 11.0–12.4
- 10.0–10.9
- 6.6–9.9

United States average is 12.3

Note: Data are for 2017.
Source: U.S. Census Bureau 2018c:Table 19.

block grants to the states to use as they wish in assisting poor and needy residents, and it permits states to experiment with ways to move people off welfare.

Other countries vary widely in their commitment to social service programs. But most industrialized nations devote higher proportions of their expenditures to housing, Social Security, welfare, health care, and unemployment compensation than the United States does. For example, in Germany, the government pays for 85 percent of health care expenditures, compared to 80 percent in the United Kingdom, 74 percent in Canada, and 52 percent in Mexico. The U.S. government pays 50 percent of health care expenditures, ranking it behind the global average of 59 percent (World Bank 2016b).

The domino effects of a lack of economic resources can be severe, as Rae McCormick's experience demonstrated at the beginning of this chapter. Poor people often also lack the social network connections to help them get good jobs, not to mention having to overcome the negative status associated with being poor. When it comes to cultural resources, they also often lack the same kind of educational credentials that can serve as a valuable asset. Journalist David Shipler (2004), in his in-depth study titled *The Working Poor: Invisible in America,* referred to the combination of factors that poor people must overcome as the "interlocking deficits of poverty." As Shipler (2004:4–5) put it,

> Breaking away and moving a comfortable distance from poverty seems to require a perfect lineup of favorable conditions. A set of skills, a

good starting wage, and a job with the likelihood of promotion are prerequisites. But so are clarity of purpose, courageous self-esteem, a lack of substantial debt, freedom from mental illness or addiction, a functional family, a network of upstanding friends, and the right help from private or governmental agencies.

The obstacles that poverty presents, and the advantages that access to wealth provides, raise questions about the degree to which a person can succeed based on his or her abilities alone or whether the social position people inherit determines their likely outcome.

THE AMERICAN DREAM

The American Dream is as much about opportunity as it is success. The existence of substantial levels of income and wealth inequality, and the persistence of poverty, are not themselves contrary to the American Dream. In the United States, 61 percent of adults believe that people who want to get ahead can make it if they are willing to work hard. This belief does not vary significantly by income level (Pew Research Center 2014e, 2018c). Even though the gap between rich and poor is wide, people in the United States are less likely to see that gap as a big problem than do people in a wide variety of other nations, including England, France, Greece, Russia, China, and Pakistan (Pew Research Center 2014f). Americans want to assume that the system is fair and that both the rich and the poor are deserving of their positions (Putnam 2015).

Meritocracy Faith in opportunity manifests itself in a commitment to meritocracy. A meritocracy is a system in which a person's social status is achieved through a combination of ability and effort. To put it in terms of stratification and social mobility, a meritocracy is an open system in which your position is earned.

The commitment to meritocracy in the United States works in tandem with the principle of equality. That value is set forth within the opening lines of the Declaration of Independence: "We hold these truths to be self-evident, that all men are created equal, that they are endowed by their Creator with certain unalienable Rights, that among these are Life, Liberty and the Pursuit of Happiness" (The U.S. National Archives and Records Administration 1776). This conviction regarding our fundamental sameness implies that everyone should have a chance for success regardless of their station in life. Our outcomes should be based on something other than having had the good fortune of being born into the right family. Differences in outcomes in terms of income, wealth, and poverty are accepted, and even valued, because they provide incentives for hard work and sacrifice, so long as everyone has an opportunity to succeed (Reeves 2015).

The desire to put the principle of meritocracy into practice was apparent early on in American history in the works of people like Benjamin Franklin and Thomas Jefferson. It provided the justification for Horace Mann's commitment to public education as the great equalizer, as we saw in the "Education in Society" section in Chapter 8. One of his goals was to have schools spread a common American culture through a shared curriculum. Values, including the importance of meritocracy, were reinforced. Children in 1843, for example, in their *McGuffey's Eclectic Readers,* one of the most commonly assigned textbook series in American history, read passages such as this:

Elnur Amikishiyev/123RF

> The road to wealth, to honor, to usefulness, and happiness, is open to all, and all who will, may enter upon it with the almost certain prospect of success. In this free community, there are no privileged orders. Every man finds his level. If he has talents, he will be known and estimated, and rise in the respect and confidence of society. (Quoted in Weiss 1969:33)

Similarly, in the late 1800s, the best-selling books by Horatio Alger, including titles such as *Struggling Upward,*

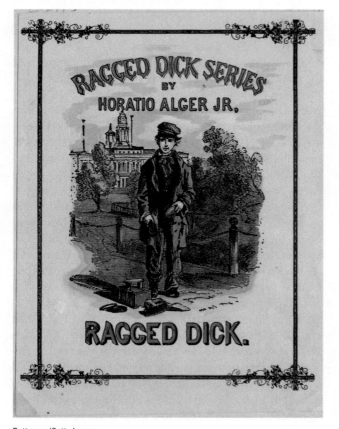

Bettmann/Getty Images

Mark the Match Boy, and *Rough and Ready,* reinforced the rags-to-riches ideal. In *Ragged Dick,* for example, the title character is told as a boy, "You know in this free country poverty in early life is no bar to a man's advancement" (Alger [1868] 1985:55). In Alger's stories, a person's character and values trump social position as superior resources all but ensuring certain success (Reeves 2014).

Faith in the American Dream remains strong. Former president Barack Obama reinforced the U.S. commitment to meritocracy in his second inaugural address. In it he declared, "We are true to our creed when a little girl born into the bleakest poverty knows that she has the same chance to succeed as anybody else, because she is an American; she is free, and she is equal, not just in the eyes of God but also in our own" (Obama 2013). There is, in the United States, an almost sacred aura that surrounds the principle of meritocracy. Violation of this principle would represent a betrayal of the public trust.

Aristocracy In many ways, commitment to meritocracy was the counterpoint to the rule by the British monarchy that early American colonists rebelled against. In an aristocracy, social status is ascribed and membership in the privileged or elite ranks is inherited. Unlike the sameness principle undergirding meritocracy, this system presupposes the existence of innate differences between people. Some are born to lead while others are destined to follow. *Aristocracy* literally means "rule by the best," and, over time, that came to mean the nobility. The principle of aristocracy undergirds both the caste and estate systems of stratification. Because differences are presumed to be inherited, there are limited opportunities for social mobility.

In the United States, people are less certain about the degree to which opportunities for social mobility remain possible. The 61 percent of people who believe that "anyone can get ahead if they work hard" has declined from 74 percent in 1999, and the percentage of people who now say that "hard work and determination are no guarantee of success for most people" rose from 23 to 36 percent (Pew Research Center 2016d).

The likelihood of children doing better than their parents, an important marker for the American Dream, has decreased, as the "Will You Earn More Than Your Parents?" graph shows. Comparing incomes for parents and children when each reached age 30, and using constant dollars to make comparison possible, 92 percent of children born in 1940 earned more than their parents did at the same age. For those born in 1984, only 50 percent outearned their parents. In other words, the odds of doing better than your parents are now no better than a coin flip (Chetty, Grusky, and Hell et al. 2016).

Resources parents possess play a significant role in shaping outcomes for their children. A parent's occupational status is a strong predictor of their children's occupational

Will You Earn More Than Your Parents?

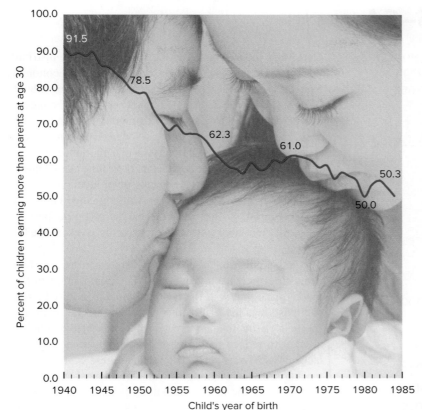

Percent of children earning more than parents at age 30 (y-axis)

- 91.5
- 78.5
- 62.3
- 61.0
- 50.0
- 50.3

Child's year of birth (x-axis): 1940, 1945, 1950, 1955, 1960, 1965, 1970, 1975, 1980, 1985

Note: Graph compares pretax income for parents and children when each reached age 30.
Source: Chetty, Grusky, and Hell et al. 2016. *Photo:* Cecilia Cartner/Cultura/Getty Images

Likelihood of Graduating from College

College Graduates (%) (y-axis)

Legend: Low — Middle — High

Poorest quarter of families: 3, 8, 29
Richest quarter of families: 30, 51, 74

8th-Grade Test Score Performance

Note: Test performance is for a standardized 8th-grade math test. Family status is based on parent's education, occupation, and income. College graduation rate measure is for 12 years after the test.
Source: Putnam 2015:190.

status as adults. Working-class parents, for example, tend to produce children who become working-class adults themselves (Hout 2018). The amount of wealth parents own is a significant predictor of how much wealth their children will possess when they are adults. Mobility can happen, but only 6 percent of children in the lowest wealth quintile make the rags-to-riches journey to the top wealth quintile (Pfeffer and Killewald 2016).

Political scientist Robert Putnam (2015) uses the expression "opportunity gap" to describe what appears to be a growing divide between the children of the well-to-do compared to children from working-class and poor families. Increased levels of neighborhood segregation, educational segregation, and social network segregation, including the increased likelihood of marrying a same-class spouse, he claims, all contribute to a growing class divide. Well-off parents provide their children with a whole host of advantages, including private schools, tutors, educational vacations, and specialized summer camps, making the divide even wider (Duncan and Murnane 2011; Finighan and Putnam 2016; Putnam 2015; Thompson 2018).

As we can see from the "Likelihood of Graduating from College" graph, a child from a high-income family who scores poorly on a standardized 8th-grade math exam is more likely to graduate from college 12 years later than a child from a low-income family who scores high on the exam. This suggests that rich kids with poor academic performance are more likely to graduate than are smart poor kids (Papageorge and Thom 2018; Putnam 2015). As one report analyzing similar outcomes regarding academic potential and educational success put it, "being born rich trumps being born gifted" (Van Dam 2018).

The economic, social, and cultural advantages children at the top receive provide a cushion that protects these children should failure occur. Putnam writes, "Parental wealth is especially important for social mobility, because it can provide informal insurance that allows kids to take more risks in search of more reward" (Putnam 2015:36). Those who do not get the opportunity to fully develop their skills through education, for example, are less likely to share in the rewards that such accomplishment conveys, as shown in the "Education Pays" graph. Over time, as those at the top transmit increased access to resources to their children, the rungs of the mobility ladder get farther apart, making it difficult for people with limited resources to reach the next level (Frank 2016; Reeves 2017; Thompson 2018). Yet seeing this reality remains a challenge, because when a society makes an overt commitment to meritocracy in principle, it becomes easy to minimize the degree to which inherited resources shape likely outcomes.

Education Pays: Full-Time, Year-Round Workers Aged 25–64

Education level	Median annual earnings
Professional degree	$110,656
Doctorate degree	$102,027
Master's degree	$77,685
Bachelor's degree	$62,100
Associate's degree	$46,629
Some college, no degree	$42,418
High school grad (includes GED)	$39,005
Some high school, no degree	$31,121

Source: U.S. Census Bureau 2018b:Table PINC-03. *Photo:* McGraw-Hill Education

>> Sociological Perspectives on Stratification

Bourgeoisie The ruling class under capitalism due to their ownership of the means of production.

Proletariat The working class under capitalism who must sell their labor power in exchange for a wage because they lack ownership of the means of production.

By paying attention to the structure of the stratification system and how resources within it are distributed, we can better understand how a society committed to the principle of meritocracy might produce the practice of aristocracy. Sociologists provide us with tools to focus our attention on key resources that enable us to discern who has power and why. As noted, three categories of resources are critical: material, social, and cultural.

MARX AND MATERIAL RESOURCES

Karl Marx focuses his attention primarily on the distribution of material resources. As we saw in the "Economic Systems" section of Chapter 9, he argues that, throughout history, power was determined by ownership of the means of production. As a result, Marx's model of class has two basic categories: owners and non-owners. During feudal times, for example, the nobility owned the land, and the peasants did not. Under capitalism, the ruling class, known as the **bourgeoisie,** own the means of production, including factories and machinery. The working class, known as the **proletariat,** do not own the means of production so must sell their labor power to the capitalist in exchange for a wage.

Marx argues that the logic of capitalism as a system determines how each group acts. The competition in the marketplace that is at the heart of capitalism initially pits capitalists against each other in their pursuit of profit. In their desire to gain greater market share, capitalists attempt to reduce the costs of production in general and labor costs in particular. They reduce these costs through mechanization (inventing new machines capable of taking over more of the labor), de-skilling (simplifying the work process by breaking it down into its most basic steps so that minimal knowledge is required), and offshoring (finding labor in other parts of the world capable of doing the work for less money). It's not that capitalists are necessarily greedier than others or have a particular desire to exploit their workers; they act based on the principles inherent in the system.

Marx argued that this downward pressure on workers' wages and working conditions is unrelenting. It ultimately leads to the development of a massive global working class of largely poor, unskilled workers competing against each other for low-wage jobs, resulting in racial, ethnic, and nationalistic conflict among the proletariat. Ironically, it is the technological innovation of capitalism that makes a better future possible, as we explored in Chapter 9. Marx praised this aspect of capitalism because it solves the problem of production like no other previous economic system. Capitalism, he writes, was "the first to show what man's activity can bring about. It has accomplished wonders far surpassing Egyptian pyramids, Roman aqueducts, and Gothic cathedrals" (Marx and Engels [1848] 1998:38). As a result, we will eventually eliminate scarcity. Even now we can produce enough so that no one in the world needs to go hungry.

Once this technological obstacle to providing for all our needs was solved, Marx felt that the only obstacle to an equitable society would be the capitalist system of social relations. Its emphasis on private property enabled the few

Source: Elkins 2018. *Photo:* Martin H. Simon/Pool/Getty Images

at the top, the bourgeoisie, to own and control much more than they could ever hope to need or want while the majority at the bottom, the proletariat, struggled. Eventually, Marx argued, the proletariat would see that they had no real interest in the existing set of social relations. They would develop **class consciousness**—a subjective awareness of common vested interests and the need for collective political action to bring about social change. This would lead to the overthrow of capitalism in favor of a system of more equitable distribution in the form of socialism and then communism.

A question that often arises in response to Marx's work is this: why hasn't that revolution happened? One answer is that Marx thought capitalists would work against the development of such class consciousness by shaping society's accepted values and norms. The term dominant ideology describes a set of cultural beliefs and practices that helps to maintain powerful social, economic, and political interests. From this perspective, one of the possible functions of meritocracy as a value is to reinforce the belief that mobility is possible even when limited opportunity exists in practice. In addition, belief in meritocracy reinforces the idea

that those at the top belong there as a consequence of ability and effort and, therefore, deserve whatever riches and power they can accumulate (Fraser 2015). As a result, workers must overcome what Marx termed **false consciousness**—an attitude held by members of a class that does not accurately reflect their objective position. A worker with false consciousness may adopt an individualistic viewpoint toward capitalist exploitation ("*I* am being exploited by *my* boss"). In contrast, the class-conscious worker realizes that all workers are being exploited by the bourgeoisie and have a common stake in revolution.

Because Marx paid attention to the structure of the system itself, he was able to identify inherent tensions between social classes based on their control over material resources. Much more recently, economist Thomas Piketty did something similar in his surprise best seller *Capital in the Twenty-First Century* (2014). In this expansive historical overview of economic growth, Piketty maintains that, in the long run, the rate of return on capital, including profits, rents, interest, and dividends, is greater than overall economic growth, including increased income and output. Piketty uses the formula $r > g$ to describe this relationship. One reviewer summarized it this way, "Simply having money is the best way to get more money" (Doctorow 2014). Yet, in the United States, the commitment to meritocracy makes it difficult to accept the consequences of this simple fact. Denial was possible, in part, because, for most of the 20th century, the economy grew faster than normal due to technological innovation, and wealth grew more slowly as a consequence of the destructive impact of both world wars and the Great Depression. According to Piketty, that anomalous period, which helped produce a prosperous middle class in the middle of the century, has come to an end. In effect, Piketty is arguing that increasing inequality is an inevitable consequence of the structure of capitalism, and this, he says, "poses a challenge to the meritocratic model" (2014:27). What we learn from both Marx and Piketty is that control over material resources conveys substantial advantages.

Class consciousness The subjective awareness held by members of a class regarding their common vested interests and need for collective political action to bring about social change.

False consciousness A term used by Karl Marx to describe an attitude held by members of a class that does not accurately reflect their objective position.

WEBER AND SOCIAL RESOURCES

Max Weber accepted Marx's premise that social class plays a substantial role in shaping outcomes, but he argued that Marx's conception of power was too narrow, because it focused almost exclusively on ownership of the means of production. Weber argued that, in addition to material resources, social resources mattered, too. In response, he proposed a multidimensional model of stratification that included three components: class, status, and party.

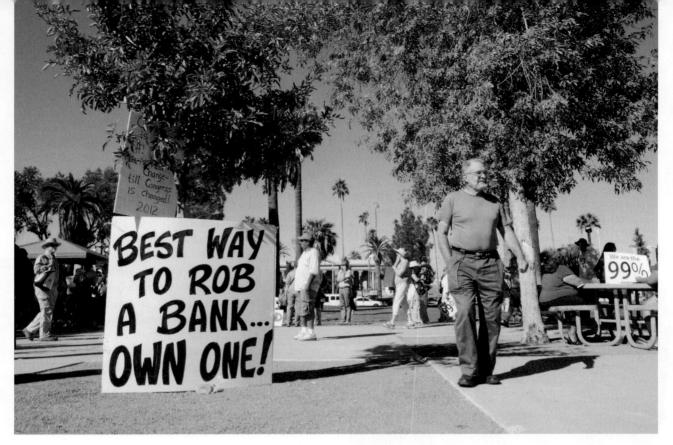

Dave Moyer

Class A group of people who have a similar level of economic resources.

Status group People who share the same perceived level of prestige.

Prestige The respect and admiration that a particular status holds in society.

Socioeconomic status (SES) A measure of social class position based on a combination of education, occupation, and income.

Weber used the term **class** to refer to a group of people who have a similar level of economic resources. He identified two core elements of class: material resources and skill knowledge in the marketplace. In the first instance, class is about how much you own. Like Marx, this included ownership of the means of production, but Weber argued that ownership of other economic resources, including land, savings, and stocks, also defined a person's class position. And, whereas Marx maintained that mechanization and extreme division of labor would make skilled labor less valuable under capitalism, Weber argued that, given the complexity of modern society, knowledge would continue to be a valuable commodity in the labor market, something that employers would reward. By developing our skill knowledge—for example, by going to college—we enhance our class position.

Whereas class represents a material resource, status is a social resource. Weber used the term **status group** to refer to people who share the same perceived level of prestige. The power that your status provides depends on how others view you, including both positive and negative estimations of honor.

Prestige refers to the respect and admiration that a particular status holds in a society. Based on national surveys, sociologists have produced the "Prestige Rankings of Occupations" table to summarize people's perceptions of the relative status of a variety of occupations. We see doctors and lawyers as more prestigious than librarians and social workers, who are higher than janitors and maids (Hout, Smith, and Marsden 2015). But prestige in a class-based system involves more than just occupation. **Socioeconomic status (SES)** is a measure of social class

5 Movies on SOCIAL CLASS

Snowpiercer
Class warfare breaks out on a post-apocalyptic train ride.

Winter's Bone
A teen living in the Ozarks investigates her father's criminal dealings.

The Florida Project
Growing up in the shadow of the Magic Kingdom.

Rich Hill
Three boys and their families struggle to get by.

Generation Wealth
No matter how much people have, they still want more.

Prestige Rankings of Occupations

Occupation	Score		Occupation	Score
Physicians and surgeons	80		Tool and die makers	38
Astronomers and physicists	75		Barbers	36
College professors	74		Printing press operators	36
Architects	73		File clerks	36
Dentists	72		Bus drivers	35
Chief executives	72		Childcare workers	35
Psychologists	71		Security guards	34
Lawyers	69		Cooks	33
Clergy	66		Office clerks	32
Aircraft pilots	65		Bartenders	32
Registered nurses	64		Waiters and waitresses	31
High school teachers	64		Hotel desk clerks	30
Computer programmers	63		Logging workers	29
Sociologists	63		Construction laborers	28
Chiropractors	61		Hunters and trappers	28
Elementary and middle school teachers	61		Laundry and dry-cleaning workers	26
Police officers	60		Taxi drivers and chauffeurs	26
Firefighters	59		Janitors	24
Actors	58		Maids	20
Dental hygienists	56		Telemarketers	18
Librarians	55			
Social workers	54			
Chefs and head cooks	50			
Electricians	49			
Insurance sales agents	47			
Bakers	45			
Carpenters	44			
Fundraisers	40			
Residential advisors	39			
Animal trainers	38			

Note: 100 is the highest and 0 the lowest possible prestige score.
Source: Hout, Smith, and Marsden 2015. Photos: *(top):* Michael N. Paras/Pixtal/age fotostock; *(bottom):* James Hardy/PhotoAlto

particular goal. This is what we mean when we talk of a political party, but such organization extends beyond politics to all spheres of life. As we have seen previously with Weber, bureaucracies represent the ideal form of this resource because they are organized explicitly to maximize available resources and to accomplish their goals in the most efficient manner possible. For Weber, party was a potential resource, available to any individuals or groups who would seize it. The civil rights movement in the United States provides a classic example. With minimal class or status resources as defined by the larger society, organization was critical to the success of this movement.

Weber maintained that, in practice, these three resources work together to shape individual and group power. People who are strong in one area can leverage that power to increase resources in the others. For example, people donate material resources to political causes in the hope that doing so will advance social and organizational interests. Those who already possess power in all three areas have advantages over those who do not.

Party The capacity to organize to accomplish some particular goal.

Cultural capital Our tastes, knowledge, attitudes, language, and ways of thinking that we exchange in interaction with others.

BOURDIEU AND CULTURAL RESOURCES

Marx emphasized material resources, and Weber highlighted the significance of social resources in the form of both status and party. Sociologist Pierre Bourdieu (1984, 1986) added to these the significance of cultural resources. He introduced the concept of **cultural capital,** by which he meant our tastes, knowledge, attitudes, language, and ways of thinking that we exchange in interaction with others. Often associated with artistic or

position that combines education, occupation, and income. Class and status are not necessarily linked. It is possible to have significant social prestige along with a low economic standing, as is the case for many clergy members who are highly regarded within their faith communities, but who often receive relatively modest incomes.

The third major element in Weber's multidimensional model of stratification focuses on organizational resources. **Party** refers to the capacity to organize to accomplish some

SOCTHINK

How might a group coordinate its class, status, and party resources to accomplish its goals? Pick a group on campus or in your community that is seeking to bring about social change, and imagine how you might advise group members using Weber's principles.

literary preferences, cultural capital goes much deeper than this because it is rooted in our perception of reality itself. For Bourdieu, because some culture is more highly valued than other culture, it represents a form of power.

Our things aren't just things. They are symbols telling stories of who we are, where we are from, and what is important to us. Whether in the form of shoes, cars, pets, or smartphones, we choose them because they fit with our tastes which are shaped by the cultural capital we come to inherit from those around us. From NASCAR to Mozart, for example, the tastes of the working class typically differ from those of the upper class. Symphonic concerts, operas, and foreign films, for instance, are considered "high culture," whereas "pop culture," including popular movies, TV shows, and most streaming music channels, is considered "middle-brow" or below. People draw distinctions, for example, between watching *Masterpiece* on PBS versus *American Ninja Warrior* and listening to Placido Domingo versus Bruno Mars. Such judgments are based on a certain level of cultural elitism in which those at the top are able to define their preferences as apparently superior to those of the masses (Accominotti, Storer, and Khan 2018; Wilson 2007). The cultural capital of people who are working class, often disparaged as redneck or ghetto, is valued least of all—until it is claimed by others as their own, as was the case with jazz, blues, rock and roll, and rap (Gans 1971).

SOCTHINK

Paul Fussell (1992), in his book *Class: A Guide through the American Status System,* argued that the writing on our clothes says a lot about our social class. What story do the logos, brands, and writing on your clothes tell about you? How might your clothing choices have differed had you been in a different class position?

When we interact with others, we draw on the cultural capital resources we possess. Such interaction is fairly easy with others who share the same basic set of resources. When interaction occurs with others who possess a different stock of cultural capital, however, it becomes more complex. We see these kinds of difficulties when executives try to interact casually with workers on the factory floor or when we find ourselves dining in a place where we aren't quite sure what the rules are.

If cultural capital preferences were only a matter of social difference between various subcultures, it might not be a big deal. But the cultural capital of the elite is also tied to their control over economic and social resources. As a result, cultural capital can be used as a form of exclusion from jobs, organizations, and opportunities. For example, a qualified applicant may not be hired because, during the interview, they used inappropriate syntax or did not seem adequately familiar with cultural references, such as current news events or the latest in the world of golf. Employers tend to hire people they feel comfortable with, and cultural capital plays a significant role in that process (Kanter 1993).

Compounding this problem of cultural inequality is the fact that our preferences and perceptions often pass down from parent to child in the same way that material capital is inherited. Parents teach their children linguistic patterns and cultural tastes, from the use of double negatives to the appreciation of literature (Lareau 2015; Rothstein 2009). Cultural capital is also reproduced in the next generation in the context of schools, where class distinctions within the community shape the curriculum and patterns of discipline. Sociologist Jessi Streib (2011) found that, already by age four, children had adopted cultural conventions based on their social class positions. For eight months she conducted research at a diverse preschool and found that children from upper-middle-class families were more talkative and demanding of the teacher's time and attention than were working-class kids. The linguistic style of the higher-class children was more consistent with the classroom culture, and, as a result, they were more likely to get their needs met.

Social mobility from this perspective involves more than just acquiring more money and better social connections. Winning the lottery, for example, does not transform a person at the bottom of the hierarchy into one at the top, or, as Bourdieu put it, "Having a million does not in itself make one able to live like a millionaire" (1984:374). Such movement requires a social and cultural transformation as well. For mobility to happen, individuals must earn and learn a different set of knowledge and skills, as well as a whole new lifestyle: new tastes, attitudes, language, and thoughts.

MATERIAL, SOCIAL, AND CULTURAL RESOURCES

Using these sociological tools enables us to better understand how social stratification operates. We learn that we must be particularly attentive to the type of social stratification system in place and to the categories of resources that determine positions within those systems. In closed systems, position is largely determined through inheritance at birth, and there is little you can do to change it. In the U.S. class-based system, some degree of mobility is possible.

> Money may be the measure of wealth, but it is far from the only form of it.
>
> Matthew Stewart (2018)

Personal Sociology

Cultural Capital

As a professor, I have seen that grades are shaped by more than just effort and inherent intellectual ability. Students with more cultural capital, including significant background educational resources, simply do not have to work as hard. Seniors in my introductory course, for example, know the rules of the game. In comparison, first-year students often have a hard time distinguishing what is essential versus what is secondary. Over time, however, most learn how to study effectively. This same principle is at work before students even arrive on campus. Students who come to college with the kinds of cultural capital that professors reward have advantages over those who lack such resources.

But it turns out that being rich or poor involves more than just having more or less money. We must be attentive to social and cultural resources as well.

When it comes to social order, it is easier for us, and for others, to continue along the same paths than to carve out new ones. In so doing, the status quo reproduces itself. Our social resources, including networks of relationships with family, friends, and coworkers, constrain the kinds of connections that might open up new pathways for us. Our cultural resources,

including preferences, tastes, and knowledge, limit what we might imagine as possible or desirable. Whereas some at the top look down on those at the bottom as irresponsible and short-sighted, members of the working class may make fun of rich people's hoity-toity preference for opera and ballet and criticize their values as materialistic and selfish, lacking commitment to family and friends (MacLeod 2009).

As a result of material, social, and cultural resource differences, changing classes may involve the difficult task of changing identities, leading some to argue that the United States is more caste-like (Fussell 1992). Mobility would involve new social networks, new lifestyles, and new tastes. Complicating matters further, changing classes requires more than just changing ourselves; it also requires recognition and acceptance by others. Just as there may be interlocking deficits of poverty, there may also be interlocking advantages of wealth. One of those privileges is exclusion, denying others access to valuable social network connections. When considering the consequences of difference, implementing meritocracy and living up to the American Dream turn out to be challenging undertakings. But an understanding and appreciation for the challenges involved can empower people to take the steps necessary to succeed.

SOCIOLOGY IS A VERB

Sociological Autobiography

Write your sociological autobiography through the lens of class. How have your life chances been shaped by your access to material resources, such as your family income and wealth? By social resources—namely, your family and friendship network connections? By cultural resources—including taste, language, artistic and pop culture preferences, and educational attainment of family members? How might your life have been totally different if you had been born into another family with a different stock of resources?

For REVIEW

I. **What is social class?**
- Like slavery, caste, and estate, it is a stratification system in which people and groups are ranked, but it places them based primarily on economic position.

II. **How does social class operate?**
- Three categories of resources are key: material, including income and wealth; social, including social networks and prestige; and cultural, including tastes, education, and knowledge. Power is based on access to and control over these resources.

III. **What are the consequences of social class?**
- Although class-based systems are more open than the others, our life chances are shaped by our inherited class position and the material, social, and cultural resources that go with it. For most people, the social mobility that does occur, whether in terms of occupation, income, or wealth, is of a relatively short distance.

SOCVIEWS on Social Class

Functionalist View

All societies have some degree of stratification in order to ensure that all of society's needs are met.

In a society with a complex **division of labor**, some positions will inevitably be more important or require more skill than others.

Those with more talent and determination fill the higher-paid and more prestigious positions, whereas those who do not develop their talents take the low-ranking jobs.

DIVISION OF LABOR, SOCIAL MOBILITY
KEY CONCEPTS

Conflict View

Stratification systems perpetuate unequal economic rewards and facilitate exploitation.

Social class standing is largely an **ascribed status**.

People in power maintain and spread their interests and influence through their hold on the **dominant ideology** in a society.

Income and wealth are **distributed unequally** in U.S. society, and the gap between the rich and the poor is steadily increasing.

KEY CONCEPTS
STRATIFICATION, INEQUALITY, DOMINANT IDEOLOGY

Interactionist View

Social mobility results from interactions in which people attempt to better their place in the class system (for example, getting degrees, **networking**, acquiring cultural capital).

When we interact with others, we **exchange** our cultural capital resources, such as knowledge, tastes, attitudes, and ways of thinking.

Our social class helps determine our taste in clothes, food, music, TV shows, and many other everyday preferences.

KEY CONCEPTS
NETWORKING, EXCHANGE

MAKE THE CONNECTION
After reviewing the chapter, answer the following questions:

1
Analyze social mobility from the point of view of the three perspectives. In what way might mobility be functional? How would conflict theory explain it? What role does interaction play in getting ahead?

2
How do the conflict and the interactionist perspectives intersect in Marx's concept of "false consciousness"?

3
How would a theorist from each perspective explain the distribution of material, social, and cultural resources in society?

4
Think about your own "life chances." Which perspectives help you see factors that shaped your opportunities and outcomes?

Pop Quiz

1. **What expression did Max Weber coin to describe the fact that our likelihood for success is shaped by our access to valued material, social, and cultural resources?**
   a. *verstehen*
   b. cultural capital
   c. social mobility
   d. life chances

2. **Which of the systems of stratification included "those who pray, those who fight, and those who work"?**
   a. slavery
   b. caste
   c. estate
   d. class

3. **A college professor whose father was a printer is an example of**
   a. downward intergenerational mobility.
   b. upward intergenerational mobility.
   c. downward intragenerational mobility.
   d. upward intragenerational mobility.

4. **What term describes money received over some period of time?**
   a. wealth
   b. material resources
   c. assets
   d. income

5. **What percentage of total income in the United States did the top quintile earn in 2017?**
   a. 17.4 percent
   b. 24.5 percent
   c. 51.5 percent
   d. 77.2 percent

6. **What does absolute poverty refer to?**
   a. income below the 10th percentile as measured globally
   b. a minimum level of subsistence that no family should be expected to live without
   c. income below the 10th percentile within any society
   d. a level of deprivation by which people at the bottom of a society are judged to be disadvantaged in comparison with the nation as a whole

7. **Approximately what percentage of the U.S. population lived in poverty in 2017?**
   a. 3.2 percent
   b. 8.4 percent
   c. 12.3 percent
   d. 22.8 percent

8. **According to Karl Marx, the class that owns the means of production is the**
   a. nobility.
   b. proletariat.
   c. Brahman.
   d. bourgeoisie.

9. **Which of the following were viewed by Max Weber as distinct components of stratification?**
   a. conformity, deviance, and social control
   b. class, status, and party
   c. class, caste, and age
   d. class, prestige, and esteem

10. **According to Pierre Bourdieu, our tastes, our education, the way we talk, and the things we like all represent forms of**
    a. social capital.
    b. esteem.
    c. cultural capital.
    d. intelligence.

1. (d), 2. (c), 3. (b), 4. (d), 5. (c), 6. (b), 7. (c), 8. (d), 9. (b), 10. (c)

Viviane Moos/Corbis Historical/Getty Images

TWO TALES OF ONE CITY

Mumbai is a city of contrasts. On the one hand, it is the entertainment and financial capital of India, home of Bollywood stars and billionaires. On the other, 5.2 million of its residents, 41 percent of the city's population, live in areas designated as slums (Abkowitz 2015; GPOBA 2014).

Nita Ambani describes Mumbai as "a city where dreams come true," and for Nita and her family, it has been (Ward 2016). Nita's husband, Mukesh Ambani, is India's wealthiest man, with a net worth of $45.4 billion. Their 27-story house—which they share with their three kids and Mukesh's mother—reportedly cost $1 billion to build, likely making it the most expensive home in the world. Named Antilia, the house contains a library, ballroom, 50-seat theater, swimming pool, spa, dance studio, terraced gardens, temple, parking garage for 160 vehicles, and reportedly

even an ice-room that produces artificial snow flurries as a place to cool off on a hot day (*Forbes* 2019; Magnier 2010; Reginato 2012).

People at the top are doing well in Mumbai. The number of residents worth $30 million or more rose 357 percent from 2005 to 2015, producing a real estate boom (Knight Frank Research 2016). To meet the increasing demand for luxury accommodations in that city, developers launched a number of high-cost residential skyscraper projects. World One, for example, will become the tallest residential building in the world when completed, with housing units costing from $2.4 million to $16 million each. Before he became president, Donald Trump, not wanting to miss out on Mumbai's high-rise boom, also jumped in. Units at Trump Tower Mumbai start at $1.6 million apiece (Abkowitz 2015). Explaining the skyscraper boom, Babulal Varma, the managing director of yet another Mumbai developer, reports, "Everyone wants to get away from the crowd. . . . People want to go up. You're away from the noise, you're away from the pollution" (Bundhun 2016). Units in Varma's project start at $1.9 million, rising to $44 million for those near the top.

Life at street level looks very different for most people in Mumbai. In order to get by, many have to scavenge at Deonar, a massive 326-acre garbage dump that is surrounded on three sides by slums. People do this to find items they might recycle into something profitable, selling them to people such as Nawab Ali Shaikh, 61, who buys foam rubber collected from the dump, mostly from discarded furniture, cuts it into cubes, and sells it as stuffing material for toymakers. These scavenging and recycling jobs offer low pay, no security, and significant health and safety risks (Bag, Seth, and Gupta 2016; McKirdy and Kapur 2016; Shrivastava and Antony 2015; Ullah and Phadke 2016).

In India as a whole, the richest 1 percent owns 58.4 percent of the nation's wealth. At the other end of the scale, 176 million people live below the international poverty line of $1.90 per day. Globally, 736 million people live below that poverty line (Shorrocks, Davies, and Lluberas 2016; World Bank 2018e). In this chapter we explore various dimensions of such global inequality.

As You READ >>

- **How do sociologists approach modernization?**
- **How significant is global stratification?**
- **Why did the global movement for universal human rights develop?**

>> Global Interdependence

The people on whom we depend are often unknown and invisible to us. We've explored this idea in a number of ways throughout these chapters. In Chapter 1, for example, we considered the notion that a hamburger is a miracle, highlighting the extent to which we take for granted the knowledge and skills others possess. Most of us don't know how to mine the ore necessary to make the steel to produce the knife we would need to kill and butcher the cow. And that's just the beginning of our ignorance. Yet we buy things like hamburgers, veggieburgers, backpacks, smartphones, textbooks, shoes, clothes, cars, and so much more without thinking twice about all the people who participated in making those

Access to life's necessities, including clean drinking water, varies substantially around the world. (Left) Steve Morgan/Photofusion Picture Library/ Alamy Stock Photo; (Right) B2M Productions/Photodisc/Getty Images

Going GLOBAL

Measuring Global Inequality

Country	HDI
Yemen	0.452
Ethiopia	0.463
Afghanistan	0.498
Haiti	0.498
India	0.640
Guatemala	0.650
China	0.752
Brazil	0.759
Russia	0.816
UAE	0.863
USA	0.924
Norway	0.953

Note: The Human Development Index combines data on health, education, and income to provide a snapshot for each of 178 countries. Scores range from 0 to 1. These data are for 2017.
Source: United Nations Development Programme 2018. *Photos: (scale):* Ryan McVay/ Getty Images; *(earth):* 1xpert/123RF

things possible. And, to push this a bit further, we think little about the living and working conditions of the people who produce those goods (Timmerman 2012). Yet we could not lead the lives we do without the contributions they make.

In order to become more aware of the taken-for-granted knowledge and skill that make our current consumption possible, American journalist A. J. Jacobs (2018a) decided to try to thank all the people who contributed to his morning cup of coffee. He started with the barista at his local coffee shop, who was a bit surprised because she sometimes feels more like a vending machine than a human being. He thanked the guy behind the scenes who selected the beans for the shop, the truck drivers who deliver the beans to the store, and, all the way down the line to the Guarnizo family farm in Colombia, South America, he thanked the farmers who grow his beans. But he didn't stop there. He thanked the workers who paved the roads the trucks drive on, those who made the asphalt for the road, and others who produce the yellow paint for the lines on the road. He thanked the

miners who gathered the ore which gets made into steel that goes into making the coffee roasters. He thanked the steelworkers, too. He ultimately learned that there is no end to this project. Every new link produces many more links that create a massive, interdependent web of people who contribute to making our everyday lives what they are. Jacobs recounts his tale in a TED talk, available online (2018b).

Along the way, Jacobs also learned some difficult lessons. As he put it, "there's incredible suffering and horror along the supply chain" (quoted in Lambert 2018). Wages played an important role in that conclusion. Jacobs concluded that, even though $3 seems like a lot to pay for a cup of coffee, if all the people involved in its production got paid even minimum wage, it would likely cost much more. The vast majority of such work takes place outside the United States, beyond the consciousness of most Americans.

People's life chances are very much shaped by the country where they are born. For example, access to clean water and modern sanitation facilities represents a daily challenge for millions of people in developing nations. The United Nations created the Human Development Index (HDI) to assess progress along three key dimensions of human development: *health,* measured by life expectancy; *knowledge,* measured by average years and expected years of schooling; and *standard of living,* measured by gross national income per capita (United Nations Development Programme 2018). As the "Going Global: Measuring Global Inequality" graph demonstrates, nations differ significantly along these dimensions. As part of its annual HDI report, the UN also explores various dimensions within these three areas, including child labor, workplace safety, labor rights, maternity leave, leisure time, child malnutrition, HIV prevalence, public expenditures on education, environmental sustainability, and gender inequality (United Nations Development Programme 2018).

Given the rise of globalization, if we are to understand why we think and act as we do, we can't focus only on what's happening within a single country. We must consider issues within the larger global context. Economic decisions made in Shenzhen, China, may well have ripple effects in small towns across America, and policies approved in corporate board rooms in Chicago may impact indigenous peoples throughout Central and South America. Sociologists explore the patterns and practices of global inequality, developing various theories to account for its development and persistence.

>> Sociological Perspectives on Globalization

Sociology developed as a discipline largely to come to terms with the transition from traditional to modern society. The norms and values that guided people's actions

THE PROGRESS OF THE CENTURY.

THE LIGHTNING STEAM PRESS.   THE ELECTRIC TELEGRAPH.   THE LOCOMOTIVE.   THE STEAMBOAT.

Source: Library of Congress Prints and Photographs Division [LC-DIG-ppmsca-17563]

were breaking down as a result of changes ushered in with the Industrial Revolution. Increasingly, people worked in factories instead of on farms, they lived in huge cities instead of rural communities, and they encountered more and more people who didn't think and act like they did. Early sociologists saw it as their mission to make sense of such change in hopes of providing guidance for how best to manage it.

MODERNIZATION AND THE FUNCTIONALIST PERSPECTIVE

In order to understand the pathway to a brighter future, sociologists drawing on the functionalist perspective looked first to the past. Émile Durkheim, for example, investigated what he saw as simpler societies, including hunting-and-gathering and horticultural societies, in order to uncover those elements of society essential for social order. Knowing what these elements are would enable sociologists, and others, to ensure that the building blocks necessary for social order get tended to, especially during times of significant social upheaval.

Durkheim, along with many other theorists of his time, believed that societies evolve from the simple to the complex. They assumed that through **modernization,** all societies would eventually progress from traditional forms of social organization—typically rural, agricultural, and religious—toward forms characteristic of post–Industrial Revolution societies. According to this perspective, characteristics of modern societies include a *complex division of labor* in which work is specialized; *institutional specialization* including the division of family, economy, government, education, and religion into largely separate spheres, each with their own experts; a *societal or global orientation,* in which the economic and political focus shifts from the local concerns toward the global; *rational decision making in the public sphere* that relies primarily on technical experts rather than religious authorities; and the spread of both *cultural diversity,* as more peoples from different backgrounds come into contact with each other, and a corresponding growth in *egalitarianism* as a value that embraces such diversity (Bruce 2000).

The road toward modernization, according to modernization theorists, would ultimately be traveled by all. People in

> **Modernization** The evolution of societies from traditional forms of social organization—typically rural, agricultural, and religious—toward forms characteristic of post–Industrial Revolution societies.

Housing for people living in poverty around the world can be precarious, as shown here from Manila in the Philippines. John Wang/Getty Images

the United States and the countries of western Europe, for example, experienced significant upheaval during their transition from traditional to modern, only later to lead more comfortable lives as the benefits of modernization became more widely shared. Countries such as China and India, they would argue, are currently undergoing this disruptive process of becoming modern societies, but the benefits of doing so will inevitably follow. They also believe that eventually, the less developed nations of the world, which are often also the poorest countries, will inevitably go through this same evolutionary process so that all nations will benefit from modernization in the long term (Lipset 1959).

Dependency theory The theory that poor, less developed nations become subservient to wealthy industrial nations, which use their economic and political might to maintain power.

SOCTHINK

Early sociologists were optimistic that positive social change was inevitable. To what extent do you think people today share this vision of the inevitable rise of the good society? How might cynicism about the possibility for change contribute to the maintenance of the status quo?

Faith in the modernization model extended well beyond sociology and became a central premise for much modern economic and political theory. Advocates of free-market competition, in keeping with the principles of capitalism we explored in the "Economic Systems" section of Chapter 9, found an ally in modernization theory. The presupposition that development follows along an inevitable evolutionary path fit well with capitalism's *laissez-faire* commitment to let the economy function freely and naturally. For both approaches, the greatest good for the greatest number will inevitably occur.

Critics of the modernization perspective do not share this rosy outlook regarding a singular path toward inevitable progress. They suggest that modernization theory contains an ethnocentric bias. The modernization perspective portrays countries not as far along on the evolutionary ladder of modernization as primitive or inferior. The unstated assumption of the modernization perspective, according to critics, is that the local, indigenous cultures around the world will die off. In place of their long-standing beliefs and practices, the peoples of the world would embrace modern, Western consumer culture, and they would do so gladly. Many groups around the world reject this modernization narrative, viewing such "development" as an attack on their way of life and a threat to their core values and norms (Césaire 1972; Hopper 2007).

STRUCTURAL INEQUALITY AND THE CONFLICT PERSPECTIVE

Sociologists drawing on the conflict perspective maintain that movement toward modernity has less to do with an inevitable evolution than it has to do with power and control over resources.

Dependency Theory According to **dependency theory,** poor, less developed nations become subservient to wealthy industrial nations, which in turn use their economic and political might to maintain power. Theorists here argue that resources flow from poor nations to rich nations. For example, rich countries take advantage of poorer nations through the extraction of raw materials and exploitation of cheap labor. According to this approach, the structure of the system determines modernity's winners and losers, not success or failure at choosing policies consistent with those established by modernized nations. Wealthy, developed nations use their use their economic, political, and military might in ways that limit possibilities for development for poorer nations.

To better understand the challenges faced by poorer countries seeking to develop, we must consider global political and economic history tied to colonialism. **Colonialism** occurs when a foreign power maintains political, social, economic, and cultural domination over a people for an extended period. In simple terms, it is rule by outsiders. The long reign of the British Empire over much of North America, parts of Africa, and India is an example of colonial domination. The same can be said of French rule over Algeria, Tunisia, and other parts of North Africa. Dependency theorists maintain that power relations between the colonial nation and the colonized people are similar to those between the dominant capitalist class and the proletariat, as described by Marx (Fanon 1963).

By the 1980s, such global political empires had largely disappeared. Most of the nations that were colonies before World War I had achieved political independence and established their own governments. However, for many of these countries, the transition to genuine self-rule was not yet complete. Colonial domination had established patterns of economic exploitation that continued even after nationhood was achieved—in part because the former colonies were unable to develop their own industry and technology (Acemoglu and Robinson 2012). Their dependence on more industrialized nations, including their former colonizers, for managerial and technical expertise, investment capital, and manufactured goods kept the former colonies in a subservient position. Such continuing dependence and foreign domination are referred to as **neocolonialism.**

Dependency theorists point out that workers in these poor nations become a source of cheap labor for major corporations based in industrialized nations. At the same time, these major corporations also exploit the raw materials of the less developed nations by using their multinational economic might to negotiate advantageous terms. Even when developing countries advance economically, they remain dependent on powerful nations and wealthy corporations in an increasingly intertwined global economy. Through dominance and exploitation, industrialized nations continue to exploit developing countries for their own gain.

World Systems Analysis World systems analysis provides a variant of the dependency theory that emphasizes

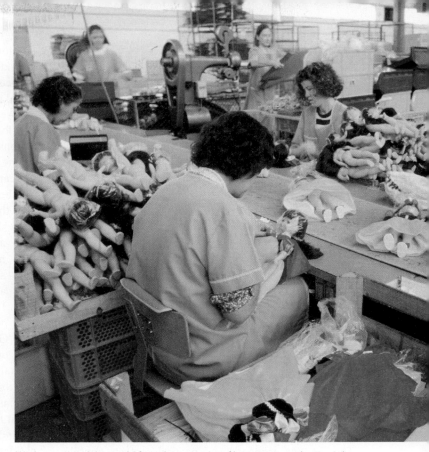

Workers around the world face the prospect of low-wage production jobs.
Siqui Sanchez/The Image Bank/Getty Images

the importance of taking into account the global economic system within which nations operate to better understand global inequality. The **world systems analysis** model, presents the global economic system as being divided between industrial nations that control wealth and developing countries that are controlled and exploited. Sociologist Immanuel Wallerstein (2000, 2004, 2010), the theorist most identified with this model, distinguished between core, periphery, and semiperiphery nations. At the core, industrialized nations, such as the United States, Japan, and Germany, use their economic and political might to their advantage. At the periphery are poor nations, including the developing countries of Asia, Africa, and Latin America that lack sufficient power to resist the advances of the core nations. Between the two are semiperiphery nations, such as China, Ireland, and India, that have experienced some degree of development but cannot go toe-to-toe with the core nations. The economic and political power core nations wield make it difficult for nations on the periphery and semiperiphery to establish and maintain their own economic and political autonomy (Hardt and Negri 2009).

> **Colonialism** The maintenance of political, social, economic, and cultural dominance over a people by a foreign power for an extended period.
>
> **Neocolonialism** Continuing dependence of former colonies on foreign countries.
>
> **World systems analysis** A view of the global economic system as one divided between certain industrialized nations that control wealth and developing countries that are controlled and exploited.

World Systems Analysis in the 21st Century

Core	Semiperiphery	Periphery
Canada	China	Afghanistan
France	India	Bolivia
Germany	Ireland	Chad
Japan	Mexico	Dominican Republic
United Kingdom	Pakistan	Egypt
United States	Panama	Haiti
		Philippines
		Vietnam

Note: Figure shows only a partial listing of countries.

The resulting economic and political conflicts transpire within the context of globalization—the worldwide integration of government policies, cultures, social movements, and financial markets through trade and the exchange of ideas. Because the forces of world financial markets often transcend governance by conventional nation-states, international organizations such as the World Bank and the International Monetary Fund have emerged as major players in the global economy. The function of these institutions, which are heavily funded and influenced by core nations, is to encourage trade and development and to ensure the smooth operation of international financial markets. As such, they are seen as promoters of modernization and defenders primarily of the interests of core nations. Critics call attention to a variety of related issues, including violations of workers' rights, the destruction of the environment, the loss of cultural identity, and discrimination against minority groups in periphery nations.

The Growth of Multinational Corporations Focusing on comparing nations can distract from the larger point made by the world systems approach that differences in outcomes have more to do with access to and control over valued resources than they do with nationality. The ruling elite of people in periphery nations, such as Niger, Pakistan, and Bolivia, increasingly identify more with the ruling elite of people in core nations, including the United States, than with people of their own country. Comparing countries represents a convenient way of contrasting when different parts of the world experienced modern economic

Multinational corporation A commercial organization that is headquartered in one country but does business throughout the world.

development. But, according to this conflict perspective, it should not get in the way of recognizing the larger struggle between the economically and politically powerful of the world relative to the poor, regardless of where they live.

We gain a better sense of the economic power of the elites by focusing on the rising power of multinational corporations whose very existence transcends, and often trumps, the power of the nation state. The term **multinational corporations** refers to commercial organizations that are headquartered in one country but do business around the world. Such private trade and lending relationships are not new; merchants have conducted business abroad for hundreds of years, trading gems, spices, garments, and other goods. Today's multinational giants are not merely buying and selling overseas; they are also producing goods all over the world (Wallerstein 1974, 2004).

These multinational corporations are huge. As the "Going Global: Top 10 Multinational Corporations Compared to National Economies" graph portrays, total revenues for these companies are equivalent to the total value of goods and services exchanged in entire nations. Foreign sales represent an important source of profit for multinational corporations, encouraging them to expand into other countries (in many cases, the developing nations). The U.S. economy is heavily dependent on foreign commerce, much of which is conducted by multinationals. In 2017 the combined value of U.S. exports and imports of goods and services was the equivalent of 27.1 percent of total economic output as measured by gross domestic product (Bureau of Economic Analysis 2018).

In an effort to reduce production costs, corporate executives used deindustrialization and offshoring strategies, thus relocating production jobs around the globe where labor costs less and health, safety, and environmental regulations are weaker. Increasingly, however, it is not only production jobs that are being relocated. Today's global factories may now have the "global office" alongside them. And multinationals based in core nations have established reservation services and centers for processing data and insurance claims in the periphery nations. As service industries become a more important part of the international marketplace, many companies are concluding that the low costs of overseas operations more than offset the

SOCTHINK

Multinational corporations have become so big that they have more economic resources than do some nations. What consequences arise from the fact that they can relocate their headquarters, offices, and production facilities anywhere in the world? How might this affect a nation's political power?

Going GLOBAL

Top 10 Multinational Corporations Compared to National Economies

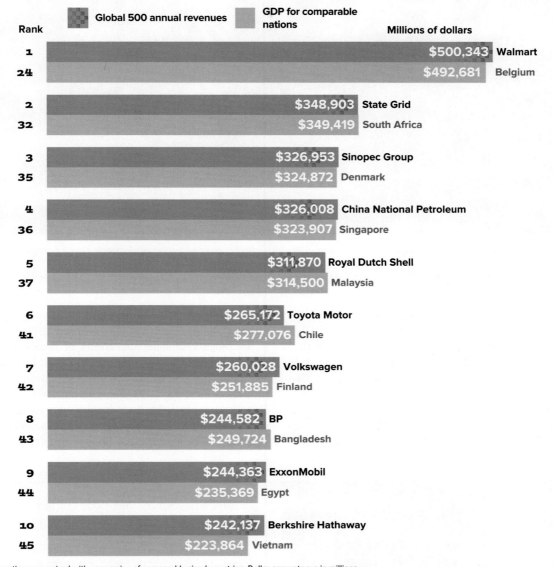

	Global 500 annual revenues	GDP for comparable nations	Millions of dollars

Rank		
1	$500,343	Walmart
24	$492,681	Belgium
2	$348,903	State Grid
32	$349,419	South Africa
3	$326,953	Sinopec Group
35	$324,872	Denmark
4	$326,008	China National Petroleum
36	$323,907	Singapore
5	$311,870	Royal Dutch Shell
37	$314,500	Malaysia
6	$265,172	Toyota Motor
41	$277,076	Chile
7	$260,028	Volkswagen
42	$251,885	Finland
8	$244,582	BP
43	$249,724	Bangladesh
9	$244,363	ExxonMobil
44	$235,369	Egypt
10	$242,137	Berkshire Hathaway
45	$223,864	Vietnam

Note: Corporations are paired with economies of comparably sized countries. Dollar amounts are in millions.
Sources: For corporate data, *Fortune* 2018; for GDP data, World Bank 2018f.

expense of transmitting information around the world (Rothstein 2016; Susskind and Susskind 2015; Sweet and Meiksins 2017).

Workers in these nations, in pursuit of better access to material resources than they would otherwise have, provide a steady stream of cheap labor for these companies. If workers or governments become too demanding, companies can up and move again. As a result, these workers often face dangerous working conditions. One particularly striking example of how unfettered capitalism can harm developing nations is found in the Democratic Republic of Congo (formerly Zaire). Congo has significant deposits of the metal columbite-tantalite—coltan, for short—which is used in the production of electronic circuit boards. U.S. manufacturers used to obtain most of their coltan from Australia, but with increasing demand for electronics, they turned to miners in Congo to increase their supply.

Predictably, the escalating price of the metal—as much as $400 per kilogram at one point, or more than three times the average Congolese worker's yearly wages—attracted undesirable attention. Soon the neighboring countries of Rwanda, Uganda, and Burundi, at war with one another

In the Democratic Republic of Congo, workers mine for coltan, a key ingredient in the production of electronic circuit boards.
Tom Stoddart/Hulton Archive/Getty Images

and desperate for resources to finance the conflict, were raiding Congo's national parks, slashing and burning to expose the coltan underneath the forest floor. In 2010 the U.S. Congress passed the Dodd-Frank Act, which included a provision requiring manufacturing companies to disclose whether they used any "conflict minerals," including coltan, cassiterite, gold, wolframite, or their derivatives, originating from the Democratic Republic of Congo or adjoining nations. According to a UN report, the result has

been reforms in how business and government operate in Congo (Lezhnev 2011; Vigo 2019; Wyatt 2012).

Sociologists studying the effects of foreign investment by multinationals have found that, although it initially may contribute to a host nation's wealth, such investment eventually increases economic inequality within developing nations. This finding holds for both income and ownership. The upper and middle classes benefit most from economic expansion; the lower classes are less likely to benefit. And because

Photo: Lifestyle pictures/Alamy Stock Photo

In an analysis of more than 1,000 U.S. films, communications professor Jack Shaheen (2006, 2009, 2012) found that only 5 percent of Arab and Muslim characters were presented in a positive light. Stereotypical portrayals continue today. Arabs are repeatedly caricatured as Bedouin bandits, seductive belly dancers, villainous oil tycoons, or fanatical terrorists. Such portrayals reinforce the dominance of the majority groups at the expense of minorities who may lack the material, social, and cultural resources to provide alternative, more nuanced narratives to broader audiences, such as the plight of Arab and Muslim children who face similar social and economic hardships as children in the West do. (Allam 2016; Choudry and Habib 2018; Curiel 2016).

POPSOC

multinationals invest in limited economic sectors and restricted regions of a nation, only some sectors benefit. The expansion of such sectors of the host nation's economy, such as hotels and high-end restaurants, appears to retard growth in agriculture and other economic sectors. Moreover, multinational corporations often buy out or force out local entrepreneurs and companies, thereby increasing economic and cultural dependence (Kerbo 2011; Wallerstein 1979, 2004).

>> Economic Inequality around the World

At the same time the gap between rich and poor nations is widening, so too is the gap between rich and poor citizens within nations. As the world systems model suggests, stratification in developing nations is closely related to their relatively weak and dependent position in the global economy. Local elites work hand in hand with multinational corporations and prosper from such alliances. As a result, significant income and wealth differences arise.

INCOME

One of the most common ways to measure average income in a way that allows for comparisons across countries is per capita **gross national income (GNI)**—which measures the total value of goods and services produced within the country plus net income from other countries. GNI encompasses all income a country's residents and businesses earn, including net income from abroad. In 2017, the global average per capita, meaning per person, GNI was $10,366. This provides a baseline for comparing incomes for countries above and below this average.

> **Gross national income (GNI)**
> A measure of the total monetary value of all goods and services produced within a country during some specified period of time.

Industrialized countries such as the United States, Canada, Switzerland, Norway, and Australia had per capita GNIs more than $40,000. By comparison, more than 30 countries, including Malawi, Ethiopia, Nepal, Rwanda, and Afghanistan, had per capita GNIs of less than $1,000. Burundi had the lowest per capita GNI at $290, in stark contrast to the United States' value of $58,270 (World Bank 2016d). As the "Gross National Income per Capita" map portrays, the poorest nations of the world are concentrated in sub-Saharan Africa and South Asia.

Income differences between the haves and have-nots within nations are substantial, as the "Quintile Distribution of Income" graph displays. In South Africa, for example, the bottom quintile earns 2.4 percent of the country's total income compared to 68.2 percent for the top quintile.

Gross National Income per Capita

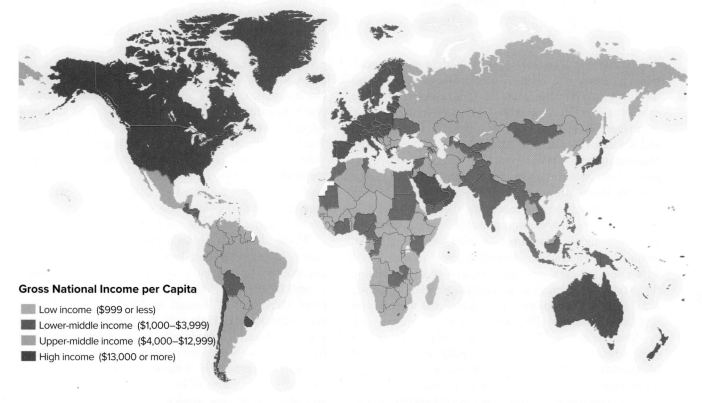

Gross National Income per Capita

- Low income ($999 or less)
- Lower-middle income ($1,000–$3,999)
- Upper-middle income ($4,000–$12,999)
- High income ($13,000 or more)

Note: Data are from 2015 with the exception of Andorra, Bermuda, and Venezuela from 2013, and Isle of Man, Puerto Rico, Gambia, Mauritania, Papua New Guinea, West Bank and Gaza, Vanuatu, and Iran from 2014.
Source: World Bank 2016d.

Quintile Distribution of Income

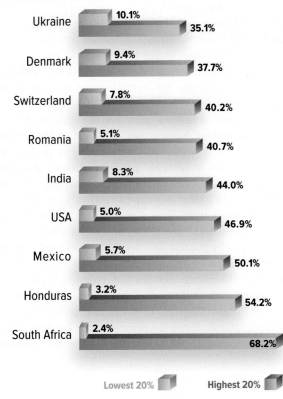

Country	Lowest 20%	Highest 20%
Ukraine	10.1%	35.1%
Denmark	9.4%	37.7%
Switzerland	7.8%	40.2%
Romania	5.1%	40.7%
India	8.3%	44.0%
USA	5.0%	46.9%
Mexico	5.7%	50.1%
Honduras	3.2%	54.2%
South Africa	2.4%	68.2%

Note: Percentage of income earned by the top and bottom quintiles.
Data are for the most recent year available.
Sources: World Bank 2018h, 2018i.

Compare that to Ukraine, where the bottom quintile takes home 5 percent of total income compared to 46.9 percent for the top. Globally, countries that consistently have substantial income inequality include, among others, Seychelles, Haiti, Colombia, Brazil, Namibia, Honduras, and Rwanda (World Bank 2018h, 2018i). As we saw with Mumbai in India, the lack of available, regular, well-paying jobs in such countries makes it extremely difficult for those at the bottom to provide for their needs.

Despite this persistent inequality, there has been good news in recent years regarding global incomes. Because the global income pie grew larger—in other words, more total income became available—average incomes in real dollars have risen for each percentile income grouping around the world. According to economist Branko Milanovic (2013, 2016), after-tax per capita household income rose significantly between 1988 and 2008 for all groups. But, as Milanovic puts it, "The gains from globalization are not evenly distributed" (2016:10). Assuming you line up all households from those earning least to those earning most, those between the 40th and 60th percentiles did best, as their incomes rose more than 60 percent during that period. People in this middle quintile, whom Milanovic calls "the emerging global middle class," live primarily in rising

Asian economies, mostly China, but also India, Thailand, Vietnam, and Indonesia (2016:19). Another group that did particularly well in terms of percentage increase included those in the top 1 percent.

While overall income grew for all quintiles, the group that saw the smallest increase in income—whose income increased less than 10 percent—fell between the 80th and 90th percentiles globally. People in this group live primarily in richer, industrialized nations, such as the United States, Japan, and Germany, and come from the lower-half of the income distribution within those nations (Lakner and Milanovic 2015; Milanovic 2013, 2016). Milanovic sums up his findings this way: "the great [globalization] winners have been the Asian poor and middle classes; the great losers, the lower middle classes of the rich world," which would also include most members of the working class in the United States (2016:20).

WEALTH

Turning to wealth, inequality is even greater than for income. Globally, the median for household wealth is $4,209 per adult, and the mean is $63,100. The difference between the two suggests that a relatively small percentage of the world's adults own a significant amount of wealth. The data support that conclusion. The top 10 percent own 85 percent of global household wealth, and the top 1 percent own 47 percent. To break into the top 1 percent globally, a person must be worth a minimum of $871,317. On the other end of the spectrum, the bottom 50 percent of the world's adults combined own less than 1 percent of global wealth (Shorrocks, Davies, and Lluberas 2018).

Focusing on wealth distribution between regions and nations, as portrayed in the "Global Wealth Distribution" graph, the bulk of the world's wealth is held by countries in North America, Europe, and the rich Asia-Pacific nations. North America has 5.4 percent of the world's adult population but owns 33.6 percent of global household wealth. The United States alone commands 31 percent of global wealth. Contrast this with India, which has 16.9 percent of the world's population but only 1.9 percent of the world's wealth. The entire continent of Africa has 12.3 percent of the world's adult population but only 0.8 percent of global wealth (Shorrocks Davies, and Lluberas 2018).

Wealth distribution within nations also varies significantly. As the "Wealth Concentration" graph shows, for example, the top 1 percent of adults in Japan owns 19 percent of total Japanese wealth, while in Russia the top 1 percent owns 82 percent of Russian wealth (Shorrocks, Davies, and Lluberas 2018:Table 6-5). Ownership of significant amounts of wealth conveys substantial advantages because those who possess it do not need to rely only on their labor to produce income. Wealth can be used to produce income through various forms of investment, which can produce both more income and more wealth.

Women in developing countries often face significant obstacles, making it difficult for them to attain economic

Global Wealth Distribution

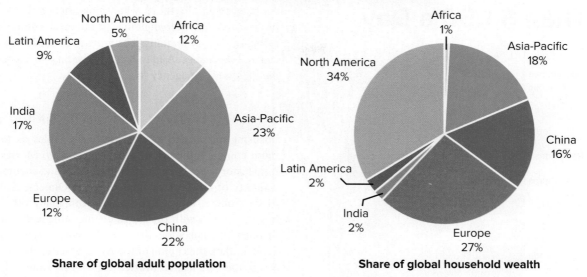

Share of global adult population

Share of global household wealth

Source: Shorrocks, Davies, and Lluberas 2018:Table 2-4.

assets. Karuna Chanana Ahmed, a sociologist from India who has studied women in developing nations, calls women "the most exploited among the oppressed" (Anderson and Moore 1993). Access to jobs represents an important pathway to valuable resources, yet participation in the labor force varies significantly by nation. In countries such as the United States, Canada, France, Iceland, Russia, and Sweden, women make up nearly 50 percent of the labor force. In other nations the rate can be significantly lower. Less than 15 percent of the labor force in in Syria, Qatar,

Oman, United Arab Emirates, and Yemen is female (World Bank 2018j). We explore more issues related to gender inequality in the next chapter.

POVERTY

In developing countries, any deterioration in the economic well-being of the least well-off threatens their very survival. The standardized measure of extreme poverty globally means living on the equivalent of $1.90 per day or less. In 2015, 10 percent of the world's population lived in extreme poverty which represents 736 million people. As the "Living on Less Than $1.90 a Day" graph shows, poverty rates vary substantially by country.

The good news globally is that, driven largely by the income increases noted above, international poverty rates have fallen significantly over recent decades. In 2017, 1.1 billion fewer people lived in extreme poverty around the world than in 1990. This decline was due primarily to decreased poverty numbers in China and India (World Bank 2018e).

Geographically speaking, even though poverty affects hundreds of millions of people worldwide, it is distributed unequally. As the "Share of Global Poor by Region" graph shows, those falling below the $1.90 per day poverty line are concentrated in two regions of the world. More than 56 percent of the world's global poor live in sub-Saharan Africa, and about one-third live in India (World Bank 2018e:40). That does not mean poverty is absent from other parts of the world, including the United States. Instead, it reflects the effect of establishing and using a universal measure of extreme poverty that can be applied in any country.

Wealth Concentration

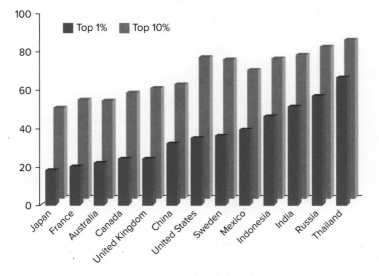

Note: Columns represent the percentage of the country's wealth held by the top 10 percent and top 1 percent.
Source: Shorrocks, Davies, and Lluberas 2018:Table 6-5.

Living on Less Than $1.90 a Day

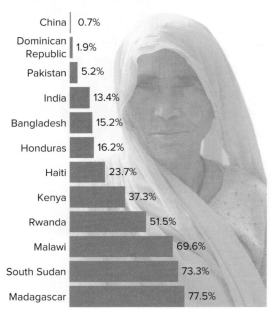

China	0.7%
Dominican Republic	1.9%
Pakistan	5.2%
India	13.4%
Bangladesh	15.2%
Honduras	16.2%
Haiti	23.7%
Kenya	37.3%
Rwanda	51.5%
Malawi	69.6%
South Sudan	73.3%
Madagascar	77.5%

Source: World Bank 2018e. *Photo:* Lissa Harrison

The success in driving down the global poverty rates was due in part to a global commitment facilitated by the United Nations. In 2000, the UN passed the Millennium Declaration, promising to "spare no effort to free our fellow men, women, and children from the abject and dehumanizing conditions of extreme poverty" (United Nations 2000). It established 2015 as a deadline for its Millennium Development Goals and, when 2015 arrived, substantial progress had been made. The goal of reducing extreme poverty by half was accomplished five years early. The target of cutting in half the proportion of people without access to improved water sources was also attained. Considerable progress also occurred in providing access to primary schools, reducing child and maternal mortality, increasing access to medical treatment for people with HIV or AIDS, and reducing rates of both tuberculosis and malaria (United Nations 2014a).

Building on the successes of goals met, and challenged by those not yet achieved, in 2015 the United Nations proposed a new program, the Sustainable Development Goals (SDGs), with a deadline of the year 2030 (United Nations 2014a). Its goals are framed to work toward a more universal and comprehensive vision of development. The SDGs include 17 goals, such as "no poverty," "no hunger," "good health," and "quality education," that in turn include 169 measurable targets to assess progress toward the goals. The goals are organized around five themes: people, planet, prosperity, peace, and partnership (L. Ford 2015; World Bank 2018k).

The success represented by both the Millennium and Sustainable Development Goals programs should provide encouragement to those who think that tackling social problems is too overwhelming to attempt. The degree of global inequality remains substantial, but social structures can and do change. And that change occurs only when people exercise their agency to act differently.

SOCIAL STRATIFICATION IN MEXICO

Focusing on Mexico as a single case enables us to get a more complete picture of global inequality. Mexican cultural history goes back thousands of years and encompasses a variety of civilizations, including the Olmecs, Zapotecs, Maya, Toltecs, and Aztecs, along with many other local cultural groups with their own distinct languages. In 1521, Spanish conquistadors led by Hernán Cortés captured Tenochtitlán, the capital of the Aztec empire, claimed it for Spain and established Mexico City on its ruins. Mexico's colonial era continued until it established independence from Spain in 1821. The consequences of that colonial rule persist in Mexican society today. After independence, for example, the more dominant, Spanish-speaking authorities

Share of Global Poor by Region

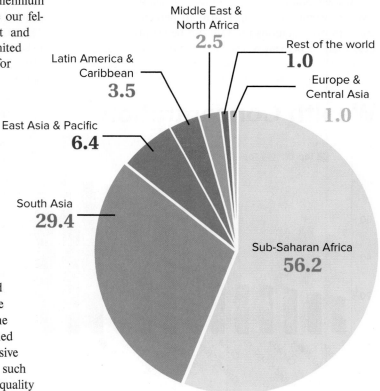

Middle East & North Africa
2.5

Rest of the world
1.0

Latin America & Caribbean
3.5

Europe & Central Asia
1.0

East Asia & Pacific
6.4

South Asia
29.4

Sub-Saharan Africa
56.2

Note: Graph shows the global distribution for the world's 736 million people living on less than $1.90 per day. Numbers represent the percentage of people in extreme poverty living in each region.
Source: World Bank 2018e:42.

Did You Know?

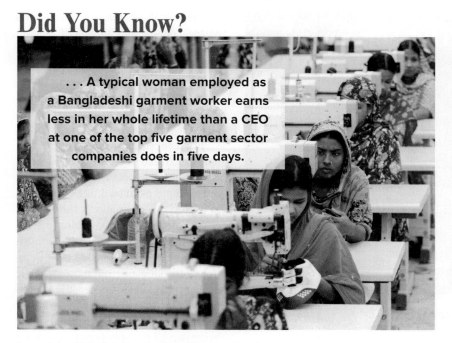

... A typical woman employed as a Bangladeshi garment worker earns less in her whole lifetime than a CEO at one of the top five garment sector companies does in five days.

Source: Oxfam 2018. *Photo:* Tomohiro Ohsumi/Bloomberg/Getty Images

sought to establish a singular Mexican culture and identity. As a result, education programs worked to establish Spanish as the country's universal language and privileged the values and norms of the dominant social groups at the expense of the indigenous populations throughout Mexico. It was not until 1992 that Mexico passed an amendment to its constitution to affirm Mexico as a multicultural and multilingual country (Despagne 2013; Hamnett 2019).

Mexico today, with its population of over 125 million people, should not be thought of in singular, homogeneous terms. Significant variation exists, for example, by region. Mexico consists of 31 states. Some—especially those near the U.S. border—have many manufacturing plants and factories, others rely extensively on tourism for their local economy, and many are quite poor. Mexico City and its surrounding area have a population of over 21 million people and offer all the amenities any modern urban center would provide. If you drive the streets of a city like Mérida on the Yucatán Peninsula, you will find areas that look very much like any U.S. suburb, with shopping malls, fast-food chains, and residential subdivisions. And in rural areas you can find towns with relatively limited development and extreme levels of poverty.

Mexico's Income, Wealth, and Poverty
If we compare Mexico's economy to that of the United States, differences in the standard of living and in life chances are quite dramatic. As we saw earlier, gross national income is a commonly used measure of an average resident's economic well-being. In 2017 the gross national income per person in the United States came to $58,270; in Mexico, it was a mere $8,610 (World Bank 2018g). Given this difference, it should come as no surprise that U.S. companies sought to establish manufacturing factories in Mexico to save on labor costs.

A substantial income gap exists between Mexico's richest and poorest citizens. The top quintile earns 50.1 percent of total income, whereas the bottom earns just 5.7 percent (World Bank 2018h, 2018i). Using the Gini coefficient as an indicator of inequality, which we explored in Chapter 10, Chiapas, Oaxaca, and Yucatán have among the highest levels of inequality of the Mexican states. All three of those states have significant populations of indigenous peoples which typically have lower incomes than do others in Mexico (Despagne 2013; INEGI 2018).

Significant differences in wealth exist between Mexico and the United States. The median amount of wealth per adult in Mexico is $5,784 compared to $61,667 in the United States. The mean wealth per adult in Mexico is $20,620 compared to $403,974 in the United States. When looking at the total wealth owned within each nation, the United States owns 31 percent of global household wealth compared to 0.5 percent by Mexico. In Mexico, the top 1 percent owns 40 percent of household wealth (Shorrocks, Davies, and Lluberas 2018). Mexico's wealthiest individual is Carlos Slim Helú whose $67 billion make him the seventh-richest person in the world (*Forbes* 2019).

Even though economic development has improved the lives of many Mexicans, poverty continues to be a major challenge. According to official statistics, 43.6 percent of people in Mexico live in poverty. When looking more specifically at extreme poverty, 4.2 million, or 3.3 percent, of Mexico's population survives on less than $1.90 per day (World Bank 2018e, 2018l). Poverty rates for the states in Mexico vary significantly. In Chiapas, Oaxaca, Guerrero, and Veracruz, more than 60 percent live in poverty. But poverty rates in Baja California Sur, Baja California, and Coahuila are all less than 25 percent with a low of 14.2 percent in Nuevo León (INEGI 2018).

Indigenous Peoples in Mexico
Indigenous peoples, sometimes referred to as first peoples, existed in a region, in this case Mexico, before colonization occurred and continue to practice and identify with their own distinct culture. Examples in Mexico would include people of Mayan or Aztec descent or any of the distinct 68 indigenous linguistic groups in Mexico (Despagne 2013). Mexico's indigenous groups account for an estimated 12.6 percent of the nation's population. In terms of income, 71 percent earn minimum wage or less. Within this group, 72 percent of Mexico's indigenous people live in poverty. The illiteracy rate in Mexico as a whole is 8.4 percent, but it hovers around 44 percent among the indigenous population (Heath 2016; Roldán 2018).

The subordinate status of Mexico's indigenous groups is but one reflection of the nation's color hierarchy, which links social class status to the appearance of racial purity. At the top of this hierarchy are the *criollos,* the 10 percent

The government of Mexico also has to deal with what to do about immigrants who enter that country illegally. In 2017, government authorities expelled more than 74,000 undocumented immigrants from Central American nations, such as Guatemala, El Salvador, and Honduras.

Source: Grillo 2018. *Photo:* Alfredo Estrella/AFP/Getty Images

of the population who are typically White, well-educated members of the business and intellectual elites, with familial roots in Spain. In the middle is the large, impoverished *mestizo* majority, most of whom have brown skin and a mixed racial lineage as a result of intermarriage. At the bottom of the color hierarchy are the destitute, full-blooded Mexican indigenous minority and a small number of African heritage, some descended from 200,000 African slaves brought to Mexico. This color hierarchy is an important part of day-to-day life—enough so that some Mexicans in the cities use hair dyes, skin lighteners, and blue or green contact lenses to appear White and European. Ironically, however, nearly all Mexicans are considered part Indian because of centuries of intermarriage (Castañeda 1995; Standish and Bell 2004).

—SOC THINK—

How might racial categories in Mexico differ from those in the United States? Why might such differences arise?

The Status of Women in Mexico Though the United Nations convened the first international conference on the status of women in Mexico in 1975, and opportunities there have improved, women still face significant obstacles. Women now constitute 36.5 percent of the labor force—an increase from 29.8 percent in 1990 (World Bank 2018m). Unfortunately, Mexican women are even more mired in the lowest-paying jobs than their counterparts in industrial nations, on average earning 50 percent of what men in similar jobs earn (World Economic Forum 2018:185). Men are still typically viewed as heads of the household, making it difficult for women to obtain credit

Borderlands The area of common culture along the border between Mexico and the United States.

and technical assistance in many parts of the country and to inherit land in rural areas. As for education, the literacy rate for women in Chiapas (71 percent) and Oaxaca (73 percent), states with high levels of indigenous populations, is well below the national average (INEGI 2009).

In recent decades, Mexican women have organized to address an array of economic, political, and health issues. For example, as far back as 1973, women in Monterrey—the nation's third-largest city—protested the continuing disruptions of the city's water supply. Through coordinated efforts, including delegations of politicians, rallies, and public demonstrations, they succeeded in improving Monterrey's water service, a major concern in developing nations. After being denied the opportunity to run for mayor in her hometown in 2007, Eufrosina Cruz organized QUIEGO (Queremos Unir Integrando por la Equidad y Género en Oaxaca), meaning "we want to come together for equity and gender in Oaxaca") to raise awareness about political rights for women in her home state and ultimately throughout Mexico (Bennett, Dávila-Poblete, and Rico 2005; Cevallos 2009).

To ensure greater political representation by women in office, Mexico passed a series of laws setting gender quotas for candidates. First established in 1996, Mexico strengthened these laws over time, now requiring that women compose at least 40 percent of the nominees. In 2014, Mexico passed an amendment to article 41 of its Federal Constitution to cement its commitment to gender parity throughout its political system. These policy changes worked. In 1990, women accounted for 3.1 percent of seats in the Senate and 8.8 percent of seats in the Chamber of Deputies. After the 2018 elections, those numbers rose to 49 percent in the Senate and 48 percent in the Chamber of Deputies. Mexico now ranks 4th among 193 nations in female representation, substantially higher than 103rd for the United States (Baldez 2004; Inter-Parliamentary Union 2018; Lucio 2014; QuotaProject 2014).

The Borderlands Growing recognition of the borderlands reflects the increasingly close and complex relationship between Mexico and the United States. The term **borderlands** refers to the area of common culture along the border between Mexico and the United States. Legal and illegal emigration from Mexico to the United States, day laborers crossing the border regularly to go to work in the United States, the ongoing trade between nations, the exchange of media across the border—all make the notion of separate Mexican and U.S. cultures obsolete in the borderlands.

The economic position of the borderlands is rather complicated, as demonstrated by the emergence of *maquiladoras.*

Personal Sociology

Study Abroad

Central College, where I teach, started its first international program in 1965. It was a leader in establishing study abroad programs for students. It now operates programs around the world, in places such as Mérida in Mexico, Bangor in Wales, and Accra in Ghana. Central instituted these programs to provide students with a prolonged experience in another country, in hopes that such exposure would enable them to go beyond being a tourist and to achieve a deep understanding of another culture. Going abroad really does make a difference. My students are often nervous to go but come back with great stories. The experience clearly changed how they understand both the world and themselves. What factors might encourage or discourage students from studying abroad?

These are foreign-owned factories, often located just across the border in Mexico, that are allowed to import parts and materials without tariffs. Typical jobs include manufacturing electronics, transportation equipment, electrical machinery, and textiles and apparel, as well as service jobs in call centers and coupon processing operations. The chief appeal for U.S. companies is less expensive labor. At $514 per month, the average wages for production workers in the border region of Mexico are lower than $629 earned by similar workers in the interior of Mexico. Wages in Ciudad Juárez, just over the border from El Paso, Texas, are even lower at $422 per month (Hunt Institute 2015).

Emigration to the United States The movement of people between Mexico and the United States significantly affects both nations. In 2017, 118,559 people who were born in Mexico became naturalized U.S. citizens, more than twice the number from India, the second-leading country. Another 170,581 gained lawful permanent resident status in the United States. However, also in 2017, 188,122 individuals from Mexico were apprehended and classified as "aliens" by U.S. immigration officials, which constituted 56 percent of those apprehended (U.S. Department of Homeland Security 2018b). This issue became a major factor in the 2016 presidential campaign. Candidate Donald Trump promised to build a wall between the United States and Mexico and make Mexico pay for it. Midway through his presidency, approving funding for the wall became a major political battle, leading to the longest government shutdown in U.S. history.

Many Mexicans, whether documented or undocumented, come to the United States in pursuit of economic opportunity. These workers frequently send a portion of their earnings back across the border to family members in Mexico. This substantial flow of money, referred to as **remittances** (or *remesas*), amounted to $30 billion in 2017. It is second only to oil as a source of foreign revenue for Mexico. Money also flowed in

> **Remittances** The monies that immigrants return to their families of origin. Also known as *remesas*.

The Borderlands

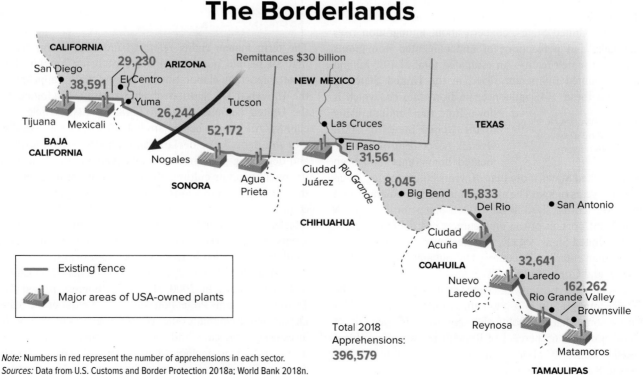

Note: Numbers in red represent the number of apprehensions in each sector.
Sources: Data from U.S. Customs and Border Protection 2018a; World Bank 2018n.

the opposite direction, with $1.8 billion going from Mexico to the United States (World Bank 2018n).

The journey to the United States in hopes of a better future can prove deadly. Many men, women, and children have died attempting to cross into the United States in search of opportunity. Although solid numbers are difficult to come by, the United States Border Patrol reported 294 border deaths in 2017. The three areas with the highest numbers were Rio Grande Valley with 104, Laredo with 83, and Tucson with 72 (U.S. Customs and Border Protection 2016a).

In the United States, concern about immigration rises and falls, and perceptions of undocumented immigrants might not match reality. An estimated total of 10.7 million undocumented immigrants lived in the United States in 2016. Of these, 5.45 million came from Mexico, which is down from the 7 million living in the United States in 2007. Overall, 66 percent of undocumented immigrants have been in the United States more than 10 years compared to 18 percent at 5 years or less. The average undocumented immigrant from Mexico has lived in the United States for 17 years. A significant portion of the undocumented immigrants came to the United States legally, but then overstayed their visas, rather than entering the country without any documentation (Passel and Cohn 2018).

Human rights Universal moral rights possessed by all people because they are human.

Overall, 75 percent of Americans say that, on the whole, immigration is a good thing for the country. This varies somewhat by political party with 85 percent of Democrats and 65 percent of Republicans agreeing. When asked specifically about legal immigration, that number rises to 84 percent (Brenan 2018).

From the Mexican point of view, the United States too often regards Mexico simply as a reserve pool of cheap labor, encouraging Mexicans to cross the border when workers are needed but discouraging and cracking down on them when they are not. Some people, then, see immigration more as a labor market issue than a law enforcement issue. Viewed from the perspective of world systems analysis and dependency theory, it is yet another example of a core industrialized nation exploiting a developing country.

>> Universal Human Rights

As globalization has spread, more people recognize and affirm our collective interdependence. Many have concluded that, if our well-being depends on the contributions of people around the world who are largely unknown and invisible to us, perhaps we bear responsibility for caring for their livelihoods as well. As a result, a movement toward ensuring universal human rights has arisen. Activists in this movement fight to preserve and protect the interests of people who lack significant power or access to resources. This movement attempts to serve as a countervailing source of power to the sheer size and economic might of multinational corporations, along with their freedom to move jobs and plants around the world without regard for the impact on national populations. The goal of human rights activists is to establish a nonnegotiable and inviolable foundation of rights that applies no matter where people are or which governments or multinational corporations are involved.

DEFINING HUMAN RIGHTS

The term **human rights** refers to universal moral rights that all people possess by virtue of being human. The most important elaboration of human rights appears in the Universal Declaration of Human Rights, adopted by the United Nations (UN) in 1948. Its first Article proclaims, "All human beings are born free and equal in dignity and rights." The declaration prohibits slavery, torture, and degrading punishment; grants everyone the right to a nationality and its culture; affirms freedom of religion and the right to vote; proclaims the right to seek asylum in other countries to escape persecution; and prohibits arbitrary interference with one's privacy and the arbitrary seizure of a person's property. It also emphasizes that mothers and children are entitled to special care and assistance.

Human trafficking represents a fundamental violation of human rights. In 2000, the U.S. Congress passed the Trafficking Victims Protection Act. The act requires the State Department to monitor other countries' efforts to vigorously investigate, prosecute, and convict individuals who participate in trafficking—including government officials. Each year the State Department reports its findings, dividing countries

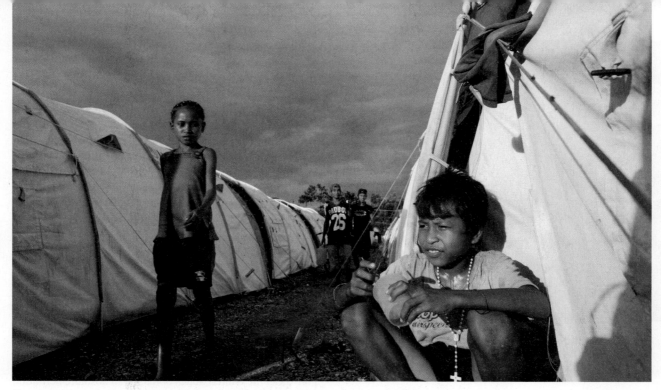

Ongoing violence in East Timor has driven children like these to seek safety in refugee camps in the country.   Paula Bronstein/Getty Images

into three groups, or tiers, depending on their level of compliance. As shown in the "Human Trafficking Report" table, Tier-1 countries are thought to be largely in compliance with the act. Tier-2 nations are making a significant effort to comply, and Tier-2 "watch" nations are making efforts to comply, although trafficking remains a real concern. Tier-3 countries are not compliant (U.S. Department of State 2018b).

In the world today, there are a variety of challenging human rights hotspots. In Yemen, for example, armed conflict broke out in March 2015, and since that time, human rights violations abound. As of late 2018, 14 million people are at risk of starvation and susceptible to diseases such as cholera. Fighters there have used banned antipersonnel landmines and cluster weapons. They have recruited child

Human Trafficking Report

Tier 1 Full Compliance	Tier 2 Significant Effort	Tier 2 Watch List Some Effort, but Trafficking Remains a Concern	Tier 3 Noncompliant, No Effort
Australia	Afghanistan	Bangladesh	Belarus
Canada	Barbados	Cuba	Belize
Denmark	Brazil	Fiji	Burundi
France	Greece	Hong Kong	Equatorial Guinea
Germany	India	Kuwait	Iran
Israel	Ireland	Malaysia	Laos
Italy	Kenya	Niger	North Korea
Norway	Malawi	Nigeria	Republic of Congo
Poland	Mexico	Saudi Arabia	Russia
South Korea	Romania	Senegal	Syria
Spain	Turkey	South Africa	South Sudan
United States	Vietnam	Zimbabwe	Venezuela

Note: Table does not include all countries; each tier lists only a sampling of nations.
Source: U.S. Department of State 2018b.

The crisis in Yemen led to mass protests as millions faced starvation. Ahmad Gharabli/AFP/Getty Images

soldiers, including boys as young as 11. They use rape and torture as instruments of war. Airstrikes have hit homes, schools, hospitals, and mosques. Citizens have been detained and disappeared. Journalists, lawyers, and aid workers have been harassed, arrested, and killed. Humanitarian aid, including food and medical supplies, has been delayed, diverted, and denied (Human Rights Watch 2019). Of the situation there, the UN Secretary-General said, "Yemen is the world's worst humanitarian crisis" (UNOG 2018). Many other countries around the world deal with human rights concerns and violations, including North Korea, South Sudan, and even the United States (Human Rights Watch 2019).

PRINCIPLE AND PRACTICE

When it comes to human rights, the balance between principle and practice can be problematic. People on opposite sides of conflicts can view practices quite differently. What one side may see as a defensive act, the other side may define as terrorism. Cultural insiders and outsiders can disagree about what constitutes a violation. For example, some argued that India's caste system, which defined whole categories of people as fundamentally unequal, as violation of human rights while others viewed it as the natural order of things. Some cultures view the subordinate

SOCTHINK

To what extent do you think violations of human rights are excusable in a time of war? At such times, how might our perception of the balance between rights and security alter what we think of as universal?

status of women as an essential element of their traditions and ordained by god. Such cultural variation creates challenges when determining who has the right to define and enforce universal human rights.

We can consider, as an example, female genital mutilation, a practice that is common in more than 30 countries around the world but that has been condemned in Western nations as a human rights abuse. This controversial practice often involves removal of the clitoris, in the belief that its excision will inhibit a young woman's sex drive, making her chaste and thus more desirable to her future husband. Though some countries have passed laws against the practice, they have gone largely unenforced. Emigrants from countries where genital mutilation is common often insist that their daughters undergo the procedure, to protect them from Western cultural norms that allow premarital sex (World Health Organization 2018). Deciding where to draw the line regarding what practices a culture has the right to define for themselves as appropriate versus when to intervene in an effort to preserve and protect human rights creates real-world challenges.

In 1993 the United States opted for an absolute definition of human rights, insisting that the Universal Declaration of Human Rights set a single standard for acceptable behavior around the world. In practice, however, interpretation still plays a role. Some human rights activists have argued that the United States practices selective enforcement of human rights. Critics contend, for example, that officials in the United States are more likely to become concerned about human rights abuses when oil is at stake, as in the Middle East, or when military alliances come into play, as in Europe.

SOCTHINK

How active should the U.S. government be in addressing violations of human rights in other countries? At what point, if any, does concern for human rights turn into ethnocentrism through failure to respect the distinctive norms, values, and customs of another culture?

HUMAN RIGHTS ACTIVISM

Many activists who work to bring about change do so through nongovernmental organizations (NGOs), which are not-for-profit groups committed to bringing about social change. These groups may be local, national, or international in scope. They are frequently funded by donations and staffed by volunteers. Examples of the best-known NGOs include Amnesty International, Human Rights Watch, Red Cross, CARE International, and Oxfam.

Efforts to protect and ensure human rights seldom come from inside governments but arise out of social movements that organize to generate economic, social, and political pressure in an effort to force change. Human Rights Watch (www.hrw.org), a premier international human rights organization, releases an annual report documenting human rights challenges around the world on a country-by-country basis. This includes coverage of efforts to bring about positive change made by NGOs, national governments, international organizations, and others (Human Rights Watch 2019).

Médecins Sans Frontières (Doctors Without Borders), the world's largest independent emergency medical aid organization, won the 1999 Nobel Peace Prize for its work. Founded in 1971 and based in Paris, the organization has thousands of doctors, nurses, and other expert volunteers working around the world. In 2017, it provided humanitarian assistance in 72 countries. It conducted more than 10.6 million outpatient consultations, treated 2.5 million malaria cases, vaccinated 886,300 people for meningitis, helped 288,900 women deliver babies, and assisted many thousands of other patients for various ailments (Doctors Without Borders 2017).

One of the things we learn from sociology is that we are embedded in larger networks in which decisions and events that happen far away, and about which we may know little or nothing, shape our daily life experiences. And the choices we make can have substantial consequences for the lives of others. Ethnic cleansing in South Sudan, human rights violations in Yemen and North Korea, female genital mutilation

SOCTHINK

Should other nations and the UN have the power to force the United States to change its laws to comply with human rights principles?

> There can be no peace as long as there is grinding poverty, social injustice, inequality, oppression, environmental degradation, and as long as the weak and small continue to be trodden by the mighty and powerful.
>
> **The Dalai Lama (2000)**

and other forms of violence against women inside and outside the family—all these are vivid reminders that social inequality can have life-and-death consequences. In each case, people recognized the consequences of global inequality, and individuals, groups, and nations took steps to address the problems. By developing a more fully formed sociological imagination, we can more readily see such issues and take necessary steps toward addressing them.

SOCIOLOGY IS A VERB

Global Perspectives

The world is huge, and there are so many places about which we know so little. Pick a country you are unfamiliar with, perhaps one you didn't even know existed. Find out all you can about its history, politics, economy, family structures, beliefs, and so on. If possible, contact an organization that assists immigrants from there to learn more about their experiences as first-generation immigrants here. What might you learn by trying to understand the world from their perspective?

FOR REVIEW

I. How do sociologists approach modernization?
   - Theorists emphasizing modernization argue that it is part of the natural evolution of societies as they pass through the effects of the Industrial Revolution and beyond. Dependency theorists argue that it is due to a fundamental power struggle between wealthy nations at the core and developing nations at the periphery.

II. How significant is global stratification?
   - Analyses of wealth, income, poverty, and social mobility demonstrate a wide gap both within and between nations.

III. Why did the global movement for universal human rights develop?
   - As global inequality became more apparent, activists worked to establish a foundational set of human rights that would protect people regardless of who or where they were.

SOCVIEWS on Global Inequality

Functionalist View

Through **modernization**, nations make the transition from traditional forms of organization to postindustrial societies for the benefit of all.

Globalization involves the worldwide **integration** of government policies, cultures, social movements, and financial markets through trade and exchange of ideas.

Multinational organizations create jobs and industries in developing countries, foster innovation, and make nations of the world **interdependent**.

MODERNIZATION, INTEGRATION
KEY CONCEPTS

Conflict View

There is significant **inequality** between the rich and the poor within as well as across nations, but the scourge of poverty is most evident in Africa and Asia.

According to world system analysis, modernization can result in political, economic, and cultural **imperialism**.

The economic success of core nations depends upon the extraction of raw materials and cheap labor from periphery nations.

KEY CONCEPTS
IMPERIALISM, INEQUALITY

Interactionist View

People undergoing modernization often experience a dramatic change in the established ways of working and interacting.

Encounters with people from different cultures open us up to alternative ways of thinking and acting.

Many women in developing nations face inequality in employment opportunities, education, and health care, thus limiting their **social interaction** in the community.

KEY CONCEPTS
SOCIAL INTERACTION, ENCOUNTERS

MAKE THE CONNECTION
After reviewing the chapter, answer the following questions:

1
How might each perspective seek to better understand the situation in cities such as Mumbai?

2
How do the modernization and world systems theories fit with the functionalist and conflict perspectives?

3
How would each perspective provide insight into the situation of immigration between the United States and Mexico?

4
What ties do you have to a developing nation—perhaps as a tourist, or a second-generation immigrant, or an activist? Which perspective best fits those ties? Why?

Pop Quiz

1. **Which of the following terms is used by contemporary social scientists to describe the far-reaching process by which nations pass from traditional forms of social organization toward those characteristic of post–Industrial Revolution societies?**

   a. dependency

   b. globalization

   c. industrialization

   d. modernization

2. **The maintenance of political, social, economic, and cultural domination over a people by a foreign power for an extended period of time is referred to as**

   a. globalization.

   b. government-imposed stratification.

   c. colonialism.

   d. dependency.

3. **The world systems analysis model focuses on**

   a. the unequal access to and control of resources between core and periphery nations.

   b. the natural evolutionary development of all societies toward the modern ideal.

   c. the rise of multinational corporations.

   d. the global pattern of inequality faced by women.

4. **Companies that are headquartered in one country but do business throughout the world are known as**

   a. global corporations.

   b. multinational corporations.

   c. *maquiladoras.*

   d. international agencies.

5. **What region of the world owns 34 percent of global household wealth?**

   a. Asia-Pacific

   b. Europe

   c. China

   d. North America

6. **What region of the world is home to 56 percent of the global poor?**

   a. South Asia

   b. East Asia & Pacific

   c. Central and South America

   d. Sub-Saharan Africa

7. **Globally, approximately how many people subsist on less than $1.90 per day?**

   a. 736 million

   b. 1.53 billion

   c. 3.07 billion

   d. 5.1 billion

8. **What is the term for the monies that immigrants return to their families of origin?**

   a. migration money

   b. remittances

   c. assistance

   d. pocket money

9. **Which of the following terms refers to the foreign-owned factories established just across the border in Mexico, where the companies that own them don't have to pay taxes or high wages, or provide insurance or benefits for their workers?**

   a. *maquiladoras*

   b. *hombres*

   c. *mujeres*

   d. *remesas*

10. **What does the acronym NGO stand for?**

    a. national governance operations

    b. normal government options

    c. nongovernmental organization

    d. necessary good options

1. (d), 2. (c), 3. (a), 4. (b), 5. (d), 6. (d), 7. (a), 8. (b), 9. (a), 10. (c)

Gender and Sexuality

DREAMING BIG

When you're a child, your imagination often runs wild. When someone asks what you want to be when you grow up, almost anything seems possible—superhero, jet pilot, ballet dancer, movie star, secret agent, Olympic athlete, or maybe even president. As we get older, reality hits, and most of us narrow our choices to something more realistic. But not everyone.

When Sheryl Sandberg was young, her mom encouraged her to work hard so she could be whatever she wanted to be. She took her mom's advice, and it paid off. She earned an economics degree at Harvard, served as chief of staff at the U.S. Department of the Treasury, and worked as the vice president of global online sales and operations at Google. Now Sandberg is second in command at Facebook, a position she accepted when she was 38 years old. Hers is a classic tale of upward mobility.

Yet when she reached the top, she found that very few women had made the journey with her. It didn't start out that way. In college and in her entry-level jobs, Sandberg's peers included equal numbers of men and women. As she climbed each rung of the career ladder, men increasingly outnumbered women. One of the most staggering examples of inequity is the disparity at the very top, among corporate leaders. In fact, only 4.8 percent of CEOs at S&P 500 firms are women (Catalyst 2019a).

In an effort to understand the challenges women face and help bring about change, Sandberg (2013), with research assistance from sociologist Marianne Cooper, wrote *Lean In: Women, Work, and the Will to Lead*, and founded LeanIn.Org. In her work, Sandberg highlights two key factors that have hindered women's progress in the workplace. First, women experience consistent patterns of discrimination. For example, in LeanIn.Org's 2018 annual report, which surveyed 279 companies employing 13 million people, researchers found that when it comes to moving up the ladder early in their careers, for every 100 men promoted to managerial jobs, 79 women are promoted. Women are less likely than their male peers to have either substantive or informal interactions with their senior leaders at work. They are also less likely to socialize with their manager outside of work. When it comes to everyday interactions, women workers are more likely to have their judgment questioned in their area of expertise, be asked to show more evidence of their competence, and be addressed in a less-than-professional way (LeanIn.Org 2018).

The second obstacle Sandberg highlights involves women's own creation and acceptance of internal barriers to their success. In their annual report, LeanIn.org researchers found that fewer women aspire to become top executives. Sandberg writes, "We hold ourselves back in ways both big and small, by lacking self-confidence, by not raising our hands, and by pulling back when we should be leaning in" (2013:8). Whether the barriers are external or internal, being a woman makes success in business and politics more challenging.

As children, anything may seem possible. The truth is that the positions we occupy in society shape the choices we make. In this chapter, we explore the ways in which both gender and sexuality play roles in who we are and what we become.

As You READ >>

- **How has our understanding of gender and sexuality shifted over time?**

- **How has opportunity for women in the United States changed over time?**

- **To what extent does gender still shape access to resources?**

>> The Social Construction of Gender

When a baby is born, one of the first questions people ask is "Is it a boy or a girl?" How parents, physicians, and others answer this question shapes one of our primary and most powerful statuses. From our earliest days, it influences how others will interact with us as newborns. Later it affects the clothes we wear, the friends we choose, the kinds of games we play, the college majors we consider, the types of jobs we have, the amount of money we earn, and much more. And increasingly, the options available to us on how we might answer that question have become more open.

In the 1970s, sociologists began drawing a more explicit distinction between sex and gender to differentiate between biology and culture. **Sex** refers to biological differences between males and females. **Gender** involves the social and cultural significance that we attach to those presumed biological differences. Sociologists did so, in part, to respond to arguments that essential biological differences existed between males and females, differences that were used to justify discrimination against women. Introducing gender highlighted the degree to which our conceptions of masculinity and femininity

Rainer Elstermann/Lifesize/Getty Images

are social constructions that vary across cultures and over time. Eventually, even the distinction between sex and gender became too limiting, which led sociologists to explore the importance of **transgender**—those whose gender identity differs from the sex they were assigned at birth. Each concept provides a different perspective through which we can better understand why we think and act as we do.

> **Sex** The biological differences between males and females.
>
> **Gender** The social and cultural significance that we attach to the biological differences of sex.
>
> **Transgender** A person whose gender identity differs from the sex he or she was assigned at birth.

SEX

Sex focuses on biological differences between males and females that occur at the cellular, hormonal, and anatomical levels. Through the lens that sex provides, females typically have XX chromosome patterns, estrogen hormones, ovaries, and a vagina; males have XY chromosomes, androgen hormones, testicles, and a penis. The presupposition is that the dividing line is clear; there is no significant biological overlap between the sexes. This model is known as a simple two-sex, or dimorphic, model, in which the line between males and females is distinct and absolute (Fausto-Sterling 2000, 2012; Richardson 2013).

The problem with such a simplistic division is that we find many exceptions to what is

After she won the gold medal in the 800-meter race at the 2016 Olympics in Rio, South African runner Caster Semenya again faced questions about her sex. During her career she has been ordered to submit to various psychological, gynecological, and endocrine tests (Boren 2016; Karkazis 2016; Karkazis et al. 2012; Maese 2016). The Asahi Shimbun/Getty Images

assumed to be the rule. Many people exhibit physical characteristics that we presume to belong to the "opposite" sex: women with facial hair, men with high voices, tall women and short men, women with narrow hips and broad shoulders, men who are slight of build or who have "breasts," women who experience "male pattern baldness," and so on. Differences go beyond these secondary sex characteristics to include people whose cellular, hormonal, and anatomical characteristics are sexually ambiguous. As geneticist Anne Fausto-Sterling (2000) points out in a critique of the simplistic male–female model, "On close inspection, absolute dimorphism disintegrates even at the level of basic biology. Chromosomes, hormones, the internal sex structures, the gonads and the external genitalia all vary more than most people realize" (p. 20). We know, for example, that both males and females have androgen and estrogen hormones and that sex hormone levels vary by individual.

Biologically, Fausto-Sterling (1993) suggests we have at least five sexes, not just two. In addition to male and female, we exhibit at least three intersexual categories. The first category includes "true hermaphrodites," who have one testis and one ovary. In other words, they are theoretically capable of producing both sperm and eggs. The second category includes "male pseudohermaphrodites." They have testes and what appear to be female genitalia, lacking a penis and ovaries. The third category includes "female pseudohermaphrodites," who have ovaries along with some male genitalia but no testes. She later suggested that even these five sexes present an overly simplistic model of the range of biological diversity, which better resembles a continuum (Fausto-Sterling 2000, 2012).

Doctors studying what have come to be known medically as disorders of sex development (DSDs) have discovered that the basic biology of sex extends well beyond the XX and XY chromosome combinations (Davis 2014; Richardson 2013). Researchers have identified more than 25 genes involved in the development of these traits. For example, XY individuals with extra copies of the *WNT4* gene, which promotes ovarian development and suppresses testicular development, can develop a rudimentary uterus and Fallopian tubes. Individuals who are XX but with the *RSPO1* gene can develop ovotestis, a gonad incorporating both ovarian and testicular development (Ainsworth 2015). When considering the biology of sex, researcher Eric Vilain, the director of the Center for Gender-Based Biology at the University of California, Los Angeles, concludes, "Biologically, it's a spectrum" (Ainsworth 2015). Because the use of "disorder" implies something negative about people born with these naturally occurring traits, medical professionals and human rights advocates are proposing the elimination of the DSD label (Council of Europe 2015; Holmes 2011).

When babies are born presenting ambiguous indicators of maleness or femaleness, even though such conditions rarely pose a health threat, physicians typically perform surgery to make the baby fit more neatly into one category or the other. In recent years, ethical questions have been raised about the appropriateness of doing so, especially when the person most affected has no voice in the matter (Ainsworth 2015; Karkazis 2008). In 2013, the United Nations issued a statement condemning such nonconsensual surgeries, and in 2015 Malta became the first nation to ban such surgeries by law (Larsson 2016; Méndez 2013). Increasingly, countries have adopted policies to recognize the complexity of sex. In 2011, Australia began allowing people to select a third sex category on their passports. In 2013, Germany allowed parents to leave the gender category on their child's birth certificate blank. In 2015, Thailand began the process of revising its constitution to formally recognize a third gender category as a human right. In 2017, Oregon became the first U.S. state to allow people to put an X when identifying their sex on their driver's licenses rather than only an M or F, and a number of other states have since followed suit. Also in 2017, California became the first state to allow parents to choose a gender-neutral category on their child's birth certificate (Commonwealth of Australia 2013; Heine 2013; Katz 2017; Levin 2019; Park and Dhitavat 2015).

SOCTHINK

Why do most women in the United States assume that shaving their legs is natural? What role does it play as a rite of passage?

GENDER

Our biological diversity calls for a more complex model of our species than the dimorphic model of sex supplies. Adding gender to a more comprehensive conception of sex, enables us to capture a wider range of expressions of our humanity. Social constructions of gender vary over time and across cultures, suggesting that biology alone does not narrowly determine maleness and femaleness. Through socialization we typically internalize the cognitive, normative, and material culture defined as appropriate or natural for men and women within the context of our societies.

Gender Displays Even before a child's birth, parents begin the socialization process that will shape their child's gender identity. The development of imaging technology, including ultrasounds and sonograms, enables parents to know the sex of their baby before birth. Parents today use this knowledge to decide what clothes to buy and how to decorate their expected baby's crib. Gender reveal parties rely on the presupposed association of pink and blue to identify share the news with others (Paoletti 2012).

As children grow, we continue to reinforce male–female differences through our actions. Even though awareness regarding such expectations has shifted, a trip down the toy aisle continues to reveal the degree to which toys are gendered. Yet, historical and sociological research suggest that such preferences are not innate. For example, in 1893, an article on baby clothes in *The New York Times* reported "Always give pink to a boy and blue to a girl" (quoted in St. Clair 2017:115). An early 20th-century article in *Ladies' Home Journal* noted, "There has been a great diversity of opinion on the subject, but the generally accepted rule is pink for the boy and blue for the girl. The reason is that pink being a more decided and stronger color is more suitable for the boy, while blue, which is more delicate and dainty, is prettier for the girl" (quoted in Frassanito and Pettorini 2008; see also Cohen 2013; Walsh 2016a, 2016b). We learn such preferences through socialization experiences with others.

Gender socialization never ends. In all our interactions, we receive positive and negative feedback based on our gender performance. It is not hard to test how rigid gender-role socialization can be. Just try breaking some gender norm—say, by smoking a cigar in public if you are female, or wearing a skirt to work if you are male. Corrective feedback will likely follow. That was exactly the assignment given to sociology students at the University of Colorado and at Luther College in Iowa. Professors asked students to behave in ways that they thought violated the norms of how a man or woman should act. Over the years that this ongoing experiment has been performed, students consistently received clear signals—ranging from amusement to disgust—that their actions were inappropriate and that they should instead behave in ways defined as appropriate by dominant heterosexual gender norms (Nielsen, Walden, and Kunkel 2000).

Artist Nickolay Lamm used crowdfunding to release Lammily, a fashion doll matching the body proportions of an average 19-year-old American woman. CB2/ZOB/WENN.com/Newscom

Most of the time we do not actually see the "parts" that biologically define someone as male or female; we rely instead on other indicators, such as clothes and shapes, to be sufficient. As sociologist Judith Lorber (1994) put it, "Clothing, paradoxically, often hides the sex but displays the gender" (p. 22). We depend on established cues (such as outfits and hairstyles) to recognize someone's sex when we interact, often taking that recognition for granted (Butler 1990; West and Zimmerman 1987).

Personal Sociology

Drawing Distinctions

When Emily and Eleanor were little, they covered our refrigerator with pictures they drew of our family. In the pictures, the girls wore dresses while I wore pants. They had long eyelashes and I did not. They had long hair, and I had what looked like a plate on my head. When she was little, I asked Eleanor, "What about the women we know with short hair and the men we know with long hair?" She replied, "Yeah, but women have long hair and men have short hair." She knew there were people who didn't fit her hair hypothesis, but she had already come to accept an image in which the line between men and women was obvious, important, and inevitable. To what extent have your hairstyles been a fairly predictable indicator of your gender?

Women's Gender Roles Parents, schools, friends, and the mass media all socialize us to internalize dominant gender norms. The positive and negative sanctions that we experience during such interactions shape the thoughts, actions, and appearances we accept as appropriate. Women, for example, continue to face pressure to be thin, beautiful, submissive, sexy, and maternal (Pai and Schryver 2015).

Films, television programs, and magazine ads all contribute to an idealized image of feminine beauty (H. Brown 2015; Kilbourne 2010, 2014). As we saw in the "Deviance and Social Stigma" section in Chapter 6, this image, dubbed the "beauty myth" by Naomi Wolf (1992), is largely unattainable for most women. It contributes to millions of cosmetic procedures each year for those seeking it. Part of the reason is that these images are often not real. Instead, they are altered with the assistance of computer programs such as Photoshop (H. Brown 2015; Grossman 2015; Gurari, Hetts, and Strube 2006). Attaining an idealized image can be particularly problematic for those who do not match the White and heterosexual assumptions upon which it is built (Milillo 2008; Reel et al. 2008; Tate 2009).

As we increasingly recognize the impact of such artificial images, attempts have been made to offer alternative images of women. In Spain, fashion designers have established a minimum body mass index (BMI) score of 18 for runway models. And Israel passed a law banning models with a BMI less than 18.5 from fashion runways

Singer Alicia Keys chose not to wear makeup as an expression of freedom and self-revelation. C Flanigan/Getty Images

and advertisements; for example, a 5-foot, 8-inch-tall model must weigh at least 119 pounds. The law also requires publications to disclose when they have digitally altered photos to make models appear thinner. Singer Alicia Keys opted to go without makeup in appearances at the VMA, BET, and Grammy Awards and in her role as a judge/coach in the NBC talent show *The Voice*. She did so, she said, because "I don't want to cover up anymore. Not my face, not my mind, not my soul, not my thoughts, not my dreams, not my struggles, not my emotional growth. Nothing" (Keys 2016; see also Izadi 2016; Park 2018).

Gendered messages about being a woman are about more than just beauty. They also project idealized images of "women's proper place," identifying some social status positions as more appropriate than others. Studies show that children's books reinforce such messages. One study of 5,618 children's books published throughout the 20th century found that male characters were represented twice as often as females. The disparity was greatest when portraying animal characters as males or females. Little Golden Books were more unequal than other series they studied. Starting in the 1970s they found a trend toward greater equity, though a significant imbalance remains. The researchers conclude, "This widespread pattern of underrepresentation of females may contribute to a sense of unimportance among girls and privilege among boys" (McCabe et al. 2011:221). Other studies have found similar gendered patterns. Males are more likely to be portrayed as leading characters, more likely to have speaking roles, and eight times as likely to be portrayed as villains. Females are more likely to appear as moms, less likely to appear in science roles, and more likely to not be present at all (Caldwell and Wilbraham 2018; Ferguson 2018; Filipović 2018; Tilley 2018).

In recent years, companies have begun to respond. Mattel added Curvy Barbie, Tall Barbie, and Petite Barbie to its lineup along with a wider array of skin tones and hair types to reflect more racial and ethnic diversity (Bates 2016). Publishers of children's literature have produced a wider range of gender portrayals in books such as Robert Munsch's *The Paper Bag Princess;* Steven Lenton's *Princess Daisy, the Dragon, and the Nincompoop Knights;* and Kate Beaton's *The Princess and the Pony.* Comic book company DC Entertainment, as part of its Super Hero Girls Initiative, intends to produce more toys, TV specials, movies, and apparel for girls, a target demographic that has been largely ignored in the superhero product category. And Marvel's film *Wonder Woman* was a blockbuster that left women and girls feeling empowered (Brown 2016; Burton 2018; Watercutter 2017).

Men's Gender Roles Conventional gender-role expectations also exist for men. For example, stay-at-home fathers are still relatively uncommon. Among married-couple families with children under 15, there are 26 times more stay-at-home moms than stay-at-home dads (U.S. Census Bureau 2018g:Table FG-8). Although it is still rare for men to stay

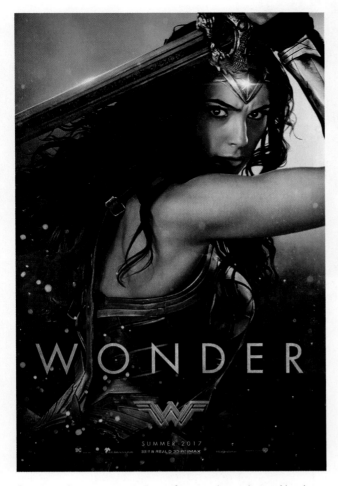

Popular culture representations of women in movies and books show signs of becoming more diverse. DC Entertainment/Warner Bros./Album/Newscom

or brothers (Katz 1999; Pascoe 2011). Such name-calling represents a form of social control that limits the likelihood of new gender norms being established. It limits the expansion of gender roles for boys and perpetuates degrading stereotypes against LGBTQ individuals (Pascoe and Bridges 2015).

We also see the effects of gendered expectations demonstrated by men in nontraditional occupations, such as preschool teacher or nurse. They may lie about their occupations when introduced to others in order to avoid negative reactions. For example, researchers interviewed a 35-year-old male nurse who reported that he would claim to be "a carpenter or something like that" when he "went clubbing," because women weren't interested in getting to know a male nurse. Subjects of the study made similar accommodations in casual exchanges with other men (Bagilhole and Cross 2006; Cottingham, Johnson, and Tayler 2016; Croft, Schmader, and Block 2015; Cross and Bagilhole 2002).

There may be a price to pay for such narrow conceptions of manhood. Boys who successfully adapt to cultural standards of masculinity may grow up to be inexpressive men who cannot share their feelings with others. They remain forceful and tough, but they are also closed and isolated. These traditional gender roles may be putting men at a disadvantage. Today girls outdo boys in high school, grabbing a disproportionate share of the leadership positions, from valedictorian to class president to yearbook editor—everything, in short, except captain of the boys' athletic teams. And their advantage continues after high school. Starting in the 1980s, girls in the United States became more likely than boys to go to college. In 2018, women accounted for 57 percent of college students nationwide (National Center for Education Statistics 2018:Table 303.10). And more women than men earned doctoral degrees in the United States

home to care for their children, in a nationwide survey, 53 percent of respondents said that if one parent stays home with the children, it makes no difference whether that parent is the mother or the father. Among the others responding, 45 percent still thought that the mother should be the one to stay home, and only 2 percent responded that it's better if the father stays home. Age played a significant role in the responses, with those over 65 most likely to say that the kids are better off if the mother stays home (Graf 2016).

Although attitudes toward parenting may be changing, traditional gender-role expectations continue to have a significant impact. Men, too, receive messages from family, peers, and the media about what it means to be masculine. One of the most powerful expectations is to be tough, both physically and emotionally, in sports, at work, and even in relationships. Males who fail to conform to such gender norms face criticism and even humiliation. Boys, for example, run the risk of being called a "chicken," "sissy," or "fag" even by fathers

Bbernard/Shutterstock

Thousands of hijras gathered for a festival near Kolkata, India. Saikat Paul/Pacific Press/ LightRocket/Getty Images

starting in 2006 (National Center for Education Statistics 2018:Table 324.20).

Increasing numbers of men in the United States have criticized the restrictive aspects of the traditional male gender role. Australian sociologist R. W. Connell (2002, 2005) has written about **multiple masculinities,** meaning that expressions of manliness can take varieties of forms beyond the culturally domi-nant, stereotypical construct of what it means to be a man. This involves the expansion of masculinity to incorporate a variety of possible expressions, including a nurturing-caring role, an effeminate-gay role, the more traditional role, and others (Connell and Messerschmidt 2005).

Multiple masculinities The idea that expressions of manliness can take varieties of forms beyond the culturally dominant, stereotypical construct of what it means to be a man.

Gender across Cultures Beginning with the path-breaking work of anthropologist Margaret Mead ([1935] 2001) and continuing through contemporary fieldwork, scholars have repeatedly shown that gender roles can vary greatly from one physical environment, economy, and politi-cal system to the next. Some cultures assume the existence of three or four gender categories. Sociologist Judith Lorber (1994) notes that "male women," biological males who live for the most part as women, and "female men," biological females who live for the most part as men, can be found in various societies. "Female men" can be found in some African and Native American societies, and in Albania, where they take on male work and family roles. "Male women" include the *berdaches,* also known as two-spirit peo-ple, of the Native Americans of the Great Plains; the *hijras* of India; and the *xanith* of Oman in the Middle East (Nanda 1997; Reddy 2005).

The Bugis people, the largest ethnic group in South Sulawesi, Indonesia, identify five distinct genders: *oroané*

(masculine man), *makkunrai* (feminine woman), *calabai* (feminine male), *calalai* (masculine female), and *bissu,* best described as a transgender shaman with physical aspects of both sexes (Davies 2007; Guy-Ryan 2016). In these societies, multiple gender categories are a well-accepted part of their social lives. Individuals who fill them are not simply tolerated or viewed as devi-ant. Two-spirit people and *bissu,* for example, have high status because they are thought to have special powers (Davies 2007; Kimmel 2004; Roscoe 1997).

The distribution of power based on gender also varies cross-culturally. In the Minangkabau society in Indonesia, for example, men and women are not com-petitors but partners for the common good. This society is characterized by a nurturing approach to the environment, blended with Islamic religious ethics. Women control the land through inheritance; in the event of a divorce, the ex-husband leaves with only his clothes. The larger community may be gov-erned by men, women, or both men and women working together (Bhanbhro 2017; Sanday 2002, 2008). The kind of cultural variation these examples provide reinforces the claim that biology is not destiny. Social relations within and between the sexes can take many different forms.

—SOC THINK—

Given that our understandings of gender vary across time and place, why are we so commit-ted to the notion that gender differences are narrowly determined by biology?

REIMAGINING SEX AND GENDER

Moving beyond a simple, dimorphic model of sex opens the door to new opportunities for both men and women. It sug-gests that the line between what anthropologist Lisa Peattie and sociologist Martin Rein refer to as the natural and the artificial shifts over time. When we say something is *natu-ral,* what we mean is that it should be accepted as given and cannot be changed. For example, when people contend that "men are more rational," or that "women are more nur-turing," they often assume that these stereotypes are deter-mined by our biology and thus immutable. Analysis of how gender is expressed across cultures and over time suggests, however, that such presumed-to-be inherent traits distin-guishing men and women are really *artificial*—that is, they are social constructions subject to change, not inevitable determinants of who we must be (Peattie and Rein 1983).

Moving the line so that something that was once con-sidered natural comes to be seen as an artificial social construction often opens up opportunities for groups facing discrimination. Even into the 20th century it was thought that women's biological makeup justified their exclusion from schools, the workplace, and politics—social locations in which women's participation is now taken for granted. For example, women were once banned from colleges and universities in the United States, because it was presumed that they were biologically incapable of succeeding. At the Jefferson Medical College in Philadelphia in 1847, Professor Charles Meigs, in a famous speech delivered to an all-male class of gynecology students, said of women, "She has a head almost too small for intellect and just big enough for love. . . . She reigns in the heart . . . the household altar is her place of worship and service" (quoted in Collins 2003:89–90). In 1874, at Harvard University, Dr. Edward Clarke, a member of its board of overseers, wrote that women were too delicate to handle the rigors of college education. The increased effort needed for thinking would sap energy from a woman's uterus and ovaries, leading these reproductive organs to shrink (Clarke 1874).

When women were finally given the opportunity to attend college, a right they had to fight hard for to win, they excelled. They now have a higher overall grade point average, and they outnumber men among college graduates. What was once thought to be natural is now recognized to have been a social construction. It turns out that the problem wasn't biology; it was the socially constructed culture that denied opportunity to women (Chee, Pino, and Smith 2005; National Center for Education Statistics 2018).

WOMAN MAY WEAR TROUSERS.

Attorney General of Kansas Rules There Is No Law Against It.

TOPEKA. Kan.. April 2S.—Gov. Stubbs received a letter yesterday from a widow at Oswego asking permission to wear men's trousers while at work at her home. It said she was supporting a large family. which necessitated outside work, and that in wearing skirts she was badly handicapped.

The letter was turned over to the Attorney General. who ruled there was no law prohibiting a woman from wearing men's trousers. especially if she were the head of the house.

It used to be considered unnatural for women to wear pants in the United States, but times change.
Source: Newspaper article "woman may wear trousers," April 29, 1910

On the flip side, the notion persists that men just aren't as nurturing as women. It appears to grow out of the presumption that women, because they give birth and nurse babies, are naturally better at providing love, care, and protection. Yet research demonstrates that when men have the primary responsibility for raising children, they do the same things conventionally associated with "mothering."

. . . In an exploratory experiment controlling college students' knowledge of the professor's gender for an online course, students gave better teaching evaluations to professors the students thought were male. This was true even when the actual professor was a woman.

Did You Know?

Source: MacNell, Driscoll, and Hunt 2014. Photo: Asia Images/PictureIndia/Getty Images reality itself, but such defiance is necessary to enact significant social change.

THE GENDER SPECTRUM

Awareness of the degree to which sex turns out to be more complex than simply XX versus XY, that we get socialized into gender roles rather than biologically determined into them, has led many people to conclude that multiple gender manifestations are possible when it comes to how we express ourselves. A person's biological sex does not inevitably determine his or her **gender identity,** which refers to a person's subjective or internal sense of his or her own gender. And this internal conception of who a person is can differ from his or her **gender expression,** the outward or public expression of a person's gender, often manifested in terms of clothes, haircuts, language, and other gendered behaviors. As noted previously, for example, a **transgender** person is someone whose gender identity differs from the sex he or she was assigned at birth. For example, a transgender person may have been born with a vagina but self-identify as male or masculine. The gender identity of a person who is **cisgender,** on the other hand, aligns more closely with the cultural expectations associated with his or her biological sex at birth. The prefix for the two words come from Latin, with *trans-* meaning "across" and *cis-* meaning "on the same side" (Tate, Ledbetter, and Youssef 2013; Tate, Youssef, and Bettergarcia 2014; Zimmer 2015).

To represent the full range of people's lived experiences, theorists have pushed even further, suggesting that we replace the existing either/or gender dimorphism implicit within conceptions of gender with a new model. The existing **gender binary**—a model in which gender roles are represented as either masculine or feminine with a clear divide between the two—constrained both sexual orientation and gender expression. The proposed alternative model portrays a **gender spectrum,** which presents gender as a continuum that incorporates a full range of possible combinations involving sex, gender, sexual orientation, gender identity, and gender expression. According to this model, gender is visualized as similar to a color wheel with no clear dividing lines between shades as opposed to an either/or check box. Many have adopted the use of the term **queer** (or genderqueer), because it reflects the rejection of sexual and gender binaries and highlights the multiple varieties of possible sexual orientations, gender identities, and gender expressions.

gender identity A person's subjective or internal sense of his or her own gender.

Gender expression The outward or public display of a person's gender.

Transgender A person whose gender identity differs from the sex he or she was assigned at birth.

Cisgender A person whose gender identity aligns more closely with the cultural expectations associated with his or her biological sex at birth.

Gender binary A dimorphic model in which gender roles are represented as either masculine or feminine with a clear divide between the two.

Gender spectrum A model of gender as a continuum that incorporates a full range of possible combinations involving sex, gender, sexual orientation, gender identity, and gender expression.

queer A term that incorporates the multiplicity of possible sexual orientations, gender identities, and gender expressions.

Research shows that single fathers effectively nurture their children, developing intimate and affectionate relationships with them, even though historically that got represented as non-masculine. Increasingly, fathers in the United States seek to find ways to more effectively engage with their children in what used to be seen as unconventional ways (Marsiglio and Roy 2012; McGill 2014; Risman 1986).

Identifying some aspect of our definitions of sex and gender as artificial reveals the complex relationship between the two. Questioning our conceptions of the natural, however, is never easy, as women who have worked for the right to vote and equal opportunity in the workplace have discovered. Confronting these notions can look like an attempt to defy

>> Working for Change: Women's Movements

One of the lessons we learn from research on gender is that change is possible. As we saw with college education for women, past norms need not determine future practices.

Change, however, seldom comes without conflict. People have fought against existing cultural assumptions about what is natural in order to advance opportunity for women in politics, the economy, and other spheres of public and private life. **Feminism** is the term for this belief in social, economic, and political equality for women.

THE FIRST WAVE

The feminist movement in the United States was born in upstate New York, in the town of Seneca Falls, in the summer of 1848. On July 19, the first women's rights convention began, attended by Elizabeth Cady Stanton, Lucretia Mott, and other pioneers in the struggle for women's rights. At the convention, members passed the "Declaration of Sentiments," which included this claim: "The history of mankind is a history of repeated injuries and usurpation on the part of man toward woman, having in direct object the establishment of an absolute tyranny over her." Echoing and expanding on the Declaration of Independence, it called for the recognition that "all men and women are created equal" (Stanton 1848). This first wave of feminists faced ridicule and scorn as they fought for legal and political equality for women. They were not afraid to risk controversy on behalf of their cause; in 1872, Susan B. Anthony was arrested for attempting to vote in that year's presidential election.

Did You Know?

. . . When it comes to science education in the United States, the fact that boys consistently score higher than girls on standardized tests has led many to assume that the difference is related to inherent differences based on sex. Yet, in a broader study of 65 countries, girls were more likely to outperform boys. Boys tend to do better in western/northern European countries and the Americas. Girls outdo boys in Asia, eastern/southern Europe, and the Middle East.

Source: Fairfield and McLean 2012. *Photo:* M. Constantini/Photoalto, Inc.

These early feminists won many victories in health care, education, and property rights. The pinnacle accomplishment of the first wave was the passage and ratification of the 19th Amendment to the Constitution in 1920, which guaranteed women's right to vote in the United States. The amendment was initially introduced to Congress in 1878, and its wording mirrored that of the 15th Amendment, which prohibits denial of the right to vote on the basis of race. After gaining this new right, however, the movement lost momentum because various factions within it disagreed about future goals, and, for a time, the women's movement became a much less powerful force for social change (Dicker 2016; Flexner and Fitzpatrick 1996).

> **Feminism** The belief in social, economic, and political equality for women.

THE SECOND WAVE

What is called the second wave of feminism in the United States emerged in the 1960s and came into full force in the 1970s. Betty Friedan's book *The Feminine Mystique* played a crucial part, as did two other pioneering books that argued for women's rights: Simone de Beauvoir's *The Second Sex* (1952) and Kate Millett's *Sexual Politics* (1970). Friedan was an upper-middle-class, White, suburban housewife who worked part-time as a freelance journalist in the 1950s. As part of a story she planned to write, she surveyed her college classmates about their lives. What she heard repeatedly from women like her was that they shared a sense of nameless, aching dissatisfaction that she famously labeled "the problem that has no name." Even though they were living what many considered the American Dream, something was missing. They mostly blamed themselves for this feeling of emptiness or incompleteness, and when they sought help, doctors and psychiatrists prescribed charity work, community activities, or perhaps tranquilizers.

In *The Feminine Mystique,* Friedan (1963) argued that the problem was not with women as individuals, but with the position they occupied in American society at the time. Friedan's realization that this was not a private trouble but a public issue represents a classic case of using the sociological imagination. Women were cut off from the public sphere, and their lack of access to valued economic, social, and cultural resources—including money and power in the workplace—was the real problem. (Friedan herself attributed part of her own relative happiness to the fact that she retained dual status as both journalist and housewife.) To challenge this structural problem, women had to fight against the cultural assumption that the primary and most "natural" goal for women was to be a wife and mother in the private sphere. As Friedan put it, "We can no longer ignore that voice within women that says, 'I want something more than my husband and my children and my home'" (1963:32).

In 1966, Friedan helped found the National Organization for Women (NOW) to fight for equality for women; she served as its president until 1970. In addition to political and legal battles, one of the organization's tools was

Betty Friedan's work as an organizer played a significant role in the second wave of feminism in the United States. B. Friedan/MPI/Archive Photos/Getty Images

....

argue it should be illegal in all or most cases. When asked about *Roe v. Wade,* the 1973 Supreme Court ruling that established the legal right to an abortion in the United States, 69 percent say it should *not* be overturned (Fingerhut 2017; Hartig 2018).

As more and more women identified existing cultural attitudes and practices as sexist—including those they themselves had accepted through socialization into traditional gender roles—they began to challenge male dominance. A sense of sisterhood, much like the class consciousness that Marx hoped would emerge in the proletariat, became evident. Individual women identified their interests with women as a whole, and they rejected the principle that their happiness depended on their acceptance of submissive and subordinate roles.

THE THIRD WAVE

In the 1980s, partially because of second-wave successes in opening up opportunities and earning greater respect for women, a sense developed that the central goals of feminism had largely been accomplished. Some scholars argued that we had entered a postfeminist era. In the early 1990s, however, a new style of feminism arose that went beyond fighting the structural obstacles that motivated the first and second waves. It ventured into the cultural sphere to embrace a multiplicity of voices, expressions, and experiences. This third wave was part of a conceptual shift away from a singular focus on equality of persons, which it takes as a given, to a celebration of difference (Brooks 1997; Lotz 2007; Showden 2009).

The third wave arose in part as a generational shift; younger women were dissatisfied with the dominant image of feminism as stodgy and uptight. It also represented a shift in message toward a more varied and pluralistic understanding of what feminism is. This was evident in two early anthologies that played a pivotal role presenting the multiplicity of voices this movement represents: Rebecca Walker's *To Be Real: Telling the Truth and Changing the Face of Feminism* (1995) and Barbara Findlen's *Listen Up: Voices from the Next Feminist Generation* (1995). Previously, feminists were characterized as White, upper-middle class, and heterosexual. Third-wave feminists place greater emphasis on agency and subjectivity;

"consciousness-raising groups." Among other goals, these groups sought to elevate awareness among women regarding the degree to which they shared "the problem that has no name." This shared consciousness could then lead to collective action and the development of a new structure with enhanced opportunities. Choice was a core value at the center of these efforts. The existing system limited options for women in many areas of social life. Feminists fought to open up structural opportunity and to ensure that women could make choices about going to college, pursuing a career based on ability rather than gender expectations, getting married or staying single, having children or remaining childless, and so on.

The question of whether women should have control over their reproductive rights and their bodies has also played a significant role in this movement. In the United States, most people support a woman's right to a legal abortion, but with reservations. According to a national survey, 58 percent say it should be legal in all or most cases, while 37 percent

Nancy Pelosi, Democrat from California, was the first female Speaker of the U.S. House of Representatives. Scott J Ferrell/Getty Images

....

own realities. This fits with the notion that our sex is not narrowly determined by biology and that our expression of our gender need not be singular in nature but is open to our creativity and control. One result is a more playful or ironic element to the movement, especially when it comes to so-called girlie feminism, which seeks to reclaim things like lipstick, high heels, and more sexualized images of women as viable emblems of feminist empowerment. Critics have argued that this rhetoric of choice inappropriately minimizes the continued power of racial, sexual, and class positions in society (Munford 2007; Renegar and Sowards 2009; Showden 2009).

INTERSECTIONALITY

One of the outgrowths of this new feminist perspective was the recognition that defining others primarily by any one position may diminish the importance of the multiple positions we all occupy. To look at the social location of Hispanic women, for example, we must pay mind to both their gender and their ethnicity (as well as other factors). Two significant theoretical developments arising out of this multiple-identity approach are standpoint theory and intersectionality.

are committed to personal empowerment; are more open about sexuality and sexual exploration; and celebrate diversity of gender, race, ethnicity, and class. Embracing a multiplicity of identities led to a commitment to social justice and a global perspective so that other voices have the opportunity to be heard (Baumgardner and Richards 2000; Groeneveld 2009; Lotz 2007; Zimmerman, McDermott, and Gould 2009).

The third wave includes a bit of the postmodern idea of self-creation, which we explored in the "Postmodern Life" section in Chapter 5. According to this idea, we can choose our identities from a buffet of possibilities and also create our

> **Standpoint theory** Because our social positions shape our perceptions, a more complete understanding of social relations must incorporate the perspectives of marginalized voices.
>
> **Intersectionality** Gender, sexuality, race, ethnicity, and class must not be studied in isolation, because they have intermingled effects on our identity, knowledge, and outcomes.

According to **standpoint theory,** our understanding of reality is shaped by the positions we occupy and the experiences we have. Given that the views of some (based on their gender, sexuality, race, ethnicity, or class) are privileged over others, this theory emphasizes the importance of listening to the voices of those who are in some way considered outsiders. Such attention provides a deeper and richer understanding of social systems (Collins 2000; Harding 2004; Hartsock 1983; Smith 1987).

Intersectionality represents a second major development. According to this approach, we cannot speak of gender or race or class or sexuality as if they exist in isolation from each other. Rather, these combine within us in ways that make it difficult to

The #MeToo movement, which provides support for survivors of sexual violence, was intentionally intersectional from the very beginning.   Mark Ralston/AFP/Getty Images

separate the effects of each. Thus research must analyze the intermingled effects of multiple social statuses on identity, knowledge, and outcomes. In her TED talk, "The Urgency of Intersectionality," law professor Kimberlé Crenshaw focused on the cultural frames we use to understand the world around us. In doing so, she suggested that these frames prevent us from seeing how the social justice inequalities people experience around gender, sexuality, race, ethnicity, and class overlap and cannot be dealt with in isolation from each other (Alimahomed 2010; Crenshaw 2016; Harding 2004; Shields 2008). For both standpoint theory and intersectionality, a narrative approach in research, in which we hear the voices of those who are other to us, is critical.

>> The Social Construction of Sexuality

The shifts that occur in how sex and gender are defined—as more complex than simple binary categories of male and female or masculine and feminine—also apply to

sexuality. In the United States, as a consequence of the dimorphic model of sex, the dominant ideology presumed heterosexual relationships, in which the idealized norm was chastity until marriage, followed by lifelong faithfulness to a single partner. This vision reached perhaps its zenith in the 1950s television portrayal of families in programs such as *Leave It To Beaver* and *Father Knows Best.* Times have changed.

When considering sexuality, we should distinguish between how we see ourselves and what we do. **Sexuality** denotes our identities and activities as sexual beings. In terms of *identity,* our sexuality represents an expression of who we are in ways similar to how gender, race, ethnicity, and class shape us. In terms of our sexual *practices,* sexuality shapes what we do (or do not do), with whom, and how often.

SEXUALITY AND IDENTITY

Sexual expression is not simply a result of biological urges and instincts. It is situated within, and an outgrowth of, existing social, cultural, and historical processes. Though alternative expressions of sexuality have a long history in the United States, their existence and practice has not always been acknowledged (Duberman, Vicinus, and Chauncy 1989; Escoffier 1997). During the 1960s, experimentation with "free love" helped open the door to more widespread recognition of such expressions. Around the same time organizations arose, such as the Gay Liberation Front in 1969 and the Gay Activist Alliance in 1970, that raised awareness that alternatives existed and sought to establish the legitimacy of alternative sexualities in the public consciousness.

As a result of such historical events, people became more aware of the concept of **sexual orientation**—the categories of people to whom we are sexually attracted—as a form of personal and community identity. Initially, in keeping with the dimorphic model of sex, the two major subcategories included **heterosexual,** those who were sexually attracted to members of the opposite sex, and **homosexual,** those who were attracted to members of the same sex. Homosexual men were identified as gay, and

U.S. Attitudes about Homosexuality

Always Wrong

Not Wrong at All

'73 '74 '76 '77 '80 '82 '84 '85 '87 '88 '89 '90 '91 '93 '94 '96 '98 2000 '02 '04 '06 '08 '10 '12 '14 '16

Note: Responses are to the question "What about sexual relationship between two adults of the same sex—do you think it is always wrong, almost always wrong, wrong only sometimes, or wrong at all?" Data are from the General Social Survey, a regularly administered national survey of the U.S. adult population.

Sources: Smith 2011; Smith et al. 2018. Photos: *(scale):* Comstock Images/Alamy Stock Photo *(two grooms):* ©Ivonne Wierink/Shutterstock.com; *(bride and groom):* ©Evgenii Zadiraka/123RF homosexual women were identified as lesbian. **Bisexual** was later added to these subcategories to include those who were attracted to both men and women. Attitudes regarding sexual orientation has shifted significantly over time. As the "U.S. Attitudes about Homosexuality" graph displays, the majority of adults surveyed now believe that homosexuality is not wrong at all.

Even though this heterosexual, homosexual, bisexual model extended awareness of sexuality beyond the 1950s version, it still presents the dividing lines as clear-cut and absolute. Classifying where you or others belong is presumed to be a simple matter of identifying your sexual practices and checking the appropriate box. But people's experiences of sexuality are more complex and varied than that. For example, what about those who have had occasional homosexual experiences but are now practicing heterosexuals? Or those who engage in same-sex practices but do not identify themselves as gay, lesbian, or bisexual (Silva 2016; Ward 2015)? Over time, additional categories were added to reflect a wider array of possibilities, such as polysexual, pansexual, and asexual.

Although awareness of the socially constructed nature of gender and sexuality has increased, a cultural expectation of heterosexuality remains dominant in the United States. Sociologists use the term **heteronormativity** to describe the cultural presupposition that heterosexuality is the appropriate standard for sexual identity and practice and that alternative sexualities are deviant, abnormal, or wrong (Chambers 2007; Jackson 2006; Warner 1993). Heteronormativity is a form of ethnocentrism that generalizes a particular cultural ideal (heterosexuality) onto all other populations, thus denying legitimacy to those outside it (Chambers 2007).

As an example of heteronormativity, a 1957 survey found that "four out of five people believed that anyone who preferred to remain single was 'sick,' 'neurotic,' or 'immoral'" (Coontz 2005:230). Additionally, homosexuality was categorized as a psychological disorder until 1972 in the American Psychiatric Association's official *Diagnostic and Statistical Manual of Mental Disorders* (*DSM*). A new edition, *DSM-5*, came out in 2013. The category "gender identity disorders," which included those who are transgender and transsexual, was removed and replaced with "gender dysphoria." The intent was to minimize the stigma attached to the diagnosis while still recognizing its existence. Some argue for the importance of maintaining these diagnoses, because transgender people who seek gender reassignment surgery might not get proper diagnosis and treatment without such a designation (Drescher 2010, 2011; Melby 2009; Winters 2012).

Socialization plays a key role in determining our sexual identity (Parker 2009). Just as was the case with gender, we face significant pressure to obey dominant norms for masculinity and femininity. In her book *Dude, You're a Fag*, sociologist C. J. Pascoe (2011) set out to understand how heteronormativity is reproduced. She conducted an ethnographic study of boys in a working-class high school. She found that one of the ways they reinforced existing masculinity norms was by casually using the term *fag* to call out anyone who deviates from the dominant masculine ideal. According to Pascoe, calling someone a fag was not so much an antigay act (though she admits it was that, too) as it was a means of keeping guys in line. Whereas it was possible to be a homosexual and still be masculine, being a fag represented a form of failed masculinity. The threat of being a fag hangs over boys like a specter or ghost that could possess them at any time; only eternal vigilance keeps it at bay. Pascoe argues that rejecting this role also represented a repudiation of femininity. So not only did this discourse support existing heteronormative standards, it also reinforced traditional conceptions of gender.

> **Bisexual** A category of sexual orientation that includes those who are attracted to both men and women.
>
> **Heteronormativity** A term that sociologists use to describe the cultural presupposition that heterosexuality is the appropriate standard for sexual identity and practice and that alternative sexualities are deviant, abnormal, or wrong.

Actor Neil Patrick Harris (right) along with his husband, David Burtka. Jason LaVeris/FilmMagic/Getty Images

─**SOC**THINK─

How is heteronormativity reinforced in the current top-rated songs and television programs? Can you think of any exceptions?

┌─ SOCTHINK ──────────────────────────┐
│ How does gendered name-calling, such as │
│ joking that a guy is a fag, maintain clear-cut │
│ gender boundaries? What consequences does │
│ it have for gays, lesbians, or heterosexual girls? │
└────────────────────────────────────┘

Such examples point to the fact that differences in sexuality are not just matters of orientation and alternative preferences; they are connected to larger systems of power in which some statuses are privileged over others (Brickell 2009). We construct our sexual identities, making sense of who we are, within the contexts of our social structures. Within these worlds, not all paths are accepted as equally legitimate. In the United States, establishing a sexual identity as something other than heterosexual has been difficult owing to the meanings attached to such identities and the lack of broader cultural support for them. These power differences contribute to discrimination and threats of violence. According to the FBI, for example, 16.9 percent of the 7,227 hate crime offenses reported in 2016 involved sexual orientation (U.S. Department of Justice 2017a:Table 1). In an effort to ensure the civil, political, and social rights of those in lesbian, gay, bisexual, transgender, and queer (LGBTQ) communities around the world, a group of human rights experts worked to establish the Yogyakarta Principles (www.yogyakartaprinciples.org). They identify 29 basic principles, including the right to equality and

nondiscrimination, the right to work, and the right to found a family.

In review, to better understand issues surrounding sexuality and identity, we must understand the complexity sexuality entails. Doing so necessitates taking into account sex (biology), gender (social, cultural, and psychological constructs), sexual orientation (partner preferences), gender identity (subjective sensibility), and gender expression (external displays). A variety of possible manifestations exists within each of these major variables—not only a simple dichotomy of male versus female for each. As a result, many combinations are possible. As alternative expressions of gender and sexuality become more accepted, their role as master status through which all identity is filtered may become less powerful. Instead, in keeping with the lessons learned regarding intersectionality, sexuality may become but one significant piece of identity among others, all of which we must take into account to better understand why we think and act as we do.

SEXUALITY IN ACTION

While our sexuality shapes our conception of who we are, it also has consequences for what we do. In sociological terms, as suggested by the Thomas theorem, our sexual identity is shaped by our interactions with others. We then act on the basis of those perceptions. In our everyday lives, our perceptions of ourselves and our sexual practices often reinforce each other. Working out our sexuality in practice includes the types of sex acts we perform and the types of sexual relationships we establish with others.

Because open discussions about sex are generally considered to be taboo, people are often both ignorant and curious about actual sexual practices. The Kinsey Reports (*Sexual Behavior in the Human Male* [1948] and *Sexual Behavior in the Human Female* [1953]) provided the earliest in-depth research studies on people's sexual practices. Compiled by American biologist Alfred C. Kinsey and his colleagues, the reports, particularly their finding that 8 percent of men had been in predominantly homosexual relationships for at least three years between ages 16 and 55, were considered shocking at the time. Both volumes became best sellers. Their studies opened the door for others to conduct additional research (Bullough 1998; Laumann et al. 1994; Smith 2006).

The National Survey of Family Growth (NSFG) provides updated data and includes detailed information on sexual practices. The survey is conducted by the National Center for Health Statistics (NCHS) and the Centers for Disease Control and Prevention (CDC) and is based on a national sample of more than 9,000 respondents (Copen, Chandra, and Febo-Vazquez 2016). Summarizing the results regarding heterosexual relationship patterns, the NSFG researchers reported that "94.2% of women and 92.0% of men aged 18–44 had ever had vaginal intercourse; 86.2% of women and 87.4% of men had ever had oral sex; and 35.9% of women and 42.3% of men had ever had anal

Alfred C. Kinsey, with the help of his team of researchers, provided unprecedented insight into people's sexual practices in the United States. Hulton Archive/Getty Images

sex)" (p. 1). In an earlier wave of research they found that the median number of total opposite-sex partners was 3.6 for women and 6.1 for men (Chandra et al. 2011).

Over the years, a contentious question in such studies has involved the percentage of homosexuals in the U.S. population. A commonly reported figure (derived from the Kinsey Reports) estimates that approximately 10 percent of the population is homosexual. The NSFG study distinguished between having had same-sex experiences and identifying with particular sexual orientations. The researchers found that among adults aged 18–44, 6.2 percent of men and 17.4 percent of women have had same-sex sexual contact in their lifetime. Likelihoods of engaging in same-sex sexual behavior varied somewhat by age. Among women, the difference was wider: 19.4 percent of 18- to 24-year-olds compared to 13.1 percent for 35- to 44-year-olds. Among men, 6.6 percent of 18- to 24-year-olds reported having had same-sex sexual contact compared to 6.0 percent for 35- to 44-year-olds (Copen, Chandra, and Febo-Vazquez 2016).

SOC THINK

Why are younger women more likely to have had same-sex experiences than either older women or men of any age?

Simply having had same-sex experiences does not necessarily result in a same-sex identity. The percentage of people who identify as homosexual and bisexual are lower than the percentage of those who have engaged in such practices. To explore sexual orientation, the NSFG researchers asked, "Do you think of yourself as a heterosexual, homosexual, or bisexual?" As the "Sexual Orientation Self-Identification" table indicates, 95.1 percent of men and 92.3 percent of women identify themselves as heterosexual. Overall, approximately 1.6 percent of men and women aged 18–44 in the United

States identify themselves as homosexual and 3.8 percent as bisexual (Copen, Chandra, and Febo-Vazquez 2016).

The age at which people have their first sexual experiences has historically been an additional interest of researchers. In terms of opposite-sex experiences, the percentage of teens who have had sexual intercourse rises with each subsequent year. At age 15, 11 percent of girls and 16 percent of boys have had vaginal sexual intercourse; by age 17, it is 42 percent for girls and 41 percent for boys; and at age 19, it is 69 percent for females and 68 percent for males (Abma and Martinez 2017). At the same time, teen birthrates in the United States have reached record lows, having fallen 51 percent since 2007. Rates are down significantly for all racial and ethnic groups (Martin et al. 2018).

Most teens who have had sex did so for the first time with someone they were in a steady relationship with. That likelihood varied by gender, however, at 74 percent for females and 51 percent for males. Among teens who have not had sex, the most common reason given was that it was against their religion or morals at 35 percent for girls and 28 percent for boys. The second most common reason for both females and males was that they hadn't found the right person yet (Abma and Martinez 2017).

When it comes to sexual activity overall, perhaps no invention in the history of human sexuality was more

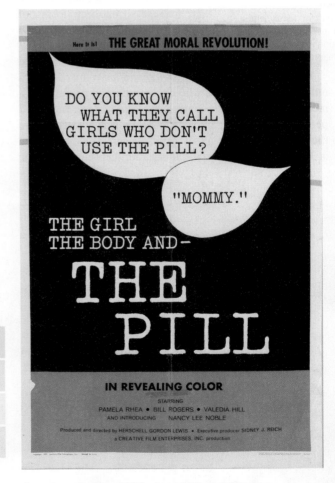

A movie poster from 1967.   Image Art/Moviepix/Getty Images

Sexual Orientation Self-Identification

	Men	Women
Heterosexual	95.1	92.3
Homosexual	1.9	1.3
Bisexual	2.0	5.5
Did Not Report	1.0	0.9

Note: Percentage is in response to the question "Do you think of yourself as a heterosexual, homosexual, or bisexual?" Age range of respondents was 18–44.
Source: Copen, Chandra, and Febo-Vazquez 2016.

important than that of the birth control pill. It was approved for use in the United States in 1960 and helped spark the sexual revolution. Together with other modern forms of birth control, the pill made it possible to engage in sex without significant risk of getting pregnant. It gave women greater control over their sexuality and their careers by allowing them to control their fertility. Effective birth control also resulted in debates about how sex should be viewed, whether primarily for procreation (that is, having babies) or recreation (for pleasure, love, and commitment) or both. Religious groups, including the Roman Catholic Church, continue to struggle with these issues (Benagiano and Mori 2009).

In the United States, 61.7 percent of women of childbearing age (15–44) use some form of contraception. Of these, 26 percent use birth control pills, 25 percent opted for female surgical sterilization, and 15 percent rely on male condoms. Among those not using contraception, 11 percent have never had intercourse and 8 percent had no intercourse recently (Daniels et al. 2015).

> **Instrumental leader** The person in the family who bears responsibility for the completion of tasks, focuses on distant goals, and manages the external relationship between one's family and other social institutions.
>
> **Expressive leader** The person in the family who bears responsibility for the maintenance of harmony and internal emotional affairs.

Internationally, birth control practices vary significantly from country to country. The overall global average for use of modern forms of birth control—condoms, the pill, and sterilization—is 57 percent among women aged 15–49 who are married or in a union. For Europe as a whole, 60 percent of women use a modern form of birth control. In Asia, China's rate is 82 percent, India's is 51 percent, and Japan's is 40. Compare these countries with all of Africa, where the overall rate is 33 percent with substantial variation between countries.

Some African nations have extremely low rates—for example, South Sudan at 6.5, Chad at 6.3 percent, and Guinea at 8.4 percent. Just as was the case for women in the United States, greater control over fertility by women internationally increases their opportunities for self-determination. It also increases the likelihood of extending basic human rights and protections to women in countries around the world (Inglehart, Norris, and Welzel 2002; Kristof and WuDunn 2009; United Nations 2018a).

SOCTHINK

How might economic, social, and cultural factors influence a society's pattern of birth control use? How might these factors influence a society's attitudes about gender?

>> Gender and Inequality

Although the work of early sociologists such as Harriet Martineau, Charlotte Perkins Gilman, and Ida B. Wells-Barnett highlighted the significance of gender inequality, in the 1950s sociologists Talcott Parsons and Robert Bales (1955) by and large accepted a dimorphic model of gender as natural. Drawing on the functionalist perspective, they maintained that families need both an instrumental and an expressive leader to function properly. The **instrumental leader** is the person in the family who bears responsibility for completion of tasks, focuses on distant goals, and manages the external relationship between the family and other social institutions. The **expressive leader** is the person in the family who bears responsibility for the maintenance of harmony and internal emotional affairs. Parson and Bales argued that this division of labor works well because women's interest in expressive goals frees men for instrumental tasks, and vice versa. Based on their theory, it seemed only natural that women become anchored in the family as wives, mothers, and household managers, while men become anchored in the occupational world outside the home.

As we saw earlier with Betty Friedan and the discussion of "The Second Wave" of women's movements, a major consequence of this supposed ideal was isolation from the public sphere's economy and politics. This separation had the effect of denying women access to financial resources and political power. Over time, as a direct consequence of activism, women have gained greater access to educational opportunities, jobs, and political positions. And yet, as we will see, women still face significant challenges.

SEXISM AND DISCRIMINATION

As is apparent in the definition of sociology, sociologists are interested in understanding the "consequences of difference"; that is, the impact the social structures we build have on the distribution

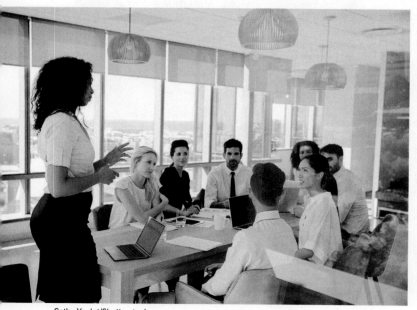

Cathy Yeulet/Shutterstock

of valued resources. When it comes to gender, sociologists investigate the degree of sexism that exists within social systems. **Sexism** is the ideology that claims one sex is superior to the other. The term generally refers to male prejudice and discrimination against women. It is not enough, however, to understand gender inequality only by looking at the attitudes and practices of individuals, such as sexist remarks and acts of aggression. We must analyze it as a characteristic of the social system itself.

Sociologists use the expression **institutional discrimination** to refer to patterns of treatment that, as part of a society's normal operations, systematically deny a group access to resources and opportunities. All the major institutions in the United States—including the government, the armed forces, large corporations, the media, universities, and the medical establishment—are controlled primarily by men. Analysis of patterns of distribution allow for some assessment of the degree to which institutional sexism exists.

WOMEN IN THE UNITED STATES

When the Declaration of Independence claimed "all men are created equal," it really meant White, property-owning, adult males. It took a long time for the United States to recognize and affirm women's political rights. The battle for their full economic rights continues.

Labor Force Participation

The labor market has opened up significantly since Betty Friedan published *The Feminine Mystique* in 1963. Today, millions of women—married or single, with or without children, pregnant or recently having given birth—are in the labor force. Overall, as shown in the "Labor Force Participation Rates" graph, the percentage of U.S. women aged 16 and older in the labor force rose from 33.9 percent in 1950 to 57 percent in 2017. By contrast, the percentages for men were 86.3 percent in 1950 and 69.1 percent in 2017. Among women with children under age 6, 39 percent were in the labor force in 1975 compared to 65.1 percent in 2017 (Bureau of

Labor Force Participation Rates

Source: Bureau of Labor Statistics 2018g. *Photo:* kristian sekulic/E Plus/Getty Images

Labor Statistics 2018g:Tables 2 and 7).

Within the labor force, we see significant differences in the jobs men and women hold. As is evident in the "Women's Representation in U.S. Occupations" table, significant

> **Sexism** The ideology that claims one sex is superior to the other.
>
> **Institutional discrimination** The systematic denial of rights and opportunities to marginalized groups as part of society's normal operations.

Women's Representation in U.S. Occupations

Underrepresented		Overrepresented	
Occupation	Percentage female	Occupation	Percentage female
Roofer	0.6	Flight attendants	72.9
Auto mechanic	2.4	Elementary teachers	79.3
Electrician	2.5	Librarians	79.5
Firefighter	3.5	Social workers	82.5
Aircraft pilot	6.2	Tellers	85.2
Mechanical engineer	9.2	Occupational therapist	87.6
Police officer	13.6	Registered nurses	89.9
Printers	17.7	Receptionists	91.0
Computer programmer	21.2	Hairdresser	92.6
Architect	28.6	Childcare workers	93.7
Lawyers	37.4	Dental hygienists	94.9
Physicians	40.0	Secretary	95.0

Note: These data are for 2017. The elementary teacher category includes middle school teachers.
Source: Bureau of Labor Statistics 2018g:Table 11. *Photo:* JupiterImage, Creatas Image/Getty Images

occupational gender segregation exists. For example, women account for 95 percent of all secretaries and 94.9 percent of all dental hygienists. Entering such sex-typed occupations often places women in "service" roles that parallel the traditional gender-role standard. At the same time, women are underrepresented in occupations historically defined as "men's jobs," which often offer much greater financial rewards and prestige than women's jobs. For example, women account for 47 percent of the paid labor force of the United States, yet they constituted only 6.2 percent of aircraft pilots, 9.2 percent of mechanical engineers, 13.6 percent of police officers, and 37.4 percent of lawyers (Bureau of Labor Statistics 2018g:Table 11).

Income Today we claim to value "equal pay for equal work," meaning that someone's sex (along with race, ethnicity, or age) shouldn't matter in determining what the person earns; the only characteristic that should matter is job performance. But in practice, women do not earn as much on average as men, even in the same occupations. When comparing individuals who worked full-time, year-round in 2017, the median income for men was $52,146 and the median for women was $41,977 (Fontenot, Semega, and Kollar 2018). In other words, women earned 80.5 cents for every dollar that men earned overall.

Taking occupational segregation into account does not explain away the wage gap. It's true, of course, that women are often more concentrated in occupations with lower average wages than men (child care worker or receptionist versus physician or civil engineer). However, in 2017, out of 125 specific jobs for which the Bureau of Labor Statistics provides sufficient data, in only 2 did women earn more on average than men: "non-farm wholesale and retail buyers" and "dining room and cafeteria attendants and bartender helpers." Significant wage gaps exist within occupations across the board. For example, wage gaps persist in the three occupations for which women receive the highest average pay: chief executive officer (79.5 percent of men's earnings), pharmacist (82.3 percent), and physician (77.3 percent). Of course, in some occupations the wage gap is significantly wider, including personal financial advisors (58.9), administrative services managers (62.2), and financial managers (71.1) (Bureau of Labor Statistics 2018g:Table 2).

Glass ceiling An invisible barrier that blocks the promotion of a qualified individual in a work environment because of the individual's gender, race, or ethnicity.

Even in occupations where women are more likely to be concentrated, they still earn less on average than do men in the same field. Examples include secretary (86.3 percent of what male secretaries earn), elementary or middle school teacher (86.7 percent), and registered nurse (90.7 percent). Being a man in a predominantly female occupation seems to be an asset, whereas the reverse does not appear to be true (Bureau of Labor Statistics 2018g:Table 2).

Additional factors to explain the wage gap include education and age. When comparing women and men who have similar levels of education—for example, a woman whose highest degree is a high school diploma to a man with the same level of education—the wage gap persists. As is portrayed in the "Gender Wage Gap by Education" table, women with some college but no degree earn 71.6 percent compared to men with the same educational attainment. There continues to be a wage gap, though not as large, for men and women with professional degrees, including medical doctors and lawyers. Within this group, women earn 78.7 percent of what men earn (U.S. Census Bureau 2018b:Table PINC-03).

When comparing women and men in similar age groups, a pattern does emerge. The wage gap between men and women under age 35 averages approximately 90 percent. But then the gap widens for age groups older than that to about 78 percent (Bureau of Labor Statistics 2018g:Table 1). A major factor suggested to explain this difference is that women are more likely than men to take time away from the workforce around that age to raise children. As a result, when they return to the labor force they have less seniority than men of equal age and thus receive lower wages (England et al. 2016; Erosa, Fuster, and Restuccia 2016; Golan and Hincapié 2016; Jee, Misra, and Murray-Close 2018).

Gender Wage Gap by Education

Education Level	Women	Men	Wage Gap (%)
High school graduates	$32,140	$42,399	75.8
Some college, no degree	$36,287	$50,662	71.6
Bachelor's degree	$52,531	$72,082	72.9
Master's degree	$67,704	$91,439	74
Professional degree	$98,780	$125,493	78.7
Doctorate degree	$91,954	$117,570	78.2

Note: Data based on median earnings for people aged 25–64 who worked full-time, year-round. High school graduates included those with GEDs.
Source: U.S. Census Bureau 2018b:Table PINC-03.

The Glass Ceiling As we saw with Sheryl Sandberg at the beginning of this chapter, the higher you look up the corporate ladder, the fewer women you see. These positions tend to have higher pay and greater power, yet women have often been passed over when it came to these jobs. The term **glass ceiling** refers to the invisible barrier that blocks the promotion of qualified individuals in a work environment because of the individual's gender, race, or ethnicity. In 1995, the federal government's Glass Ceiling Commission family. Who does the housework when women become productive wage earners? In dual-income families, fathers do an average of 9.4 hours of housework per week compared to 15.7 hours for women. Even in households where she works and he does not, wives still do more housework (Parker and Wang 2013). Researchers have found that sharing housework equally improves both overall relationship satisfaction and levels of sexual intimacy. When not shared equally, the task most likely to reduce relationship satisfaction for women is the mundane daily chore of doing dishes (Carlson, Miller, and Sassler 2018).

Sociologist Arlie Hochschild (1989, 1990, 2005) has used the phrase **second shift** to describe the double burden of working outside the home followed by child care and housework. On the basis of interviews with and observations of 52 couples over an eight-year period, Hochschild reported that the wives (and not their husbands) drive home from the office while planning domestic schedules and play dates for children—and then begin their second shift. Drawing on national studies, she concluded that women spend 15 fewer hours each week in leisure activities than their husbands. In a year, these women work an extra month of 24-hour days because of the second shift; over a dozen years, they work an extra year of 24-hour

Second shift The double burden of working outside the home followed by child care and housework.

(1995) offered the first comprehensive study of the barriers in hiring decisions. It concluded that prejudice against women and minority group candidates plays a substantial role in hiring outcomes. It also concluded that the supply of qualified top-level candidates is limited by the cumulative effects of similar practices throughout the career path, limiting access to the training and experiences necessary to be considered for top-level jobs.

In recent years, corporations have made a concerted effort to increase their executive-level diversity, but they still have a long way to go if their goal is balanced representation between men and women. In 2015, only 3.9 percent of the chief executive officers (CEOs) and 14.1 percent of chief financial officers (CFOs) globally were women. Only 14.7 percent of board of director seats globally are occupied by women. To put it another way, men hold 85 percent of the seats on these boards, a source of a significant amount of power and influence. Board representation varies significantly between countries. In Norway, women occupy 46.7 percent of board seats; in the United States it's 16.6 percent; and in Japan women represent only 3.5 percent of board members (Dawson, Natella, and Kersley 2016).

Home and Work Today, many women face the challenge of trying to juggle work and

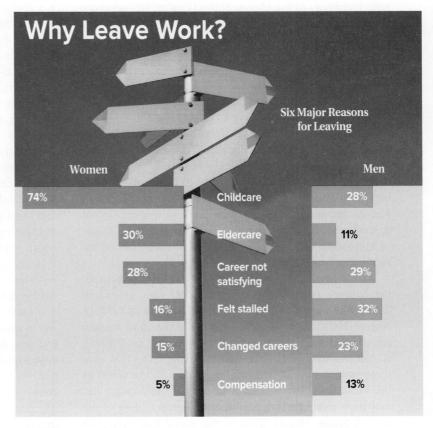

Why Leave Work?

Six Major Reasons for Leaving

	Women	Men
Childcare	74%	28%
Eldercare	30%	11%
Career not satisfying	28%	29%
Felt stalled	16%	32%
Changed careers	15%	23%
Compensation	5%	13%

Note: Reasons cited as major factors in voluntarily leaving their jobs in a survey of "highly qualified" workers, aged 28–55, defined as those with a graduate degree, a professional degree, or a bachelor's degree with honors.

Source: Hewlett, Foster, Sherbin, Shiller, and Sumberg 2010. *Photo:* Narvikk/Getty Images days. Hochschild found that the married couples she studied were fraying at the edges, and so were their careers and their marriages. With such reports in mind, many feminists have advocated greater governmental and corporate support for child care, more-flexible family leave policies, and other reforms designed to ease the burden on the nation's families (Mann, Sullivan, and Gershuny 2011; Moen and Roehling 2005).

Politics Turning to political involvement, after years of struggle, women won the right to vote with the passage of the 19th Amendment in 1920. Looking at voter participation rates, we can see that they have taken advantage of that opportunity. In fact, a higher percentage of women turn out to vote than do men. This has been true in every presidential election since 1980 (Center for American Women and Politics 2017).

When it comes to holding elected office, however, we find the same kind of underrepresentation in positions of power by women as is evident in the workplace. Even though women make up slightly more than half of the population, they make up a significantly smaller proportion of elected officials. In 2019, for example, only 9 of the nation's 50 states had a female governor. Also at the state level, women make up 28.6 percent of all 7,383 state legislators in the United States (Center for American Women and Politics 2019).

Women have made slow but steady progress in certain political arenas. In 1971, only 3 percent of members of Congress were women. By 2019, that number rose to 23.7 percent, a record number of 127 members: 102 in the House and 25 in the Senate. In 2007, Nancy Pelosi became the first ever woman to serve as Speaker of the House, a post she returned to in 2019. In the 2018 midterm elections, 4 states elected their first woman ever to the Senate leaving 18 states never to have done so. In the House, the number of women of color rose to a record 43 members. Deb Haaland of New Mexico and Sharice Davids of Kansas became the first Native American women elected to Congress. Rashida Tlaib of Michigan and Ilhan Omar of Minnesota became the first Muslim women (Center for American Women and Politics 2018, 2019).

At the Supreme Court, Sandra Day O'Connor became the nation's first female justice in 1981 (and retired in 2006). She was joined by Ruth Bader Ginsberg in 1993. In August 2009, Sonia Sotomayor became the third woman and first Hispanic on the Court. In August 2010 Elena Kagan was sworn in to the Court, making it the first time three women have ever served as justices on the Court at the same time. In the executive branch, no woman has ever been elected either president or vice president of the United States. Hillary Clinton challenged that barrier in 2016, winning the popular vote with 2,868,692 more votes but losing the Electoral College vote to Donald Trump (Wasserman 2016).

5 Movies on GENDER AND SEXUALITY

Love, Simon
Announcing who you are to the world is pretty terrifying.

The Fits
What does being a girl mean?

Moonlight
An African American man faces questions about love, friendship, and sexuality.

What Men Want
She knows what men think.

Transformer
A transgender woman's journey to acceptance.

Violence against Women Violence against women is a global problem. The full extent of such violence, both in the United States and abroad, is unknown because such crimes often go unreported and unrecognized. Globally, the World Health Organization estimates that 35.6 percent of women have been victims of sexual or physical violence by an intimate partner. Rates vary significantly by region, including 65.6 percent in central sub-Saharan Africa and 41.7 percent in South Asia to 16.3 percent in East Asia and 19.3 percent in western Europe (World Health Organization 2013b).

Violence against women in the United States remains a significant problem. According to the National Crime Victimization Survey, women were the victims of 298,410 rapes and sexual assaults in 2016. Overall, only 23.2 percent of these rapes and sexual assaults were reported to police, which works out to 1.3 million rapes and sexual assaults that year. Other studies suggest that the likelihood of reporting such acts to police may be significantly lower (Morgan and Kena 2018).

Research shows that women and girls of all ages are subject to acts of violence. Among high school girls, 9.1 percent had been hit, slapped, or physically hurt on purpose by their boyfriend or girlfriend in the previous year, and 10.7 percent had been kissed, touched, or forced to have sexual intercourse when they did not want to (Kann et al. 2018:Table 38, Table 40). In a survey of college women, 19 percent experienced either an attempted or completed sexual assault while in college. Overall, 3.4 percent of college women had been forcibly raped and 8.5 percent had been raped while incapacitated—drunk, passed out, drugged, or asleep.

Nice Nailantei Leng'ete, an advocate for the elimination of female genital mutilation, was one of Time magazine's 100 Most Influential People in the World in 2018.   Taylor Hill/FilmMagic/Getty Images

Among college women who were victims of a forced sexual assault, only 13 percent reported it to police or campus security, although 69 percent disclosed the incident to a family member or friend (Krebs et al. 2007). In a national survey of adult women in the United States, researchers found that 18 percent had been raped at some point in their lifetime. Only 16 percent of these women had reported it to law enforcement officials (Kilpatrick et al. 2007). And in the most extreme form of violence, 549 wives and 488 girlfriends were murdered by their intimate partners in 2017 according to FBI data (U.S. Department of Justice 2018d:Table 10).

WOMEN AROUND THE WORLD

The likelihood of violence against women is shaped in part by cultural attitudes about them, along with the relative lack of power they possess in society. As Nicholas Kristof and Sherly WuDunn (2009) put it in their book *Half the Sky,* "People get away with enslaving village girls for the same reason that people got away with enslaving blacks two hundred years ago: The victims are perceived as discounted humans" (p. 24). Increased education and opportunity for women, they suggest, lead to a curtailing of violence.

Women face significant oppression, violence, and discrimination in nations around the globe. Whether in the form of sex trafficking, socially condoned rape, or denial of medical services, the simple fact of being a woman is enough to justify such practices in some countries. In the case of Woineshet Zebene, for example, a group of men came for her at 11:30 at night. She was in a deep sleep, but they took her from her home in the Ethiopian countryside and battered and raped her over the next two days. Afterward, it was expected that she would marry the man who led the assault. When she refused, she was again kidnapped, beaten, and raped. A court official to whom she pleaded for help advised her to "get over it" and marry her attacker. She was 13 years old (Kristof and WuDunn 2009).

Women are particularly vulnerable to sex trafficking, gender-based violence (including honor killings and mass rape), and death or serious injury during childbirth due to inadequate medical care. For example, in Ghana, 21 percent of women report that their first sexual experience was by rape. Regarding inadequate health care, 1 in 7 women in Nigeria, 1 in 22 in sub-Saharan Africa, and 1 in 70 in India die during childbirth, compared to 1 in 4,800 in the United States (Kristof and WuDunn 2009).

Such practices often go unnoticed because they represent "quotidian cruelties"—the everyday practice of violence and discrimination that is largely invisible and considered inevitable or even natural. Fortunately, women around the world have successfully fought to change local attitudes and practices. In India, for example, Ruchira Gupta founded Apne Aap Women Worldwide, with its mission to end sex trafficking (www.apneaap.org). In Pakistan, Mukhtar Mai used settlement money she received after having been gang

In Kenya, Myla Rodgers established Mama Hope as an organization to provide girls a greater sense of agency and opportunity.   ©Bryce Yukio Adolphson

Going GLOBAL

Time Spent in Unpaid Labor

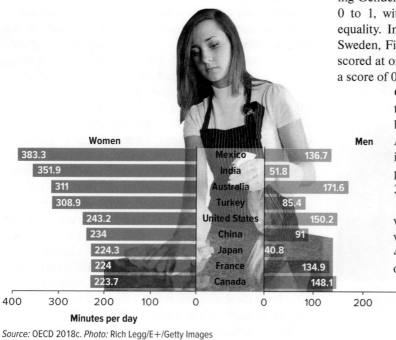

Women		Men
383.3	Mexico	136.7
351.9	India	51.8
311	Australia	171.6
308.9	Turkey	85.4
243.2	United States	150.2
234	China	91
224.3	Japan	40.8
224	France	134.9
223.7	Canada	148.1

400 300 200 100 0   0 100 200 300 400

Minutes per day

Source: OECD 2018c. *Photo:* Rich Legg/E+/Getty Images

Opportunities for women vary significantly around the world. In an attempt to quantify the degree of global gender inequality, the World Economic Forum releases an annual report ranking nations in four areas: educational attainment, health and survival, economic participation and opportunity, and political empowerment. The resulting Gender Gap Index score for each country ranges from 0 to 1, with a higher score representing greater gender equality. In 2018 only seven countries—Iceland, Norway, Sweden, Finland, Nicaragua, Rwanda, and New Zealand—scored at or above 0.8. The United States ranked 51st, with a score of 0.72, behind nations such as South Africa, Cuba, Canada, and Bangladesh. Ten nations, among them Yemen, Pakistan, Iraq, and Syria, scored below 0.6. Countries in the Middle East and Africa had the lowest average rankings, primarily because of their low scores on economic and political indicators (World Economic Forum 2018).

Although people in most nations agree that women should have equal rights, significant variation exists. For example, in Tanzania, 48 percent of men agree, compared to 73 percent of women, a gap of 25 percent. In Pakistan the gap is 24 percent, and in Uganda it is 23. In Japan the gap is actually reversed, with 67 percent of men versus 53 percent of women saying that it is very important for women to have the same rights as men (Zainulbhai 2016).

Change is possible. In an effort to address some of the structural inequality that exists, legislators in Norway established minimum quotas for the number of female members of boards of directors for companies. As the architects of the plan put it, "Instead of assuming what people *can't* do at work, provide opportunities for employees to prove what they can do." Norway now has the highest average percentage of female board members of any nation (Dawson, Natella, and Kersley 2016). Setting clear workplace and political representation goals makes a difference. Looking forward, the Rockefeller Foundation (2016) has established a goal of 100 women CEOs of Fortune 500 companies by 2025, a significant increase over the current 21.

raped to establish her School for Girls; she later expanded it to include a free legal clinic, a public library, and a women's shelter. And in Kenya, Myla Rodgers established the organization Mama Hope. In addition to helping build health clinics, poultry farms, drip irrigation gardens, and other projects, the group produced a number of viral videos designed to show African people as active, engaged, intelligent, and multidimensional. The videos portray the people of Kenya, Uganda, Tanzania, Ghana, and elsewhere not as objects to be manipulated or subjects to be studied, but as participants who, when given access to and control over even limited amounts of economic resources, have the vision and ability to transform their futures for the better (Kristof and WuDunn 2009).

Sociology often confronts us with things that can make us uncomfortable, such as gender inequality. The point of doing so is a more complete understanding of what we do and why we do it. Such knowledge can lead us to new and better practices that provide greater understanding, fairness, equality, and opportunity. Through practicing the sociological imagination, as Betty Friedan did in the case of gender, we can make the world a better place.

SOCIOLOGY IS A VERB

The Bechdel Test

According to the Bechdel Test, developed by cartoonist Alison Bechdel, a movie fails if three criteria are not met: (1) It has to have at least two women in it, (2) who talk to each other, (3) about something besides a man. Go to BechdelTest.com to see how some of your favorite movies fared. Pick out a movie that has not been added to the site; watch and evaluate it according to the criteria, and upload your results.

For REVIEW

I. How has our understanding of gender and sexuality shifted over time?
- The presumption that gender and sexuality are narrowly determined by our biology has given way to an understanding of both as socially constructed, complex, and multidimensional.

II. How has opportunity for women in the United States changed over time?
- In the 1950s, women's primary roles were wife and mother. Since that time, largely because of the efforts of the second wave of the women's movement, their labor force participation and income have risen significantly.

III. To what extent does gender still shape access to resources?
- Women continue to be paid less than men in the same occupations, tend to be segregated into a narrower range of female-dominated occupations, bear greater responsibility for housework, and are underrepresented as elected officials, though outcomes in all areas have improved.

Functionalist View

Gender roles establish the proper behavior, attitudes, and activities expected of men and women for a stable society.

Shifts in sexuality are a consequence of changes in what modern societies need, especially in terms of reproduction, to maintain social order.

Families need both an **instrumental leader** and an **expressive leader**; historically, women's natural gravitation to expressive goals freed men for instrumental tasks, and vice versa.

GENDER ROLES, INSTRUMENTAL LEADER, EXPRESSIVE LEADER
KEY CONCEPTS

Conflict View

The presumption that gender is determined by nature results in a belief that biology is destiny, an ideology that reinforces the existing system of gender inequality.

Heteronormativity is a form of power that limits alternative expressions of sexuality and contributes to discrimination.

Even after the feminist movements produced substantial changes, women still face significant **discrimination** in wages, occupations, and politics.

KEY CONCEPTS
IDEOLOGY, DISCRIMINATION, SEXISM

Interactionist View

Our conceptions of gender and sexuality are not determined by biology but, rather, are the consequences of historical, social, and cultural practices over time.

Male–female differences and heterosexual preferences get reinforced through **everyday interaction**, such as giving trucks to boys and dolls to girls.

The negative responses people have when gender and sexuality norms are broken—reinforce existing dominant roles.

KEY CONCEPTS
SOCIAL CONSTRUCTION, GENDER NORMS, ROLES

MAKE THE CONNECTION

After reviewing the chapter, answer the following questions:

1
How would each of the perspectives seek to explain Sheryl Sandberg's career experiences?

2
How would each of the three perspectives look at the supposition that differences between men and women are "natural" and always have been?

3
How would the macro approaches of the conflict and functionalist perspectives study gender and sexuality differently than the micro approach of the interactionist perspective?

4
How does each perspective contribute to your understanding of your own gender-role socialization?

Pop Quiz

1. **What term do sociologists use to describe the presumed biological differences between males and females?**
   a. gender
   b. sexism
   c. anatomy
   d. sex

2. **What term does geneticist Anne Fausto-Sterling use to describe those who have biological characteristics typically associated with both males and females?**
   a. sex
   b. gender
   c. intersexual
   d. gender displays

3. **When college students conducted an experiment in which they violated expected gender norms, they demonstrated the power of**
   a. gender-role socialization.
   b. biological determinism.
   c. instrumental leadership.
   d. the glass ceiling.

4. **What is the expression used when claiming that gender for men is not narrowly limited to traditional conceptions of masculinity?**
   a. intersexual
   b. gender modification
   c. sex
   d. multiple masculinities

5. **What do groups such as the *berdaches, hijras,* and *xanith* reveal about the nature of sex and gender?**
   a. All societies share the same dimorphic, male–female model of sex.
   b. The number of sex and gender categories varies across cultures.
   c. Socialization plays a significant role in modern societies, but a more limited role in traditional societies.
   d. Sex categories vary across cultures, but expressions of gender are universal.

6. **The primary accomplishment of the first wave of the women's movement was**
   a. making women citizens.
   b. gaining the right to an abortion.
   c. earning the right to nondiscrimination in the workplace.
   d. winning the right to vote.

7. **What term describes the categories of people to whom we are sexually attracted?**
   a. heteronormativity
   b. sexual orientation
   c. sexuality
   d. sexual displays

8. **According to early sociologists Talcott Parsons and Robert Bales, which type of leader bears responsibility for completion of tasks, focuses on more-distant goals, and manages the external relationship between the family and other social institutions?**
   a. expressive
   b. charismatic
   c. instrumental
   d. traditional

9. **Overall, when comparing full-time, year-round workers, how much do women earn compared to every dollar men earn?**
   a. 42 cents
   b. 63 cents
   c. 80 cents
   d. 94 cents

10. **The expression "second shift" refers to**
    a. doing the emotional work of maintaining family relationships.
    b. maintaining the household, including housework in addition to a job outside the home.
    c. having a work shift ranging approximately between 4:00 p.m. and midnight.
    d. doing paid labor at the workplace.

1. (d), 2. (c), 3. (a), 4. (d), 5. (b), 6. (d), 7. (b), 8. (c), 9. (c), 10. (b)

Design Elements: *Going Global (Earth):* ©Studio Photogram/Alamy Stock Photo; *Personal Sociology (drawing of author):* McGraw-Hill Education; *5 Movies (popcorn):* ©D. Hurst/Alamy Stock Photo; *Sociology Is a Verb (overlapping hands):* ©Jeff DeWeerd/Imagezoo/Getty Images

Race and Ethnicity

Kim Kim Foster/The State/MCT/Getty Images

BLACK LIVES MATTER

On August 9, 2014, in Ferguson, Missouri, Michael Brown was stopped by Officer Darren Wilson because Brown matched the just-broadcast description of a suspect who stole cigarillos from a nearby convenience store. A confrontation ensued. By the time it was over, Wilson had fired 12 shots, and Brown, who was unarmed, lay dead in the street. Eyewitness accounts of the encounter conflicted, some arguing Brown turned at one point and raised his hands in surrender. Wilson claimed that Brown reached for what might have been a weapon and charged at him. Huge protests broke out in the days that followed that ultimately ignited what we know today as the Black Lives Matter movement.

In the years since Michael Brown's death, there have been many high-profile incidents involving police officers killing unarmed African American males. On March 18, 2018, for example, in Sacramento, California, 22-year-old Stephon Clark was shot and killed by police in the backyard of his grandparents' home. Two officers fired a total of 20 rounds at Clark, hitting him 8 times, most of them in the back. Police were responding to a 911 call regarding a man in a hoodie breaking car windows in the neighborhood and a helicopter surveillance camera had seemingly tracked the perpetrator to that yard. According to a police statement, "At the time of the shooting, the officers believed the suspect was pointing a firearm at them. After an exhaustive search, scene investigators did not locate any firearms. The only item found near the suspect was a cell phone" (Sacramento Police Department 2018). Clark was pronounced dead at the scene.

Tamir Rice, Rumain Brisbon, Walter Scott, Philando Castile, Terence Crutcher, and Keith Scott are but just a few of the unarmed black men who have suffered the same fate. Very often the police officers involved in these shootings receive relatively minor punishment—or no punishment at all.

African American men between the ages of 15 and 34 are 10 to 15 times more likely to be killed by police compared to all other races (Fryer 2018). To provide perspective on the loss that results from deaths such as these, researchers analyzed each case where a person was killed by police. Based on their age at the time of death compared to their estimated life expectancy, those who died in 2016 lost an estimated 54,754 years of life. Of these, 51.5 percent were lost by people of color (Bui, Coates, and Mathay 2018).

When it comes to the consequences of difference, one of the lessons we learn, over and over again, is that African American men too often pay with their lives.

As You READ >>

- **How do sociologists define race and ethnicity?**
- **What are prejudice and discrimination, and how do they operate?**
- **What are the consequences of race and ethnicity for opportunity?**

>> The Social Construction of Race and Ethnicity

Are we defined more by our similarities or differences? That question rests at the heart of our discussions about race—and those discussions usually revolve around biology. Perhaps surprisingly, most biologists do not view race as a meaningful scientific concept when it comes to humans. The Human Genome Project (HGP), the scientific team that mapped human DNA, found that 99.9 percent of human genetic sequences are identical (Roth and Ivemark 2018; Venter 2000). Biologist Craig Venter, one of the HGP's lead scientists, summarized its findings this way: "Race is a social concept, not a scientific one" (Angier 2000). Even if those statistical estimates get modified slightly as scientists come to better understand the complexity of the human genome (Redon et al. 2006), the underlying premise will remain the same: We humans are vastly more biologically alike than we are different. And yet, when it comes to race, especially in the United States, there exists a long history of focusing on difference rather than sameness.

In this chapter, we will explore the way sociologists have come to understand race and ethnicity as social constructs to which people assign significant meaning. As a sociological concept, **race** refers to *presumed biological* differences between humans to which people attach meaning resulting in the creation of *supposed genetically* distinct subgroups within the population. Racial differences people assign significance to include variations in skin color, facial features, hair texture, hair color, eye color, and the like. **Ethnicity** refers to the *presumed cultural* differences between humans to which people attach meaning resulting in the creation of

Race Presumed *biological* differences between humans to which people attach meaning resulting in the creation of supposed *genetically* distinct subgroups within the population.

Ethnicity Presumed cultural differences between humans to which people attach meaning resulting in the creation of supposed socially distinct subgroups within the population.

Tuul/Bruno Morandi/Photolibrary/Getty Images

Racial and Ethnic Groups in the United States

Classification	Number in Thousands	Percentage of Total Population
Racial Groups		
Whites (non-Hispanic)	197,285,202	60.6
Blacks/African Americans	40,129,593	12.3
Asian Americans	17,999,846	5.5
Chinese	4,344,981	1.3
Asian Indians	4,094,539	1.3
Filipinos	2,911,668	0.9
Vietnamese	1,826,998	0.6
Koreans	1,477,282	0.5
Japanese	770,546	0.2
American Indians, Alaska Natives	2,145,162	0.7
Native Hawaiians/Pacific Islanders	546,778	0.2
Some other race	833,898	0.3
Ethnic Groups		
Hispanics (or Latinx)	58,846,134	18.1
Mexican Americans	36,668,018	11.3
Puerto Ricans	5,588,664	1.7
Cubans	2,315,863	0.7
Salvadorans	2,310,784	0.7
Dominicans	2,081,419	0.6
Whites (single or mixed, non-Hispanic)		
Germans	43,093,766	13.2
Irish	31,479,232	9.7
English	23,074,947	7.1
Italians	16,650,674	5.1
Poles	9,012,085	2.8
Scottish and Scotch-Irish	8,407,093	2.6
French	7,673,619	2.4
Total (all groups)	**325,719,178**	

Source: U.S. Census Bureau 2018a:Table S0201.

supposed socially distinct subgroups within the population. Ethnic differences include indicators such as language, customs, food preferences, religion, and so on. Perception of the existence and significance of difference, by insiders and outsiders alike, plays an important role in the impact race and ethnicity have in our lives (Roth & Ivemark 2018).

THE ROOTS OF RACIAL CLASSIFICATION

Our conception of race is rooted in time and place. How we think about it changes, as does the degree to which it is important or unimportant. For much of human history, race as we conceive of it now didn't exist. Historically, groups were conquered and enslaved, but that had more to do with cultural and tribal differences. Encounters with people who lived on the other side of the continent or world were rare, but when they did occur, differences in physical characteristics were more likely seen as a consequence of their different climate or geography rather than some innate and fundamental biological attribute (Tattersall and DeSalle 2011).

We can trace efforts to categorize race on biological terms back to Swedish botanist Carolus Linnaeus who, in the mid-1700s, created a taxonomy to organize all of life (including plants, animals, microbes, and more) into a single classification system with nested hierarchies and a standardized naming system. It was Linnaeus who coined the term *Homo sapiens* for humans which established our relationship to other living things (Koerner 1999; Linnaeus 1758). As part of his system, Linnaeus identified four varieties of humans that became the foundation for what people now think of as races: *Afer* (Native Africans), *Americanus* (Native Americans), *Asiaticus* (Native Asians), and *Europeaus* (Native Europeans). But Linnaeus didn't stop at simple classification. In a controversial move, he went on to attribute essential character traits to each racial group. He described Africans as slow, relaxed and contented; Native Americans as energetic, combative, and governed by custom; Asians as gloomy, thoughtful, and greedy; and Europeans as gentle, inventive, and governed by laws (DeSalle and Tattersall 2018; Tattersall and DeSalle 2011).

The belief that it was possible to categorize millions, and later billions, of human beings into a handful of meaningful categories set the stage for debates on how best to define race. After Linneaus, the chase was on to identify both the number of races and the possible consequences of those differences. And scientists couldn't seem to agree. In Germany, Johann Blumenbach ([1776] 1865) identified 5 races: Caucasians (Europeans including Lapps), Mongolians (Asians), Ethiopians (Africans), Americans (Native Americans), and Malaysians (Pacific Islanders); in France, Georges Cuvier ([1817] 1832) said there were 3: Caucasian, Mongolian, and Ethiopian; Swiss American Louis Agassiz distinguished 11 human types; Louis-Antoine Desmoulins claimed there were 11 human species which he later raised to 16; Samuel George Morton divided humans into 5 races which he subdivided into 22 families; and, there were many others with varying sum totals of categories. Some thought the differences between races were sharp and uncrossable while others believed them to be ambiguous and transitory. Historian Nell Irvin Painter points out, "No consensus has ever been formed on the number of human races or even on the number of white races" (2010a:383). Whole populations of people, such as the Celts, Italians, or Asian Indians, were placed in different racial groups according to different racial models (Baum 2006; Jackson and Weidman 2004; Lurie 1954; Painter 2010a; Tuttle 1866:35).

This lack of consensus in racial categorization highlights the scientific reality that there are no clear biological dividing lines between racial groups. Rather, race is a social construction imposed upon the biological data.

This map from 1849 portrayed the distribution of races of the world as understood at that time.
Lake Erie Maps and Prints/Alamy Stock Photo

Whatever number of categories we might choose, we can then find evidence in the human population to support that model. We can do so because biological variation is more continuous than categorical. This is most obvious when it comes to skin color, which exists as a gradational spectrum with no clear boundaries marking where one category of skin color ends and another begins. Our continued use of those color categories, however, results in a kind of self-fulfilling prophecy through which we perpetuate the myth that they are biologically meaningful.

The historical reality is that existing biological variation is a consequence of distance and time. Throughout human history, as groups migrated to other parts of the world, which limited contact between them over many generations, physical changes occurred that resulted in differences in skin color, hair, texture, body type, and the like, as people adapted to the terrain and climate of their particular environments. For example, individuals who lived in hotter climates would necessarily develop more melanin (what makes our skin lighter or darker) to protect them from the sun than would individuals who inhabited colder climates with less sun exposure.

Even though distances between groups seemed great, very few cultures have lived completely isolated from the rest of the world. As one scientific report put it, "No large group is known to have maintained reproductive isolation for extended periods" (Rohde, Olson, and Chang 2004:565). Or, to put it in simple terms, humans have always been sleeping with people from the next tribe over (Rutherford 2016). Sharing partners across boundaries means humans have also always been sharing DNA and passing it along from generation to generation.

When it comes to genetic variation, the biological differences within what we think of as racial groups are actually greater than the differences between those groups. Genetic researchers Luca Cavalli-Sforza, Paolo Menozzi, and Alberto Piazza (1994), for example, point out that people from northeast China are genetically closer to Europeans, Eskimos, and North American Indians than they are to people from south China (p. 84). Biologically, the overall degree of human genetic variation is quite small when compared with genetic variation among other large mammals—due primarily to the fact that communities of human beings have always interacted and reproduced, even across great distances (Greenwood 2013; MacEachern 2003:20).

When we look at photos from people around the world, we see a wide spectrum of physical differences. Brazilian artist Angélica Dass paired more than 4,000 portraits of people from 18 different countries with the Pantone color code that matched their skin tone. Collectively, her photos portray a continuous spectrum of human skin colors with no clear dividing lines at any point. Dass discussed her project, "Humanae," in an online TED Talk.

POPSOC

Sources: Dass 2016; Strochlic 2018. Photo: Kivilcim Pinar/iStock/Getty Images

THE ERA OF PSEUDOSCIENTIFIC RACISM

Despite the problems and contradictions inherent in the categorization of race on biological terms, many scientists continued to categorize race in this way. A group of scientists—most notably American scientists—then took it even further: They argued that races didn't just *differ* based on biology, but that races could be *ranked* from superior to inferior. They claimed that humans didn't all descend from common ancestors. In doing so, this group of scientists rejected the commonly held monogenesis model, a version of which maintained that all humans could trace their ancestry back to Adam and Eve as the parents of us all. Instead, they advocated a polygenesis model in which the various human races arose out of multiple origins. The consequences of such unsupported claims would prove to be very dangerous and, ultimately, tragic.

The motivations of these scientists appear clear. They sought to claim the legitimacy of scientific authority to justify their racist ideology. In 1847, for example, scientist and polygenism advocate Louis Agassiz argued that separate human origins resulted in superior and inferior races. He claimed that "The brain of the Negro is that of the imperfect brain of a seven month's old infant in the womb of a White" (quoted in Menand 2001:109). Claims such as these are sociologically important because they tell us more about the motivations of the so-called scientists than they do about the supposed facts on which they based their conclusions (Lurie 1954).

One-drop rule The principle that, if a person had even one Black African ancestor, no matter how many generations back, the person was labeled Black—even if he or she appeared to be White.

Early claims of inherent racial superiority or inferiority existed largely to justify the practice of slavery. If all humans were not, as stated in the Declaration of Independence, "created equal" and "endowed by their Creator with certain unalienable Rights," then consigning a whole race of people to a lifetime of servitude gained greater legitimacy. Alexander H. Stephens, speaking as the vice president of the newly established Confederate States of America in 1861, argued that, "Our new government is founded upon exactly the opposite ideas [of the equality of all]; its foundations are laid . . . upon the great truth that the negro is not equal to the white man; that slavery . . . is his natural and normal condition" (Cleveland 1866:721). This philosophical difference regarding our fundamental sameness gave rise to the Civil War.

Slavery wouldn't be the only oppressive force legitimized in part by the pseudoscience of biological racial difference. If the races were truly biologically distinct and hierarchical, it should come as no surprise that those who viewed their race as superior would seek to limit the amount of interracial mixing so as not to contaminate their gene pool. As a result, there was an increasing outcry for racial purity. This impulse gave rise to what came to be the **one-drop rule,** which held that if a person had even one Black African ancestor, no matter how many generations back, the person was labeled Black—even if he or she appeared to be White. According to this premise, even a "single drop of Black blood" was presumed sufficient to make a person "Black."

After slavery was officially abolished in 1865, the consequences of the one-drop rule would help institute alternative ways to divide and oppress people of color in the United States, including the practice known as "Separate but Equal." The infamous *Plessy v. Ferguson* Supreme Court decision in 1896 affirmed the legality of "Separate but Equal" accommodations for Blacks and Whites based on the premise of biological racial purity. In that case, Homer Plessy, who under the one-drop rule was classified as Black due to his one-eighth African American ancestry, could easily pass for White based on his appearance. Plessy was arrested for sitting in a "Whites-only" train car in Louisiana after he reportedly revealed to the conductor that he was only seven-eighth's White and refused to sit in the "Coloreds-only" car in hopes of challenging such laws in court. In the end, however, the Supreme Court decided against Plessy (Hoffer 2012; Medley 2003). This ruling had the effect of legitimizing the practice of racial segregation of public places including drinking fountains, restrooms, restaurants, buses, and

White nationalist rallies have a long history in the United States, from those of the Ku Klux Klan, founded in 1865, to 2017's Unite the Right rally in Charlottesville, Virginia. (Ku Klux Klan): William Campbell/Sygma/Corbis/Getty Images; (Unite the Right): Samuel Corum/Anadolu Agency/Getty Images schools throughout the United States. It took until 1954 for the Supreme Court to overturn that principle with its *Brown v. Board of Education* decision in which it ruled that "separate educational facilities are inherently unequal."

The quest for racial separation in pursuit of biological purity also manifested itself through bans on interracial marriage, referred to as anti-miscegenation laws. From the nation's founding, numerous U.S. states, mostly in the South, banned interracial marriage. As the United States expanded, so also did the number of states with bans. As of 1947, 30 states still imposed such laws. It wasn't until the 1960s that the U.S. Supreme Court finally banned such laws as unconstitutional in the *Loving v. Virginia* case, declaring, "Under our Constitution, the freedom to marry, or not marry, a person of another race resides with the individual and cannot be infringed by the State" (Pascoe 2009; Romano 2006; Wallenstein 2014).

The early 20th-century eugenics movement represented perhaps the ultimate manifestation of this racial purity crusade in the United States. The *eugenics* movement sought to improve human genetic stock through selective breeding (Galton 1883). Eugenicists encouraged people they identified as racially superior to have more babies. The flip side to the eugenics movement involved discouraging, inhibiting, or outright banning reproduction between people identified as part of a biologically inferior race. The United States was at the forefront of this movement.

In 1927, in an 8–1 ruling, the U.S. Supreme Court upheld Virginia's Eugenical Sterilization Act, and in doing so, legitimized eugenics laws nationally. By 1940, 32 states enacted such laws, empowering officials to prevent individuals identified biologically deficient from passing on those traits to the next generation (Stern 2016). Perhaps it should come as no surprise that Adolf Hitler and the Nazis looked to the work of eugenicists in their pursuit of a "master race" and their justification for the wholesale massacre of millions of people deemed racially inferior (Black 2012; Burleigh and Wippermann 1991). We still hear echoes of eugenics in political discourse today when concerns are raised about changing demographics and the respective birthrates, whether high or low, among various subgroups in the population.

REJECTING RACIAL PSEUDOSCIENCE

Although a number of scholars, including Frederick Douglass (1854) and Franz Boas (1911, 1940), had questioned the biological premise of race from early on, it took until World War II to reach a critical turning point in how we view race and ethnicity. Hitler's racist ideology led many to reevaluate their assumptions about race and ethnicity. In the run-up to the war, anthropologist Ashley Montagu, in his book *Man's Most Dangerous Myth: The Fallacy of Race* (1942), anticipated the conclusions of the Human Genome Project by decades by arguing that race was a social construction rather than a biological determinant.

In recent years, countries with low birthrates have established campaigns to encourage people in their country to have more babies. Denmark's provocative "Do it for Denmark" videos, which can be viewed online, may have worked. Birthrates in Denmark rose in the years since the ads ran (Sims 2016). To what extent might this represent a form of eugenics?

POPSOC

Source: Sims 2016. *Photo:* FlamingoImages/iStock/Getty Images

Did You Know?

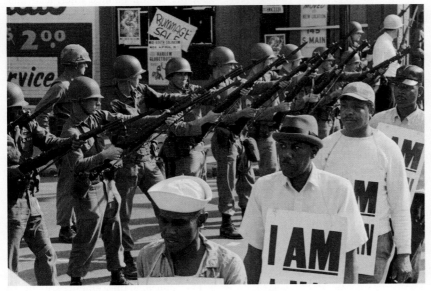

. . . In 1854, Frederick Douglass, in response to racial pseudoscience during his time, wrote, "Tried by all the usual, and all the unusual tests, whether mental, moral, physical, or psychological, the negro is a MAN." In so doing, he presaged appeals regarding the fundamental humanity of African Americans echoed 100 years later as part of the civil rights movement.

Source: Douglass 1854. *Photo:* Bettmann/Getty Images

After World War II, as part of a team of sociologists and anthropologists, Montagu helped write the United Nations Educational, Scientific, and Cultural Organization (UNESCO) statement *The Race Question,* which asserted, "For all practical social purposes 'race' is not so much a biological phenomenon as a social myth. The myth [of] 'race' has created an enormous amount of human and social damage" (UNESCO 1950:8). Because of the problematic use of the term *race,* the authors went so far as to recommend "when the term 'race' is used in popular parlance, it would be better when speaking of human races to drop the term 'race' altogether and speak of *ethnic groups*" (UNESCO 1950:6).

The appeal to take up the use of ethnic groups takes us back to where we started. The attempts to categorize all of humanity into a handful of racial boxes failed to adequately account for biological, social, and cultural variety manifested around the world. Adding ethnicity to the mix creates the possibility that we might move beyond

Martin Luther King Jr. at the March on Washington for Jobs and Freedom on August 28, 1963. Francis Miller/Time Life Pictures/Getty Images

conceptualizing races as homogeneous groups within which exist a singular identity or culture. Saying someone is Black means something different than saying they are from Kenya, and saying someone is from Kenya is different than saying someone is from the Mbeere ethnic group, which itself is distinct from the Kikuyu, Embu, or Maasai. In the same way, saying someone is White means something different than saying they are from the Netherlands, and saying someone is from the Netherlands is different than saying they are from Zeeland, which is distinct from Freesland or Groningen. The racial categories we use fail to reflect the degree of difference that exists within presumed racial groups and sociologists have a responsibility to reflect the diversity of the world as it is.

The U.S. Census, reflecting our shifting conceptions of race and ethnicity over time, has made numerous modifications in the categories it has used to classify the American population. The "U.S. Race Categories, 1790–2010" table provides a selection of the models the Census has used over the years. To get an accurate population count, the Census Bureau needs categories that are both mutually exclusive and exhaustive, meaning each individual fits in only one and that there's a place for everyone to fit. Children with biological parents from two different racial categories proved particularly challenging to taken-for-granted Census assumptions.

In recognition of the growing diversity of the U.S. population, and the growing numbers of interracial marriages, for the first time in 2000 and again in 2010 the U.S. Census allowed people to select more than 1 category when identifying their race. People can now choose from 5 major race categories—White, Black, Asian, Native American, and Native Hawaiian or Other Pacific Islander—in addition to "Some other race." Considering all the combinations people might select, a total of 63 race categories are now possible (Humes, Jones, and Ramirez 2011). In the 2010 Census more than 9 million people in the United States, 2.9 percent overall, reported that they were of 2 or more races. Of these, 20.4 percent chose both Black and White, the most frequent combination. Within racial categories, more than half of those who chose Native Hawaiian or Other Pacific Islander also selected another race, whereas those who self-identified as White were least likely to do so (Humes, Jones, and Ramirez 2011).

When faced with the decision about which Census category to choose, former president Barack Obama, who had a Black father, originally from Kenya, and a White mother, originally from Kansas, chose to self-identify as African American. He could just as easily have chosen White, both Black and White, or "some other race" (Roberts and Baker 2010). When asked why he chose African American, Obama responded, "I self-identify as African American—that's how I'm treated and that's how I'm viewed. I'm proud of it" (Folley 2016). Not everyone with the same genetic ancestry makes the same choice. In a study of biracial college students, researchers found that 71 percent of children with a Black–White combination of

U.S. Race Categories, 1790–2010

Race Categories

1790	Free white males
	Free white females
	All other free persons
	Slaves
1890	White
	Black
	Mulatto
	Chinese
	Indian
1940	White
	Negro
	Indian
	Chinese, Japanese, Filipino, Hindu, Korean
	Other
1990	White
	Black or Negro
	American Indian
	Eskimo
	Aleut
	Asian or Pacific Islander, Chinese, Filipino, Hawaiian, Korean, Vietnamese, Japanese, Asian Indian, Samoan, Guamanian, other Asian or Pacific Islander
	Other race
2010	White
	Black, African American, or Negro
	American Indian or Alaska Native (print name of tribe)
	Asian: Asian Indian, Chinese, Filipino, Japanese, Korean, Vietnamese, Other Asian (print race)
	Native Hawaiian, Guamanian or Chamorro, Samoan, or Other Pacific Islander (print race)
	Some other race (print race)

Sources: Nobles 2000:1739; U.S. Census Bureau 2010c. *Photo:* Markus Mainka/Shutterstock

Barack Obama self-identifies as African American rather than multiracial or White. Theo Wargo/WireImage/Getty Images

parents self-identified as multiracial, 25 percent as Black, and 5 percent as White (Davenport 2016).

The Census Bureau faces additional challenges when dealing with ethnicity, the resolution of which provide additional support for considering a more multiplex model than our conventional models of race and ethnicity permit. It treats race and ethnicity as separate items, but in its ethnicity question, the only category recognized is "Hispanic, Latino, or Spanish origin." This situation creates difficulties for groups that see themselves as a distinct ethnicity and find the race options inadequate to describe who they are. In such circumstances, many people choose "Some other race" and then write in an ethnicity or nationality (such as Mexican, Iranian, or Saudi Arabian) as their race. In the 2010 Census, of those who selected "Other," 97 percent also selected Hispanic as their ethnicity. In fact, 41 percent of those who self-identified as Hispanic also selected "Some other race" (Humes, Jones, and Ramirez 2011; U.S. Commission on Civil Rights 2009:4).

We now know that the earlier pseudoscientific claims regarding race were wrong. Today, the science of ancestry enables scientists to explore how far back in time we need to go to identify what they refer to as our Most Recent Common Ancestor (MRCA). Based on informed statistical estimates, and backed up by genetic analysis, researchers estimate that a person to whom all people alive on earth today can trace their direct ancestry lived approximately 3,400 years ago. Our MRCA probably lived in east Asia likely near a port anywhere from the Bering Strait on down to Malaysia, facilitating the migration of their descendants east to the Americas as well as to remote Pacific Islands. If we go back just a few thousand years before our MRCA, there even comes a point when everyone alive then (if they have any descendants alive today) is a direct descendant to everyone alive today (Chang 1999; Ralph and Coop 2013; Rohde, Olson, and Chang 2004).

This MRCA research is distinct from, but consistent with, the scientific evidence that points toward a common maternal ancestor even further back and located in Africa, frequently referred to as "Mitochondrial Eve," to whom we can trace specific DNA, shared by all humans living today (Chang 1999; Lewin 1987). Any biological differences that have developed between us as a consequence of migration and environmental adaptation are insufficient to justify any claims of fundamental racial difference. To put it simply, all are related to all.

>> Sociological Perspectives on Race and Ethnicity

Sociologists provide us with tools to better understand how race and ethnicity operate within society. The interactionist perspective helps us see how and why the social construction of race and ethnicity occur. The functionalist perspective provides insight into why we attach significance to racial categories. And the conflict perspective enables us to explore the consequences of those categorizations when it comes to power and access to resources.

THE INTERACTIONIST PERSPECTIVE: RACE AS MULTIDIMENSIONAL

Sociology's interactionist perspective pays particular attention to the social construction of race. As we have already seen, race isn't simply given. It is a social construction that varies by both time and place. Because the simplistic biological racial categorization of the past seems inadequate to the task of describing human diversity, numerous sociologists and others have moved toward a more nuanced model that presents race as multidimensional. This involves viewing race not as singular and fixed, but as something fluid, changing based on when and where people live (Roth 2016; Saperstein, Kizer, and Penner 2016).

In order to come to terms with the multiple ways in which we conceptualize, institutionalize, and internalize race, sociologist Wendy Roth (2016) constructed a multidimensional typology of racial classification. As we learn from the Thomas theorem, we must take into account both our self-perception along with the perceptions of others if we are to understand why we act as we do. And our perceptions are shaped by the cultural expectations we have been socialized to accept as natural.

Roth's multidimensional typology of race includes the following factors:

- *Racial Self-Classification:* Self-identification according to standardized, fixed-response race questionnaires such as those on a college application form, a survey, or the Census form.

- *Racial Self-Narrative:* A person's subjective self-identification in response to open-ended questions regarding his or her race; this dimension allows for greater nuance and self-expression, enabling an individual to clarify his or her self-assessment that goes beyond the limits of just the boxes; it also opens up the possibility that a person may self-identify differently in different contexts.
- *Observed Appearance-Based Race:* The race others perceive a person to be based on observed characteristics including skin color, but also clothing, hairstyle, and so on.
- *Observed Interaction-Based Race:* The race others perceive a person to be based on information they gain through interaction, including his or her name, language, accent, cultural references, and more.
- *Reflected Race:* The race a person believes others perceive him or her to be; a difference can exist between (a) how a person categorizes himself or herself, (b) how others categorize him or her, and (c) how a person thinks they categorize him or her; this aspect of race ties back to Cooley's concept of the looking-glass self, according to which we develop our sense of self based on our perceptions of how we think others perceive us, and then we act based on those self-perceptions.
- *Racial Phenotype:* A person's visible biological indicators of racial classification, including factors such as skin color, hair texture, facial structure, eye color, and so on.
- *Racial Family History:* The racial groups of a person's ancestors, which may be known through oral tradition, according to family history (including family genealogies).
- *Racial Genetic Ancestry:* The racial groups of a person's biological ancestors as revealed through genetic testing; this has become a significant issue due to the increased availability of such tests through companies such as 23andMe.com and AncestryDNA.com; the results from such tests can come as a surprise.

An important element of this typology is that a person's racial classification may differ significantly across the dimensions, or even within categories over time and across place. Roth provides an example, based on her research, to highlight this reality. According to Roth, "Salvador, a restaurant worker in New York, identifies his race as Puerto Rican. Phenotypically, he is dark-skinned with indigenous features, leading some Americans to view him as Black. He believes that Americans view him as Hispanic, based on his accent and name. Yet, on the Census, Salvador checks White for his race because no listed option fits his identity and in Puerto Rico his mixed racial ancestry allows him to consider himself closer to White than to Black" (Roth 2016:1310–1311). Recognizing racial multidimensionality enables us to better understand how race functions in

Get Out
When meeting the parents really is a nightmare.

Zootopia
A bunny and a fox explore whether or not biology is destiny.

Crazy Rich Asians
Race encounters class all in the name of romance.

The Hate U Give
Straddling two worlds, a young African American woman stands up for what's right.

13th
Slavery, in the form of imprisonment, remains legal in the United States via the 13th Amendment.

5 Movies on RACE AND ETHNICITY

practice and the effect it can have on an individual's life chances (Roth 2016; Saperstein and Penner 2012, 2016).

As is so often the case in sociology, we learn more about how mainstream culture works by paying attention to people on the margins. For example, there is a long history in the United States of **passing** in which people whose genetic ancestry and family history convey membership in one racial category but who are perceived to belong to another race in the eyes of others (passing also occurs in other areas, including gender, sexuality, social class, and so on). In the early to mid-1900s in the United States, an African American who could pass as White might be able to avoid some of the consequences of racial discrimination. In the 1940s, sociologist Robert Stuckert (1958) estimated that each year an additional 15,550 people with African ancestry were added to the rolls of those who passed as White in the United States. Passing enabled people to secure access to valued material, social, and cultural resources, but often at the price of turning their backs on their family, community, and culture (Dawkins 2012; Hobbs 2014; Larsen 1929).

> **Passing** When people whose genetic ancestry and family history convey membership in one racial category but who are perceived to belong to another race in the eyes of others.

Another example of conflicting racial dimensions occurs when a person's racial self-narrative is at odds with their racial genetic ancestry, family history, and phenotype. Rachel Doležal presented a controversial and headline-grabbing case of what sometimes gets called "reverse passing," which occurs when a member of a majority group claims membership in a minority group. Doležal's racial self-narrative was African American, but her phenotype and ancestry were White. She successfully passed as African American to coworkers and friends, working as a civil rights activist, serving as the president of the NAACP chapter in Spokane, Washington, and teaching a variety of courses in the Africana Studies Program at the local university. In 2015, her case became national news when reporters uncovered her racial family history. Even though her parents were of White, European descent, at some point in her life she had embraced an African American heritage and identity. Even after her ancestry became known, she continued to assert her African American identity as part of her racial self-narrative. In a TEDx Talk given after the controversy erupted, consistent with the multidimensional nature of race, she asserted, "Race is a political reality, but not a biological one." She went on to ask, "Is the identity that you were assigned at birth the best description of who you really are and what your purpose is for being in this world?" (Doležal 2016). Although her case is more sensational than most, it did raise important questions about taken-for-granted conceptions of race.

The multidimensionality of race also manifests itself through transracial adoption, which refers to cases when parents adopt a child from a racial or ethnic background different

Rachel Doležal, whose racial genetic ancestry is White, self-identifies as African American. Nicholas K. Geranios/AP Images

than their own. Between 20 and 25 percent of U.S. adoptions among children aged two and under each year are transracial (Marr 2017). As they grow up, these children frequently face what psychologist Richard M. Lee calls the transracial adoption paradox: "[transracial] adoptees are racial/ethnic minorities in society, but they are perceived and treated by others, and sometimes themselves, as if they are members of the majority culture (i.e., racially White and ethnically European) due to adoption into a White family" (2003:711). Transracial adoptive parents must decide whether or not to expose their children to the culture associated with their child's birth culture. Although some parents opt for what they describe as a color-blind approach by minimizing the significance of their racial differences, the more common practice now involves enculturation. Through books, culture camps, relationships with same-race mentors, and so on they provide their children opportunities to explore the culture most associated with their genetic ancestry. Increasingly, transracial adoptive parents also explore with their children the racial discrimination they will likely face as they grow up, seeking to provide them with the coping skills necessary to deal with it (Lindholm 2018; Reed 2018).

As they grow into adulthood, transracial adoptees often give voice to a feeling of cognitive dissonance about who they are and whether or not they fit in. Throughout their lives they have faced questions about whose family they belong to, whether or not they are foreign exchange students, or even how much it cost their family to adopt them (Docan-Morgan 2010; Lee 2003; Lee et al. 2006; Reed 2018). Kaylee Domzalski, adopted as an infant from South Korea by a White midwestern American couple, very much loves her adopted parents, but regrets that "They never taught me anything about my Korean heritage or language or thought to surround me with people who could. That's left me with a sense of loss, placelessness" (Domzalski 2018). Chad Goller-Sojourner, a man of African descent who'd been adopted into a White family in 1972, highlighting the importance of connecting kids to social networks associated with their birth culture, advised White parents considering adopting children of African descent, "Your child should not be your first black friend" (Martin 2014).

DNF Style/Shutterstock

Examples such as these highlight the importance of culture, family history, and identity when it comes to race.

Given the limits of biological definitions of race and the potential a multidimensional perspective provides, it makes sense to explore the inclusion of even more dimensions. Political scientists Maya Sen and Omar Wasow (2016) recommend that we conceptualize race as a composite variable—they use the analogy of a "bundle of sticks." Race, they suggest, should be thought of as an aggregate of a number of distinct elements that come together in varieties of ways. Elements Sen and Wasow highlight as part of race include, among others, genes, skin color, region of ancestry, norms, diet, dialect, education, religion, neighborhood, wealth, social status, and class.

THE FUNCTIONALIST PERSPECTIVE: HOW RACIAL CATEGORIZATION WORKS

Given that race is a social construction and not a biological inevitability, why do we construct it in the first place? As we have already learned, we construct culture to make sense of, and impose order on, the world around us. Culture provides us with an understanding of where we fit in relationship to nature and with each other (as we explored in Chapter 3). In defining who we are in relationship to others, we not only identify with and *include* people like ourselves, we also *exclude* people whom we decide differ from us.

Even though science suggests that there are no essential differences between groups that we identify as races—no clear dividing lines that separates one group from the other—that doesn't stop us from elevating the significance of perceived physical differences in order to segregate insiders and outsiders. As we already explored through the research of social psychologist Henri Tajfel and others (Tajfel 1981; Tajfel and Turner 1979; see Chapter 4), three elements of this process appear common: (1) *social categorization:* dividing the world into in-groups ("us") and out-groups ("them"); (2) *social identification:* tying our identity, or sense of self, to our connection with our fellow insiders by thinking, acting, and speaking alike; and (3) *social comparison:* ranking our group and its members as superior and outsiders as inferior. In-group members tend to privilege each other and deny in-group benefits to outsiders, and, frequently, they don't even know they are doing so (Banaji and Greenwald 2013; Staats et al. 2016).

Two important functions result from this in-group/out-group process: solidarity and identity. Identifying more closely with others like ourselves provides in-group members with an enhanced sense of collective solidarity, a perception of "we"-ness. We see this process at work in appeals to, and expressions of, patriotism: "We hold these truths to be self-evident . . .," or "America, love it or leave it." This process also provides individuals with a stronger sense of identity: "I'm a Yankee doodle dandy . . . ," or "I'm proud to be an American." Allegiance to the whole makes it possible for the group to demand more from individual members.

What's important about race from this perspective isn't the biological or physical, it's our attribution of significance to such differences in ways that provide us with a sense of solidarity and identity. In the words of historian Nell Irvin Painter (2010b), "Race functions to identify difference. . . . It says, 'These are people who are permanently this way and these are people who are permanently that way. . . . Race is a tool of differentiation and separation." The simple three- or five-category models of race make drawing the lines between "us" and "them" easier, even if those divisions don't hold up well under careful scrutiny.

When it comes to race, going down this path can get ugly fairly quickly. Choosing to identify with "your people" routinely turns into prejudice and discrimination. Add power

Civil rights activist Rosa Parks being fingerprinted upon her arrest in 1955 for her act of civil disobedience in refusing to give up her seat on a bus to a White man.   Gene Herrick/AP Images

to the equation, in which one racial group has the capacity to deny access to resources to others, and the consequences, as we will see below, become tragic. Historically, racial and ethnic tragedies have played out infamously in the grotesqueness of systematic slavery and genocide, but we also need to understand the everyday reality of racial and ethnic discrimination in less obvious ways in the lives of millions. Examples of everyday indignities racial and ethnic minorities face include being singled out by police for traffic stops, getting denied a mortgage, being followed by security while shopping, and a whole host of others.

Sociologists do know that one potential way to reduce in-/out-group tension is through regularized interaction with others unlike ourselves. According to the **contact hypothesis,** interaction with people unlike ourselves decreases negative attitudes we may have about them. Researchers initially suggested that two characteristics were necessary for a change in attitudes to occur. First, the context for the interaction had to be cooperative, rather than competitive. Second, the people interacting needed to be of relatively equal status (Allport 1979; Fine 2008). Contact hypothesis researchers assumed that when workers from different racial and ethnic groups compete with each other for valued resources, rather than cooperate toward shared goals, hostilities would increase. This was particularly likely in cases when significant power imbalances existed. More recent research suggests that, even in cases when interaction does not take place in cooperative circumstances between relative equals, attitudes about, and actions toward, the "others" often still improves (Pettigrew and Tropp 2006).

One way various organizations, including schools, government agencies, and corporations, have sought to reduce intergroup conflict is through the establishment of affirmative action programs. **Affirmative action** refers to proactive efforts to recruit minority group members or women for jobs, promotions, and educational opportunities. In addition to providing opportunity to those who had systematically been denied it, the intent is to increase the diversity of the organization which has positive benefits for all. It widens the talent pool from which individuals are drawn and expands the knowledge, skills, experiences, and perspectives of in-group members. In keeping with the principles of the contact hypothesis, the hope is that increased interaction with people from diverse backgrounds can increase understanding and decrease prejudice. However, in practice, this solution can have the unintended consequence of heightening tensions between groups. In-group members sometimes resent these programs, arguing that advancing out-group members' interests occurs at the expense of in-group members' already established control over resources.

Contact hypothesis The theory that interaction with people unlike ourselves decreases negative attitudes we may have about them.

Affirmative action Positive efforts to recruit minority group members or women for jobs, promotions, and educational opportunities.

Racial formation A sociohistorical process in which racial categories are created, inhibited, transformed, and destroyed.

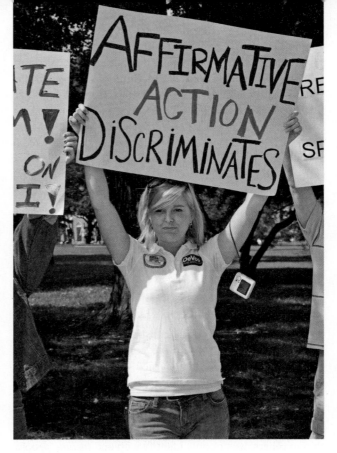

Jim West/The Image Works

─**SOC**THINK─

What are the costs and benefits of establishing hiring quotas based on race, ethnicity, or gender to ensure greater opportunity?

THE CONFLICT PERSPECTIVE: RACIAL INEQUALITY

Harriet Martineau ([1837] 1962), one of sociology's founders, argued that we can and should ask whether or not the *principles* we hold to be true are in alignment with the *practices* we engage in during our everyday lives. With regard to race, she pointed to the U.S. foundational principles of equality and liberty and contrasted them with the practice of slavery. Today, no matter where we come from, we can still raise questions regarding the degree to which we live up to the ideals to which we aspire.

The ability to define things as real represents a source of immense power. Defining race as a biological reality enabled political and economic leaders to justify practices such as slavery and eugenics, and continues to justify the practice of unequal treatment of certain groups, as well as the outcomes suffered by those groups. In other words, even though race should not be understood simplistically as a direct consequence of biology, its consequences are no less real. To address this reality, sociologists Michael Omi and Howard Winant (1994) developed the concept of **racial formation,** which refers to the sociohistorical process in which categories are created, inhibited, transformed, and destroyed.

Omi and Winant argue that race is neither fundamentally biological nor an illusion that can be simply ignored. To understand race, one must pay careful attention to the social, economic, and political forces that have established it as a basic distinction among human beings. Historically, those in positions of power have categorized whole groups of people as fundamentally distinct from each other (for example, when the one-drop rule was instituted) and then used their control over resources to treat people differently based on those distinctions. The result is a social structure that reinforces presumed racial differences and justifies unequal treatment on the basis of race. The creation of a reservation system for Native Americans in the late 1800s is one example of racial formation. Federal officials combined what were distinctive tribes into a single racial group, which we refer to today as Native Americans.

In the same way that "Native Americans" became a singular category out of what previously were multiple and diverse tribal ethnic groups, the concept of the White race, along with who gets included in it, has varied significantly over time. The massive influx of immigrants in the 19th century complicated the supposed simplicity of the Black–White divide. Immigrants that were initially counted as members of inferior races, including Germans, Italians, and the Irish, over time came to be seen as White ethnics. This was accomplished in part by these groups positioning themselves relative to, and distinct from, African Americans in order to identify more closely with the White majority (Guglielmo 2003; Ignatiev 1995; Painter 2010a; Roediger 2005).

Using race to justify the unequal treatment of others becomes a self-fulfilling prophecy. Identifying a group as biologically inferior leads to that group having unequal access to valued resources which reduces that group's opportunities to excel which reinforces stereotypes regarding that group's inherent inferiority. Frederick Douglass, speaking about the African experience of his day, put it this way: "His faculties and powers, uneducated and unimproved, have been contrasted with those of the highest cultivation; and the world has then been called upon to behold the immense and amazing difference between the man admitted, and the man disputed" (1854:7). Lack of access to resources produces racial and ethnic inequality.

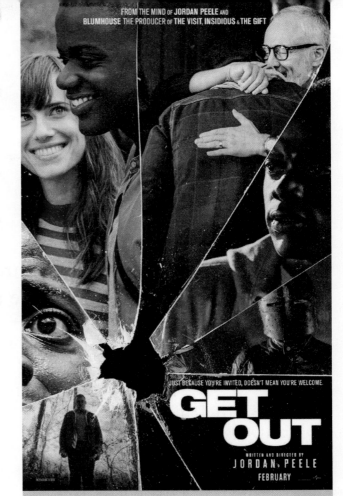

As part of their annual study of the top 100 films, researchers at USC's Annenberg School for Communication and Journalism found that out of the 4,454 speaking or named roles in films released in 2017, 70.7 percent were White characters. The percentage of Black characters, at 12.1, closely approximated their proportion of the U.S. population, but Hispanics, at 6.2 percent, were significantly underrepresented in these films.

POPSOC

Source: Smith, Choueiti, Pieper, Case, and Choi 2018. *Photo:* Moviestore collection Ltd/Alamy Stock Photo

Federal troops were needed to support the Supreme Court decision that led to the integration of schools in the 1950s. Bettmann/Getty Images

>> The Consequences of Racial and Ethnic Difference

Race may be a social construct, but its consequences are quite real. In the United States, a person's race, in conjunction with their ethnicity, shapes their access to valued resources. In the words of political scientist Bruce Baum, "Race . . . is an effect of power" (2006:8). Those in positions of power, both knowingly and unknowingly, have used their authority to institutionalize persistent patterns of unequal outcomes based on racial and ethnic categorization. To understand how this happens, we must take into account both perception and action.

> It is the province of
> prejudice to blind.
>
> ───────────
>
> Frederick Douglass (1854)

PREJUDICE AND DISCRIMINATION

According to the Thomas theorem, perception shapes action. When it comes to race and ethnicity, prejudice often shapes discrimination. Sociologists define **prejudice** as a preconceived and unjustified judgment of individuals, whether positive or negative, based on their membership in a particular group. In other words, prejudice involves the belief that the outcomes others experience in life are primarily a consequence of inherent differences among groups, whether based in race, ethnicity, gender, disability, age, or other statuses. Frequently, prejudice results from ethnocentrism—the tendency to assume that one's own culture and way of life represent the norm or are superior to all others. Ethnocentric people judge other cultures by the standards of their own group without taking into account the perspectives and experiences of others. This often leads to prejudice against cultures they view as inferior.

Prejudicial attitudes often work in conjunction with **stereotypes,** which are unreliable generalizations about all members of a group that do not recognize individual differences within that group. Stereotypes can be applied to members of any out-group we might define as different than "us," but they are particularly common with regard to race because the differences among groups are frequently defined as essential, meaning that those differences are inherited,

Prejudice A preconceived and unjustified judgment of individuals, whether positive or negative, based on their membership in a particular group.

Stereotype An unreliable generalization about all members of a group that does not recognize individual differences within the group.

Implicit bias The automatic and unconscious association of value, whether positive or negative, with particular groups, subgroups, or characteristics of people.

Discrimination The practice of denying equal access to opportunities and resources on the basis of group membership rather than merit or rights.

immutable, and inevitable (Bastian and Haslam 2006; Omi and Winant 1994; Painter, Holmes, and Bateman 2015). One of the challenges we face with regard to stereotypes is that we are frequently unaware of our underling **implicit biases** and the consequences they have in our treatment of others (as we saw in Chapter 4).

Prejudice often leads to **discrimination,** the practice of denying equal access to opportunities and resources on the basis of group membership rather than merit or rights. Whereas prejudice involves belief, discrimination entails action. Discrimination is experienced at the individual level by people whose opportunities are limited as a consequence of the actions of others. It occurs when a person in a position of relative power acts, whether consciously or unconsciously, to deny someone something of value—for example, a job, a promotion, an opportunity to volunteer, or a seat on a bus. But discrimination cannot be understood at the individual level alone. It occurs as

Did You Know?

. . . Perception of policing varies by race. When asked if police in their community do an excellent or good job, 75 percent of Whites said they did compared to 33 percent among African Americans. When asked if local police treat racial and ethnic groups equally, only 35 percent of Blacks responded positively compared to 75 percent of Whites.

Source: Morin and Stepler 2016. *Photo:* Don Farrall/Getty Images

Perceptions of Discrimination

Black respondents

0 20 40 60 80 100%

Hispanic respondents

0 20 40 60 80 100%

White respondents

0 20 40 60 80 100%

How often do Blacks face discrimination when . . . ?

Applying to a college or university

Applying for a job

Almost always/frequently

Renting an apartment or buying a house

Eating at a restaurant or shopping in a retail store

Not often/hardly ever

Source: Pew Research Center 2007:30.

a consequence of collectively held beliefs about the significance of group membership. As such, we must analyze discrimination within the context of the existing culture and corresponding social structure.

Sociologists handle the contextual nature of discrimination by emphasizing the significance of **institutional discrimination,** which refers to the systematic denial of

rights and opportunities to marginalized groups as part of society's normal operations. Persistent patterns of inequality indicate that such discrimination represents what Mills called a "public issue" rather than a "personal trouble" (concepts we explored in Chapter 1). Institutional discrimination is a consequence of the social structure impacting how we think and act.

─SOCTHINK─

Why might institutional discrimination be an even greater concern than interpersonal discrimination?

A telltale sign of institutional discrimination is the ongoing presence of racial and ethnic income inequality. As we saw with the gender wage gap in the "Women in the United States" section of Chapter 12, a person's ascribed social status frequently predicts his or her income level. As the accompanying "Median Income by Race, Ethnicity, and Gender" graph demonstrates, a clear difference exists when taking race, gender, and income into account. Those who are Asian or White make more money, on average, than those from other racial and ethnic groups. A variety of factors, including educational attainment, occupation, and seniority, likely explain some of those gaps. At the very least, however, the income differences point to the fact that the lived experience of individuals—the opportunities presented to them and obstacles they face—varies significantly based on the group to which they belong.

RACISM

Addressing institutional discrimination leads directly into a consideration of racism. When most people think of racism, they do so in terms of negative beliefs individuals have about racial groups. In other words, we tend to define racism as an extreme form of an individual's personal prejudice. Sociologists take a more comprehensive approach (Clair and Denis 2015; Wellman 1993). Sociologically, **racism** combines cultural beliefs regarding inherent racial superiority and inferiority with normative practices of advantage or disadvantage which get built into a structure that reproduces patterns of unequal outcomes.

Racism both presupposes and reproduces a racial hierarchy. Racism does not need to involve overt prejudice, deliberate ill-will, or conscious intent. Even if personal prejudice at an interpersonal level seems low, at a societal level, enduring inequality based on race can be substantial (DiAngelo 2018; Oluo 2018; Wellman 1993).

> **Institutional discrimination** The systematic denial of rights and opportunities to marginalized groups as part of society's normal operations.
>
> **Racism** The combination of cultural beliefs regarding inherent racial superiority and inferiority with normative practices of advantage or disadvantage which get built into a structure that reproduces patterns of unequal outcomes.

Median Income by Race, Ethnicity, and Gender

Median income

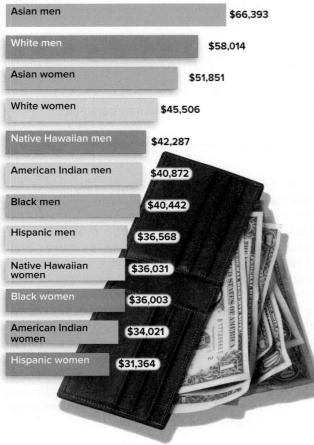

Asian men	$66,393
White men	$58,014
Asian women	$51,851
White women	$45,506
Native Hawaiian men	$42,287
American Indian men	$40,872
Black men	$40,442
Hispanic men	$36,568
Native Hawaiian women	$36,031
Black women	$36,003
American Indian women	$34,021
Hispanic women	$31,364

Note: Data represent people working full-time, year-round in the United States. Race groups do not include Hispanics.
Source: U.S. Census Bureau 2018a:Table S0201. *Photo:* Comstock Images/ Jupiter Images

In an effort to clarify issues surrounding racism, sociologists Matthew Desmond and Mustafa Emerbayer (2009) have identified five fallacies, misunderstandings, or misconceptions about it. First, the *individualistic fallacy* is that racism springs from the "bad" ideas of a few prejudiced individuals. This approach is fallacious because it doesn't come to terms with racism's social, cultural, and institutional dimensions. Second, according to the *legalistic fallacy,* we will inevitably eliminate racism in practice by establishing the principle of racial equality in the law; for example, through the *Brown v. Board of Education* decision in 1954 or the Civil Rights Act of 1964. But principle and practice do not always align. Third, via the *tokenistic fallacy,* people assert that the success of a few individuals, such as Barack Obama, Oprah Winfrey, or Beyoncé, demonstrates that racial obstacles no longer exist. But exceptions to not prove the rule. Fourth, according to the *fixed fallacy,* the definition of racism is narrow and extreme and always takes the same horrifying forms, such as slavery or genocide, whereas in reality racism takes different forms over time and can occur in ways both big and small, such as a hate crime or the hiring practices of a corporation. And fifth, according to the *ahistorical fallacy,* the patterns of the past, especially the legacy of slavery, do not have any significant impact on the present. But this assertion fails to fully appreciate the degree to which historical precedents become embedded in the social structure, shaping opportunities for generations to come. Racism in the United States has deep historical roots.

The establishment of the first permanent English settlement in the Americas at Jamestown in 1607 began a long-running rocky relationship between the European settlers and the already present Native Americans. The settlement would likely not have survived had it not been for the assistance it received from the Powhatan tribe, including Pocahontas, the daughter of Chief Powhatan (Price 2003). To make money, the settlers turned toward planting tobacco—a skill taught them by the Powhatans—which resulted in their seizing more and more land, leading to a cycle of back-and-forth violence which continued over the centuries and across the continent (Woolley 2007).

Concurrently, African slaves were brought to Point Comfort, near Jamestown, in 1619. The Africans were purchased from Captain John Colyn Jope, a Calvinist minister and ship commander, in exchange for food "at the best and easyest rate they could [obtain]" (Sluiter 1997:396). Jamestown's labor-intensive tobacco economy required many workers. It is likely that at least some of these enslaved Africans were treated as indentured servants who later gained their freedom, whereas others may have been enslaved for life (Hashaw 2007; Thornton 1998; Wood 1997). The practice of slavery continued in the United States until 1865, and institutional discrimination against African Americans continues today.

Despite the very real and profound consequences

> One day our descendants will think it incredible that we paid so much attention to things like the amount of melanin in our skin or the shape of our eyes or our gender instead of the unique identities of each of us as complex human beings.
>
> **Franklin Thomas**

past injustices have on present equality and opportunity, many people choose to ignore such impacts. One way they do so is through the practice of what sociologists call **color-blind racism,** in which the principle of race neutrality perpetuates a racially unequal status quo (Bonilla-Silva 2018). In such cases, commitment to the principle of equality leads some people to argue that any attempt to address unequal racial outcomes implies racial bias because such efforts seek to benefit members of disadvantaged groups at the expense of others. But in a system where inequality based on race and ethnicity is built into the structure of society, unwillingness to address these issues explicitly in those terms serves to perpetuate the status quo. Some nations, in pursuit of equal opportunity, have established quotas in political representation and hiring

Hate Crime Offenses

. . . President George Washington inherited 10 slaves when he was 11 years old. At the time of his death, he owned 123 slaves and leased another 40 from a neighbor. Martha, his wife, effectively owned another 153 through her first husband's estate.

Photo: Library of Congress Prints and Photographs Division [LC-DIG-pga-02419]

Gender and gender identity **2.3%** Disability **1.1%**

16.9%

Sexual orientation

21.3%

Religion

Race/Ethnicity **58.5%**

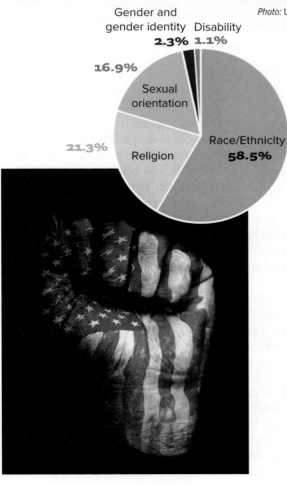

Source: U.S. Department of Justice 2017a:Table1
Photo: Duncan Walker/Getty Images

to reduce institutional discrimination. Such practices are controversial in the United States and are subject to charges of reverse discrimination.

Sociologist Devah Pager explored the consequences of racism at the interpersonal level in her research on the hiring process, as we explored in the "Experiments" section of Chapter 2. To test the impact of both race and a criminal record on the likelihood of getting a job, Pager sent out White and Black applicants with similar characteristics and resumes, varying whether or not they reported having been convicted. In repeated experiments in a number of cities, the results consistently showed the same thing. White applicants received significantly more job callbacks than did African Americans. But what was particularly surprising was the fact that White job applicants who reported having a prison record received slightly more job callbacks than did Black applicants with no criminal record (Pager 2003, 2007; Pager and Pedulla 2015; Pager and Western 2012). Over time, the cumulative impact of such differential treatment contributes to significant differences in access to critical resources.

In addition to examples of everyday discrimination, overt racist acts also continue in the United States. In 1990, Congress passed the Hate Crime Statistics Act to track such encounters. A **hate crime** is a criminal offense committed

Color-blind racism When race-neutral principles perpetuate a racially unequal status quo.

Hate crime A criminal offense committed because of the offender's bias against an individual based on race, religion, ethnicity, national origin, or sexual orientation.

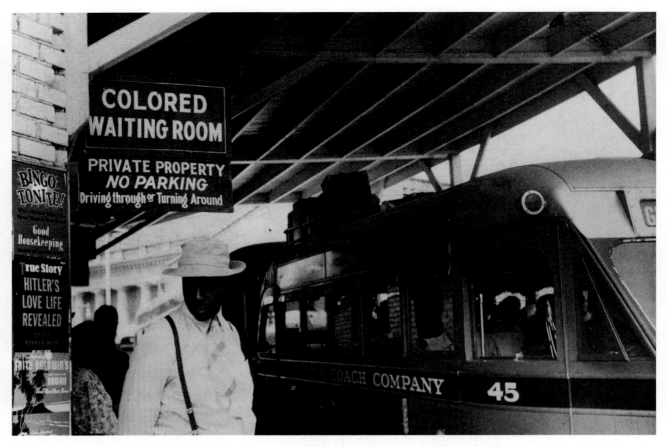

Before passage of the Civil Rights Act in 1964, segregation of public accommodations was the norm throughout the South.   Jack Delano/ Library of Congress Prints and Photographs Division [LC-DIG-ppmsc-00199]

because of the offender's bias against an individual based on race, religion, ethnicity, national origin, or sexual orientation. The act was amended in 2009 to also include gender and gender identity. In 2016, 7,227 hate crime offenses were reported to authorities. Overall, 58.5 percent of those crimes involved racial or ethnic bias (Department of Justice 2017a:Table 1). Offenses include crimes against individuals (including murder, rape, and assault) and crimes against property (such as vandalism, theft, and arson).

Racial profiling Any police-initiated action based on race, ethnicity, or national origin rather than on a person's behavior.

Another form of discrimination involves **racial profiling,** which is any arbitrary action initiated by an authority based on race, ethnicity, or national origin rather than on a person's behavior. Generally, racial profiling occurs when law enforcement officers, including customs officials, airport security, and police, assume that people who fit a certain description are likely to engage in illegal activities. For example, whether in the form of Driving While Black covered in the "Labeling Theory" section of Chapter 6, or as we saw with police shootings of African American males at the beginning of this chapter and the possible life-and-death consequences of an encounter with police that goes bad, African American males live in fear that police officers are out to get them.

Researchers investigating arrests for marijuana use found that, even when controlling for factors such as prior arrests, prior hard drug use, prior property crimes, prior assault, prior gun carrying, and neighborhood reputation, African Americans were still substantially more likely to be arrested. As the researchers put it, "the racial disparity in drug arrests between blacks and whites cannot be explained by race differences in the *extent* of drug offending or the *nature* of drug offending. In fact, in this sample, African-Americans (and Hispanics) were no more, and often less, likely to be involved in drug offending than whites" (Mitchell and Caudy 2015:22). The strength of this relationship between race and arrest increased with age, peaking for suspects in their twenties.

In analyses of the role of skin tone, sociologist Ellis Monk found that the darker a person's skin, the more likely he or she is to face unequal outcomes. In other words, in keeping with the multidimensional model of race, racial inequality involves more than just membership in either "Black" or "White" categories, as if each is internally homogeneous. According to Monk (2015), "darker-skinned African Americans have less income, lower occupational prestige, and even worse mental and physical health outcomes." When it comes to encounters with the criminal justice system, Monk (2018) found that the

Tom Carter/PhotoEdit

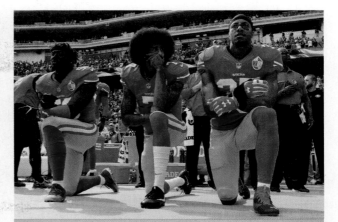

NFL quarterback Colin Kaepernick sparked a movement when, in 2016, he took a knee during the national anthem in order to bring attention to racial injustice. He became a free agent after that season. As of mid 2019, not a single NFL team offered him a contract, despite the fact that he was still young and had a better record of accomplishment than many other quarterbacks still in the league.

POPSOC

Photo: Thearon W. Henderson/Getty Images Sport/Getty Images

darker a person's skin, the more likely he or she was to be both arrested and incarcerated. This difference exists even after taking into account factors such as socioeconomic status, neighborhood conditions, drug use, and childhood delinquency.

After Michael Brown was killed in Ferguson, Missouri, the U.S. Justice Department conducted an investigation of the police department there. In an analysis of traffic stops, 85 percent of the stops, 90 percent of the citations, and 93 percent of the arrests involved African Americans, even though Blacks represent only 67 percent of the population. During vehicle stops, Black drivers in Ferguson were more than twice as likely to be searched, but were 26 percent less likely to have contraband. Based on the study, U.S. Attorney General Eric Holder concluded, "Our investigation showed that Ferguson police officers routinely violate the Fourth Amendment in stopping people without reasonable suspicion, arresting them without probable cause, and using unreasonable force against them" (U.S. Department of Justice 2015a, 2015b).

The protests following the deaths of Michael Brown and others brought attention to the persistent pattern of differential outcomes for African Americans when encountering police in the United States. In 2017, 1,147 people were killed by police. Of these 27 percent were African American and 21 percent were Hispanic. Of the total killed, 149 people were unarmed, the majority of whom were people of color, including 49 African Americans and 34 Hispanics (Mapping Police Violence 2018). In an analysis of FBI records of deadly police shootings, researchers found that 15- to 19-year-old Black males were killed at a much higher rate than White males of the same age: 31.17 per million compared to 1.47 million (Gabrielson, Grochowski Jones, and Sagara 2014).

In seeking to uncover underlying factors affecting such differential treatment, researchers analyzed fatal police shootings of unarmed Black victims and found that rates for such encounters varied based on systemic racial inequality (Mesic et al. 2018). States with higher scores on the structural racism index—which measures Black–White residential segregation along with racial disparities in economic status, employment status, educational attainment, and incarceration rates—had higher rates of fatal police shootings. This relationship held even after taking into account differential arrest rates based on race. Results such as these point toward the significance of the structural nature of the problem. In other words, we cannot understand the problem solely by focusing on individuals and attitudes alone.

PATTERNS OF INTERGROUP RELATIONS

The nature of relationships among racial and ethnic groups within societies varies across time and place. Sociologists have identified six characteristic patterns of intergroup relations. Which type of pattern prevails often depends on the relationship between dominant groups and **minority groups,** which refers to subordinate groups whose members, even if they represent a numeric majority, lack access to and control over valued resources in society.

> **Minority group** A subordinate group whose members, even if they represent a numeric majority, lack access to, and control over, valued resources in society.

EXECUTION OF THE THIRTY-EIGHT SIOUX INDIANS
AT MANKATO, MINNESOTA, DECEMBER 26,1862.

Photo: Source: Library of Congress, Prints and Photographs Division (LC-USZ62-193)

recently, as a result of Syria's civil war involving a variety of ethnic and religious groups, 5.6 million people had fled the country as refugees as of late 2018 (United Nations High Commission for Refugees 2018).

Segregation represents a less extreme form of division. **Segregation** refers to the physical separation of two groups of people in terms of residence, workplace, and social events. South Africa practiced an institutionalized form of segregation, known as apartheid, from 1948 to 1990, after which it was abolished due largely to the work of long-standing resistance movements whose most prominent leader, Nelson Mandela, was later elected president of the country.

In the United States, historically, overt forms of racial segregation took the form of separate schools, separate washrooms, even

Separation The first three types of intergroup relations focus on difference and separation between majority and minority groups. Genocide represents perhaps the most extreme type of dominant versus minority groups relationship. **Genocide** involves the systematic killing of an entire group of people or nation. The term is most commonly associated with Nazi Germany's murder of 6 million European Jews, along with Slavs, Romani, gays and lesbians, and others during World War II. The term also describes the United States' policies toward Native Americans in the 19th century. In California, for example, between 1846 and 1873, the Native American population dropped from approximately 150,000 to about 30,000 as a consequence of state-sanctioned violence (Madley 2016). Ongoing concerns about genocide persist in nations such as Sudan, Myanmar, and Syria (Genocide Watch 2018).

Expulsion represents another extreme type of dominant versus minority group relationship. **Expulsion** involves the systematic removal of a group of people from society. Also known as population transfer, this can include the isolation of groups into internment camps, as happened to more than 120,000 Japanese Americans in the United States during World War II (Daniels 2004; Reeves 2015). In 1979, Vietnam expelled nearly 1 million ethnic Chinese, partly as a result of hostility between Vietnam and neighboring China. More

Genocide The systematic killing of an entire people or nation.

Expulsion The systematic removal of a group of people from society.

Segregation The physical separation of two groups of people in terms of residence, workplace, and social events.

Former South African president Nelson Mandela oversaw that country's transition from a segregated society. Daniel Berehulak/ Getty Images

Did You Know?

Source: Fischer 2011. *Photo:* Bill Rankin (Yale University), www.radicalcartography.net. Color version reprinted with permission of Eric Fisher

Jennifer Aniston changed her name from Jennifer Anastassakis, which represents a form of assimilation. Steve Granitz/WireImage/Getty Images

separate drinking fountains. Even though laws now ban these more public forms of segregation, analyses of neighborhood composition suggest that it continues in practice. According to the index of dissimilarity, when looking at segregation between Blacks and Whites, Milwaukee was the most segregated urban area in the United States, with a dissimilarity index of 81.5, meaning 81.5 percent of either Blacks or Whites would have to move to a different neighborhood to completely eliminate segregation. The next four most segregated large metro areas were New York City (78.0), Chicago (76.4), Detroit (75.3), and Cleveland (74.1). When comparing counties across the United States as a whole for Whites versus African Americans, 47.2 percent of either group would have to move to a different county to eliminate segregation (Frey 2017; Lichter, Parisi, and De Valk 2016).

Segregation has consequences for social interaction between groups. In an analysis of friendship networks in the United States, researchers found that among Whites, 91 percent of their friends are White and only 1 percent are Black. Among African Americans, 83 percent of their friends are Black and 8 percent are White (Cox and Jones 2016).

Consolidation The three remaining models of intergroup relations focus less on separation and more on consolidation between majority and minority groups. Groups can come together in a variety of ways. **Assimilation** involves the process through which a person forsakes his or her own cultural tradition to become part of a different culture. Generally, it is practiced by minority group members who want to, or are expected to, conform to the standards of the dominant group. Assimilation can be described as a pattern in which $A + B + C \rightarrow A$. The majority group, A, dominates in such a way that members of minority groups B and C imitate it and attempt to become indistinguishable from it (Newman 1973).

> **Assimilation** The process through which a person forsakes his or her own cultural tradition to become part of a different culture.

Assimilation results in the devaluation of minority group culture and the elevation of the dominant culture. We see such processes at work in the United States when immigrants change their ethnic-sounding family names to names that fit more easily with the dominant White Protestant culture. Jennifer Anastassakis, for example, changed her name to Jennifer Aniston, Ralph Lipschitz became Ralph Lauren,

Natalie Hershlag is now Natalie Portman, and the Academy Award-winning British actress Helen Mirren gave up her birth name of Ilyena Vasilievna Mironova. Name changes, switches in religious affiliation, and the dropping of native languages can obscure one's roots and heritage. Especially across generations, assimilation can lead to the virtual death of a culture in that family's history. For example, many second- or third-generation western Europeans have little knowledge or understanding of their roots in Ireland, Italy, or Germany, and so on. In such cases, individuals from these lineages now may just consider themselves "American."

Amalgamation The process through which a majority group and a minority group combine to form a new group.

Pluralism Mutual respect for one another's cultures among the various groups in a society, which allows minorities to express their own cultures without experiencing prejudice.

Amalgamation occurs when majority and minority groups combine to form a new group. This pattern can be expressed as $A + B + C \rightarrow D$, where A, B, and C represent different groups in a society, and D signifies the end result, a unique cultural-racial group unlike any of the initial groups (Newman 1973). In the United States, early founders gave voice to this ideal by adopting the Latin phrase *e pluribus unum,* meaning "out of many, one." Considered the early motto of the United States, it was approved by Congress in 1782 and still appears on the Great Seal of the United States. The belief in the United States as a "melting pot" became compelling in the early 20th century, particularly since that image suggested that the nation had an almost divine mission to amalgamate various groups into one people (Zangwill 1909). In actuality, however, many residents were not willing to include Native Americans, Jews, Blacks, Asians, and Irish Roman Catholics in the melting pot. Therefore, this pattern does not adequately describe dominant–subordinate relations in the United States.

The final model of intergroup relations maintains group identity within the larger context of a multicultural society. **Pluralism** refers to mutual respect for one another's culture among the various groups within a society, which allows minority groups to express their own cultures without experiencing prejudice. This pattern can be expressed as $A + B + C \rightarrow A + B + C$, meaning that all groups coexist within the same society (Newman 1973). In this case, the analogy of the "melting pot" gets replaced with that of the "salad bowl." We see evidence of pluralism in the United States to the extent that ethnic groups maintain their cultural identity and heritage yet still act as full participants in the larger society without fear of prejudice or discrimination. One way

Personal Sociology

Celebrating Ethnicity

I live in Pella, Iowa, a small town with a strong Dutch heritage. The first weekend each May, Pella holds its annual Tulip Time festival (www.pellatuliptime.com). Hundreds of thousands of tourists come to the three-day celebration to watch the parades, eat the food, and see people scrub streets in their Dutch costumes. In 2015, my daughter Eleanor was crowned Pella's 80th Tulip Queen. She, along with four other girls on the Royal Court, represented Pella as goodwill ambassadors, performing at numerous locations around the region to help promote Tulip Time and celebrate Pella's Dutch heritage. Like other ethnic celebrations in other communities, Tulip Time plays a significant role in fostering a sense of community solidarity.

Andrew B. Graham/Library of Congress Prints and Photographs Division [LC-USZC4-2108]

Communities throughout the United States celebrate their ethnic heritage with local festivals such as Cinco de Mayo, Octoberfest, and Pella's (Iowa) Tulip Time Festival (shown here). Cyndi Atkins

we see pluralism expressed is through community events that celebrate ethnic group culture and tradition.

In practice, pluralism represents a challenge because some degree of shared culture, such as the capacity to communicate with each other, seems necessary for society to operate. Members of the dominant group can also feel threatened by the arrival of groups whose beliefs and actions—for example, the new group's language, diet, clothes, or religion—differ significantly from those of the majority group. Concerns such as these drove many voters in the United States to support Donald Trump for president, who pledged to crack down on immigration and build a wall along the border with Mexico (Corasanti 2016).

INEQUALITY AMONG RACIAL AND ETHNIC GROUPS IN THE UNITED STATES

In the United States, racism violates the principle of meritocracy, the idea that our outcomes should be based on ability, training, and effort. Where racism exists, life chances vary significantly among racial groups to the persistent advantage of some and the detriment of others. Evidence comes in the form of a systemic pattern of unequal outcomes in access to, and possession of, valued material, social, and cultural resources on the basis of perceived racial categorization. In the words of sociologist David Wellman, "racism today remains essentially what it has always been: a defense of racial privilege" (1993:4). In the battle over resources, when it comes to race, winners and losers can be found in a wide array of areas including income, wealth, job opportunities, promotions, criminal justice treatment, housing choices, loan rates, school quality, medical care, infant mortality, life expectancy, political representation, and more (Alexander 2012; Oluo 2018).

Comparing relative differences in terms of measurable outcomes allows us to see the degree to which racial and ethnic categorization impacts our life chances. At the same time, one of the lessons we learn from the multidimensional model of race is that significant variation might exist within these broad categories, so we should tend to that as well. The three largest racial minority groups in the United States currently are African Americans, Native Americans, and Asian Americans.

African Americans According to the U.S. Census, African Americans comprise 12.3 percent of the total U.S. population. When looking at key indicators of life chances, African Americans as a group often end up with access to, and possession of, fewer resources. In terms of educational attainment, 86 percent of African Americans aged 25 and older have attained at least a high school degree compared to 93 percent for non-Hispanic Whites. The gap widens further when considering college degrees, with 21.4 percent of African Americans possessing a bachelor's degree or

Racial and Ethnic Groups in the United States, 1790–2060 (Projected)

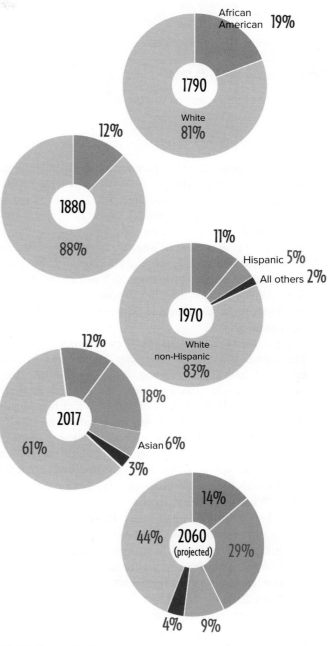

Note: U.S. Census categories vary over time.
Sources: Colby and Ortman 2015; Gibson and Jung 2002:Table 1; U.S. Census Bureau 2018a:Table S0201.

Poverty Rates by Race and Ethnicity

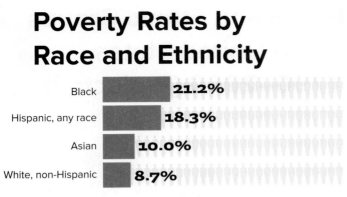

Black	**21.2%**
Hispanic, any race	**18.3%**
Asian	**10.0%**
White, non-Hispanic	**8.7%**

Source: Fontenot, Semega, and Kollar 2018:Table 3.

higher compared to 35.8 percent among non-Hispanic Whites (U.S. Census Bureau 2018a). The median income for African American households is $40,258, compared to $68,145 for non-Hispanic Whites. In other words, a substantial wage gap exists, with African American households making 59 percent of what the typical non-Hispanic White household takes home, a difference of $27,887 per year. When it comes to poverty, 21.2 percent of African Americans are below the official poverty line, compared to 8.7 percent of non-Hispanic Whites (Fontenot, Semega, and Kollar 2018).

Significant wealth differences between groups also exist. The median for African American families was $17,600 compared to $171,000 among White families in 2016, meaning that the typical African American household has wealth worth 10 percent of that of White households (Bricker et al. 2017). Wealth also varies within the African American community based on educational level. African American families with a bachelor's degree or higher have a median net worth of $68,200 compared to $11,600 for families with less than a bachelor's degree (Dettling et al. 2017). When it comes to home ownership, a significant form of wealth in the United States, 41.3 percent of African American households own their own homes compared to 71.9 percent for Whites. African Americans are more likely to be turned down for a mortgage and, on average, pay a higher interest rate for the mortgages they do get (DeSilver and Bialik 2017; Fry and Brown 2016).

Substantial variation exists in the types of occupations African Americans hold. Overall, African Americans make up 12.1 percent of persons employed in the labor force. Using this number as a baseline, it is possible to highlight jobs in which African Americans are underrepresented and overrepresented. For example, African Americans compose only 2.1 percent of veterinarians, 3.7 percent of dentists, 3.8 percent of chief executives, and 5.6 percent of lawyers. By contrast, they constitute 24 percent of social workers, 27 percent of bus drivers, 38 percent of nurses' aides, and 38 percent of barbers (Bureau of Labor Statistics 2018a:Table 11).

In politics, the number of African American elected officials has increased over time. Between 1969 and 2018, the number of African Americans in Congress rose from 6 to 50, and the election of Barack Obama as president in 2008 represented a major breakthrough in the political glass ceiling. However, even though the 115th Congress was the most diverse ever, at 9.3 percent of Congress, African Americans remain underrepresented compared to their proportion in the overall population (Bialik and Krogstad 2017).

Inequality also exists within the African American population. Focusing on three major categories highlights these differences. The first group, American African Americans, trace their heritage back to the transatlantic slave trade's horrific Middle Passage in the 17th and 18th centuries, and all that followed after it involving legacy of slavery in the United States, including the Civil War, Emancipation, Reconstruction, Jim Crow, Civil Rights, and more. The second group, African African Americans, are more recent immigrants from African countries such as Kenya, Ghana, Somalia, and Sudan, with limited cultural identification with the legacy of slavery, identifying instead with the African culture from which they more recently arrived. There are just under 2.3 million people born in Africa living in the United States, not all of whom are Black (U.S. Census Bureau 2018a:Table S0201). The third group, Caribbean African Americans, also arrived more recently, but mainly from countries such as the Dominican Republic, Haiti, and Jamaica. There are more than 4.4 million people born in the Caribbean living in the United States, not all of whom are Black. Populations for these latter two groups spiked in the United States after U.S. immigration changed in 1965 with the passage of the Immigration and Nationality Act (U.S. Census Bureau 2018a:Table S0201).

The post-1965 increase in immigrants from Africa and the Caribbean undercuts the already problematic notion of a homogeneous Black experience in the United States. To address these differences, political scientist Christina Greer highlights what she calls the "dual identities of race

Did You Know?

. . . With the release of *The Princess and the Frog* in 2009, Princess Tiana became Disney's first African American princess in a feature film. At the same time, Disney was criticized for drawing on racial stereotypes of 1920s New Orleans in the film.

Photo: Walt Disney Pictures/Album/Alamy Stock Photo

and ethnicity" (2013:3). In racial terms, these three groups share a common biological ancestry, but in terms of ethnicity, they do not share a common cultural history. As a result, they do not see themselves as a singular people. Not all American African Americans, for example, recognize all Africans in America as African Americans. Those in the historic African American community sometimes portray recent African and Caribbean immigrants as fundamentally different because they lack that defining American heritage rooted in a history of slavery and oppression (Berlin 2010; Greer 2013).

On the flip side, Greer (2013) argues that these African and Caribbean groups frequently highlight their "otherness" relative to the historic African American community. This can take a variety of forms including community ethnic celebrations, such as New York City's West Indian American Day Carnival, Houston's Nigerian Day Festival, or Chicago's African/Caribbean International Festival of Life. Many maintain "foreign markers" including accents and native styles of dress to distinguish themselves from historic African Americans. In so doing, they are explicitly rejecting assimilation into the African American community by, as Greer puts it, "remaining perpetual outsiders and forever foreign" (2013:27). One of their motivations for drawing these lines is their hope, both for themselves and their children, of avoiding the historic discrimination associated with being African American in the United States.

Yet, in the United States, because all three groups share a common skin color, all members still get lumped together by others who assume that those with a common skin color also share other things in common. This can be a challenge for Africans who may never have thought about themselves as "Black" before migrating, only to be confronted with the reality of its significance in the United States where they become "American with a modifier" (Greer 2013:138). In the words of novelist Chimamanda Ngozi Adichie, herself a Nigerian immigrant, "Dear Non-American Black, when you make the choice to come to America, you become black. Stop arguing. Stop saying I'm Jamaican or I'm Ghanaian. America doesn't care" (2013). This will likely remain the case so long as Americans of African descent continue to be seen through the singular lens of race.

American Indians and Alaska Natives
Starting in 1492, when European explorers "discovered" what would later be called the Americas, they encountered people already living there for whom the notion of their discovery

> ## I came from a country where race was not an issue; I did not think of myself as black and I only became black when I came to America
>
> Chimamanda Ngozi Adichie (2014)

might come as a surprise. As European immigrants arrived to establish settlements in the lands that would become the United States, they came to refer to the native people as "American Indians." Encounters between the indigenous populations and European settlers resulted in the deaths of tens of millions of native peoples on the American continents, largely as a consequence of the spread of diseases for which the local populations had limited resistance, though warfare killed many, too. Taking responsibility for such atrocities was long in coming, but one step in that direction came in 2015 when Pope Francis acknowledged that "Grave sins were committed against the native peoples of America in the name of God" and apologized for the role the Catholic Church played (Boren 2015).

SOCTHINK

To what extent do race and ethnicity influence the opportunities you have and obstacles you face? How conscious are you of your race and ethnicity and their possible influences on your life?

The effects of the racism, displacement, and discrimination suffered by the American Indians at the hands of European settlers are still apparent today. According to the U.S. Census, there are 2.1 million American Indian and Alaska Natives who make up 0.7 percent of the total U.S. population (U.S. Census Bureau 2018a:Table S0201). Native Americans represent a diverse array of cultures distinguishable by language, family organization, religion, and livelihood. There are 567 federally recognized American Indian tribal groups in the United States. The 2 largest Native American groupings are the Navajo and Cherokee. Alaska Native groups include, among others, the Inupiat, Yup'ik, and Aleut (Department of Interior 2018).

The median household income for American Indian and Alaska Natives is $40,936, meaning these household earn 60 percent of what the median non-Hispanic White household takes home. Overall, 26.5 percent of American Indians and Alaska Natives fall below the official poverty line. When it comes to education, 72 percent of American Indian and Alaska Native students graduate with a regular diploma within four years of starting ninth grade, compared to 88 percent among non-Hispanic Whites. When it comes to higher education, 15.1 percent of Native Americans and

Ethnic enclaves in urban areas, such as Koreatown in Los Angeles, demonstrate cultural pluralism in the United States.
David McNew/Getty Images

Alaska Natives aged 25 and older have at least a bachelor's degree (National Center for Education Statistics 2018:Table 219.46; U.S. Census Bureau 2018a:Table S0201).

Asian Americans The Asian population in the United States, including 18 million people at 5.5 percent of the population, is the fastest-growing major racial or ethnic group in the country, having grown by 72 percent since 2000 (López, Ruiz, and Patten 2017). Most of that growth is a product of immigration. At 78 percent, the proportion of Asian adults who are foreign-born exceeds that of any of the other major racial or ethnic groups, the next closest being Hispanic adults, 47 percent of whom are foreign-born. Only 5 percent of non-Hispanic Whites are foreign-born. Between 1970 and 2016, immigrants accounted for 81 percent of the growth in the Asian adult population (Kochhar and Cilluffo 2018).

Asian Americans are often held up as a model minority group, meaning that their members supposedly have succeeded economically, socially, and educationally despite past prejudice and discrimination. For example, the median household income for Asian Americans is $81,331, the highest income for any racial or ethnic group, which represents 119 percent of what non-Hispanic White households make. Yet this representation minimizes the degree of difference that exists within the Asian American category. For example, the poverty rate for Asian Americans is 10 percent, which is higher than the 8.7 rate for non-Hispanic Whites (Fontenot, Semega, and Kollar 2018). The income for Asians at the 90th percentile is 10.7 times greater than those at the 10th percentile (Kochhar and Cilluffo 2018). This difference is larger than that for Hispanics, Blacks, or non-Hispanic Whites.

Even though they all fall within the same racial category, groups identifying with various Asian nationalities have significantly different education and income levels. Among Asian Indians, 72 percent hold at least a bachelor's degree as do 60 percent of Malaysians. This represents a significant contrast with Laotians at 16 percent and Bhutanese at 9 percent (López, Ruiz, and Patten 2017). And when it comes to income, Asian Americans who identify their heritage as Indian ($114,261), Filipino ($90,815), Japanese ($79,504), and Chinese ($77,136) have median household incomes significantly higher than the incomes reported by those who identify as Bangladeshi ($57,606), Nepalese ($54,853), or Burmese ($39,730) (U.S. Census Bureau 2018a:Table S0201).

Hispanic Americans At 18 percent of the population, which includes 58.8 million people, Hispanics make up the largest minority group in the United States, an increase

Major Asian American Groups in the United States

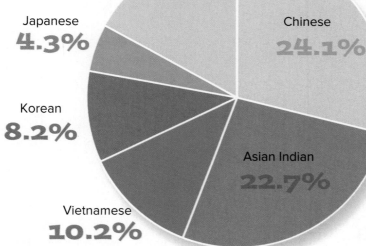

Other Asian
14.3%

Japanese
4.3%

Chinese
24.1%

Korean
8.2%

Asian Indian
22.7%

Vietnamese
10.2%

Source: U.S. Census Bureau 2018a:Table S0201.

Age Variation by Race and Ethnicity

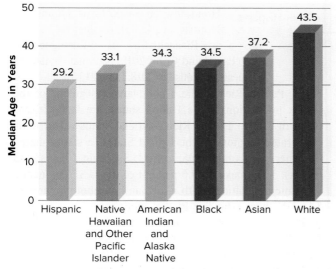

Median Age in Years

Hispanic	29.2
Native Hawaiian and Other Pacific Islander	33.1
American Indian and Alaska Native	34.3
Black	34.5
Asian	37.2
White	43.5

Note: Hispanics are included only in the Hispanic category, even though they can be of any race.
Source: U.S. Census Bureau 2018a:Table S0201.

from 35.3 million in 2000. The fastest-growing subgroups in terms of percentages are those who come from the Central American nations of El Salvador, Honduras, and Guatemala (Cohn, Passel, and Gonzalez-Barrera 2017). The majority of the overall Hispanic population increase, however, is due not to immigration. Instead, the median age for Hispanics is younger than the other groups—as is shown in the "Age Variation by Race and Ethnicity" graph—meaning that more Hispanics are of childbearing age which, combined with the fact that Hispanics overall have higher birthrates, results in more babies (Humes, Jones, and Ramirez 2011; Johnson and Lichter 2010; Patten 2016; U.S. Census Bureau 2018a:Table S0201).

Although the growth in the Hispanic population has been a national phenomenon, the five states with the largest Hispanic population are California, Texas, Florida, New York, and Illinois. In New Mexico, 47.7 percent of the population is Hispanic (Stepler and Brown 2016:Table 44). Major urban areas have also experienced substantial expansion. As the "Hispanic Population and Percent in U.S. Metro Areas" graph depicts, Los Angeles is home to the largest number of Hispanics. Within the top metro areas, however, the population of San Antonio, at 55.7 percent, has the highest percentage of Hispanics (Pew Research Center 2016e).

The educational challenges facing the Latinx population is reflected in the fact that 67 percent of Hispanics aged 25 and older have completed high school, compared to 93 percent for non-Hispanic Whites. At the college level, 16 percent of Hispanics have at least a bachelor's degree, whereas 36 percent of non-Hispanic Whites have the same.

Educational attainment of Hispanics is, however, on the rise. Dropout rates for Latinx youths fell dramatically from 32.4 percent in 1990 to 8.6 percent in 2016. And the percentage of Hispanics who went directly to college after high school exceeded the rate for non-Hispanic Whites for the first time in 2012 (Gramlich 2017; National Center for Education Statistics 2018:Table 219.70).

In economic terms, median household income for Hispanics is $50,486, which represents 74 percent of what the typical non-Hispanic White household earns. Put another way, the typical Hispanic household must get by on almost $18,000 less per year (Fontenot, Semega, and Kollar 2018). In terms of net worth, the median wealth for Hispanic families is $20,700 compared to a median of $171,000 for non-Hispanic White families. In other words, the typical Hispanic family owns 11 percent as much wealth as non-Hispanic White families. Education plays a significant role when it comes to wealth. Hispanic families with a bachelor's degree or more have a net worth of $77,900 compared to $17,500 in families with less than a college degree (Dettling et al. 2017).

Hispanic Population and Percent in U.S. Metro Areas

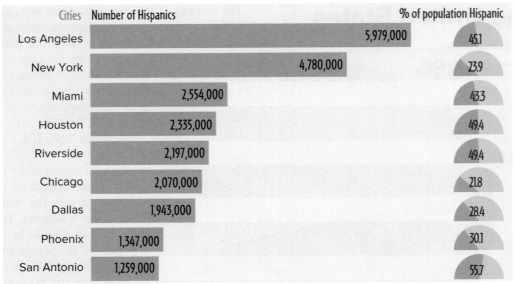

Cities	Number of Hispanics	% of population Hispanic
Los Angeles	5,979,000	45.1
New York	4,780,000	23.9
Miami	2,554,000	43.3
Houston	2,335,000	49.4
Riverside	2,197,000	49.4
Chicago	2,070,000	21.8
Dallas	1,943,000	28.4
Phoenix	1,347,000	30.1
San Antonio	1,259,000	55.7

Source: Pew Research Center 2016e.

Major Hispanic Groups in the United States

Puerto Rican **9.5%**
Salvadoran **3.9%**
Cuban **3.9%**
Dominican **3.5%**
Guatemalan **2.5%**
Jamaican **1.9%**
Haitian **1.8%**
Other Hispanic **10.6%**
Mexican **62.3%**

Source: U.S. Census Bureau 2018a:Table S0201. *Photo:* PhotoDisc/Getty Images

As was the case for the previous race groupings, significant variation exists among U.S. Hispanic groups. Mexican Americans, for example, make up the largest proportion of the Hispanic population in the United States, comprising 62.3 percent of the whole. Their median household income is $49,439 and 19.9 percent fall below the poverty line. Of the 11 million unauthorized immigrants living in the United States, 50 percent are from Mexico. The median income levels for Mexican Americans contrasts with those originally from Honduras, at $41,824, or Dominican Republic, at $43,851, on the lower end or Costa Rica with $62,769 on the higher end (Passel and Cohn 2018; National Center for Education Statistics 2018:Table 219.70).

Puerto Ricans, the second-largest segment of the Latinx population in the United states, are U.S. citizens by birth due to Puerto Rico's official status as an unincorporated territory of the United States (a status shared by American Samoa, Guam, the U.S. Virgin Islands, and others). They make up 9.5 percent of the U.S. continental Hispanic population. With a median household income of $44,731, those who live in the continental United States make 68 percent of what non-Hispanic White households earn. They have a poverty rate of 22.5 percent (National Center for Education Statistics 2018:Table 219.70). Although there has been much discussion in Puerto Rico for decades, the question of whether or not to petition for admission to the United States as the 51st state remains unresolved (Garrett 2017).

Jewish Americans The Jewish population in the United States includes 6.9 million people, which represents approximately 2.1 percent of the total U.S. population. Historically, the Jewish population in the United States centered in New York City, which remains largely true, though the population is now more dispersed with 26 percent living in New York, 18 percent in California, and 10 percent in Florida (Sheskin and Dashefsky 2017). Within the Jewish community, commitment to the Jewish faith that provided a significant cultural foundation is varied. The majority of people in the United States who identify as Jewish say that being Jewish is mainly a matter of ancestry or culture, which is significantly more than those who say it is primarily a matter of religion. However, 78 percent of those who self-identify as Jewish also say that they do so on the basis of religion (Pew Research Center 2013b).

Historically, **antisemitism**—a form of racism directed toward Jewish people—has resulted in some of the most horrific acts of persecution and discrimination in modern history. The most extreme example came in the form the Holocaust, which, as noted earlier, sought the extermination of the entire Jewish population in and around Germany as part of World War II. In the United States, until the late 1960s, many prestigious universities maintained restrictive quotas that limited Jewish enrollment. Private social clubs and fraternal groups frequently denied membership to Jews, a practice upheld by the Supreme Court in the 1964 case *Bell v. Maryland*. The Anti-Defamation League (ADL) of B'nai B'rith produces an annual report of anti-Semitic incidents in the United States. In 2017, the total reported incidents of harassment, threats, vandalism, and assaults came to 1,986, a 164 percent increase from 2013 (Anti-Defamation League 2018).

Arab Americans Arab Americans include those whose ancestors hail from the 22 nations of what's known as the Arab world. This group highlights the limitations of the broad geographically based race categories, because these nations include both northern Africa and western Asia (known as the Middle East) countries. Not all residents of those countries are Arab; for example, the Kurds of northern Iraq are not Arab. And some Arab Americans may have immigrated to the United States from non-Arab countries, such as Great Britain or France, where

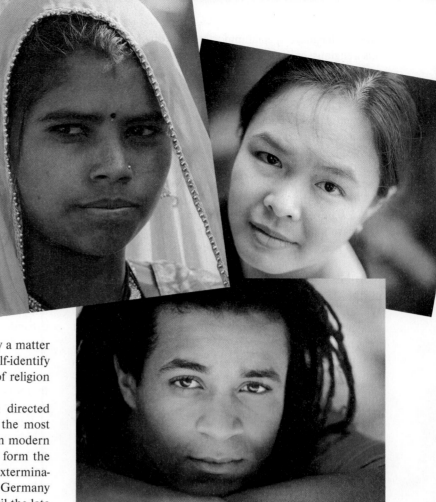

(Top left): Greta6/123RF; *(top right):* Pitinan/123RF *(bottom):* liquidlibrary/PictureQuest

their families have lived for generations (Kayyali 2006; Orfalea 2006). Estimates of the size of the Arab American population vary widely. According to the U.S. Census Bureau (2018a:Table S0201), 2 million people of Arab ancestry reside in the United States. The Arab American Institute Foundation (2014), building on Census data, places that number at 3.7 million. The top four Arab countries of origin for the foreign-born population in the United States are Iraq, Egypt, Lebanon, and Saudi Arabia (U.S. Census Bureau 2018a:Table B05006).

> **Antisemitism** A form of racism directed toward Jewish people.

The Arabic language is the single most unifying force among Arabs, although not all Arabs, and certainly not all Arab Americans, can read and speak Arabic. Moreover, the language has evolved over the centuries so that people in different parts of the Arab world speak different dialects. The fact that the Muslim holy book, the Qur'an, was originally written in Arabic

> A fully functional multiracial society cannot be achieved without a sense of history and open, honest dialogue.
>
> ———
>
> **Cornel West (2009)**

gave the language special importance to Muslims. Despite this religious cultural foundation, most Arab Americans are not Muslim and not all practice religion. In fact, the majority of Arab Americans are Christian (Arab American Institute 2008; David 2004).

Significant differences exist within the Arab American populace when it comes to economic resources. Overall, the median household income for Arab Americans is $58,581 and the poverty rate is 22.2 percent. Among those who trace their roots to Lebanon, the median household income is $76,805 with a poverty rate of 11.3 percent. This represent a significant difference compared to those from Iraq who have a median income of $35,421 and a poverty rate of 34.3 percent (U.S. Census Bureau 2018a:Table S0201).

Non-Hispanic White Americans Overall, 60.6 percent of the U.S. population is composed of non-Hispanic Whites. The nation's non-Hispanic White ethnic population includes approximately 43 million people who claim at least partial German ancestry, 31 million Irish Americans, 23 million with English roots, 17 million Italian Americans, and 9 million Polish Americans, among others. As we saw earlier in the "Age Variation by Race and Ethnicity" graph, non-Hispanic White's represent the oldest of the major race and ethnicity groups, with an average age of 43.5. Among non-Hispanic Whites, 19.8 percent are 65 and older compared to only 7.1 percent among Hispanics. To put it plainly, in addition to their percentages of the population decreasing, the absolute numbers for most of these non-Hispanic White ethnic groups are also going down as members of these groups get older and die and are not replaced by a comparable number of children or immigrants who identify with the same European ancestries (Hixson, Hepler, and Kim 2011; U.S. Census Bureau 2018a:Table S0201).

As noted earlier, access to economic resources overall for those in this category tends to be greater than for most groups. Median income for non-Hispanic White households is $68,145. Their poverty rate is 8.7 percent (Fontenot, Semega, and Kollar 2018). In terms of net worth, their median wealth is $171,000. As with all the previous groups, education matters in non-Hispanic White households when it comes to wealth. Households that include a bachelor's degree holder have a median net worth of $397,100 compared to $98,100 in households with less than a bachelor's degree (Dettling et al. 2017).

Many non-Hispanic White ethnics today identify only sporadically with their ethnic cultural past. They adopt a form of **symbolic ethnicity** meaning they view their cultural heritage not as a core part of their identity but as an emblematic marker pointing toward their family's ancestral homeland. According to sociologist Herbert Gans (1979, 2009), the diminishing significance of one's ethnic heritage occurs over the course of several generations due

Symbolic ethnicity An ethnic identity that emphasizes concerns such as ethnic food or political issues rather than deeper ties to one's ethnic heritage.

to acculturation and assimilation. Over time, the strong attachment to the homeland culture among first-generation immigrants subsides so that by the third or fourth generation there is limited firsthand familiarity with the original cultural traditions. Symbolic ethnicity may manifest itself in occasional home decor choices, ethnic festivals, or vacation destinations, but it doesn't appear to shape everyday interactions or limit opportunities. Those who experience ethnicity in this way treat ethnicity as optional, paying little heed to possible constraints built into the surrounding social environment that might limit others from doing the same. The ability to embrace or distance oneself from ethnicity is not equally available to all (Waters 1990). For members of the dominant majority, ethnicity is less likely to have negative consequences when it comes to access to valued economic, social, and material resources.

A sizable number of non-Hispanic Whites feel excluded and even threatened by increasing multiculturalism and expanding diversity (Hochschild 2016; Plaut et al. 2011). According to a national survey, 50 percent of Whites now believe that the level of anti-White discrimination is at least as common as discrimination against Blacks and other minority groups. That number rises to 60 percent among members of the White working class. When it comes to political party, 64 percent of Republicans agree that discrimination against Whites is at least as common and 71 percent of Democrats disagree. Researchers suggest that belief in reverse discrimination functions to bolster Whites' self-esteem (Jacobs 2016; Jones et al. 2015).

The Multiplicity of Race Diversity within all of these racial and ethnic groups highlights the limitations of broad racial categories. Within the African American community, we need to be aware of distinctions among African African Americans, Caribbean African Americans, and American African Americans (Greer 2013). Within the Asian American populace, we should recognize that substantial differences exist among groups based on nation of origin and time of immigration. Technically, Israel is in Asia, which would make most people of Jewish ancestry Asian American, yet we don't typically place them there. The main Arab states are in both Africa and Asia, and again, we don't usually refer to Arabs as either African American or Asian American, thinking of them as a distinct cultural group. No matter which major racial or ethnic group we consider, we need to be careful about missing out on the fact that differences within these categories are often as great as, if not greater than, differences among these categories.

IMMIGRATION

There are 258 million immigrants around the world, people who left their country of birth and now reside in another. The United States is the top destination for these migrants with 49.8 million, or 19 percent of the world's total, residing there. Germany and Saudi Arabia are tied for a distant

Going GLOBAL

World Immigration Since 1500

Source: Allen 2008.

second place as the destination location for the world's immigrants with 12.2 million each. International migrants now account for 15.3 percent of the total U.S. population. Other countries have a higher percentage of immigrants, including Austria at 19 percent, Canada at 21.5 percent, and Australia at 28.8 percent. Globally, the top country of origin, from which immigrants departed, is India, followed by Mexico, the Russian Federation, and China (United Nations 2017a).

Immigration Trends The migration of people is not uniform across time or space. At certain times, war or famine may precipitate large movements of people, either temporarily or permanently. As noted earlier when discussing expulsion, for example, the civil war in Syria led at least 5.6 million people to leave that country (United Nations High Commission for Refugees 2018). Temporary dislocations occur when people wait until it is safe to return to their home areas. However, more and more migrants who cannot eke out an adequate living at home are making permanent moves to developed nations. The major migration streams flow into North America, the oil-rich areas of the Middle East, and the industrial economies of western Europe and Asia. Currently, seven of the world's wealthiest nations (including Germany, France, the United Kingdom, and the United States) shelter about one-third of the world's migrant population but less than one-fifth of the world's

total population. As long as disparities in job opportunities exist among countries, this international trend is not likely to reverse.

Even though the sending nation loses a significant source of labor and talent due to emigration, the process does contribute to its economy. For example, it reduces the size of the population that an economy with limited resources has a difficult time supporting, and it leads to an economic infusion in the form of remittances—monies that immigrants send back to their home nations. Worldwide, immigrants send more than $581 billion a year back home to their relatives—an amount that represents a major source of income for developing nations. In 2017, over $148 billion was sent from the United States to other countries in the form of remittances. The single largest recipient was Mexico with $30 billion, followed by China with $16.1 billion, and India at $11.7 billion (World Bank 2018a).

Immigrants continue to face obstacles owing to their relative lack of resources. Immigrant women, for example, face all the challenges that immigrant men do, plus some additional ones. Typically, they bear the responsibility for obtaining services for their families, particularly their children. Women are often left to navigate the bureaucratic tangle of schools, city services, and health care, as well as the unfamiliar stores and markets they must shop at to feed their families. Women who need special medical services or are victims of domestic violence are often reluctant to

Going GLOBAL

Legal Migration to the United States, 1820–2017

Millions of immigrants

| 1820s | 1840s | 1860s | 1880s | 1900s | 1920s | 1940s | 1960s | 1980s | 2000s | 2010s |

0.1
0.5
1.4
2.1
2.8
2.7
3.7
5.2
6.3
Europe and Canada
All Others
8.2
0.7
0.9
4.3
2.5
3.2
4.2
6.2
8.5
9.8
10.3

Source: U.S. Department of Homeland Security 2018:Table 2. *Photo:* pixhook/Getty Images

1924 set restrictive quotas on the number of immigrants allowed from various countries, with a particular emphasis on limiting entry to southern and eastern Europeans, such as Italians, Greeks, and Russians. In the late 1930s and early 1940s, the federal government refused to loosen restrictive immigration quotas to allow Jewish refugees to escape the terror of Nazi Germany. In keeping with this policy, in 1939, the MS *St. Louis,* with more than 900 Jewish refugees on board, was denied permission to dock in the United States. The ship was forced back to Europe, where at least a few hundred of its passengers later died at the hands of the Nazis (Ogilvie and Miller 2010; G. Thomas and Morgan-Witts 2010).

The fate of the *St. Louis* passengers has served as a cautionary tale regarding immigration policy in the United States ever since, though debates continue about how inclusive policy should be. The principle of not denying entry to those who might face torture or death was embedded in U.S. amnesty and asylum policies which provide safe haven for those who face persecution, or its imminent threat, in their home countries. However, the processes for qualifying for amnesty or asylum are lengthy and involve significant legal maneuvering (Good 2007; Hamlin 2014; Mahmood 1996).

The United States opened its doors more widely to immigrants with the passage of the Immigration and Nationality Act of 1965. Although per-country immigration limits still existed, this bill abolished the quota system based on national origins. It also instituted a preferences system which gave priority to relatives of U.S. citizens and to those with specialized skills. As a result, increased numbers of immigrants arrived from Asia, Africa, and the Middle East. This inflow of immigrants from places other than Europe and Canada—portrayed in the "Legal Migration to the United States, 1820-2017" graph—substantially changed the demographic makeup of the United States (U.S. Department of Homeland Security 2018).

In many nations, including the United States, people are concerned that the new arrivals do not reflect and will not embrace their own cultural and racial heritage. Others fear that immigrants represent an economic threat because they increase the supply of available workers, which effectively

seek outside help. Finally, because many new immigrants view the United States as a dangerous place to raise a family, women must be especially watchful over their children's lives (Ruiz, Zong, and Batalva 2015).

Immigration Policies Countries establish national policies in order to address immigration. The United States has a long history of immigration laws that reflect changing attitudes regarding race over time. In 1882, Congress passed the Chinese Exclusion Act banning virtually all immigration from that country. The Immigration Act of

Detention facilities, such as this one in Tornillo, Texas, housed thousands of migrant children. Andres Leighton/AP Images

reduces available job opportunities and depresses wages for natives. In 1986, the U.S. Congress passed the Immigration Reform and Control Act which outlawed the recruiting and hiring of undocumented immigrants and subjected employers to fines and even imprisonment if they violated the law. Under both the George W. Bush and Barack Obama administrations, significant efforts were made to crack down on those entering the country illegally (U.S. Department of Homeland Security 2018).

Battles over immigration continue. During the second week of his administration, President Donald Trump signed an Executive Order severely restricting immigration from seven predominantly Muslim nations, temporarily suspending admission of all refugees and barring refugees from Syria indefinitely (Calamur 2017). Protesters streamed into airports around the country to make their displeasure known, and a legal battle ensued (Dolan 2017). After the Executive Order was reworked so as not to focus narrowly on Muslim nations, in June 2018 the U.S. Supreme Court ruled 5–4 that the president does have the authority to institute such bans. The new policy severely restricted travel to the United States from Iran, Libya, North Korea, Somalia, Syria, Venezuela, and Yemen (Liptak and Shear 2018).

The president justified immigration curbs by claiming they were in the interests of national security—that is, to reduce the likelihood that a terrorist might come to the United States and stage an attack. Protesters claimed that, instead, it amounted to a Muslim ban, which ran counter to both U.S. law and values. Corporate executives claimed that these curbs would create competitive disadvantages by limiting their ability to hire talented and skilled workers from around the world (Newmeyer 2017). Part of the reason that

such conflicts over immigration continue is that Congress has had difficulty reaching a bipartisan compromise on how to update and reform immigration policies.

A similar controversy arose over the treatment of undocumented children who, with or without their parents, crossed the southern border illegally into the United States. As of September 2018, a total of 12,800 such children were being held in custody (Dickerson 2018). This number rose significantly due in part to the Trump administration's zero tolerance border enforcement policy. In an effort to deter immigration, this policy separated immigrant children from their parents at the border, sending the children to detention centers, including the temporary Tornillo, Texas, "Tent City" facility capable of housing up to 3,800 children, while their parents got sent to federal jails and faced prosecution and possible deportation (Dickerson 2018). This policy was later suspended due to the controversy that resulted but may be reenacted in a different form at a later date.

PRIVILEGE

Topics involving race and ethnicity can challenge our sense of fairness and opportunity. Yet, in keeping with the sociological imagination, we should recognize that our tendency to take seriously, or to ignore, issues related to racism is shaped by our relative positions in the social structure. This is especially challenging for those who may not have experienced the consequences of racial inequality personally or directly. For example, we tend to focus more on the difficulty women have balancing career and family than on the ease with which men avoid household chores and advance in the workplace. Similarly, we concentrate more on discrimination against racial and ethnic minorities than on the advantages members of the White majority enjoy. Indeed, most White people rarely think about their "Whiteness," taking their status for granted. However, sociologists and other social scientists are becoming increasingly interested in what it means to be "White," because White privilege is the other side of the proverbial coin of racial discrimination (Painter 2010a).

Feminist scholar Peggy McIntosh (1988) became interested in White privilege after noticing that most men would not acknowledge the privileges attached to being male—even if they would agree that being female had its disadvantages. She wondered whether White people suffer from a similar blind spot regarding their own racial privilege. Intrigued, McIntosh began to list all the ways in which she benefited from her Whiteness. She soon realized that the list of unspoken advantages was long and significant.

McIntosh found that as a White person, she rarely needed to step out of her comfort zone, no matter where she went. If she wished to, she could spend most of her time with people of her own race. She could find a good place to live in a pleasant neighborhood, buy the foods she liked to eat from almost any grocery store, and get her hair styled in almost any salon. She could attend a public meeting without feeling that she did not belong or that she was different from everyone else.

McIntosh discovered, too, that her skin color opened doors for her. She could cash checks and use credit cards without suspicion, and she could browse through stores without being shadowed by security guards. She could be seated without difficulty in a restaurant. If she asked to see the manager, she could assume he or she would be of her own race. If she needed help from a doctor or a lawyer, she could get it.

McIntosh also realized that her Whiteness made the job of parenting easier. She did not need to worry about protecting her children from people who didn't like them because of their race. She could be sure that their books would show pictures of people who looked like them and that their history texts would describe White people's achievements. She knew that the television programs they watched would include White characters.

SOCTHINK

McIntosh's model implies the possibility of earned and unearned advantages and disadvantages. What might be an example of an earned advantage? An unearned advantage? An earned disadvantage? An unearned disadvantage?

Finally, McIntosh had to admit that others did not constantly evaluate her in racial terms. When she appeared in public, she didn't need to worry that her clothing or behavior might reflect poorly on White people. If she was recognized for an achievement, it was seen as her own accomplishment, not that of an entire race. And no one ever assumed that the personal opinions she voiced should be those of all White people. Because McIntosh blended in with the people around her, she wasn't always onstage.

The concept of privilege makes many people uncomfortable, but one of the tasks of sociology is to explore all elements of our social systems, including those that might challenge us. Power has consequences. In the words of Max Weber, "The fortunate is seldom satisfied with the fact of being fortunate. Beyond this, he needs to know that he has a right to his good fortune. He wants to be convinced that he 'deserves' it, and above all, that he deserves it in comparison with others. Good fortune thus wants to be 'legitimate' fortune" ([1922] 1958d: 271). We create racial and ethnic difference in part to assert superiority and justify existing inequality (Oluo 2018). Sociology calls us to recognize the consequences of difference we construct. Doing so enables us to better see and understand such patterns so that we might make more informed decisions about what to do about them.

> Whites of course have the privilege of not caring, of being colorblind. Nobody else does.
>
> Ursula K. Le Guin (2004)

SOCIOLOGY IS A VERB

Privilege

As an experiment in personal sociology, and in the spirit of Peggy McIntosh's work on privilege, make a list of the unearned advantages and disadvantages that flow out of your racial and ethnic heritage. Doing so can make us more aware of both the opportunities and obstacles that are not a consequence of our individual effort or merit. How and why might such a list be more challenging for some groups than others?

FOR REVIEW

I. How do sociologists define race and ethnicity?

- Race is defined by the social significance that groups attach to external physical characteristics. Ethnicity is rooted in cultural and national traditions that define a population. Sociologists emphasize the significance of culture and its consequences for both.

II. What are prejudice and discrimination, and how do they operate?

- Prejudice involves attitudes and beliefs, whereas discrimination involves actions. In both cases, they represent a negative response to a group of people that denies them full equality as persons. Institutional discrimination is built into the structure of society itself, systematically denying some groups access to key resources.

III. What are the consequences of race and ethnicity for opportunity?

- Racial and ethnic groups in the United States—including African Americans, Native Americans, Asian Americans, Hispanic Americans, Jewish Americans, and White ethnic Americans—face differing levels of opportunity based on their relative position in society. Groups within each of these categories continue to face significant structural inequality.

Functionalist View

Historically, race and ethnicity have contributed to **social integration** and **identity** by providing clear boundaries between groups.

Amalgamation, assimilation, and pluralism function to bring **order** to society. Immigration is functional for the host nation if it gains needed workers and for the sending nation when remittances are sent back.

KEY CONCEPTS
INTEGRATION, IDENTITY, ORDER

Conflict View

Prejudice, discrimination, ethnocentrism, stereotyping, racism, and hate crimes are all manifestations of perceived **superiority** of a dominant group over subordinate minority groups.

Institutional discrimination denies opportunities and equal rights to individuals and groups as part of the normal operations of society.

Exploitation theory holds that prejudice and discrimination help preserve inequality in the economic system as a whole.

KEY CONCEPTS
DISCRIMINATION, EXPLOITATION, RACISM

Interactionist View

According to the **contact hypothesis**, interracial contact between people in cooperative circumstances will lessen prejudice and stereotyping.

Racial **profiling** occurs when arbitrary actions are taken by authorities based on a person's perceived racial or ethnic identity.

Being White in the United States represents an often unacknowledged form of privilege in everyday encounters.

KEY CONCEPTS
CONTACT, INTERACTION

MAKE THE CONNECTION

After reviewing the chapter, answer the following questions:

1

How would each perspective approach the issue of African American deaths at the hands of police?

2

How would each perspective explain the pseudoscientific attempts to use race to justify inequality?

3

How do the functionalist and conflict perspectives intersect in both color-blind racism and affirmative action?

4

Using the interactionist perspective, describe an example of interracial contact you have experienced along with its consequences.

Pop Quiz

1. **According to the findings of the Human Genome Project, race**

   a. determines intellectual ability.

   b. is a biological, not a social, concept.

   c. explains significant social outcomes.

   d. has no genetic or scientific basis.

2. **How do sociologists define race?**

   a. genetic differences between categories of humans based on clear chromosomal markers that specify a person's race

   b. the presumed biological differences between humans to which people attach meaning resulting in the creation of supposed genetically distinct subgroups within the population

   c. the presumed cultural differences between humans to which people attach meaning resulting in the creation of supposed socially distinct subgroups within the population

   d. levels of melatonin, which shape skin color and divide the human population into distinct groups

3. **How did the scientific community respond in the years after Linnaeus created his model defining the biological categorization of racial groups?**

   a. Scientists reached widespread consensus that his four-category model accurately captured human racial differences.

   b. Scientists revised his model and reached widespread agreement that a three-category model was best.

   c. Scientists revised his model and reached widespread agreement that a five-category model was best.

   d. Scientists could not reach widespread consensus regarding how many biologically based human races exist.

4. **What legal principle regarding race was reaffirmed in the 1896 *Plessy v. Ferguson* Supreme Court decision?**

   a. equal voting rights

   b. anti-miscegenation

   c. separate but equal

   d. expulsion

5. **Starting with the 2000 U.S. Census, there were a total of _____ possible race combinations you could choose from to identify yourself.**

   a. 3

   b. 6

   c. 42

   d. 63

6. **According to Roth's multidimensional typology of race, which category focuses on a person's subjective sense of which race he or she identifies with?**

   a. racial self-classification

   b. racial self-narrative

   c. reflected race

   d. racial family history

7. **Working together as computer programmers for an electronics firm, a Hispanic woman and a Jewish man overcome their initial prejudices and come to appreciate each other's strengths and talents. This scenario is an example of**

   a. the contact hypothesis.

   b. a self-fulfilling prophecy.

   c. amalgamation.

   d. reverse discrimination.

8. **What term do sociologists use to describe the combination of cultural beliefs regarding inherent racial superiority and inferiority with normative practices of advantage or disadvantage that get built into a structure that reproduces patterns of unequal outcomes?**

   a. prejudice

   b. segregation

   c. racism

   d. discrimination

9. **Which of the following is the largest overall minority group in the United States?**

   a. African Americans

   b. Asian Americans

   c. Latinx Americans

   d. Arab Americans

10. **What term does Peggy McIntosh use to describe the unearned advantages that those in the majority take for granted?**

    a. privilege

    b. discrimination

    c. racism

    d. institutional discrimination

1. (d), 2. (b), 3. (d), 4. (c), 5. (d), 6. (b), 7. (a), 8. (c), 9. (c), 10. (a)

Michael Nigro/Pacific Press/LightRocket/Getty Images

14

Population, Health, and Environment

WATER IS LIFE

In fall of 2016, approximately 10,000 people made their way to the Standing Rock Sioux Reservation in North Dakota to stand in solidarity against the construction of the Dakota Access Pipeline (DAPL). The proposed 1,172-mile-long, $3.8 billion pipeline project would carry over 500,000 barrels of crude oil per day from North Dakota's Bakken oil fields to southern Illinois, where it would be refined and distributed. The two primary concerns for the Standing Rock Sioux were that the pipeline represented a potential threat to the reservation's water supply and that construction would desecrate ancestral lands, including tribal burial grounds and sacred cultural artifacts (Allard 2016; Bengal 2016; Healy 2016).

The protest started small. In February 2016, Jasilyn Charger, Joseph White Eyes, and a handful of friends heard about DAPL and headed to Standing Rock to see if they could make a difference. They lived about two hours away and had already founded a youth group to provide counseling, organize events, and build solidarity around issues their fellow Native American teens faced. In their meeting with representatives from Standing Rock, Ladonna Brave Bull Allard, who owned property adjacent to the pipeline project, volunteered her land and herself to the cause (Elbein 2017; Goodman 2017; Merlan 2016). Together they established Sacred Stone Camp (sacredstonecamp.org) on Allard's property as a prayer camp focused on ceremony and activism. In July, after the Army Corps of Engineers approved the easement that would allow the pipeline to cross under the Missouri River just upriver of the reservation, word spread about both the protest and the camp, and people streamed in (Elbein 2017).

The movement's rallying cry became "Mni wiconi!" (pronounced "mini we-choh-nee") which means "Water is life," and the protesters referred to themselves as water protectors (Healy and Fandos 2016). Although water served as a unifying symbol, the group conceived of this fight as part of a larger struggle for Native American culture, environmental sustainability, and the survival of the planet (Elbein 2017). As fall turned to winter, through back-and-forth legal maneuverings along with protests in which participants were subjected to tear gas, pepper spray, and rubber bullets, President Obama directed the Army Corps of Engineers on December 4, 2016, to deny the easement necessary for the project to move forward (Healy and Fandos 2016). The Standing Rock Sioux effectively declared victory and encouraged the protesters to go home. Some stayed, in part to continue the larger fight, but also because they feared that although the battle was won, the war was not over. On February 7, 2017, President Trump, just weeks after his inauguration, announced that the deputy secretary of the army, who oversees the Army Corps of Engineers, would approve the easement enabling the project to move forward (Eilperin and Dennis 2017).

Such battles—of local versus corporate interests or cultural tradition versus social change—highlight the interdependent nature of people and interests in our world today. For the sake of our public health, we must understand the web of relationships between our natural and social environments. In this chapter we explore such interconnections in the areas of population, health, and environment.

As You READ >>

- **What role do population dynamics play in shaping our lives?**
- **What does sociology contribute to something as seemingly biological as health?**
- **What environmental lessons do we learn from sociology?**

>> Population

One strength of the sociological imagination is that it helps us understand the big picture of society and where we fit in it. It does so by contextualizing our beliefs and practices within a larger social framework, one that is often invisible to us. We have already seen this at work with regard to various components of social structure, including family, religion, education, economy, and politics. In sociology, place matters. This is no less true when it comes to the topics of population, health, and environment. Approaching these issues with a big-picture perspective allows us to see how the positions we occupy shape our individual outcomes.

Today, more than 7.5 billion people live on Earth, a number that goes up by 212,587 each day and 148 every minute, as the "World Population Clock" shows (U.S. Census Bureau 2017a, 2019a). Every one of us must live off the limited resources the planet provides. To better understand our life chances, as well as those of others, we must take into account the direction of population trends. **Demography**—the statistical study of population dynamics— is the discipline committed to studying such patterns. It focuses on how populations change over time, with particular attention to whether they are growing, shrinking, or staying the same. It also includes analysis of the composition of those populations—particularly age and sex, with special emphasis on the degree to which a group's makeup influences its likelihood for population change. For example, if the population is young, there is more potential for women to bear children, increasing the possibility for future population growth.

Demography The statistical study of population dynamics.

In their analysis, demographers begin by specifying the population to be studied. They might select a city, county,

World Population Clock

	Births	Deaths	Population Increase
Year	135,374,175	57,780,066	77,594,110
Day	370,888	158,302	212,587
Minute	258	110	148

Source: U.S. Census Bureau 2017a. *Photos: (clock):* Dimedrol68/Shutterstock; *(Earth):* Source: NOAA/NASA GOES Project state, or, most often, a nation—although they could choose any group with a specified population boundary. They then gather data about that group over some specified period of time, usually per year, to see how many new members join and how many existing members leave. New arrivals come via birth and immigration, while departures occur through death and emigration. Demographers can then use their results to show how a population changes from one point in time to another or to contrast differences between populations.

BIRTH

Births are the primary means by which a population replaces its members from one generation to the next. Yet the likelihood of each of our births was shaped by population dynamics above and beyond the desires of our biological parents. The rate at which women give birth varies significantly over time and place. To better understand these patterns—whether studying England in the Middle Ages, the United States in the late 19th century, or Afghanistan today—demographers analyze trends in **fertility,** the number of children born in a given period of time. The two primary measures they use to do so are the crude birthrate and the total fertility rate.

A population's **crude birthrate** refers to the number of live births per 1,000 people in the population in a given year. It is described as crude because it provides a simple measure, without taking additional factors into consideration, thus allowing for straightforward comparisons between populations. In the United States, for example, the crude birthrate dropped from 23.7 in 1960 to 15.7 in 1985 to 12.4 in 2016, suggesting the long-term possibility of declining population size. Contrast this with the 2016 rates in a variety of other nations, such as Niger at 49.1, Afghanistan at 33.2, China at 12, Germany at 9.3, and a global rate of 18.9 (World Bank 2018o). One variable in isolation, however, is not sufficient to understand the full scope of population change.

Fertility The number of children born in a given period of time.

Crude birthrate The number of live births per 1,000 people in the population in a given year.

Total fertility rate The average number of children a woman would have during her lifetime given current birthrates and assuming she survives through her childbearing years.

Replacement fertility rate The minimum number of children a woman would need to average in her lifetime to reproduce the population in the next generation.

A second indicator is a population's **total fertility rate,** which measures the average number of children a woman would have during her lifetime given current birthrates and assuming she survives through her childbearing years. This indicator is, in some ways, easier to understand because we may already be familiar with the notion that "the average family has 2.5 children." To provide a more precise count, rather than tying the indicator to particular family situations

Total Fertility Rates

Average number of births per woman*

Niger
Afghanistan
Rwanda
Algeria
Cambodia
India
United States
Iran
China
Germany

1960   1970   1980   1990   2000   2010   2016

*If the woman survives to the end of her childbearing years.

Source: Google 2018a.

that are subject to change, this benchmark measures it per woman regardless of her family status. Doing so provides a more universally comparable statistic. As the "Total Fertility Rates" graph portrays, especially in the case of Iran and China, rates can vary significantly over time. In the United States in 1960, the average number of children a woman had in her lifetime was 3.65. The rate fell to 1.74 in 1976 before rising again to 1.8 in 2016. This rate varies widely by country, with Niger at 7.24, Somalia at 6.27, Iraq at 4.37, and Bosnia and Herzegovina at 1.36 in 2016 (World Bank 2018p).

To sustain a population over time—apart from the addition of immigrants who join from the outside—the total fertility rate must fall no lower than approximately 2.1, which is known as the **replacement fertility rate.** This is considered the minimum number of children a woman would need to average in her lifetime to reproduce the population in the next generation. The reason for this number is fairly simple. Because men can't have babies, the average woman must have at least two children so that two parents are replaced in the next generation by two children. The number is boosted a bit to account for the fact that not all females survive through their childbearing years and because the ratio between males and females is not exactly 50–50. The global total fertility rate fell from 4.98 in 1960 to the point where the average woman now has 2.44 children in her lifetime. This decline suggests a slowing in the overall population growth rate and, if trends continue, the possibility of zero population growth, or even global population decline, at some point in the future (World Bank 2018p).

DEATH

Just as new arrivals occur through birth, departures occur through death. And just as with birth, demographers use a simple measure of mortality to allow for comparisons between populations. The **crude death rate** is a measure of the number of deaths per 1,000 people in a population in a given year. In the United States the crude death rate fell from 9.5 in 1960 to 8.4 in 2016. That rate compares with a high of 15.1 in Bulgaria and a low of 1.59 in Qatar (World Bank 2018q). Overall, this measure is more difficult to interpret because it is influenced by the age composition of the population. For example, in a society in which the population is on average older, the death rate may be higher, even though people are living longer. Because of this, demographers often turn to two additional measures: infant mortality and life expectancy.

A population's **infant mortality rate** measures the number of deaths in infants less than one year old per 1,000 live births per year. It is considered a major indicator of the overall well-being of a population, because it is a reflection of available health care, economic opportunity, and inequality. The fact that the numbers vary substantially also suggests that actions can be taken to improve the likelihood that a baby survives infancy. The rate in the United States in 1960 was 25.9. It fell to 10.6 by 1985 and then to 5.7 in 2016 owing to improved prenatal care and medical innovations. Internationally, the global rate fell from 121.9 in 1960 to 29.4 in 2016. Central African Republic had the highest rate in 2016 at 87.6, followed by Sierra Leone (81.7) and Somalia (79.7). At the other end of the scale, Iceland has the lowest rate at 1.6, followed by Slovenia at 1.7 and Japan at 1.9 (World Bank 2018r).

The mortality statistic that is perhaps easiest for us to identify with is **life expectancy,** the projected number of years a person can expect to live based on his or her year of birth. It represents an often unwelcome reminder that factors beyond our individual control influence our life chances. For example, a baby born in Sierra Leone in 2016 has an average life expectancy of 51.8 years, but one born in Japan at the same time can anticipate living until the age of 84. The global average in 2016 was 72 years, a significant increase from 1960, when it was 52.5. Again, such differences point to the sociological fact that place matters. The same is true of time. In the case of Cambodia and Rwanda, for example, specific historical events, such as war and ethnic cleansing, can dramatically affect outcomes, as the "Life Expectancy" graph shows. In the United States life expectancy has increased from 69.8 in 1960 to 78.7 in 2016, owing to such factors as advances in health care, reductions in smoking rates, and increases in exercise and fitness (World Bank 2018s). As life expectancy expands,

Life Expectancy

The average number of years a newborn is expected to live*

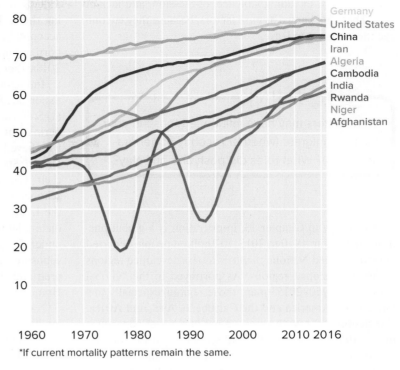

Germany
United States
China
Iran
Algeria
Cambodia
India
Rwanda
Niger
Afghanistan

*If current mortality patterns remain the same.

Source: Google 2018b.

population size typically increases, because the number of people departing in any given year goes down.

MIGRATION

In addition to birth and death, arrivals and departures occur through **migration,** the movement of people from one population group to another. **Immigration** occurs when someone joins a population group of which they were not previously a member. **Emigration** occurs when a member of a population leaves that group. In other words, an immigrant is someone who arrives, and an emigrant is someone who departs.

Reasons for joining or leaving a population group can be varied. Sometimes an immigrant joins a new group because of the opportunities that doing so provides. This might include new job opportunities, connections with families, freedom of religious expression, or other factors that make migration appealing.

Crude death rate The number of deaths per 1,000 people in a population in a given year.

Infant mortality rate The number of deaths of infants under one year old per 1,000 live births in a given year.

Life expectancy The projected number of years a person can expect to live based on his or her year of birth.

Migration The movement of people from one population group to another.

Immigration When individuals join a population group of which they were not previously a member.

Emigration When members of a population leave that group.

Such influences are known as *pull* factors, because they serve as a sort of magnet attracting the immigrant to the new place. At other times people leave locations because they seek to get away from unappealing features in their home country, including violence, oppression, and lack of jobs. These are known as *push* factors, because they encourage the emigrant to leave.

---SOC THINK---

What factors may have influenced those in your family to migrate (whether recently or generations ago)? What roles did push and pull play?

As we saw in Chapter 13, immigration is a global phenomenon. From 1950 to 2015, 102 million people departed what the United Nations classifies as less developed regions to more developed regions. As portrayed in the "Global Migration, 1950–2015" map, those regions especially included Latin America and the Caribbean, Asia, and Africa. The nation that saw the greatest net number of departures during that period was Bangladesh with 14.6 million, followed by Mexico with 13.5 million and China with 10.4 million. The country with the most arrivals by far was the United States with 48.9 million, more than all of Europe combined (United Nations 2017b).

In the United States, 13.9 percent of the population is foreign born. As depicted in the "U.S. Foreign-Born Population" graph, 50.4 percent were born in Latin America, and 31.2 percent came from Asia. As indicated in Chapter 13, Mexico leads the way as the source country, accounting for 25.3 percent, followed by India at 5.9 percent, China at 5 percent, and Philippines at 4.5 percent (U.S. Census Bureau 2018a:Table S0201). California is the most common destination for these immigrants, with 10.7 million, or 23.9 percent, of the foreign-born population living there. Texas, New York, and Florida come next, each accounting for approximately 10 percent of the foreign-born population in the United States (U.S. Census Bureau 2018a:Table S0201).

Immigrants in the United States are classified into four major categories by the Department of Homeland Security (U.S. Department of Homeland Security 2018). Lawful permanent residents, as the name suggests, are those who have been granted lawful permanent residence in the United States. Sometimes referred to as having received their "Green Card," they can legally get a job, attend public schools or colleges, and even join the military. In 2017, of the 1,127,167 such recipients, 66 percent were either immediate relatives of U.S. citizens, including spouses, children under 21 years old, and parents, or they were family-sponsored immigrants, including adult siblings, adult children and their spouses, and others (U.S. Department of Homeland Security 2018:Table 6).

Naturalized citizens, the second category of immigrants, include foreign citizens who have become U.S. citizens. In 2017 there were 707,265 new naturalized citizens. North America accounted for 36.5 percent, making it the most common region of origin, followed closely by Asia. Mexico was the most common country of origin, accounting for 16.8 percent of new naturalized citizens (U.S. Department of Homeland Security 2018:Table 21).

The third immigrant category consists of those seeking residence in the United States because they face persecution, or its imminent threat, in their home country. The two subgroups here are refugees and people seeking asylum. Refugees make their request for protection while located outside the United States, and those seeking asylum make the request while located within some U.S. territory. In 2016, 84,989 people living outside the country were granted refugee status, enabling admission into the United States, and another 11,729 were granted asylum status. The three top countries from which refugees came were Democratic Republic of Congo, Syria, and Burma. The leading sources of asylees were China, El Salvador, Guatemala, and Honduras (U.S. Department of Homeland Security 2017:Tables 14, 17, 19).

The final category of immigrants includes people entering the United States in violation of U.S. immigration laws. In 2016, a total of 530,250 individuals were apprehended by U.S. immigration officials and barred from

Global Migration, 1950–2015

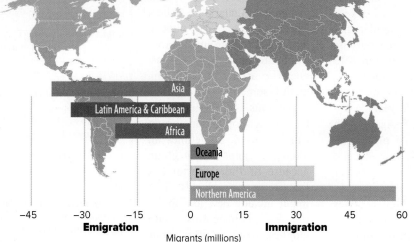

Source: United Nations 2017b.

U.S. Foreign-Born Population

Other regions **2.4%**

Africa **5.1%**

Europe **10.8%**

Asia **31.2%**

Latin America **50.4%**

Foreign born **13.9%**

Native **86.1%**

Source: U.S. Census Bureau 2018a:Table S0201.

is growing or shrinking. Growth rates can vary significantly from country to country. From 2010 to 2015, Qatar grew by an average of 6.7 percent per year followed by Oman at 6.5 percent and Lebanon at 6 percent. At the other end of the scale, the population of some nations actually shrunk, including Syria, which lost 2.3 percent per year, followed by Andorra at 2.1 percent and Georgia at 1.6 percent (United Nations 2017c).

Globally, the world's population increases each year, because the overall birthrate rate exceeds the overall death rate. From 2010 to 2015, the world's population grew an average of 1.2 percent per year.

This rate represents a decline from the 2.1 percent annual increase during the late 1960s, but it is still significantly higher than the projected annual rate of 0.1 percent by the year 2100. In other words, even though the population will continue to rise by several billion over the next several decades, projections show a substantial decline in the rate of the overall population increase (United Nations 2017c). This prediction of a leveling off of total population after generations of growth is consistent with the population model known as the demographic transition.

DEMOGRAPHIC TRANSITION

The most defining characteristic of population dynamics in the past 100 years or so is its explosive growth. Throughout most of human history, global population levels were relatively stable. The world's total population 2,000 years ago was approximately 300 million people. It took 1,500 years for it to reach the 500 million mark and another 300 years to surpass 1 billion in 1804. At that point, population growth began accelerating rapidly, as the "World Population Growth" graph demonstrates, from 2 billion in 1927, 3 billion in 1960, to 7 billion in 2011. According to projections, it will top the 10 billion mark in 2055 (United Nations 1999, 2017d).

Perhaps the best-known attempt to come to terms with the population explosion was offered early on by English economist Thomas Malthus (1766–1834). In 1798 he published the first edition of his book *An Essay on the Principle of Population,* in which he argued that there are natural limits to the number of people the environment can sustain. He claimed that, even though total food production expands to provide for a growing population, it does so at an arithmetic rate (1 → 2 → 3 → 4 → 5). The problem is that population grows at a geometric rate (1 → 2 → 4 → 8 → 16). Ultimately, population will grow so fast there won't be sufficient land to provide enough food for everyone. Crises would inevitably occur—including poverty, famine, disease, and war—and people would die as a result, reducing the population size to a more sustainable level.

Growth rate The overall percentage change in a population per year.

For Malthus, history is a never-ending struggle over resources in which people attempt to escape want, a battle

entering the United States. Of these, 265,747 arrived from Mexico and another 84,649 came from Guatemala. U.S. Border Patrol agents apprehended 78 percent of these immigrants, and Immigration and Customs Enforcement (ICE) officials apprehended the rest (U.S. Department of Homeland Security 2016:Tables 33, 34, 35).

By combining data on births, deaths, and migration, we can create a single indicator that provides a more complete picture of population dynamics. One such measure is a population's **growth rate,** which represents the overall percentage change in a population per year. It is important to consider this overall rate in conjunction with the other measures, because the internal population dynamics at any given time can vary. For example, birthrates and death rates might both rise or fall over a given time period, or one might go up while the other goes down, and migration rates can be similarly variable. The growth rate measure provides a snapshot of whether the population as a whole that those who control resources are more likely to win. As a result, the burden of this misery falls more heavily on the poor. Though he did argue that people could and should exercise moral restraint to rein in population growth by delaying marriage and practicing celibacy, ultimately, Malthus's emphasis was on control of population through the increased mortality rates that result from crises over resources (Malthus 1878).

An alternative, and somewhat less dismal, model of population change is known as the **demographic transition.** According to this model, as societies transform from preindustrial to postindustrial, their population size shifts from small but stable, with high birthrates and death rates, through a period of significant population growth, to large but stable, when both birthrates and death rates are low (Notestein 1945; Thompson 1929, 1948). Unlike Malthus, theorists here do not see elevated death rates through disease and war as inevitable checks on population growth. Instead, they argue that a natural decline in fertility rates occurs owing to technological, social, and economic changes. In basic terms, they portray the transition from a population with large families but short life spans to one with small families and long life spans as virtually inevitable (Bongaarts 2009; Kirk 1996; Myrskylä, Kohler, and Billari 2009). This transition has four primary stages.

> **Demographic transition** As societies transform from preindustrial to postindustrial, their population size shifts from small but stable with high birthrates and death rates, through a period of significant population growth, to large but stable, when both birthrates and death rates are low.

Stage 1: Preindustrial Society

This is the stage humans occupied throughout most of our history. As is evident in the "World Population Growth" graph, global population size was steady for a very long time. In terms of demographic factors, nations at this stage are characterized by high fertility rates and high death rates. The economies of such nations are primarily agricultural, and more children means more workers to produce the food necessary for survival. Because infant and child mortality rates are high in this stage, having more children ensures that some will make it to adulthood. Life expectancy in such nations tends to be short. To provide a visual representation of this distribution, demographers use population pyramids to show the ratio of the population by both age groupings (usually in five-year increments) and sex. As the "Population Pyramids" graphs portray, pyramids for nations at this stage tend to have a wide base, indicating a large percentage of children in the population, and to narrow quickly at the top, showing the relatively small percentage of those who are elderly.

Stage 2: Early Industrial Society

In this stage, death rates fall while birthrates remain high. More babies survive infancy and additional children make it to adulthood. Because there are more young adults, and the birthrate stays high, even more babies are born. On top of that, overall life expectancy increases. The result is a population explosion. This occurs as a consequence of innovations taking place in the society. Advances in technology lead to increased food supplies, cleaner water, improved sanitation, and better medical care. Developments in

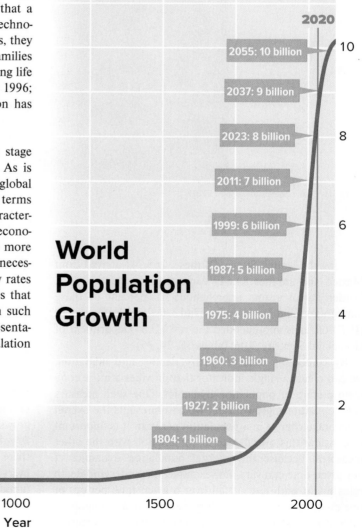

World Population (billions)

2020

2055: 10 billion — 10

2037: 9 billion

2023: 8 billion — 8

2011: 7 billion

1999: 6 billion — 6

1987: 5 billion

1975: 4 billion — 4

1960: 3 billion

1927: 2 billion — 2

1804: 1 billion

World Population Growth

Year: 0 — 50 — 1000 — 1500 — 2000

Year

Sources: United Nations 1999, 2017d.

Population Pyramids

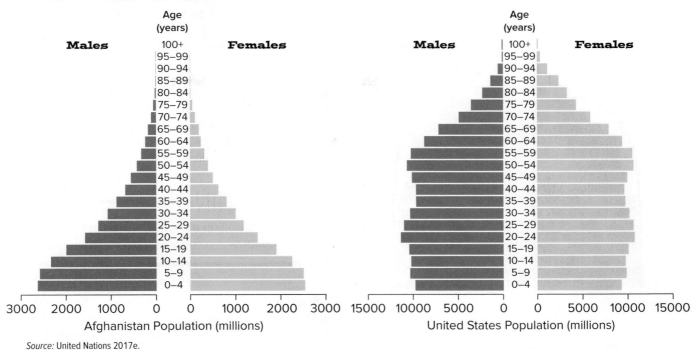

Age
(years)

Males   100+   **Females**

Afghanistan Population (millions)

United States Population (millions)

Source: United Nations 2017e.

agricultural technology and techniques, such as crop rotation, are particularly important. In population pyramid terms, the base widens as the total number of children grows and the top both expands and gets taller owing to more people living longer. Historically, nations that entered this phase early on in the Industrial Revolution, such as the United States or Germany, saw slower population growth rates during this stage than have more recent developing nations. Gaining access to existing advances in medical technology often plays a critical role for developing nations because it can dramatically decrease death rates (Bongaarts 2009).

Stage 3: Late Industrial Society Over time, fertility rates also begin to drop. People start to realize that, with mortality rates falling, having many children is no longer necessary to ensure that some survive into adulthood. Additionally, as the economy transitions away from agriculture, children are no longer needed as workers to assist in food production. In fact, especially with the establishment of child labor laws, children can become a liability rather than an asset. They are no longer primarily producers who contribute, becoming instead consumers whose needs must be met. Advances in contraception technology facilitate this choice to have fewer children. One effect of declining fertility rates is increased opportunity for women. As they spend less time bearing children, women have more opportunity to play expanded roles in the public spheres of politics and the economy. Because the adult population is relatively young, without an overwhelming number of

children or elderly people to support, the economy often thrives, creating what is sometimes referred to as a demographic dividend (Bongaarts 2009).

Stage 4: Postindustrial Society Eventually the demographic transition is complete and population size becomes stable once again. This occurs because birthrates and death rates both reach low levels. Globally this takes a long time, but within a country the amount of time can vary: longer in early industrializing nations but less time for more recent developing nations. Total fertility rates reached replacement levels in Europe and North America by 1980 and were anticipated to do so in Asia and Latin America by 2020 (Bongaarts 2009). As a result of these changes, the population pyramid develops sides that are more vertical before they angle in to its pinnacle, as portrayed in the "Global Population Pyramid" graph. According to this theory, as these trends spread it is just a matter of time, perhaps by the end of this century, until we reach a global population peak and stability (Scherbov, Lutz, and Sanderson 2011).

Some demographers have suggested that the demographic transition model needs to be extended to include additional stages to adequately describe recent demographic trends. In a possible Stage 5, fertility rates would continue falling below replacement levels, contributing to population decline. This has already occurred in numerous nations, including Germany and China (Bloom et al. 2010; Hvistendahl 2010; Myrskylä, Kohler, and Billari 2009). In such cases, as the number of people

Global Population Pyramid

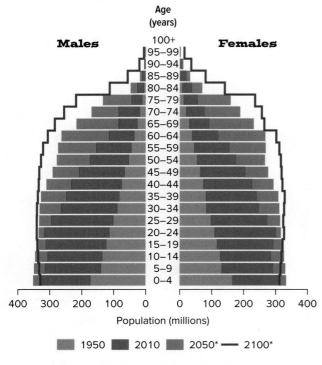

Age
(years)

Males   100+   **Females**
95–99
90–94
85–89
80–84
75–79
70–74
65–69
60–64
55–59
50–54
45–49
40–44
35–39
30–34
25–29
20–24
15–19
10–14
5–9
0–4

400 300 200 100   0   0 100 200 300 400

Population (millions)

■ 1950 ■ 2010 ■ 2050* ▬ 2100*

*Numbers for 2050 and 2100 are projections based on existing birthrate
and death rate trends.
Source: United Nations 2017e.

who retire increases relative to the working-age population, questions arise about how to care for the needs of an aging population. In the United States, ongoing political struggles over health care are driven, to some extent, by concerns about the ability to pay for increased Medicare costs caused by the demographic surge in retirees in the coming years (OASDI 2018). Some countries, such as Japan, have begun taking steps to boost fertility by establishing programs, such as extended paid maternity leave and subsidized day care, that encourage people to have more children (Suzuki 2009).

In recent years, some of these nations with below-replacement birthrates have experienced a fertility rebound, a possible Stage 6 of the demographic transition model. Demographers suggest that this is most likely to

Did You Know?

. . . Chinese officials instituted a one-child policy in 1979 and claim their one-child policy reduced the current population by 400 million. Demographers counter that total fertility rates would have fallen substantially even without the policy, as they have in other nations.

Sources: Cai 2010; Hvistendahl 2010.

occur in countries with the highest scores on the United Nations Human Development Index (HDI). As we saw in the "Measuring Global Inequality" graph in Chapter 11, this index ranges from 0 to 1 and is based on three societal dimensions, including health, education, and income. Countries with an HDI score of greater than 0.86, such as Norway, the Netherlands, and the United States, are most likely to experience this rebound (Myrskylä, Kohler, and Billari 2009; United Nations Development Programme 2018). Parents in such countries can worry less about having sufficient individual and collective resources to provide for the needs of their children.

SOCTHINK

What factors do you think might explain the fertility rebound in countries with high HDI scores?

Studying population dynamics is important because the world into which we are born is not of our own choosing, yet it shapes our life chances. When we were born, how long we live, and our likelihood for migration are all part of larger social trends. Understanding the nature and direction of these patterns can empower us to create new pathways in hopes of a better future. Such informed innovation has contributed to advances in health care, education, and environmental protection, substantially improving the life chances of people all around the world.

>> Sociological Perspectives on Health and Illness

To understand health, we cannot focus on biology alone. We also must think beyond medicine, doctors, and hospitals. We must consider relationships, contexts, and the significance and impact of culture and society. Whether we are considered "healthy" or "ill" is not our decision alone to make. Family, friends, coworkers, physicians, and others all shape how we perceive the state of our health. A sociological understanding must take into account how society defines health and illness, what the consequences of such definitions are, and how social position and access to resources shape health outcomes.

CULTURE, SOCIETY, AND HEALTH

Our conceptions of what it means to be healthy vary over time and across cultures. In an attempt to provide a more universally applicable definition, the World Health Organization (WHO), in the preamble to its constitution, defined health as a "state of complete physical, mental, and social well-being, and not merely the absence of disease and infirmity" (World Health Organization 1948). Based on this absolute standard, most of us are probably not fully healthy most of the time. In practice, people fall somewhere along a continuum between this ideal at one extreme and death on the other.

Researchers have shown that diseases and disorders are rooted in the shared meanings of particular cultures. The term **culture-bound syndrome** refers to a disease or illness that cannot be understood apart from some specific social context. This means that there is something particular about the culture—how it is organized, what it believes, what is expected of members—that contributes to that malady (Burns 2013; Romans et al. 2012; Wedge 2012). Examples include amok in Malaysia, in which a knife- or spear-wielding male goes on a seemingly random and totally unanticipated rampage followed by amnesia about doing so (Carr and Tan 1976; Saint Martin 1999; Spores 1988; Williamson 2007). Another is koro, in countries such as China, India, and Malaysia, in which men come to believe their penis is shrinking and that after it fully retracts into their body, they will die (Garlipp 2008; Kumar, Phookun, and Datta 2014).

In our globalized world, the lines between societies have become increasingly permeable so that culture-bound syndromes can now cross boundaries, where they can transform local conceptions of disease (Ventriglio, Ayonrinde, and Bhugra 2016). This seems to have occurred with anorexia nervosa. Formally named as a medical disorder in 1873 by English physician William Gull, people in the United States now commonly associate anorexia with the fear of being fat and a misperception of one's actual body weight. But in the 1990s, psychiatrist Sing Lee wondered why he didn't see such manifestations in Hong Kong. Cases of anorexia were exceedingly rare, and when they did appear, the patients did not exhibit the same kinds of symptoms as in the West. Most did not express a fear of fatness or misperceive themselves to be overweight. In fact, they expressed a desire to return to a normal body weight. They did not obsess over food portions or suppress a strong desire to eat. They weren't enamored with pop culture visions of thinness or hooked on diet books or exercise fads. They just didn't feel hungry or said they had an upset stomach (Lee 1991; Lee, Chiu, and Chen 1989; Lee, Ho, and Hsu 1993; Watters 2010a, 2010b).

This Chinese manifestation of anorexia changed quickly, however, after 14-year-old Charlene Hsu Chi-Ying passed out and died on a busy street in downtown Hong Kong on her way home from school in 1994. She weighed 75 pounds. In an effort to make sense of what had happened, the media covering her death paid significant attention to the way anorexia nervosa was diagnosed in the West, including its emphasis on the fear of fatness and body misperception. Not long after Charlene's death, the number of Lee's patients who exhibited the symptoms more typical of the Western diagnosis rose dramatically. By the late 1990s, as many as 3 to 10 percent of Hong Kong's

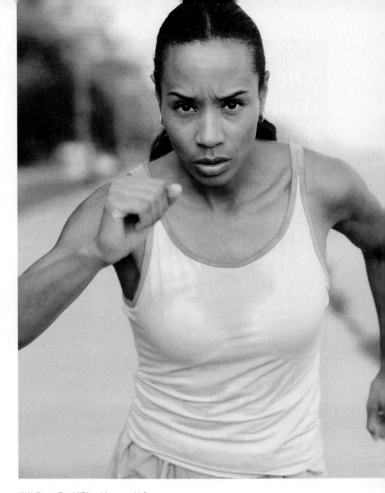

LWA/Dann Tardif/Blend Images LLC

young women exhibited symptoms and, by 2007, 90 percent of Lee's anorexia patients reported a fear of getting fat (Watters 2010a, 2010b). Lee attributes this shift largely to the dominant power the Western medical model has attained in matters of health and illness. The legitimacy of medical books and diagnostic manuals overwhelms alternative conceptions of health and illness. In turn, such models affect what doctors perceive and what patients describe (Watters 2010a).

> **Culture-bound syndrome** A disease or illness that cannot be understood apart from some specific social context.

The fact that culture affects how anorexia nervosa presents itself doesn't make the disease any less real; people die from it. But what it does suggest is that diseases and disorders get manifested, identified, and treated through the lenses culture provides. As noted in the "Constructing Culture" section of Chapter 3, we never interact with nature directly. Culture always mediates, even when it comes to how we understand our bodies. Psychological or physical distress gets manifested through culture-specific symptoms recognized as available within a culture (Watters 2010a). We have no choice but to express things through culture, but we should remember that culture not only enables us to see—and Western medicine's way of seeing has produced amazing results—it also limits what we can see, or give voice to, when it comes to health and illness.

Did You Know?

... The average American adult woman wears a Misses size 16–18 or its equivalent, a Women's Plus size 20W. Her average waist is 39.7 inches.

Source: Christel and Dunn 2016. *Photo:* Alberto Pellaschiar/AP Images

┌─ **SOC**THINK ──────────────────────

What factors shape your likelihood of doing all you can to avoid "being sick"? How might the power others have over you influence your actions? What positions do they occupy relative to you?

└──────────────────────────────────────

can violate the norms that regularly guide their everyday actions, whether as student, parent, or employee. They have a right to expect that others will not blame them for failure to conduct their usual responsibilities and that they will be given space and time to recover. That does not mean they are exempt from social obligations. Those who are deemed legitimately sick have a responsibility to get better as soon as possible, which includes seeking competent professional care. Failure to do so can result in negative sanctions (Parsons 1951, 1975). In fact, especially in the context of competitive work environments, we often look down on those who seem to get sick too easily or frequently, suspecting that they are either lazy or weak. Such attitudes present significant difficulties for those facing chronic health problems.

Physicians and nurses have the power to label people as healthy or sick and, thus, to function as gatekeepers for the sick role. For example, instructors often require students to get a note from a health care professional to verify a claim of illness as a legitimate excuse for missing a paper or an exam. The ill person becomes dependent on the doctor or nurse, because physicians and nurses control the resources that patients need, whether it be a note for a professor or a prescription for medication. We look to such professionals

ILLNESS AND SOCIAL ORDER

From a functionalist perspective, social order is paramount and illness represents a threat to the normal processes of society. To maintain order, we place social pressure on people to continue to perform their normal roles even when they feel sick. As a result, we debate about what it means to be "sick enough" to be considered truly ill. At what point, for example, do we stay home from school or work due to illness, and who gets to decide? All of us have likely faced this dilemma, sometimes dragging ourselves out of bed and going anyway because we felt we needed to be there, whether for the sake of ourselves or for others.

Sick role A form of legitimate deviance in which the person who becomes ill has a corresponding set of rights and responsibilities associated with that status.

When people cross the line into illness, they take on what sociologists call the **sick role,** a form of legitimate deviance in which the person who becomes ill has a corresponding set of rights and responsibilities associated with that status. A sick person

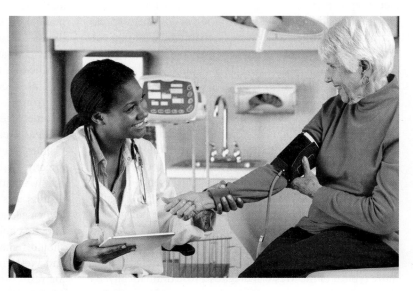

Monkey Business Images/Shutterstock

to solve our health care needs, trusting that they have sufficient expertise and experience to diagnose and treat our problems.

POWER, RESOURCES, AND HEALTH

The faith we place in physicians to heal what ails us has helped them attain significant levels of prestige and power. Over time, the jurisdiction over which medical professionals have authority has expanded. Theorists use the phrase "medicalization of society," taking this extension of medical legitimacy into new realms thus granting medical professional greater power (Conrad 2007; Zola 1972, 1983).

The Medicalization of Society The process of **medicalization** involves redefining new areas of social life as the legitimate domain for medical expertise by converting them into treatable medical conditions. This includes aspects we used to take for granted as involving natural human processes, such as childbirth, aging, menopause, sex, diet, mental health, addictions, sexuality, and even parenting and childhood (Cacchioni and Tiefer 2012; Chavigny 2014; Fainzang 2013; Francis 2012; Shaw 2013). We accept, and even encourage, the expansion of the boundaries of medicine because we hope that these experts can provide factual and effective cures to complex human problems, as they have to various infectious diseases.

This transference of authority to medical professionals is not without consequences. The presumed expertise of these specialists—and the specialized discourse that goes with it—makes it more difficult for common people to join in the discussion and exert their influence, even though their lives may be significantly affected by decisions the experts make. In addition, the natural science orientation of this model makes it more difficult to view these issues as also being shaped by social, cultural, or psychological factors (Davis 2006; Starr 1982; Watters 2010a).

As medical professionals expand their authority, they also engage in boundary maintenance to ensure that only those with appropriate knowledge and training are certified to practice medicine. One of the effects historically was to place some practitioners, such as chiropractors and nurse-midwives, outside the domain of legitimate medicine. Despite the fact that midwives first brought professionalism to child delivery, they have been portrayed by doctors as having invaded the "legitimate" field of obstetrics, in both the United States and Mexico. Nurse-midwives have sought licensing as a way to achieve professional respectability, but physicians continue to exert power to ensure that midwifery remains a subordinate occupation (Scharnberg 2007; Shaw 2013).

Inequities in Health Care Another serious concern regarding power and resources in the context of contemporary medicine involves the glaring inequities that exist in health care. In 1978, at the International Conference on

Primary Health Care, convened by WHO and UNICEF, global health leaders reaffirmed their commitment to health as "a fundamental human right" in the Alma-Ata Declaration. In doing so, they called on all nations to provide sufficient primary health care for all people of the world, a goal that in many respects remains aspirational (Gillam 2008; Hall and Taylor 2003). Around the world, poor areas tend to be underserved because medical services concentrate where the wealth is. The United States, for example, has 117.3 skilled health care professionals, including physicians, nurses, and midwives, per 10,000 people, whereas other nations have much lower rates, such as Sierra Leone with 3.4 per 10,000, Ethiopia with 2.8, Niger with 1.6, and Somalia with 1.1 (World Health Organization 2018c).

The supply of health care in poorer countries is further reduced by what is referred to as **brain drain**—the immigration to the United States and other industrialized nations of skilled workers, professionals, and technicians who are needed in their home countries. As part of this brain drain, physicians, nurses, and other health care professionals have come to the United States from developing

> **Medicalization** The process of redefining new areas of social life as the legitimate domain for medical expertise by converting them into treatable medical conditions.
>
> **Brain drain** The immigration to the United States and other industrialized nations of skilled workers, professionals, and technicians who are needed in their home countries.

Going GLOBAL

Infant Mortality Rates in Selected Countries

Infant deaths per 1,000 live births

Central African Republic 87.6

Sierra Leone 81.7

Somalia 79.7

Haiti 53.9

India 32.0

World 29.4

Mexico 11.5

United States 5.7

Canada 4.5

France 3.5

Japan 1.9

Iceland 1.6

Source: World Bank 2018r.

Mortality Rates in Selected Countries" graph depicts, infant mortality rates in developing countries, such as Central African Republic, Sierra Leone, and Somalia, differ dramatically from those in industrialized nations, such as Iceland, Japan, and France. Such differences reflect unequal distribution of health care resources based on the wealth or poverty of various nations as seen, for example, in prenatal nutrition, delivery procedures, and infant screening measures. An additional way that developing countries suffer the consequences of health care inequality is in reduced life expectancy. Average life expectancy in sub-Saharan African nations is 60 compared to 81 in European Union nations. By comparison, in the United States it is 79 years (World Bank 2018r, 2018s).

Labeling and Power Sometimes the power to label and the power to oppress go hand in hand. A historical example illustrates perhaps the ultimate extreme in labeling social behavior as a sickness. As enslavement of Africans in the United States came under increasing attack in the 19th century, medical authorities provided new rationalizations for the oppressive practice. Noted physicians published articles stating that the skin color of Africans deviated from "healthy" white skin coloring because Africans suffered from congenital leprosy. Moreover, physicians classified the continuing efforts of enslaved Africans to escape from their White masters as an example of the "disease" of drapetomania (or "crazy runaways"). In 1851 the prestigious *New Orleans Medical and Surgical Journal* suggested that the remedy for this "disease" was to treat slaves kindly, as one might treat children. Apparently, these medical authorities would not entertain the view that it was healthy and sane to flee slavery or join in a slave revolt (Szasz 1971).

When AIDS first emerged on the national stage, being labeled "HIV positive" functioned as a master status that overshadowed other aspects of a person's life, creating a stigma for the person diagnosed. Ignorance about its underlying biological causes and fear of catching the deadly disease only made things worse. The fact that a significant proportion of AIDS patients were homosexuals or drug users led critics to say that those who came down with the disease got what they deserved. People wanted to isolate and quarantine patients to keep the disease from spreading (France 2016; Shilts 1987). As a result, a person with AIDS had to deal not only with the serious medical consequences of the disease, but also with the distressing social consequences of the label.

Over time, as medical knowledge increased and social perceptions changed, the stigma associated with AIDS decreased. Today, drugs can reduce the likelihood that the disease progresses from the initial stage of HIV infection to the stage known as AIDS, in which the immune system is badly compromised (Hardin 2012). People's perceptions about its symbolic significance have also shifted. This happened in part due to public figures whose very existence

countries such as India, Pakistan, and various African states. Their emigration represents yet another way in which the world's core industrialized nations enhance their quality of life at the expense of developing countries (Firsing 2016; List 2009).

Such inequities in health care have clear life-and-death consequences. For example, as the "Going Global: Infant

344 · SOC 2020

called into question the stereotypes of AIDS patients, such as NBA superstar Magic Johnson who was diagnosed in 1991 and Ryan White, a 13-year-old with hemophilia who contracted HIV as a result of a blood transfusion in 1984. Attitudes also changed as a result of grassroots activists who worked hard to change the narrative, education campaigns in schools, a change in media coverage, and an overall shift in cultural values regarding homosexuality (France 2016; Shilts 1987). Our perceptions shape the labels we use to define others. As we learned with the Thomas theorem, as those perceptions change, the ways we respond also change. AIDS represents a case where its medicalization as primarily a biological contagion, along with its humanization, reduced the stigma attached to the disease (Drescher 2015).

According to labeling theorists, we can choose whether to view a variety of life experiences as illnesses. The medical community now recognizes premenstrual syndrome, posttraumatic stress disorder,

Ryan White's public battle with AIDS in the late 1980s changed perceptions regarding the disease. Bettmann/Getty Images

and hyperactivity as medical disorders. Homosexuality represents perhaps the most noteworthy medical example of labeling. For years, psychiatrists classified being gay or lesbian as a mental disorder subject to treatment. This official diagnosis by the psychiatry profession became an early target of the growing gay and lesbian rights movement in the United States. In 1974 members of the American Psychiatric Association voted to drop homosexuality from their standard diagnostic manual on mental disorders (Drescher 2015).

NEGOTIATING CURES

In practice, we seek to strike a balance between the authority of the physician and the agency of the patient. Physicians use cues to reinforce their prestige and power. According to medical sociologist Brenda Beagan (2001, 2003), and consistent with Goffman's dramaturgical approach, the technical language students learn in medical school becomes the basis for the script they follow as novice physicians. The familiar white coat and stethoscope is their costume—one that helps them appear confident and professional at the same time that it identifies them as doctors to patients and other staff members. Beagan found that many medical students struggle to project the appearance of competence they think their role demands, but over time most become accustomed to expecting respect and deference.

Patients, however, are not passive. Active involvement in health care can have positive or negative consequences. Sometimes, patients play an active role in health care by choosing not to follow a physician's advice. For example, some patients stop taking medications long before they should. Some decrease or increase the dosage on purpose (because they think they know better what they need), and others never even fill their prescriptions. Such noncompliance results in part from the prevalence of self-medication in our society; many people are accustomed to self-diagnosis and self-treatment.

Patients' active involvement in their health care can have very positive consequences. Some patients consult books, magazines, and websites about preventive health care techniques, attempt to maintain a healthful and nutritious diet, carefully monitor any side effects of medication, and adjust the dosage based on perceived side effects. Recognizing this change, pharmaceutical firms are advertising their prescription drugs directly to potential customers. For their part, medical professionals are understandably suspicious of these new sources of information.

> **Social epidemiology** The study of the role social factors play in the development and distribution of disease throughout the population.
>
> **Prevalence** The total number of cases of a specific disorder that exist at a given time.
>
> **Incidence** The number of new cases of a specific disorder that occur within a given population during a stated period.

It is a lot harder to keep people well than it is to just get them over a sickness.

DeForest Clinton Jarvis (2013)

Studies, including one published in the *Journal of the American Medical Association,* found that health information on the Internet can be incomplete and inaccurate, even on the best sites. Nevertheless, there is little doubt that Internet research is transforming patient–physician encounters (Adams and de Bont 2007; Arora et al. 2008; Fox and Duggan 2013).

>> Health and the Significance of Place

By looking at patterns of health and illness throughout society, we can better understand which factors are at work in shaping health outcomes. **Social epidemiology** investigates the role social factors play in the development and distribution of disease throughout the population. The social positions we occupy shape our chances for a healthy life. Analysis of biological factors alone is insufficient. We must also consider the impact factors such as social class, ethnicity, race, and gender have on our overall health. Statuses such as these influence our access to material, social, and cultural resources. Having enough money to afford health insurance or to purchase foods for a healthy diet; having social connections that open doors in times of crisis or concern; having knowledge about where to get medical information, what to ask the doctor, and what foods to consume are all examples of how our social position shapes our health care outcomes. And yet we tend to minimize the consequences of such differences when considering health care solutions.

To describe how widespread a disease is and how fast it is spreading, social epidemiologists report on rates of prevalence and incidence. **Prevalence** refers to the *total* number of cases of a specific disorder that exist at a given time. At the end of 2016, for example, a total of 991,447 people in the United States were living with a diagnosed HIV infection, and of these cases a total of 525,374 people had advanced to the AIDS stage of the disease (Centers for Disease Control and Prevention 2018b:Tables 22a, 23a). Rather than counting all the cases of a disease in a population, **incidence** refers only to the number of *new* cases of a specific disorder that occur within a given population during a specified period

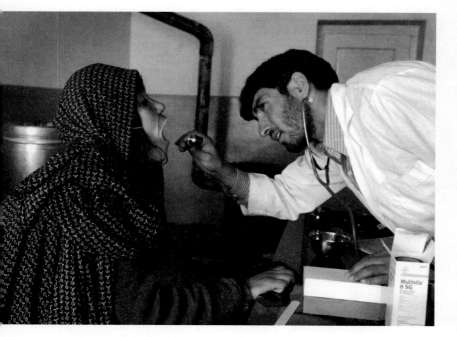

©Jean Marc Giboux/Getty Images

of time, usually a year. For example, 38,281 people were newly diagnosed with HIV infection in 2017 in the United States and 17,604 were people newly diagnosed with AIDS (Centers for Disease Control and Prevention 2018b:Tables 1a, 2a). Globally, in 2017, the prevalence of HIV infections amounted to an estimated 36.9 million people around the world living with the disease, as represented in the "Going Global: HIV Prevalence and Mortality" graph. When it comes to incidence, there were an estimated 1.8 million new HIV cases globally in 2017 (UNAIDS 2018a).

To better understand and measure the prevalence and incidence of disease within and between cultures, researchers rely on rates to provide standardized measures. Two indicators they use to do so include morbidity and mortality. **Morbidity rates** measure the occurrences of illness in a given population over some period of time. These rates can be calculated for both prevalence and incidence. For example, when considering prevalence of HIV infections, the HIV morbidity rate is 306.6 per 100,000 people in the United States at the end of 2016. When considering incidence, the morbidity rate was 11.8 new HIV diagnoses per 100,000 people in 2017 (Centers for Disease Control and Prevention 2018b:Tables 1a, 22a). Globally, by the end of 2017, an estimated 59 percent of HIV-infected patients

around the world were receiving antiretroviral therapy compared to 22.5 percent in 2010 (UNAIDS 2018a).

Whereas morbidity focuses on illness, mortality deals with death. The **mortality rate** refers to the incidence of death in a given population over some period of time. In 2016, 12,287 people in the United States who had been diagnosed with AIDS died, a rate of 3.8 per 100,000 people in the population. The morbidity and mortality rates for both HIV and AIDS in the United States have declined in recent years (Centers for Disease Control and Prevention 2018b:Table 19a). Globally, as depicted in the "Going Global: HIV Prevalence and Mortality" graph, 940,000 AIDS-related deaths occurred in 2017, and the distribution of those deaths varied significantly by region (UNAIDS 2018b).

SOCIAL CLASS

Morbidity and mortality rates vary significantly based on one's social positions, including factors such as social class, race, ethnicity, gender, and age (Barr 2014; National Center for Health Statistics 2018a).

Morbidity rate The occurrences of illness in a given population over some period of time.

Mortality rate The incidence of death in a given population over some period of time.

When it comes to social class, for example, studies in the United States and other countries have consistently shown that people in the lower classes have higher rates of mortality and disability than those in higher classes. And studies of educational attainment, an indicator of both income

Going **GLOBAL**

HIV Prevalence and Mortality

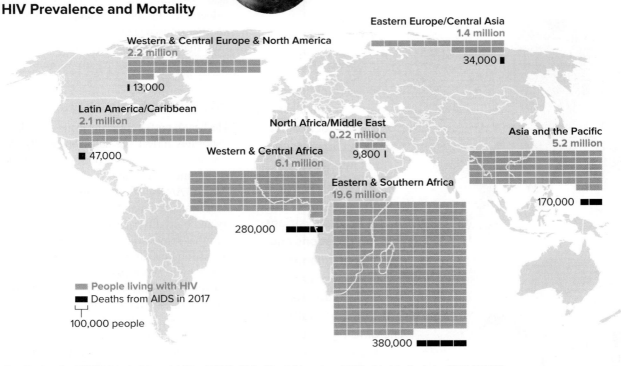

Note: Total number of HIV-infected adults and children in 2017, 36.9 million; total number of AIDS-related deaths during 2017, 940,000.
Source: UNAIDS 2018b.

People without Health Insurance

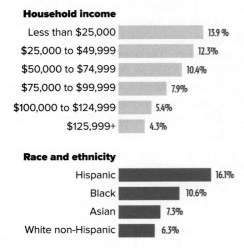

Household income

Less than $25,000	13.9%
$25,000 to $49,999	12.3%
$50,000 to $74,999	10.4%
$75,000 to $99,999	7.9%
$100,000 to $124,999	5.4%
$125,999+	4.3%

Race and ethnicity

Hispanic	16.1%
Black	10.6%
Asian	7.3%
White non-Hispanic	6.3%

Note: Numbers represent the percentage of people without health insurance for the full calendar year.
Source: Berchick, Hood, and Barnett 2018:Tables 4, 5.

and class, show that those with with more education have significantly lower mortality rates than do those with less (Buckles et al. 2016).

A number of factors appear to influence the effect class has on health. Crowded living conditions, substandard housing, poor diet, and stress all contribute to the ill health of many low-income people in the United States. In certain instances, poor education may lead to a lack of awareness of measures necessary to maintain good health. Financial strains are certainly a major factor in the health problems of less-affluent people.

People who are poor—many of whom belong to racial and ethnic minorities—are less able than others to afford quality medical care, as the "People without Health Insurance" graph portrays. Not surprisingly, those with high incomes are significantly more likely to have health insurance, either because they can afford it or because they have jobs that provide it (Berchick, Hood, and Barnett 2018). The ultimate price to pay for a lack of health insurance is the increased risk of early death.

Income level also affects likely life expectancy. Researchers found that the life expectancy for men in the top 1 percent was 14.6 years longer than men in the bottom 1 percent. For women, those in the top 1 percent lived 10.1 years longer on average. Between 2000 and 2014, life expectancy went up for virtually all income groups, but it went up faster for those nearer the top, so the life expectancy gap between the top and bottom income groups got wider over that time (Chetty, Stepner, and Abraham et al. 2016).

Coming from the conflict perspective, Karl Marx would have argued that capitalist societies such as the United States care more about maximizing profits than they do about the health and safety of workers. As a result, government agencies in the United States do not take forceful action to regulate conditions in the workplace, and workers suffer many preventable job-related injuries and illnesses (Centers for Disease Control and Prevention 2018c; Rest 2018). As we will see later in this chapter, research also shows that the lower classes are more vulnerable to environmental pollution, another consequence of capitalist production, than are the affluent, not only where they work but where they live as well.

RACE AND ETHNICITY

The health profiles of many racial and ethnic minorities reflect the social inequality evident in U.S. society. The poor economic and environmental conditions of groups such as African Americans, Hispanics, and Native Americans are manifested in high morbidity and mortality rates for these groups. It is true that some afflictions, such as sickle cell disease among African Americans, are influenced by genetics, but in most instances, environmental factors contribute to the differential rates of disease and death.

As noted in the "Population" section earlier in this chapter, infant mortality is regarded as a primary indicator of health care. There is a significant gap in the United States between the infant mortality rates of African Americans and Whites.

Did You Know?

... In research looking at how social class operates, sociologist Annette Lareau found that middle-class parents and children were more likely to engage with physicians, asking questions and questioning diagnoses. Working-class patients were more deferential to the doctor's authority. The difference between the two affects health outcomes.

Source: Lareau 2003, 2011. *Photo:* UpperCut Images/SuperStock

Infant Mortality Rates in the United States

Race and ethnicity	Infant deaths per 1,000 live births
Black, non-Hispanic	11.21
American Indian or Alaska Native	8.61
Hispanic	4.96
White, non-Hispanic	4.87
Asian or Pacific Islander	3.97

Note: Rates represent the number of infant deaths per 1,000 live births.
Source: Ely, Driscoll, and Mathews 2018.

As the "Infant Mortality Rates in the United States" graph depicts, on average, the rate of infant death is more than twice as high among African Americans. Lack of adequate medical coverage among African Americans, which contributes to low birth weight, plays a major part in that difference (Ely, Driscoll, and Mathews 2018).

Considering mortality rates, African Americans have higher death rates from heart disease, strokes, pneumonia, and diabetes than do Whites (Xu et al. 2018:Table B). Such epidemiological findings are related to the social class effects noted previously—the fact that average income for African Americans is lower than that for Whites. The effect of these factors can be seen in terms of life expectancy. According to statistics from the Centers for Disease Control and Prevention, for babies born in 2016, the life expectancy for non-Hispanic Whites is 78.5 years compared to 74.8 years for non-Hispanic Blacks (National Center for Health Statistics 2018b:Table 15).

The medical establishment is not exempt from institutional discrimination. There is evidence that minorities receive inferior care even when they are insured. Despite having access to care, African Americans, Latinxs, and American Indians are treated unequally as a result of differences in the quality of various health care plans. Furthermore, national clinical studies have shown that even allowing for differences in income and insurance coverage, racial and ethnic minorities are less likely than other groups to receive both standard health care and life-saving treatment (Benjamins and Whitman 2013; Cooper et al. 2012; Schroeder 2016).

Mexican Americans and many other Latinx populations adhere to cultural beliefs that make them less likely to use the established medical system. They may interpret their illnesses according to traditional Latinx folk medicine, or *curanderismo*—a form of holistic health care and healing. *Curanderismo* influences how one approaches health care and even how one defines illness. Although most Hispanics use folk healers, or *curanderos,* infrequently, perhaps 20 percent rely on home remedies. Some define such illnesses as *susto* (fright sickness) and *atague* (fighting attack) according to folk beliefs. Because these complaints often have biological bases, sensitive medical practitioners need to deal with them carefully to diagnose and treat illnesses accurately (Hendrickson 2014; Sanchez 2018; Tafur, Crowe, and Torres 2009).

> **Curanderismo** Latino folk medicine, a form of holistic health care and healing.

Also affecting Latinx morbidity rates is the fact that Latinx individuals are much more likely to wait to seek treatment. This may be due in part, as the previous "People without Health Insurance" graph demonstrates, to their relative lack of health insurance. As a result, Hispanics often seek treatment for pressing medical problems at clinics and emergency rooms rather than receiving regular preventive care through a family physician. Such delays in treatments increase the severity of the consequences of illness and disease (Berchick, Hood, and Barnett 2018).

GENDER

Men and women do differ in their overall health. For example, women live longer than men. Girls born in 2016 can anticipate an average life expectancy of 81.1 years, compared to 76.1 for boys. The good news for men is that, although life expectancy continues to rise for both men and women, rates have been rising even faster for men. As a result, the life expectancy gap between men and women has declined from 7.6 years for those born in 1970 to 5 years in 2016 (National Center for Health Statistics 2018b:Table 15).

Peter Frank/Fancy Photography/Veer

Smoking Rates by Gender

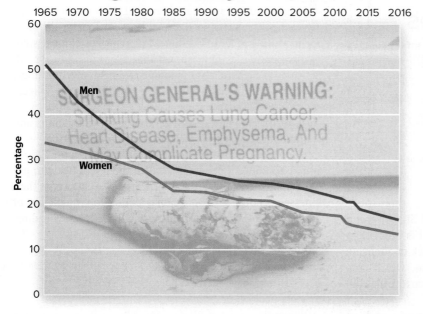

1965 1970 1975 1980 1985 1990 1995 2000 2005 2010 2015 2016

Men

Women

Percentage

60

50

40

30

20

10

0

Source: National Center for Health Statistics 2018b:Table 47. *Photo:* Dan Brandenburg/Getty Images

Greater longevity for women appears to be tied to lifestyle differences between men and women that grow out of gendered norms. Historically, women's lower rate of cigarette smoking (reducing their risk of heart disease, lung cancer, and emphysema), lower consumption of alcohol (reducing the risk of auto accidents and cirrhosis of the liver), and lower rate of employment in dangerous occupations explain about one-third of their greater longevity than men. Researchers argue that women are much more likely than men to seek treatment, to be diagnosed as having a disease, and thus to have their illnesses reflected in the data examined by epidemiologists (National Center for Health Statistics 2018a). Changes in lifestyle do matter. As the "Smoking Rates by Gender" graph shows, the gap in smoking rates between men and women has declined, accounting for some of the reduction in the difference in life expectancy between men and women.

With everything from birth to beauty being treated in an increasingly medical context, women have been particularly vulnerable to the medicalization of society. Ironically, even given the increased power of the medical establishment in women's lives, medical researchers have often excluded them from clinical studies. Female physicians and researchers charge that sexism lies at the heart of such research practices and insist there is a desperate need for studies of female subjects (Johnson et al. 2014; Pinnow et al. 2009).

AGE

Health is the overriding concern of older adults. Most older people in the United States report having at least one chronic illness, but only some of those conditions are potentially life threatening or require medical care. The quality of life among older people is of particular concern in the face of potentially escalating health problems. A substantial number of older people in the United States are troubled by arthritis and other chronic diseases, and many have visual or hearing impairments that can interfere with the performance of everyday tasks (Hootman et al. 2006; National Center for Health Statistics 2018a).

Older people are also especially vulnerable to certain mental health problems. Alzheimer's disease, the leading cause of dementia in the United States, afflicts 10 percent of people aged 65 years and older. In terms of prevalence, that works out to 5.7 million Americans in 2018. That number is projected to grow to 13.8 million in 2050 as the U.S. population ages (Alzheimer's Association 2018).

Because of their increased health risks, the rate at which older people in the United States (aged 75 and older) use health services is more than three times greater than that for younger people (aged 15–24). This heightened use level is tied to health insurance coverage, with people over age 65 the most likely to be covered, as the "Health Insurance Rates by Age" graph portrays. The disproportionate use of the U.S. health

Health Insurance Rates by Age

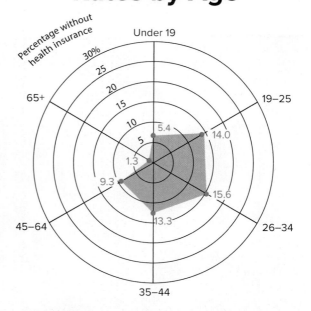

Percentage without health insurance

Under 19

30%

25

20

15

10

5

65+

5.4

14.0

1.3

19–25

9.3

15.6

45–64

13.3

26–34

35–44

Note: Numbers represent the percentage of people without health insurance for the full calendar year.
Source: Berchick, Hood, and Barnett 2018:Table 2.

Availability of Physicians by State

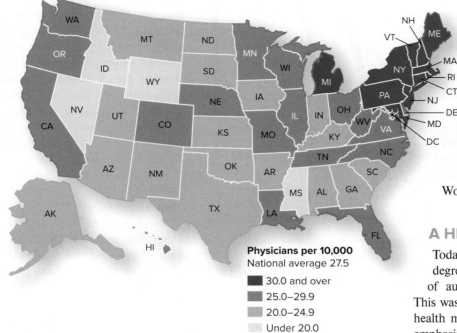

Physicians per 10,000
National average 27.5

- 30.0 and over
- 25.0–29.9
- 20.0–24.9
- Under 20.0

Source: National Center for Health Statistics 2018b:Table 83.

spending to health care, 16.8 percent as measured by GDP, than does any other country in the world. Contrast the U.S. rate with those of countries such as Sweden (11 percent), France (11.1), Japan (10.9), Canada (10.4), or the United Kingdom (9.9). In spite of these expenditure differences, these five nations provide universal health coverage for all their people, while the United States does not (OECD 2018d; World Bank 2018t).

A HISTORICAL VIEW

Today, state licensing and medical degrees confer a widely recognized level of authority on medical professionals. This was not always the case. The "popular health movement" of the 1830s and 1840s emphasized preventive care and what is termed "self-help." It voiced strong criticism of "doctoring" as a paid occupation. New medical philosophies or sects established their own medical schools and challenged the authority and methods of traditional doctors. By the 1840s

care system by older people is a critical factor in all discussions about the cost of health care and possible reforms of the health care system. Many younger people choose not to purchase health insurance in order to save money, and their decision to opt out means fewer people paying in, which means higher costs. The Affordable Care Act, also known as Obamacare, sought to make participation mandatory for this reason (Berchick, Hood, and Barnett 2018:Table 2).

A person's odds of good health are shaped by her or his class, race and ethnicity, gender, and age. Even geography matters, because there are significant differences in the number of physicians from one state to the next. Health care professionals and program advisers need to take such differential effects into account when considering what constitutes equitable health care coverage. Any attempts to do so, however, are constrained by the cost of health care.

>> Health Care in the United States

The costs of health care have skyrocketed over the past few decades. Total expenditures for health care in the United States broke the $500 million barrier in 1987. They quickly went on to reach other milestones, including $1 trillion in 1995, $2 trillion in 2005, and $3 trillion in 2014. In 2017, expenditures worked out to an average of $10,739 per person (Centers for Medicare & Medicaid Services 2018a:Table 1). The United States devotes a greater proportion of its total

Total Health Care Expenditures in the United States

Total expenditure in billions of dollars

$75	$255	$721	$1,369	$2,599	$3,492		$5,370
1970	1980	1990	2000	2010	2017		2025 (projected)

Sources: Centers for Medicare & Medicaid Services 2018a, 2018b.
Photo: Comstock Images/Alamy Stock Photo

most states had repealed medical licensing laws, and the health care field was largely unregulated (Porter 1998, 2004).

In response, through the leadership of the American Medical Association (AMA), founded in 1848, "regular" doctors marginalized lay practitioners, sectarian doctors, and female physicians in general. They institutionalized their authority through standardized programs of education and licensing. Only those who successfully completed AMA programs gained legitimate authority as medical practitioners. The authority of the physician no longer depended on lay attitudes or on the person occupying the sick role; increasingly, it was built into the structure of the medical profession and the health care system.

Jules Frazier/Getty Images

As the institutionalization of health care proceeded, the medical profession gained control over both the market for its services and the various organizational hierarchies that govern medical practice, financing, and policy making. By the 1920s physicians controlled hospital technology, the division of labor of health personnel, and indirectly, other professional practices, such as nursing and pharmaceutical services (Coser 1984; Starr 1982; Whorton 2002).

THE ROLE OF GOVERNMENT

Not until the 20th century did health care receive federal aid in conjunction with the expansion of medicine as a social institution. The first significant government involvement was the 1946 Hill-Burton Act, which provided subsidies for building and improving hospitals, especially in rural areas. An even more important development was the enactment in 1965 of two wide-ranging government assistance programs: Medicare and Medicaid. Medicare provides insurance primarily for those 65 and older in the United States. It is administered by the federal government and funded primarily by a payroll tax on all U.S. workers. In 2018, Medicare covered 59.1 million people. Medicaid, a joint federal and state insurance plan, provides coverage for eligible people who lack sufficient income to pay for their own health care. In 2019, Medicaid covered 75.1 million people (Centers for Medicare & Medicaid Services 2018c).

As health care costs rose, political debates about how best to provide for the public health of the nation became commonplace. In 1993 the Clinton administration proposed health care reform designed to provide universal coverage, but the legislation failed to pass. Throughout the George W. Bush administration, the United States remained the only wealthy, industrialized nation that did not provide some form of universal coverage. Then, following Barack Obama's election as president—after significant debate and against substantial Republican opposition—Congress passed, and President Obama signed, the Patient Protection and Affordable Care Act and the Health Care and Education Reconciliation Act in March 2010 (Brill 2015).

In terms of its structure, the Affordable Care Act (ACA), also referred to as Obamacare, has three main elements and has been described as a three-legged stool, meaning if you remove any of the three, the whole thing will collapse. The first leg is known as a community rating, which means that premiums customers pay will be based on age, geographic location, size of family, and tobacco use rather than their underlying physical condition. In other words, insurance companies cannot discriminate against people with preexisting conditions by refusing them coverage or charging them higher rates. To compensate for the increased insurance costs that result from this, the second leg mandates that everyone must obtain insurance, whether through their employer, the government, or the marketplace. Those who don't would have to pay a penalty. The third leg involves providing subsidies to those who cannot afford to purchase insurance on their own. The combination of all three elements distributes the costs of health care across a larger pool of participants while assisting those who would otherwise lack the means to pay for it (Gruber 2010).

President Barack Obama signs the Affordable Care Act into law. Chip Somodevilla/Getty Images

To ensure that all three elements were provided for, the Affordable Care Act contained the following provisions:

- Young adults may stay on their parents' health care plans until age 26.
- Coverage for checkups and other preventive care does not require copays.
- Annual caps and lifetime limits on the cost of benefits patients can receive were eliminated.
- People with preexisting conditions cannot be denied coverage, and companies are no longer able to cut employees from a plan when they get sick.
- Most Americans are required to purchase some form of health insurance.
- Tax credits for the purchase of insurance are available for individuals and families between 100 and 400 percent of the poverty level.
- Companies with more than 50 employees are required to provide an employer-sponsored health plan that provides a mandated level of minimal coverage.
- Small businesses are eligible to receive tax credits to assist them in providing coverage.
- State-based insurance exchanges offer a choice of plans for small businesses and people who lack employer-supplied coverage.
- Insurance companies are required to provide greater transparency regarding spending on overhead costs.

After the Affordable Care Act was fully implemented, the rate of Americans without insurance began to fall, as the "U.S. Uninsured Rate, 1997–2018" graph shows. This was true for people at all income levels and from all racial and ethnic groups (Berchick, Hood, and Barnett 2018). In spite of this, however, many Republicans continued to prefer market-based solutions, arguing that free-market capitalism would lead to greater efficiency and cost control.

> **Holistic medicine** Therapies in which the health care practitioner considers the person's physical, mental, emotional, and spiritual characteristics.

In 2016, Republicans running for Congress, along with presidential candidate Donald Trump, pledged to repeal and replace Obamacare on the first day of the new term. Once elected, however, they ran into the challenge presented by the three-legged stool. The first leg, which ensured people with preexisting conditions would not be discriminated against, was quite popular. Elimination of the second leg, the mandate requiring the purchase of insurance, a particularly unpopular element of the ACA, meant fewer people paying into the system, which would mean higher prices for those who remain. Elimination of the subsidies, the third leg, meant those without means to afford insurance drop out, again reducing the number of people participating in the system and raising costs (Gruber 2010). Efforts at outright repeal failed, but the requirement that people pay a penalty if they lack some form of insurance coverage, the second leg of the stool, was eliminated effective January 1, 2019. This change raised questions about the stability of the overall system moving forward. As noted in the discussion regarding citizenship rights in the "Balancing Economic and Political Power" section of Chapter 9, the questions regarding how best to approach health insurance hinge on the question of whether health should be considered a social right, something guaranteed for all (Marshall 1950).

U.S. Uninsured Rate, 1997–2018

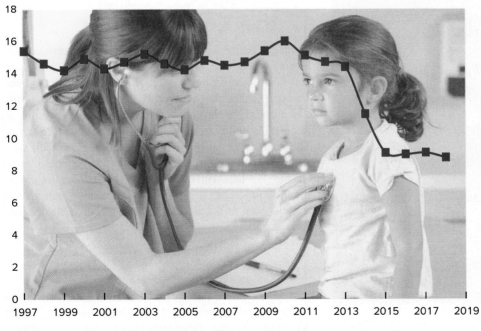

Note: Percentage of all persons without health insurance at the time of the interview. Data come from the National Health Interview Survey.
Sources: Martinez, Zammitti, and Cohen 2018:Table 1; Ward et al. 2016:Table 1.1b. *Photo:* Cathy Yeulet/Stockbroker/123RF

COMPLEMENTARY AND ALTERNATIVE MEDICINE

In modern forms of health care, people rely on physicians and hospitals for the treatment of illness. Yet a significant proportion of adults in the United States attempt to maintain good health or respond to illness through the use of alternative health care techniques. For example, in recent decades, interest has been growing in holistic medical principles, first developed in China. **Holistic medicine** refers to therapies in which the health care practitioner considers the person's physical, mental, emotional, and spiritual characteristics. The individual is regarded as a totality rather than a collection of interrelated organ systems. Treatment methods include massage, chiropractic medicine, acupuncture, respiratory exercises, and the use of herbs as remedies. Nutrition, exercise, and visualization may also be used to treat ailments (Barnes, Bloom, and Nahin 2008; Stratton and McGivern-Snofsky 2008).

The medical establishment—professional organizations, research hospitals, and medical schools—continues to zealously protect its authority. However, a major breakthrough occurred in 1992 when the federal government's National Institutes of Health (NIH)—the nation's major funding source for biomedical research—opened the National Center for Complementary and Alternative Medicine and empowered it to accept grant requests. An NIH-sponsored national study found that 33.2 percent of adults in the United States had used some form of complementary or alternative medicine within the previous year. As the "Complementary and Alternative Medicine Use" graph demonstrates, examples include natural dietary supplements (such as fish oil, glucosamine, echinacea, or ginseng), deep breathing, and

Anthropocene A geological epoch in which human actions, even at a micro level, have global environmental consequences.

Human ecology The area of study concerned with the interrelationships between people and their environment.

meditation. When private or communal prayer was included as part of the NIH-sponsored 2002 study, the number rose to 62.1 percent (Barnes et al. 2004; Clarke et al. 2015).

On the international level, the World Health Organization (WHO) has begun to monitor the use of alternative medicine around the world. According to the WHO, 80 percent of people in some African and Asian countries use alternative medicine, from herbal treatments to the services of a faith healer. In most countries, these treatments are largely unregulated, even though some of them can be fatal. For example, kava kava, an herbal tea used in the Pacific Islands to relieve anxiety, can be toxic to the liver in concentrated form. Other alternative treatments have been found to be effective in the treatment of serious diseases, such as malaria and sickle-cell anemia. WHO's goal is to compile a list of such practices, as well as to encourage the development of universal training programs and ethical standards for practitioners of alternative medicine (World Health Organization 2005, 2013a).

Sociological analysis of health and illness suggests that if we are to understand sickness we must look beyond biology. Society and culture, family and friends, the medical profession, and social position all help shape medical outcomes. Given the increasing costs of health care, and the fact that different groups experience different outcomes, this issue becomes one of equality and fairness. Lives are at stake. It is precisely such concerns that drive debates about the expansion of health care coverage as a social right.

Complementary and Alternative Medicine Use

Dietary supplements	17.7
Deep breathing	10.9
Yoga	10.1
Chiropractic	8.4
Meditation	8.0
Massage therapy	6.9
Special diets	3.0
Homeopathic treatment	2.2
Progressive relaxation	2.1
Guided imagery	1.7

Note: Dietary supplements include nonvitamin and nonmineral supplements such as fish oil, glucosamine, and probiotics. Special diets include vegetarian, vegan, macrobiotic, and others.
Source: Clarke et al. 2015. *Photo:* Anthony Saint James/Photodisc/Getty Images

>> Sociological Perspectives on the Environment

Humans' interdependent relationships with one another also extend to the natural environment. The choices we make are constrained by available natural resources. Through technology we modify nature to suit our needs, and throughout history humans have demonstrated an astonishing ability to do so, but not without consequences. The benefits of the Industrial Revolution came with costs such as air pollution, water pollution, and global climate change. We have entered an era of what some are calling the **Anthropocene,** a geological epoch in which human actions, even at a micro level, have global environmental consequences (Sample 2014).

HUMAN ECOLOGY

Human ecology is an area of study that is concerned with interrelationships between people and their environment. As biologist and environmentalist Barry Commoner (1971:39) put it during the early stages of the modern environmental movement, "Everything is connected to everything else." Human ecologists focus on how the physical environment shapes people's lives and on how people influence the surrounding environment.

In an application of the human ecological perspective, sociologists and environmentalists have identified several relationships between the environment and people. Among them are the following:

- *The environment provides the resources essential for life.* These include air, water, and materials used to create shelter, transportation, and needed products. If human societies exhaust these resources—for example, by polluting the water supply or cutting down rain forests—the consequences could be dire.
- *The environment serves as a waste repository.* More so than other living species, humans produce a huge quantity and variety of waste products—bottles, cans, boxes, paper, sewage, garbage, and so on. Various types of pollution have become more common because human societies are generating more wastes than the environment can safely absorb.
- *The environment "houses" our species.* It is our home, our living space, the place where we reside, work, and play. At times we take this truism for granted, but not when day-to-day living conditions become unpleasant and problematic. If our air is polluted, if our tap water turns brown, or if toxic chemicals seep into our neighborhood, we remember why it is vital to live in a healthful environment.

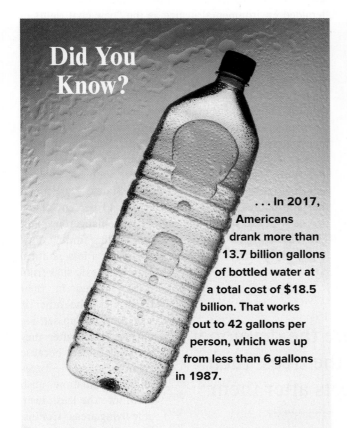

Did You Know?

. . . In 2017, Americans drank more than 13.7 billion gallons of bottled water at a total cost of $18.5 billion. That works out to 42 gallons per person, which was up from less than 6 gallons in 1987.

Source: Arthur 2018. *Photo:* Digital Vision/PictureQuest

There is no shortage of illustrations of the interconnectedness of humans and the environment. For example, scientific research has linked pollutants in the environment to people's health and behavior. The increasing prevalence of asthma, lead poisoning, and cancer has been tied to human alterations to the environment. Similarly, the rise in melanoma (skin cancer) diagnoses has been linked to global climate change. And ecological changes in our food and diet have been related to childhood obesity and diabetes (Demeneix 2017; Hill 2010).

With its view that "everything is connected to everything else," human ecology stresses the trade-offs inherent in every decision that alters the environment. In facing the environmental challenges of the 21st century, government policy makers and environmentalists must determine how they can fulfill humans' pressing needs for food, clothing, and shelter while preserving the environment as a source of resources, a waste repository, and a home.

POWER, RESOURCES, AND THE ENVIRONMENT

Analyzing environmental issues from a world systems approach allows us to better understand the global consequences of differential access to resources. This approach highlights the difference in relative power between core nations, which control wealth and so dominate the global economy, and developing countries, which lack control and whose resources are exploited. This process only intensifies the destruction of natural resources in poorer regions of the world. Less affluent nations are being forced to exploit their mineral deposits, forests, and fisheries to meet their debt obligations. People in developing nations often end up turning to the only means of survival available to them, including plowing mountain slopes, burning sections of tropical forests, and overgrazing grasslands. The resulting reduction of the rain forest, for example, affects worldwide weather patterns, heightening the gradual warming of the Earth (Jorgenson 2015; Parks and Roberts 2010; Pollini 2009).

Although destruction of the rain forest has long been a concern, only in the past few decades have policy makers begun to listen to the indigenous peoples who live in these areas. Preservation of the rain forests may make sense at the global level, but for many local peoples, it limits their ability to cultivate crops or graze cattle. Even though it harms the global environment, they feel they have no choice but to take advantage of their available resources. In 2008, native peoples from Brazil to the Congo to Indonesia convened to make the case that wealthier countries should compensate them for conservation of the tropical rain forests (Barrionuevo 2008; Birdsall and Kuczynski 2015).

There is, in fact, a certain amount of ethnocentrism involved when people in industrialized countries insist that those developing nations change their practices to save the planet. In calling for the poverty-stricken and "food-hungry" populations of the world to sacrifice, they should also consider the lifestyle consequences for the "energy-hungry" nations. The industrialized nations of North America and Europe account for only 12 percent of the world's population but are responsible for 60 percent of worldwide consumption. The money their residents spend on ocean cruises each year could provide clean drinking water for everyone on the planet. Ice cream expenditures in Europe alone could be used to immunize every child in the world. The global consumer represents a serious environmental threat, but it is often difficult to look in the mirror and blame ourselves because our individual contribution to the problem seems so small. Collectively, however, the choices we make have a significant global impact (Diamond 2008; Gardner, Assadourian, and Sarin 2004).

The rise in global consumption is tied to a capitalist system that depends on growth for its survival. Capitalism creates a "treadmill of production" (Baer 2008; Gould, Pellow, and Schnaiberg 2008). Cutting back on consumption means cutting back on purchases, which leads to reduced production and the loss of profits and jobs. This treadmill necessitates creating an increasing demand for products, obtaining natural resources at minimal cost, and manufacturing products as quickly and cheaply as possible—no matter what the long-term environmental consequences.

Environmental justice A legal strategy based on claims that racial minorities are subjected disproportionately to environmental hazards.

ENVIRONMENTAL JUSTICE

In the autumn of 1982, nearly 500 African Americans participated in a six-week protest against a hazardous waste landfill containing cancer-causing chemicals in Warren County, North Carolina. Their protests and legal actions continued until 2002, when decontamination of the site finally began. This 20-year battle can be seen as yet another "not-in-my-backyard" (NIMBY) event in which people desire the benefits of growth but want someone else to pay for its negative effects. In any event, the Warren County struggle is viewed as a transformative moment in contemporary environmentalism: the beginning of the environmental justice movement (Hager 2017; McGurty 2007; Wong 2016).

Environmental justice is a legal strategy based on claims that racial minorities are subjected disproportionately to environmental hazards. Some observers have heralded environmental justice as the "new civil rights of the 21st century" (Kokmen 2008:42). Since the advent of the environmental justice movement, activists and scholars have identified other environmental disparities that break along racial and social class lines. In general, poor people and people of color are much more likely than others to be victimized by the everyday consequences of economic development, including air pollution from expressways and incinerators (Sandler and Pezzullo 2007; Schlosberg 2013).

Sociologists Paul Mohai and Robin Saha (2007) examined more than 600 hazardous waste treatment, storage, and disposal facilities in the United States. They found that non-Whites and Latinxs make up 43 percent of the people who live within one mile of these dangerous sites. There are two possible explanations for this finding. One is that racial and ethnic minorities possess less political power than others, so they cannot prevent toxic sites from being located in their backyards. The other is that they end up settling near the sites after they are constructed, because economics and the forces of discrimination push them into the least desirable living areas (Collins, Munoz, and JaJa 2016).

> Suburbia is where the developer bulldozes out the trees, then names the streets after them.
>
> **Bill Vaughan**

Public Perception of Environmental Issues

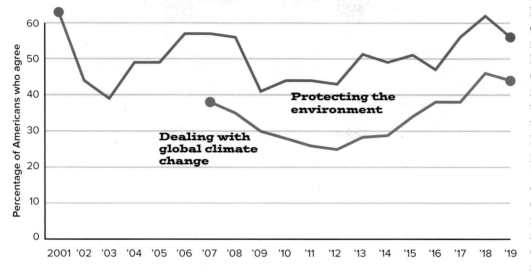

Note: When asked to identify priorities for Congress and the president, response options included top priority, important but lower priority, not too important. After 2014, wording changed from "global warming" to "global climate change."
Source: Pew Research Center 2019a.

AIR POLLUTION

Worldwide, an estimated 4.2 million premature deaths occurred due to outdoor air pollution in 2016. Of these, 91 percent lived in low- and middle-income countries. Another 3.8 million died due to household air pollution (World Health Organization 2018d). Unfortunately, in cities around the world, residents have come to accept polluted air as normal. Urban air pollution is caused primarily by emissions from automobiles and secondarily by emissions from electric power plants and heavy industries. Air pollution not only limits visibility, but also can lead to health problems as uncomfortable as eye irritation and as deadly as lung cancer. Such problems are especially severe in developing countries (United Nations Environment Programme 2014, 2018).

People are capable of changing their behavior, but they are also often unwilling to make such changes permanent. During the 1984 Olympics in Los Angeles, authorities

When it comes to public concern about the environment, as the "Public Perception of Environmental Issues" graph shows, attitudes have shifted over time. People distinguish between general concern about environmental issues and global climate change more specifically. In surveys asking about future development of U.S. energy supplies, Americans showed stronger support for alternative sources than conventional ones. Given the option, 65 percent preferred wind, solar, and the like compared to 27 percent who preferred expanding production of oil, coal, and natural gas. A clear political divide existed in their responses, with 81 percent of Democrats preferring alternative sources compared to 45 percent of Republican (Kennedy 2017; Pew Research Center 2019a).

>> Environmental Problems

Until, in some distant future, humans colonize another planet, Earth is our only home. The natural environment provides for all our needs. But in consuming, we inevitably also produce waste. Some leftovers from consumption are biodegradable and some get recycled, but others can last for hundreds of years and more. Some go into the air, into the water, and still more into the Earth.

Movies 5 ON THE ENVIRONMENT

Anthropocene
Consequences of human environmental domination.

WALL-E
A robot in the year 2700 discovers his destiny.

Age of Consequences
The intersection of climate change, resource scarcity, migration, and conflict.

Rodents of Unusual Size
The nutrias are taking over but not without a fight.

Chasing Ice
A climate change skeptic's doubts melt through the lens of his camera.

asked residents to carpool and stagger their work hours to relieve traffic congestion and improve the quality of the air athletes would breathe. These changes resulted in a remarkable 12 percent drop in ozone levels. After the Olympics ended, however, people reverted to their normal behavior, and the ozone levels climbed again. Similarly, China took drastic action to ensure that Beijing's high levels of air pollution did not mar the 2008 Olympic Games. Construction work in the city ceased, polluting factories and power plants closed down, and workers swept roads and sprayed them with water several times a day. This temporary solution, however, has not solved China's ongoing pollution problem (*The Economist* 2008).

WATER POLLUTION

Throughout the United States, waste materials dumped by industries and local governments have polluted streams, rivers, and lakes. Consequently, many bodies of water have become unsafe for fishing and swimming, let alone drinking. Around the world, pollution of the oceans is an issue of growing concern. For example, when the Deepwater Horizon oil-well explosion occurred in the Gulf of Mexico in 2010, 4.2 million barrels of oil poured into the water. The spill affected birds, fish, mammals, and their habitats.

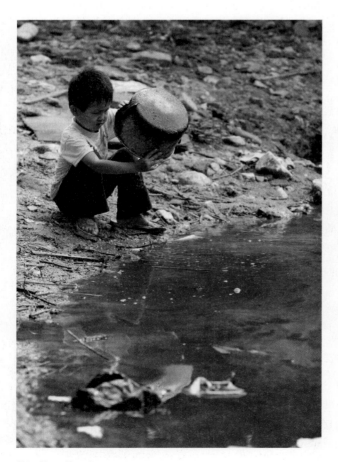

China Photos/Getty Images

In the two years following its occurrence, 675 dolphins were stranded in the northern Gulf of Mexico compared to an annual average of 74 before the spill; deep-water corals experienced significant stress; the nitrogen cycle for microorganisms was inhibited; and 102 species of birds were harmed (Cornwall 2015; *National Geographic* 2012).

This incident is one among many water-based accidents that have resulted in significant environmental harm. When the oil tanker *Exxon Valdez* ran aground in Prince William Sound, Alaska, in 1989, its cargo of 11 million gallons of crude oil spilled into the sound and washed onto the shore, contaminating 1,285 miles of shoreline. Altogether, about 11,000 people joined in a massive cleanup effort that cost more than $2 billion. Globally, oil spills occur regularly. In 2002 the oil tanker *Prestige* spilled twice as much fuel as the *Valdez,* greatly damaging coastal areas in Spain and France (ITOPF 2006).

Less dramatic than large-scale accidents or disasters, but more common in many parts of the world, are problems with the basic water supply. Worldwide, more than 844 million people lack safe and adequate drinking water, and 2 billion rely on a drinking water source contaminated with feces. When it comes to sanitation facilities, 2.3 billion lack access—a problem that further threatens the quality of water supplies. The health costs of unsafe water are enormous (World Health Organization 2018e, 2018f).

Given such water concerns, it should not come as a surprise that water is now a highly contested commodity in many parts of the world. In the United States, competition over water is intense, especially in the Southwest including cities such as Las Vegas. In the Middle East, the immense political challenges posed by ethnic and religious conflict are often complicated by battles over water. There, competing nations accuse each other of taking unfair advantage of existing water supplies, and water tanks are a likely target for both military forces and terrorists (Carmichael 2007; Scott 2018).

GLOBAL CLIMATE CHANGE

The scientific evidence for global climate change is clear, consistent, and compelling, yet public opinion polls show that people remain skeptical. Global warming, one of the key indicators of global climate change, refers to the significant rise in the Earth's surface temperatures that occurs when industrial gases such as carbon dioxide turn the planet's atmosphere into a virtual greenhouse. As the "Global Temperature, 1850–2018" graph shows, the warmest global temperatures in the era for which we have detailed meteorological measurements around the world have all come in the most recent decades. Globally, 8 of the warmest years on record occurred in the last 10 years. Even one additional degree of warmth in the planet's average temperature increases the likelihood of wildfires, shrinking rivers and lakes, desert expansion, and torrential downpours, including typhoons and hurricanes (Climatic Research Unit, University of East Anglia 2019).

Global Temperature, 1850–2018

Note: The base line (0°C) is the average global air temperature from 1961 to 1990. Temperatures beneath that line are below that average and temperatures above that line are above that average. The hottest years on record have all occurred within the past two decades.

Source of data: Climatic Research Unit, University of East Anglia 2019.

Scientists now track carbon dioxide emissions around the world and can map the current and projected contribution each country makes. As the "Going Global: CO_2 Emissions per Capita" graph portrays, the United States produces a sizable amount of carbon dioxide per person relative to other nations, ranking 11th of 250 nations for which there are data (World Bank 2016r). Data on temperature and carbon dioxide emissions contribute to the scientific consensus regarding global climate change. In a study of 24,210 articles published in peer-reviewed scientific journals from 2013 to 2014 and written by a total of 69,406 authors, only 5 articles with a total of 4 authors rejected the conclusion that human-caused global warming is happening (Powell 2015). By contrast, when looking at public opinion, only 48 percent of Americans think that global climate change is due to human activity, and another 31 percent attribute climate change to natural causes (Funk and Kennedy 2016).

We can again draw on world systems analysis when it comes to seeing who pays the highest price for global climate changes. Historically, core nations have been the major emitters of greenhouse gases. Today, much manufacturing has moved to semiperiphery and periphery nations, where greenhouse gas emissions are escalating. Ironically, many of those who are now calling for a reduction in the human activity that contributes to global climate change are located in core nations, which have contributed disproportionately to the problem. We want our hamburgers, but we decry the destruction of the rain forests to create grazing land for cattle. We want inexpensive clothes and toys, but we condemn developing countries for depending

on coal-fired power plants, the number of which are expected to increase 46 percent by 2030. The challenge of global climate change, then, is closely tied to global inequality (Jenkins 2008; Leonard 2010; Roberts, Grines, and Manale 2003).

Of course, the consequences of environmental change, whether in the form of pollution or climate change, are extensive. The impacts of plastics, detergents, synthetic fibers, pesticides, herbicides, and chemical fertilizers challenge the ecosystems necessary for the survival of some species. Some environmentalists express concern that we may be entering a new age of extinction (Kolbert 2014). As the "Threatened and Endangered Species" graph shows, fish and amphibians are particularly vulnerable.

THE GLOBAL RESPONSE

Globalization can be both good and bad for the environment. On the negative side, it can create a race to the bottom as polluting companies relocate to countries with

CO_2 Emissions Per Capita

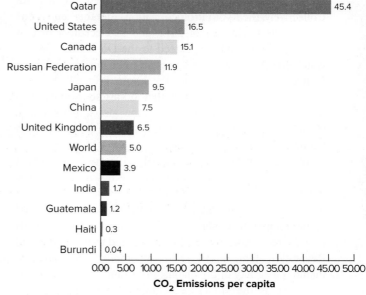

Note: Annual emissions per capita measured in metric tons.
Source: World Bank 2018u.

Threatened and Endangered Species

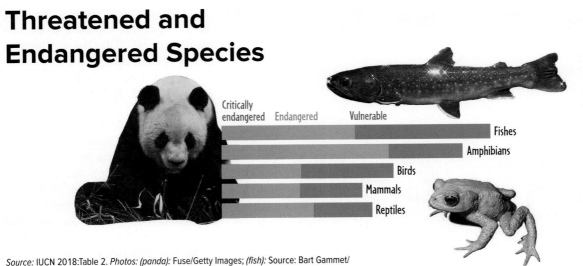

Source: IUCN 2018:Table 2. Photos: (panda): Fuse/Getty Images; (fish): Source: Bart Gammet/ USFWS; (toad): Source: U.S. Fish and Wildlife Service, Charles H. Smith

less stringent environmental standards. Also of concern is that globalization allows multinationals to exploit the resources of developing countries for short-term profit. From Mexico to China, the industrialization that often accompanies globalization has increased pollution of all types.

Yet globalization can have a positive impact as well. As barriers to the international movement of goods, services, and people fall, multinational corporations have an incentive to carefully consider the cost of natural resources. The Kyoto Protocol, for example, demonstrated that countries around the world can come together to take action that makes a significant difference. Established in 1997 and enacted in 2005, the Kyoto Protocol intended to provide a unified response to reducing global emissions of greenhouse gases. Nearly 200 countries ratified the accord. Collectively, the Kyoto Protocol nations met their emissions goal by the target year of 2012, and in December of that year some of the nations agreed to the Doha Amendment, which established a new set of goals to be met by 2020. The United States did not ratify the Kyoto Protocol, because U.S. political leaders feared that doing so would place the nation at a disadvantage in the global marketplace (Clark 2012; United Nations Framework Convention on Climate Change 2015a,2015b).

In Paris, on December 12, 2015, 195 countries agreed to a new international climate pact. Known as the Paris Agreement, it went into effect on November 4, 2016. The agreement commits the nations of the world to limiting the global temperature increase to less than 2 degrees Celsius (3.6 degrees Fahrenheit) when compared to pre-Industrial Revolution temperatures. To accomplish this goal, it includes a variety of provisions. For example, it encourages and rewards the reduction of deforestation. The nations also agreed to provide sufficient funding, including public funds, to make progress possible. Further, they agreed to

Global Concern Regarding Climate Change

Spain 89%
Greece 79%
Kenya 76%
France 72%
Mexico 72%
Brazil 67%
Canada 60%
United States 56%
Turkey 53%
India 47%
Russia 35%

Note: Percentage of people responding that global climate change represents a "major threat" to their country.
Source: Poushter and Manevich 2017. Photos: (top): Kim Steele/Photographer's Choice/Getty Images; (bottom): Stockbyte/Punchstock/Getty Images

transparency in how progress would be measured. And they affirmed that it will take developing nations longer to reduce their emissions, but it did not exempt such nations from moving in that direction (as occurred with the Kyoto Protocol). Overall, the nations committed to minimizing the loss and damage that results from climate change, noting that such losses are inevitable even with this agreement in place, especially for vulnerable nations. And they committed to meeting every five years to review progress and establish new emission-reduction targets.

The agreement was hailed a historic milestone in international cooperation. However, in June 2017, President Trump announced that the United States would begin the process of withdrawing from the accord which, according to the agreement, cannot be completed until November 2020 at the earliest. In response, 18 states, representing 43 percent of the U.S. population, joined together to form the United States Climate Alliance. Together they intend to implement policies in keeping with the Paris Agreement goals (Bradsher 2016; Davenport et al. 2015; United Nations 2016c; United States Climate Alliance 2018).

Perhaps, as Émile Durkheim argued long ago, by recognizing our mutual interdependence, we will take the steps necessary to bring about positive social change. Sociology helps us better see the ways we are interconnected by highlighting the significance of the system as a whole, as well as raising awareness about the inequalities that are a consequence

Jonas Marcos B. San Luis/Cutcaster

of the global system we have constructed. Such analysis can prepare us to more effectively respond to the global challenges we face.

SOCIOLOGY IS A VERB

Health and Environment

Conduct a mini-survey of 10 friends, family members, and/or classmates. How concerned are they about global climate change? How concerned are they about health care? What do they think are the major issues in each? What are the obstacles to positive change in each? Record their responses. How did answers vary depending on how old they are, how much education they have, whether they are male or female, or other possible variables?

For REVIEW

I. **What role do population dynamics play in shaping our lives?**
    - Population dynamics provide a context within which we are born, live, move, and even die, and population trends vary significantly across time and between nations, shaping our life chances.

II. **What does sociology contribute to something as seemingly biological as health?**
    - Our understanding of what counts as health and illness is shaped by the society to which we belong. Similarly, our social position and control over resources shape our likelihood of exposure to illness and our access to health care.

III. **What environmental lessons do we learn from sociology?**
    - The natural environment represents our human home, within which all social interaction occurs, and the way we organize our social relations influences the effects we have on the environment. Countries that control a larger amount of resources have a bigger impact and therefore bear a greater responsibility for those effects.

SOCVIEWS on Population, Health, and Environment

Functionalist View

Over time, population levels naturally reach a balance that maximizes social order.

Health care is a social institution that provides for our health and welfare and thus preserves **social order.**

As we become more socially, economically, and environmentally **interdependent**, new, more global conscious, norms and values arise.

SOCIAL ORDER, INTERCONNECTEDNESS
KEY CONCEPTS

Conflict View

Population crises are driven more by battles over resources than by natural processes.

Core nations **exploit** the natural resources of developing nations on the periphery without taking responsibility for the consequences.

Poor people and minorities suffer disproportionately from **inequities** in health care and exposure to environmental hazards, such as toxic waste and air and water pollution.

KEY CONCEPTS
CONTROL, INEQUALITY, EXPLOITATION

Interactionist View

Changes in population trends show the importance of the choices we make in shaping society.

Patients can play an **active role** in their health both by seeking out a physician's services and by choosing whether or not to follow a doctor's orders.

The degree to which we think significant environmental problems exist is a consequence of **socialization** by family, friends, teachers, television, and so on.

KEY CONCEPTS
ACTIVITY, INTERACTION

MAKE THE CONNECTION

After reviewing the chapter, answer the following questions:

1
How would each perspective approach the study of the protests over the Dakota Access Pipeline?

2
How would each of the perspectives approach the demographic transition model, and how would their insights differ?

3
What insights would we gain from each perspective regarding the current state of health care in the United States, including recent health care reform efforts?

4
Look at your experience with the medical world from an interactionist perspective. What were your interactions with the doctors and nurses like? Have you taken an active role or a passive role as a patient?

Pop Quiz

1. **How is the total fertility rate defined?**
   a. number of children born over a given period of time
   b. number of live births per 1,000 people in the population in a given year
   c. average number of children a woman would have during her lifetime given current birthrates and assuming she survives through her childbearing years
   d. minimum number of children a woman would need to average in her lifetime to reproduce the population in the next generation

2. **What term is used when people leave a population group to which they had belonged?**
   a. immigration
   b. replacement
   c. emigration
   d. transition

3. **What was the relationship between birthrates and death rates throughout most of human history as described by the demographic transition model?**
   a. Both were low.
   b. Death rates were low; birthrates were high.
   c. Birthrates were low; death rates were high.
   d. Both were high.

4. **A disease that cannot be understood apart from its specific social context is an example of**
   a. human ecology.
   b. culture-bound syndrome.
   c. the sick role.
   d. holistic medicine.

5. **Which of the following represents a form of legitimate deviance in which the person who becomes ill has a corresponding set of rights and responsibilities associated with that status?**
   a. medicalization
   b. the sick role
   c. brain drain
   d. social epidemiology

6. **In the area of social epidemiology, what does prevalence refer to?**
   a. the rate at which key indicators change over time
   b. the total number of cases of a specific disorder that exist at a given period of time
   c. the likelihood that a disease or illness will be labeled as such in a given cultural context
   d. the number of new cases of a specific disorder that occur within a given population during a stated period

7. **The age group that is most likely to be covered by some form of health insurance is**
   a. under 18.
   b. 18–34.
   c. 35–64.
   d. 65 and older.

8. **Which of the following is *not* one of the three main elements of the Affordable Care Act (also known as Obamacare)?**
   a. a mandate requiring coverage
   b. subsidies for those who cannot afford insurance
   c. community rating pricing
   d. Medicare for all

9. **What is the term used for the geological epoch in which human actions affect the environment on a global scale?**
   a. Jurassic
   b. Homocene
   c. demographic
   d. Anthropocene

10. **What is the international treaty that sought to reduce global emissions of greenhouse gases?**
    a. Valdez Treaty
    b. Paris Agreement
    c. Port Huron Statement
    d. Gore Accord

1. (c), 2. (c), 3. (d), 4. (b), 5. (b), 6. (b), 7. (d), 8. (d), 9. (d), 10. (b)

Design Elements: *Going Global (Earth):* ©Studio Photogram/Alamy Stock Photo; *Personal Sociology (drawing of author):* McGraw-Hill Education; *5 Movies (popcorn):* ©D. Hurst/Alamy Stock Photo; *Sociology Is a Verb (overlapping hands):* ©Jeff DeWeerd/Imagezoo/Getty Images

CHANGING THE WORLD
ONE STUDENT AT A TIME

"We've had enough. We are the generation that was born after Columbine. We have lived with this our entire lives and now it happened at my school. I spent two hours in a closet just hiding and I am done hiding. We're done hiding. America is done hiding" (quoted in Sreenivasan 2018).

Ryan Deitsch, a senior at Marjorie Stoneman Douglas High School, spoke these words just a few days after the school shooting that killed 17 in Parkland, Florida. As we explored in Chapter 6, many like him were willing to stand up and fight for the things they believed in. They did so by rallying together in the March for Our Lives, lobbying politicians in both the Florida legislature and the U.S. Capitol, appearing on news programs, sharing posts through social media, and participating in many other activities. Their primary mission was to move people from feelings of compassion to acts of justice, including the passage of laws, so that no shooting like that would happen ever again.

Throughout American history, over and over again, people have stood up for what they believed was right. Individuals came together to march in hopes of bringing attention to their concerns. Examples abound of people committed to causes and working hard to bring about substantial change, some of which we have explored in other chapters: the antislavery movement of the 1800s; the woman's suffrage movement, resulting in women's right to vote in 1920; the civil rights movement that fought for political, social, and economic rights for African Americans; the student-led protests over the Vietnam War; the 1960s women's rights movement that sought equality and respect; the pro-life and pro-choice movements that followed, battling over the question of abortion; the Tea Party movement that raised concerns about the encroaching size and power of government. More recent examples include the Black Lives Matter movement concerned about life, liberty, and justice for African Americans; the Women's March and #MeToo movement that continue to fight against sexual violence and unequal treatment of women; the school walkouts around the country in response to the Parkland shootings; and, along the way, many other movements and moments in which individuals acted together to fight for change.

Students often find sociology appealing because they feel that it can help them make a difference in the world. And it can. Since sociology's founding, sociologists have been committed to understanding social change. We learn, for example, that when we act the ways we always have, we reproduce the status quo. By acting differently, we have the power to change the world. We can use the knowledge we gain from sociology to improve our odds for bringing about the kind of change we hope to see.

As You READ >>

- **What factors shape the success of a social movement?**
- **How and why does social change happen?**
- **What does it mean to practice sociology?**

>> Social Movements

Change occurs when we alter how we act. If a sufficient number of us do so, what begins as something new at the micro level can have consequences at the macro level, leading to a new social structure. Social movements are committed to bringing about such change in an intentional manner. Sociologists use the term **social movements** to refer to groups of individuals and organizations collectively committed to bringing about, or resisting, fundamental societal change in a systematic way.

The power to change is rooted in our agency. Most of the time, the choices we make are predictable based on the social positions we occupy, and the socialization we have experienced. We take in information from a variety of sources, and then we make a judgment about which pathway we prefer. In doing so, however, we typically do what is expected of us. We follow established norms, both big and small, primarily because it is much easier to do so. Yet, in each and every moment of our lives, we can choose to act differently.

Social movements are committed to providing us with information so that we can better understand the consequences of the choices we make. They seek to convince people to choose a new path. And the more people that do so, the more viable that new pathway becomes for others. Initially, for example, people viewed the ideas of Margaret Sanger and other early advocates of birth control as radical, yet contraceptives are now widely available in the United States.

> **Social movement** Groups of individuals and organizations collectively committed to bringing about, or resisting, fundamental societal change in a systematic way.

When it comes to better understanding social change through collective action, sociologists have pursued a variety of theoretical pathways. Starting in the 1890s, when social scientists considered social movements, they tended to focus on rallies and the crowds that attended them, with a particular emphasis on emotional manipulation of crowds by leaders, rather than focusing on movement organizations dedicated to bringing about significant social change. In the 1950s, theorists focused on the impact people's perceptions of their own situation might have on their willingness to participate in social movements. Starting in the

Did You Know?

... In 1916 Margaret Sanger opened a family planning and birth control clinic. Nine days later, it was raided by police, and she served 30 days in jail as a result. She was undeterred and continued working to dispense birth control information.

Photo: Source: Library of Congress, Prints and Photographs Division [LC-USZ62-29808]

1960s, in part due to the many movements active at the time, sociologists' focus shifted from the characteristics of the participants to how the movements operated and the factors that were more or less influential in determining success. More recently, sociologists have explored the motivations of the individuals involved in the organizations to better understand why people devote their time and energy to such movements, with particular attention paid to the role of sympathy and compassion. We will explore all four of these approaches in this section.

EARLY SOCIAL SCIENCE CROWD THEORY

For a long time, social scientists studying social movements focused less on organizations and their accomplishments and more on anomalous events that seemed to occur outside the bounds of normal social behavior. In their more extreme form, this included riots and mobs, but it also included fads and got extended to include protests and rallies. Of particular concern was the relative power the group could wield over the individual (Smelser 1962; Turner and Killian 1957).

In the late 1890s, psychologist Gustave Le Bon established a theory of crowd psychology that largely held sway until the 1960s (Goodwin, Jasper, and Polletta 2000). In his bestselling book *The Crowd,* Le Bon argued that people in crowds are susceptible to manipulative leaders, writing, "Whoever can supply them with illusion is easily their master" (1896:110). Le Bon argued that leaders especially used appeals to emotion to their advantage, claiming, "Given to exaggeration in its feelings, a crowd is only impressed by excessive sentiments" (p. 36). This theory seemed particularly salient in the 1930s and 1940s, with the rise of Adolf Hitler in Germany (Goodwin, Jasper, and Polletta 2000).

Relative deprivation People's perception that they lack the resources necessary to lead the kind of life they believe they deserve.

This understanding of crowd psychology pitted emotion and rationality against each other in a way that makes them seem incompatible. Protest is portrayed as irrational behavior on the part of impressionable and unthinking people. In the context of the crowd, they get swept up in the moment to believe and do things they might not otherwise consider (Goodwin, Jasper, and Polletta 2000). People today continue to appeal to a version of this theory when they raise concerns about charismatic leaders, whether religious or political, who critics accuse of manipulating, deceiving, or brainwashing their followers into belief.

With its focus on crowds and manipulation, this theory especially appealed to people in positions of power who sought to delegitimize the claims of participants. When the woman's suffrage movement held rallies to fight for women's right to vote or labor unions gathered to demand fair pay and better working conditions, this theory provided those in power with a tool enabling them to dismiss those claims. Those in power instead blamed a few rabble-rousers for riling up the crowds. Rather than focusing on the legitimacy of the protestors claims, they accused the leaders of being spinsters or radicals, and sometimes even used violence to break up their rallies and did so in the name of social order (Dray 2010; McConnaughy 2013; O'Neill 1969).

Sociologists today largely reject this theory because it does not appear compatible with what they found when studying how social movements operate in practice. Starting especially in the 1960s, due to their research on, and sometimes their participation in, the movements at that time, sociologists recognized that the people who engaged in those movements were no more irrational or susceptible than those who did not. These researchers turned their attention toward the ways in which control over resources impacted social movement failure or success (Beckford 1985; Goodwin, Jasper, and Polletta 2000; Lofland and Stark 1965; Stark and Bainbridge 1980).

RELATIVE DEPRIVATION

To better understand why people might participate in social movements, sociologists began focusing on people's perceptions. They found that those members of society who feel most frustrated with and disgruntled by social and economic conditions are not necessarily the worst off in an objective sense. Social scientists have long recognized that people's perceptions of their situation are often more important than their actual objective situation.

The theory known as **relative deprivation** refers to people's perception that they lack the resources necessary to lead the kind of life they believe they deserve. The relative part refers to comparing one's self to others, and the deprivation part involves lack of resources such as money, property, or power. A relatively deprived person is dissatisfied because he or she feels unfortunate relative to some appropriate reference group. They have a desire for more, but can't get what they want. And even if they try, just getting what they need is not enough. Thus, blue-collar workers who live in modest homes on small plots of land—though hardly destitute—may nevertheless feel deprived in comparison to corporate managers and professionals who live in lavish homes in exclusive suburbs (Stewart 2006).

In addition to the feeling of relative deprivation, however, two other elements must be present before discontent will be channeled into a social movement. First, people must feel that they have a right to their goals, that they deserve better than what they have. For example, the struggle against European colonialism in Africa intensified when growing numbers of Africans decided that it was legitimate for them to have political and economic independence. Second, the disadvantaged group must perceive that its goals cannot be attained through conventional means. This belief may or may not be correct. In any case, the group will not mobilize into a social movement unless there is a shared perception that members can end their relative deprivation only through collective action (Walker and Smith 2002).

One of the challenges this perspective faced was explaining why some people who feel discontent or deprived do

5 **Movies** on SOCIAL MOVEMENTS AND SOCIAL CHANGE

2 Fists Up
Students fight for racial equality at the University of Missouri.

BlacKkKlansman
The power of activism at a micro level.

Freedom Riders
Young activists challenge segregation in the American South.

An Inconvenient Sequel: Truth to Power
Global climate change motivates people to act.

Beasts of the Southern Wild
When you're small, you gotta fix what you can.

not take action or join social movements, while others do. And then there are those who feel no significant deprivation yet still act. As a result of such issues, in the 1960s, emphasis shifted away from attempts to explain internal motivations and focused more on how access to resources affected social movement outcomes.

RATIONAL ACTION AND RESOURCE MOBILIZATION

The 1960s provided many opportunities for sociologists to study social movements. A new wave of theorists turned their attention away from why people do or don't participate, and toward how movements operate with a particular emphasis on the importance of rational calculation. Desire matters, but having access to money, political influence, the media, and personnel makes things much easier. These theorists called this approach **resource mobilization** which refers to the rational management of resources to accomplish a social movement's organizational goals. From this perspective, the success of a movement in bringing about change depends on what resources it has and how effectively it utilizes them. The leadership of a social movement must be able to both access valued resources and activate potential followers (McCarthy and Zald 1977, 2002).

Max Weber laid a foundation for this model with his work on social power. As we explored in the "Weber and Social Resources" section in Chapter 10, Weber argued that class, status, and party represent three types of resources.

Access to each shapes relative social power within society. Class involves ownership and control of material resources. Status entails control over social resources, including both the relative perception people have of an individual or group's prestige and the power of social network connections. And party refers to the capacity to organize to accomplish some specific goal. According to Weber, groups can utilize their relative power in one of these areas to gain greater power in another. In the United States, for example, the civil rights movement effectively used its organizational power to alter the relative standing of African Americans in terms of both class and status (Ling 2006).

Sociologist Anthony Oberschall (1973:199) argued that to sustain social protest or resistance, there must be both an "organizational base and continuity of leadership." As people become part of a social movement, norms develop to guide their behavior. Members of the movement may be expected to attend regular meetings of organizations, pay dues, recruit new adherents, and boycott "enemy" products or speakers. Leadership is a central factor in the mobilization of the discontented into social movements. Often, a movement will be led by a charismatic figure, such as occurred in the civil rights movement with Dr. Martin Luther King Jr. Charismatic authority alone, however, may not be enough.

—SOCTHINK**—**

Online sites such as changemakers.net serve as information clearinghouses and networking hubs for social activists. How might the existence of such online resources shape social activism both positively and negatively?

If a group is to succeed, coordinated action is essential. Recent movements have worked to negotiate how best to accomplish this. For example, after the Parkland shootings, in addition to the marches, walkouts, lobbying, and interviews, the students established the Never Again MSD political action committee in order to better deal with the organizational details that activism can require. Social movements sometimes debate about the degree to which they want to take advantage of the efficiency that bureaucratic structures provide. Some groups fear that doing so entails taking on some of the characteristics of the groups they were organized to protest. For example, leaders might dominate the decision-making process without directly consulting followers.

> **Resource mobilization** The rational management of resources to accomplish a social movement's organizational goals.

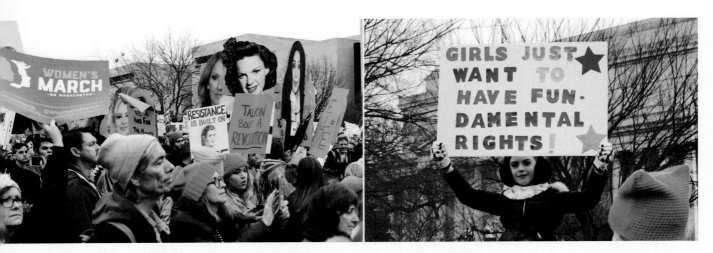

The Women's March on Washington drew more than 500,000 participants in January 2017. Many others marched at alternative locations around the country and around the world. (left): Amanda Edwards/FilmMagic/Getty Images; (right): Jenny Anderson/FilmMagic/Getty Images

One of the key resources social movements need to mobilize involves media exposure. Innovations in social networking technologies, including Instagram, Twitter, Facebook, and a variety of messaging apps, can serve as important resources, facilitating the organization and success of mass movements. The capacity to capture and share video of apparent brutality played an important part in the development and expansion of the Black Lives Matter movement. Social networking apps made it possible to successfully organize and carry out the March for Our Lives events, held around the country, only five-and-a-half weeks after the Parkland school shootings. Such technologies continue to play a role in the ongoing activities of these movements and others.

⌐SOCTHINK⌐

Are there any issues on your campus or in your community that people persistently complain about? If so, what factors might inhibit them from organizing to bring about social change?

THE POWER OF COMPASSION

A more recent turn in social movement theory returns to the question of motivations, but does so informed by recent research in the sociology of emotions. The resource mobilization model emphasizes *how* social movements operate and succeed; these newer theories, on the other hand, focus on the question of *why* people participate and what keeps them engaged. Theorists from this perspective reject the premise that emotions equal irrationality. Feminist theorists especially called this false equivalence into question,

recognizing the ways that it had been used to delegitimize women's knowledge and experience (Goodwin, Jasper, and Polletta 2000). In the words of sociologist James Jasper, "Emotions can be helpful, functional, and sometimes even wise" (2018:1).

According to this perspective, people will fight for the things they believe in, not just because they are focused on the instrumental rationality tied to access to resources, but because they believe it is right to do so. Their sense of justice, along with an almost guttural response when they see someone treated unfairly, provide important motivations. To see their values put into practice provides a sense of pride, accomplishment, and worth (Jasper 2014, 2018).

When it comes to social movements, the range of emotions involved varies. Sometimes the most important emotions are the visceral reactions people have to a tragic event. We've seen this over and over again when it comes to school shootings. In the words of Parkland shooting survivor Delaney Tarr, "This movement, created by students, led by students, is based in emotion. It is based in passion. It is based in pain" (Burke 2018). One of the things that made the Parkland case different was the fact that the students involved began to organize right away, enabling them to draw on these immediate emotions in a way that led to action. But movements cannot rely on these types of emotions alone (Jasper 2018).

At their heart, reactions such as these are rooted in more fundamental emotional commitments tied to people's sense of morality. We often express these commitments in the forms of narratives, such as morality plays or fairy tales, that can help us to better articulate what we believe. These stories often include victims, villains, heroes, and minions. And when some event comes along that challenges our sense of social justice, we can more easily identify who is who in the current crisis. Effective social movements will often find ways to tell such tales (Jasper 2014).

Moral emotions get to the very heart of what we believe is true, just, good, and right. Sociologist James Jasper (2018) highlights three categories of moral emotions. The first, *pride,* highlights the importance we attach to the reputation of our group and ourselves. We want to be able to feel good about those whom we consider our people. An attack against any of them can feel like on attack on ourselves. A shameful action by one of our own can also bring shame to us. The second, *compassion,* involves our capacity for both empathy and sympathy. Empathy means we can understand what others are feeling. Sympathy goes beyond empathy to affirm and support the others, caring about the fact that they are feeling bad. Third, *justice,* means that we care about how people are treated. It is from here that a sense of indignation, or righteous anger, grows. Jasper uses the expression "indignation gap" to describe the difference between how things are and how they should be according to our beliefs (2018:158).

> # Every time you spend money, you're casting a vote for the kind of world you want.
>
> Anna Lappé (2003)

When the Columbine school shootings happened in 1999, long before hashtags were created, the slogan "We are Columbine" became a rallying cry, giving voice to the sense of *pride* and identity present in that community. One of the reasons people participate in social movements is to feel that sense of connection to something bigger and more important than themselves. Perhaps because the scale of the shooting was unprecedented at the time, the outpouring of *compassion* toward the Columbine community came from all corners of the country. And, in keeping with the principle of *justice,* and the deep-in-the-marrow sense of unfairness this act provoked, people said "Never again" (Cullen 2009). Sadly, that plaintive cry has since been heard many times after repeated mass shootings, including those at Sandy Hook Elementary School, the Pulse nightclub in Orlando, and the Harvest Music Festival in Las Vegas.

Combining elements of the resource mobilization perspective with these more compassion-based models enables us to better understand what makes a social movement work. If a movement is to succeed, it must tend to people's sense of social justice and their perception of possibility. Asking people to sacrifice their time, money, and effort should invoke both their emotional sense of right and wrong and their rational sense about the most efficient and effective pathways forward.

>> Assessing Social Change

Studying social movements enables us to focus our attention on intentional efforts to bring about or resist change, but the general topic of social change is much broader. Change is the norm. As the "Social Change in the USA" table shows, in the past century or so, the U.S. population has more than doubled, the percentage of people finishing high school and attending college has skyrocketed, women have entered the paid labor force in significant numbers, life expectancy has risen, technological innovation has exploded, men and women have been marrying later, and family size has shrunk.

A comprehensive understanding of social change, inclusive of that brought about by social movements, should explore how each of the major elements of culture—material, cognitive, and normative—shift over time. Material culture involves our our physical modification of the natural environment to suit our purposes; cognitive culture concerns our mental and symbolic representations of reality; and, normative culture consists of the ways we establish, abide by, and enforce principles of conduct.

Did You Know?

. . . Women played an active role in the antiwar and civil rights movements but were often blocked from positions of leadership. Symbolizing this exclusion perhaps better than any other example was Student Nonviolent Coordinating Committee leader Stokely Carmichael's infamous line: "The only position for women in SNCC is prone." Such sexism and discrimination led women to start their own organizations to fight for women's rights.

Photo: Bettmann/Getty Images

Social Change in the USA

Population	1850	1940	1960	2017
Total in millions	23.3	132.1	179.3	326.0
Percentage under age 15	41%	25%	31%	19%

Education	1850	1940	1960	2017
Percentage aged 25+ who have not completed high school	88%	75%	59%	10%
Percentage aged 19–24 enrolled in higher education	<1%	8%	24%	40%

Labor Force Participation	1850	1940	1960	2018
Men working in their 20s	94%	86%	86%	81%
Women working in their 20s	22%	51%	74%	73%

Health	1850	1940	1960	2016
Physicians per 100,000 population	176	133	150	292
Life expectancy at birth, in years	38	63	70	79

Technology	1870	1940	1960	2015
Copyrights issued	5,600	176,997	243,926	443,823
Patents issued	12,137	42,238	47,170	325,979

Family	1890	1940	1960	2018
Men median age at first marriage	26	24	23	30
Women median age at first marriage	22	22	20	28
Birthrate for women aged 20–24 per 1,000	168.4	135.6	258.1	74

Note: Data are comparable, although definitions vary somewhat across time. Earliest birthrate is from 1905.
Sources: Bureau of Labor Statistics 2019c; Carter et al. 2006:vol. 1: 28–29, 401–402, 440, 541, 685, 697, 709, vol. 2: 441–442, vol. 3: 422–425, 427–428; National Center for Health Statistics 2018a:Tables 3, 15, 83; National Center for Education Statistics 2018:Tables 104.10, 302.60; U.S. Census Bureau 2010a:Table 80, 2016e:Table MS-2, 2018a:Table S0201; U.S. Copyright Office 2016; U.S. Patent and Trademark Office 2016.
Photo: Nisian Hughes/Getty Images

Social change Shifts in how humans think and act within society that alter material, cognitive, and normative culture.

Our definition of social change incorporates all three. **Social change** refers to shifts in how humans think and act within society that alter material, cognitive, and normative culture. Understanding how and why change has occurred in each of these areas better equips us to bring about the kinds of change we desire.

MATERIAL CULTURE AND CHANGE

Technology represents one of the core elements of material culture. Changes in technology today seem constant. It wasn't always that way. The development of new technologies throughout most of human history was relatively flat. But then the Industrial Revolution happened, and since then, the world has never been the same. Karl Marx recognized capitalism's contributions to technological innovation. And we continue to reap the benefits of new technologies in our everyday lives. Yet one of the lessons we should have already learned from sociology is that we should regularly stand back and ask questions about advantages and disadvantages that are gained and lost as a consequence of technological change.

Technology's Benefits and Costs Technological innovations are, in fact, emerging and being accepted with remarkable speed. And there are many ways in which technology makes our lives better. The list of possible examples seems endless, but would certainly include innovations in health and health care. Examples might include pacemakers, contact lenses, defibrillators, insulin pumps, robot-assisted surgery, vaccines, and a whole host of others.

In our Internet age, digital technologies have transformed how we live. Driven in part by the spread of mobile phones around the world, for example, Internet access has gone global. In 2018, the Internet reached 4.2 billion users, or 55.1 percent of the world's population. If we look at global Internet use, Asia alone represents more than 2 billion users. However, in terms of access, as the "Internet Use and Penetration by World Region" graph shows, a larger proportion of the population in North America—95 percent—can connect to the Internet than on any other continent. Contrast that with Africa where only 36 percent have access (Internet World Stats 2018).

In developing nations, whole populations can move quite rapidly from having limited access to technologies to adopting them in their more advanced forms. An example of such leapfrogging occurs when countries skip landlines, with all the wiring infrastructure installation that entails, and move directly to widespread access to cell phones. Or when they go straight to e-commerce for financial transactions, such as those provided by the M-Pesa app in places such as Kenya, Afghanistan, and India (Harford 2017).

Technological change does not come without costs. Already in the mid-1800s, for example, Karl Marx predicted that technological innovation would cost people their jobs as machines took over work previously done by humans. Concerns about mechanization, computerization, and robotization continue today. Technology analysts Thomas Davenport and Julia Kirby (2016) suggest that jobs particularly susceptible to automation include those that have clearly delineated rules for performance, involve

Internet Use and Penetration by World Region

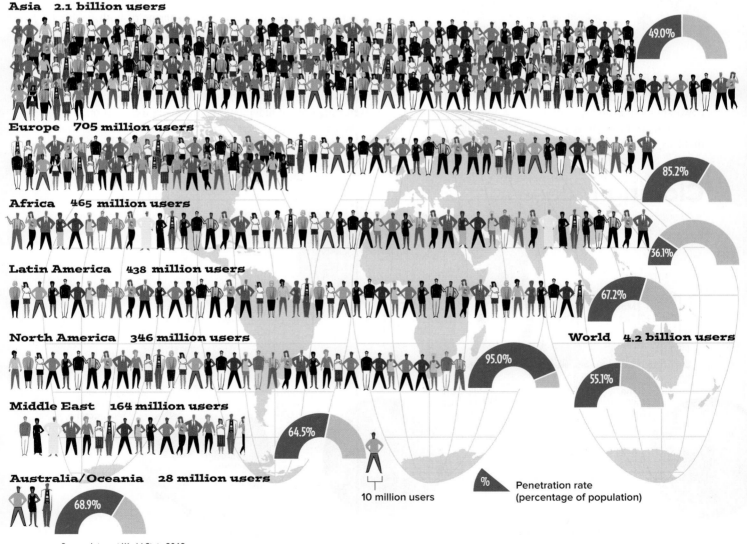

Asia 2.1 billion users — 49.0%

Europe 705 million users — 85.2%

Africa 465 million users — 36.1%

Latin America 438 million users — 67.2%

North America 346 million users — 95.0%

Middle East 164 million users — 64.5%

Australia/Oceania 28 million users — 68.9%

World 4.2 billion users — 55.1%

10 million users

% Penetration rate (percentage of population)

Source: Internet World Stats 2018.

simple content transmission, require quantitative analysis, or necessitate little face-to-face contact with customers or coworkers. For example, radiologists who read x-ray images and CT scans to diagnose tumors are susceptible to replacement by technology that can draw on pattern-recognition databases to do the job. This kind of social change raises economic concerns about what happens if the supply of workers looking for good jobs exceeds the demand of employers looking to hire them (M. Ford 2015; Frey and Osborne 2017).

As technology spreads, we may also lose control over other areas of our lives, including our privacy. In 2019, Marriott International reported the theft of 383 million of its guests' private data, including 5 million unencrypted passport numbers. In 2017, Equifax, a credit reporting agency, reported a data breach affecting 148 million customers. And in 2016, FriendFinder reported the theft of usernames, passwords, and email addresses for 339 million users of its AdultFriendFinder site—which describes itself as "the world's largest sex & swinger community" (Greenberg 2016).

Scientific research provides another area of concern when it comes to technological innovation. Genetic modification of plants, animals, and microorganisms leads people to raise questions about how much change here is appropriate. For example, many people fear that genetically modified food may result in unintended consequences in terms of both health and the environment. Yet, genetically modified food, because it can be adapted to challenging environmental contexts, can help alleviate hunger and starvation in countries around the world (Jenkins 2018). Balancing the advantages and disadvantages of such changes involves exercising critical judgment and adequate information.

When it comes to genetic modifications of animals, the first major milestone occurred in 1997 when scientists in

Cloning Milestones

Dolly, Sheep Feb. '97

Cumulina, Mouse Oct. '97

Mira, Goat Oct. '98

CC, Cat Dec. '01

Taz, Mule
Dewey, Deer
Prometea, Horse May '03

Snuppy, Dog Aug. '05

1997   1998   1999   2000   2001   2002   2003   2004   2005   2018

Gene, Calf Aug. '97

Millie, Christa, Alexis, Carrel, & Dotcom, Piglets Mar. '00

Ralph, Rat Sept. '03

Zhong Zhong and Hua Hua, Macaque monkeys Dec.'17

Photos: *(sheep):* PA Images/Getty Images; *(goat):* G.K.&Vikki Hart/Photodisc/Yuri Kevhiev/Getty Images; *(cat):* G.K.&Vikki Hart/Photodisc/Getty Images; *(pig):* Image Source/PunchStock; *(monkeys):* Jin Liwang/Xinhua News Agency/Getty Images

Scotland announced that they had cloned a sheep, which they named Dolly. Since then many other species have been successfully cloned, as can be seen in the "Cloning Milestones" timeline. It is now possible to get your pet cat or dog cloned, though doing is costly. Scientists have even begun work on "de-extinction," the cloning of extinct species such as the woolly mammoth and passenger pigeon (McCauley et al. 2016; Schultz 2016).

In 2015, scientists announced that they had succeeded in genetically modifying human embryos, though none were brought to term. In 2017, scientists successfully cloned the first primates ever, a pair of macaque monkeys named Zhong Zhong and Hua Hua. And in 2018, the first gene-edited human babies were born making them less susceptible to contracting HIV (Cyranoski and Reardon 2015; Greshko 2018). When asked, 81 percent of Americans responded that cloning humans is morally wrong. And, even though cloning nonhuman mammals has become routine, 51 percent reject it as morally wrong (Gallup 2018b).

Questioning Technology Given the consequences of technological change, it should come as no surprise that, through the ages, there have been those who questioned whether technological innovation equals progress. Inventions that grew out of the Industrial Revolution, for example, led to strong resistance in some countries. In England, beginning in 1811, masked craftworkers took extreme measures: They mounted nighttime raids on factories and destroyed some of the new machinery. The government hunted these rebels, known as **Luddites,** and ultimately banished or hanged them. In a similar effort in France, angry workers threw their wooden shoes (sabots) into factory machinery to destroy it, giving rise to the term *sabotage.* Although the resistance of the Luddites and the French workers was short-lived and unsuccessful, they have come to symbolize resistance to technology. It would be a mistake, however, to simply dismiss the actions of these resisters as anti-technology or irrational. Their primary concern was with the impact such technology had on their employment, their communities, and their way of life. Today the Amish do much the same thing (Hostetler 1993; Hurst and McConnell 2010; Kraybill, Johnson-Weiner, and Nolt 2013).

Sociologist Jacques Ellul (1964, 1980, 1990) argued that the key factor to consider when analyzing our modern technological society is not simply the *technology,* by which he meant the physical tools we create as we modify our material environment, but what he referred to more generally as *technique.* By this he meant our systemic commitment to maximizing efficiency and increasing productivity in all areas of human endeavor. Success, whether in business, education, or love, is increasingly measured in quantitative terms. That which cannot be measured is suspect. For example, we see evidence of this at work in the No Child Left Behind education reforms. Performance on particular kinds of tests, in a narrow range of subjects, is becoming the primary indicator of learning. Although living in a technique-focused system has the advantage of technical

progress, we lose something human in the process—art, beauty, and qualitative, as opposed to quantitative, values. Ellul's concerns echo those of Max Weber about the dehumanizing consequences of bureaucracy.

Most of us today automatically adopt the latest technologies without taking time to step back and ask what consequences they might have for social order and meaning. On the one hand, smartphones facilitate the establishment and success of social movements, as we saw after the Parkland shootings. On the other hand, they impact our everyday interactions with others. Communications professor Neil Postman (1988, 1993, 1999) argues that, instead of passively accepting technological innovations, we should critically examine whether we really need them and investigate what consequences adoption might have on ourselves, our relationships, and our society. He identified five questions we should ask whenever we consider adopting a new technology or technique—when buying a new smartphone or car, or when implementing a new management or organizational plan, for example—which are highlighted in the "Five Questions to Ask When Adopting New Technology" feature.

COGNITIVE CULTURE AND CHANGE

Cognitive culture represents the second element of culture. Change here involves new values, beliefs, and knowledge. Education has been a powerful tool for advancing both our individual and collective knowledge. We have exposure to more ideas and ways of doing things than ever before. Sociology calls us always to seek out new ways of understanding the world around us so that we might better explain why we think and act as we do. Based on their research, sociologists bring this new knowledge to us so that we, too, can expand our understanding. Of course we can also pursue our own research and contribute to that common stock of knowledge, too.

> **Luddites** Rebellious craftworkers in 19th-century England who destroyed new factory machinery as part of their resistance to the Industrial Revolution.
>
> **social evolution** A theory of social change that holds that societies progress from simple to complex over time.

The Evolution of Societies Some sociologists argue that change in society follows a fairly predictable path. We've already encountered one version of this approach in the form of modernization theory in Chapter 11. Inspired in part by Charles Darwin's (1859) evolutionary model of nature, and rooted in the functionalist perspective, these sociologists proposed a **social evolution** model of social change, according to which societies progress from simple to complex over time. This approach encourages a certain level of passivity. Change is inevitable and follows a predictable path, which reduces the perceived need to fight for positive social change.

Auguste Comte, for example, whose contributions to early sociology we explored in the "Sociology's Roots" section of Chapter 1, also posited the Law of Three Stages

Five Questions to Ask When Adopting New Technology

- What is the problem for which this technology is the solution?

- Whose problem is it?

- What new problems might be created because we solve the problem?

- Which people and institutions might be most seriously harmed?

- Which people and institutions might acquire special economic and political power?

Source: Postman 1988. *Photo:* Ariel Skelley/Blend Images LLC

Equilibrium model The theory that society's natural tendency is toward social order with change in one part of society counterbalanced by adjustments in others.

to describe social change over time. During the *theological* stage, people base their knowledge and decision making on religious principles. To explain why things happen, people turn toward the direct involvement in our daily lives of supernatural or divine beings—gods, demons, and the like. During this stage, according to Comte, people are irrational and superstitious. In the *metaphysical* stage, worship of concrete, active beings gives way to the belief that abstract forces guide what happens in the world. This perspective assumes that there is an underlying logic built within the universe. Knowledge is advanced by studying the fundamental essence of things. In Comte's *positive* stage, knowledge is built on facts revealed using the scientific method. Natural and social scientists seek to uncover the underlying laws that govern the universe. Empirical investigation trumps philosophical reflection, and researchers adhere to the Missouri principle of "don't just tell me, show me." During this stage, according to Comte, people are rational, guided by logic and reason, making progress not only possible, but inevitable. Most sociologists today have rejected the simplistic and ethnocentric elements of this model, but most also affirm the importance of understanding how past developments shape future outcomes.

Equilibrium and Social Order Another sociological theory to explain social change, also rooted in the functionalist perspective, portrays societies as naturally tending toward stability or social order. Sociologist Talcott Parsons, an advocate of this model, maintained that even seemingly significant social disruptions, such as protests and riots, are but temporary interruptions along the pathway to enhanced social stability. According to his **equilibrium model,** society's

natural tendency is toward social order with change in one part of society counterbalanced by adjustments in others. This model, too, encourages some degree of passivity. The system will function, reaching a natural balance, without a seeming need for agency or activism.

Parsons (1966) maintained that four processes of social change are inevitable. The first, *differentiation,* refers to the division of society, into specialized subsystems, such as institutions, as occurs when the overlapping functions associated with family, education, religion, politics, and the economy in traditional societies become increasingly separate in modern times. The second process, *adaptive upgrading,* refers to increased specialization of tasks, also known as the division of labor. Such specialization allows for greater productivity and efficiency. The third process, *inclusion,* ensures that the various elements of the social system work together by building links between those elements. Finally, *value generalization,* involves the development of new values to legitimate the broader range of activities that arose within the system. All four processes identified by Parsons stress consensus—societal agreement on the nature of social organization and values (Gerhardt 2002).

SOCTHINK

Why might the equilibrium model have a difficult time addressing such issues as inequality and poverty as social problems to be solved?

Resources, Power, and Change Karl Marx, who utilized the conflict perspective, accepted elements of an evolutionary argument, believing that societies develop along predictable paths. But Marx argued that people with power and control over valued resources play a pivotal role in shaping the direction of social change, at least in the short term. Major social change happens, according to Marx, when a revolution in social relations occurs, leading to a new stage of economic and social development. Ultimately, as we saw in the "Economic Systems" section of Chapter 9, Marx predicted that, after the problem of production is solved—meaning we had the technological capacity to produce enough enough for everyone to survive and thrive—human society would move toward the final stage of social development: a classless communist society, or "community of free individuals" who control their own labor power and are able to exercise it freely (Marx [1867] 2000:478).

Alex Brandon/AP Images

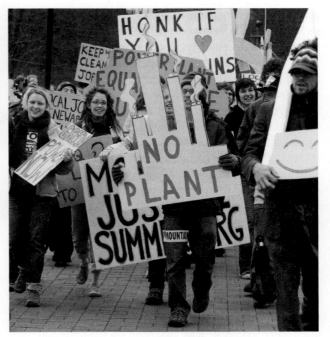

David Crigger/Bristol Herald Courier/AP Images

Marx argued that conflict is a normal and desirable aspect of social change. In fact, change must be encouraged if social inequality is to be eliminated. In his view, people are not restricted to a passive role in responding to inevitable cycles or changes in the material culture. Rather, Marxist theory offers a tool for those who want to seize control of the historical process and gain their freedom from injustice. Social movements today continue to maintain this same hope. Efforts to promote social change are, however, likely to meet with resistance. Battles over resources, which can involve government, unions, social movement organizations, and more, all shape likely outcomes.

Individuals and groups in positions of power have a stake in maintaining the status quo. Social economist Thorstein Veblen (1857–1929) coined the term **vested interests** to refer to those people or groups who benefit most from the existing social, political, and economic system. They are the ones who have the most to lose should social change take place. For example, historically the American Medical Association (AMA) has taken strong stands against universal health insurance and the professionalization of midwives. National health insurance was seen as a threat to physicians' income and authority, and a rise in the status of midwives could undercut the doctors' expertise, and therefore also their authority and prestige, as deliverers of babies. In general, people with a disproportionate share of society's wealth, status, and power have a vested interest in preserving the status quo (Furedi 2006; Scelfo 2008; Veblen 1919).

Communities also work to protect their vested interests, often in the name of "protecting property values." As noted in Chapter 14, the abbreviation NIMBY stands for "not in my backyard," a cry often heard when people protest landfills, prisons, nuclear power facilities, and even bike trails and group homes for people with developmental disabilities. The targeted community may not challenge the need for the facility, but may simply insist that

it be located elsewhere. The NIMBY attitude has become so common that it is almost impossible for policy makers to find acceptable locations for facilities such as hazardous waste dumps. Unfortunately, it is often those with the fewest resources who end up on the losing end of such battles (Scally 2015; Wonjun et al. 2016).

> **Vested interests** Those people or groups who benefit most from the existing social, political, and economic structure.

NORMATIVE CULTURE AND CHANGE

Normative culture represents the third element of culture. Change here involves how we act and the rules we establish for governing behavior. As we think about change in this area, we should consider the importance of agency. We have the capacity to choose how to act. As the world changes, we might want to consider how changes in the contexts within which we live might open up new possibilities for us. For example, we can now establish relationships with people on the other side of the globe. Given sufficient resources, we can communicate with them instantly at any time, day or night via texts, social media apps, video conferencing technology, and more. Increasingly, we take these abilities for granted and as a result often fail to realize their full potential.

Expanding our social network ties beyond those most like ourselves, and, perhaps even more important, intentionally to those not like us, provides significant advantages. It exposes us to new ways of acting and thinking, allows us to consider possible new pathways for our futures, and makes us more

> ## Ignorance is the parent of fear.
>
> ——————————
>
> Herman Melville

accepting of others, as we learned with the contact hypothesis in Chapter 13. Surrounding ourselves with others just like ourselves, on the other hand, can have the opposite effects. For example, too much homogeneity within decision-making groups produces less effective outcomes (Surowiecki 2004).

When constructing groups, we might want to be more deliberate about their composition. James Surowiecki, in his book *The Wisdom of Crowds,* maintained that groups can be quite smart. As he put it, "under the right circumstances, groups are remarkably intelligent, and are often smarter than the smartest people in them" (2004:xiii). The diversity of perspectives in the group represents one of the most important factors. People drawing on alternative experiences are also more likely to see limitations or holes in the plans and programs we propose. Existing in groups and networks of only like-minded people creates the danger of living in an echo chamber or bubble in which the only perspectives we hear are those with which we already agree.

Even though social media provide us with the potential to interact with a wide variety of others, one of their unintended consequences has been to reinforce our preconceived notions about what count as facts. Political discourse today seems more divided than ever. Analysis of interaction patterns on Twitter, Facebook, and a variety of other platforms confirms that the political social network worlds people occupy have become quite distinct and disconnected. People in these social network bubbles do not hear the same facts or narratives, and as a result can come to very different conclusions about what is wrong and what should be done to fix it (Kahn and Bowyer 2018; Kelly and François 2018; Pew Research Center 2018c).

In terms of new norms, embracing diversity has clear advantages, even if implementing it can prove challenging in practice. One of the benefits of taking intersectionality seriously is that it enables us to more fully recognize and affirm the varieties of backgrounds and experiences the people around us have. Early on, for example, the students organizing the March for Our Lives events recognized that the mainstream media seemed to give more time and attention to gun violence victims who were mostly White and upper-middle class. In response, at the rally that preceded the March, the organizers were intentional about giving opportunities to speak to those who might not otherwise be heard, especially young Black women. Doing so provides more people access to the kinds of diverse voices necessary for more informed decision making (Grinberg and Muaddi 2018; Johnson 2018; Talbot 2018).

In today's world, change is inevitable. From sociology we learn that we should challenge ourselves to continually expand our ideas about what's possible. As we better understand factors influencing the nature and direction of changes in technology, ideas, and norms, we can use that knowledge to make more informed choices as we move into the future. After all, the choices we make today establish the foundation for the society we will live in tomorrow.

>> Sociology Is a Verb

Ultimately, social change happens because we begin to act in new ways. Change involves our stepping off expected paths and, in doing so, creating new sets of norms. Although external changes in our technological and environmental contexts do influence social change, it still takes people willing to do things differently to bring about such shifts.

Sociology is a tool that helps open up new pathways for us. By enabling us to see things we might have missed before, it helps us view ourselves and the world around us differently. Sociology allows us to recognize how the distribution of social, cultural, and material resources gives advantage to some and disadvantage to others. It helps us understand whether the things we do are consistent with what we claim to believe. It can inform our conversation of whether we are headed where we want to go. It does these things by getting us to pay attention to the world around us in a new way.

We need to move from thinking of sociology as only something we learn about to thinking of sociology as something we *do.* In our daily lives, sociology can help us better understand our own individual actions and the actions of those around us. In the context of our larger society and the world, it also enables us to better appreciate the forces at work shaping outcomes—knowledge that we can then use to act in ways that make the world a better place. In both our personal and public lives, we need to practice sociology in the same way that doctors practice medicine.

Did You Know?

. . . Martin Luther King Jr. graduated with a BA in sociology from Morehouse College in Atlanta, Georgia, in 1948.

Photo: Popperfoto/Getty Images

PERSONAL SOCIOLOGY

Sociology can help us in our everyday lives to better understand our beliefs and actions and to make more informed choices. We learn from sociology that we are in society and society is in us. Self and society are not two separate things. Being an individual necessitates understanding the importance of place, of position, of connection, and of interaction. Though we like to believe that any choice is available to us, in reality, our options are limited.

Practicing sociology means asking uncomfortable questions and not settling for easy answers. It means taking into account the significance of both the individual and society, of both action and structure, of both freedom and constraint. It means recognizing the significance of power and the impact that access to material, social, and cultural resources has on the choices available to us. In short, as we saw in Chapter 1, doing **personal sociology** means recognizing the impact our individual position has on who we are and how we think and act, and then taking responsibility for the impacts our actions have on others.

From the beginning, sociologists wanted to understand our constraints so that we might be able to change them. As sociologist Pierre Bourdieu (1998b) put it, "To those who always tax the sociologist with determinism and pessimism, I will only say that if people became fully aware of them, conscious action aimed at controlling the structural mechanisms that engender moral failure would be possible" (p. 56). In other words, we need to be honest with ourselves about the degree to which society limits our choices so that we might be empowered to make choices that are more informed and therefore more effective in helping us attain our goals.

As individuals, we need to learn to see the degree to which we follow visible and invisible rules. We need to ask whether our current paths represent the values, norms, and goals that we really want to follow. As we have seen, the movies we watch, the things we buy, our likelihood for suicide, our chances of facing a wage gap, our perception of reality, our very selves—all are shaped by the positions we occupy. Understanding these influences empowers us to change.

PUBLIC SOCIOLOGY: TOOLS FOR CHANGE

Beyond providing a more informed understanding of why we as individuals act and think the way we do, sociology calls on us to look beyond ourselves to the world around us and ask, What might we do to make the world a better place? Since the discipline was founded, sociologists have sought to understand and explain social processes for the purpose of shaping the future of society. **Public sociology** involves bringing the insights gained through sociological observation and analysis into the public sphere, thereby seeking to bring about positive social change. As Michael Burawoy, former president of the American Sociological Association, put it, public sociology seeks to speak to a

Personal Sociology

Past, Present, and Future

Each year, on our road trip to Wisconsin to visit family for the holidays, we listen to Charles Dickens's classic tale, *A Christmas Carol*. Near the end, after Ebenezer Scrooge, a miserly businessman, has been visited by the Ghosts of Christmas Past, Present, and Yet to Come, he repents of having selfishly cut himself off from everyone. At that moment he says, "I will live in the Past, the Present, and the Future! The Spirits of all Three shall strive within me." This is the sociological imagination in a nutshell. We need to learn from the past, understanding that the choices made then, by ourselves and others, shape options available to us in today's social structure, while at the same time looking forward to the future, envisioning the world we hope is to come, knowing that the choices we make today shape the structure of tomorrow.

wide audience, aiming to "enrich public debate about moral and political issues by infusing them with sociological theory and research" (Burawoy 2004:1603).

Because we construct the existing social structures through our collective and recurring actions, we bear responsibility for their consequences. Existing systems—the structure and culture we create—are not inevitable. We can choose to change them; we can act differently, as the accompanying table "Citizen Activities in a Democratic Society" suggests. It can be difficult to step off the "paths of least resistance" that support the existing system (Johnson 1997), and the consequences for action and belief that run counter to the status quo can be severe. But we can do so.

What we cannot do is absolve ourselves of responsibility for the systems we end up with. In fact, to not act differently is to support the existing system of inequality. As sociologist Scott Schaffer (2004) points out, we can no longer ignore practices that violate our basic beliefs, trying to wash our hands of responsibility. Writes Schaffer: "Our hands are already dirty; the question I leave here is whether our hands will be dirtied through action intended to bring concrete, actual, enacted freedom into the world, or through our choice to preserve ourselves at the cost of all others

> **Personal sociology** The practice of recognizing the impact the positions we occupy have on who we are and how we think and act.
>
> **Public sociology** The process of bringing the insights gained through sociological observation and analysis into the public sphere, thereby seeking to bring about positive social change.

in the here and now and in the future" (pp. 271–272). Our cynicism and resignation only reinforce systems of oppression and violence. To not act to bring about positive change still represents a choice, and we bear responsibility either way.

By helping us see why we think and act as we do, by helping us clarify the relationship between belief and practice, and by helping us better understand the consequences of difference, personal and public sociology can encourage discussion that can lead to a better future. We can use the tools of sociology to allow ourselves to enter into conversations in which we share our stories with others (both positive and negative), clarifying places where we agree and disagree, and opening ourselves up to our blind spots. We often want to avoid uncomfortable conflict, opting instead for polite discourse, but to fail to be more genuinely engaged in our cultural and structural differences virtually ensures a lack of progress toward implementing our core principles (Schaffer 2004).

PRACTICING SOCIOLOGY

Change comes because people continue not only to believe that it is possible but also to act on their hopes and dreams. As ethnographer Studs Terkel (2003) put it, "In all epochs, there were at first doubts and the fear of stepping forth and speaking out, but the attribute that spurred the warriors on was hope. And then *act*" (p. xviii). We can change the world for the better. We can do so by becoming more informed about ourselves and others and then acting on that knowledge. Here are some possibilities for action:

- *Practice personal sociology.* Become more conscious of the factors that shape your beliefs and actions.
- *Become more aware of privilege.* Identify the advantages you have, especially relative to the rest of the world; you likely have sufficient food, clothes, and shelter; you can read this; you can plan for the future; and so on.
- *Become more informed.* We have access to more information about our world now than ever. Seek it out; find out what's going on.
- *Interpret what you learn.* Analyze the information you receive. Remember that data never speak for themselves; they aren't just facts but are embedded in networks and systems that have their own interests.
- *Vote.* Elected leaders in a democracy, whether local, state, or national, are chosen by voters. It may not seem like your individual vote is significant, but the simple

Citizen Activities in a Democratic Society

PRIVATE LIFE	CIVIC LIFE	
Individual activity	**Civic engagement activities**	
	Nonpolitical activities	Political participation
Family School Work	Recycling Fellowship meetings Service activities	Voting Attending political meetings Political campaigning
Cultivates personal relationships, serves individual needs—e.g., getting an education, earning a living	Provides community services and acts as a training ground for political participation	Fulfills demands of democratic citizenship

Functions

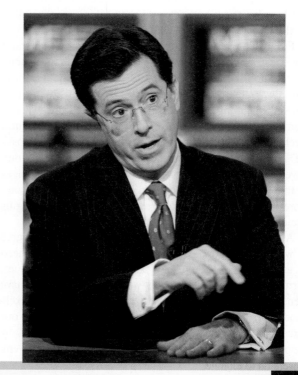

Before his current role as host of the *Late Show* on CBS, Stephen Colbert became famous for spoofing TV talking heads on his Comedy Central show, *The Colbert Report.* He was quite serious, however, when he gave advice in a 2006 commencement speech at Knox College. He challenged students not to give in to cynicism, telling them, "Cynicism masquerades as wisdom, but it is the farthest thing from it. Because cynics don't learn anything. Because cynicism is a self-imposed blindness, a rejection of the world because we are afraid it will hurt us or disappoint us. Cynics always say 'no.' But saying 'yes' begins things. Saying 'yes' is how things grow. Saying 'yes' leads to knowledge. 'Yes' is for young people. So for as long as you have the strength to, say 'yes.'"

POPSOC

Source of quote: Stephen Colbert. *Photo*: Alex Wong/Getty Images fact is that all those votes still add up to a winner. And even if your candidate cannot win, you can still make a statement; for example, if you don't think any of the candidates would make a good choice, write in someone who would.

- *Participate in local politics.* Think of politics as a contact sport: Go to rallies, protests, school board meetings, city council meetings, and more. You might be surprised how much of a difference a single voice can make, especially on the local level.
- *Run for office.* Don't assume that such positions of leadership are only for others who are somehow better or more informed than you. We need more people to believe that they can lead so that we get more diversity in our leaders.
- *Volunteer.* There are local organizations in every community seeking to bring about positive social change. You might contact a local school to see if you can read to kids, work at a homeless shelter, or help build houses with Habitat for Humanity.
- *Join.* There are many organizations that provide long-term outreach opportunities, such as AmeriCorps, the Peace Corps, and the American Red Cross, in which you provide assistance to people with varieties of needs, in communities near and far.
- *Organize.* Work to bring about the world you envision; there are undoubtedly others out there who share your views. Find them and work with them, both inside and outside existing institutions, to bring about change.
- *Fight for change.* Regardless of where you are, whether in your relationships, your family, your workplace, your

> ## Another world is not only possible; she is on her way. On a quiet day, I can hear her breathing.
>
> Arundhati Roy

community, or elsewhere, work to bring about positive social change. We have the power to change the world; we can't do so in a vacuum, but if sociologists are at all correct about the social construction of reality, things could be otherwise.

As Comte wrote at sociology's very founding, "Science leads to foresight, and foresight leads to action" (quoted in Bourdieu 1998b:55). It is only by seeing those things that limit us that we can move toward freedom.

Sociology is more than just a noun. Sociology is a verb. It is something we do, not something we possess. Our overreliance on individualistic models, and our failure to appreciate the impact of social forces, presents a distorted picture of our freedom. An appreciation of the relationship between self and society and of the consequences of difference allows us to make more informed choices and to shape the future. It allows us to provide answers to the questions "Why do we think the way we think?" and "Why do we act the way we act?" Sociology shouldn't be something confined to college classrooms. It shouldn't be left only to professionals. We are all sociologists now, and there is work to be done.

SOCIOLOGY IS A VERB

Sociology as a Way of Life

Sociology is a rich and complex discipline with so much more than can possibly be covered in an introductory course. Consider exploring what else is out there and take another sociology course in an area that sparks your interest. Even if you don't, try to engage your sociological imagination every day. Investigate. Learn. Vote. Organize. Run for office. Fight for change. Practice sociology. Make a difference.

For
REVIEW

I. **What factors shape the success of a social movement?**

- Sociologists argue that both rational planning and compassionate engagement matter. The capacity to organize some specific goal, along with the commitment to core values, increase the likelihood for success.

II. **How and why does social change happen?**

- Social change affects our material, normative, and cognitive culture. By paying attention to technological innovation, shifts in knowledge, and diverse social networks we can better understand, and engage with, social change today.

III. **What does it mean to practice sociology?**

- Personal sociology involves better understanding the influence social factors have on our thoughts and actions and using this information to our advantage. Public sociology means taking responsibility for the collective impacts our individual actions have in shaping society and opportunity and working for positive social change.

Monkey Business Images/Shutterstock

SOCVIEWS on Social Change

Functionalist View

Social change is a way for society to make adjustments in order to return to a state of **stability** or balance.

The four processes of social change identified by Parsons—differentiation, adaptive upgrading, inclusion, and value generalization—stress **consensus** in society.

Social movements and protests enable us to see the dysfunctions of the existing system, and thus facilitate positive social change.

EQUILIBRIUM, CONSENSUS, STABILITY
KEY CONCEPTS

Conflict View

Groups in society that **control** valued resources can either inhibit or facilitate social change more effectively than other groups.

Though new technology can provide tools that facilitate greater freedom, those in positions of power can use it to exert greater control and surveillance.

Social change should be encouraged as a way of eliminating **inequality** and correcting social **injustice**.

KEY CONCEPTS CONTROL, SURVEILLANCE, VESTED INTERESTS

Interactionist View

Every individual has the power to change society through the everyday **choices** he or she makes and **actions** he or she takes (i.e., words we use, relationships we build, voting, volunteering, organizing for change).

Technological innovations in communication allow us to **connect** and interact with people around the world but may also cut us off from those right next to us.

Social movements consist of the **collective activities** of individuals in search of change.

KEY CONCEPTS ACTION, ORGANIZATION, CONNECTION

MAKE THE CONNECTION

After reviewing the chapter, answer the following questions:

1
How would each perspective explain the activism in the varieties of social movements described in the opening vignette?

2
How might an interactionist approach a study of the importance of pride, compassion, and justice in social movements?

3
According to each perspective, what effects have new communication technologies (for example, the Internet, cell phones, and so on) had on our interactions, relationships, and communities?

4
How would drawing an insight from each perspective enable you to more effectively bring about social change?

Pop Quiz

1. **What term do sociologists use to describe "groups of individuals and organizations collectively committed to bringing about, or resisting, fundamental societal change in a systematic way"?**
   a. engaged action
   b. social movements
   c. mobility organizations
   d. social change

2. **What three categories of moral emotions did sociologist James Jasper identify as important when studying the role of emotions in social movements?**
   a. life, liberty, and the pursuit of happiness
   b. pride, compassion, and justice
   c. material, social, and cultural
   d. joy, fear, and hope

3. **It takes more than desire to start a social movement; it helps to have money, political influence, access to the media, and workers. The ways in which a social movement uses such things are referred to collectively as**
   a. relative deprivation.
   b. false consciousness.
   c. resource mobilization.
   d. economic independence.

4. **You are a student and do not own a car. All your close friends who are attending your college or university have vehicles of their own. You feel downtrodden and dissatisfied. You are experiencing**
   a. relative deprivation.
   b. resource mobilization.
   c. false consciousness.
   d. depression.

5. **According to the definition, what is social change?**
   a. tumultuous, revolutionary alterations that lead to changes in leadership
   b. shifts in how humans think and act within society that alter material, cognitive, and normative culture
   c. regular alterations in a consistent social frame of reference
   d. subtle alterations in any social system

6. **What percentage of the world's population now has Internet access?**
   a. 36.1 percent
   b. 55.1 percent
   c. 68.9 percent
   d. 95.0 percent

7. **What name was given to the rebellious craftworkers in 19th-century England who destroyed new factory machinery as part of their resistance to the Industrial Revolution?**
   a. traitors
   b. Marxists
   c. technophobes
   d. Luddites

8. **According to Talcott Parsons's equilibrium model, during which process do social institutions become more specialized to improve performance?**
   a. differentiation
   b. adaptive upgrading
   c. inclusion
   d. value generalization

9. **What term did sociologist Jacques Ellul use to describe our systematic commitment to maximizing efficiency and increasing human productivity in all areas of human life?**
   a. technology
   b. management
   c. technique
   d. kaizen

10. **Recognizing the impact our individual position has on who we are and how we think and act and then taking responsibility for the effects our actions have on others is known as**
    a. resource mobilization.
    b. false consciousness.
    c. public sociology.
    d. personal sociology.

1. (b), 2. (b), 3. (c), 4. (a), 5. (b), 6. (b), 7. (d), 8. (b), 9. (c), 10. (d)

A

Absolute poverty   A minimum level of subsistence that no family should be expected to live below.

Accomplishment of natural growth   A style of parenting that provides broad guidelines for behavior, allowing children greater freedom to navigate the world on their own.

Achieved status   A social position that is within our power to change.

Activity theory   A theory of aging that suggests that those elderly people who remain active and socially involved will have an improved quality of life.

Adoption   The socially recognized and affirmed transfer of the legal rights, responsibilities, and privileges of parenthood.

Affirmative action   Positive efforts to recruit minority group members or women for jobs, promotions, and educational opportunities.

Ageism   Prejudice and discrimination based on a person's age.

Agency   Our freedom as individuals to think and act as we choose.

Agrarian society   The most technologically advanced form of preindustrial society. Members are engaged primarily in the production of food, but they increase their crop yields through technological innovations such as the plow.

Alienation   Loss of control over our creative human capacity to produce, separation from the products we make, and isolation from our fellow producers.

Amalgamation   The process through which a majority group and a minority group combine to form a new group.

Anomie   A weak sense of social solidarity due to a lack of agreed-upon rules to guide behavior.

Anthropocene   A geological epoch in which human actions, even at a micro level, have global environmental consequences.

Anticipatory socialization   Processes of socialization in which a person "rehearses" for future positions, occupations, and social relationships.

Antisemitism   A form of racism directed toward Jewish people.

Applied sociology   The use of the discipline of sociology with the specific intent of yielding practical applications for human behavior and organizations.

Argot   Specialized language used by members of a group or subculture.

Ascribed status   A social position assigned to a person by society without regard for the person's unique talents or characteristics.

Assimilation   The process through which a person forsakes his or her own cultural tradition to become part of a different culture.

Authority   Power that is recognized as legitimate by the people over whom it is exercised.

B

Bilateral descent   A kinship system in which both sides of a person's family are regarded as equally important.

Bisexual   A category of sexual orientation that includes those who are attracted to both men and women.

Borderlands   The area of common culture along the border between Mexico and the United States.

Bourgeoisie   The ruling class under capitalism due to their ownership of the means of production.

Brain drain   The immigration to the United States and other industrialized nations of skilled workers, professionals, and technicians who are needed in their home countries.

Broken windows hypothesis   The theory that physical signs of decline in a community or neighborhood indicate a corresponding breakdown of social order within which crime and deviance are likely to thrive

Bureaucracy   A formal organization built on the principle of maximum efficiency.

Bureaucratization   The process by which a group, organization, or social movement increasingly relies on technical-rational decision making in the pursuit of efficiency.

C

Capitalism   An economic system in which owners of private property compete in the marketplace in pursuit of profit.

Caste   A stratification system in which boundaries between strata are clear, relations between levels are regulated, and social status is ascribed.

Causal logic   A relationship exists between variables in which change in one brings about change in the other.

Charismatic authority   Power made legitimate by a leader's exceptional personal or emotional appeal to his or her followers.

Cisgender   A person whose gender identity aligns more closely with the cultural expectations associated with his or her biological sex at birth.

Class   A group of people who have a similar level of economic resources.

Class consciousness   The subjective awareness held by members of a class regarding their common vested interests and need for collective political action to bring about social change.

Clinical sociology   The use of the discipline of sociology with the specific intent of altering social relationships or restructuring social institutions.

Closed system   A society with a system of stratification that does not allow for social mobility between strata.

Coalition   A temporary or permanent alliance geared toward a common goal.

Code of Ethics   The standards of acceptable behavior developed by and for members of a profession.

Cognitive culture   Our mental and symbolic representations of reality.

Cohabitation   Two adults living in a committed relationship with an unmarried partner.

Colonialism   The maintenance of political, social, economic, and cultural dominance over a people by a foreign power for an extended period.

Color-blind racism   When race-neutral principles perpetuate a racially unequal status quo.

Concerted cultivation   A style of parenting that involves active engagement with, and sustained supervision over, children in order to foster their growth and development.

Conflict perspective   A sociological paradigm that focuses on power and the allocation of valued resources in society.

Conformity   Abiding by the norms of our peers even though they have no direct authority over us.

Contact hypothesis   The theory that interaction with people unlike ourselves decreases negative attitudes we may have about them.

Content analysis   The systematic coding and objective recording of data, guided by some rationale.

Control group   The subjects in an experiment who are not introduced to the independent variable by the researcher.

Control variable   A factor that is held constant to test the relative impact of an independent variable.

Correlation   A relationship between two variables in which a change in one coincides with a change in the other.

Correspondence principle   Schools' reproduction of the existing class structure through socializing students to embrace their social class position.

Counterculture   A subculture that deliberately opposes certain aspects of the larger culture.

Credentialism   An increase in the lowest level of education required to enter a field.

Crime   A violation of criminal law for which some governmental authority applies formal penalties.

Crude birthrate   The number of live births per 1,000 people in the population in a given year.

Crude death rate   The number of deaths per 1,000 people in a population in a given year.

Cultural capital   Our tastes, knowledge, attitudes, language, and ways of thinking that we exchange in interaction with others.

Cultural lag   The general principle that technological innovation occurs more quickly than does our capacity to perceive, interpret, and respond to that change.

Cultural relativism   The viewing of other people's behavior from the perspective of those other people's culture.

Cultural transmission   A school of criminology that argues that criminal behavior is learned through social interactions.

Cultural universal   A common belief or practice shared by all societies.

Culture   Everything humans create in establishing our relationships to nature and with each other.

Culture shock   The feelings of disorientation, uncertainty, and even fear that people experience when they encounter unfamiliar cultural practices.

Culture-bound syndrome   A disease or illness that cannot be understood apart from some specific social context.

Curanderismo   Latino folk medicine, a form of holistic health care and healing.

D

Degradation ceremony   An aspect of the socialization process within some total institutions, in which people are subjected to humiliating rituals.

Deindustrialization   The systematic and widespread reduction of investment in domestic manufacturing and material production.

Democracy   In a literal sense, government by the people.

Demographic transition   As societies transform from preindustrial to postindustrial, their population size shifts from small but stable with high birthrates and death rates, through a period of significant population growth, to large but stable, when both birthrates and death rates are low.

Demography   The statistical study of population dynamics.

Denomination   A large, organized religion that is not officially linked to the state or government.

Dependency theory   The theory that poor, less developed nations become subservient to wealthy industrial nations, which use their economic and political might to maintain power.

Dependent variable   The variable in a causal relationship that is subject to the influence of another variable.

Deviance   Behavior that violates the standards of conduct or expectations of a group or society.

Dictatorship   A government in which one person has nearly total power to make and enforce laws.

Differential association   A theory of deviance that holds that violation of rules results from exposure to attitudes favorable to criminal acts.

Differential justice   Variations in the way social control is exercised over different groups.

Diffusion   The process by which a cultural item spreads within and between societies.

Discovery   The process of revealing a previously unknown aspect of reality.

Discrimination   The practice of denying equal access to opportunities and resources on the basis of group membership rather than merit or rights.

Disengagement theory   A theory of aging that suggests that society and the aging individual mutually sever many of their relationships.

Dominant ideology   A set of cultural beliefs and practices that legitimates existing powerful social, economic, and political interests.

Downsizing   Organizational restructuring to reduce the size of a company's workforce.

Dramaturgical approach   A view of social interaction in which people are seen as actors on a stage attempting to put on a successful performance.

Dyad   The most basic building block of a social network, it consists of two nodes and the relationship between them.

E

Ecclesia   A religious organization that claims to include most or all members of a society and is recognized as the national or official religion.

Economy   A social institution dedicated to the production, distribution, and consumption of goods and services.

Education   A social institution dedicated to the formal process of transmitting culture from teachers to students.

Egalitarian family   An authority pattern in which spouses are regarded as equals.

Elite model   A view of society as being ruled by a small group of individuals who share a common set of political and economic interests.

Emigration   When members of a population leave that group.

Endogamy   The restriction of mate selection to people within the same group.

Environmental justice   A legal strategy based on claims that racial minorities are subjected disproportionately to environmental hazards.

Equilibrium model   The theory that society's natural tendency is toward social order with change in one part of society counterbalanced by adjustments in others.

Established sect   A religious group that is the outgrowth of a sect, yet remains isolated from society.

Estate system   A system of stratification that divides power in society into three primary sectors: the church, the nobility, and the commoners.

Ethnicity   Presumed cultural differences between humans to which people attach meaning resulting in the creation of supposed socially distinct subgroups within the population.

Ethnocentrism   The tendency to assume that one's own culture and way of life represent what's normal or is superior to all others.

Ethnography   The study of an entire social setting through extended systematic observation.

Exogamy   The requirement that people select a mate outside certain groups.

Experiment   An artificially created situation that allows a researcher to manipulate variables.

Experimental group   The subjects in an experiment who are exposed to an independent variable introduced by a researcher.

Expressive leader   The person in the family who bears responsibility for the maintenance of harmony and internal emotional affairs.

Expulsion   The systematic removal of a group of people from society.

Extended family   A family in which relatives—such as grandparents, aunts, or uncles—live in the same or adjacent households as parents and their children.

F

Face-work   Altering our presentation of self in order to maintain a proper image and avoid public embarrassment.

False consciousness   A term used by Karl Marx to describe an attitude held by members of a class that does not accurately reflect their objective position.

Familism   Placing the interests of the family before those of the individual.

Feminism   The belief in social, economic, and political equality for women.

Fertility   The number of children born in a given period of time.

Folkways   Norms governing everyday behavior, whose violation raises comparatively little concern.

Force   The actual or threatened use of coercion to impose one's will on others.

Formal norm   A norm that generally has been written down and that specifies strict punishments for violators.

Formal social control   The imposition of sanctions, whether positive or negative, by officially recognized authorities in order to to enforce norms.

Functionalist definition of families   A definition of families that focuses on how families provide for the physical, social, and emotional needs of individuals and of society as a whole.

Functionalist perspective   A sociological paradigm that sees society as like a living organism in which its various parts work together for the good of the whole.

Fundamentalism   Rigid adherence to core religious doctrines, often accompanied by a literal application of scripture or historical beliefs to today's world.

G

Gemeinschaft   A close-knit community, often found in rural areas, in which strong personal bonds unite members.

Gender   The social and cultural significance that we attach to the biological differences of sex.

Gender binary A dimorphic model in which gender roles are represented as either masculine or feminine with a clear divide between the two.

Gender expression The outward or public display of a person's gender.

gender identity A person's subjective or internal sense of his or her own gender.

Gender roles The normative expectations regarding proper behavior, attitudes, and activities associated with maleness and femaleness.

Gender spectrum A model of gender as a continuum that incorporates a full range of possible combinations involving sex, gender, sexual orientation, gender identity, and gender expression.

Generalized other The attitudes, viewpoints, and expectations of society as a whole that individuals take into account when interacting with others.

Genocide The systematic killing of an entire people or nation.

Gerontology The study of the sociological and psychological aspects of aging and the problems of aging adults.

Gesellschaft Consists of a large, impersonal, task-oriented society, typically urban, in which individuals have a limited commitment to the group.

Glass ceiling An invisible barrier that blocks the promotion of a qualified individual in a work environment because of the individual's gender, race, or ethnicity.

Globalization The worldwide integration of government policies, cultures, social movements, and financial markets through trade and the exchange of ideas.

Goal displacement Overzealous conformity to official regulations of a bureaucracy.

Gross national income (GNI) A measure of the total monetary value of all goods and services produced within a country during some specified period of time.

Group Two or more people, united by a shared sense of identity or purpose, who interact with each other over time in ways that distinguish them from outsiders.

Growth rate The overall percentage change in a population per year.

H

Hate crime A criminal offense committed because of the offender's bias against an individual based on race, religion, ethnicity, national origin, or sexual orientation.

Hawthorne effect The unintended influence that observers of experiments can have on their subjects.

Heteronormativity A term that sociologists use to describe the cultural presupposition that heterosexuality is the appropriate standard for sexual identity and practice and that alternative sexualities are deviant, abnormal, or wrong.

Heterosexual A category of sexual orientation that includes those who are sexually attracted to members of the opposite sex.

Hidden curriculum Teaching students to submit to authority and accept society's dominant ideology.

Holistic medicine Therapies in which the health care practitioner considers the person's physical, mental, emotional, and spiritual characteristics.

Homogamy The conscious or unconscious tendency to select a mate with personal and social characteristics similar to one's own.

Homophily Our tendency to establish close social network relationships with others who share our same knowledge, beliefs, practices, and characteristics.

Homosexual A category of sexual orientation that includes those who are attracted to members of the same sex.

Horizontal mobility The movement of an individual from one social position to another of the same rank.

Horticultural society A preindustrial society in which people plant seeds and crops rather than merely subsist on available foods.

Hospice care Treatment of terminally ill individuals in their own homes, or in special hospital units or other facilities, with the goal of helping them die comfortably, without pain.

Human ecology The area of study concerned with the interrelationships between people and their environment.

Human relations management An approach to the study of formal organizations that emphasizes the role of people, communication, and participation in a bureaucracy and tends to focus on the informal structure of the organization.

Human rights Universal moral rights possessed by all people because they are human.

Hunting-and-gathering society A preindustrial society in which people rely on whatever foods and fibers are readily available in order to survive.

Hypothesis A testable statement about the relationship between two or more variables.

I

I The acting self that exists in relation to the Me.

Ideal norms Guidelines for behavior that people agree should be followed.

Ideal type An abstract model of the essential characteristics of a phenomenon.

Immigration When individuals join a population group of which they were not previously a member.

Implicit bias The automatic and unconscious association of value, whether positive or negative, with particular groups, subgroups, or characteristics of people.

Impression management The altering of the presentation of the self in order to create distinctive appearances and satisfy particular audiences.

In-group A category of people who share a common identity and sense of belonging.

Incest taboo   The prohibition of sexual relationships between certain culturally specified relatives.

Incidence   The number of new cases of a specific disorder that occur within a given population during a stated period.

Income   Money received over some period of time.

Independent variable   The variable in a causal relationship that causes or influences a change in a second variable.

Index crimes   The eight types of crime reported annually by the FBI in the *Uniform Crime Reports:* murder, forcible rape, robbery, aggravated assault, burglary, larceny-theft, motor vehicle theft, and arson.

Industrial society   A society that depends on mechanization to produce its goods and services.

Infant mortality rate   The number of deaths of infants under one year old per 1,000 live births in a given year.

Informal norm   A norm that is generally understood but not precisely recorded.

Informal social control   The use of interpersonal cues through everyday interaction to enforce norms.

Innovation   The process of introducing a new idea or object to a culture through discovery or invention.

Institutional discrimination   The systematic denial of rights and opportunities to marginalized groups as part of society's normal operations.

Instrumental leader   The person in the family who bears responsibility for the completion of tasks, focuses on distant goals, and manages the external relationship between one's family and other social institutions.

Interactionist perspective   A sociological paradigm that maintains that society is a product of our everyday encounters with others through which we establish shared meanings and thus construct order.

Intergenerational mobility   Changes in the social position of children relative to their parents.

Intersectionality   Gender, sexuality, race, ethnicity, and class must not be studied in isolation, because they have intermingled effects on our identity, knowledge, and outcomes.

Interview   A face-to-face or telephone questioning of a respondent to obtain desired information.

Intragenerational mobility   Changes in social position within a person's adult life.

Invention   The combination of existing materials to create something new.

Iron law of oligarchy   The principle that all organizations, even democratic ones, tend to develop into bureaucracies ruled by an elite few.

K

Kinship   The state of being related to others.

L

Labeling theory   An approach to deviance that attempts to explain why certain people are viewed as deviants while others engaged in the same behavior are not.

Laissez-faire   The principle that people should be able to compete freely, without government interference, in the capitalist marketplace.

Language   A system of shared symbols; it includes speech, written characters, numerals, symbols, and nonverbal gestures and expressions.

Laws   Formal norms enforced by the state.

Liberation theology   Use of a church, primarily Roman Catholic, in a political effort to eliminate poverty, discrimination, and other forms of injustice from a secular society.

Life chances   The likelihood that our success is shaped by our access to valued material, social, and cultural resources.

Life course approach   A research orientation in which sociologists and other social scientists look closely at the social factors that influence people throughout their lives, from birth to death.

Life expectancy   The projected number of years a person can expect to live based on his or her year of birth.

Looking-glass self   A theory that we become who we are based on how we think others see us.

Luddites   Rebellious craftworkers in 19th-century England who destroyed new factory machinery as part of their resistance to the Industrial Revolution.

M

Macrosociology   Sociological investigation that concentrates on large-scale phenomena or entire civilizations.

Master status   A status that dominates others and thereby determines a person's general position in society.

Material culture   Our physical modification of the natural environment to suit our purposes.

Matriarchy   A society in which women dominate in family decision making.

Matrilineal descent   A kinship system in which only the mother's relatives are significant.

McDonaldization   The process by which the principles of efficiency, calculability, predictability, and control shape organization and decision making, in the United States and around the world.

Me   The socialized self that plans actions and judges performances based on the standards we have learned from others.

Mean   A number calculated by adding a series of values and then dividing by the number of values.

Mechanical solidarity   Social cohesion based on shared experiences, knowledge, and skills in which things function more or less the way they always have, with minimal change.

Median   The midpoint, or number that divides a series of values into two groups of equal numbers of values.

Medicalization   The process of redefining new areas of social life as the legitimate domain for medical expertise by converting them into treatable medical conditions.

Microsociology   Sociological investigation that stresses the study of small groups and the analysis of our everyday experiences and interactions.

Midlife crisis   A stressful period of self-evaluation that begins at about age 40.

Migration   The movement of people from one population group to another.

Minority group   A subordinate group whose members, even if they represent a numeric majority, lack access to, and control over, valued resources in society.

Mixed economy   An economic system that combines elements of both capitalism and socialism.

Mode   The most common value in a series of scores.

Modernization   The evolution of societies from traditional forms of social organization—typically rural, agricultural, and religious—toward forms characteristic of post-Industrial Revolution societies.

Monarchy   A form of government headed by a single member of a royal family, usually a king, queen, or some other hereditary ruler.

Monogamy   A form of marriage in which two people are married only to each other.

Monopoly   Control of a market by a single business firm.

Morbidity rate   The occurrences of illness in a given population over some period of time.

Mores   Norms deemed highly necessary to the welfare of a society.

Mortality rate   The incidence of death in a given population over some period of time.

Multinational corporation   A commercial organization that is headquartered in one country but does business throughout the world.

Multiple masculinities   The idea that expressions of manliness can take varieties of forms beyond the culturally dominant, stereotypical construct of what it means to be a man.

N

Natural science   The systematic study of the physical features of nature and the ways in which they interact and change.

Neocolonialism   Continuing dependence of former colonies on foreign countries.

New religious movement (NRM)   A small, alternative faith community that represents either a new religion or a major innovation in an existing faith.

Nonverbal communication   The use of gestures, facial expressions, and other visual images to communicate.

Norm   An established standard of behavior maintained by a society.

Normative culture   Consists of the ways we establish, abide by, and enforce principles of conduct.

Nuclear family   A married couple and their unmarried children living together.

O

Obedience   Doing what a person in a position of authority over you says you should.

Observation   A research technique in which an investigator collects information through direct participation and/or by closely watching a group or community.

Offshoring   Outsourcing of work to foreign contractors.

Oligarchy   A form of government in which a few individuals rule.

One-drop rule   The principle that, if a person had even one Black African ancestor, no matter how many generations back, the person was labeled Black—even if he or she appeared to be White.

Open system   A society with a system of stratification that allows for social mobility between strata.

Operational definition   Transformation of an abstract concept into indicators that are observable and measurable.

Organic solidarity   Social cohesion based on mutual interdependence in the context of extreme division of labor.

Organized crime   The work of a group that regulates relations among criminal enterprises involved in illegal activities, including prostitution, gambling, and the smuggling and sale of illegal drugs.

Out-group   A category of people who do not belong or do not fit in.

P

Party   The capacity to organize to accomplish some particular goal.

Passing   When people whose genetic ancestry and family history convey membership in one racial category but who are perceived to belong to another race in the eyes of others.

Patriarchy   A society in which men dominate in family decision making.

Patrilineal descent   A kinship system in which only the father's relatives are significant.

Peace   The absence of war, or, more broadly, a proactive effort to develop cooperative relations among nations.

Personal sociology   The practice of recognizing the impact the positions we occupy have on who we are and how we think and act.

Pluralism   Mutual respect for one another's cultures among the various groups in a society, which allows minorities to express their own cultures without experiencing prejudice.

Pluralist model   A view of society in which many competing groups within the community have access to government so that no single group is dominant.

Politics   The competition between individuals or groups over the allocation of valued resources.

Polity   The social institution that establishes and enforces rules within a society and negotiates relationships with other societies.

Polyandry   A form of polygamy in which a woman may have more than one husband at the same time.

Polygamy   A form of marriage in which an individual may have several husbands or wives simultaneously.

Polygyny   A form of polygamy in which a man may have more than one wife at the same time.

Postindustrial society   A society whose economic system is engaged primarily in the processing and control of information.

Postmodern society   A technologically sophisticated, pluralistic, interconnected, globalized society.

Power   The ability to exercise one's will over others even if they resist.

Power elite   A small group of military, industrial, and government leaders who control the fate of the United States.

Prejudice   A preconceived and unjustified judgment of individuals, whether positive or negative, based on their membership in a particular group.

Prestige   The respect and admiration that a particular status holds in society.

Prevalence   The total number of cases of a specific disorder that exist at a given time.

Primary groups   Small group characterized by intimate, face-to-face association and cooperation.

Primary sector   The segment of the economy involving activities that extract products directly from the natural environment.

Private troubles   Problems we face in our immediate relationships with particular individuals in our personal lives.

Profane   The ordinary and commonplace elements of life, as distinguished from the sacred.

Proletariat   The working class under capitalism who must sell their labor power in exchange for a wage because they lack ownership of the means of production.

Protestant ethic   Max Weber's term for the disciplined commitment to worldly labor driven by a desire to bring glory to God, shared by followers of Martin Luther and John Calvin.

Public issues   Problems we face as a consequence of the positions we occupy within the larger social structure.

Public sociology   The process of bringing the insights gained through sociological observation and analysis into the public sphere, thereby seeking to bring about positive social change.

Q

Qualitative research   Descriptive research that relies on narrative accounts rather than statistical procedures.

Quantitative research   Research that collects and reports data primarily in numerical form.

Queer   A term that incorporates the multiplicity of possible sexual orientations, gender identities, and gender expressions.

Questionnaire   A respondent completes a printed or computerized form and returns it to the researcher.

R

Race   Presumed *biological* differences between humans to which people attach meaning resulting in the creation of supposed *genetically* distinct subgroups within the population.

Racial formation   A sociohistorical process in which racial categories are created, inhibited, transformed, and destroyed.

Racial profiling   Any police-initiated action based on race, ethnicity, or national origin rather than on a person's behavior.

Racism   The combination of cultural beliefs regarding inherent racial superiority and inferiority with normative practices of advantage or disadvantage which get built into a structure that reproduces patterns of unequal outcomes.

Random sample   A sample for which every member of an entire population has the same chance of being selected.

Rational-legal authority   Authority based on formally agreed-upon and accepted rules, principles, and procedures of conduct that are established in order to accomplish goals in the most efficient manner possible.

Real norms   Rules of conduct generated from people's actual behavior.

Reference group   Any group that individuals use as a standard for evaluating themselves and their own behavior.

Relative deprivation   People's perception that they lack the resources necessary to lead the kind of life they believe they deserve.

Relative poverty   A floating standard of deprivation by which people at the bottom of a society are judged to be disadvantaged in comparison with the nation as a whole.

Reliability   The extent to which a measure produces consistent results.

Religion   A social institution dedicated to establishing a shared sense of identity, encouraging social integration, and offering believers a sense of meaning and purpose.

Religious belief   A statement to which members of a particular religion adhere.

Religious experience   The feeling or perception of being in direct contact with the ultimate reality, such as a divine being, or of being overcome with religious emotion.

Religious ritual   A practice required or expected of members of a faith.

Remittances   The monies that immigrants return to their families of origin. Also known as *remesas*.

Replacement fertility rate   The minimum number of children a woman would need to average in her lifetime to reproduce the population in the next generation.

Representative democracy   A system of government in which citizens elect political leaders to make decisions on behalf of the people.

Research design   A detailed plan or method for obtaining data scientifically.

Resocialization   The process of discarding former behavior patterns and accepting new ones as part of a transition in one's life.

Resource mobilization   The rational management of resources to accomplish a social movement's organizational goals.

Rite of passage   A ritual marking the symbolic transition from one social position to another, dramatizing and validating changes in a person's status.

Role conflict   The situation that occurs when incompatible expectations arise from two or more social statuses held by the same person.

Role exit   The process of disengagement from a role that is central to one's self-identity in order to establish a new role and identity.

Role strain   The difficulty that arises when role expectations within the same social status clash.

Role taking   The process of mentally assuming the perspective of another and responding from that imagined viewpoint.

S

Sacred   Elements beyond everyday life that inspire respect, awe, and even fear.

Sample   A selection from a larger population that is statistically representative of that population.

Sanction   A penalty or reward for conduct concerning a social norm.

Sandwich generation   The generation of adults who simultaneously try to meet the competing needs of their parents and their children.

Sapir-Whorf hypothesis   The structure and vocabulary of language shapes our perception of reality and therefore also our actions.

Scientific management   Theory of management that measures all aspects of the work process to eliminate any inefficiencies.

Scientific method   The systematic observation of empirical, this-worldly evidence to assess and refine ideas about what happens and why.

Second shift   The double burden of working outside the home followed by child care and housework.

Secondary analysis   A variety of research techniques that make use of existing data for the purpose of new analysis.

Secondary groups   Formal, impersonal groups created to accomplish specific, shared goals.

Secondary sector   The segment of the economy consisting of activities that transform raw or intermediate materials into finished products.

Sect   A relatively small religious group that has broken away from some other religious organization to renew what it considers the original vision of the faith.

Secularization   Religion's diminishing influence in the public sphere, especially in politics and the economy.

Segregation   The physical separation of two groups of people in terms of residence, workplace, and social events.

Self   Our sense of who we are, distinct from others, and shaped by the unique combination of our social interactions.

Serial monogamy   A form of marriage in which a person may have several spouses in his or her lifetime, but only one spouse at a time.

Sex   The biological differences between males and females.

Sexism   The ideology that claims one sex is superior to the other.

Sexual orientation   The categories of people to whom we are sexually attracted.

Sexuality   Denotes our identities and activities as sexual beings.

Sick role   A form of legitimate deviance in which the person who becomes ill has a corresponding set of rights and responsibilities associated with that status.

Significant other   An individual who is most important in the development of the self, such as a parent, friend, or teacher.

Single-parent family   A family in which only one parent is present to care for the children.

Slavery   A system of enforced servitude in which some people are owned by others as property.

Social change   Shifts in how humans think and act within society that alter material, cognitive, and normative culture.

Social class   A system of stratification primarily based on socioeconomic status, both real and perceived.

Social construction of reality   The ongoing interdependent relationship within which individuals create society through our actions and, at the same time, become products of the society we construct.

Social control   Society's power to limit deviance by enforcing conformity to expected norms and values.

Social control theory   A theory of deviance that posits that the social bonds we share with other members of society lead us to conform to society's norms

Social disorganization theory   The theory that attributes increases in crime and deviance to the absence or breakdown of communal relationships and social institutions, such as the family, school, church, and local government.

Social epidemiology   The study of the role social factors play in the development and distribution of disease throughout the population.

Social evolution   A theory of social change that holds that societies progress from simple to complex over time.

Social facts   Manners of acting, thinking, and feeling external to the individual with coercive power to shape how we act, think, and feel.

Social inequality   A condition in which members of society have different amounts of wealth, prestige, or power.

Social institution   An integrated and persistent social network dedicated to ensuring that society's core needs are met.

Social interaction   A reciprocal exchange in which two or more people read, react, and respond to each other.

Social mobility   Movement within or between society's strata.

Social movement   Groups of individuals and organizations collectively committed to bringing about, or resisting, fundamental societal change in a systematic way.

Social network   A web of relationships through which people interact both directly and indirectly to accomplish formal and informal goals.

Social role   A set of expected behaviors for people who occupy a given social status.

Social science   The systematic study of human behavior, interaction, and change.

Social structure   The underlying framework of society consisting of the positions people occupy and the relationships between them.

Socialism   An economic system under which the means of production and distribution are collectively owned.

Socialization   The lifelong process through which people learn the attitudes, values, and behaviors appropriate for members of a particular culture.

Societal-reaction approach   Another name for *labeling theory*.

Society   The structure of relationships within which culture is created and shared through regularized patterns of social interaction.

Sociobiology   The systematic study of how biology affects human social behavior.

Socioeconomic status (SES)   A measure of social class position based on a combination of education, occupation, and income.

Sociological imagination   Our exploration of the interdependent relationship between who we are as individuals and the social forces that shape our lives.

Sociology   The systematic study of the relationship between the individual and society and of the consequences of difference.

Standpoint theory   Because our social positions shape our perceptions, a more complete understanding of social relations must incorporate the perspectives of marginalized voices.

Status   The social positions we occupy relative to others.

Status group   People who share the same perceived level of prestige.

Stereotype   An unreliable generalization about all members of a group that does not recognize individual differences within the group.

Stigma   Labeling individuals or members of a group as less than whole persons due to some attribute that marks them as different in the eyes of others.

Strain theory of deviance   Robert Merton's theory of deviance as an adaptation of socially prescribed goals or of the means governing their attainment, or both.

Stratification   A structured ranking of entire groups of people that perpetuates unequal economic rewards and power in a society.

Subculture   A segment of society that shares a distinctive pattern of mores, folkways, and values that differs from the pattern of the larger society.

Substantive definition of families   A definition of families in terms of blood, connecting people biologically, and law, connecting people through formal social recognition.

Survey   A predefined series of questions designed to collect information about people's particular attributes, beliefs, and actions.

Symbol   A gesture, object, or word that forms the basis of human communication.

Symbolic ethnicity   An ethnic identity that emphasizes concerns such as ethnic food or political issues rather than deeper ties to one's ethnic heritage.

T

Teacher-expectancy effect   The impact that a teacher's expectations about a student's performance may have on the student's actual achievements.

Technology   A form of material culture in which humans convert natural resources into tools to accomplish practical ends.

Terrorism   The use or threat of violence against random or symbolic targets in pursuit of political aims.

Tertiary sector   The segment of the economy consisting of activities that provide services rather than produce tangible goods.

Theory   In sociology, a set of statements that seeks to explain problems, actions, or behavior.

Thomas theorem   What we perceive as real is real in its consequences.

Total fertility rate   The average number of children a woman would have during her lifetime given current birthrates and assuming she survives through her childbearing years.

Total institution   An institution that regulates all aspects of a person's life under a single authority, such as a prison, the military, a mental hospital, or a convent.

Totalitarianism   Virtually complete government control and surveillance over all aspects of a society's social and political life.

Tracking   The practice of placing students in specific curriculum groups on the basis of their test scores and other criteria.

Traditional authority   Legitimate power conferred by custom and accepted practice.

Transgender   A person whose gender identity differs from the sex he or she was assigned at birth.

Transnational crime   Crime that occurs across multiple national borders.

Triad   Within a social network, it consists of three nodes and the direct and indirect relationships among them.

V

Validity   The degree to which a measure or scale truly reflects the phenomenon under study.

Value   A collective conception of what is considered good, desirable, and proper—or bad, undesirable, and improper—in a culture.

Value neutrality   Max Weber's term for objectivity of sociologists in the interpretation of data.

Variable   A measurable trait or characteristic that is subject to change under different conditions.

Vertical mobility   The movement of an individual from one social position to another of a different rank.

Vested interests   Those people or groups who benefit most from the existing social, political, and economic structure.

Victimization surveys   Questionnaires or interviews that ask representative samples of the population whether or not they have been victims of crime.

Victimless crime   A term used by sociologists to describe the willing exchange among adults of widely desired, but illegal, goods and services.

W

War   Conflict between organizations that possess trained combat forces equipped with deadly weapons.

Wealth   The total value of all material assets minus debts at a single point in time.

White-collar crime   Illegal acts committed by high-status individuals who use their positions of power and influence for their own benefit.

World systems analysis   A view of the global economic system as one divided between certain industrialized nations that control wealth and developing countries that are controlled and exploited.

A

Aaronson, Daniel, and Bhashkar Mazumder. 2007. "Intergenerational Economic Mobility in the U.S., 1940 to 2000." FRB Chicago Working Paper No. WP 2005-12, revised February 2007. Federal Reserve Bank of Chicago. Accessed June 21, 2008 (http://ssrn.com/abstract5869435).

AAUP. 2018. "Data Snapshot: Contingent Faculty in US Higher Education." American Association of University Professors, October 11. Accessed December 22, 2018 (www.aaup.org/sites/default/files/10112018%20Data%20Snapshot%20Tenure.pdf).

Abercrombie, Nicholas, Stephen Hill, and Bryan S. Turner. 1980. *The Dominant Ideology Thesis.* London: George Allen and Unwin.

———. 2006. *The Penguin Dictionary of Sociology,* 5th ed. New York: Penguin Books.

Aberle, David E., A. K. Cohen, A. K. Davis, M. J. Leng Jr., and F. N. Sutton. 1950. "The Functional Prerequisites of a Society." *Ethics* 60 (January): 100-111.

Abkowitz, Alyssa. 2015. "A High-Rise Race in Mumbai." *The Wall Street Journal,* April 2. Accessed January 14, 2017 (www.wsj.com/articles/a-high-rise-race-in-mumbai-1427988257).

Abma, Joyce C., and Gladys M. Martinez. 2017. "Sexual Activity and Contraceptive Use among Teenagers in the United States, 2011-2015." NCHS Data Brief, No. 104, June 22. Hyattsville, MD: National Center for Health Statistics. Accessed February 1, 2017 (www.cdc.gov/nchs/data/nhsr/nhsr104.pdf).

Accominotti, Fabien, Adam Storer, and Shamus R. Khan. 2018. "How Cultural Capital Emerged in Guilded Age America: Musical Purification and Cross-Class Inclusion at the New York Philharmonic." *American Journal of Sociology* 123 (6): 1743-1783

Acemoglu, Daron, and James A. Robinson. 2012. *Why Nations Fail: The Origins of Power, Prosperity, and Poverty.* New York: Crown Business.

Adair-Toteff, Christopher. 2005. "Max Weber's Charisma." *Journal of Classical Sociology* 5 (2): 189-204.

Adams, Jimi. 2007. "Stained Glass Makes the Ceiling Visible: Organizational Opposition to Women in Congregational Leadership." *Gender and Society* 21 (February): 80-115.

Adams, Samantha, and Antoinette de Bont. 2007. "Information Rx: Prescribing Good Consumerism and Responsible Citizenship." *Health Care Analysis* 15 (4): 273-290.

Addams, Jane. 1910. *Twenty Years at Hull-House.* New York: Macmillan.

———. 1930. *The Second Twenty Years at Hull-House.* New York: Macmillan.

Adichie, Chimamanda Ngozi. 2014. *Americanah.* London: Fourth Estate.

Adler, Patricia A., and Peter Adler. 1996. "Preadolescent Clique Stratification and the Hierarchy of Identity." *Sociological Inquiry* 66 (2): 111-142.

———. 2012. "Tales from the Field: Reflections on Four Decades of Ethnography." *Qualitative Sociology Review* 7 (1): 10-32.

Adler, Patricia A., Steve J. Kless, and Peter Adler. 1992. "Socialization to Gender Roles: Popularity among Elementary School Boys and Girls." *Sociology of Education* 65 (July): 169-187.

Agar, Jon. 2013. *Constant Touch: A Global History of the Mobile Phone.* Revised and Updated. London: Icon Books, Ltd.

Agrawal, Nadya. 2013. "Dye-ing Culture: Color Run, White-washing Holi Since 2012." *Brown Girl Magazine,* April. Accessed September 30, 2016 (www.browngirlmagazine.com/2013/04/color-run-controversy/).

Ahler, Douglas J., and Guarav Sood. 2018. "The Parties in Our Heads: Misperceptions about Party Composition and Their Consequences." *The Journal of Politics* 80 (3): 964-981.

Ahnonen, Tomi T. 2008. *Mobile as 7th of the Mass Media: Cellphone, Cameraphone, Smartphone.* London: Futuretext Ltd.

Ainsworth, Claire. 2015. "Sex Redefined." *Nature* 518: 288-291.

Akseer, Tabasum, Zachary Warren, and John Rieger, eds. 2017. "Afghanistan in 2017: A Survey of the Afghan People." San Francisco: The Asia Foundation. Accessed November 11, 2018 (https://asiafoundation.org/wp-content/uploads/2017/11/2017_AfghanSurvey_report.pdf).

Alba, Richard. 2015. "The Myth of a White Minority." *The New York Times,* June 11. Accessed February 4, 2017 (www.nytimes.com/2015/06/11/opinion/the-myth-of-a-white-minority.html).

Alexander, Michelle. 2012. *The New Jim Crow: Mass Incarceration in the Age of Colorblindness.* New York: New Press.

Alger, Horatio, Jr. [1868] 1985. *Ragged Dick and Struggling Upward.* New York: Penguin Books.

Alimahomed, Sabrina. 2010. "Thinking outside the Rainbow: Women of Color Redefining Queer Politics and Identity." *Social Identities* 16 (2): 151-168.

Allam, Hannah. 2016. "Muslim Stereotyping in Pop Culture Is Worse Than Ever." *McClatchyDC,* April 26. Accessed January 18, 2017 (www.mcclatchydc.com/news/nation-world/national/article73969887.html).

Allard, Ladonna Brave Bull. 2016. "Why the Founder of Standing Rock Sioux Camp Can't Forget the Whitestone Massacre." *Yes! Magazine,* September 3. Accessed February 8, 2017 (www.yesmagazine.org/people-power/why-the-founder-of-standing-rock-sioux-camp-cant-forget-the-whitestone-massacre-20160903).

Allen, John L. 2008. *Student Atlas of World Politics,* 8th ed. New York: McGraw-Hill.

Allen, Robert C. 2017. *The Industrial Revolution: A Very Short Introduction.* New York: Oxford University Press.

Allport, Gordon W. 1979. *The Nature of Prejudice,* 25th anniversary ed. Reading, MA: Addison-Wesley.

Althoff, Tim, Ryen W. White, and Eric Horvitz. 2016. "Influence of Pokemon Go on Physical Activity: Study and Implications." *arXiv* 1610.02085. Accessed October 24, 2016 (https://arxiv.org/pdf/1610.02085v1.pdf).

Alzheimer's Association. 2018. "2018 Alzheimer's Disease Facts and Figures." *Alzheimer's & Dementia* 14 (3). Accessed January 26, 2019 (www.alz.org/facts/overview.asp).

Amato, Paul R., and Alan Booth. 1997. *A Generation at Risk.* Cambridge, MA: Harvard University Press.

American Society of Plastic Surgeons. 2018. "2017 Plastic Surgery Statistics Report." ASPS National Clearing House of Plastic Surgery Procedural Statistics. Arlington Heights, IL: American Society of Plastic Surgeons. Accessed December 3, 2018 (www.plasticsurgery.org/news/plastic-surgery-statistics/).

American Sociological Association. 1999. *Code of Ethics and Policies and Procedures of the ASA Committee on Professional Ethics.* Washington, DC: American Sociological Association. Accessed May 1, 2013 (www.asanet.org/images/asa/docs/pdf/CodeofEthics.pdf).

Amnesty International. 1994. *Breaking the Silence: Human Rights Violations Based on Sexual Orientation.* New York: Amnesty International.

———. 2009. "Sexual Orientation and Gender Identity." Accessed June 15, 2009 (www.amnesty.org/en/sexual-orientation-and-gender-identity).

———. 2011. "Annual Report 2011: The State of the World's Human Rights." Accessed May 28, 2012 (www.amnesty.org/en/annual-report/2011).

———. 2015. *Amnesty International Report 2014/15: The State of the World's Human Rights.* London: Amnesty International, Ltd. Accessed April 15, 2015 (www.amnesty.org/en/documents/pol10/0001/2015/en/).

Anagnostou, Yiorgos. 2009a. "A Critique of Symbolic Ethnicity: The Ideology of Choice?" *Ethnicities* 9 (1): 94-122.

———. 2009b. "About Facts and Fictions: Reply to Herbert Gans and Mary Waters." *Ethnicities* 9 (1).

Anderson, John Ward, and Molly Moore. 1993. "Born Oppressed: Women in the Developing World Face Cradle-to-Grave Discrimination, Poverty." *The Washington Post,* February 14, p. A1.

Anderson, Terry H. 2007. *The Sixties,* 3rd ed. Englewood Cliffs, NJ: Prentice Hall.

Andrews, Wilson, Josh Katz, and Jugal Patel. 2016. "Latest Election Polls 2016." *The New York Times,* November 8. Accessed December 13, 2016 (www.nytimes.com/interactive/2016/us/elections/polls.html).

Angier, Natalie. 2000. "Do Races Differ? Not Really, Genes Show." *The New York Times,* August 22, p. F6. Accessed June 30, 2008 (http://query.nytimes.com/gst/fullpage.html?res59E07E7DF1E3EF931A1575BC0A9669C8B63&scp52&sq5natalie1angier&st5nyt).

Anti-Defamation League. 2018. "Audit of Anti-Semitic Incidents: Year in Review 2017." Accessed October 13, 2018 (www.adl.org/media/11174/download).

Applebaum, Binyamin. 2015. "Behaviorists Show the U.S. How to Improve Government Operations." *The New York Times,* September 29. Accessed November 1, 2018 (www.nytimes.com/2015/09/30/business/behaviorists-show-the-us-how-to-improve-government-operations.html).

Arab American Institute. 2008. "Arab Americans: Demographics." Accessed July 1, 2008 (www.aaiusa.org/arab-americans/22/demographics).

Arab American Institute Foundation. 2014. "Demographics." Accessed October 10, 2018 (www.aaiusa.org/demographics).

Arendt, Hannah. 1951. *The Origins of Totalitarianism.* New York: Harcourt, Brace, and Co.

Arora, Neeraj K., Bradford W. Hesse, Barbara K. Rimer, K. Viswanath, Marla L. Clayman, and Robert T. Croyle. 2008. "Frustrated and Confused: The American Public Rates Its Cancer-Related Information-Seeking Experiences."*Journal of General Internal Medicine* 23 (3): 223–228.

Arthur, Rachel. 2018. "'Bottled Water Is America's Favorite Drink!' Bottled Water Takes Top Spot in US." *Beverage Daily,* June 1. Accessed January 26, 2019 (www.beveragedaily.com/Article/2018/06/01/Bottled-water-takes-top-spot-in-US-in-2017).

Aslan, Reza. 2010. *Beyond Fundamentalism: Confronting Religious Extremism in the Age of Globalization.* New York: Random House.

Association of Theological Schools. 2018. "2017–2018 Annual Data Tables." The Commission on Accrediting, Association of Theological Schools in the United States and Canada, Pittsburgh. Accessed December 22, 2018 (www.ats.edu/uploads/resources/institutional-data/annual-data-tables/2017-2018-annual-data-tables.pdf).

Atchley, Robert C. 1976. *The Sociology of Retirement.* New York: Wiley.

Atkinson, Anthony B. 2015. *Inequality: What Can Be Done?* Cambridge, MA: Harvard University Press.

Avise, John C. 2004. *The Hope, Hype, and Reality of Genetic Engineering: Remarkable Stories from Agriculture, Industry, Medicine, and the Environment.* New York: Oxford University Press.

B

Backhaus, Peter. 2013. "The Japanese Traffic Light Blues: Stop on Red, Go on What?" *The Japan Times,* February 25. Accessed January 19, 2015 (www.japantimes.co.jp/life/2013/02/25/language/the-japanese-traffic-light-blues-stop-on-red-go-on-what/#.VMgFdC6fnjY).

Bacon, Perry, Jr. 2018. "Democrats Are Wrong about Republicans. Republicans Are Wrong about Democrats." *FiveThirtyEight.* June 26. Accessed November 17, 2018 (https://fivethirtyeight.com/features/democrats-are-wrong-about-republicans-republicans-are-wrong-about-democrats/).

Baer, Drake. 2016. "English Could Use Swedish's Untranslatable Words for Relationships." *New York Magazine,* October 19. Accessed November 22, 2016 (http://nymag.com/scienceofus/2016/10/english-could-use-swedishs-words-for-relationships.html).

Baer, Hans. 2008. "Global Warming as a By-product of the Capitalist Treadmill of Production and Consumption—the Need for an Alternative Global System." *Australian Journal of Anthropology* 19 (1): 58–62.

Bag, Sugata, Suman Seth, and Anish Gupta. 2016. "A Comparative Study of Living Conditions in Slums of Three Metro Cities in India." Centre for Development Economics, Delhi School, Delhi School of Economics, Working Paper No. 253, ISSN No. 2454-1427. Accessed January 14, 2017 (https://papers.ssrn.com/sol3/papers.cfm?abstract_id=2727005).

Bagilhole, Barbara, and Simon Cross. 2006. "It Never Struck Me as Female: Investigating Men's Entry into Female-Dominated Occupations." *Journal of Gender Studies* 15 (1): 35–48.

Bahadur, Amar. 2008. "Sanskritization and Caste Opposition: A Shift from Ritual to Political-Economic Power." *Himalayan Journal of Sociology and Anthropology* 3: 1–10.

Bahr, Peter Riley. 2008. "*Cooling Out* in the Community College: What Is the Effect of Academic Advising on Students Chances of Success?" *Research in Higher Education* 49: 704–732.

Bain-Selbo, Eric. 2012. *Game Day and God: Football, Faith, and Politics in the American South.* Macon, GA: Mercer University Press.

Baio, Andy. 2015. "Pirating the 2015 Oscars: HD Edition." *The Message,* January 22. Accessed February 19, 2015 (https://medium.com/message/pirating-the-2015-oscars-hd-edition-6c78e0cb471d).

———. 2016. "Pirating the Oscars 2016." *Waxy,* January 19. Accessed November 11, 2016 (http://waxy.org/2016/01/pirating_the_oscars_2016/).

———. 2017. "Oscar Screener Piracy: 2003–2017." Waxy.org. Accessed May 25, 2017 (https://docs.google.com/spreadsheets/d/1H8eds6jEeBXoXIFH1RdbgigVtWdpyc8A9gyqHUt4Do/edit#gid=0).

———. 2018. "Pirating the Oscars." Updated. *Waxy.* Accessed December 1, 2018 (http://waxy.org/2016/01/pirating_the_oscars_2016/).

Baldez, Lisa. 2004. "Elected Bodies: The Gender Quota Law for Legislative Candidates in Mexico." *Legislative Studies Quarterly* 29: 231–258.

Baldwin, James. [1965] 1985. "White Man's Guilt." Pp. 409–414 in *The Price of the Ticket: Collected Nonfiction, 1948–1985.* New York: St. Martin's Press.

Balfour, Gillian. 2006. "Re-imagining a Feminist Criminology." *Canadian Journal of Criminology & Criminal Justice* 48 (5): 735–752.

Banaji, Mahzarin R., and Anthony G. Greenwald. 2013. *Blindspot: Hidden Biases of Good People.* New York: Delacorte Press.

Banks, Duren, Lance Couzens, Caroline Blanton, and Devon Cribb. 2015. "Arrest-Related Deaths Program Assessment: Technical Report." U.S. Department of Justice, Office of Justice Programs, NCJ 248543, March. Accessed April 27, 2015 (www.bjs.gov/content/pub/pdf/ardpatr.pdf).

Banks, Pauline, and Maggie Lawrence. 2006. "The Disability Discrimination Act, a Necessary, but Not Sufficient Safeguard for People with Progressive Conditions in the Workplace? The Experiences of Younger People with Parkinson's Disease." *Disability and Rehabilitation* 28 (1): 13–24.

Barnes, Patricia M., Barbara Bloom, and Richard L. Nahin. 2008. "Complementary and Alternative Medicine Use Among Adults and Children: United States, 2007." *National Health Statistics Reports* 12. Hyattsville, MD: National Center for Health Statistics. Accessed May 20, 2010 (http://nccam.nih.gov/news/2008/nhsr12.pdf).

Barnes, Patricia M., Eve Powell-Griner, Kim McFann, and Richard L. Nahin. 2004. "Complementary and Alternative Medicine Use among Adults, United States, 2002." Advance data from *Vital and Health Statistics* 343. Hyattsville, MD: National Center for Health Statistics. Accessed July 5, 2008 (http://nccam.nih.gov/news/camsurvey_fs1.htm).

Barr, Donald A. 2014. *Health Disparities in the United States: Social Class, Race, Ethnicity, and Health,* 2nd ed. Baltimore, MD: Johns Hopkins University Press.

Barrionuevo, Alexei. 2008. "Amazons Forest Peoples Seek a Role in Striking Global Climate Agreements." *The New York Times,* April 6, p. 6.

Basinger, Jeanine. 2012. *I Do and I Don't: A History of Marriage in the Movies.* New York: Knopf.

Bastian, Brock, and Nick Haslam. 2006. "Psychological Essentialism and Stereotype Endorsement." *Journal of Experimental Psychology* 42: 228–235.

Bates, Claire. 2016. "How Does 'Curvy Barbie' Compare with an Average Woman?" *BBC News,* March 3. Accessed January 30, 2017 (www.bbc.com/news/magazine-35670446).

Baudrillard, Jean. [1981] 1994. *Simulacra and Simulation.* Ann Arbor: University of Michigan Press.

Bauer, Roxanne. 2015. "Media (R)evolutions: Skipping the Landline, Going Straight for a Mobile Phone." People, Spaces, Deliberation, The World Bank, April 1. Accessed November 20, 2018 (https://blogs.worldbank.org/publicsphere/media-revolutions-skipping-landline-going-straight-mobile-phone).

Baum, Bruce. 2006. *The Rise and Fall of the Caucasian Race: A Political History of Racial Identity.* New York: New York University Press.

Baumgardner, Jennifer, and Amy Richards. 2000. *Manifesta: Young Women, Feminism and the Future.* New York: Farrar, Straus and Giroux.

Beagan, Brenda. 2001. "Even If I Don't Know What I'm Doing I Can Make It Look Like I Know What I'm Doing: Becoming a Doctor in the 1990s." *Canadian Review of Sociology and Anthropology* 38: 275–292.

————. 2003. "Teaching Social and Cultural Awareness to Medical Students: It's All Very Nice to Talk about It in Theory, but Ultimately It Makes No Difference." *Academic Medicine* 78 (6): 605–614.

Bearman, Peter S., James Moody, and Katherine Stovel. 2004. "Chains of Affection: The Structure of Adolescent Romantic and Sexual Networks." *American Journal of Sociology* 110 (July): 44–91.

Beauvoir, Simone de. 1952. *The Second Sex.* New York: Knopf.

Becker, Howard S. 1963. *The Outsiders: Studies in the Sociology of Deviance.* New York: Free Press.

————, ed. 1964. *The Other Side: Perspectives on Deviance.* New York: Free Press.

Beckford, James A. 1985. *Cult Controversies: The Societal Response to the New Religious Movements.* New York: Tavistock.

Beeghley, Leonard. 2007. *The Structure of Social Stratification in the United States,* 5th ed. Boston: Allyn & Bacon.

Bell, Daniel. 1953. "Crime as an American Way of Life." *Antioch Review* 13 (Summer): 131–154.

————. 1999. *The Coming of Post-industrial Society: A Venture in Social Forecasting.* With new foreword. New York: Basic Books.

————. 2001. *Liberation Theology after the End of History: The Refusal to Cease Suffering.* New York: Routledge.

Benagiano, Giuseppe, and Maurizio Mori. 2009. "The Origins of Human Sexuality: Procreation or Recreation?" *Reproductive Bio-Medicine Online* 18 (S1): 50–59.

Bengal. Rebecca. 2016. "Standing Rock Rising: Inside the Movement to Stop the Dakota Access Pipeline." *Vogue,* November 22. Accessed February 8, 2017 (www.vogue.com/projects/13505511/standing-rock-movement-dakota-access-pipeline/).

Benhorin, Shira, and Susan D. McMahon. 2008. "Exposure to Violence and Aggression: Protective Roles of Social Support among Urban African American Youth." *Journal of Community Psychology* 36 (6): 723–743.

Benjamins, Maureen R., and Steven Whitman. 2013. "Relationships between Discrimination in Health Care and Health Care Outcomes among Four Race/Ethnic Groups." *Journal of Behavioral Medicine* 37 (3): 402–413.

Bennett, Asa. 2016. "Did Britain Really Vote Brexit to Cut Immigration?" *The Telegraph,* June 29. Accessed February 4, 2017 (www.telegraph.co.uk/news/2016/06/29/did-britain-really-vote-brexit-to-cut-immigration/).

Bennett, Drake. 2010. "This Will Be on the Midterm. You Feel Me? Why So Many Colleges Are Teaching *The Wire.*" *Slate,* March 24. Accessed April 9, 2010 (www.slate.com/id/2245788/).

Bennett, V., S. Dávila-Poblete, and M. N. Rico, eds. 2005. *Opposing Currents: The Politics of Water and Gender in Latin America.* Pittsburgh, PA: University of Pittsburgh Press.

Berchick, Edward R., Emily Hood, and Jessica C. Barnett. 2018. *Health Insurance Coverage in the United States: 2017. Current Population Reports,* P60-264. Washington, DC: U.S. Government Printing Office. Accessed January 26, 2019 (www.census.gov/content/dam/Census/library/publications/2018/demo/p60-264.pdf).

Berenson, Alex, and Diana B. Henriques. 2008. "Look at Wall St. Wizard Finds Magic Had Skeptics." *The New York Times,* December 12. Accessed May 21, 2009 (www.nytimes.com/2008/12/13/business/13fraud.html).

Berg, Scott W. 2012. *38 Nooses: Lincoln, Little Crow, and the Beginning of the Frontier's End.* New York: Pantheon Books.

Bergen, Raquel Kennedy. 2006. *Marital Rape: New Research and Directions.* Harrisburg, PA: VAW Net.

Berger, Peter. 1969. *The Sacred Canopy: Elements of a Sociological Theory of Religion.* Garden City, NY: Anchor Books.

Berger, Peter, and Thomas Luckmann. 1966. *The Social Construction of Reality.* New York: Doubleday.

Berlin, Brent, and Paul Kay. 1991. *Basic Color Terms: Their Universality and Evolution.* Berkeley: University of California Press.

Berlin, Ira. 2010. *The Making of African America: The Four Great Migrations.* New York: Viking.

Bernburg, Jón Gunnar, Marvin D. Krohn, and Craig Rivera. 2006. "Official Labeling, Criminal Embeddedness, and Subsequent Delinquency: A Longitudinal Test of Labeling Theory." *Journal of Research in Crime & Delinquency* 43 (1): 67–88.

Best, Steven, and Douglas Kellner. 2001. *The Postmodern Adventure: Science, Technology, and Cultural Studies at the Third Millennium.* New York: Guilford Press.

Bevir, George. 2017. "Cost of Online Piracy to Hit $52bn." IBC, October 30. Accessed December 2, 2018 (www.ibc.org/delivery/cost-of-online-piracy-to-hit-52bn/2509.article).

Bezrukova, Katerina, Karen A. Jehn, and Chester S. Spell. 2012. "Reviewing Diversity Training: Where We Have Been and Where We Should Go." *Academy of Management Learning & Education* 11 (2): 207–227.

Bhanbhro, Sadiq. 2017. "Indonesia's Minangkabau Culture Promotes Empowered Women." *The Conversation,* January 12. Accessed January 24, 2019 (https://theconversation.com/indonesias-minangkabau-culture-promotes-empowered-muslim-women-68077).

Bhatia, Aatish. 2012. "The Crayola-fication of the World: How We Gave Colors Names, and It Messed with Our Brains (Part I)." *Wired,* June 5. Accessed January 19, 2015 (www.wired.com/2012/06/the-crayola-fication-of-the-world-how-we-gave-colors-names-and-it-messed-with-our-brains-part-i/).

Bhrolcháin, Máire Ní. 2001. "Divorce Effects and Causality in the Social Sciences." *European Sociological Review* 17 (1): 33–57.

Bialik, Kristin, and Jens Manuel Krogstad. 2017. "115th Congress Sets New High for Racial, Ethnic Diversity." Pew Research Center, January 24. Accessed February 6, 2017 (www.pewresearch.org/fact-tank/2017/01/24/115th-congress-sets-new-high-for-racial-ethnic-diversity/).

Bianchi, Suzanne M., John P. Robinson, and Melissa A. Milkie. 2006. *Changing Rhythms of American Family Life.* New York: Sage.

Bijker, Wiebe E., Thomas P. Hughes, and Trevor Pinch, eds. 2012. *The Social Construction of Technological Systems: New Directions in the Sociology and History of Technology,* Anniversary Edition. Cambridge, MA: MIT Press.

Birdsall, Nancy, and Pedro Pablo Kuczynski. 2015. "Climate Talks: Rich Countries Should Pay to Keep Tropical Forests Standing." *The Guardian,* December 2. Accessed January 26, 2019 (www.theguardian.com/global-development/2015/dec/02/climate-talks-rich-countries-should-pay-to-keep-tropical-forests-standing).

Bivens, Josh. 2012. "Inequality, Exhibit A: Walmart and the Wealth of American Families." Economic Policy Institute, July 17. Accessed January 10, 2019 (www.epi.org/blog/inequality-exhibit-wal-mart-wealth-american/).

Black, Edwin. 2012. *War Against the Weak: Eugenics and America's Campaign to Create a Master Race.* Washington, DC: Dialog Press.

Blair, J. Pete, and Katherine W. Schweit. 2014. "A Study of Active Shooter Incidents, 2000–2013." Texas State University and Federal Bureau of Investigation, U.S. Department of Justice, Washington, DC. Accessed February 19, 2015 (www.fbi.gov/news/stories/2014/september/fbi-releases-study-on-active-shooter-incidents/pdfs/a-study-of-active-shooter-incidents-in-the-u.s.-between-2000-and-2013).

Blass, Thomas. 1999. "The Milgram Paradigm after 35 Years: Some Things We Now Know about Obedience to Authority." *Journal of Applied Psychology* 29: 955–978.

Blauner, Robert. 1972. *Racial Oppression in America.* New York: Harper and Row.

References

Bloemraad, Irene, Anna Korteweg, and Gökçe Yurdakul. 2008. "Citizenship and Immigration: Multiculturalism, Assimilation, and Challenges to the Nation-State." *Annual Review of Sociology* 34: 153–179.

Bloom, David E., David Canning, Günther Fink, and Jocelyn E. Finlay. 2010. "The Cost of Low Fertility in Europe." *European Journal of Population* 26: 141–158.

Bluestone, Barry, and Bennett Harrison. 1982. *The Deindustrialization of America: Plant Closings, Community Abandonment, and the Dismantling of Basic Industry.* New York: Basic Books.

Blumenbach, Johann Friedrich. [1776] 1865. *On the Natural Variety of Mankind,* ed. and trans. Thomas Bendyshe in *The Anthropological Treatises of Johann Friedrich Blumenbach.* London: Anthropological Society.

Blumer, Herbert. 1955. "Collective Behavior." Pp. 165–198 in *Principles of Sociology,* 2nd ed., ed. Alfred McClung Lee. New York: Barnes and Noble.

Boas, Franz. 1911. *The Mind of Primitive Man.* New York: Macmillan.

———. 1940. *Race, Language, and Culture.* New York: Macmillan.

———. 1945. *Race and Democratic Society.* New York: J. J. Augustin Publishers.

Boaz, Rachel Floersheim. 1987. "Early Withdrawal from the Labor Force." *Research on Aging* 9 (December): 530–547.

Bolt, Gideon, A. Sule Ozuekren, and Deborah Phillips. 2010. "Linking Integration and Residential Segregation." *Journal of Ethnic & Migration Studies* 36 (2): 169–186.

Bongaarts, John. 2009. "Human Population Growth and the Demographic Transition." *Philosophical Transactions of the Royal Society, Series B, Biological Sciences* 364: 2985–2990.

Booth, Alan, and Paul R. Amato. 2001. "Parental Predivorce Relations and Offspring Postdivorce Well-Being." *Journal of Marriage and Family* 62: 197–212.

Boren, Cindy. 2016. "For Two Olympians, a Humiliating Journey to Rio Filled with Gender-Questioning." *The Washington Post,* August 16. Accessed January 26, 2017 (www.washingtonpost.com/news/early-lead/wp/2016/08/16/for-two-olympians-a-humiliating-journey-to-rio-filled-with-gender-questioning/).

Boren, Zachary Davies. 2015. "Pope Francis Apologizes for Catholic Crimes against Indigenous Peoples during the Colonisation of the Americas." *The Independent,* July 10. Accessed October 9, 2018 (www.independent.co.uk/news/world/americas/pope-francis-apologises-for-catholic-crimes-against-indigenous-peoples-during-the-colonisation-of-10380319.html).

Boshara, Ray, William R. Emmons, and Bryan J. Noeth. 2015. "Race, Ethnicity, and Wealth." The Demographics of Wealth: How Age, Education, and Race Separate Thrivers from Strugglers in Today's Economy, Essay No. 1, February. Accessed February 6, 2017 (www.stlouisfed.org/~/media/Files/PDFs/HFS/essays/HFS-Essay-1-2015-Race-Ethnicity-and-Wealth.pdf).

Bouis, Howarth E. 2007. "The Potential of Genetically Modified Food Crops to Improve Human Nutrition in Developing Countries." *Journal of Development Studies* 43 (1): 79–96.

Bourdieu, Pierre. 1962. *The Algerians.* Preface by Raymond Aron. Boston: Beacon Press.

———. 1984. *Distinction: A Social Critique of the Judgment of Taste.* Cambridge, MA: Harvard University Press.

———. 1986. "The Forms of Capital." Pp. 241–258 in *Handbook of Theory and Research for the Sociology of Education,* ed. J. G. Richardson. New York: Greenwood Press.

———. 1998a. *Acts of Resistance: Against the Tyranny of the Market.* New York: New Press.

———. 1998b. *On Television.* New York: New Press.

Bowles, Samuel, and Herbert Gintis. 1976. *Schooling in Capitalistic America: Educational Reforms and the Contradictions of Economic Life.* New York: Basic Books.

Bradsher, Keith. 2016. "The Paris Agreement on Climate Change Is Official. Now What?" *The New York Times,* November 3. Accessed February 13, 2017 (www.nytimes.com/2016/11/04/business/energy-environment/paris-climate-change-agreement-official-now-what.html).

Brand, Jennie E., and Yu Xie. 2010. "Who Benefits Most from College? Evidence for Negative Selection in Heterogeneous Economic Returns to Higher Education." *American Sociological Review* 75 (2): 273–302.

Brandon, Emily. 2012. "The New Ideal Retirement Age: 67." Planning to Retire, Money, *U.S. News & World Report,* May 8. Accessed May 22, 2012 (http://money.usnews.com/money/blogs/planning-to-retire/2012/05/08/the-new-ideal-retirement-age-67).

Brands, H. W. 2008. "15 Minutes That Saved America." *American History* 43 (4): 34–41.

Brannigan, Augustine, and William Zwerman. 2001. "The Real Hawthorne Effect." *Society* 38 (January/February): 55–60.

Brenan, Megan. 2018. "Record-High 75% of Americans Say Immigration Is Good Thing." Gallup, June 21. Accessed January 22, 2019 (https://news.gallup.com/poll/235793/record-high-americans-say-immigration-good-thing.aspx).

Brewer, Rose M., and Nancy A. Heitzeg. 2008. "The Racialization of Criminal Punishment." *American Behavioral Scientist* 51 (January): 625–644.

Brickell, Chris. 2009. "Sexuality and the Dimensions of Power." *Sexuality & Culture* 13 (2): 57–74.

Bricker, Jesse, Lisa J. Dettling, Alice Henriques, Joanne W. Hsu, Lindsay Jacobs, Kevin B. Moore, Sarah Pack, John Sabelhaus, Jeffrey Thompson, and Richard A. Windle. 2017. "Changes in U.S. Family Finances from 2013 to 2016: Evidence from the Survey of Consumer Finances." *Federal Reserve Bulletin* 103 (3). Accessed October 6, 2018 (www.federalreserve.gov/publications/files/scf17.pdf).

Brill, Steven. 2015. *America's Bitter Pill: Money, Politics, Backroom Deals, and the Fight to Fix Our Broken Healthcare System.* New York: Random House.

Brooks, Ann. 1997. *Postfeminisms: Feminism, Cultural Theory, and Cultural Forms.* New York: Routledge.

Brown, Ashley. 2015. "Picture [Im]Perfect: Photoshop Redefining Beauty in Cosmetic Advertisements, Giving False Advertising a Run for the Money." *Texas Review of Entertainment and Sports Law* 16 (2): 87–105.

Brown, Curt. 2015. "In Little Crow's Wake, Horrors for the Dakota." *Minneapolis Star Tribune,* April 29. Accessed February 4, 2017 (www.startribune.com/in-little-crow-s-wake-horrors-for-the-dakota/166163736/).

Brown, Harriet. 2015. *Body of Truth: How Science, History, and Culture Drive Our Obsession with Weight—and What We Can Do about It.* Boston: Da Capo Press.

Brown, Luke. 2016. "Providing Role Models for Young Girls Could Make DC Super Hero Girls a Billion-Dollar Brand." *Comics Alliance,* May 25. Accessed January 30, 2017 (http://comicsalliance.com/dc-super-hero-girls-diane-nelson-billion-dollars/).

Brown, Robert McAfee. 1980. *Gustavo Gutierrez.* Atlanta, GA: John Knox.

Brown, Susan L., and I-Fen Lin. 2012. "The Gray Divorce Revolution: Rising Divorce among Middle-Aged and Older Adults, 1990–2010." *The Journals of Gerontology: Series B* 6 (1): 731–741.

Brown, Wyatt, and Wesley G. Jennings. 2014. "A Replication and an Honor-Based Extension of Hirschi's Reconceptualization of Self-Control Theory and Crime and Analogous Behaviors." *Deviant Behavior* 35: 297–310.

Bruce, Steve. 2000. *Choice and Religion: A Critique of Rational Choice Theory.* New York: Oxford University Press.

Buck, Christopher G. 2006. "'Never Again': Kevin Gover's Apology for the Bureau of Indian Affairs." *Wicazo Sa Review* 21 (1): 97–126.

Buckles, Kasey, Andreas Hagemann, Ofer Malamud, Melinda Morrill, and Abigail Wozniak. 2016. "The Effect of College Education on Mortality." *Journal of Health Economics* 50: 99–114.

Buffett, Warren E. 2010. "Pretty Good for Government Work." *The New York Times,* November 16. Accessed June 3, 2015 (www.nytimes.com/2010/11/17/opinion/17buffett.html).

Bui, Anthony L., Matthew M. Coates, and Ellicott C. Matthay. 2018. "Years of Life Lost Due to Encounters with Law Enforcement in the USA, 2015–2016." *Journal Epidemiological & Community Health* 72 (8): 715–718.

Bui, Quoctrung, and Claire Cain Miller. 2018. "The Age That Women Have Babies: How a Gap Divides America." *The New York Times*, August 4. Accessed December 15, 2018 (www.nytimes.com/interactive/2018/08/04/upshot/up-birth-age-gap.html).

Bullough, Vern L. 1998. "Alfred Kinsey and the Kinsey Report: Historical Overview and Lasting Contributions." *Journal of Sex Research* 35 (2): 127–131.

Bundhun, Rebecca. 2016. "Supertall Buildings Lure Mumbai's Elite." *The New York Times*, March 3. Accessed January 14, 2017 (www.nytimes.com/2016/03/04/realestate/supertall-buildings-lure-mumbais-elite.html).

Burawoy, Michael. 2004. "Public Sociologies: Contradictions, Dilemmas, and Possibilities." *Social Forces* 82: 1603–1618.

———. 2009. *The Extended Case Method: Four Countries, Four Decades, Four Great Transformations, and One Theoretical Tradition.* Berkeley: University of California Press.

Bureau of Economic Analysis. 2018. "Gross Domestic Product: Fourth Quarter and Annual 2017 (Second Estimate)." U.S. Department of Commerce, Washington, DC, BEA 18-08, February 28. January 20, 2019 (www.bea.gov/system/files/2018-02/gdp4q17_2nd.pdf).

Bureau of Labor Statistics. 2010. "Civilian Labor Force, 2019–2050." Employment Projections, Labor Force (Demographic) Data. Accessed April 20, 2010 (www.bls.gov/emp/ep_data_labor_force.htm).

———. 2015a. "Number of Jobs, Labor Market Experience, and Earnings Growth: Results from a Longitudinal Survey." *Economic New Release*, March 31. Accessed October 25, 2016 (www.bls.gov/news.release/nlsoy.toc.htm).

———. 2015b. "Women in the Labor Force: A Databook." U.S. Department of Labor, U.S. Bureau of Labor Statistics, Report 1059, December. Accessed December 14, 2016 (www.bls.gov/opub/reports/womens-databook/archive/women-in-the-labor-force-a-databook-2015.pdf).

———. 2015c. "Labor Force Characteristics by Race and Ethnicity, 2015." U.S. Department of Labor, U.S. Bureau of Labor Statistics, September. Accessed December 14, 2016 (www.bls.gov/opub/reports/race-and-ethnicity/2015/pdf/home.pdf).

———. 2016e. "2016 Employment & Earnings Online: Household Survey Data." U.S. Department of Labor. Accessed December 7, 2016 (www.bls.gov/opub/ee/2016/cps/annual.htm).

———. 2016h. "Household Activities." American Time Use Survey, December 20. Accessed February 2, 2017 (www.bls.gov/tus/charts/household.htm).

———. 2016i. "Labor Force Statistics from the Current Population Survey: 2015." U.S. Department of Labor, Washington, DC. Accessed February 6, 2017 (www.bls.gov/cps/tables.htm).

———. 2017b. "Women in the Labor Force: A Databook." U.S. Department of Labor, U.S. Bureau of Labor Statistics, Report 1065, April. Accessed June 1, 2017 (www.bls.gov/opub/reports/womens-databook/2016/pdf/home.pdf).

———. 2017c. "Number of Jobs, Labor Market Experience, and Earnings Growth among Americans at 50: Results from a Longitudinal Survey." U.S. Department of Labor, USDL-17-1158, August 24. Accessed November 20, 2018 (www.bls.gov/news.release/pdf/nlsoy.pdf).

———. 2017d. "Number of Jobs, Labor Market Experience, and Earnings Growth Among Americans at 50: Results from a Longitudinal Study." U.S. Department of Labor, News Release, USDL-17-1158. Accessed April 17, 2019 (www.bls.gov/news.release/pdf/nlsoy.pdf).

———. 2018a. "Labor Force Statistics from the Current Population Survey: 2017." U.S. Department of Labor, Washington, DC. Accessed October 6, 2018 (www.bls.gov/cps/tables.htm).

———. 2018b. "Unemployment: Rates for States." Local Area Unemployment Statistics. Washington, DC: U.S. Department of Labor. Accessed October 29, 2018 (www.bls.gov/web/laus/laumstrk.htm).

———. 2018c. "Unemployment: Rates & Levels—Labor Force Statistics including the National Unemployment Rate." Current Population Survey, Databases, Tables & Calculators by Subject. Washington, DC: U.S. Department of Labor. Accessed October 29, 2018 (www.bls.gov/data/#unemployment).

———. 2018d. "Employment Characteristics of Families—2017." U.S. Department of Labor, USDL-18-0589, April 19. Accessed December 15, 2018 (www.bls.gov/news.release/pdf/famee.pdf).

———. 2018e. "College Enrollment and Work Activity of Recent High School and College Graduates." U.S. Department of Labor, USDL-18-0635, April 26. Accessed December 20, 2018 (www.bls.gov/news.release/pdf/hsgec.pdf).

———. 2018f. "2018 Employment & Earnings Online." U.S. Department of Labor, March 9. Accessed December 22, 2018 (www.bls.gov/opub/ee/2018/cps/annual.htm).

———. 2018g. "Women in the Labor Force: A Databook." U.S. Department of Labor, U.S. Bureau of Labor Statistics, Report 1077, December. Accessed January 7, 2019 (www.bls.gov/opub/reports/womens-databook/2018/home.htm).

———. 2018h. "Labor Force Characteristics by Race and Ethnicity, 2017." U.S. Department of Labor, U.S. Bureau of Labor Statistics, Report 1076, September. Accessed January 7, 2019 (www.bls.gov/opub/reports/race-and-ethnicity/2017/home.htm).

———. 2018i. "Consumer Expenditure Survey: CE Tables—Table 1101 Quintiles of Income before Taxes," September. Accessed January 13, 2019 (www.bls.gov/cex/tables.htm).

———. 2019a. "Average Hourly Earnings of Production and Nonsupervisory Employees, 1982–84 Dollars, Total Private, Seasonally Adjusted." U.S. Department of Labor, Employment, Hours, and Earnings from the Current Employment Statistics survey (National), Series Id: CES0500000032. Accessed January 10, 2019 (https://data.bls.gov/timeseries/CES0500000032).

———. 2019b. "Average Hourly Earnings of Production and Non-supervisory Employees, Total Private, Not Seasonally Adjusted." U.S. Department of Labor, Employment, Hours, and Earnings from the Current Employment Statistics Survey (National), Series Id: CEU0500000008. Accessed January 10, 2019 (https://data.bls.gov/timeseries/CEU0500000008).

———. 2019c. "Employment Status of the Civilian Noninstitutional Population by Age, Sex, and Race." Labor Force Statistics from the Current Population Survey. Washington, DC: U.S. Department of Labor. Accessed January 30, 2019 (www.bls.gov/cps/cpsaat03.htm).

Burger, Jerry M. 2009. "Replicating Milgram: Would People Still Obey Today?" *American Psychologist* 64: 1–11.

Burgoon, Judee K., Laura K. Guerrero, and Kory Floyd. 2010. *Nonverbal Communication.* New York: Allyn & Bacon.

Burleigh, Michael, and Wolfgang Wippermann. 1991. *The Racial State: Germany 1933-1945.* New York: Cambridge University Press.

Burke, Moira, Carlos Greg Diuk, and Adrien Friggeri. 2015. "Cupid in Your Network." Facebook Research. Accessed May 6, 2015 (https://research.facebook.com/blog/448802398605370/cupid-in-your-network/).

Burke, Peter. 2018. "Marjory Stoneman Douglas High School Students Give Impassioned Speeches in Tallahassee." *Local 10 News*, February 21. Accessed January 30, 2019 (www.local10.com/news/parkland-school-shooting/marjory-stoneman-douglas-high-school-students-give-impassioned-speeches-in-tallahassee).

Burns, Corinne. 2013. "Are Mental Illnesses Such as PMS and Depression Culturally Determined?" *The Guardian*, May 20. Accessed June 7, 2013 (www.guardian.co.uk/science/blog/2013/may/20/mental-illnesses-depression-pms-culturally-determined?CMP=twt_fd).

Burns, Crosby, Kimberly Barton, and Sophia Kerby. 2012. "The State of Diversity in Today's Workforce." Center for American Progress, Washington, DC, July. Accessed June 1, 2013 (www.americanprogress.org/wp-content/uploads/issues/2012/07/pdf/diversity_brief.pdf).

Burton, Bonnie. 2018. "Wonder Woman Really Does Boost Girls' Self Esteem, according to a New Study." *Insider*, October 9. Accessed January 23, 2019 (www.thisisinsider.com/wonder-woman-female-superheroes-boost-girls-self-esteem-2018-10).

Butler, Judith. 1990. *Gender Trouble: Feminism and the Subversion of Identity.* New York: Routledge.

Butler, Rhett. 2016. "Calculating Deforestation Figures for the Amazon." Mongabay, January 23. Accessed February 13, 2017 (http://rainforests.mongabay.com/amazon/deforestation_calculations.html).

Butler, Robert N. 1990. "A Disease Called Ageism." *Journal of American Geriatrics Society* 38 (February): 178–180.

C

Cacchioni, Thea, and Leonore Tiefer. 2012. "Why Medicalization? Introduction to the Special Issue on the Medicalization of Sex." *Journal of Sex Research* 49: 307–310.

Cacioppo, John T., Stephanie Cacioppo, Gian C. Gonzaga, Elizabeth L. Ogburn, and Tyler J. VanderWeele. 2013. "Marital Satisfaction and Break-Ups Differ across On-Line and Off-Line Meeting Venues." *PNAS* 110: 10135–10140.

Cai, Yong. 2010. "China's Below-Replacement Fertility: Government Policy or Socioeconomic Development?" *Population and Development Review* 36: 419–440.

Calamur, Krishnadev. 2017. "What Trump's Executive Order on Immigration Does—and Doesn't Do." *The Atlantic,* January 30. Accessed February 7, 2017 (www.theatlantic.com/news/archive/2017/01/trump-immigration-order-muslims/514844/).

Calderón, Laura, Octavio Rodríguez Ferreira, and David A. Shirk. 2018. *Drug Violence in Mexico: Data and Analysis through 2017.* Justice in Mexico Project, Special Report, April. Accessed December 4, 2018 (https://justiceinmexico.org/wp-content/uploads/2018/04/180411_DrugViolenceinMexico-12mb.pdf).

Caldwell, Elizabeth F., and Susan Jane Wilbraham. 2018. "Hairdressing in Space: Depiction of Gender in Science Books for Children." *Journal of Science & Popular Culture* 1 (2): 101–118.

Camp, Roderic Ai. 2010a. *The Metamorphosis of Leadership in a Democratic Mexico.* New York: Oxford University Press.

————. 2010b. "Armed Forces and Drugs: Public Perceptions and Institutional Challenges." Pp. 291–325 in *Shared Responsibility: U.S.-Mexico Policy Options for Confronting Organized Crime,* ed. Eric L. Olson, David A. Shirk, and Andrew Selee. San Diego: University of San Diego Trans-Border Institute.

Campos, Belinda, Jodie B. Ullman, Adrian Aguilera, and Christine Dunkel Schetter. 2014. "Familism and Psychological Health: The Intervening Role of Closeness and Social Support." *Cultural Diversity and Ethnic Minority Psychology* 20 (2): 191–201.

Caplow, Theodore, and Louis Hicks. 2002. *Systems of War and Peace,* 2nd ed. Lanham, MD: University Press of America.

Carey, Kate B., Lori A. J. Scott-Sheldon, Jennifer C. Elliott, Lorra Garey, and Michael P. Carey. 2012. "Face-to-Face versus Computer-Delivered Alcohol Interventions for College Drinkers: A Meta-Analytic Review, 1998 to 2010." *Clinical Psychology Review* 32 (8): 690–703.

Carlson, Daniel L., Amanda Jayne Miller, and Sharon Sassler. 2018. "Stalled for Whom? Change in the Division of Particular Housework Tasks and Their Consequenes for Middle- to Low-Income Couples." *Socius* 4: 1–17. Accessed January 25, 2019 (https://journals.sagepub.com/doi/pdf/10.1177/2378023118765867).

Carmichael, Mary. 2007. "Troubled Waters." *Newsweek* 149 (June 4): 52–56.

Carothers, Bobbi J., and Harry T. Reis. 2013. "Men and Women Are from Earth: Examining the Latent Structure of Gender." *Journal of Personality and Social Psychology* 104 (2): 385–407.

Carr, John E., and Eng K. Tan. 1976. "In Search of the True Amok: Amok as Viewed within the Malay Culture." *American Journal of Psychiatry* 133 (11): 1295–1299.

Carr, Nicholas. 2010. *The Shallows: What the Internet Is Doing to Our Brains.* New York: Norton.

————. 2014. *The Glass Cage: Automation and Us.* New York: Norton.

Carroll, Aaron E. 2015. "No, You Do Not Have to Drink 8 Glasses of Water a Day." *The New York Times,* August 24. Accessed September 12, 2016 (www.nytimes.com/2015/08/25/upshot/no-you-do-not-have-to-drink-8-glasses-of-water-a-day.html).

Carroll, Aaron E., and Rachel C. Vreeman. 2009. *Don't Swallow Your Gum! Myths, Half-Truths and Outright Lies about Your Body and Health.* New York: St. Martin's Press.

Carroll, Rory. 2016. "Starved, Tortured, Forgotten: Genie, the Feral Child Who Left a Mark on Researchers." *The Guardian,* July 14. Accessed October 17, 2016 (www.theguardian.com/society/2016/jul/14/genie-feral-child-los-angeles-researchers).

Carson, Rachel. 1962. *Silent Spring.* Boston: Houghton Mifflin.

Carter, Susan B., Scott Sigmund Gartner, Michael R. Haines, Alan L. Olmstead, Richard Sutch, and Gavin Wright. 2006. *Historical Statistics of the United States: Earliest Times to the Present, Millennial Edition.* 5 vols. Cambridge, UK: Cambridge University Press.

Carty, Victoria, and Jake Onyett. 2006. "Protest, Cyberactivism and New Social Movements: The Reemergence of the Peace Movement Post 9/11." *Social Movement Studies* 5 (3): 229–249.

Cassandra. 2015. "No Kid(ding)." Ages & Stages, Cassandra Report, Summer. Accessed November 22, 2016 (https://cassandra.co/2015/ages-and-stages/no-kidding).

Casselman, Ben. 2016. "Stuck in Your Parents' Basement? Don't Blame the Economy." *FiveThirtyEight,* May 27. Accessed November 22, 2016 (http://fivethirtyeight.com/features/stuck-in-your-parents-basement-dont-blame-the-economy/).

Catalyst. 2019a. "Women CEOs of the S&P 500." Catalyst Knowledge Center, January 16. Wednesday, January 23, 2019 (www.catalyst.org/knowledge/women-ceos-sp-500).

Cavalli-Sforza, L. Luca, Paolo Menozzi, and Alberto Piazza. 1994. *The History and Geography of Human Genes.* Princeton, NJ: Princeton University Press.

Center for American Women and Politics. 2018. "Results: Women Candidates in the 2018 Elections." Eagleton Institute of Politics, Rutgers, University, New Brunswick, NJ. Accessed January 25, 2019 (http://cawp.rutgers.edu/sites/default/files/resources/results_release_5bletterhead5d_1.pdf).

————. 2019. "Women in Elective Office 2019." Eagleton Institute of Politics, Rutgers, University, New Brunswick, NJ. Accessed January 25, 2019 (www.cawp.rutgers.edu/women-elective-office-2019).

Centers for Disease Control and Prevention. 2016b. "Youth Risk Behavior Surveillance—United States, 2015." Surveillance Summaries, June 10. *Morbidity and Mortality Weekly Report* 65 (6). Accessed February 2, 2017 (www.cdc.gov/healthyyouth/data/yrbs/pdf/2015/ss6506_updated.pdf).

————. 2018a. "Marriages and Divorces—Detailed State Tables." National Center for Health Statistics, Atlanta, GA. Accessed December 13, 2018 (www.cdc.gov/nchs/nvss/marriage-divorce.htm).

————. 2018c. "Traumatic Occupation Injuries: Data and Statistics." National Institute for Occupational Health and Safety. Accessed January 26, 2019 (www.cdc.gov/niosh/injury/data.html).

Centers for Medicare & Medicaid Services. 2018a. "National Health Expenditure Data: Historical." Department of Health and Human Services. Accessed January 26, 2019 (www.cms.gov/Research-Statistics-Data-and-Systems/Statistics-Trends-and-Reports/NationalHealthExpendData/NationalHealthAccountsHistorical.html).

————. 2018b. "National Health Expenditure Data: Projected." Department of Health and Human Services. Accessed January 26, 2019 (www.cms.gov/Research-Statistics-Data-and-Systems/Statistics-Trends-and-Reports/NationalHealthExpendData/NationalHealthAccountsProjected.html).

————. 2018c. "Fast Facts: CMS Program Data—Populations." Department of Health and Human Services. Accessed January 26, 2019 (www.cms.gov/fastfacts/).

Césaire, Aimé. 1972. *Discourse on Colonialism.* New York: Monthly Review Press.

Chalabi, Mona, and Andrew Flowers. 2014. "Dear Mona, What's the Most Popular Name in America?" *FiveThirtyEight Life,* November 20. Accessed January 10, 2015 (http://fivethirtyeight.com/features/whats-the-most-common-name-in-america/).

Chambers, Samuel. 2007. "An Incalculable Effect: Subversions of Heteronormativity." *Political Studies* 55 (3): 656–679.

Chambliss, William. 1973. "The Saints and the Roughnecks." *Society* 11 (November/December): 24–31.

Chandra, Anjani, Casey E. Copen, and William D. Mosher. 2013. "Sexual Behavior, Sexual Attraction, and Sexual Identity in the United States: Data from the 2006–2010 National Survey of Family Growth." *International Handbook on the Demography of Sexuality, International Handbooks of Population* 5: 45–66.

Chandra, Anjani, William D. Mosher, Casey Copen, and Catlainn Sionean. 2011. "Sexual Behavior, Sexual Attraction, and Sexual Identity in the United States: Data from the 2006–2008 National Survey of Family Growth." National Center for Health Statistics. *National Health Statistics Reports* 36, March 3. Accessed August 9, 2011 (www.cdc.gov/nchs/data/nhsr/nhsr036.pdf).

Chang, Joseph T. 1999. "Recent Common Ancestors of All Present-Day Individuals." *Advances in Applied Probability* 31: 1002–1026.

Charney, Leo, and Vanessa R. Schwartz, eds. 1995. *Cinema and the Invention of Modern Life.* Berkeley: University of California Press.

Chavigny, Katherine A. 2014. "An Army of Reformed Drunkards and Clergymen: The Medicalization of Habitual Drunkenness, 1857–1910." *Journal of the History of Medicine & Allied Sciences* 69: 383–425.

Chee, Kyong Hee, Nathan W. Pino, and William L. Smith. 2005. "Gender Differences in the Academic Ethic and Academic Achievement." *College Student Journal* 39 (3): 604–618.

Chen, Victor Tan. 2016. "The Spiritual Crisis of the Modern Economy." *The Atlantic,* December 21. Accessed December 22, 2016 (www.theatlantic.com/business/archive/2016/12/spiritual-crisis-modern-economy/511067/).

Cheng, Shu-Ju Ada. 2003. "Rethinking the Globalization of Domestic Service." *Gender and Society* 17 (2): 166–186.

Chenoweth, Erica. 2017. "This Is What We Learned by Counting the Women's Marches." *The Washington Post,* February 7. Accessed November 27, 2018 (www.washingtonpost.com/news/monkey-cage/wp/2017/02/07/this-is-what-we-learned-by-counting-the-womens-marches/?utm_term=.58b902ee0a9f).

Cherlin, Andrew. 2008. *Public and Private Families: An Introduction,* 5th ed. New York: McGraw-Hill.

———. 2009. *The Marriage-Go-Round: The State of Marriage and the Family in America Today.* New York: Knopf.

Chesney-Lind, Meda. 1989. "Girls' Crime and Woman's Place: Toward a Feminist Model of Female Delinquency." *Crime and Delinquency* 35: 5–29.

Chesney-Lind, Meda, and Lisa Pasko. 2004. *The Female Offender: Girls, Women, and Crime,* 2nd ed. Thousand Oaks, CA: Sage.

Chettiar, Inimai M. 2015. "The Many Causes of American Crime." *The Atlantic,* February 11. Accessed November 12, 2016 (www.theatlantic.com/politics/archive/2015/02/the-many-causes-of-americas-decline-in-crime/385364/).

Chetty, Raj, David Grusky, Maximilian Hell, Nathaniel Hendren, Robert Manduca, and Jimmy Narang. 2016. "The Fading American Dream: Trends in Absolute Income Mobility Since 1940." NBER Working Paper Series, Number 22910, December. Accessed December 22, 2016 (www.equality-of-opportunity.org/papers/abs_mobility_paper.pdf).

Chetty, Raj, Michael Stepner, Sarah Abraham, Shelby Lin, Benjamin Scuderi, Nicholas Turner, Augustin Bergeron, and David Cutler. 2016. "The Association between Income and Life Expectancy in the United States, 2001–2014." *JAMA* 315 (16): 1750–1766.

Choudry, Shaf, and Sadia Habib. 2018. "Shows Like Bodyguard Perpetuate Muslim Stereotypes. We Created the Riz Test to Show How Dire Representation Is." *Metro,* September 16. Accessed January 20, 2019 (https://metro.co.uk/2018/09/16/shows-like-bodyguard-perpetuate-muslim-stereotypes-we-created-the-riz-test-to-show-how-dire-representation-is-7944626/).

Christakis, Nicholas A., and James H. Fowler. 2009. *Connected: The Surprising Power of Our Social Networks and How They Shape Our Lives.* New York: Little, Brown and Company.

Christel, Deborah A., and Susan C. Dunn. 2016. "Average American Women's Clothing Size: Comparing National Health and Nutritional Examination Surveys (1988–2010) to ASTM International Misses & Women's Plus Size Clothing." *International Journal of Fashion Design, Technology, and Education,* August: 1–8.

Christian, Joseph. 2009. "Coffee Culture: A Symbol of Middle-Class Lifestyle." *China Daily,* November 3. Accessed April 1, 2010 (www.chinadaily.com.cn/cndy/2009-11/03/content_8903174.htm).

Chua, Amy. 2011. *The Battle Hymn of the Tiger Mother.* New York: Penguin Press.

Chun, Helen, Maria I. Tavarez, Grace E. Dann, and Michael P. Anastario. 2011. "Interviewer Gender and Self-Reported Sexual Behavior and Mental Health among Male Military Personnel." *International Journal of Public Health* 56 (2): 225–229.

Cigar, Norman. 1995. *Genocide in Bosnia: The Policy of "Ethnic Cleansing."* College Station: Texas A&M University Press.

CIRCLE. 2016. "Young People Reject Trump, but Older Voters Propel Him to Unexpected Victory." The Center for Information & Research on Civic Learning & Engagement, Medford, MA, November 9. Accessed December 15, 2016 (http://civicyouth.org/too-close-to-call-young-people-reject-trump-older-voters-key-to-his-unexpectedly-strong-performance/).

———. 2018. "Young People Dramatically Increase Their Turnout to 31%, Shape 2018 Midterm Elections." The Center for Information & Research on Civic Learning and Engagement, November 7. Accessed January 8, 2019 (https://civicyouth.org/young-people-dramatically-increase-their-turnout-31-percent-shape-2018-midterm-elections/).

Clair, Matthew, and Jeffrey S. Denis. 2015. "Racism, Sociology of." *International Association of the Social and Behavioral Sciences,* 2nd ed, 19: 857–863.

Clammer, John. 2009. "Sociology and Beyond: Towards a Deep Sociology." *Asian Journal of Social Science* 37 (3): 332–346.

Clark, Burton. 1960. "The Cooling-Out Function in Higher Education." *American Journal of Sociology* 65: 569–576.

———. 1980. "The Cooling-Out Function Revisited." *New Directions for Community Colleges* 32: 15–31.

Clark, Duncan. 2012. "Has the Kyoto Protocol Made Any Difference to Carbon Emissions?" *The Guardian,* November 26. Accessed May 3, 2015 (www.theguardian.com/environment/blog/2012/nov/26/kyoto-protocol-carbon-emissions).

Clark, Jonathan R., Robert S. Huckman, and Bradley R. Staats. 2013. "Learning from Customers: Individual and Organizational Effects in Outsourced Radiological Services." *Organization Science* 24: 1539–1557.

Clarke, Edward H. 1874. *Sex in Education; or, A Fair Chance for the Girls.* Boston: James R. Osgood.

Clarke, Tainya C., Lindsey I. Black, Barbara J. Stussman, Patricia M. Barnes, and Richard L. Nahin. 2015. "Trends in the Use of Complementary Health Approaches among Adults: United States, 2002–2012." *National Health Statistics Reports,* no. 79. Hyattsville, MD: National Center for Health Statistics, February 10. Accessed February 13, 2017 (www.cdc.gov/nchs/data/nhsr/nhsr079.pdf).

Cleveland, Henry. 1866. Alexander H. Stephens, in *Public and Private with Letters and Speeches, Before, During, and Since the War.* Philadelphia: National Publishing Company.

Climatic Research Unit, University of East Anglia. 2017. "Temperature: HadCRUT4 – GL." Accessed February 13, 2017 (https://crudata.uea.ac.uk/cru/data/temperature/).

Climatic Research Unit, University of East Anglia. 2019. "Temperature: HadCRUT4 – GL." Accessed January 26, 2019 (https://crudata.uea.ac.uk/cru/data/temperature/).

Clinard, Marshall B., and Robert F. Miller. 1998. *Sociology of Deviant Behavior,* 10th ed. Fort Worth, TX: Harcourt Brace.

Coates, Ta-Nehisi. 2014. "The Case for Reparations." *The Atlantic,* June. Accessed February 5, 2017 (www.theatlantic.com/magazine/archive/2014/06/the-case-for-reparations/361631/).

Cohen, Philip. 2018. "The Coming Divorce Decline." *SocArXiv,* November 14. Accessed December 17, 2018 (https://osf.io/preprints/socarxiv/h2sk6/).

Cohen, Philip N. 2013. "Children's Gender and Parent's Color Preferences." *Archives of Sexual Behavior* 42 (3): 393–397.

_____. 2016. "Life Table Says Divorce Rate Is 52.7%." *Family Inequality,* June 8. Accessed November 23, 2016 (https://familyinequality. wordpress.com/2016/06/08/life-table-says-divorce-rate-is-52-7/).

Cohn, D'Vera. 2011. "Multi-Race and the 2010 Census." Pew Research Center, April 6. Accessed June 18, 2011 (http://pewresearch.org/ pubs/1953/multi-race-2010-census-obama).

_____. 2016. "Federal Officials May Revamp How Americans Identify Race, Ethnicity on Census and Other Forms." Pew Research Center, October 4. Accessed February 2, 2017 (www.pewresearch.org/fact-tank/2016/10/04/federal-officials-may-revamp-how-americans-identify-race-ethnicity-on-census-and-other-forms/).

Cohn, D'Vera, and Jeffrey S. Passel. 2018. "A Record 64 Million Americans Live in Multigenerational Households." Pew Research Center, April 5. Accessed December 16, 2018 (www.pewresearch. org/fact-tank/2018/04/05/a-record-64-million-americans-live-in-multigenerational-households/).

Cohn, D'Vera, Jeffrey S. Passel, and Ana Gonzalez-Barrera. 2017. "Rise in U.S. Immigrants from El Salvador, Guatemala, and Honduras Outpaces Growth from Elsewhere." Hispanic Trends, Pew Research Center, December 7. Accessed October 10, 2018 (www.pewhispanic.org/2017/12/07/rise-in-u-s-immigrants-from-el-salvador-guatemala-and-honduras-outpaces-growth-from-elsewhere/).

Cohn, Nate. 2016. "Why Trump Won: Working-Class Whites." *The New York Times.* November 9. Accessed December 13, 2016 (www. nytimes.com/2016/11/10/upshot/why-trump-won-working-class-whites.html).

Colby, Sandra L., and Jennifer M. Ortman. 2015. "Projections of the Size and Composition of the U.S. Population: 2014 to 2060." *Current Population Reports,* P25-1143, U.S. Census Bureau, March. Accessed February 4, 2017 (www.census.gov/content/dam/Census/ library/publications/2015/demo/p25-1143.pdf).

Coleman, James William. 2006. *The Criminal Elite: Understanding White-Collar Crime,* 6th ed. New York: Worth.

College Board. 2016a. "Trends in Student Aid 2016." *Trends in Higher Education Series,* October. Accessed December 5, 2016 (https://trends.collegeboard.org/student-aid).

_____. 2018a. "Trends in Student Aid 2018." *Trends in Higher Education Series.* Accessed December 21, 2018 (https://trends. collegeboard.org/student-aid).

_____. 2018b. "Trends in College Pricing 2018." *Trends in Higher Education Series,* October. Accessed December 21, 2018 (https:// trends.collegeboard.org/college-pricing).

Collins, Gail. 2003. *America's Women.* New York: HarperCollins.

Collins, Mary B., Ian Munoz, and Joseph JaJa. 2016. "Linking 'Toxic Outliers' to Environmental Justice Communities." *Environmental Research Letters* 11(1): 015004.

Collins, Patricia Hill. 2000. *Black Feminist Thought,* 2nd ed. New York: Routledge.

Commoner, Barry. 1971. *The Closing Circle.* New York: Knopf.

Commonwealth of Australia. 2013. "Australian Government Guidelines on the Recognition of Sex and Gender." July. Accessed April 19, 2015 (www.ag.gov.au/Publications/Documents/AustralianGovern-mentGuidelinesontheRecognitionofSexandGender/AustralianG-overnmentGuidelinesontheRecognitionofSexandGender.PDF).

Connell, R. W. 2002. *Gender.* Cambridge, UK: Polity Press.

_____. 2005. *Masculinities,* 2nd ed. Berkeley: University of California Press.

Connell, R. W., and James W. Messerschmidt. 2005. "Hegemonic Masculinity: Rethinking the Concept." *Gender & Society* 19 (6): 829–859.

Connolly, Ceci. 2008. "As Latin Nations Treat Gays Better, Asylum Is Elusive." *The Washington Post,* August 12. Accessed May 28, 2010 (www.washingtonpost.com/wp-dyn/content/article/2008/08/11/ AR2008081102038.html).

Conrad, Peter. 2007. *The Medicalization of Society: On the Transformation of Human Conditions into Treatable Disorders.* Baltimore, MD: Johns Hopkins University Press.

Cooley, Charles H. 1902. *Human Nature and the Social Order.* New York: Scribner.

Cooley, Charles H. 1983. *Human Nature and the Social Order.* New York: Routledge.

Coontz, Stephanie. 1992. *The Way We Never Were: American Families and the Nostalgia Trap.* New York: Basic Books.

_____. 2005. *Marriage, a History: From Obedience to Intimacy or How Love Conquered Marriage.* New York: Viking.

_____. 2006. "A Pop Quiz on Marriage." *The New York Times,* February 19, p. 12.

_____. 2008. "The Future of Marriage." *Cato Unbound,* January 14. Accessed August 2, 2010 (www.cato-unbound.org/2008/01/14/ stephanie-coontz/the-future-of-marriage).

_____. 2011. *A Strange Stirring: The Feminine Mystique and American Women at the Dawn of the 1960s.* New York: Basic Books.

Cooper, Bruce S., and John Sureau. 2007. "The Politics of Homeschooling: New Developments, New Challenges." *Educational Policy* 21 (January and March): 110–131.

Cooper, K., S. Day, A. Green, and H. Ward. 2007. "Maids, Migrants and Occupational Health in the London Sex Industry." *Anthropology and Medicine* 14 (April): 41–53.

Cooper, Lisa A., Debra L. Roter, Kathry A. Carson, Mary Catherine Beach, Janice A. Sabin, Anthony G. Greenwald, and Thomas S. Inui. 2012. "The Associations of Clinicians' Implicit Attitudes about Race with Medical Visit Communication and Patient Ratings of Interpersonal Care." *American Journal of Public Health* 102 (5): 979–987.

Copen, Casey E., Anjani Chandra, and Isaedmarie Febo-Vazquez. 2016. "Sexual Behavior, Sexual Attraction, and Sexual Orientation among Adults Aged 18–44 in the United States: Data from the 2011–2013 National Survey of Family Growth." *National Health Statistics Reports,* No. 88. Hyattsville, MD: National Center for Health Statistics. Accessed February 1, 2017 (www.cdc.gov/nchs/data/nhsr/ nhsr088.pdf).

Copen, Casey E., Kimberly Daniels, Jonathan Vespa, and William D. Mosher. 2012. "First Marriages in the United States: Data from the 2006–2012 National Survey of Family Growth." *National Health Statistics Reports* 49, March 22. Accessed November 21, 2016 (www. cdc.gov/nchs/data/nhsr/nhsr049.pdf).

Corak, Miles. 2006. "Do Poor Children Become Poor Adults? Lessons from a Cross Country Comparison of Generational Earnings Mobility." Institute for the Study of Labor (IZA) Discussion Paper No. 1993, March. Accessed June 24, 2008 (http://papers.ssrn.com/ sol3/papers.cfm?abstract_id5889034).

_____. 2016. "Inequality from Generation to Generation: The United States in Comparison." IZA Discussion Paper No. 9929, May. Accessed January 20, 2017 (https://papers.ssrn.com/sol3/papers. cfm?abstract_id=2786013).

Corasanti, Nick. "Donald Trump Focuses on Immigration in His First Ad of General Election." *The New York Times,* August 20. Accessed February 4, 2017 (www.nytimes.com/2016/08/21/us/politics/donald-trump-focuses-on-immigration-in-his-first-ad-of-general-election. html).

Cornwall, Warren. 2015. "*Deepwater Horizon:* After the Oil." *Science,* April 3, 22–29.

Coser, Rose Laub. 1984. "American Medicine's Ambiguous Progress." *Contemporary Sociology* 13 (January): 9–13.

Côté, James E. 2000. *Arrested Adulthood: The Changing Nature of Identity and Maturity in the Late World.* New York: New York University.

Cottingham, Marci D., Austin H. Johnson, and Tiffany Taylor. 2016. "Heteronormative Labour: Conflicting Acountability Structures among Men in Nursing." *Gender, Work, and Organization* 23 (6): 535–550.

Council of Europe. 2015. *Human Rights and Intersex People.* Commissioner for Human Rights, Issue Paper, September. Accessed January 26, 2017 (https://rm.coe.int/CoERMPublicCommon-SearchServices/DisplayDCTMContent?documentId=0900001680 6da5d4).

Courvertier, Dave. 2016. "Investigative Update Regarding Pulse Nightclub Shooting." FBI Tampa, June 20. Accessed November 4, 2016 (www.fbi.gov/contact-us/field-offices/tampa/news/press-releases/ investigative-update-regarding-pulse-nightclub-shooting).

Cox, Daniel, and Robert P. Jones. 2016. "Race, Religion, and Political Affiliation of American's Core Social Networks." PRRI, Washington, DC, August 3. Accessed February 4, 2017 (www.prri.org/research/poll-race-religion-politics-americans-social-networks/).

Cox, Oliver C. 1948. *Caste, Class, and Race: A Study in Social Dynamics.* Detroit, MI: Wayne State University Press.

Crenshaw, Kimberlé. 2016. "The Urgency of Intersectionality." Video. TEDWomen, October. Accessed January 31, 2017 (www.ted.com/talks/kimberle_crenshaw_the_urgency_of_intersectionality).

Croft, Alyssa, Toni Schmader, and Katharina Block. 2015. "An Under-examined Inequality: Cultural and Psychological Barriers to Men's Engagement with Communal Roles." *Personality and Social Psychology Review* 19 (4): 343–370.

Cross, Christina J., Robert Joseph Taylor, and Linda M. Chatters. 2018. "Family Social Support Networks of African American and Black Caribbean Adolescents." *Journal of Child and Family Studies* 27 (9): 2757–2771.

Cross, Simon, and Barbara Bagilhole. 2002. "Girls' Jobs for the Boys? Men, Masculinity, and Non-Traditional Occupations." *Gender, Work, and Organization* 9: 204–226.

CTIA. 2018. "Background on CTIA's Wireless Industry Survey." CTIA—The Wireless Association. Accessed November 13, 2018 (https://api.ctia.org/wp-content/uploads/2018/07/CTIA_ToplineWirelessIndustrySurvey.pdf).

Cullen, Dave. 2009. *Columbine.* New York: Twelve.

Cumming, Elaine, and William E. Henry. 1961. *Growing Old: The Process of Disengagement.* New York: Basic Books.

Curiel, Jonathan. 2016. "A Is for Arab." *AramcoWorld,* March/April. Accessed January 18, 2017 (www.aramcoworld.com/en-US/Articles/March-2016/A-Is-For-Arab).

Currie, Elliott. 1985. *Confronting Crime: An American Challenge.* New York: Pantheon Books.

———. 1998. *Crime and Punishment in America.* New York: Metropolitan Books.

Curtiss, Susan. 1977. *Genie: A Psycholinguistic Study of a Modern Day "Wild Child."* New York: Academic Press.

Cusack, Carole M., and Justine Digance. 2009. "The Melbourne Cup: Australian Identity and Secular Pilgrimage." *Sport in Society* 12 (7): 876–889.

Cuvier, Georges. [1817] 1832. *The Animal Kingdom: Arranged in Conformity with Its Organization,* trans. H. M'Murtire. New York: Carvill.

Cyranoski, David, and Sara Reardon. 2015. "Chinese Scientists Genetically Modify Human Embryos." *Nature,* April 22. Accessed May 5, 2015 (www.nature.com/news/chinese-scientists-genetically-modify-human-embryos-1.17378).

D

Dahl, Robert A. 1961. *Who Governs?* New Haven, CT: Yale University Press.

Daisey, Mike. 2002. *21 Dog Years: Doing Time @ Amazon.com.* New York: Free Press.

Dalai Lama. 2000. Dalai Lama message at religious summit, United Nations, August 30, 2000.

Daly, Mary C., Andrew J. Oswald, Daniel Wilson, and Stephen Wu. 2011. "Dark Contrasts: The Paradox of High Rates of Suicide in Happy Places." *Journal of Economic Behavior & Organization* 80: 435–442.

Daly, Mary C., Daniel J. Wilson, and Norman J. Johnson. 2013. "Relative Status and Well-Being: Evidence from U.S. Suicide Deaths." *The Review of Economics and Statistics* 95 (5): 1480–1500.

Daniels, Kimberly, Jill Daugherty, Jo Jones, and William Mosher. 2015. "Current Contraceptive Use and Variation by Selected Characteristics among Women Aged 15–44: United States, 2011–2013." *National Health Statistics Reports,* No. 86, November 10. Hyattsville, MD: National Center for Health Statistics. Accessed February 1, 2017 (www.cdc.gov/nchs/data/nhsr/nhsr086.pdf).

Daniels, Roger. 2004. *Prisoners without Trial: Japanese Americans in World War II,* revised edition. New York: Hill and Wang.

Dao, James. 1995. "New York's Highest Court Rules Unmarried Couples Can Adopt." *The New York Times,* November 3, pp. A1, B2.

Darwin, Charles. 1859. *On the Origin of Species.* London: John Murray.

Dass, Angélica. 2016. "The Beauty of Human Skin in Every Color." Video. *TED Talk,* February. Accessed July 27, 2018 (www.ted.com/talks/angelica_dass_the_beauty_of_human_skin_in_every_color).

Davenport, Coral, Justin Gillis, Sewell Chan, and Melissa Eddy. 2015. "Inside the Paris Climate Deal." *The New York Times,* December 12. Accessed February 13, 2017 (www.nytimes.com/interactive/2015/12/12/world/paris-climate-change-deal-explainer.html).

Davenport, Thomas H., and Julia Kirby. 2016. *Only Humans Need Apply: Winners and Losers in the Age of Smart Machines.* New York: HarperCollins.

David, Gary. 2004. "Scholarship on Arab Americans Distorted Past 9/11." *Al Jadid,* Winter/Spring, 26–27.

David, Pierre. 2015. *Nuancier.* Paris: RVB Books.

Davenport, Lauren D. 2016. "The Role of Gender, Class, and Religion in Biracial Americans' Racial Labeling Decisions." *American Sociological Review* 81 (1): 57–84.

Davies, Sharyn Graham. 2007. *Challenging Gender Norms: Five Genders among Bugis in Indonesia.* Belmont, CA: Wadsworth, Cengage Learning.

Davis, Angela. 1998. "Masked Racism: Reflection on the Prison Industrial Complex." *Colorlines,* September 10. Accessed November 10, 2016 (www.colorlines.com/articles/masked-racism-reflections-prison-industrial-complex).

Davis, Darren W., and Brian D. Silver. 2003. "Stereotype Threat and Race of Interviewer Effects in a Survey on Political Knowledge." *American Journal of Political Science* 47 (1): 33–45.

Davis, F. James. 1991. *Who Is Black? One Nation's Definition.* University Park: Pennsylvania University Press.

Davis, Georgiann. 2014. "The Power in a Name: Diagnostic Terminology and Diverse Experiences." *Psychology & Sexuality* 5: 15–27.

Davis, Joseph E. 2006. "How Medicalization Lost Its Way." *Society* 43 (6): 51–56.

Davis, Kingsley, and Wilbert E. Moore. 1945. "Some Principles of Stratification." *American Sociological Review* 10 (April): 242–249.

Dawkins, Marcia Alesan. 2012. *Clearly Invisible: Racial Passing and the Color of Cultural Identity.* Waco, TX: Baylor University Press.

Dawson, Julia, Stefano Natella, and Richard Kersley. 2016. *The CS Gender 3000: The Reward for Change.* Zurich: Credit Suisse AG. Accessed February 2, 2017 (http://publications.credit-suisse.com/index.cfm/publikationen-shop/research-institute/cs-gender-3000/).

Dawson, Lorne. 2009. "Church-Sect-Cult: Constructing Typologies of Religious Groups." Pp. 525–544 in *The Oxford Handbook of the Sociology of Religion,* ed. Peter B. Clarke. New York: Oxford University Press.

Death Penalty Information Center. 2018. "Facts about the Death Penalty." Washington, DC, December 5. Accessed December 5, 2018 (www.deathpenaltyinfo.org/documents/FactSheet.pdf).

Debczak, Michele. 2018. "25 of the New Words Merriam-Webster Is Adding to the Dictionary in 2018." Mental Floss, September 5. Accessed November 13, 2018 (http://mentalfloss.com/article/556420/25-new-words-merriam-webster-adding-dictionary-2018).

Deflem, Mathieu. 2005. "Wild Beasts without Nationality: The Uncertain Origins of Interpol, 1898–1910." Pp. 275–285 in *Handbook of Transnational Crime and Justice,* ed. Philip Rerchel. Thousand Oaks, CA: Sage.

de Freytas-Tamura, Kimiko. 2016. "After 'Brexit' Vote, Immigrants Feel a Town Turn against Them." *The New York Times,* July 9. Accessed February 4, 2017 (www.nytimes.com/2016/07/10/world/europe/brexit-immigrants-great-britain-eu.html).

DeGregory, Lane. 2008. "The Girl in the Window." *St. Petersburg Times,* July 31. Accessed May 14, 2013 (www.tampabay.com/features/humaninterest/the-girl-in-the-window/750838).

———. 2011. "Three Years Later, The Girl in the Window Learns to Connect." *Tampa Bay Times,* August 19. Accessed May 14, 2013 (www.tampabay.com/features/humaninterest/three-years-later-the-girl-in-the-window-learns-to-connect/1186860).

DeGregory, Lane. 2017. "The Girl in the Window 10 Years Later." *Tampa Bay Times,* November 29. Accessed November 18, 2018 (www.tampabay.com/projects/girl-in-the-window/neglect-feral-child-ten-years-later/).

Demeneix, Barbara. 2017. *Toxic Cocktail: How Chemical Pollution Is Poisoning Our Brains.* New York: Oxford University Press.

Denyer, Simon. 2016. "China's Scary Lesson to the World: Censoring the Internet Works." *The Washington Post,* May 23. Accessed February 15, 2017 (www.washingtonpost.com/world/asia_pacific/chinas-scary-lesson-to-the-world-censoring-the-internet-works/2016/05/23/413afe78-fff3-11e5-8bb1-f124a43f84dc_story.html).

DeNavas-Walt, Carmen, and Bernadette D. Proctor. 2014. "Income and Poverty in the United States: 2013." *Current Population Reports,* P60-249. Washington, DC: U.S. Government Printing Office. Accessed January 7, 2015 (www.census.gov/content/dam/Census/library/publications/2014/demo/p60-249.pdf).

Department of Defense. 2016. "Active Duty Military Personnel by Service by Rank/Grade: October 2016 (Women Only)." DoD Personnel, Workforce Reports & Publications. Accessed December 16, 2016 (www.dmdc.osd.mil/appj/dwp/dwp_reports.jsp).

Department of Interior. 2018. "Indian Entities Recognized and Eligible to Receive Services from the United States Bureau of Indian Affairs." *Federal Register* 83 (20): 4235–4241. Accessed October 9, 2018 (www.gpo.gov/fdsys/pkg/FR-2018-01-30/pdf/2018-01907.pdf).

DePaulo, Bella. 2014. "A Singles Studies Perspective on Mount Marriage." *Psychological Inquiry* 25: 64–68.

DeSalle, Rob, and Ian Tattersall. 2018. *Troublesome Science: The Misuse of Genetics and Genomics in Understanding Race.* New York: Columbia University Press.

DeSilver, Drew. 2015. "The Fading of the Teen Summer Job." Pew Research Center, June 23. Accessed October 25, 2016 (www.pewresearch.org/fact-tank/2015/06/23/the-fading-of-the-teen-summer-job/).

_____. 2016. "Increase in Living with Parents Driven by Those Ages 25–34, Non-College Grads." Pew Research Center, June 8. Accessed November 22, 2016 (www.pewresearch.org/fact-tank/2016/06/08/increase-in-living-with-parents-driven-by-those-ages-25-34-non-college-grads/).

DeSilver, Drew, and Kristen Bialik. 2017. "Blacks and Hispanics Face Extra Challenges in Getting Home Loans." Pew Research Center, January 10. Accessed February 6, 2017 (www.pewresearch.org/fact-tank/2017/01/10/blacks-and-hispanics-face-extra-challenges-in-getting-home-loans/).

Desmond, Matthew. 2016. *Evicted: Poverty and Profit in the American City.* New York: Crown.

Desmond, Matthew, and Mustafa Emerbayer. 2009. "What Is Racial Domination?" *Du Bois Review* 6 (2): 335–355.

Desmond, Matthew, and Ruth N. López Turley. 2009. "The Role of Familism in Explaining the Hispanic–White College Application Gap." *Social Problems* 56 (2): 311–334.

Despagne, Colette. 2013. "Indigenous Education in Mexico: Indigenous Students' Voices." *Diaspora, Indigenous, and Minority Education* 7: 114–129.

Dettling, Lisa J., Joanne W. Hsu, Lindsay Jacobs, Kevin B. Moore, and Jeffrey P. Thompson. 2017. "Recent Trends in Wealth-Holding by Race and Ethnicity: Evidence from the Survey of Consumer Finances." Board of Governors of the Federal Reserve System, *FEDS Notes,* September 27. Accessed October 6, 2018 (www.federalreserve.gov/econres/notes/feds-notes/recent-trends-in-wealth-holding-by-race-and-ethnicity-evidence-from-the-survey-of-consumer-finances-20170927.htm).

Diamond, Jared. 2008. "What's Your Consumption Factor?" *The New York Times,* January 2. Accessed May 21, 2010 (www.nytimes.com/2008/01/02/opinion/02diamond.html).

DiAngelo, Michelle. 2018. *White Fragility: Why It's So Hard to Talk to White People about Racism.* Boston: Beacon Press.

Dickens, Charles. 1843. *A Christmas Carol.* London: Chapman and Hall. Accessed July 7, 2008 (www.gutenberg.org/dirs/4/46/46-h/46-h.htm).

Dicker, Rory. 2016. *A History of U.S. Feminisms.* Berkeley, CA: Seal Press.

Dickerson, Caitlin. 2018. "Detention of Migrant Children Has Skyrocketed to Highest Levels Ever." *The New York Times,* September 12. Accessed October 11, 2018 (www.nytimes.com/2018/09/12/us/migrant-children-detention.html).

Docan-Morgan, Sara. 2010. "'They Don't Know What It's Like to Be in My Shoes': Topic Avoidance about Race in Transracially Adopted Families." *Journal of Social and Personal Relationships* 28 (3): 336–355.

Doctorow, Cory. 2014. "Thomas Pikettys Capital in the 21st Century." *BoingBoing,* June 24. Accessed June 8, 2015 (http://boingboing.net/2014/06/24/thomas-pikettys-capital-in-t.html).

Doctors Without Borders. 2017. *U.S. Annual Report 2017.* New York, September 12. Accessed June 4, 2019 (www.doctorswithoutborders.org/us-annual-reports).

Dolan, Maura. 2017. "A Flurry of Legal Arguments as Appeals Court Decides Whether Trump's Immigration Ban Will Be Enforced." *Los Angeles Times,* February 6. Accessed February 7, 2017 (www.latimes.com/nation/la-na-immigration-order-legal-20170206-story.html).

Doležal, Rachel. 2016. "Rachel Doležal's TEDx Talk." *TED Blog,* November 2. Accessed August 29, 2018 (https://blog.ted.com/rachel-dolezals-tedx-talk/).

Domhoff, G. William. 1978. *Who Really Rules? New Haven and Community Power Reexamined.* New Brunswick, NJ: Transaction.

_____. 2009. "The Power Elite and Their Challengers: The Role of Nonprofits in American Social Conflict." *American Behavioral Scientist* 52 (7): 955–973.

_____. 2014. *Who Rules America?: The Triumph of the Corporate Rich.* 7th ed. New York: McGraw-Hill.

Domzalski, Kaylee. 2018. "The Complicated, Messy Identity of a Transracial Adoptee." *Slate,* August 31. Accessed September 4, 2018 (https://slate.com/human-interest/2018/08/david-frenchs-atlantic-essay-on-adoption-invalidates-the-experiences-of-transracial-adoptees-like-me.html).

Doress, Irwin, and Jack Nusan Porter. 1977. *Kids in Cults: Why They Join, Why They Stay, Why They Leave.* Brookline, MA: Reconciliation Associates.

Dostoevsky, Fyodor. [1879] 1985. *The House of the Dead.* London: Penguin Classics.

Dotinga, Randy. 2014. "When Parents Need Care, Daughters Carry the Burden." *CBS News,* August 19. Accessed February 2, 2015 (www.cbsnews.com/news/when-parents-need-care-daughters-carry-the-burden-study-says/).

Douglass, Frederick. 1854. *The Claims of the Negro, Ethnologically Considered : an Address Before the Literary Societies of Western Reserve College.* Rochester, NY: Lee, Mann & Co.

Dray, Philip. 2010. *There Is Power in a Union: The Epic Story of Labor in America.* New York: Doubleday.

Drescher, Jack. 2010. "Queer Diagnoses: Parallels and Contrasts in the History of Homosexuality, Gender Variance, and the *Diagnostic and Statistical Manual.*" *Archives of Sexual Behavior* 39 (2): 427–460.

_____. 2011. "The Removal of Homosexuality from the DSM: Its Impact on Today's Marriage Equality Debate." *Journal of Gay & Lesbian Mental Health* 16 (2): 124–135.

_____. 2015. "Out of DSM: Depathologizing Homosexuality." *Behavioral Sciences* 5 (4): 565–575.

Druckman, James N. 2003. "The Power of Television Images: The First Kennedy–Nixon Debate Revisited." *The Journal of Politics* 65 (2): 559–571.

Duberman, Martin Bauml, Martha Vicinus, and George Chauncey Jr., eds. 1989. *Hidden from History: Reclaiming the Gay and Lesbian Past.* New York: New American Library.

Du Bois, W. E. B. 1899. *The Philadelphia Negro: A Social Study.* Philadelphia: University of Pennsylvania.

_____. 1903. *The Souls of Black Folk: Essays and Sketches.* Chicago: A. C. McClurg & Co.

_____. [1909] 1970. *The Negro American Family.* Cambridge, MA: MIT Press.

Dufton, Emily. 2012. "The War on Drugs: How President Nixon Tied Addiction to Crime." *The Atlantic,* March 26. Accessed November 10, 2016 (www.theatlantic.com/health/archive/2012/03/the-war-on-drugs-how-president-nixon-tied-addiction-to-crime/254319/).

Dunbar-Ortiz, Roxanne. 2014. *An Indigenous Peoples' History of the United States.* Boston: Beacon Press.

Duncan, Greg J., and Richard J Murnane. 2011. "Introduction: The American Dream, Then and Now." Pp. 3–23 in *Whither Opportunity?: Rising Inequality, Schools, and Children's Life Chances,* ed. Greg J. Duncan and Richard J. Murnane. New York: Russell Sage Foundation.

Duong, Thi Hoa, Ulla-Britt Jansson, and Ann-Lena Hellström. 2013. "Vietnamese Mothers Experiences with Potty Training Procedure for Children from Birth to 2 Years of Age." *Journal of Pediatric Urology* 9: 808–814.

Durkheim, Émile. [1887] 1972. "Religion and Ritual." Pp. 219–238 in *Émile Durkheim: Selected Writings,* ed. A. Giddens. Cambridge, UK: Cambridge University Press.

———. [1893] 1933. *Division of Labor in Society,* trans. George Simpson. New York: Free Press.

———. [1895] 1964. *The Rules of Sociological Method,* trans. Sarah A. Solovay and John H. Mueller. New York: Free Press.

———. [1895] 1982. *The Rules of Sociological Method and Selected Texts on Sociology and Its Method,* trans. W. D. Halls. New York: Free Press.

———. [1897] 1951. *Suicide,* trans. John A. Spaulding and George Simpson. New York: Free Press.

E

Eagan, Kevin, Ellen Bara Stolzenberg, Hilary B. Zimmerman, Melissa C. Aragon, Hanna Whang Sayson, and Cecilia Rios-Aguilar. 2017. *The American Freshman: National Norms Fall 2016.* Los Angeles: Higher Education Research Institute, UCLA. Accessed November 17, 2018 (https://heri.ucla.edu/publications-tfs/).

Ebaugh, Helen Rose Fuchs. 1988. *Becoming an Ex: The Process of Role Exit.* Chicago: University of Chicago Press.

Eckert, Penelope, and Sally McConnell-Ginet. 2003. *Language and Gender.* New York: Cambridge University Press.

The Economist. 2008. "A Ravenous Dragon: A Special Report on China's Quest for Resources." March 15, 1–22.

Edgerton, Gary R. 2007. *The Columbia History of American Television.* New York: Columbia University Press.

Edin, Kathryn, and Maria Kefalas. 2005. *Promises I Can Keep: Why Poor Women Put Motherhood before Marriage.* Berkeley: University of California Press.

Edin, Kathryn, and H. Luke Shaefer. 2015. *$2.00 a Day: Living on Almost Nothing in America.* Boston: Houghton Mifflin Harcourt.

Edmondson, Catie, and Jasmine C. Lee. 2019. "Meet the New Freshmen in Congress." *The New York Times,* January 3. Accessed January 8, 2019 (www.nytimes.com/interactive/2018/11/28/us/politics/congress-freshman-class.html).

Edwards, Mark U., Jr. 1994. *Printing, Propaganda, and Martin Luther.* Berkeley: University of California Press.

EEOC. 2014. "Age Discrimination Employment Act (Includes Concurrent Charges with Title VII, ADA and EPA) FY 1997–FY 2014." U.S. Equal Employment Opportunity Commission. Accessed February 2, 2015 (www.eeoc.gov/eeoc/statistics/-enforcement/adea.cfm).

eHarmony. 2014. "Who We Are." Accessed February 26, 2014 (www.eharmony.com/about/eharmony/).

Eilperin, Juliet, and Brady Dennis. 2017. "Trump Administration to Approve Final Permit for Dakota Access Pipeline." *The Washington Post,* February 7. Accessed February 8, 2017 (www.washingtonpost.com/news/energy-environment/wp/2017/02/07/trump-administration-to-approve-final-permit-for-dakota-access-pipeline/).

Elbein, Saul. 2017. "The Youth Group That Launched a Movement at Standing Rock." *The New York Times Magazine,* January 31. Accessed February 8, 2017 (https://nytimes.com/2017/01/31/magazine/the-youth-group-that-launched-a-movement-at-standing-rock.html).

Elgin, Suzette Haden. 1984. *Native Tongue.* New York: Feminist Press.

———. 1988. *A First Dictionary and Grammar of Láadan,* 2nd ed. Madison, WI: Society for the Furtherance and Study of Fantasy and Science Fiction.

Eliot, George. 1859. *Adam Bede.* New York: Harper & Brothers Publishers, p. 491.

Elkins, Kathleen. 2018. "Median CEO Pay Reachers $12.1 Million—Here's How Much the 5 Highest-Paid Leaders Earn." *CNBC,* May 9. Accessed January 13, 2019 (www.cnbc.com/2018/05/09/how-much-the-5-highest-paid-ceos-earn.html).

Elliott, Michael. 2005. "Hopelessly Devoted: Being a Fan Is Like Having Your Own Personal Time Machine." *Time,* June 20, p. 76.

Ellison, Ralph. 1952. *Invisible Man.* New York: Random House.

Ellul, Jacques. 1964. *The Technological Society.* New York: Knopf.

———. 1980. *The Technological System.* New York: Continuum.

———. 1990. *The Technological Bluff.* Grand Rapids, MI: Eerdmans.

Ely, Danielle M., Anne K. Driscoll, and T. J. Mathews. 2018. "Infant Mortality by Age at Death in the United States, 2016." National NCHS Data Brief, No. 326, November. Accessed January 26, 2019 (www.cdc.gov/nchs/data/databriefs/db326-h.pdf).

Emerson, Michael O., David Hartman, Karen Cook, and Douglas Massey. 2006. "The Rise of Religious Fundamentalism." *Annual Review of Sociology* 32: 127–144.

Engels, Friedrich. [1884] 1959. "The Origin of the Family, Private Property, and the State." Pp. 392–394 in *Marx and Engels: Basic Writings on Politics and Philosophy,* ed. Lewis Feuer. Garden City, NY: Anchor Books.

England, Paula, Jonathan Bearak, Michelle J. Budig, and Melissa J. Hodges. 2016. "Do Highly Paid, Highly Skilled Women Experience the Largest Motherhood Penalty?" *American Sociological Review* 81 (6): 1161–1189.

Enriquez, Juan, and Steve Gullans. 2015. *Evolving Ourselves: Redesigning the Future of Humanity—One Gene at a Time.* New York: Current.

Eom, Young-Ho, and Hang-Hyun Jo. 2014. "Generalized Friendship Paradox in Complex Networks: The Case of Scientific Collaboration." *Scientific Reports* 4: 4603. Accessed February 11, 2015 (www.nature.com/srep/2014/140408/srep04603/pdf/srep04603.pdf).

Equilar. 2016. "200 Highest-Paid CEOs 2016." Redwood City, CA, May 27. Accessed December 22, 2016 (www.equilar.com/reports/38-new-york-times-200-highest-paid-ceos-2016.html).

Erosa, Andres, Luisa Fuster, and Diego Restuccia. 2016. "A Quantitative Theory of the Gender Gap in Wages." *European Economic Review* 85: 165–187.

Escoffier, Jeffrey. 1997. "Homosexuality and the Sociological Imagination: The 1950s and 1960s." Pp. 248–261 in *A Queer World: The Center for Lesbian and Gay Studies Reader,* ed. Martin Duberman. New York: New York University Press.

Estin, Ann Laquer. 2017. "Marriage and Divorce Conflicts in International Perspective." *Duke Journal of Comparative & International Law* 27: 485–517.

Etzioni, Amitai. 1965. *Political Unification.* New York: Holt, Rinehart and Winston.

———. 2007. "Are New Technologies the Enemy of Privacy?" *Knowledge, Technology & Policy* 20 (2): 115–119.

F

Fahs, Breanne, Jax Gonzalez, Rose Coursey, and Stephanie Robinson-Cestaro. 2014. "Cycling Together: Menstrual Synchrony as a Projection of Gendered Solidarity." *Women's Reproductive Health* 1 (2): 90–105.

Fainzang, Sylvie. 2013. "The Other Side of Medicalization: Self-Medicalization and Self-Medication." *Culture, Medicine, & Psychiatry* 37: 488–504.

Fairfield, Hannah, and Alan McLean. 2012. "Girls Lead in Science Exam, but Not in the United States." *The New York Times,* February 4. Accessed June 5, 2013 (www.nytimes.com/interactive/2013/02/04/science/girls-lead-in-science-exam-but-not-in-the-united-states.html).

Fanon, Frantz. 1963. *The Wretched of the Earth.* New York: Grove.

Farley, Melissa, and Victor Malarek. 2008. "The Myth of the Victimless Crime." *The New York Times,* March 12. Accessed May 20, 2009 (www.nytimes.com/2008/03/12/opinion/12farley.html).

Farr, Grant M. 1999. *Modern Iran.* New York: McGraw-Hill.

Fass, Paula S. 2016. *The End of American Childhood: A History of Parenting on the Frontier to the Managed Child.* Princeton, NJ: Princeton University Press.

Faulkner, William. 2013. *Requiem for a Nun.* New York: Random House.

Fausset, Richard , Serge F. Kovaleski, and Patricia Mazzei. 2018. "On a Day Like Any Other at a Florida School, 6 Minutes of Death and Chaos." *The New York Times,* February 16. Accessed December 1, 2018 (www.nytimes.com/2018/02/16/us/stoneman-douglas-shooting.html).

Fausto-Sterling, Anne. 1993. "The Five Sexes: Why Male and Female Are Not Enough." *The Sciences,* July/August, 18–23.

———. 2000. "The Five Sexes, Revisited." *The Sciences,* July/August, 18–23.

———. 2012. *Sex/Gender: Biology in a Social World.* New York: Routledge.

Fearon, James D., and David D. Laitin. 2003. "Ethnicity, Insurgency, and Civil War." *American Political Science Review* 97 (March): 75–90.

Federal Bureau of Investigation. 2016. "Organized Crime." U.S. Department of Justice, Washington, DC. Accessed November 15, 2016 (www.fbi.gov/investigate/organized-crime).

Feld, Scott L. 1991. "Why Your Friends Have More Friends Than You Do." *American Journal of Sociology* 96: 1464–1477.

Felson, David, and Akis Kalaitzidis. 2005. "A Historical Overview of Transnational Crime." Pp. 3–19 in *Handbook of Transnational Crime and Justice,* ed. Philip Reichel. Thousand Oaks, CA: Sage.

Fenske, James. 2013. "African Polygamy: Past and Present." Vox, The Centre for Economic Policy Research, November 9. Accessed November 21, 2016 (http://voxeu.org/article/african-polygamy-past-and-present).

Ferguson, Donna. 2018. "Must Monsters Always Be Male? Huge Gender Bias Revealed in Children's Books." *The Guardian,* January 20. Accessed January 23, 2019 (www.theguardian.com/books/2018/jan/21/childrens-books-sexism-monster-in-your-kids-book-is-male).

Ferree, Myra Marx, and David A. Merrill. 2000. "Hot Movements, Cold Cognition: Thinking about Social Movements in Gendered Frames." *Contemporary Society* 29 (May): 454–462.

File, Thom. 2013. "The Diversifying Electorate—Voting Rates by Race and Hispanic Origin in 2012 (and Other Recent Elections)." Current Population Survey, P20–568, U.S. Census Bureau, Accessed June 1, 2013 (www.census.gov/prod/2013pubs/p20-568.pdf).

———. 2018. "Characteristics of Voters in the Presidential Election of 2016." *Current Population Reports,* P20-582, U.S. Census Bureau, September. Accessed January 8, 2019 (www.census.gov/content/dam/Census/library/publications/2018/demo/P20-582.pdf).

Filipović, Katarina. 2018. "Gender Representation in Children's Books: Case of an Early Childhood Setting." *Journal of Research in Childhood Education* 32: 310–325.

Finder, Alan. 2006. "For Some, Online Persona Undermines a Résumé." *The New York Times,* June 11. Accessed June 30, 2009 (www.nytimes.com/2006/06/11/us/11recruit.html).

Findlen, Barbara, ed. 1995. *Listen Up: Voices from the Next Feminist Generation.* Seattle, WA: Seal Press.

Fine, Gary C. 2008. "Robbers Cave." Pp. 1163–1164 in *Encyclopedia of Race, Ethnicity, and Society,* vol. 3, ed. Richard T. Schaefer. Thousand Oaks, CA: Sage.

Fingerhut, Hannah. 2017. "About Seven-in-Ten Americans Oppose Overturning Roe v. Wade." Pew Research Center, January 3. Accessed January 31, 2017 (www.pewresearch.org/fact-tank/2017/01/03/about-seven-in-ten-americans-oppose-overturning-roe-v-wade/).

Finighan, Reuban, and Robert Putnam. 2016. "A Country Divided: The Growing Opportunity Gap in America." Pp. 139–173 in *Economic Mobility: Research & Ideas on Strengthening Families, Communities, & the Economy.* St. Louis, MO: Federal Reserve Bank of St. Louis.

Accessed December 22, 2016 (www.stlouisfed.org/~/media/Files/PDFs/Community%20Development/EconMobilityPapers/Section2/EconMobility_2-2FinighanPutnam_508.pdf).

Firsing, Scott. 2016. "How Severe Is Africa's Brain Drain?" *Quartz,* January 21. Accessed February 10, 2017 (https://qz.com/599140/how-severe-is-africas-brain-drain/).

Fischer, Eric. 2011. "Race and Ethnicity 2010." Accessed April 28, 2015 (www.flickr.com/photos/walkingsf/sets/72157626354149574/).

Fisher, Gordon M. 1992. "The Development and History of the Poverty Thresholds." *Social Security Bulletin* 55 (4): 3–14. Accessed April 25, 2010 (www.ssa.gov/history/fisheronpoverty.html).

———. 2008. "Remembering Mollie Orshansky—the Developer of the Poverty Thresholds." *Social Security Bulletin* 68 (3): 79–83. Accessed April 25, 2010 (www.ssa.gov/policy/docs/ssb/v68n3/v68n3p79.pdf).

Fisher, Max. 2012. "The Middle East Didn't Really Get Any Freer in 2011." *The Atlantic,* January 19. Accessed May 28, 2012 (www.theatlantic.com/international/archive/2012/01/the-middle-east-didnt-really-get-any-freer-in-2011/251653/).

Fishman, Charles. 2006. *The Wal-Mart Effect: How the World's Most Powerful Company Really Works—and How It's Transforming the American Economy.* New York: Penguin Books.

Five Year Plan. 2006. "55: A Meditation on the Speed Limit." Video. Campus MovieFest, Atlanta, GA. Accessed October 6, 2016 (www.campusmoviefest.com/movies/924-a-meditation-on-the-speed-limit).

Flexner, Eleanor, and Ellen Fitzpatrick. 1996. *Century of Struggle: The Woman's Rights Movement in the United States, Enlarged Edition.* Cambridge, MA: Belknap Press of Harvard University Press.

Flora, Stephen Ray, and Courtney Allyn Polenik. 2013. "Effects of Sugar Consumption on Human Behavior and Performance." *The Psychological Record* 63: 513–524.

Flynt, Larry. n.d. *Larry Flynt Quotes.*

Folley, Aris. 2016. "Biracial Sons More Likely Than Daughters to Identify as Black." *NBC News,* February 1. Accessed August 28, 2018 (www.nbcnews.com/news/nbcblk/biracial-sons-more-likely-daughters-identify-black-n505311).

Follman, Mark, Gavin Aronsen, and Deanna Pann. 2016. "US Mass Shootings, 1982–2016." *Mother Jones,* September 24. Accessed November 4, 2016 (www.motherjones.com/politics/2012/12/mass-shootings-mother-jones-full-data).

Fontenot, Kayla, Jessica Semega, and Melissa Kollar. 2018. "Income and Poverty in the United States: 2017." *Current Population Reports,* P60–263. Washington, DC: U.S. Government Printing Office. Accessed November 10, 2018 (www.census.gov/content/dam/Census/library/publications/2018/demo/p60-263.pdf).

Forbes. 2019. "The World's Billionaires." January 17. Accessed January 16, 2019 (www.forbes.com/billionaires/list/).

Force, W. R. 2011. "Another Two Cents on England (and Crawley): Masculinity, Culture, and Tucson." Sociology Lens, The Society Pages, April 26. Accessed March 10, 2012 (http://thesocietypages.org/sociologylens/2011/04/26/another-two-cents-on-england-and-crawley-masculinity-culture-and-tucson/).

Ford, Liz. 2015. "Sustainable Development Goals: All You Need to Know." *The Guardian,* January 19. Accessed April 14, 2015 (www.theguardian.com/global-development/2015/jan/19/sustainable-development-goals-united-nations).

Ford, Martin. 2015. *Rise of the Robots: Technology and the Threat of a Jobless Future.* New York: Basic Books.

Forsythe, David P. 1990. "Human Rights in U.S. Foreign Policy: Retrospect and Prospect." *Political Science Quarterly* 105 (3): 435–454.

Fortune. 2018. "Global 500." July 19. Accessed January 20, 2019 (http://fortune.com/global500/).

Fowler, Danielle. 2018. "Claire Foy Won't Receive Back Pay for Her Role in 'The Crown' after Gender Pay Dispute." *Harper's Bazaar,* July 29. Accessed October 30, 2018 (www.harpersbazaar.com/uk/culture/culture-news/a22582948/claire-foy-gender-pay-gap-back-pay-the-crown/).

Fox, Liana. 2018. "The Supplemental Poverty Measure: 2017." *Current Population Reports,* P60-265, September. Accessed January 13, 2019 (www.census.gov/content/dam/Census/library/publications/2018/demo/p60-265.pdf).

Fox, Susannah, and Maeve Duggan. 2013. "Health Online 2013." Pew Research Center, Internet, Science, & Tech, January 15. Accessed February 11, 2017 (www.pewinternet.org/2013/01/15/health-online-2013/).

France, David. 2016. *How to Survive a Plague: The Inside Story of How Citizens and Science Tamed AIDS.* New York: Knopf.

Francis, Ara. 2012. "Stigma in an Era of Medicalization and Anxious Parenting: How Proximity and Culpability Shape Middle-Class Parents Experiences of Disgrace." *Sociology of Health & Illness* 34: 927–942.

Frank, Robert H. 2016. *Success and Luck: Good Fortune and the Myth of Meritocracy.* Princeton, NJ: Princeton University Press.

Franklin, Delano R., and Samuel W. Zwickel. 2018. "Record-Low 4.59 Percent of Applicants Accepted to Harvard Class of 2022." *The Harvard Crimson,* March 29. Accessed December 21, 2018 (www.thecrimson.com/article/2018/3/29/harvard-regular-admissions-2022/).

Franklin, John Hope, and Alfred A. Moss. 2000. *From Slavery to Freedom: A History of African Americans,* 8th ed. Upper Saddle River, NJ: Prentice Hall.

Fraser, Steve. 2015. *The Age of Acquiescence: The Life and Death of American Resistance to Organized Wealth and Power.* New York: Little, Brown.

Frassanito, Paolo, and Benedetta Pettorini. 2008. "Pink and Blue: The Color of Gender." *Child's Nervous System* 24 (8): 881–882.

Frey, Carl Benedikt, and Michael A. Osborne. 2017. "The Future of Employment: How Susceptible Are Jobs to Computerisation?" *Technological Forecasting and Social Change* 114: 254–280.

Frey, William H. 2011. "White–Black Segregation." Brookings Institution and University of Michigan Social Science Data Analysis Networks Analysis of 2010 Census Data, CensusScope. Accessed April 28, 2015 (www.censusscope.org/2010Census/index.php).

————. 2015. *Diversity Explosion: How New Racial Demographics Are Remaking America.* Washington, DC: Brookings Institution.

————. 2017. "Race Segregation for Largest Metro Areas (Population over 500,000): Brookings Institution and University of Michigan Social Science Data Analysis Network's Analysis of 1990, 2000, and 2010 Census Decennial Census Tract Data." Population Studies Center, Institute for Social Research, University of Michigan. Accessed February 5, 2017 (www.psc.isr.umich.edu/dis/census/segregation2010.html).

Friedan, Betty. 1963. *The Feminine Mystique.* New York: Dell.

Friedrich, Carl J., and Zbigniew K. Brzezinski. 1956. *Totalitarian Dictatorship and Autocracy.* Cambridge, MA: Harvard University Press.

Friend, Christian, Andrea Hunter, and Anne Fletcher. 2011. "Parental Racial Socialization and the Academic Achievement of African American Children: A Cultural-Ecological Approach." *Journal of African American Studies* 15: 40–57.

Friman, H. Richard. 2004. "The Great Escape? Globalization, Immigrant Entrepreneurship and the Criminal Economy." *Review of International Political Economy* 11 (1): 98–131.

Fry, Richard. 2016. "For the First Time in Modern Era, Living with Parents Edges Out Other Living Arrangements for 18- to 34-Year-Olds." Pew Research Center, May 24. Accessed December 16, 2018 (www.pewsocialtrends.org/2016/05/24/for-first-time-in-modern-era-living-with-parents-edges-out-other-living-arrangements-for-18-to-34-year-olds/).

————. 2017. "The Share of Americans Living without a Partner Has Increased, Especially among Young Adults." Pew Research Center, October 11. Accessed December 17, 2018 (www.pewresearch.org/fact-tank/2017/10/11/the-share-of-americans-living-without-a-partner-has-increased-especially-among-young-adults/).

Fry, Richard, and Anna Brown. 2016. "In a Recovering Market, Homeownership Rates Are Down Sharply for Blacks, Young Adults." Pew Research Center, Social & Demographic Trends December 15. Accessed February 6, 2017 (www.pewsocialtrends.org/2016/12/15/in-a-recovering-market-homeownership-rates-are-down-sharply-for-blacks-young-adults/).

Fry, Richard, and Jeffrey S. Passel. 2014. "In Post-Recesson Era, Young Adults Drive Continuing Rise in Multi-Generational Living." Washington, DC: Pew Research Centers Social and Demographic Trends project, July 17. Accessed February 26, 2015 (www.pewsocialtrends.org/files/2014/07/ST-2014-07-17-multigen-households-report.pdf).

Fryer, Roland G. 2018. "Reconciling Results on Racial Differences in Police Shootings." *American Economic Association Papers and Proceedings* 108: 228–233

Fu, Furio. 2017. "The List of Blocked Websites in China." *Sapore di Cina,* January 4. Accessed February 15, 2017 (www.saporedicina.com/english/list-of-blocked-websites-in-china/).

Funk, Cary, and Brian Kennedy. 2016. "The Politics of Climate." Pew Research Center, Internet, Science, & Tech October 4. Accessed February 13, 2017 (www.pewinternet.org/2016/10/04/public-views-on-climate-change-and-climate-scientists/).

Furedi, Frank. 2006. "The End of Professional Dominance." *Society* 43 (6): 14–18.

Furstenberg, Frank F., Jr. 2010. "On a New Schedule: Transitions to Adulthood and Family Change." *The Future of Children* 20 (1): 67–87.

Fussell, Paul. 1992. *Class: A Guide through the American Status System.* New York: Touchstone.

G

Gabler, Neal. 2006. *Walt Disney: The Triumph of the American Imagination.* New York: Knopf.

Gabrielson, Ryan, Ryann Grochowski Jones, and Eric Sagara. 2014. "Deadly Force, in Black and White." *ProPublica,* October 10. Accessed April 26, 2015 (www.propublica.org/article/deadly-force-in-black-and-white).

Galbraith, John K. 1952. *American Capitalism: The Concept of Countervailing Power.* New York: Houghton Mifflin.

Gallup. 2018a. "Military and National Defense." Washington, DC: Gallup, Inc. Accessed January 8, 2019 (www.gallup.com/poll/1666/military-national-defense.aspx).

————. "Cloning." Washington, DC: Gallup, Inc. Accessed January 30, 2019 (www.gallup.com/poll/6028/Cloning.aspx).

Galton, Francis. 1883. *Inquiries into Human Faculty and Its Development.* New York: Macmillan and Co.

————. 1904. "Eugenics: Its Definition, Scope, and Aims." *The American Journal of Sociology* 10 (1): 1–25.

Gane, Mike. 2006. *Auguste Comte.* New York: Routledge.

Gans, Herbert. 1971. "The Uses of Poverty: The Poor Pay All." *Social Policy,* July/August, 20–24.

————. 1979. "Symbolic Ethnicity: The Future of Ethnic Groups and Cultures in America." *Ethnic and Racial Studies* 2: 1–20.

————. 2009. "Reflections on Symbolic Ethnicity: A Response to Y. Anagnostou." *Ethnicities* 9 (1): 123–130.

Gao, George. 2015. "How Do Americans Stand Out from the Rest of the World?" Pew Research Center, March 12. Accessed May 28, 2015 (www.pewresearch.org/fact-tank/2015/03/12/how-do-americans-stand-out-from-the-rest-of-the-world/).

Gardner, Gary, Erik Assadourian, and Radhika Sarin. 2004. "The State of Consumption Today." Pp. 3–21 in *State of the World 2004,* ed. Brian Halweil and Lisa Mastny. New York: Norton.

Garfinkel, Harold. 1956. "Conditions of Successful Degradation Ceremonies." *American Journal of Sociology* 61 (March): 420–424.

Garlipp, Petra. 2008. "Koro—a Culture-Bound Phenomenon: Intercultural Psychiatric Implications." *German Journal of Psychiatry* 11:21–28.

Garrett, R. Sam. 2017. "Political Status of Puerto Rico: Brief Background and Recent Developments for Congress." *Congressional Research Service* R44721. Accessed October 10, 2018 (https://fas.org/sgp/crs/row/R44721.pdf).

Garrett, Ruth Irene. 2003. *Crossing Over: One Woman's Escape from Amish Life.* New York: HarperOne.

Gaviria, Marcela, and Martin Smith. 2009. "The Madoff Affair." *PBS Frontline,* May 12. Accessed May 21, 2009 (www.pbs.org/wgbh/pages/frontline/madoff).

Gay, Chloe. 2018. "Bumble Sociologist Says 85% of Users Looking for a Relationship." *Global Dating Insights,* April 25. Accessed December 13, 2018 (https://globaldatinginsights.com/2018/04/25/bumble-sociologist-says-85-users-looking-relationship/).

Geggel, Laura. 2016. "Does Sugar Make Kids Hyper?" *LiveScience,* August 15. Accessed September 12, 2016 (www.livescience.com/55754-does-sugar-make-kids-hyper.html).

Gelman, Andrew, Jeffrey Fagan, and Alex Kiss. 2007. "An Analysis of the New York City Police Department's 'Stop-and-Frisk' Policy in the Context of Claims of Racial Bias." *Journal of the American Statistical Association* 102 (479): 813–823.

Gelvin, James L. 2012. *The Arab Uprisings: What Everyone Needs to Know.* New York: Oxford University Press.

Genocide Watch. 2018. "Countries at Risk: Recent Alerts." Accessed September 29, 2018 (http://genocidewatch.net/alerts-2/new-alerts/).

Gerhardt, Uta. 2002. *Talcott Parsons: An Intellectual Biography.* New York: Cambridge University Press.

Gheytanchi, Elham. 2009. "Iranian Women Lead the Protests." *San Francisco Chronicle,* June 29. Accessed June 30, 2009 (www.sfgate.com/cgi-bin/article.cgi?f5/c/a/2009/06/29/ED8618EMUC.DTL).

Ghitis, Frida. 2011. "Women of Arab Spring Still Fighting for Liberation." *Salt Lake Star Tribune,* June 21. Accessed August 12, 2011 (www.startribune.com/opinion/otherviews/124292204.html).

Gibson, Campbell, and Kay Jung. 2002. "Historical Census Statistics on Population Totals by Race, 1790 to 1990, and by Hispanic Origin, 1970 to 1990, for the United States, Regions, Divisions, and States." Population Division, U.S. Census Bureau, Washington, DC, September, Working Paper Series No. 56. Accessed May 17, 2010 (www.census.gov/population/www/documentation/twps0056/twps0056.html).

Gillam, Stephen. 2008. "Is the Declaration of Alma Ata Still Relevant to Primary Health Care?" *BMJ* 336: 536–539.

Ginder, Scott, A., Janice E. Kelly-Reid, and Farrah B. Mann. 2014. *Enrollment in Postsecondary Institutions, Fall 2011; Financial Statistics, Fiscal Year 2011; and Graduation Rates, Selected Cohorts, 2003–08.* U.S. Department of Education, NCES 2012-174rev. Washington, DC: National Center for Education Statistics. Accessed May 30, 2013 (http://nces.ed.gov/pubs2012/2012174rev.pdf).

Gitlin, Todd. 1993. *The Sixties: Years of Hope, Days of Rage.* New York: Bantam Books.

Glass Ceiling Commission. 1995. "Good for Business: Making Full Use of the Nations Human Capital—the Environmental Scan." A Fact-Finding Report of the Federal Glass Ceiling Commission, Washington, DC. Accessed June 19, 2011 (www.dol.gov/oasam/programs/history/reich/reports/ceiling.pdf).

Glassner, Barry. 2010. "Still Fearful." *Chronicle of Higher Education* 56 (January 22): B11–B12.

Glaude, Eddie, Jr. 2016. *Democracy in Black: How Race Still Enslaves the American Soul.* New York: Crown.

Global Slavery Index. 2018. "Unravelling the Numbers." The Walk Free Foundation, Perth, Australia. Accessed January 10, 2019 (www.globalslaveryindex.org/2018/findings/highlights/).

Goffman, Alice. 2014a. *On the Run: Fugitive Life in an American City.* Chicago: University of Chicago Press.

————.2014b. "Surveillance City: The War on Drugs in Urban Neighborhoods." The 2014 Nathan Levin Lecture on Public Policy, Public Policy Forums, the Center for New York City Affairs, New School, New York City, June 18, 2014. Accessed January 10, 2015 (http://blogs.newschool.edu/cnyca/2014/05/21/surveillance-city-the-war-on-drugs-in-urban-neighborhoods/).

Goffman, Erving. 1959. *The Presentation of Self in Everyday Life.* New York: Doubleday.

————. 1961. *Asylums: Essays on the Social Situation of Mental Patients and Other Inmates.* Garden City, NY: Doubleday.

————. 1963. *Stigma: Notes on Management of Spoiled Identity.* Englewood Cliffs, NJ: Prentice Hall.

————. 1979. *Gender Advertisements.* Cambridge, MA: Harvard University Press.

Golan, Limor, and Andrés Hincapié. 2016. "Breaking Down the Gender Wage Gap by Age and Hours Worked." *The Regional Economist,* October: 6–7, 13. Accessed February 2, 2017 (www.stlouisfed.org/~/media/Publications/Regional%20Economist/2016/October/gender_wage.pdf).

Goldring, Rebecca, Soheyla Taie, Minsun Riddles, and Chelsea Owens. 2014. "Teacher Attrition and Mobility: Results from the 2012–13 Teacher Follow-Up Survey." U.S. Department of Education, National Center for Education Statistics, NCES 2014-77, September. Accessed December 6, 2016 (http://nces.ed.gov/pubs2014/2014077.pdf).

Goldstein, Amy. 2017. *Janesville: An American Story.* New York: Simon & Schuster.

Goldstein, Melvyn C., and Cynthia M. Beall. 1981. "Modernization and Aging in the Third and Fourth World: Views from the Rural Hinterland in Nepal." *Human Organization* 40 (Spring): 48–55.

Gonzales, Suzannah, and Steve Holland. 2018. "Trump Advocates 'Stop-and-Frisk' to Curtail Chicago Crime." Reuters, October 8. Accessed December 4, 2018 (www.reuters.com/article/us-usa-trump-chicago/trump-advocates-stop-and-frisk-to-curtail-chicago-crime-idUSKCN1MI2BV).

Gonzalez-Barrera, Ana. 2015. "More Mexicans Leaving Than Coming to the U.S." Pew Research Center Hispanic Trends, November 19. Accessed January 20, 2017 (www.pewhispanic.org/2015/11/19/more-mexicans-leaving-than-coming-to-the-u-s/).

Good, Anthony. 2007. *Anthropology and Expertise in the Asylum Courts.* New York: Routledge-Cavendish.

Goode, William J. 1960. "A Theory of Role Strain." *American Sociological Review* 25 (4): 483–496.

Goodman, Amy. 2017. "From Keystone XL Pipeline to #DAPL: Jasilyn Charger, Water Protector from Cheyenne River Reservation." Interview. *Democracy Now,* January 4. Accessed February 8, 2017 (www.democracynow.org/2017/1/4/from_keystone_xl_pipeline_to_dapl).

Goodwin, Jeff, James M. Jasper, and Francesca Polletta. 2000. "The Return of the Repressed: The Fall and Rise of Emotions in Social Movement Theory." *Mobilization: An International Journal* 5 (1): 65–83.

Goodwin, Paula Y., William D. Mosher, and Anjani Chandra. 2010. "Marriage and Cohabitation in the United States: A Statistical Portrait Based on Cycle 6 (2002) of the National Survey of Family Growth." *Vital and Health Statistics* 23 (28). National Center for Health Statistics, Washington, DC.

Google. 2018a. "Fertility Rate." World Bank Development Indicators, Public Data Visualization Program, July 6. Accessed January 25, 2019 (www.google.com/publicdata/explore?ds=d5bncppjof8f9_&ctype=l&strail=false&bcs=d&nselm=h&met_y=sp_dyn_tfrt_in&scale_y=lin&ind_y=false&rdim=country&idim=country:NER:AFG:RWA:KHM:IND:DZA:USA:IRN:CHN:DEU&ifdim=country&hl=en&dl=en&ind=false).

————. 2018b. "Life Expectancy." World Bank Development Indicators, Public Data Visualization Program. Accessed April 30, 2015 (www.google.com/publicdata/explore?ds=d5bncppjof8f9_&ctype=l&strail=false&bcs=d&nselm=h&met_y=sp_dyn_le00_in&scale_y=lin&ind_y=false&rdim=country&idim=country:AFG:KHM:CHN:DEU:IND:IRN:DZA:USA:NER:RWA&ifdim=country&hl=en&dl=en&ind=false).

Gough, E. Kathleen. 1959. "The Nayars and the Definition of Marriage." *The Journal of the Royal Anthropological Institute of Great Britain and Ireland* 89: 23–34.

Gould, Kenneth A., David N. Pellow, and Allan Schnaibert. 2008. *The Treadmill of Production: Injustice and Unsustainability in the Global Economy.* New York: Routledge.

Gouldner, Alvin. 1960. "The Norm of Reciprocity." *American Sociological Review* 25 (April): 161–177.

————. 1970. *The Coming Crisis of Western Sociology.* New York: Basic Books.

Gover, Kevin. 2000. "Remarks of Kevin Gover, Department of the Interior Assistant Secretary of Indian Affairs." *Congressional Record* 146 (107): E1453-E1454. Accessed October 9, 2018 (www.gpo.gov/fdsys/pkg/CREC-2000-09-13/html/CREC-2000-09-13-pt1-PgE1453-3.htm).

GPOBA. 2014. "Challenges in Formalizing the Supply of Electricity in Mumbai's Slums." The Global Parternship on Output-Based Aid, Note Number 6, October. Accessed January 16, 2017 (http://documents.worldbank.org/curated/en/594161468033306544/pdf/938370BRI0Box300MumbaiElectricity01.pdf).

Graf, Nikki. 2016. "Most Americans Say Children Are Better Off with a Parent Home." Pew Research Center, October 10. Accessed January 30, 2017 (www.pewresearch.org/fact-tank/2016/10/10/most-americans-say-children-are-better-off-with-a-parent-at-home/).

Gramlich, John. 2017. "Hispanic Dropout Rate Hits New Low, College Enrollment at New High." Pew Research Center, September 29. Accessed October 10, 2018 (www.pewresearch.org/fact-tank/2017/09/29/hispanic-dropout-rate-hits-new-low-college-enrollment-at-new-high/).

Gramsci, Antonio. 1929. Selections from the Prison Notebooks, ed. and trans. Quintin Hoare and Geoffrey Nowell Smith. London: Lawrence and Wishort.

Granovetter, Mark S. 1973. "The Strength of Weak Ties." American Journal of Sociology 78: 1360–1380.

Green, Emma. 2016. "Tom Brady, Sociologist of Religion." The Atlantic, November 30. Accessed December 22, 2018 (www.theatlantic.com/entertainment/archive/2016/11/religion-of-sports-gotham-chopra-tom-brady-michael-strahan/508913/).

Greenberg, Andy. 2016. "Hack Brief: 412M Accounts Breached on FriendFinder Sex Sites." Wired, November 11. Accessed February 15, 2017 (www.wired.com/2016/11/hack-brief-412m-accounts-breached-friendfinder-sex-sites/).

Greenfield, Patrick. 2018. "The Crown's Claire Foy Paid Less Than Male Co-Star, Producers Admit." The Guardian, March 13. Accessed October 30, 2018 (www.theguardian.com/society/2018/mar/13/the-crowns-claire-foy-paid-less-than-male-co-star-producers-admit).

Greenhouse, Steven. 2008. "Queens Factory Is Found to Owe Workers $5.3 Million." The New York Times, July 23. Accessed June 20, 2009 (http://cityroom.blogs.nytimes.com/2008/07/23/a-queens-sweatshop-found-to-owe-workers-53-million/).

Greenwald, Glenn. 2013. "NSA Collecting Phone Records of Millions of Verizon Customers Daily." The Guardian, June 5. Accessed June 7, 2013 (www.guardian.co.uk/world/2013/jun/06/nsa-phone-records-verizon-court-order).

Greenwald, Glenn, and Ewen MacAskill. 2013. "NSA PRISM Program Taps in to User Data of Facebook, Yahoo and Others." The Guardian, June 6. Accessed June 7, 2013 (www.guardian.co.uk/world/2013/jun/06/us-tech-giants-nsa-data).

Greenwood, Veronique. 2013. "We Are All Princes, Paupers, and Part of the Human Family." Nautilus, May 17. Accessed June 6, 2013 (http://nautil.us/blog/we-are-all-princes-paupers-and-part-of-the-human-family).

Greer, Christina M. 2013. Black Ethnics: Race, Immigration, and the Pursuit of the American Dream. New York: Oxford University Press.

Greshko, Michael. 2018. "Monkey Clones Created in the Lab. Now What?" National Geographic, January 24. Accessed January 30, 2019 (https://news.nationalgeographic.com/2018/01/monkey-clones-dolly-sheep-china-medicine-science/).

Grillo, Ioan. 2018. "Mexico's Own Refugee Surge." U.S. News & World Report, July 10. Accessed June 4, 2019 (www.usnews.com/news/best-countries/articles/2018-07-10/mexico-faces-its-own-surge-of-refugees-entering-the-country).

Grinberg, Emanuella, and Nadeem Muaddi. 2018. "How the Parkland Students Pulled Off a Massive National Protest in Only 5 Weeks." CNN, March 26. Accessed January 30, 2019 (www.cnn.com/2018/03/26/us/march-for-our-lives/index.html).

Groeneveld, Elizabeth. 2009. "Be a Feminist or Just Dress Like One: BUST, Fashion and Feminism as Lifestyle." Journal of Gender Studies 18 (2): 179–190.

Gross, Jane. 2005. "Forget the Career. My Parents Need Me at Home." The New York Times, November 24, pp. A1, A20.

Grossman, Samantha. 2015. "This Time-Lapse Video Shows How Much Photoshop Is Used in High Fashion Photography." Time, May 4. Accessed January 26, 2017 (http://time.com/3845647/high-fashion-photo-retouching-time-lapse-video/).

Gruber, Jonathan. 2010. "Health Care Reform Is a 'Three-Legged Stool': The Costs of Partially Repealing the Affordable Care Act." Center for American Progress, August 5. Accessed February 12, 2017 (www.americanprogress.org/issues/healthcare/reports/2010/08/05/8226/health-care-reform-is-a-three-legged-stool/).

Guglielmo, Jennifer. 2003. "White Lies, Dark Truths." Pp. 1–14 in Are Italians White? How Race Is Made in America, ed. Jennifer Guglielmo and Salvatore Salerno. New York: Routledge.

Gurari, Inbal, John Hetts, and Michael Strube. 2006. "Beauty in the I of the Beholder: Effects of Idealized Media Portrayals on Implicit Self-Image." Basic & Applied Social Psychology 28 (3): 273–282.

Gutiérrez, Gustavo. 1988. A Theology of Liberation: History, Politics, and Salvation (15th Anniversary Edition with New Introduction by Author). Maryknoll, NY: Orbis Books, 17–18.

———. 1990. "Theology and the Social Sciences." Pp. 214–225 in Liberation Theology at the Crossroads: Democracy or Revolution? ed. Paul E. Sigmund. New York: Oxford University Press.

Guy-Ryan, Jessie. 2016. "In Indonesia, Non-Binary Gender Is a Centuries-Old Idea." Atlas Obscura, June 18. Accessed June 6, 2016 (www.atlasobscura.com/articles/in-indonesia-nonbinary-gender-is-a-centuriesold-idea).

H

Hager, Carol. 2017. "Grassroots Protest and Innovation: A New Look at NIMBY." Social Science Research Council. Items, October 17. Accessed January 26, 2019 (https://items.ssrc.org/grassroots-protest-and-innovation-a-new-look-at-nimby/).

Hall, John J., and Richard Taylor. 2003. "Health for All beyond 2000: The Demise of the Alma-Ata Declaration and Primary Health Care in Developing Countries." The Medical Journal of Australia 178: 17–20.

Halper, Mark. 2013. "Hooking China on Coffee." SmartPlanet, May 3. Accessed May 7, 2013 (www.smartplanet.com/blog/bulletin/hooking-china-on-coffee/18742).

Hamlin, Rebecca. 2014. Let Me Be a Refugee: Administrative Justice and the Politics of Asylum in the United States, Canada, and Australia. New York: Oxford University Press.

Hamnett, Brian R. 2019. A Concise History of Mexico, 3rd ed. New York: Cambridge University Press.

Harari, Yuval Noah. 2017. Homo Deus: A Brief History of Tomorrow. New York: Harper Press.

Hardin, Victoria A. 2012. AIDS at 30: A History. Dulles, VA: Potomac Books.

Harding, Sandra. 2004. "Introduction: Standpoint Theory as a Site of Political, Philosophic, and Scientific Debate." Pp. 1–16 in The Feminist Standpoint Theory Reader: Intellectual and Political Controversies, ed. Sandra Harding. New York: Routledge.

Harding, Sandra, ed. 2003. The Feminist Standpoint Theory Reader: Intellectual and Political Controversies. New York: Routledge.

Hardt, Michael, and Antonio Negri. 2009. Commonwealth. Cambridge, MA: Belknap Press.

Harford, Tim. 2017. "Money via Mobile: The M-Pesa Revolution." BBC World Service, February 13. Accessed February 16, 2017 (www.bbc.com/news/business-38667475).

Harlow, Harry F. 1971. Learning to Love. New York: Ballantine Books.

Harrington, Michael. 1962. The Other America: Poverty in the United States. Baltimore, MD: Penguin Books.

———. 1980. "The New Class and the Left." Pp. 123–138 in The New Class, ed. B. Bruce Briggs. New Brunswick, NJ: Transaction.

Harris, Deborah A. 2015. "'You Just Have to Look at It as a Gift': Low-Income Single Mothers' Experiences of the Child Support System." Journal of Poverty 19: 88–108.

Hart, Betty, and Todd R. Risley. 1995. Meaningful Differences in the Everyday Experience of Young American Children. Baltimore, MD: Paul H. Brookes.

Hart, Zachary P., Vernon D. Miller, and John R. Johnson. 2003. "Socialization, Resocialization and Communication Relationships in the Context of an Organizational Change." *Communication Studies* 54 (4): 483–495.

Hartig, Hannah. 2018. "Nearly Six-in-Ten Americans Say Abortion Should Be Legal in All or Most Cases." Pew Research Center, October 17. Accessed January 24, 2019 (www.pewresearch. org/fact-tank/2018/10/17/ nearly-six-in-ten-americans-say-abortion-should-be-legal/).

Hartig, Hannah, and Abigail Geiger. 2018. "About Six-in-Ten Americans Support Marijuana Legalization." Pew Research Center, Fact Tank, October 8. Accessed December 1. (www.pewresearch.org/ fact-tank/2018/10/08/americans-support-marijuana-legalization/).

Hartsock, Nancy C. M. 1983. "The Feminist Standpoint: Developing the Ground for a Specifically Feminist Historical Materialism." Pp. 283–310 in *Discovering Reality: Feminist Perspectives in Epistemology, Methodology, and Philosophy of Science,* ed. Sandra Harding and Merrill B. Hintikka. Dordrecht, The Netherlands: Reidel.

Hashaw, Tim. 2007. *The Birth of Black America: The First African Americans and the Pursuit of Freedom at Jamestown.* New York: Carroll & Graf.

Haslam, Nick, Steve Loughnan, and Gina Perry. 2014. "Meta-Milgram: An Empirical Synthesis of the Obedience Experiments." *PLoS ONE* 9 (4): e93927. Accessed February 19, 2015 (http://journals.plos. org/plosone/article?id=10.1371/journal.pone.0093927).

Haviland, William A., Harald E. L. Prins, Dana Walrath, and Bunny McBride. 2005. *Cultural Anthropology: The Human Challenge,* 11th ed. Belmont, CA: Wadsworth.

Hawkins, Stephen, Daniel Yudkin, Miriam Juan-Torres, and Tim Dixon. 2018. *Hidden Tribes: A Study of America's Polarized Landscape.* New York: More in Common. Accessed November 17, 2018 (https:// hiddentribes.us).

Hayden, H. Thomas. 2004. "What Happened at Abu Ghraib." Accessed September 19, 2011 (www.military.com/NewContent/0,13190,Hayden_090704,00.html).

Hayes, Christopher. 2012. *Twilight of the Elites: America after Meritocracy.* New York: Crown.

He, Wan, Manisha Sengupta, Victoria A. Velkoff, and Kimberly A. DeBarros. 2005. "651 in the United States: 2005." *Current Population Reports,* P23-209. Washington, DC: U.S. Government Printing Office.

Healy, Jack. 2016. "Occupying the Prairie: Tensions Rise as Tribes Move to Block a Pipeline." *The New York Times,* August 23. Accessed February 8, 2017 (www.nytimes.com/2016/08/24/us/occupying-the-prairie-tensions-rise-as-tribes-move-to-block-a-pipeline.html).

Healy, Jack, and Nicholas Fandos. 2016. "Protesters Gain Victory in Fight over Dakota Access Oil Pipeline." *The New York Times,* December 4. Accessed February 8, 2017 (https://www.nytimes. com/2016/12/04/us/federal-officials-to-explore-different-route-for-dakota-pipeline.html).

Heath, Hilary. 2016. "Mexico's Indigenous Population Continues to Face High Rates of Poverty." *Panoramas,* June 15. Accessed January 22, 2019 (www.panoramas.pitt.edu/health/ mexicos-indigenous-population-continues-face-high-rates-poverty).

Heckman, James. 2013. *Giving Kids a Fair Chance.* Boston: Boston Review Books.

Heidrick & Struggles International. 2016. *Mapping Incoming Boardroom Talent: The Heidrick & Struggles Board Monitor.* New York: Heidrick & Struggles International, Inc. Accessed February 3, 2017 (www. heidrick.com/~/media/Publications%20and%20Reports/Mapping%20incoming%20talent.pdf).

Heine, Friederike. 2013. "M, F or Blank: Third Gender Official in Germany from November." Spiegel Online International, August 16. Accessed April 19, 2015 (www.spiegel.de/international/ germany/third-gender-option-to-become-available-on-german-birth-certificates-a-916940.html).

Helliwell, John F., Richard Layard, and Jeffrey D. Sachs. 2018. *World Happiness Report 2018.* New York: Sustainable Development Solutions Network. Accessed October 30, 2018 (http://worldhappiness. report/ed/2018/).

Helms, Sarah W., Sophia Choukas-Bradley, Laura Widman, Matteo Giletta, Geoffrey L. Cohen, and Mitchell J. Prinstein. 2014.

"Adolescents Misperceive and Are Influenced by High-Status Peers Health Risk, Deviant, and Adaptive Behavior." *Developmental Psychology* 50: 2697–2714.

Henderson, Anita. 2003. "What's in a Slur?" *American Speech* 78 (1): 52–74.

Hendrickson, Brett. 2014. *Border Medicine: A Transcultural History of Curanderismo.* New York: NYU Press.

Henriques, Diana B., and Jack Healy. 2009. "Madoff Goes to Jail after Guilty Pleas." *The New York Times,* March 12. Accessed May 21, 2009 (www.nytimes.com/2009/03/13/business/13madoff.html).

Hetherington, E. Mavis, and John Kelly. 2002. *For Better or for Worse: Divorce Reconsidered.* New York: Norton.

Hewlett, Sylvia Ann, Diana Foster, Laura Sherbin, Peggy Shiller, and Karen Sumberg. 2010. *Off-Ramps and On-Ramps Revisited.* New York: Center for Work-Life Policy.

Higginbottom, Karen. 2017. "Board Diversity Still Unusual in a Fortune 500 Firm." *Forbes,* January 30. Accessed February 3, 2017 (www.forbes.com/sites/karenhigginbottom/2017/01/30/ board-diversity-still-unusual-in-a-fortune-500-firm/).

Higgins, George E., Richard Tewksbury, and Elizabeth Mustaine. 2007. "Sports Fan Binge Drinking: An Examination Using Low Self-Control and Peer Association." *Sociological Spectrum* 27 (4): 389–404.

Higher Education Research Institute. 2016. "College Students' Commitment to Activism, Political and Civic Engagement Reach All-Time Highs." UCLA Newsroom, February 10. Accessed February 14, 2017 (http://newsroom.ucla.edu/releases/college-students-commitment-to-activism-political-and-civic-engagement-reach-all-time-highs).

Hill, Marquita K. 2010. *Understanding Environmental Pollution,* 3rd ed. Cambridge, UK: Cambridge University Press.

Hirschi, Travis. 1969. *Causes of Delinquency.* Berkeley: University of California Press.

————. 2004. "Self-Control and Crime." Pp. 537–552 in *Handbook of Self-Regulation: Research, Theory, and Applications,* ed. Roy F. Baumeister and Kathleen D. Vohs. New York: Guilford Press.

Hirschman, Charles, and Irina Voloshin. 2007. "The Structure of Teenage Employment: Social Background and the Jobs Held by High School Seniors." *Research in Social Stratification and Mobility* 25: 189–203.

Hirschman, Daniel, Ellen Berrey, and Fiona Rose-Greenland. 2016. "Dequantifying Diversity: Affirmative Action and Admissions at the University of Michigan." *Theory & Society* 45 (3): 265–301.

Hixson, Lindsay, Bradford B. Hepler, and Myoung Ouk Kim. 2011. "The White Population: 2010." 2010 Census Briefs, Report C2010BR-05, September. Accessed May 27, 2012 (www.census.gov/ prod/cen2010/briefs/c2010br-05.pdf).

Hobbs, Allyson. 2014. *A Chosen Exile: A History of Racial Passing in American Life.* Cambridge, MA: Harvard University Press.

Hobsbawm, Eric. 1999. *Industry and Empire: The Birth of the Industrial Revolution.* New York: New Press.

Hochschild, Arlie Russell. 1989. *The Second Shift: Working Parents and the Revolution at Home.* New York: Viking Press.

————. 1990. "The Second Shift: Employed Women Are Putting in Another Day of Work at Home." *Utne Reader* 38 (March/April): 66–73.

————. 1997. *The Time Bind: When Work Becomes Home and Home Becomes Work.* New York: Henry Holt.

————. 2005. *The Commercialization of Intimate Life: Notes from Home and Work.* Berkeley: University of California Press.

————. 2016. *Strangers in Their Own Land: Anger and Mourning on the American Right.* New York: New Press.

Hoffer, Williamjames Hull. 2012. *Plessy v. Ferguson: Race and Inequality in Jim Crow America.* Lawrence: University of Kansas Press.

Holloway, Daniel. 2017a. "'Game of Thrones' Season 7 Pirated More than 1 Billion Times." *Variety,* September 7. Accessed December 2, 2018 (https://variety.com/2017/tv/news/ game-of-thrones-piratacy-1202550723/).

————. 2017b. "Networks Beef Up Press-Screener Security as Piracy Increases." *Variety,* September 6. Accessed December 2, 2018 (https://variety.com/2017/digital/news/ tv-piracy-screeners-security-intensifies-1202548437/).

Holmes, Morgan. 2011. "The Intersex Enchiridion: Naming and Knowledge." *Somatechnics* 1 (2): 388–411.

Hootman, J., J. Bolen, C. Helmick, and G. Langmaid. 2006. "Prevalence of Doctor-Diagnosed Arthritis and Arthritis-Attributable Activity Limitation—United States, 2003–2005." *Morbidity and Mortality Weekly Report* 55 (40): 1089–1092.

Hoover, Daniel W., and Richard Millich. 1994. "Effects of Sugar Ingestion Expectancies on Mother-Child Interactions." *Journal of Abnormal Child Psychology* 22 (4): 501–515.

Hopper, Paul. 2007. *Understanding Cultural Globalization.* Malden, MA: Polity Press.

Hostetler, John A. 1993. *Amish Society,* 4th ed. Baltimore, MD: Johns Hopkins University Press.

Hout, Michael. 2018. "Americans' Occupational Status Reflects the Status of Both of Their Parents." *PNAS* 115 (38): 9527–9532. Accessed January 13, 2019 (https://www.pnas.org/content/115/38/9527).

Hout, Michael, Tom W. Smith, and Peter V. Marsden. 2015. "Prestige and Socioeconomic Scores for the 2010 Census Codes: Supplemental File." GSS Methodological Report No. 124. Chicago: NORC. Accessed December 22, 2016 (http://gss.norc.org/Documents/other/PRESTG10SEI10_supplement.xls).

Howard, Russell D., and Reid L. Sawyer. 2003. *Terrorism and Counterterrorism: Understanding the New Security Environment.* Guilford, CT: McGraw-Hill/Dushkin.

Hughes, Everett. 1945. "Dilemmas and Contradictions of Status." *American Journal of Sociology* 50 (March): 353–359.

Hulbert, Ann. 2003. *Raising America: Experts, Parents, and a Century of Advice about Children.* New York: Knopf.

Human Rights Campaign. 2009. "Maps of State Laws & Policies." Accessed May 27, 2009 (www.hrc.org/about_us/state_laws.asp).

———. 2015. "Marriage Center." Washington, DC. Accessed February 26, 2015 (www.hrc.org/marriage-center).

Human Rights Watch. 2019. *World Report: 2019.* New York: Seven Stories Press. Accessed January 22, 2019 (www.hrw.org/world-report/2019).

Humes, Karen R., Nicholas A. Jones, and Robert R. Ramirez. 2011. "Overview of Race and Hispanic Origin: 2010." 2010 Census Briefs, C2010BR-02, March. Accessed March 25, 2015 (www.census.gov/prod/cen2010/briefs/c2010br-02.pdf).

Humphrey, Carol Sue. 2013. *The American Revolution and the Press: The Promise of Independence.* Evanston, IL: Northwestern University Press.

Hunter, Herbert M., ed. 2000. *The Sociology of Oliver C. Cox: New Perspectives: Research in Race and Ethnic Relations,* vol. 2. Stamford, CT: JAI Press.

Hunt Institute. 2015. "Paso del Norte Economic Indicator Review." Hunt Institute for Global Competitiveness, University of Texas at El Paso, Spring. Accessed April 16, 2015 (http://d31hzlhk6di2h5.cloudfront.net/20150413/d0/5b/25/92/6bd1e2c334d8287995ff5036/PASO_DEL_NORTE_ECONOMIC_INDICATOR_REVIEW.pdf).

Hurrell, Scott A., Dora Scholarios, and Paul Thompson. 2013. "More Than a 'Humpty Dumpty' Term: Strengthening the Conceptualization of Soft Skills." *Economic and Industrial Democracy* 34 (1):161–182.

Hurst, Charles E., and David L. McConnell. 2010. *An Amish Paradox: Diversity and Change in the World's Largest Amish Community.* Baltimore, MD: Johns Hopkins University Press.

Hvistendahl, Mara. 2010. "Has China Outgrown the One-Child Policy?" *Science* 329 (September 17): 1458–1461.

Hymowitz, Kay, Jason S. Carroll, W. Bradford Wilcox, and Kelleen Kay. 2013. *Knot Yet: The Benefits and Costs of Delayed Marriage in America.* Charlottesville, VA: The National Marriage Project at the University of Virginia. Accessed December 15, 2018 (http://nationalmarriageproject.org/wp-content/uploads/2013/03/KnotYet-FinalForWeb.pdf).

I

Ignatiev, Noel. 1995. *How the Irish Became White.* New York: Routledge.

Illinois State Board of Education. 2018. "Illinois Report Card 2017–2018." Springfield, IL. Accessed December 20, 2018 (http://illinois-reportcard.com/Default.aspx).

INEGI. 2009. "Mujeres y Hombres en México 2005. Anexo estadístico." Instituto Nacional de Estadística y Geografía. Accessed June 14, 2009 (www.inegi.org.mx/inegi/contenidos/espanol/bvinegi/productos/integracion/sociodemografico/mujeresyhombres/2005/anexo_2005.xls).

———. 2018. "Indicadores de Bienestar por Entidad Federativa." Instituto Nacional de Estadística y Geografía. Accessed January 21, 2019 (www.beta.inegi.org.mx/app/bienestar/#grafica).

Inglehart, Ronald, Pippa Norris, and Christian Welzel. 2002. "Gender Equality and Democracy." *Comparative Sociology* 1 (3/4): 321–346.

Innocence Project. 2018. "DNA Exonerations in the United States." Accessed December 4, 2018 (www.innocenceproject.org/free-innocent/improve-the-law/fact-sheets/dna-exonerations-nationwide).

INPE. 2018. "Annual Deforestation Rate in Brazilian Legal Amazon (AMZ)." Instituto Nacional de Pesquisas Espaciais, Brazil. Accessed January 26, 2019 (www.obt.inpe.br/prodes/dashboard/prodes-rates.html).

Institute for Criminal Policy Research. 2018. "Highest to Lowest—Prison Population Rate." London: World Prison Brief. December 4, 2018 (www.prisonstudies.org/highest-to-lowest/prison-population-total?field_region_taxonomy_tid=All).

Institute for Economics & Peace. 2018. *Global Terrorism Index 2018: Measuring and Understanding the Impact of Terrorism.* Sydney: Institute for Economics and Peace. Accessed January 8, 2019 (http://visionofhumanity.org/app/uploads/2018/12/Global-Terrorism-Index-2018-1.pdf).

Internal Revenue Service. 2018. "Number of Returns, Shares of AGI, Selected Income Items, Credits, Total Income Tax, AGI Floor on Percentiles, and Average Tax Rates: 2016." IRS Statistical Information Services, Washington, DC, October. Accessed January 12, 2019 (www.irs.gov/statistics/soi-tax-stats-individual-income-tax-rates-and-tax-shares).

International Institute for Democracy and Electoral Assistance. 2016b. "Quota Database." Quota Project. Accessed December 16, 2016 (www.quotaproject.org/searchDb.cfm).

———. 2019a. "Voter Turnout Database: Voter Turnout." International IDEA, Stockholm, Sweden. Accessed January 8, 2019 (www.idea.int/data-tools/data/voter-turnout).

———. 2019b. "Quota Database." Quota Project. Accessed January 8, 2019 (www.idea.int/data-tools/data/gender-quotas/database).

International Telecommunications Union. 2015. "Explore Key ICT Statistics." ITUs ICT Eye. Accessed February 2, 2015 (www.itu.int/net4/itu-d/icteye/).

International Telecommunications Union. 2017. "Explore Key ICT Statistics." ITUs ICT Eye. Accessed November 20, 2018 (www.itu.int/net4/itu-d/icteye/).

Internet World Stats. 2018. "Internet Usage Statistics: The Internet Big Picture." June 30 Update. Accessed January 30, 2019 (www.internetworldstats.com/stats.htm).

Inter-Parliamentary Union. 2016. "Women in National Parliaments: Situation as of 1st November 2016." Geneva, Switzerland. Accessed December 16, 2016 (www.ipu.org/wmn-e/arc/classif011116.htm).

———. 2018. "Women in National Parliaments: Situation as of 1st November 2018." Geneva, Switzerland. Accessed January 8, 2019 (http://archive.ipu.org/wmn-e/classif.htm).

Ipsos MORI. 2014. "Perceptions Are Not Reality: Things the World Gets Wrong." Ipsos MORI Perils of Perception Survey, London, October 29. Accessed January 10, 2015 (www.ipsos-mori.com/researchpublications/researcharchive/3466/Perceptions-are-not-reality-10-things-the-world-gets-wrong.aspx).

Irdeto. 2015. "Irdeto Piracy and Business Intelligence Quick Read Report: 2015 Academy Award Nominated Films," Irdeto Technology, Eagan, MN, February 19. Accessed February 19, 2015 (www.irdeto.com/documents/pr_quickread_oscars_piracy_and_BI_feb2015.pdf).

———. 2018. "The Piracy Landscape: Has Web Video Replaced Peer-to-Peer?" August 7. Accessed 12/2/2018 (https://resources.irdeto.com/white-papers-e-books-reports/the-piracy-landscape-has-web-video-replaced-peer-to-peer).

Irwin, Neil. 2015. "Global Debt Has Risen by $57 Trillion Since the Financial Crisis." *The New York Times,* February 5. Accessed January 17, 2017 (www.nytimes.com/2015/02/06/upshot/global-debt-has-risen-by-57-trillion-since-the-financial-crisis-heres-why-that-is-scary.html).

Isaacs, Julia B. 2008. "Economic Mobility of Black and White Families." *Economic Mobility Project,* Pew Charitable Trusts, November. Accessed July 15, 2017 (www.brookings.edu/wp-content/uploads/2016/07/02_economic_mobility_sawhill_ch6.pdf).

Isaacs, Julia B., Isabel V. Sawhill, and Ron Haskins. 2008. *Getting Ahead or Losing Ground.* Washington, DC: Economic Mobility Project, Pew Charitable Trusts.

Isaacson, Walter. 2014. *The Innovators: How a Group of Hackers, Geniuses, and Geeks Created the Digital Revolution.* New York: Simon & Schuster.

ITOPF. 2006. "Statistics: International Tanker Owners Pollution Federation Limited." Accessed May 2, 2007 (www.itopf.com/stats.html).

IUCN. 2016. "Summary Statistics." *The IUCN Red List of Threatened Species.* Cambridge, UK: International Union for Conservation of Nature and Natural Resources. Accessed February 13, 2017 (www.iucnredlist.org/about/summary-statistics).

———. 2018. "Summary Statistics." *The IUCN Red List of Threatened Species.* Cambridge, UK: International Union for Conservation of Nature and Natural Resources. Accessed June 13, 2019 (www.iucnredlist.org/about/summary-statistics).

Izadi, Elahe. 2016. "Why Alicia Keys Isn't Wearing Makeup on 'The Voice.'" *The Washington Post,* August 22. Accessed January 30, 2017 (www.washingtonpost.com/news/arts-and-entertainment/wp/2016/08/22/why-alicia-keys-isnt-wearing-makeup-on-the-voice/).

J

Jackson, John P., Jr., and Nadine M. Weidman. 2004. *Race, Racism, and Science: Social Impact and Interaction.* Santa Barbara, CA: ABC-CLIO, Inc.

Jackson, Stevi. 2006. "Interchanges: Gender, Sexuality, and Heterosexuality: The Complexity (and Limits) of Heteronormativity." *Feminist Theory* 7: 105–121.

Jacobs, A. J. 2018a. *Thanks a Thousand: A Gratitude Journey.* New York: Simon & Schuster.

———. 2018b. "My Journey to Thank All the People Responsible for My Morning Coffee." TED Salon: Brightline Initiative, June. Accessed January 18, 2019 (www.ted.com/talks/aj_jacobs_my_journey_to_thank_all_the_people_responsible_for_my_morning_coffee).

Jacobs, David, Zhenchao Qian, Jason T. Carmichael, and Stephanie L. Kent. 2007. "Who Survives on Death Row? An Individual and Contextual Analysis." *American Sociological Review* 72 (August): 610–632.

Jacobs, Tom. 2016. "Belief in Reverse Dicrimination Bolsters Whites' Self-Esteem." *Pacific Standard,* March 29. Accessed February 6, 2017 (https://psmag.com/belief-in-reverse-discrimination-bolsters-whites-self-esteem-4e2890ef1699).

Jamison, Andrew. 2006. "Social Movements and Science: Cultural Appropriations of Cognitive Praxis." *Science as Culture* 15 (1): 45–59.

Janssen, Sarah, ed. 2019. *The World Almanac and Book of Facts 2019.* New York: World Almanac Books.

Jarvis, D.C. 2013. *Folk Medicine.* Redditch, UK: Read Books Ltd.

Jasper, James M. 2014. *Protest: A Cultural Introduction to Social Movements.* Malden, MA: Polity Press.

———. 2018. *The Emotions of Protest.* Chicago: University of Chicago Press.

Jayson, Sharon. 2012a. "Young Parents, Older Adults Change Face of Cohabitation." *USA Today,* October 17. Accessed May 29, 2013 (www.usatoday.com/story/news/nation/2012/10/17/cohabitation-divorced-families-parents/1623117/).

———. 2012b. "Living Together Not Just for the Young, New Data Show." *USA Today,* October 17. Accessed May 29, 2013 (www.usatoday.com/story/news/nation/2012/10/17/older-couples-cohabitation/1630681/).

Jee, Eunjung, Joya Misra, and Marta Murray-Close. 2018. "Motherhood Penalties in the U.S., 1986–2104." *Journal of Marriage and Family,* December 21 (https://doi.org/10.1111/jomf.12543).

Jefferson, Thomas. 1787. *Notes on the State of Virginia.* London: John Stockdale.

———. [1816] 1905. "To Colonel Charles Yancey." Pp. 493–497 in *The Works of Thomas Jefferson,* Vol. XI, ed. Paul Leicester Ford. New York: G. P. Putnam's Sons.

Jenkins, Matt. 2008. "A Really Inconvenient Truth." *Miller-McCure* 1 (March/April): 38–41.

Jenkins, McKay. 2018. *Food Fight: GMOs and the Future of the American Diet.* New York: Avery.

Jenness, Valerie, David A. Smith, and Judith Stepan-Norris. 2006. "Pioneer Public Sociologist C. Wright Mills, 50 Years Later." *Contemporary Sociology* 35 (6): 7–8.

Jin, Beatrice. 2019. "Congress's Incoming Class Is Younger, Bluer, and More Diverse Than Ever." *Politco,* January 7. Accessed January 8, 2019 (www.politico.com/interactives/2018/interactive_116th-congress-freshman-younger-bluer-diverse/).

Jindra, Michael. 1994. "Star Trek Fandom as a Religious Phenomenon." *Sociology of Religion* 55 (1): 27–51.

Joffe-Walt, Chana. 2015. "Three Miles." *This American Life,* March 13. Accessed November 29, 2016 (www.thisamericanlife.org/radio-archives/episode/550/three-miles).

Johnson, Allan G. 1997. *The Forest and the Trees: Sociology as Life, Practice, and Promise.* Philadelphia: Temple University Press.

Johnson, Jason. 2018. "Yes, the March for Our Lives Was about Black People, Too—and It's about Time." *The Root,* March 26. Accessed January 30, 2019 (www.theroot.com/yes-the-march-for-our-lives-was-about-black-people-too-1824082682).

Johnson, Kenneth M., and Daniel T. Lichter. 2010. "Growing Diversity among America's Children and Youth: Spatial and Temporal Dimensions." *Population and Development Review* 36 (1): 151–176.

Johnson, Paula A., Therese Fitzgerald, Alina Salganicoff, Susan F. Wood, and Jill M. Goldstein. 2014. "Sex Specific Medical Research: Why Women's Health Can't Wait." Brigham and Women's Hospital. Accessed February 12, 2017 (www.brighamandwomens.org/Departments_and_Services/womenshealth/ConnorsCenter/Policy/ConnorsReportFINAL.pdf).

Johnston, David Cay. 1994. "Ruling Backs Homosexuals on Asylum." *The New York Times,* June 12, pp. D1, D6.

Jones, Jeffrey M. 2017. "In U.S., 10.2% of LGBT Adults Now Married to Same-Sex Spouse." Gallup June 22. Accessed May 21, 2019 (https://news.gallup.com/poll/212702/lgbt-adults-married-sex-spouse.aspx).

———. 2018. "Most in U.S. Say Consuming Alcohol, Marijuana Morally OK." Gallup June 4. Accessed December 14, 2018 (https://news.gallup.com/poll/235250/say-consuming-alcohol-marijuana-morally.aspx).

———. 2018b. "Michelle Obama Ends Hillary Clinton's Run as Most Admired." Gallup December 27. Accessed January 7, 2019 (https://news.gallup.com/poll/245669/michelle-obama-ends-hillary-clinton-run-admired.aspx).

Jones, Robert P., Daniel Cox, Betsy Cooper, and Rachel Lienesch. 2015. *Anxiety, Nostalgia, and Mistrust: Findings from the 2015 American Values Survey.* Washington, DC: Public Religion Research Institute. Accessed February 6, 2017 (www.prri.org/wp-content/uploads/2015/11/PRRI-AVS-2015-Web.pdf).

Jordan, Miriam. 2011. "More Silent Raids over Immigration." *The Wall Street Journal,* June 16. Accessed June 21, 2011 (http://online.wsj.com/article/SB10001424052702304186404576387843087137216.html).

Jorgenson, Andrew K. 2015. "Five Points on Sociology, PEWS, and Climate Change." *Journal of World-Systems Research* 21(2): 271–275.

Josephson Institute of Ethics. 2012. "2012 Report Card on the Ethics of American Youth." Josephson Institute, Center for Youth Ethics,

Los Angeles, November 20. Accessed May 8, 2013 (http://-charactercounts.org/pdf/reportcard/2012/Report-Card-2012-DataTables-HonestyIntegrityCheating.pdf).

Juergensmeyer, Mark. 2003. *Terror in the Mind of God: The Global Rise of Religious Violence,* 3rd ed. Berkeley: University of California Press.

Justice Policy Institute. 2000. "The Punishing Decade: Prison and Jail Estimates at the Millennium." Washington, DC, May. Accessed November 10, 2016 (www.justicepolicy.org/images/upload/00-05_rep_punishingdecade_ac.pdf). 16.

K

Kaeble, Danielle, and Mary Cowhig. 2018. "Correctional Populations in the United States, 2016." Bureau of Justice Statistics Bulletin, April, NCJ 251211. Accessed December 1, 2018 (www.bjs.gov/content/pub/pdf/cpus16.pdf).

Kahn, Joseph, and Bowyer, Benjamin. 2018. "The Political Significance of Social Media Activity and Social Networks." *Political Communication* 35(3): 470–493.

Kalev, Alexandria, Frank Dobbin, and Erin Kelly. 2006. "Best Practices or Best Guesses? Assessing the Efficacy of Corporate Affirmative Action and Diversity Policies." *American Sociological Review* 71: 589–617.

Kalish, Richard A. 1985. *Death, Grief, and Caring Relationships,* 2nd ed. Monterey, CA: Brooks/Cole.

Kalita, S. Mitra. 2006. "On the Other End of the Line." *The Washington Post National Weekly Edition,* January 9, pp. 20–21.

Kalmijn, Matthijs. 1998. "Intermarriage and Homogamy: Causes, Patterns, Trends." *Annual Review of Sociology* 24: 395–412.

Kamp, Marianne. 2008. *The New Woman in Uzbekistan.* Seattle: University of Washington Press.

Kann, Laura, Tim McManus, William A. Harris, et al. 2018. "Youth Risk Behavior Surveillance—United States, 2017." Centers for Disease Control and Prevention, Morbidity and Mortality Weekly Report, 67(8). Accessed January 25, 2019 (www.cdc.gov/healthyyouth/data/yrbs/pdf/2017/ss6708.pdf).

Kanter, Rosabeth Moss. 1993. *Men and Women of the Corporation.* New York: Basic Books.

Karkazis, Katrina. 2008. *Fixing Sex: Intersex, Medical Authority, and Lived Experience.* Durham, NC: Duke University Press.

————. 2016. "The Ignorance Aimed at Caster Semenya Flies in the Face of the Olympic Spirit." *The Guardian,* August 23. Accessed January 27, 2017 (www.theguardian.com/commentisfree/2016/aug/23/caster-semenya-olympic-spirit-iaaf-athletes-women).

Karkazis, Katrina, Rebecca Jordan-Youn, Georgiann Davis, and Silvia Camporesi. 2012. "Out of Bounds? A Critique of the New Policies of Hyperandrogenism in Elite Female Athletes." *American Journal of Bioethics* 12: 3–16.

Katz, Brigit. 2017. "California Becomes First State to Introduce Gender-Neutral Birth Certificates." *Smithsonian,* October 20. Accessed January 23, 2019 (www.smithsonianmag.com/smartnews/california-becomes-first-state-introduce-gender-neutral-birth-certificates-180965343/).

Katz, Jason. 1999. *Tough Guise: Violence, Media, and the Crisis in Masculinity.* Video. Directed by Sut Jhally. Northampton, MA: Media Education Foundation.

Kay, Katty, and Claire Shipman. 2014. "The Confidence Gap." *The Atlantic,* May. Accessed January 7, 2013 (www.theatlantic.com/features/archive/2014/04/the-confidence-gap/359815/).

Kayyali, Randa. 2006. *The Arab Americans.* Westport, CT: Greenwood Press.

Keith, Fritha. 2008. "10 Modern Cases of Feral Children." *Listverse,* March 7. Accessed October 18, 2016 (http://listverse.com/2008/03/07/10-modern-cases-of-feral-children/).

Kelling, George L. 2015. "Don't Blame My 'Broken Windows' Theory for Poor Policing". *Politico Magazine,* August 11. Accessed November 16, 2016 (www.politico.com/magazine/story/2015/08/broken-windows-theory-poor-policing-ferguson-kelling-121268).

Kelling, George L., and Catherin M. Coles. 1996. *Fixing Broken Windows: Restoring Order and Reducing Crime.* New York: Martin Kessler Books.

Kelly, John, and Camille François. 2018. "This Is What Filter Bubbles Actually Look Like." *MIT Technology Review,* August 22. Accessed January 30, 2019 (www.technologyreview.com/s/611807/this-is-what-filter-bubbles-actually-look-like/).

Kelly, Robert J., and Sharona L. Levy. 2012. "The Endangered Empire: American Responses to Transnational Organized Crime." *Journal of Social Distress and the Homeless* 21: 44–110.

Kennedy, Brian. 2017. "Two-Thirds of Americans Give Priority to Developing Alternative Energy Over Fossil Fuels." Pew Research Center, January 23. Accessed June 9, 2017 (www.pewresearch.org/fact-tank/2017/01/23/two-thirds-of-americans-give-priority-to-developing-alternative-energy-over-fossil-fuels/).

Kerbo, Harold R. 2011. *Social Stratification and Inequality: Class Conflict in Historical, Comparative, and Global Perspective,* 8th ed. New York: McGraw-Hill.

Keynes, John Maynard. 1930a. "Economic Possibilities for Our Grandchildren I." *The Nation and Athenaeum* 48(2): 36–37.

————. 1930b. "Economic Possibilities for Our Grandchildren II." *The Nation and Athenaeum* 48(3): 96–98.

Keys, Alicia. 2016. "Alicia Keys: Time to Uncover." *Lenny,* May 31. Accessed June 6, 2017 (www.lennyletter.com/style/a410/alicia-keys-time-to-uncover/).

Khan, Shamus Rahman. 2011. *Privilege: The Making of an Adolescent Elite at St. Paul's School.* Princeton, NJ: Princeton University Press.

Khorasani, Noushin Ahmadi. 2009. "How Social Movements Can Change Iran." *The Mark,* June 11. Accessed June 30, 2009 (www.themarknews.com/articles/290-how-social-movements-can-change-iran).

Kiatpongsan, Sorapop, and Michael I. Norton. 2014. "How Much (More) Should CEOs Make? A Universal Desire for More Equal Pay." *Perspectives on Psychological Science* 9: 587–593. Accessed January 7, 2015 (www.hbs.edu/faculty/Publication%20Files/kiatpongsan%20norton%202014_f02b004a-c2de-4358-9811-ea273d372af7.pdf).

Kilbourne, Jean. 2010. *Killing Us Softly 4: Advertisings Image of Women.* Video. Produced and directed by Sut Jhally. Northampton, MA: Media Education Foundation.

————. 2014. "The Dangerous Ways Ads See Women." TEDx Lafayette College March 25. Accessed January 27, 2017 (www.tedxlafayettecollege.com/jean-kilbourne/).

Kilpatrick, Dean G., Heidi S. Resnick, Kenneth J. Ruggiero, Lauren M. Conoscenti, and Jenna McCauley. 2007. "Drug-Facilitated, Incapacitated, and Forcible Rape: A National Study." National Institute of Justice Grant No. 2005-Wg-BX-0006. Accessed June 1, 2010 (www.ncjrs.gov/pdffiles1/nij/grants/219181.pdf).

Kim, Kwang Chung. 1999. *Koreans in the Hood: Conflict with African Americans.* Baltimore, MD: Johns Hopkins University Press.

Kim, Su Yeong, Yijie Wang, Diana Orozco-Lapray, Yishan Shen, and Mohammed Murtuza. 2013. "Does Tiger Parenting Exist? Parenting Profiles of Chinese Americans and Adolescent Developmental Outcomes." *Asian American Journal of Psychology* 4: 7–18.

Kimmel, Michael. 2004. *The Gendered Society,* 2nd ed. New York: Oxford University Press.

————. 2012. *Manhood in America: A Cultural History.* 3rd ed. New York: Oxford University Press.

Kindy, Kimberly, and Kimbriell Kelly. 2015. "Thousands Dead, Few Prosecuted." *The Washington Post,* April 11. Accessed April 26, 2015 (www.washingtonpost.com/sf/investigative/2015/04/11/thousands-dead-few-prosecuted/).

Kinsey, Alfred C., Wardell B. Pomeroy, and Clyde E. Martin. 1948. *Sexual Behavior in the Human Male.* Philadelphia: Saunders.

Kinsey, Alfred C., Wardell B. Pomeroy, and Paul H. Gebhard. 1953. *Sexual Behavior in the Human Female.* Philadelphia: Saunders.

Kirk, Dudley. 1996. "Demographic Transition Theory." *Population Studies* 50: 361–387.

Kleinknecht, William. 1996. *The New Ethnic Mobs: The Changing Face of Organized Crime in America.* New York: Free Press.

Kleinman, Sherryl. 2002. "Why Sexist Language Matters." *Qualitative Sociology* 25(2): 299–304.

Klemens, Guy. 2010. *The Smartphone: The History and Technology of the Gadget that Changed the World.* Jefferson, NC: McFarland & Company.

Kliewer, Wendy, and Terri N.Sullivan. 2009. "Community Violence Exposure, Threat Appraisal, and Adjustment in Adolescents." *Journal of Clinical Child & Adolescent Psychology* 37 (4): 860–873.

Klinenberg, Eric. 2002. *Heat Wave: A Social Autopsy of Disaster in Chicago.* Chicago: University of Chicago Press.

————. 2012. *Going Solo: The Extraordinary Rise and Surprising Appeal of Living Alone.* New York: Penguin Books.

Knight Frank Research. 2016. *The Wealth Report 2016,* 10th ed. London: Knight Frank. Accessed January 17, 2017 (www.knightfrank.com/wealthreport).

Knudson, Tom. 2006. "Promises and Poverty: Starbucks Calls Its Coffee Worker-Friendly—but in Ethiopia, a Day's Pay Is a Dollar." *Sacramento Bee,* September 23. Accessed June 12, 2009 (www.sacbee.com/502/story/393917.html).

Kochhar, Rakesh, and Anthony Cilluffo. 2018. "Income Inequality in the U.S. Is Rising Most Rapidly Among Asians." Pew Research Center, Social & Demographic Trends, July 12 2018. Accessed October 6, 2018 (www.pewsocialtrends.org/2018/07/12/income-inequality-in-the-u-s-is-rising-most-rapidly-among-asians/).

Kochhar, Rakesh, and Richard Fry. 2014. "Wealth Inequality Has Widened Along Racial, Ethnic Lines Since End of Great Recession." Pew Research Center, Fact Tank: News in the Numbers, December 12. Accessed January 7, 2015 (www.pewresearch.org/fact-tank/2014/12/12/racial-wealth-gaps-great-recession/).

Kochel, Tammy Rinehart, David B. Wilson, and Stephen D. Mastrofski. 2011. "Effect of Suspect Race on Officers' Arrest Decisions." *Criminology* 49(2): 473–512.

Koerner, Brendan I. 2003. "What Does a Thumbs Up Mean in Iraq?" *Slate,* March 28. Accessed May 3, 2009 (www.slate.com/id/2080812).

Koerner, Lisbet. 1999. *Linnaeus: Nature and Nation.* Cambridge: Harvard University Press.

Kokmen, Leyla. 2008. "Environmental Justice for All." *Utne Reader,* March/April, pp. 42–46.

Kolbert, Elizabeth. 2014. *The Sixth Extinction: An Unnatural History.* New York: Henry Holt and Company.

Kooti, Farshad, Hathan O. Hodas, and Kristina Lerman. 2014. "Network Weirdness: Exploring the Origins of Network Paradoxes." *arXiv:* 1403.7242. Accessed February 11, 2015 (http://arxiv.org/abs/1403.7242).

Kottak, Conrad. 2004. *Anthropology: The Explanation of Human Diversity.* New York: McGraw-Hill.

Kozol, Jonathan. 1991. *Savage Inequalities: Children in Americas Schools.* New York: Crown.

————. 2005. *The Shame of the Nation: The Restoration of Apartheid Schooling in America.* New York: Crown.

————. 2012. *Fire in the Ashes: Twenty-Five Years Among the Poorest Children in America.* New York: Crown.

Kozubek, Jim. 2016. *Modern Prometheus: Editing the Human Genome with Crispr-Cas9.* Cambridge: Cambridge University Press.

Kraus, Sidney. 1996. "Winners of the First 1960 Televised Presidential Debate between Kennedy and Nixon." *Journal of Communication* 46 (4): 78–96.

Kraybill, Donald. 2001. *The Riddle of Amish Culture,* rev. ed. Baltimore, MD: Johns Hopkins University Press.

Kraybill, Donald B., Karen M. Johnson-Weiner, and Steven M. Nolt. 2013. *The Amish.* Baltimore, MD: Johns Hopkins University Press.

Krebs, Christopher P., Christine H. Lindquist, Tara D. Warner, Bonnie S. Fisher, and Sandra L. Martin. 2007. "The Campus Sexual Assault (CSA) Study, Final Report." National Institute of Justice Grant No. 2004-WG-BX-0010. Accessed June 1, 2010 (www.ncjrs.gov.pdffiles1/nij/grants/221153.pdf).

Kreider, Rose M. 2010. "Increase in Opposite-Sex Cohabiting Couples from 2009 to 2010 in the Annual Social and Economic Supplement (ASEC) to the Current Population Survey (CPS)." Housing and Household Economic Statistics Division Working Paper. Washington, DC: U.S. Bureau of the Census. Accessed June 1, 2011 (www.census.gov/population/www/socdemo/Inc-Opp-sex-2009-to-2010.pdf).

Kreider, Rose M., and Renee Ellis. 2011. "Number, Timing, and Duration of Marriages and Divorces: 2009." *Current Population Reports,* P70–125. Washington, DC: U.S. Census Bureau. Accessed September 19, 2011 (www.census.gov/prod/2011pubs/p70–125.pdf).

Kristof, Nicholas D., and Sheryl WuDunn. 2009. *Half the Sky: Turning Oppression into Opportunity for Women Worldwide.* New York: Knopf.

Krogstad, Jens Manuel. 2016. "Five Facts about Mexico and Immigration to the U.S." Pew Research Center February 11. Accessed January 20, 2017 (www.pewresearch.org/fact-tank/2016/02/11/mexico-and-immigration-to-us/).

Krogstad, Jens Manual, and D'Vera Cohn. 2014. "U.S. Census Looking at Big Changes in How It Asks About Race and Ethnicity." Pew Research Center, Fact Tank, March 14. Accessed April 26, 2015 (www.pewresearch.org/fact-tank/2014/03/14/u-s-census-looking-at-big-changes-in-how-it-asks-about-race-and-ethnicity/).

Krogstad, Jens Manuel, Mark Hugo Lopez, and Drew DeSilver. 2015. "Puerto Rico's Losses Are Not Just Economic, but in People, Too." Pew Research Center, July 1. Accessed February 6, 2017 (www.pewresearch.org/fact-tank/2015/07/01/puerto-ricos-losses-are-not-just-economic-but-in-people-too/).

Krueger, Patrick M., Melanie K. Tran, Robert A. Hummer, and Virginia W. Chang. 2015. "Mortality Attributable to Low Levels of Education in the United States." *PLoS One* 10(7): e0131809.

Kruttschnitt, Candace. "Gender and Crime." *Annual Review of Sociology* 39: 291–308.

Kübler-Ross, Elisabeth. 1969. *On Death and Dying.* New York: Macmillan.

Kuhl, Patricia K. 2004. "Early Language Acquisition: Cracking the Speech Code." *Nature Reviews Neuroscience* 5: 831–843.

Kumar, Rajesh, Hemendra Ram Phookun, and Arunya Datta. 2014. "Epidemic of Koro in North East India: An Observational Cross-Sectional Study." *Asian Journal of Psychiatry* 12: 113–117.

Kutateladze, Besike L., Nancy R. Andiloro, Brian D. Johnson, and Cassia C. Spohn. 2014. "Cumulative Disadvantage: Examining Racial and Ethnic Disparity in Prosecution and Sentencing." *Criminology* 52(3): 514–551.

Kuumba, M. Bahati. 2001. *Gender and Social Movements.* Lanham, MD: AltaMira Press.

L

Ladner, Joyce. 1973. *The Death of White Sociology.* New York: Random Books.

LaFrance, Adrienne. 2016. "A Quest to Save America's Dying Regional Slang." *The Atlantic,* September 8. Accessed October 5, 2016 (www.theatlantic.com/technology/archive/2016/09/bat-hides-and-frog-stranglers/499046/).

Lakner, Christoph, and Branko Milanovic. 2015. "Global Income Distribution: From the Fall of the Berlin Wall to the Great Recession." *World Bank Economic Review* 30(2): 203–232.

Lambert, Phineas. 2018. "A. J. Jacobs: Gratitude and the Global Supply Chain." *Guernica,* November 20. Accessed January 18, 2019 (www.guernicamag.com/a-j-jacobs-gratitude-and-the-global-supply-chain/).

Lancy, David F. 2017. *Raising Children: Surprising Insights from Other Cultures.* New York: Cambridge University Press.

Lappé, Anna. 2003. "3 Questions for Anna Lappé." *O Magazine* 4(6): 72

Lareau, Annette. 2003. *Unequal Childhoods: Class, Race, and Family Life.* Berkeley: University of California Press.

————. 2011. *Unequal Childhoods: Class, Race, and Family Life, 2nd ed., with an update a decade later.* Berkeley: University of California Press.

————. 2015. "Cultural Knowledge and Social Inequality." *American Sociological Review* 80(1): 1–27.

Larsen, Nella. 1929. *Passing.* New York: Alfred A. Knopf.

Larsson, Naomi. 2016. "Is the World Finally Waking Up to Intersex Rights?" *The Guardian,* February 10. Accessed January 26, 2017 (www.theguardian.com/global-development-professionals-network/2016/feb/10/intersex-human-rights-lgbti-chile-argentina-uganda-costa-rica).

Laughlin, Harry Hamilton. 1922. *Eugenical Sterilization in the United States.* Chicago: Psychopathic Laboratory of the Municipal Court of Chicago.

Laughlin, Lynda. 2013. "Who's Minding the Kids? Child Care Arrangements: Spring 2011." U.S. Census Bureau, *Household Economic Studies,* pp. 70–135, April. Accessed May 20, 2013 (www.census.gov/prod/2013pubs/p70-135.pdf).

Laumann, Edward O., John H. Gagnon, Robert T. Michael, and Stuart Michaels. 1994. *The Social Organization of Sexuality: Sexual Practices in the United States.* Chicago: University of Chicago Press.

Lawless, John. 2005. "Nigel Newton: Is There Life After Harry? You Can Bet Your Hogwarts There Is." *The Independent,* July 3. Accessed February 2, 2015 (www.independent.co.uk/news/people/profiles/nigel-newton-is-there-life-after-harry-you-can-bet-your-hogwarts-there-is-296317.html).

Lazarsfeld, Paul F. 1949. "*The American Soldier*—An Expository Review." *The Public Opinion Quarterly* 13(3): 377–404.

LeanIn.Org. 2018. *Women in the Workplace: 2018.* Palo Alto, CA: LeanIn.Org. Accessed January 23, 2019 (https://womenintheworkplace.com/Women_in_the_Workplace_2018.pdf).

Le Bon, Gustav. 1895. *The Crowd: A Study of the Popular Mind.* New York: Macmillan.

Lebowitz, Shana. 2016. "Tinder's Sociologist Reveals an Easy Way to Get More People to Message You." *Business Insider,* September 19. Accessed May 31, 2017 (www.businessinsider.com/tinder-sociologist-how-to-get-more-people-to-message-you-2016-9).

Lee, Don. 2015. "Rising Global Debt Is Increasing the Risk of Another Financial Crisis." *Los Angeles Times,* July 20. Accessed January 17, 2017

Lee, Erika. 2015. *The Making of Asian America: A History.* New York: Simon & Schuster.

Lee, Helena. 2013. "The Babies Who Nap in Sub-Zero Temperatures." *BBC News Magazine,* February 21. Accessed February 2, 2015 (www.bbc.com/news/magazine-21537988).

Lee, Richard M. 2003. "The Transracial Adoption Paradox: History, Research, and Counseling Implications of Cultural Socialization." *The Counseling Psychologist* 31 (6): 711–744.

Lee, Richard M., Harold D. Grotevant, Wend L. Hellerstedt, Megan R. Gunnar, and The Minnesota International Adoption Project Team. 2006. "Cultural Socialization in Families with Internationally Adopted Children." *Journal of Family Psychology* 20 (4): 571–580.

Lee, Sing. 1991. "Anorexia Nervosa in Hong Kong: A Chinese Perspective." *Psychological Medicine* 21(3): 703–711.

Lee, Sing, H. F. K. Chiu, and Char-Nie Chen. 1989. "Anorexia Nervosa in Hong Kong: Why Not More Chinese?" *British Journal of Psychiatry* 154: 683–688.

Lee, Sing, T. P. Ho, and L. K. Hsu. 1993. "Fat Phobic and Non-Fat Phobic Anorexia Nervosa: A Comparative Study of 70 Chinese Patients in Hong Kong." *Psychological Medicine* 23(4): 999–1017.

Lefevre, Romana. 2011. *Rude Hand Gestures of the World: A Guide to Offending Without Words.* San Francisco: Chronicle Books.

Le Goff, Jacques. 1990. "Introduction: Medieval Man." Pp. 1–35 in *Medieval Callings,* ed. Jacques Le Goff. Chicago: University of Chicago Press.

Le Guin, Ursula K. 2004. *A Whitewashed Earthsea.* Washington, DC: The Slate Group LLC.

Lencioni, Patrick. 2006. *Silos, Politics, and Turf Wars: A Leadership Fable About Destroying the Barriers That Turn Colleagues into Competitors.* San Francisco: Jossey-Bass.

Lengermann, Patricia Madoo, and Jill Niebrugge-Brantley. 1998. *The Women Founders: Sociology and Social Theory, 1830–1930.* Boston: McGraw-Hill.

Leonard, Annie. 2010. *The Story of Stuff: How Our Obsession with Stuff Is Trashing the Planet, Our Communities, and Our Health—and a Vision for Change.* New York: Free Press.

Levin, Sam. 2019. "'We Exist': California Begins Issuing State IDs with a Third Gender Option." *The Guardian,* January 2. Accessed January 23, 2019 (www.theguardian.com/world/2019/jan/02/california-non-binary-identification-lgbtq).

Levine, Kenneth J., and Cynthia A. Hoffner. 2006. "Adolescents Conceptions of Work: What Is Learned from Different Sources During Anticipatory Socialization?" *Journal of Adolescent Research* 21 (6): 647–669.

Levitz, Eric. 2016. "Trump Won a Lot of White Working-Class Voters Who Backed Obama." *New York Magazine,* November 9. Accessed December 13, 2016 (http://nymag.com/daily/intelligencer/2016/11/trump-won-a-lot-of-white-working-class-obama-voters.html).

Lewin, R. 1987. "The Unmasking of Mitochondrial Eve." *Science* 238 (4823): 24–26.

Lewis, Michael. 2003. *Moneyball: The Art of Winning an Unfair Game.* New York: Norton.

Lezhnev, Sasha. 2011. "New U.N. Report: U.S. Conflict Minerals Law Having Impact in Congo." *Enough,* June 16. Accessed August 8, 2011 (www.enoughproject.org/blogs/new-un-report-us-conflict-minerals-law-having-impact-congo).

Liang, Bin, and Hong Lu. 2010. "Internet Development, Censorship, and Cyber Crimes in China." *Journal of Contemporary Criminal Justice* 26 (1): 103–120.

Lichter, Daniel T., Domenico Parisi, and Helga De Valk. 2016. "Residential Segregation." *Pathways,* Special Issue, The Poverty and Inequality Report: 65–75. Accessed February 5, 2017 (http://inequality.stanford.edu/sites/default/files/Pathways-SOTU-2016.pdf).

Lierow, Diane. 2011. *Danis Story: A Journey from Neglect to Love.* Hoboken, NJ: Wiley.

Lind, Dara. 2015. "The FBI Is Trying to Get Better Data on Police Killings. Here's What We Know Now." *Vox,* April 26. Accessed April 26, 2015 (www.vox.com/2014/8/21/6051043/how-many-people-killed-police-statistics-homicide-official-black).

Lindholm, Marika. 2018. "The Pain of White Privilege and Racism in Transracial Adoption." ESME. Accessed September 4, 2018 (https://esme.com/single-mom-resources/content/adoption/the-pain-of-white-privilege-and-racism-in-transracial-adoption).

Ling, Peter. 2006. "Social Capital, Resource Mobilization and Origins of the Civil Rights Movement." *Journal of Historical Sociology* 19 (2): 202–214.

Link, Bruce G., and Jo C. Phelan. 2001. "Conceptualizing Stigma." *Annual Review of Sociology* 27: 363–385.

Linnaeus, Caroli. 1758. *Systema Naturae,* 10th ed. Stockholmiae: Laurentius Salvius.

Lino, Mark, Kevin Kuczynski, Nestor Rodriguez, and TusaRebecca Schap. 2017. *Expenditures on Children by Families, 2015.* Center for Nutrition Policy and Promotion, Miscellaneous Publication No. 1528-2015. U.S. Department of Agriculture, Washington, DC. Accessed May 31, 2017 (www.cnpp.usda.gov/sites/default/files/crc2015_March2017.pdf).

Lipset, Seymour Martin. 1959. "Some Social Requisites of Demozcracy: Economic Development and Political Legitimacy." *American Political Science Review* 53: 69–105.

Liptak, Adam, and Michael D. Shear. 2018. "Trump's Travel Ban Is Upheld by Supreme Court." *The New York Times,* June 26. Accessed October 11, 2018 (www.nytimes.com/2018/06/26/us/politics/supreme-court-trump-travel-ban.html).

List, Justin M. 2009. "Justice and the Reversal of the Healthcare Worker Brain-Drain." *American Journal of Bioethics* 9 (3): 10–12.

Livingston, Gretchen. 2015. "It's No Longer a 'Leave It to Beaver' World for American Families—But It Wasn't Back Then, Either." Pew Research Center December 30. Accessed November 22, 2016 (www.pewresearch.org/fact-tank/2015/12/30/its-no-longer-a-leave-it-to-beaver-world-for-american-families-but-it-wasnt-back-then-either/).

Livingston, Gretchen, and Anna Brown. 2017. "Intermarriage in the U.S. 50 Years after *Loving v. Virginia.*" Pew Research Center, May 18. Accessed December 14, 2018 (http://assets.pewresearch.org/wp-content/uploads/sites/3/2017/05/19102233/Intermarriage-May-2017-Full-Report.pdf).

Lofland, John, and Rodney Stark. 1965. "Becoming a World-Saver: A Theory of Conversion to a Deviant Perspective." *American Sociological Review* 30(6): 862–875.

Logan, John R. 2014. "Separate and Unequal in Suburbia." Census Brief prepared for Project US2010, December 1. Accessed February 4, 2017 (https://s4.ad.brown.edu/Projects/Diversity/Data/Report/report12012014.pdf).

Lopata, Helena Znaniecki. 1971. *Occupation: Housewife.* New York: Oxford University Press.

López, Gustavo, Neil G. Ruiz, and Eileen Patten. 2017. "Key Facts about Asian Americans, a Diverse and Growing Population." Pew Research Center, September 8. Accessed October 6, 2018 (www.pewresearch.org/fact-tank/2017/09/08/key-facts-about-asian-americans/).

Lorber, Judith. 1994. *Paradoxes of Gender.* New Haven, CT: Yale University Press.

Lotz, Amanda D. 2007. "Theorising the Intermezzo: The Contributions of Postfeminism and Third Wave Feminism." Pp. 71–85 in *Third Wave Feminism: A Critical Exploration,* expanded 2nd ed., ed. Stacy Gillis, Gillian Howie, and Rebecca Munford. New York: Palgrave Macmillan.

Louie, Miriam Ching Yoon. 2001. *Sweatshop Warriors: Immigrant Women Workers Take on the Global Factory.* Cambridge, MA: South End Press.

Lovell, Joel, and Ryan Pfluger. 2014. "The Tale of Two Schools." *The New York Times Magazine,* May 4. Accessed March 10, 2015 (www.nytimes.com/interactive/2014/05/04/magazine/tale-of-two-schools.html).

Loxcel Geomatics. 2018. "How Many Starbucks Are Out There?" June 14. Accessed November 13, 2018 (www.loxcel.com/sbux-faq.html).

Lucio, José Miguel Cabrales. 2014. "Gender and Constitutionalism in Mexico: From Quotas to Parity?" ConstitutionNet, April 28. Accessed April 16, 2015 (www.constitutionnet.org/news/gender-and-constitutionalism-mexico-quotas-parity).

Lukács, Georg. 1923. *History and Class Consciousness.* London: Merlin.

Lumpe, Lora. 2003. "Taking Aim at the Global Gun Trade." *Amnesty Now* (Winter): 10–13.

Lurie, Edward. 1954. "Louis Agassiz and the Races of Man." *Isis* 45 (3): 227–242.

Lyall, Sarah. 2002. "For Europeans, Love, Yes; Marriage, Maybe." *The New York Times,* March 24, pp. 1–8.

M

MacEachern, Scott. 2003. "The Concept of Race in Anthropology." Pp. 10–35 in *Race and Ethnicity: An Anthropological Focus on the United States and the World,* ed. R. Scupin. Upper Saddle River, NJ: Prentice Hall.

MacFarquhar, Neil. 2008. "Resolute or Fearful, Many Muslims Turn to Home Schooling." *The New York Times,* March 26, p. A1.

MacLeod, Jay. 2009. *Ain't No Makin' It: Aspirations and Attainment in a Low-Income Neighborhood,* 3rd ed. Boulder, CO: Westview Press.

MacNell, Lillian, Adam Driscoll, and Andrea N. Hunt. 2014. "What's in a Name: Exposing Gender Bias in Student Ratings of Teachers." *Innovative Higher Education,* December.

Madley, Benjamin. 2016. *An American Genocide: The United States and the California Indian Catastrophe.* Yale University Press.

Maese, Rick. 2016. "Whispers in Rio: Is a Female Runner Gaining an Unfair Edge from Naturally High Testosterone?" *The Washington Post,* August 17. Accessed January 26, 2017 (www.washingtonpost.com/sports/olympics/whispers-on-the-track-in-rio-does-caster-semenya-have-an-unfair-edge/2016/08/17/840cf088-6486-11e6-be4e-23fc4d4d12b4_story.html).

Magnier, Mark. 2010. "Mumbai Billionaire's Home Boasts 27 Floors, Ocean and Slum Views." *Los Angeles Times,* October 24. Accessed January 16, 2017 (http://articles.latimes.com/2010/oct/24/world/la-fg-india-rich-20101025).

Mahmood, Cynthia Keppley. 1996. "Asylum, Violence and the Limits of Advocacy." *Human Organization* 55(4): 498--505.

Malacrida, Claudia. 2005. "Discipline and Dehumanization in a Total Institution: Institutional Survivors Descriptions of Time-Out Rooms." *Disability & Society* 20 (5): 523–537.

Malcolm X, with Alex Haley. 1964. *The Autobiography of Malcolm X.* New York: Grove.

Malkiel, Nancy Weiss. 2016. *"Keep the Damned Women Out": The Struggle for Coeducation.* Princeton, NJ: Princeton University Press.

Malthus, Thomas R. 1878. *An Essay on the Principle of Population: Or, A View of Its Past and Present Effects on Human Happiness, with an Inquiry into Our Prospects Respecting the Future Removal or Mitigation of the Evils Which It Occasions,* 8th ed. London: Reeves and Turner.

Mann, Horace. [1848] 1957. "Report No. 12 of the Massachusetts School Board." Pp. 79–97 in *The Republic and the School: Horace Mann on the Education of Free Men,* ed. L. A. Cremin. New York: Teachers College.

Mann, Yee Kan, Oriel Sullivan, and Jonathan Gershuny. 2011. "Gender Convergence in Domestic Work: Discerning the Effects of Interactional and Institutional Barriers from Large-Scale Data." *Sociology* 45 (2): 234–251.

Mapel, Tim. 2007. "The Adjustment Process of Ex-Buddhist Monks to Life After the Monastery." *Journal of Religion & Health* 46 (1): 19–34.

Mapping Police Violence. 2018. "2017 Police Violence Report." Accessed September 18, 2018 (https://policeviolencereport.org).

March, David D. 1998. "Sobriquets of Missouri and Missourians." *Missouri Historical Review* 92(2): 149–167.

Mare, Robert D. 2016. "Educational Homogamy in Two Gilded Ages: Evidence from Inter-generational Social Mobility Data." *The Annals of the American Academy of Political and Social Science* 663: 117–139.

Marist. 2017. "Yahoo News/Marist Poll: Weed & the American Family." Marist College Institute for Public Opinion April 17. Accessed December 1, 2018 (http://maristpoll.marist.edu/wp-content/misc/Yahoo%20News/20170417_Summary%20Yahoo%20News-Marist%20Poll_Weed%20and%20The%20American%20Family.pdf).

Markowitz, David M., and Jeffrey T. Hancock. 2018. "Deception in Mobile Dating Conversations." *Journal of Communication* 68: 547–569.

Marks, Nadine F., and James David Lambert. 1998. "Marital Status Continuity and Change Among Young and Midlife Adults: Longitudinal Effects on Psychological Well-Being." *Journal of Family Issues* 19(6): 652–686.

Marlow, Eugene, and Eugene Secunda. 1991. *Shifting Time and Shifting Space: The Story of Videotape.* New York: Praeger.

Marquis, Alice Goldfarb. 1984. "Written on the Wind: The Impact of Radio during the 1930s." *Journal of Contemporary History* 19 (3): 385–415.

Marr, Elisha. 2017. "U.S. Transracial Adoption Trends in the 21st Century." *Adoption Quarterly* 20(3): 222–251.

Marshall, T. H. 1950. *Citizenship and Social Class and Other Essays.* Cambridge, UK: Cambridge University Press.

Marsiglio, William, and Roy, Kevin. 2012. *Nurturing Dads: Social Initiatives for Contemporary Fatherhood.* New York: Russell Sage.

Martin, Joyce A., Brady E. Hamilton, Michelle J. K. Osterman, Anne K. Driscoll, and Patrick Drake. 2018. "Births: Final Data for 2016." *National Vital Statistics Reports* 67(1). Hyattsville, MD: National Center for Health Statistics. Accessed December 15, 2018 (www.cdc.gov/nchs/data/nvsr/nvsr67/nvsr67_01.pdf).

Martin, Rachel. 2014. "Growing Up 'White,' Transracial Adoptee Learned to Be Black." NPR Weekend Edition, January 26. Accessed September 4, 2018 (www.npr.org/2014/01/26/266434175/growing-up-white-transracial-adoptee-learned-to-be-black).

Martineau, Harriet. 1837. *Society in America.* New York: Saunders and Otley.

———. 1838. *How to Observe: Morals and Manners.* London: Charles Knight and Co.

Martinez, Michael E., Emily P. Zammitti, and Robin A. Cohen. 2018. "Health Insurance Coverage: Early Release of Estimates from the National Health Interview Survey, January–June 2018." National Center for Health Statistics. November. Accessed January 26, 2019 (www.cdc.gov/nchs/data/nhis/earlyrelease/insur201811.pdf).

Marx, Karl. [1843] 1978. "Contribution to the Critique of Hegel's *Philosophy of Right:* Introduction." Pp. 53–65 in Robert C. Tucker, ed. *The Marx-Engels Reader,* 2nd ed. New York: W. W. Norton & Company.

———. [1845] 2000. "German Ideology." Pp. 175–208 in *Karl Marx: Selected Writings,* 2nd ed., ed. David McLellan. New York: Oxford University Press.

———. [1867] 2000. "Capital." Pp. 452–546 in *Karl Marx: Selected Writings,* 2nd ed. David McLellan. New York: Oxford University Press.

Marx, Karl, and Friedrich Engels. [1847] 1955. *Selected Works in Two Volumes.* Moscow: Foreign Languages Publishing House.

———. [1848] 1998. *The Communist Manifesto: A Modern Edition.* New York: Verso.

Mason, Lilliana. 2018. *Uncivil Agreement: How Politics Became Our Identity.* Chicago: The University of Chicago Press.

Mather, Mark, Linda A. Jacobsen, and Kelvin M. Pollard. 2015. "Aging in the United States." Population Reference Bureau, *Population Bulletin* 70 (2). Accessed October 25, 2016 (www.prb.org/pdf16/aging-us-population-bulletin.pdf).

Maugham, W. Somerset. 2010. *The Summing Up.* New York: Random House, August 31, 2010, 285.

Mayo, Elton. 1933. *The Human Problems of an Industrial Civilization.* London: Macmillan.

McCabe, Janice. 2016a. "Friends with Academic Benefits." *Contexts* 15(3): 22–29.

———. 2016b. *Connecting in College: How Friendship Networks Matter for Academic and Social Success.* Chicago: University of Chicago Press.

McCabe, Janice, Emily Fairchild, Liz Grauerholz, Bernice A. Pes-cosolido, and Daniel Tope. 2011. "Gender in Twentieth-Century Childrens Books: Patterns of Disparity in Titles and Central Characters." *Gender & Society* 25 (2): 197–226.

McCarthy, John D., and Mayer N. Zald. 1977. "Resource Mobilization and Social Movements: A Partial Theory." *AJS* 82(6): 1212–1241.

———. 2002. "The Enduring Vitality of the Resource Mobilization Theory of Social Movement." Pp. 533–565 in *Handbook of Sociological Theory,* Jonathan H. Turner, ed. New York: Academic/Plenum Publishers.

McCarthy, Justin. 2018. "Two in Three Americans Support Same-Sex Marriage." Gallup, May 23. Accessed December 15, 2018 (https://news.gallup.com/poll/234866/two-three-americans-support-sex-marriage.aspx).

McCauley, Douglas J., Molly Hardesty-Moore, Benjamin S. Halpern, and Hillary S. Young. 2016. "A Mammoth Undertaking: Harnessing Insight from Functional Ecology to Shape De-Extinction Priority Setting." *Functional Ecology* September 12. Accessed February 15, 2017 (https://labs.eemb.ucsb.edu/young/hillary/PDF/McCauley_et_al-2016-Functional_Ecology.pdf).

McConnaughy, Corrine M. 2013. *The Woman Suffrage Movement in America: A Reassessment.* New York: Cambridge University Press.

McConnell-Ginet, Sally. 2011. *Gender, Sexuality, and Meaning: Linguistic Practice and Politics.* New York: Oxford University Press.

McDonald, Michael. 2009. "Election of a Century?" United States Elections Project. Accessed June 2, 2009 (http://elections.gmu.edu/Election_of_a_Century.html).

———. 2016. "2016 November General Election Turnout Rates." United States Elections Project. Accessed December 15, 2016 (www.electproject.org/2016g).

McDonald, Michael P. 2018. "National General Election VEP Turnout Rates, 1789–Present." United States Elections Project. November 20, 2018. Accessed November 20, 2018 (www.electproject.org/national-1789-present).

McDonald's Corporation. 2018. "2017 Annual Report." McDonald's Corporation: Oak Brook, IL. Accessed November 13, 2018 (https://corporate.mcdonalds.com/corpmcd/investors-relations/financial-information/annual-reports.html).

McDowell, David J., and Ross D. Parke. 2009. "Parental Correlates of Childrens Peer Relations: An Empirical Test of a Tripartite Model." *Developmental Psychology* 45 (1): 224–235.

McGill, Brittany S. 2014. "Navigating the New Norms of Involved Fatherhood: Employment, Fathering Attitudes, and Father Involvement." *Journal of Family Issues* 35(8): 1089–1106.

McGurty, Eileen. 2007. *Transforming Environmentalism: Warren County, PCBs, and the Origins of Environmental Justice.* Piscataway, NJ: Rutgers University Press.

McIntosh, Peggy. 1988. "White Privilege and Male Privilege: A Personal Account of Coming to See Correspondence Through Work and Women's Studies." Working Paper No. 189, Wellesley College Center for Research on Women, Wellesley, MA.

McKirdy, Euan, and Mallika Kapur. 2016. "Poor Suffer as Mumbai Chokes on Garbage Dump Haze." *CNN,* February 5. Accessed January 16, 2017 (www.cnn.com/2016/02/05/asia/mumbai-giant-garbage-dump-fire/).

McKown, Clark, and Rhona S. Weinstein. 2008. "Teacher Expectations, Classroom Context, and the Achievement Gap." *Journal of School Psychology* 46 (3): 235–261.

McLellan, David, ed. 2000. *Karl Marx, Selected Writings,* rev. ed. New York: Oxford University Press.

McNamee, Stephen J., and Robert K. Miller Jr. 2014. *The Meritocracy Myth,* 3rd ed. Lanham, MD: Rowman & Littlefield.

McPherson, Miller, Lynn Smith-Lovin, and James M. Cook. 2001. "Birds of a Feather: Homophily in Social Networks." *Annual Review of Sociology* 27: 415–222.

Mead, George H. 1934. *Mind, Self and Society,* ed. Charles W. Morris. Chicago: University of Chicago Press.

———. 1964a. *On Social Psychology,* ed. Anselm Strauss. Chicago: University of Chicago Press.

———. 1964b. "The Genesis of the Self and Social Control." Pp. 267–293 in *Selected Writings: George Herbert Mead,* ed. Andrew J. Reck. Indianapolis: Bobbs-Merrill.

Mead, Margaret. [1935] 2001. *Sex and Temperament in Three Primitive Societies.* New York: Perennial, HarperCollins.

Medina, Jennifer. 2018. "A New Report on the Las Vegas Gunman Was Released. Here Are Some Takeaways." *The New York Times,* January 19. Accessed December 1, 2018 (www.nytimes.com/2018/01/19/us/las-vegas-attack-shooting-paddock.html).

Medley, Keith Weldon. 2003. *We as Freemen: Plessy v. Ferguson.* Gretna, LA: Pelican Publishing Company, Inc.

Meier, Emily A., Jarred V. Gallegos, Lori P. Montross Thomas, Colin A. Depp, Scott A. Irwin, and Dilip V. Jeste. 2016. "Defining a Good Death (Successful Dying): Literature Review and a Call for Research and Public Dialogue." *The American Journal of Geriatric Psychiatry* 24 (4): 261–271.

Meier, Robert F., and Gilbert Geis. 1997. *Victimless Crime? Prostitution, Drugs, Homosexuality, Abortion.* Los Angeles: Roxbury Books.

Melby, Todd. 2009. "Creating the DSM-V." *Contemporary Sexuality* 43 (3): 1, 4–6.

Menand, Louis. 2001. *The Metaphysical Club: A Story of Ideas in America.* New York: Farrar, Strauss and Giroux.

Méndez, Juan E. "Report of the Special Rapporteur on Torture and Other Cruel, Inhuman or Degrading Treatment or Punishment." United Nations, Human Rights Council, Twenty-Second Session, February. Accessed April 19, 2015 (http://daccess-dds-ny.un.org/doc/UNDOC/GEN/G13/105/77/PDF/G1310577.pdf).

Merlan, Anna. 2016. "Meet the Brave, Audacious, Astonishing Women Who Built the Standing Rock Movement." *Jezebel,* December 8. Accessed February 8, 2017 (http://jezebel.com/meet-the-brave-audacious-astonishing-women-who-built-1789756669).

Merton, Robert. 1968. *Social Theory and Social Structure.* New York: Free Press.

Merton, Robert K., and Alice S. Kitt. 1950. "Contributions to the Theory of Reference Group Behavior." Pp. 40–105 in *Continuities in Social Research: Studies in the Scope and Methods of the American Soldier,* ed. Robert K. Merton and Paul L. Lazarsfeld. New York: Free Press.

Mesic, Aldina, Lydia Franklin, Alev Cansever, Fiona Potter, Anika Sharma, Anita Knopov, and Michael Siegel. 2018. "The Relationship between Structural Racism and Black-White Disparities in Fatal Police Shootings." *Journal of the National Medical Association* 110 (2): 106–116.

Michels, Robert. [1915] 1949. *Political Parties.* Glencoe, IL: Free Press.

Mika, Mike. 2013. "Why I Hacked Donkey Kong for My Daughter." *Wired,* March 11. Accessed May 20, 2013 (www.wired.com/gamelife/2013/03/donkey-kong-pauline-hack/).

Milanovic, Branko. 2013. "Global Income Inequality in Numbers: In History and Now." *Global Policy* 4(2): 198–208.

———. 2016. *Global Inequality: A New Approach for the Age of Globalization.* Cambridge: Harvard University Press.

Milgram, Stanley. 1963. "Behavioral Study of Obedience." *Journal of Abnormal and Social Psychology* 67 (October): 371–378.

———. 1974a. *Obedience to Authority: An Experimental View.* New York: Harper & Row.

———. 1974b. "We Are All Obedient." *The Listener,* October 31: 567–568.

Mililo, Diana. 2008. "Sexuality Sells: A Content Analysis of Lesbian and Heterosexual Women's Bodies in Magazine Advertisements." *Journal of Lesbian Studies* 12 (4): 381–392.

Millard, Andre. 2005. *America on Record: A History of Recorded Sound,* 2nd ed. New York: Cambridge University Press.

Miller, Claire Cain. 2015. "Single Motherhood, in Decline Over All, Rises for Women 35 and Older." *The New York Times,* May 8. Accessed November 22, 2016 (www.nytimes.com/2015/05/09/upshot/out-of-wedlock-births-are-falling-except-among-older-women.html).

Millett, Kate. 1970. *Sexual Politics.* Garden City, NY: Doubleday.

Mills, C. Wright. [1956] 2000. *The Power Elite.* New edition with afterword by Alan Wolfe. New York: Oxford University Press.

———. [1959] 2009. *The Sociological Imagination.* New York: Oxford University Press.

Milner, Greg. 2009. *Perfecting Sound Forever: An Aural History of Recorded Music.* New York: Faber and Faber.

Mitchell, Ojmarrh, and Michael S. Caudy. 2015. "Examining Racial Disparities in Drug Arrests." *Justice Quarterly* 32: 288–313.

Moen, Phyllis, and Patricia Roehling. 2005. *The Career Mystique: Cracks in the American Dream.* Lanham, MD: Rowman & Littlefield.

Mohai, Paul, and Robin Saha. 2007. "Racial Inequality in the Distribution of Hazardous Waste: A National-Level Reassessment." *Social Problems* 54 (3): 343–370.

Monaghan, Peter. 2012. "Our Storehouse of Knowledge About Social Movements . . . Is Going to Be Left Bare." *The Chronicle of Higher Education,* February 19. Accessed March 14, 2012 (http://chronicle.com/article/5-Minutes-With-a-Sociologist/130849/).

Monk, Ellis P., Jr. 2015. "The Cost of Color: Skin Color, Discrimination, and Health among African Americans." *American Journal of Sociology* 121 (2): 396–444.

———. 2018. "The Color of Punishment: African Americans, Skin Tone, and the Criminal Justice System." *Ethnic and Racial Studies* (https://doi: 10.1080/01419870.2018.1508736).

Montagu, M. F. Ashley. 1942. *Man's Most Dangerous Myth: The Fallacy of Race.* New York: Columbia University Press.

Monte, Lindsay M., and Renee R. Ellis. 2014. "Fertility of Women in the United States: June 2012." *Current Population Reports,* P20–575, U.S. Census Bureau, Washington, DC. Accessed Feb-ruary 26, 2015 (www.census.gov/content/dam/Census/library/publications/2014/demo/p20-575.pdf).

Moore, Molly. 2006. "Romance, but Not Marriage." *The Washington Post National Weekly Edition,* November 27, p. 18.

Moore, Robert B. 1976. *Racism in the English Language: A Lesson Plan and Study Essay.* New York: The Racism and Sexism Resource Center for Educators.

Morgan, Philip D. 2005 "'To Get Quit of Negroes': George Washington and Slavery." *Journal of American Studies* 39(3): 403–429.

Morgan, Rachel E., and Grace Kena. 2018. "Criminal Victimization, 2016: Revised." *Bureau of Justice Statistics Bulletin,* October, NCJ 252121. Accessed December 3, 2018 (www.bjs.gov/content/pub/pdf/cv16re.pdf).

Morgan, Sue. 2009. "Theorising Feminist History: A Thirty-Year Retrospective." *Women's History Review* 18 (3): 381–407.

Morin, Rich, and Renee Stepler. 2016. "The Racial Confidence Gap in Police Performance." Pew Research Center, Social & Demographic Trends September 29. Accessed February 3, 2017 (www.pewsocialtrends.org/2016/09/29/the-racial-confidence-gap-in-police-performance/).

Morris, Aldon D. 2015. *The Scholar Denied: W. E. B. Du Bois and the Birth of Modern Sociology.* Oakland, CA: University of California Press.

Morselli, Carlo, Pierre Tremblay, and Bill McCarthy. 2006. "Mentors and Criminal Achievement." *Criminology* 44 (1): 17–43.

Mortimer, Jeylan T., and Michael J. Shanahan, eds. 2006. *Handbook of the Life Course.* New York: Springer Science and Business Media.

Moyer, Michael. 2010. "Internet Ideology War." *Scientific American* 302 (4): 14–16.

Mullins, Justin. 2014. "Can Facebook Make You Sad?" *BBC,* February 6. Accessed February 11, 2015 (www.bbc.com/future/story/20140206-is-facebook-bad-for-you).

Munford, Rebecca. 2007. "Wake Up and Smell the Lipgloss: Gender, Generation, and the (A)Politics of Girl Power." Pp. 266–279 in *Third Wave Feminism: A Critical Exploration,* expanded 2nd ed., ed. Stacy Gillis, Gillian Howie, and Rebecca Munford. New York: Palgrave Macmillan.

Murdock, George P. 1945. "The Common Denominator of Cultures." Pp. 123–142 in *The Science of Man in the World Crisis,* ed. Ralph Linton. New York: Columbia University Press.

———. 1949. *Social Structure.* New York: Macmillan.

———. 1957. "World Ethnographic Sample." *American Anthropologist* 59 (August): 664–687.

Myrskylä, Mikko, Hans-Peter Kohler, and Francesco C. Billari. 2009. "Advances in Development Reverse Fertility Declines." *Nature,* 460 (August 6): 741–743.

N

NAEP. 2016. "2015 Mathematics Assessment." NAEP Data Explorer, U.S. Department of Education, Institute of Education Sciences, National Center for Education Statistics, National Assessment of Educational Progress (NAEP). Accessed December 5, 2016 (http://nces.ed.gov/nationsreportcard/naepdata/dataset.aspx).

Nanda, Serena. 1997. "The Hijras of India." Pp. 82–86 in *A Queer World: The Center for Lesbian and Gay Studies Reader,* ed. Martin Duberman. New York: New York University Press.

Naples, Nancy. 2003. *Feminism and Method: Ethnography, Discourse Analysis, and Activist Research.* New York: Routledge.

National Center for Access to Justice. 2016. "The Justice Index 2016." Fordham Law School, New York. Accessed November 16, 2016 (http://justiceindex.org/).

National Center for Education Statistics. 2016. *Digest of Education Statistics—Most Current Digest Tables.* Washington, DC: Institute of Education Services, U.S. Department of Education. September 6, 2016 (http://nces.ed.gov/programs/digest/current_tables.asp).

———. 2018. *Digest of Education Statistics—Most Current Digest Tables.* Washington, DC: Institute of Education Services, U.S. Department of Education. Accessed October 9, 2018 (http://nces.ed.gov/programs/digest/current_tables.asp).

National Center for Health Statistics. 2018a. *Health, United States, 2017: With Special Feature on Mortality.* Hyattsville, MD. Accessed November 20, 2018 (www.cdc.gov/nchs/hus.htm).

———. 2018b. "*Health, United States, 2017*– Data Finder." Hyattsville, MD. Accessed January 26, 2019 (www.cdc.gov/nchs/hus/contents2017.htm).

National Center for State Courts. 2015. "The Landscape of Civil Litigation in State Courts." Civil Justice Initiative, Williamsburg, Virginia. Accessed November 16, 2016 (www.ncsc.org/~/media/Files/PDF/Research/CivilJusticeReport-2015.ashx).

National Conference of State Legislatures. 2018a. "Marijuana Overview." November 8. Accessed December 1, 2018 (www.ncsl.org/research/health/state-medical-marijuana-laws.aspx).

———. 2018b. "State Medical Marijuana Laws." November 8. Accessed December 1, 2018 (www.ncsl.org/research/health/state-medical-marijuana-laws.aspx).

National Education Association. 2018. "Rankings of the States 2017 and Estimates of School Statistics 2018." NEA Research, April. Accessed December 21, 2018 (www.nea.org/home/73145.htm).

National Geographic. 2012. "Gulf Spill Pictures: Ten New Studies Show Impact on Coast." *National Geographic,* April. Accessed May 28, 2012 (http://news.nationalgeographic.com/news/energy/2012/04/pictures/120420-gulf-oil-spill-impact-studies/).

National Human Trafficking Resource Center. 2018. "Hotline Statistics: National Statistics." June 30. Accessed January 10, 2019 (https://humantraffickinghotline.org/states).

National Institute of Justice. 2007. "Transnational Organized Crime." U.S. Department of Justice. Accessed May 20, 2009 (www.ojp.usdoj.gov/nij/topics/crime/transnational-organized-crime/welcome.htm).

NCAA. 2018. "NCAA Sports Sponsorship and Participation Rates Report." Indianapolis, IN: The National Collegiate Athletic Association. Accessed December 21, 2018 (www.ncaa.org/about/resources/research/sports-sponsorship-and-participation-research).

Negoianu, Dan, and Stanley Goldfarb. 2008. "Just Add Water." *Journal of the American Society of Nephrology* 19: 1041–1043.

Neiwert, David A. 2005. *Strawberry Days: How Internment Destroyed the Japanese Community.* New York: Palgrave Macmillan.

Nelson, Laura J. 2016. "The Worst Mass Shooting? A Look Back at Massacres in U.S. History." *Los Angeles Times,* June 14. Accessed November 4, 2016 (www.latimes.com/nation/la-na-mass-shooting-20160614-snap-story.html).

Newman, William M. 1973. *American Pluralism: A Study of Minority Groups and Social Theory.* New York: Harper & Row.

Newmyer, Tory. 2017. "Trump's Immigration Ban Ruptures Truce with Business, as Tech Leaders Speak Out." *Fortune,* January 29. Accessed February 7, 2017 (http://fortune.com/2017/01/28/tech-execs-criticize-trump-immigrant-ban/).

Newport, Frank. 2013. "In U.S., 87% Approve of Black-White Marriage, vs. 4% in 1958." Gallup, July 25. Accessed February 3, 2017 (www.gallup.com/poll/163697/approve-marriage-blacks-whites.aspx).

———. 2015. "Americans Continue to Shift Left on Key Moral Issues." Gallup Social Issues, May 26. Accessed November 21, 2016 (www.gallup.com/poll/183413/americans-continue-shift-left-key-moral-issues.aspx).

———. 2018. "Democrats More Positive About Socialism Than Capitalism." Gallup August 13. Accessed May 30, 2019 (https://news.gallup.com/poll/240725/democrats-positive-socialism-capitalism.aspx).

Newton, Michael. 2002. *Savage Girls and Wild Boys: A History of Feral Children.* London: Faber and Faber.

The New York Times. 2006. "Questions Couples Should Ask (or Wish They Had) Before Marrying." *The New York Times,* December 17. Accessed August 6, 2009 (www.nytimes.com/2006/12/17/fashion/weddings/17FIELDBOX.html).

NFHS. 2018. "2017–18 High School Athletics Participation Survey." National Federation of State High School Associations, Indianapolis, IN. Accessed December 21, 2018 (www.nfhs.org/ParticipationStatistics/ParticipationStatistics/).

NHPCO. 2018. "NHPCO's Facts and Figures: Hospice Care in America: 2017 Edition." National Hospice and Palliative Care Organization, April. Accessed November 20, 2018 (www.nhpco.org/sites/default/files/public/Statistics_Research/2017_Facts_Figures.pdf).

Nickerson, Raymond S. 1998. "Confirmation Bias: A Ubiquitous Phenomenon in Many Guises." *Review of General Psychology* 2 (2): 175–220.

Nielsen. 2012. "State of the Media: U.S. Digital Consumer Report—Q3–Q4 2011." Accessed April 5, 2012 (www.nielsen.com/content/dam/corporate/us/en/reports-downloads/2012-Reports/Digital-Consumer-Report-Q4-2012.pdf).

———. 2017. "The Nielsen Comparable Metrics Report: Q2 2017." New York: The Nielsen Company. Accessed November 20, 2018 (www.nielsen.com/content/dam/corporate/us/en/reports-downloads/2017-reports/q2-2017-comparable-metrics-report.pdf).

Nielsen, Joyce McCarl, Glenda Walden, and Charlotte A. Kunkel. 2000. "Gendered Heteronormativity: Empirical Illustrations in Everyday Life." *Sociological Quarterly* 41 (2): 283–296.

Nishime, Leilani. 2012. "The Case for Cablinasian: Multiracial Naming from *Plessy* to Tiger Woods." *Communication Theory* 22(1): 92–111.

NOAA. 2017. "State of the Climate: Global Analysis for Annual 2016." NOAA Centers for Environmental Information, January. Accessed February 13, 2017 (www.ncdc.noaa.gov/sotc/global/201613).

Nobles, Melissa. 2000. "History Counts: A Comparative Analysis of Racial/Color Categorization in U.S. and Brazilian Censuses." *American Journal of Public Health* 90: 1738–1745.

Nofziger, Stacey, and Hye-Ryeon Lee. 2006. "Differential Associations and Daily Smoking of Adolescents: The Importance of Same-Sex Models." *Youth & Society* 37 (4): 453–478.

Nolan, Patrick, and Gerhard Lenski. 2006. *Human Societies: An Introduction to Macrosociology,* 10th ed. Boulder, CO: Paradigm.

Norton, Michael I., and Francesca Gino. 2013. "Rituals Alleviate Grieving for Loved Ones, Lovers, and Lotteries." *Journal of Experimental Psychology: General* 143 (1): 266–272. Accessed May 31, 2013 (http://francescagino.com/pdfs/norton_gino_jesp_2013.pdf).

Notestein, Frank. 1945. "Population: The Long View." Pp. 36–57 in *Food for the World,* ed. Theodore W. Schultz. Chicago: University of Chicago Press.

Noueihed, Lin, and Alex Warren. 2012. *The Battle for the Arab Spring: Revolution, Counter-Revolution and the Making of a New Era.* New Haven, CT: Yale University Press.

O

Oakes, Jeannie. 2008. "Keeping Track: Structuring Equality and Inequality in an Era of Accountability." *Teachers College Record* 110 (3): 700–712.

OASDI. 2018. "The 2018 Annual Report of the Board of Trustees of the Federal Old-Age and Survivors Insurance and Federal Disability Insurance Trust Funds." Social Security Administration, June 5. Washington, DC: U.S. Government Printing Office. Accessed January 25, 2019 (www.ssa.gov/OACT/TR/2018/tr2018.pdf).

Obach, Brian K. 2004. *Labor and the Environmental Movement: The Quest for Common Ground.* Cambridge, MA: MIT Press.

Obama, Barack. 2013. "Inaugural Address by President Barack Obama." The White House, Office of the Press Secretary, Washington, DC, January 21. Accessed March 28, 2015 (www.whitehouse.gov/the-press-office/2013/01/21/inaugural-address-president-barack-obama).

Obergefell v. Hodges. 2015. 576 U.S. _ (2015). Supreme Court of The United States.

Oberschall, Anthony. 1973. *Social Conflict and Social Movements.* Englewood Cliffs, NJ: Prentice Hall.

O'Brien, Valerie. 2012. "The Benefits and Challenges of Kinship Care." *Child Care in Practice* 18: 127–146.

OECD. 2016c. "Net Official Development Assistance." OECD Data. Accessed January 20, 2017 (https://data.oecd.org/oda/net-oda.htm).

———. 2018a. *Education at a Glance 2016: OECD Indicators.* Paris: OECD Publishing. Accessed December 20, 2018 (www.oecd.org/education/education-at-a-glance/).

———. 2018b. "OECD Family Database: Child Outcomes." Directorate for Employment, Labour, and Social Affairs. Accessed January 13, 2019 (www.oecd.org/els/family/database.htm).

———. 2018c. "Employment: Time Spend in Unpaid Work, by Sex." OECD Employment Database. Accessed January 25, 2019 (http://stats.oecd.org/index.aspx?queryid=54757).

———. 2018d. "Social Protection." *OECD Health Statistics.* Accessed January 26, 2019 (https://stats.oecd.org/viewhtml.aspx?datasetcode=HEALTH_PROT&lang=en).

Ogburn, William F. 1922. *Social Change with Respect to Culture and Original Nature.* New York: Huebsch (reprinted 1966, New York: Dell).

Ogburn, William F., and Clark Tibbits. 1934. "The Family and Its Functions." Pp. 661–708 in *Recent Social Trends in the United States,* ed. Research Committee on Social Trends. New York: McGraw-Hill.

Ogilvie, Sarah A., and Scott Miller. 2010. *Refuge Denied: The St. Louis Passengers and the Holocaust.* Madison, WI: University of Wisconsin Press.

O'Harrow, Robert Jr. 2005. "Mining Personal Data." *The Washington Post National Weekly Edition* (February 6), pp. 8-10.

Okrent, Arika. 2009. *In the Land of Invented Languages: Esperanto Rock Stars, Klingon Poets, Loglan Lovers, and the Mad Dreamers Who Tried to Build a Perfect Language.* New York: Spiegel and Grau.

Okun, Arthur. 1975. *Equality and Efficiency: The Big Tradeoff.* Washington, DC: Brookings Institution.

Olofsson, Parvin Tavakol, Peter Aspelin, Lott Bergstrand, and Lennart Blomqvist. 2014. "Patients Experience of Outsourcing and Care Related to Magnetic Resonance Examinations." *Upsala Journal of Medical Sciences* 119: 343-349.

Oluo, Ijeoma. 2018. *So You Want to Talk about Race.* New York: Seal Press.

Omi, Michael, and Howard Winant. 1994. *Racial Formation in the United States: From the 1960s to the 1990s,* 2nd ed. New York: Routledge.

O'Neill, William L. 1969. *Everyone Was Brave: The Rise and Fall of Feminism in America.* New York: HarperCollins.

The Oprah Winfrey Show. 2006. "Failing Grade." What Bill and Melinda Gates Want You to Know, April 11. Accessed March 10, 2015 (www.oprah.com/world/Failing-Grade).

Orfalea, Gregory. 2006. *The Arab Americans: A History.* Northampton, MA: Olive Branch Press.

Orshansky, Mollie. 1965. "Counting the Poor: Another Look at the Poverty Profile." *Social Security Bulletin* 28 (1): 3-29.

Ortman, Jennifer M., Victoria A. Velkoff, and Howard Hogan. 2014. "An Aging Nation: The Older Population in the United States." *Current Population Reports* P25-1140, May. Accessed February 2, 2015 (www.census.gov/prod/2014pubs/p25-1140.pdf).

OWN. 2015. "How 'The Girl in the Window' Is Doing 9 Years after Her Rescue from Horrific Neglect." *The Huffington Post* September 18. Accessed October 18, 2016 (www.huffingtonpost.com/2014/06/18/girl-in-the-window-danielle-oprah-lierow_n_5505079.html).

Oxfam. 2018. "Reward Work, Not Wealth." Oxfam Briefing Paper, January. Accessed January 21, 2019 (www.oxfam.org/en/research/reward-work-not-wealth).

P

Packer, George. 2013. *The Unwinding: An Inner History of the New America.* New York: Farrar, Straus and Giroux.

Pager, Devah. 2003. "The Mark of a Criminal Record." *American Journal of Sociology* 108 (March): 937-975.

———. 2007 *Marked: Race, Crime, and Finding Work in an Era of Mass Incarceration.* Chicago: University of Chicago Press.

Pager, Devah, and David S. Pedulla. 2015. "Race, Self-Selection and the Job Search Process." *AJS* 120 (4): 1005-1054.

Pager, Devah, and Bruce Western. 2012. "Identifying Discrimination at Work: The Use of Field Experiments." *Journal of Social Issues* 68: 221-237.

Pager, Devah, Bruce Western, and Bart Bonikowski. 2009. "Discrimination in a Low Wage Labor Market: A Field Experiment." *American Sociological Review* 74: 777-799.

Pager, Devah, Bruce Western, and Naomi Sugie. 2009. "Sequencing Disadvantage: Barriers to Employment Facing Young Black and White Men with Criminal Records." *Annals of the American Academy of Political and Social Sciences* 623: 195-213.

Pai, Seeta, and Kelly Schryver. 2015. *Children, Teens, Media, and Body Image: A Common Sense Media Research Brief.* San Francisco: Common Sense Media. Accessed April 19, 2015 (www.commonsensemedia.org/file/csm-body-image-report-012615-interactivepdf/download).

Painter, Matthew A., II, Malcolm D. Holmes, and Jenna Batemen. 2015. "Skin Tone, Race/Ethnicity, and Wealth Inequality among New Immigrants." *Social Forces* 94 (3): 1153-1185

Painter, Nell Irvin. 2010a. *The History of White People.* New York: Norton.

———. 2010b. "The History of White People." Video. *C-Span,* September 25. Accessed July 23, 2018 (www.c-span.org/video/?295631-9/the-history-white-people).

Panagopoulos, Costas. 2009. "Polls and Elections: Preelection Poll Accuracy in the 2008 General Elections." *Presidential Studies Quarterly* 39 (4): 896-907.

Panagopoulos, Costas, and Benjamin Farrer. 2014. "Polls and Elections: Preelection Poll Accuracy and Bias in the 2012 General Elections." *Presidential Studies Quarterly* 44: 352-363.

Paoletti, Jo B. 2012. *Pink and Blue: Telling the Boys from the Girls in America.* Bloomington, IN: Indiana University Press.

Papageorge, Nicholas W., and Kevin Thom. 2018. "Genes, Education, and Labor Market Outcomes: Evidence from the Health and Retirement Study." NBER Working Paper No. 25114 September. Accessed January 13, 2019 (www.nber.org/papers/w25114).

Park, Andrea. 2018. "Alicia Keys Looked Incredibly Radiant Without Makeup at the 2018 Grammy Awards." *Allure,* January 29. Accessed January 23, 2019 (www.allure.com/story/alicia-keys-no-makeup-2018-grammys).

Park, Madison, and Kiki Dhitavat. 2015. "Thailand's New Constitution Could Soon Recognize Third Gender." CNN, January 15. Accessed June 6, 2015 (www.cnn.com/2015/01/16/world/third-gender-thailand/index.html).

Parker, Alison. 2004. "Inalienable Rights: Can Human-Rights Law Help to End U.S. Mistreatment of Noncitizens?" *American Prospect,* October, pp. A11-A13.

Parker, Kim, and Gretchen Livingston. 2018. "Seven Facts about American Dads." Pew Research Center, June 13. Accessed December 14, 2018 (www.pewresearch.org/fact-tank/2018/06/13/fathers-day-facts/).

Parker, Kim, and Eileen Patten. 2013. "The Sandwich Generation: Rising Financial Burdens for Middle-Aged Americans." Pew Research Center, January 30. Accessed February 2, 2015 (www.pewsocialtrends.org/2013/01/30/the-sandwich-generation/).

Parker, Kim, and Renee Stepler. 2017. "As U.S. Marriage Rate Hovers at 50%, Education Gap in Marital Status Widens." Pew Research Center, September 14. Accessed December 14, 2018 (www.pewresearch.org/fact-tank/2017/09/14/as-u-s-marriage-rate-hovers-at-50-education-gap-in-marital-status-widens/).

Parker, Kim, and Wendy Wang. 2013. "Modern Parenthood: Roles of Moms and Dads Converge as They Balance Work and Family." Pew Research Center, Washington, DC, March 14. Accessed June 6, 2013 (www.pewsocialtrends.org/files/2013/03/FINAL_modern_parenthood_03-2013.pdf).

Parker, Richard. 2009. "Sexuality, Culture and Society: Shifting Paradigms in Sexuality Research." *Culture, Health & Sexuality* 11 (3): 251-266.

Parks, Bradley C., and J. Timmons Roberts. 2010. "Climate Change, Social Theory, and Justice." *Theory, Culture, & Society* 27: 134-166.

Parry, Marc. 2013. "The American Police State: A Sociologist Interrogates the Criminal-Justice System and Tries to Stay Out of the Spotlight." *The Chronicle of Higher Education,* November 18. Accessed January 10, 2015 (http://chronicle.com/article/The-American-Police-State/142965/).

Parsons, Talcott. 1951. *The Social System.* New York: Free Press.

———. 1966. *Societies: Evolutionary and Comparative Perspectives.* Englewood Cliffs, NJ: Prentice Hall.

———. 1975. "The Sick Role and the Role of the Physician Reconsidered." *Milbank Medical Fund Quarterly Health and Society* 53 (Summer): 257-278.

Parsons, Talcott, and Robert Bales. 1955. *Family, Socialization and Interaction Process.* Glencoe, IL: Free Press.

Pascoe, C. J., and Tristan Bridges, eds. 2015. *Exploring Masculinities: Identity, Inequality, Continuity, and Change.* Cambridge, MA: Oxford University Press.

Pascoe, C. J. 2011. *Dude, You're a Fag: Masculinity in High School,* with a new preface. Berkeley, CA: University of California Press.

Pascoe, Peggy. 2009. *What Comes Naturally: Miscegenation Law and the Making of Race in America.* New York: Oxford University Press.

Passel, Jeffrey S., and D'Vera Cohn. 2016. "Overall Number of U.S. Unauthorized Immigrants Holds Steady Since 2009." Pew Research Center's Hispanic Trends Project, Washington, D.C., September 20.

Accessed February 6, 2017 (http://assets.pewresearch.org/wp-content/uploads/sites/7/2016/09/31170303/PH_2016.09.20_Unauthorized_FINAL.pdf).

————. 2018. "U.S. Unauthorized Immigrant Total Dips to Lowest Level in a Decade." Pew Research Center, Hispanic Trends, November 27. Accessed January 22, 2019 (www.pewhispanic.org/wp-content/uploads/sites/5/2018/11/Pew-Research-Center_U-S-Unauthorized-Immigrants-Total-Dips_2018-11-27.pdf).

Patten, Eileen. 2016. "The Nation's Latino Population Is Defined by Its Youth." Pew Research Center, Hispanic Trends, April 20. Accessed February 6, 2017 (www.pewhispanic.org/2016/04/20/the-nations-latino-population-is-defined-by-its-youth/).

Patterson, Thomas E. 2003. *We the People,* 5th ed. New York: McGraw-Hill.

Paxton, Pamela, Sheri Kunovich, and Melanie M. Hughes. 2007. "Gender in Politics." Pp. 263–285 in *Annual Review of Sociology 2007.* Palo Alto, CA: Annual Reviews.

Pazzanese, Christina. 2018. "Parkland Students: The Violence Must Stop Here." *The Harvard Gazette,* March 20. Accessed December 1, 2018 (https://news.harvard.edu/gazette/story/2018/03/parkland-students-the-violence-must-stop-here/).

Peattie, Lisa, and Martin Rein. 1983. *Women's Claims: A Study in the Political Economy.* New York: Oxford University Press.

Peek, Lori. 2005. "Becoming Muslim: The Development of a Religious Identity." *Sociology of Religion* 66: 215–242.

Pemberton, David. 2015. "Statistical Definition of 'Family' Unchanged Since 1930." Random Samplings, Census Blogs, U.S. Census Bureau January 28. Accessed May 31, 2017 (www.census.gov/newsroom/blogs/random-samplings/2015/01/statistical-definition-of-family-unchanged-since-1930.html).

Perrow, Charles. 1986. *Complex Organizations,* 3rd ed. New York: Random House.

Peterson, David. J. 2015. *The Art of Language Invention: From Horse-Lords to Dark Elves, the Words Behind World Building.* New York: Penguin Books.

Petrovic, Drazen. 1994. "Ethnic Cleansing—an Attempt at Methodology." *EJIL* 5: 1–19.

Pettigrew, Thomas F., and Linda R. Tropp. 2006. "A Meta-Analytic Test of Intergroup Contact Theory." *Journal of Personality and Social Psychology* 90 (5): 751–783.

Pettit, Michael, and Jana Vigor. 2015. "Pheromones, Feminism and the Many Lives of Menstrual Synchrony." *BioSocieties* 10 (3): 271–294.

Pew Charitable Trusts. 2012. "A Year or More: The High Cost of Long-Term Unemployment—Addendum." Pew Fiscal Analysis Initiative, May 2. Accessed May 22, 2012 (www.pewtrusts.org/uploadedFiles/wwwpewtrustsorg/Reports/-Fiscal_Analysis/Addendum_Long-Term_Unemployment_May2012.pdf).

Pew Research Center. 2007. "Optimism About Black Progress Declines: Blacks See Growing Values Gap Between Poor and Middle Class." Washington, DC: Pew Research Center. Accessed July 1, 2008 (http://pewsocialtrends.org/assets/pdf/Race.pdf).

————. 2009a. "The Stronger Sex—Spiritually Speaking." Pew Forum on Religion & Public Life, February 26. Accessed April 19, 2010 (http://pewforum.org/docs/?DocID5403).

————. 2009b. "End of Communism Cheered but Now with More Reservations: Two Decades After the Walls Fall." Pew Global Attitudes Project, November 2. Accessed April 23, 2010 (http://pewglobal.org/reports/pdf/267.pdf).

————. 2010. "The Return of the Multi-Generational Family Household." Washington, DC: Pew Research Centers Social and Demographic Trends project, March 18. Accessed February 26, 2015 (www.pewsocialtrends.org/files/2010/10/752-multi-generational-families.pdf).

————. 2011. "Muslim Americans: No Signs of Growth in Alienation or Support for Extremism." U.S. Politics & Policy, August 30. Accessed February 2, 2017 (www.people-press.org/2011/08/30/muslim-americans-no-signs-of-growth-in-alienation-or-support-for-extremism/).

————. 2013. "U.S. Christians Views on the Return of Christ." The Pew Forum on Religion & Public Life, March 26. Accessed May 31,

2013 (www.pewforum.org/Christian/US-Christians-Views-on-the-Return-of-Christ.aspx).

————. 2013b. "A Portrait of Jewish Americans." Pew Research Center's Religion & Public Life Project, October 1. Accessed October 10, 2018 (www.pewresearch.org/wp-content/uploads/sites/7/2013/10/jewish-american-full-report-for-web.pdf).

————. 2014a. "Emerging and Developing Economies Much More Optimistic Than Rich Countries About the Future." Global Attitudes Project, October 9. Accessed January 22, 2015 (www.pewglobal.org/files/2014/10/Pew-Research-Center-Inequality-Report-FINAL-October-17-2014.pdf).

————. 2014c. "The Rising Cost of Not Going to College." Washington, DC: Social & Demographic Trends project, February 11. Accessed February 26, 2015 (www.pewsocialtrends.org/files/2014/02/SDT-higher-ed-FINAL-02-11-2014.pdf).

————. 2014d. "The Rising Cost of Not Going to College." Social & Demographic Trends, February 11. Accessed March 10, 2015 (www.pewsocialtrends.org/files/2014/02/SDT-higher-ed-FINAL-02-11-2014.pdf).

————. 2014e. "Most See Inequality Growing, but Partisans Differ over Solutions." U.S. Politics & Policy, January 23. Accessed March 26, 2015 (www.people-press.org/files/legacy-pdf/1-23-14%20Poverty_Inequality%20Release.pdf).

————. 2014f. "Global Public Downbeat about Economy." Global Attitudes & Trends, September 9. Accessed December 22, 2016 (www.pewglobal.org/2014/09/09/global-public-downbeat-about-economy/).

————. 2014g. "The Shifting Religious Identity of Latinos in the United States." Religion & Public Life, May 7. Accessed April 28, 2015 (www.pewforum.org/files/2014/05/Latinos-Religion-07-22-full-report.pdf).

————. 2015a. "Most Say Government Policies Since Recession Have Done Little to Help Middle Class, Poor." U.S. Politics & Policy Project, March 4. Accessed March 22, 2015 (www.people-press.org/files/2015/03/03-04-15-Economy-release.pdf).

————. 2015d. "Parenting in America." Washington, DC: Social & Demographic Trends Project, December 17. Accessed November 21, 2016 (www.pewsocialtrends.org/files/2015/12/2015-12-17_parenting-in-america_FINAL.pdf).

————. 2015e. "Raising Kids and Running a Household: How Working Parents Share the Load." Washington, DC: Social & Demographic Trends Project, November 4. Accessed November 22, 2016 (www.pewsocialtrends.org/files/2015/11/2015-11-04_working-parents_FINAL.pdf).

————. 2015f. "America's Changing Religious Landscape." Religion & Public Life, May 12. Accessed December 7, 2016 (www.pewforum.org/files/2015/05/RLS-08-26-full-report.pdf).

————. 2015g. "The Future of World Religions: Population Growth Projections, 2010–2050." Religion & Public Life, April. Accessed December 7, 2016 (www.pewforum.org/files/2015/03/PF_15.04.02_ProjectionsFullReport.pdf).

————. 2015i. "Party Identification." Accessed December 15, 2016 (www.pewresearch.org/data-trend/political-attitudes/party-identification/).

————. 2016a. "Budget Deficit Slips as Public Priority." The Pew Research Center for the People & the Press January 22. Accessed November 4, 2016 (www.people-press.org/2016/01/22/budget-deficit-slips-as-public-priority/).

————. 2016c. "The State of American Jobs." Social & Demographic Trends, October 6. Accessed December 14, 2016 (http://assets.pewresearch.org/wp-content/uploads/sites/3/2016/10/ST_2016.10.06_Future-of-Work_FINAL4.pdf).

————. 2016d. "Campaign Exposes Fissures Over Issues, Values, and How Life Has Changed in the U.S." U.S. Politics & Policy, March. Accessed December 22, 2016 (www.people-press.org/2016/03/31/campaign-exposes-fissures-over-issues-values-and-how-life-has-changed-in-the-u-s/).

————. 2016e. "Hispanic Population and Origin in Select U.S. Metropolitan Areas, 2014." Hispanic Trends, September 6. Accessed February 6, 2017 (www.pewhispanic.org/interactives/hispanic-population-in-select-u-s-metropolitan-areas/).

_____. 2016f. "Obama Leaves Office on High Note, But Public Has Mixed Views of Accomplishments." U.S. Politics & Policy, December 14. Accessed Thursday, May 4, 2017 (http://assets.pewresearch.org/wp-content/uploads/sites/5/2016/12/14133019/12-14-16-Obama-legacy-release.pdf).

_____. 2017. "After Seismic Political Shift, Modest Changes in Public's Policy Agenda." U.S. Politics and Policy, Pew Research Center, January 24. Accessed June 9, 2017 (www.people-press.org/2017/01/24/after-seismic-political-shift-modest-changes-in-publics-policy-agenda/).

_____. 2017a. "Changing Attitudes on Gay Marriage." Religion & Public Life, June 26. Accessed December 15, 2018 (www.pewforum.org/fact-sheet/changing-attitudes-on-gay-marriage/).

_____. 2017b. "Public Trust in Government: 1958–2017." U.S. Politics & Policy, December 14. Accessed January 8, 2019 (www.people-press.org/2017/12/14/public-trust-in-government-1958-2017/).

_____. 2018a. "For Most Trump Voters, 'Very Warm' Feelings for Him Endured." U.S. Politics & Policy, August 9. Accessed January 4, 2019 (www.people-press.org/wp-content/uploads/sites/4/2018/08/8-9-2018-Validated-voters-release-with-10-17-correction.pdf).

_____. 2018b. "Party Identification Trends: 1992–2017." U.S. Politics & Policy, August 9. Accessed January 8, 2019 (www.people-press.org/2018/03/20/party-identification-trends-1992-2017/).

_____. 2018c. "The Partisan Divide on Political Values Grows Even Wider." U.S. Politics & Policy, October 5. January 13, 2019 (www.people-press.org/2017/10/05/the-partisan-divide-on-political-values-grows-even-wider/).

_____. 2019a. "Public's 2019 Priorities: Economy, Health Care, Education, and Security All Near Top of List." U.S. Politics and Policy, January 24. Accessed January 26, 2019 (www.people-press.org/2019/01/24/publics-2019-priorities-economy-health-care-education-and-security-all-near-top-of-list/).

_____. 2019b. "Changing Attitudes on Gay Marriage." Religion & Public Life, June 26. Accessed May 22, 2019 (www.pewforum.org/fact-sheet/changing-attitudes-on-gay-marriage/).

Pfeffer, Carla A. 2017. Queering Families: The Postmodern Partnerships of Cisgender Women and Transgender Men. New York: Oxford University Press.

Pfeffer, Fabian T., and Alexdra Killewald. 2016. "Intergenerational Correlations in Wealth." Pp. 175–201 in Economic Mobility: Research & Ideas on Strengthening Families, Communities, & the Economy. St Louis, MO: Federal Reserve Bank of St. Louis. Accessed December 22, 2016 (www.stlouisfed.org/~/media/Files/PDFs/Community%20Development/EconMobilityPapers/Section2/EconMobility_2-3PfefferKillewald_508.pdf).

Pfeifer, Mark. 2008. "Vietnamese Americans." Pp. 1365–1368 in Encyclopedia of Race, Ethnicity, and Society, vol. 3, ed. Richard T. Schaefer. Thousand Oaks, CA: Sage.

Pierce, Jennifer L. 2013. "White Racism, Social Class, and the Backlash against Affirmative Action." Sociology Compass 7(11): 914–926.

Piketty, Thomas. 2014. Capital in the Twenty-First Century. Cambridge, MA: Belknap Press of Harvard University.

Piketty, Thomas, Emmanuel Saez, and Gabriel Zucman. 2016. "Distributional National Accounts: Methods and Estimates for the United States." National Bureau of Economic Research, Working Paper 22945, December. Accessed December 21, 2016 (http://gabriel-zucman.eu/usdina/).

_____. 2018. "Distributional National Accounts: Methods and Estimates for the United States." The Quarterly Journal of Economics 133(2): 553–609.

Pinderhughes, Dianne. 1987. Race and Ethnicity in Chicago Politics: A Reexamination of Pluralist Theory. Urbana: University of Illinois Press.

Pinnow, Ellen, Pellavi Sharma, Ameeta Parekh, Natalie Gevorkian, and Kathleen Uhl. 2009. "Increasing Participation of Women in Early Phase Clinical Trials Approved by the FDA." Women's Health Issues 19 (2): 89–92.

Planty, M., W. Hussar, T. Snyder, G. Kena, A. Kewal-Ramani, J. Kemp, K. Bianco, and R. Dinkes. 2009. The Condition of Education 2009. NCES 2009-081. Washington, DC: National Center for Education Statistics, Institute of Education Sciences, U.S. Department of Education. Accessed May 29, 2009 (http://nces.ed.gov/pubs2009/2009081.pdf).

Planty, M., W. Hussar, T. Snyder, S. Provasnik, G. Kena, R. Dinkes, A. Kewal-Ramani, and J. Kemp. 2008. The Condition of Education 2008. NCES 2008-031. Washington, DC: National Center for Education Statistics, Institute of Education Sciences, U.S. Department of Education. Accessed June 14, 2008 (http://nces.ed.gov/pubs2008/2008031.pdf).

Plaut, Victoria C., Flannery G. Garnett, Laura E. Buffardi, and Jeffrey Sanchez-Burks. 2011. "What About Me? Perceptions of Exclusion and Whites Reactions to Multiculturalism." Journal of Personality and Social Psychology 101(2): 337–353.

Pollini, Jacques. 2009. "Agroforestry and the Search for Alternatives to Slash-and-Burn Cultivation: From Technological Optimism to a Political Economy of Deforestation." Agriculture, Ecosystems & Environment 133 (1/2): 48–60.

Pollster. 2016b. "Donald Trump Favorable Rating." The Huffington Post. Accessed December 15, 2016 (http://elections.huffingtonpost.com/pollster/donald-trump-favorable-rating).

_____. 2016c. "Party Identification." The Huffington Post. Accessed December 15, 2016 (http://elections.huffingtonpost.com/pollster/party-identification).

Population Reference Bureau. 2016. 2016 World Population Data Sheet. Washington, DC: Population Reference Bureau. Accessed October 25, 2016 (www.prb.org/Publications/Datasheets/2016/2016-world-population-data-sheet.aspx).

Porter, Roy. 1998. The Greatest Benefit to Mankind: A Medical History of Humanity. New York: HarperCollins.

_____. 2004. Blood and Guts: A Short History of Medicine. New York: Norton.

Postman, Neil. 1988. "Questioning the Media." Video. The January Series, January 12. Grand Rapids, MI: Calvin College.

_____. 1993. Technopoly: The Surrender of Culture to Technology. New York: Vintage Books.

_____. 1999. Building a Bridge to the 18th Century: How the Past Can Improve Our Future. New York: Knopf.

Potts, John. 2009. A History of Charisma. New York: Palgrave Macmillan.

Poushter, Jacob, Caldwell Bishop, and Hanyu Chwe. 2018. "Social Media Use Continues to Rise in Developing Countries but Plateaus Across Developed Ones." Pew Research Center, Global Attitudes & Trends, June 19. Accessed November 27, 2018 (www.pewglobal.org/2018/06/19/social-media-use-continues-to-rise-in-developing-countries-but-plateaus-across-developed-ones/).

Poushter, Jacob, and Dorothy Manevich. 2017. "Globally, People Point to ISIS and Climate Change as Leading Security Threats." Global Attitudes & Trends, Pew Research Center August 1. Accessed January 26, 2019 (www.pewglobal.org/2017/08/01/globally-people-point-to-isis-and-climate-change-as-leading-security-threats/).

Powell, James Lawrence. 2015. "Climate Scientists Virtually Unanimous: Anthropogenic Global Warming Is True." Bulletin of Science, Technology, and Society 35(5–6); 121–124.

Price, David A. 2003. Love and Hate in Jamestown: John Smith, Pocahontas, and the Heart of a New Nation. New York: Knopf.

Prichard, James Cowles. 1843. Natural History of Man. London: H. Baillière.

Prior, Karen Swallow. 2013. "The Case for Getting Married Young." The Atlantic, March 22. Accessed February 26, 2015 (www.theatlantic.com/sexes/archive/2013/03/the-case-for-getting-married-young/274293/).

Prohaska, Ariane, and Jeannine Gailey. 2010. "Achieving Masculinity Through Sexual Predation: The Case of Hogging." Journal of Gender Studies 19 (1): 13–25.

Provasnik, S., and Planty, M. 2008. Community Colleges: Special Supplement to the Condition of Education 2008. NCES 2008-033. Washington, DC: National Center for Education Statistics, Institute of

Education Sciences, U.S. Department of Education. Accessed May 31, 2009 (http://nces.ed.gov/pubs2008/2008033.pdf).

Pryor, John H., Sylvia Hurtado, Victor B. Saenz, José Luis Santos, and William S. Korn. 2007. *The American Freshman: Forty-Year Trends.* Los Angeles: Higher Education Research Institute, UCLA.

Putnam, Robert D. 2015. *Our Kids: The American Dream in Crisis.* New York: Simon & Schuster.

Putnam, Robert D., and David E. Campbell. 2012. *American Grace: How Religion Divides and Unites Us.* New York: Simon & Schuster.

Q

Qian, Yue. 2018. "Educational Assortative Mating and Income Dynamics in Couples: A Longitudinal and Dyadic Perspective." *Journal of Marriage and Family* 80 (3): 607–621.

Quinnell, Kenneth. 2018. "Executive Paywatch 2018: The Gap Between CEO and Worker Compensation Continues to Grow." AFL-CIO Executive Paywatch May 22. Accessed March 13, 2019 (https://aflcio.org/2018/5/22/executive-paywatch-2018-gap-between-ceo-and-worker-compensation-continues-grow).

Quinney, Richard. 1970. *The Social Reality of Crime.* Boston: Little, Brown.

———. 1974. *Criminal Justice in America.* Boston: Little, Brown.

———. 1979. *Criminology,* 2nd ed. Boston: Little, Brown.

———. 1980. *Class, State and Crime,* 2nd ed. New York: Longman.

Quinnipiac. 2016. "Overwhelming Support for No-Fly, No-Buy Gun Law, Quinnipiac University National Poll Finds; Support for Background Checks Tops 90 Percent Again." Quinnipiac University Poll, June 30. Accessed November 7, 2016 (https://poll.qu.edu/images/polling/us/us06302016_U37mhwbr.pdf/).

QuotaProject. 2014. "Mexico." Global Database of Quotas for Women. Accessed April 16, 2015 (www.quotaproject.org/uid/countryview.cfm?CountryCode=MX).

R

Raghavan, Sudarsan. 2011. "Inspired by Tunisia and Egypt, Yemenis Join in Anti-government Protests." *The Washington Post,* January 27. Accessed May 28, 2012 (www.washingtonpost.com/wp-dyn/content/article/2011/01/27/AR2011012702081.html).

Ralph, Peter, and Graham Coop. 2013. "The Geography of Recent Genetic Ancestry across Europe." *PLoS Biol* 11(5): e1001555. Accessed August 7, 2018 (http://journals.plos.org/plosbiology/article/file?id=10.1371/journal.pbio.1001555).

Rand, Robert. 2006. *Tamerlanes Children: Dispatches from Contemporary Uzbekistan.* Oxford: Oneworld.

Rank, Mark Robert, Thomas A. Hirschl, and Kirk A. Foster. 2014. *Chasing the American Dream: Understanding What Shapes Our Fortunes.* New York: Oxford University Press.

Raphelson, Samantha. 2017. "Countries Around the World Move to Repeal 'Marry Your Rapist' Laws." All Things Considered, National Public Radio, August 9. Accessed December 4, 2018 (www.npr.org/2017/08/09/542468265/countries-around-the-world-move-to-repeal-marry-your-rapist-laws).

Ravitz, Jessica. 2009. "Neda: Latest Iconic Image to Inspire." *CNN,* June 24. Accessed June 30, 2009 (www.cnn.com/2009/WORLD/meast/06/24/neda.iconic.images/).

Reardon, Sean F. 2011. "The Widening Academic Achievement Gap Between the Rich and the Poor: New Evidence and Possible Explanations." Pp. 91–115 in *Whither Opportunity?: Rising Inequality, Schools, and Childrens Life Chances,* ed. Greg J. Duncan and Richard J. Murnane. New York: Russell Sage Foundation.

Reddy, Gayatri. 2005. *With Respect to Sex: Negotiating Hijra Identity in South India.* Chicago: University of Chicago Press.

Redford, Jeremy, Danielle Battle, and Stacey Bielick. 2017. "Homeschooling in the United States: 2012." U.S. Department of Education, National Center for Education Statistics, NCES 2016-096. REV, April. Accessed December 6, 2016 (https://nces.ed.gov/pubs2016/2016096rev.pdf).

Redon, Richard, et al. 2006. "Global Variation in Copy Number in the Human Genome." *Nature* 444 (23): 444–454.

Reed, Sunny J. 2018. "Five Potential Side Effects of Transracial Adoption." *Medium,* January 17. Accessed September 4, 2018 (https://medium.com/all-beige/five-potential-side-effects-of-transracial-adoption-f0beeb4b6fb8).

Reel, Justine J., Sonya SooHoo, Julia Franklin Summerhays, and Diane Gill. 2008. "Age Before Beauty: An Exploration of Body Image in African-American and Caucasian Adult Women." *Journal of Gender Studies* 17 (4): 321–330.

Reeves, Richard. 2015. *Infamy: The Shocking Story of the Japanese American Internment in World War II.* New York: Henry Holt and Company.

Reeves, Richard V. 2014. *Saving Horatio Alger: Equality, Opportunity, and the American Dream.* New York: Brookings Institution.

———. 2015. "Wealth, Inequality, and the Me? I'm Not Rich! Problem." *The Wall Street Journal,* February 27. Accessed March 22, 2015 (http://blogs.wsj.com/washwire/2015/02/27/wealth-inequality-and-the-me-im-not-rich-problem/).

Reeves, Richard V. 2017. *Dream Hoarders: How the American Upper Middle Class Is Leaving Everyone in the Dust, Why that Is a Problem, and What to Do About It.* Washington, DC: Brookings Institution Press.

Reginato, James. 2012. "The Talk of Mumbai." *Vanity Fair,* May 8. Accessed January 14, 2017 (www.vanityfair.com/style/2012/06/ambani-residence-photos-inside-architecture).

Reich, David. 2018. *Who We Are and How We Got Here: Ancient DNA and the New Science of the Human Past.* New York: Pantheon Books.

Reid, Luc. 2006. *Talk the Talk: The Slang of 65 American Subcultures.* Cincinnati, OH: Writers Digest Books.

Reinharz, Shulamit. 1992. *Feminist Methods in Social Research.* New York: Oxford University Press.

Reitman, Meredith. 2006. "Uncovering the White Place: Whitewashing at Work." *Social & Cultural Geography* 7 (2): 267–282.

Reitzes, Donald C., and Elizabeth J. Mutran. 2004. "The Transition to Retirement: Stages and Factors That Influence Retirement Adjustment." *International Journal of Aging & Human Development* 59 (1): 63–84.

Relerford, Patrice, Chao Xiong, Michael Rand, and Curt Brown. 2008. "42 Students Questioned, 13 Disciplined." *Minneapolis Star-Tribune,* January 10. Accessed June 30, 2009 (www.startribune.com/local/west/13663951.html).

Renegar, Valerie R., and Stacey K. Sowards. 2009. "Contradiction as Agency: Self-Determination, Transcendence, and Counter-imagination in Third Wave Feminism." *Hypatia* 24 (2): 1–20.

Rest, Kathleen. 2018. "The Health and Safety of America's Workers Is at Risk." *Scientific American,* April 27. Accessed January 26, 2019 (https://blogs.scientificamerican.com/observations/the-health-and-safety-of-americas-workers-is-at-risk/).

Reynolds, John R., and Chardie L. Baird. 2010. "Is There a Downside to Shooting for the Stars? Unrealized Educational Expectations and Symptoms of Depression." *American Sociological Review* 75 (1): 151–172.

Richardson, Sarah S. 2013. *Sex Itself: The Search for Male and Female in the Human Genome.* Chicago: University of Chicago Press.

Richtel, Matt. 2006. "The Long-Distance Journey of a Fast-Food Order." *The New York Times,* April 11. Accessed May 13, 2009 (www.nytimes.com/2006/04/11/technology/11fast.html).

Rideout, Victoria. 2015. *The Common Sense Census: Media Use by Tweens and Teens.* San Francisco: Common Sense. Accessed October 25, 2016 (www.commonsensemedia.org/sites/default/files/uploads/research/census_researchreport.pdf).

Risman, Barbara J. 1986. "Can Men Mother? Life as a Single Father." *Family Relations* 35 (1): 95–102.

Ritzer, George. 2019. *The McDonaldization of Society: Into the Digital Age,* 9th edition. Thousand Oaks, CA: SAGE Publications, Inc.

Roberson, Debi, Ian Davies, and Jules Davidoff. 2000. "Color Categories Are Not Universal: Replications and New Evidence from Stone Age Culture." *Journal of Experimental Psychology* 129 (3): 369–398.

Roberts, Andrew W., Stella U. Ogunwole, Laura Blakeslee, and Megan A. Rabe. 2018. "The Population 65 Years and Older in the

United States: 2016." *American Survey Reports,* ACS-38, October. Accessed November 20, 2018 (www.census.gov/content/dam/Census/library/publications/2018/acs/ACS-38.pdf).

Roberts, J. Timmons, Peter E. Grines, and Jodie L. Manale. 2003. "Social Roots of Global Environmental Change: A World-Systems Analysis of Carbon Dioxide Emissions." *Journal of World-Systems Research* 9 (Summer): 277–315.

Roberts, Sam, and Peter Baker. 2010. "Asked to Declare His Race, Obama Checks 'Black.'" *The New York Times,* April 2. Accessed August 28, 2018 (www.nytimes.com/2010/04/03/us/politics/03census.html).

Roberts, Sharon E., and James E. Côté. 2014. "The Identity Issues Inventory: Identity Stage Resolution in the Prolonged Transition to Adulthood." *Journal of Adult Development* 21: 225–238.

Rockefeller Foundation. 2016. "100x25: Achieving Gender Inclusivity in the Workplace." Accessed February 2, 2017 (www.rockefellerfoundation.org/our-work/initiatives/100x25/).

Rodriguez, Richard. 2002. *Brown: The Last Discovery of America.* New York: Penguin Books.

Roeder, Oliver, Lauren-Brooke Eisen, and Julia Bowling. 2015. *What Caused the Crime Decline?* New York: Brennan Center for Justice at New York University School of Law. Accessed November 14, 2016 (www.brennancenter.org/publication/what-caused-crime-decline).

Roediger, David R. 2005. *Working Toward Whiteness: How Americas Immigrants Became White.* New York: Basic Books.

Rohde, Douglas L. T., Steve Olson, and Joseph T. Chang. 2004. "Modelling the Recent Common Ancestry of All Living Things." *Nature* 431: 562–566.

Roldán, Mariluz. 2018. "Over 70% of Indigenous People in Mexico Live in Poverty." *El Univeral,* September 8. Accessed January 22, 2019 (www.eluniversal.com.mx/english/over-70-indigenous-people-mexico-live-poverty).

Romano, Renee C. 2006. *Race Mixing: Black-White Marriage in Postwar America.* Gainesville, FL: University of Florida Press.

Romans, Sarah, Rose Clarkson, Gillian Einstein, Michele Petrovic, and Donna Stewart. 2012. "Mood and the Menstrual Cycle: A Review of Prospective Data Studies." *Gender Medicine* 9 (5): 361–384.

Rootes, Christopher. 2007. "Acting Locally: The Character, Contexts and Significance of Local Environmental Mobilisations." *Environmental Politics* 16 (5): 722–741.

Roscoe, Will. 1997. "Gender Diversity in Native North America: Notes Toward a Unified Analysis." Pp. 65–81 in *A Queer World: The Center for Lesbian and Gay Studies Reader,* ed. Martin Duberman. New York: New York University Press.

Rose, Arnold. 1951. *The Roots of Prejudice.* Paris: UNESCO.

Rosen, William. 2010. *The Most Powerful Idea in the World: A Story of Steam, Industry, and Invention.* New York: Random House.

Rosen, Yereth. 2016. "Exxon Valdez Oil Spill Reaches Anticlimactic End in Federal Court." *Anchorage Daily News,* September 28. Accessed November 11, 2018 (www.adn.com/environment/article/exxon-valdez-saga-reaches-anticlimatic-end-federal-court/2015/10/16/).

Rosenfeld, Michael J., and Reuben J. Thomas. 2012. "Searching for a Mate: The Rise of the Internet as a Social Intermediary." *American Sociological Review* 77: 523–547.

Rosenfeld, Richard, and Robert Fornango. 2014. "The Impact of Police Stops on Precinct Robbery and Burglary Rates in New York City, 2003-2010." *Justice Quarterly* 31(1): 96–122.

Rosenthal, Robert, and Lenore Jacobson. 1968. *Pygmalion in the Classroom.* New York: Henry Holt.

Rosin, Hanna. 2014. "The Overprotected Kid." *The Atlantic,* April. Accessed February 2, 2015 (www.theatlantic.com/features/archive/2014/03/hey-parents-leave-those-kids-alone/358631/).

Rossi, Alice S. 1968. "Transition to Parenthood." *Journal of Marriage and Family* 30 (February): 26–39.

———. 1984. "Gender and Parenthood." *American Sociological Review* 49 (February): 1–19.

Rossi Del Corso, Annalisa, and Margherita Lanz. 2013. "Felt Obligation and the Family Cycle: A Study on Intergenerational Relationships." *International Journal of Psychology* 48: 1196–1200.

Roth, Wendy D. 2016. "The Multiple Dimensions of Race." *Ethnic and Racial Studies* 39 (8): 1310–1338.

Roth, Wendy D., and Biorn Ivemark. 2018. "Genetic Options: The Impact of Genetic Ancestry Testing on Consumers' Racial and Ethnic Identities." *American Journal of Sociology* 124 (1): 150–184).

Rothman, Joshua. 2016. "How to Restore Your Faith in Democracy." *The New Yorker,* November 11. Accessed December 13, 2016 (www.newyorker.com/culture/persons-of-interest/how-to-restore-your-faith-in-democracy).

Rothstein, Jeffrey S. 2016. *When Good Jobs Go Bad: Globalization, De-Unionization, and Declining Job Quality in the North American Auto Industry.* New Brunswick, NJ: Rutgers University Press.

Rothstein, Richard. 2009. "Equalizing Opportunity: Dramatic Differences in Children's Home Life and Health Mean That Schools Can't Do It Alone." *American Educator* 33 (2): 4–7, 45–46. Accessed April 26, 2010 (http://archive.aft.org/pubs-reports/american_educator/issues/summer2009/equalizingopportunity.pdf).

Rotman, David. 2013. "How Technology Is Destroying Jobs." *MIT Technology Review,* June 12. Accessed March 17, 2015 (www.technologyreview.com/featuredstory/515926/how-technology-is-destroying-jobs/).

Rowland, Christopher, ed. 2007. *The Cambridge Companion to Liberation Theology,* 2nd ed. New York: Cambridge University Press.

Rowling, J. K. 2014. *Harry Potter and the Chamber of Secrets* (Harry Potter Series #2). London: Bloomsbury Press.

Rubie-Davies, Christine M. 2010. "Teacher Expectations and Perceptions of Student Attributes: Is There a Relationship?" *British Journal of Educational Psychology* 80 (1): 121–135.

Rubin, Alissa J. 2003. "Pat-Down on the Way to Prayer." *Los Angeles Times,* November 25, pp. A1, A5.

Rubin, Mark, Nida Denson, Sue Kilpatrick, Kelly E. Matthews, Tom Stehlik, and David Zyngier. 2014. "I Am Working Class: Subjective Self-Definition as a Missing Measure of Social Class and Socioeconomic Status in Higher Education Research." *Educational Researcher* 43: 196–200.

Ruetschlin, Christina M., and Abdul Karim Bangura. 2012. "Transnational Organized Crime: A Global Concern." *International Journal of Diversity* 2012 (3): 94–102.

Ruiz, Ariel G., Jie Zong, and Jeanne Batalova. 2015. "Immigrant Women in the United States." Migration Policy Institute March 20. Access February 7, 2017 (www.migrationpolicy.org/article/immigrant-women-united-states).

Rutherford, Adam. 2016. *A Brief History of Everyone Who Ever Lived: The Stories in Our Genes.* London: Weidenfeld & Nicolson.

Rutter, Michael. 2010. "Gene Environment Interplay." *Depression and Anxiety* 27: 1–4.

Rutter, Michael, Terrie E. Moffitt, and Avshalom Caspi. 2006. "Gene-Environment Interplay and Psychopathology: Multiple Varieties but Real Effects." *Journal of Child Psychology and Psychiatry* 47 (3/4): 226–261.

Rymer, Russ. 1993. *Genie: An Abused Child's Flight from Science.* New York: HarperCollins.

S

Saad, Lydia. 2004. "Divorce Doesn't Last." *Gallup Poll Tuesday Briefing,* March 30 (www.gallup.com/poll/11161/divorce-doesnt-last.aspx).

Sacks, Peter. 2007. *Tearing Down the Gates: Confronting the Class Divide in American Education.* Berkeley: University of California Press.

Sacramento Police Department. 2018. "Update to the 29th Street Officer-Involved Shooting Incident." Media Advisory/News Release, March 19. Accessed September 18, 2018 (www.sacpd.org/newsroom/releases/liveview.aspx?release_id=20180319-027).

Sadat, Sayed Masood, Christina Satkowski, Renard Shamim Sarabi, Sandy Feinzig, Shahim Kabuli, Charlotte Maxwell-Jones, and Zachary Warren. 2015. *Afghanistan in 2015: A Survey of the Afghan People.* San Francisco: The Asia Foundation. Accessed September 23, 2016 (https://asiafoundation.org/resources/pdfs/Afghanistanin2015.pdf).

Saey, Tina Hesman. 2018. "News of First Gene-Edited Babies Ignited a Firestorm." *Science News,* December 17. Accessed January 31, 2019 (www.sciencenews.org/article/gene-edited-babies-top-science-stories-2018-yir).

Saez, Emmanuel. 2016. "Striking It Richer: The Evolution of Top Incomes in the United States (Updated with 2015 preliminary estimates)." Center for Equitable Growth, June 30. Accessed December 14, 2016 (http://eml.berkeley.edu/_saez/saez-UStopincomes-2015.pdf).

Saez, Emmanuel, and Gabriel Zucman. 2016. "Wealth Inequality in the United States since 1913: Evidence from Capitalized Income Tax Data." *Quarterly Journal of Economics* 131(2): 519–578. Accessed December 22, 2016 (http://gabriel-zucman.eu/uswealth/).

Saint Martin, Manuel L. 1999. "Running Amok: A Modern Perspective on a Culture-Bound Syndrome." *The Primary Care Companion to the Journal of Clinical Psychiatry* 1(3): 66–70.

Salganik, Matthew J., Peter Sheridan Dodds, and Duncan J. Watts. 2006. "Experimental Study of Inequality and Unpredictability in an Artificial Cultural Market." *Science* 311: 854–856.

Salinas, Brenda. 2014. "'Columbusing': The Art of Discovering Something That Is Not New." *NPR Code Switch,* July 6. Accessed September 30, 2016 (www.npr.org/sections/codeswitch/2014/07/06/328466757/columbusing-the-art-of-discovering-something-that-is-not-new).

Sample, Ian. 2014. "Anthropocene: Is This the New Epoch of Humans?" *The Guardian,* October 16. Accessed May 2, 2015 (www.theguardian.com/science/2014/oct/16/-sp-scientists-gather-talks-rename-human-age-anthropocene-holocene).

Sampson, Robert J., and Stephen W. Raudenbush. 2004. "Seeing Disorder: Neighborhood Stigma and the Social Construction of 'Broken Windows.'" *Social Psychology Quarterly* 67(4): 319–342.

SAMSHA. 2018. "Results from the 2017 National Survey on Drug Use and Health: Detailed Tables." Substance Abuse and Mental Health Services Administration, U.S. Department of Health & Human Services, November 1. Accessed December 1, 2018 (www.samhsa.gov/data/sites/default/files/cbhsq-reports/NSDUHDetailedTabs2017/NSDUHDetailedTabs2017.htm).

Sanchez, Angela A. 2018. "An Examination of the Folk Healing Practice of *Curanderismo* in the Hispanic Community." *Journal of Community Health Nursing* 35(3): 148–161.

Sanday, Peggy Reeves. 2002. *Women at the Center: Life in a Modern Matriarchy.* Ithaca, NY: Cornell University Press.

————. 2008. Homepage. Accessed March 15 (www.sas.upenn.edu/_psanday).

Sandberg, Sheryl. 2013. *Lean In: Women, Work, and the Will to Lead.* New York: Alfred A. Knopf.

Sandler, Ronald, and Phaedra C. Pezzullo, eds. 2007. *Environmental Justice and Environmentalism: The Social Justice Challenge to the Environmental Movement.* Cambridge, MA: MIT Press.

Saperstein, Aliya, Jessica M. Kizer, and Andrew M. Penner. 2016. "Making the Most of Multiple Measures: Disentangling the Effects of Different Dimensions of Race in Survey Research." *American Behavioral Scientist* 60 (4): 519–537.

Saperstein, Aliya, and Andrew M. Penner. 2012. "Racial Fluidity and Inequality in the United States." *American Journal of Sociology* 118 (3): 676–727.

————. 2016. "Still Searching for a True Race?: Reply to Kramer et al. and Alba et al." *American Journal of Sociology* 122 (1): 263–285.

Sarachild, Kathie. 1978. "Consciousness-Raising: A Radical Weapon." Pp. 144–150 in *Feminist Revolution.* New York: Random House. Accessed June 30, 2009 (http://scriptorium.lib.duke.edu/wlm/fem/sarachild.html).

Sarkeesian, Anita. 2013. "Damsel in Distress (Part 1) Tropes vs Women." *Feminist Frequency: Conversations with Pop Culture,* March 7. Accessed May 20, 2013 (www.feministfrequency.com/2013/03/damsel-in-distress-part-1/).

Sarkisian, Natalia, and Naomi Gerstel. 2016. "Does Singlehood Isolate or Integrate? Examining the Link Between Marital Status and Ties to Kin, Friends, and Neighbors." *Journal of Social and Personal Relationships* 33(3): 361–384.

Sawhill, Isabel V. 2006. "Teenage Sex, Pregnancy, and Nonmarital Births." *Gender Issues* 23 (4): 48–59.

Scally, Corianne Payton. 2015. "Democracy in Action?: NIMBY as Impediment to Equitable Affordable Housing Siting." *Housing Studies* 30(5): 749–69.

Scarce, Rik. 1994. "(No) Trial (but) Tribulations: When Courts and Ethnography Conflict." *Journal of Contemporary Ethnography* 23 (July): 123–149.

————. 1995. "Scholarly Ethics and Courtroom Antics: Where Researchers Stand in the Eyes of the Law." *American Sociologist* 26 (Spring): 87–112.

————. 2005a. "A Law to Protect Scholars." *Chronicle of Higher Education,* August 12, p. 324.

————. 2005b. *Contempt of Court: A Scholars Battle for Free Speech from Behind Bars.* Lanham, MD: AltaMira Press.

Scelfo, Julie. 2008. "Baby, You're Home." *The New York Times,* November 12. Accessed June 29, 2009 (www.nytimes.com/2008/11/13/garden/13birth.html).

Schachtman, Tom. 2006. *Rumspringa: To Be or Not to Be Amish.* New York: North Point Press.

Schaefer, Richard T. 1998a. "Differential Racial Mortality and the 1995 Chicago Heat Wave." Paper presented at the annual meeting of the American Sociological Association, August, San Francisco.

Schaefer, Richard T., and William W. Zellner. 2007. *Extraordinary Groups,* 8th ed. New York: Worth.

Schaffer, Scott. 2004. *Resisting Ethics.* New York: Palgrave Macmillan.

Scharnberg, Kirsten. 2007. "Black Market for Midwives Defies Bans." *Chicago Tribune,* November 25, pp. 1, 10.

Scherbov, Sergei, Wolfgang Lutz, and Warren C. Sanderson. 2011. "The Uncertain Timing of Reaching 7 Billion and Peak Population." International Institute for Applied Systems Analysis, Interim Report IR-11-002, February 21. Accessed June 29, 2011 (www.iiasa.ac.at/Admin/PUB/Documents/IR-11-002.pdf).

Schlosberg, David. 2013. "Theorising Environmental Justice: The Expanding Sphere of a Discourse." *Environmental Politics* 22(1): 37–55.

Schmeeckle, Maria. 2007. "Gender Dynamics in Stepfamilies: Adult Stepchildren's Views." *Journal of Marriage and Family* 69 (February): 174–189.

Schmeeckle, Maria, Roseann Giarrusso, Du Feng, and Vern L. Bengtson. 2006. "What Makes Someone Family? Adult Children's Perceptions of Current and Former Stepparents." *Journal of Marriage and Family* 68 (August): 595–610.

Schneier, Bruce. 2015. *Data and Goliath: The Hidden Battles to Collect Your Data and Control Your World.* New York: W. W. Norton & Company.

Schroeder, Michael O. 2016. "Racial Bias in Medicine Leads to Worse Care for Minorities." *U.S. News & World Report* February 11. Accessed February 12, 2017 (http://health.usnews.com/health-news/patient-advice/articles/2016-02-11/racial-bias-in-medicine-leads-to-worse-care-for-minorities).

Schultz, David. 2016. "Should We Bring Extinct Species Back from the Dead?" *Science* September 26. Accessed February 15, 2017 (www.sciencemag.org/news/2016/09/should-we-bring-extinct-species-back-dead).

Schur, Edwin M. 1965. *Crimes Without Victims: Deviant Behavior and Public Policy.* Englewood Cliffs, NJ: Prentice Hall.

————. 1985. "Crimes Without Victims: A 20-Year Reassessment." Paper presented at the annual meeting of the Society for the Study of Social Problems.

Schwartz, Pepper. 2006. *Finding Your Perfect Match.* New York: Perigee Books.

Scott, Greg. 2005. "Public Symposium: HIV/AIDS, Injection Drug Use and Men Who Have Sex with Men." Pp. 38–39 in *Scholarship with a Mission,* ed. Susanna Pagliaro. Chicago: De Paul University.

Scott, Katy. 2018. "Can the Middle East Solve Its Water Problem?" CNN, July 11. Accessed January 26, 2019 (www.cnn.com/2018/07/11/middleeast/middle-east-water/index.html).

Semigran, Hannah L., Jeffrey Linder, Courtney Gidengil, and Ateev Mehrotra. 2015. "Evaluation of Symptom Checkers for Self Diagnosis and Triage: Audit Study." *BMJ* 351: H3480.

References

Sen, Maya and Omar Wasow. 2016. "Race as a Bundle of Sticks: Designs that Estimate Effects of Seemingly Immutable Characterisitics." *Annual Review of Political Science* 19: 499–522.

Sengupta, Somini. 2017. "One by One, Marry-Your-Rapist Laws Are Falling in the Middle East." *The New York Times,* July 22. Accessed December 4, 2018 (www.nytimes.com/2017/07/22/world/middleeast/marry-your-rapist-laws-middle-east.html).

Senter, Mary S. 2016. "Individual Salary Is Not Enough: Measuring the Well-Being of Recent College Graduates in Sociology." Bachelors and Beyond Series, August. Washington, DC: American Sociological Association. Accessed August 30, 2016 (www.asanet.org/research-and-publications/research-sociology/research-briefs/individual-salary-not-enough).

Senter, Mary S., Roberta Spalter-Roth, and Nicole Van Vooren. 2015. "Jobs, Careers, & Sociological Skills." Bachelors and Beyond Series, February. Washington, DC: American Sociological Association. Accessed August 30, 2016 (www.asanet.org/research-and-publications/research-sociology/research-briefs/jobs-careers-sociological-skills-early-employment-experiences-2012-sociology-majors)

Shaheen, Jack. 2006. *Reel Bad Arabs: How Hollywood Vilifies a People.* Video. Directed by Sut Jhally. 50 minutes. Northampton, MA: Media Education Foundation.

———. 2009. *Reel Bad Arabs: How Hollywood Vilifies a People,* 2nd ed. New York: Olive Branch Press.

———. 2012. "The Making of the Green Menace." *The Nation,* July 2–9: 15–17.

Shakespeare, William. 1984. *Shakespeare's Comedy of As You Like It.* Woodstock, IL: Dramatic Publishing, 64.

Shankar, Maya. 2016. "How Behavioral Science Is Serving the American People." Office of Science and Technology Policy, The Whitehouse, September 15. Accessed November 1, 2018 (https://obamawhitehouse.archives.gov/blog/2016/09/15/learn-how-behavioral-science-being-used-better-serve-american-people).

Shannon-Missal, Larry. 2015. "More than Ever, Pets Are Members of the Family." The Harris Poll, July 16. Accessed November 21, 2016 (www.theharrispoll.com/health-and-life/Pets-are-Members-of-the-Family.html).

Shapiro, Thomas M. 2004. *The Hidden Cost of Being African American: How Wealth Perpetuates Inequality.* New York: Oxford University Press.

Sharp, Gwen. 2011. "Two News Stories About Gabrielle Giffords' Shooting . . . and Husband." *Sociological Images,* January 9. Accessed March 10, 2012 (http://thesocietypages.org/socimages/2011/01/09/two-news-stories-about-gabrielle-giffords-shooting-and-husband/).

Shaw, Clifford R., and Henry D. McKay. 1969. *Juvenile Delinquency and Urban Areas.* Chicago: University of Chicago Press.

Shaw, Jessica C. 2013. "The Medicalization of Birth and Midwifery as Resistance." *Health Care for Women International* 34: 522–536.

Shenk, David. 2010. *The Genius in All of Us: Why Everything You've Been Told About Genetics, Talent, and IQ Is Wrong.* New York: Doubleday.

Shenker, Jack, Angelique Chrisafis, Lauren Williams, Tom Finn, Giles Tremlett, and Martin Chulov. 2011. "Young Arabs Who Can't Wait to Throw Off Shackles of Tradition." *The Guardian,* February 14. Accessed May 28, 2012 (www.guardian.co.uk/world/2011/feb/14/young-arabs-throw-off-shackles-tradition).

Sheskin, Ira M., and Arnold Dashefsky. 2017. "United States Jewish Population, 2016." *Current Jewish Population Reports,* No. 16. Accessed October 10, 2018 (www.jewishdatabank.org/databank/search-results/study/831).

Shi, Yu. 2008. "Chinese Immigrant Women Workers: Everyday Forms of Resistance and Coagulate Politics." *Communication and Critical/Cultural Studies* 5 (4): 363–382.

Shields, Stephanie A. 2008. "Gender: An Intersectionality Perspective." *Sex Roles* 59 (5/6): 301–311.

Shilts, Randy. 1987. *And the Band Played On: Politics, People, and the AIDS Epidemic.* New York: St. Martin's Press.

Shipler, David K. 2004. *The Working Poor: Invisible in America.* New York: Knopf.

Shirky, Clay. 2008. *Here Comes Everybody: The Power of Organizing Without Organizations.* New York: Penguin Books.

Shorrocks, Anthony, James B. Davies, and Rodrigo Lluberas. 2016. *Global Wealth Databook 2016.* Zurich: Credit Suisse Research Institute. Accessed January 14, 2017 (http://publications.credit-suisse.com/tasks/render/file/index.cfm?fileid=AD6F2B43-B17B-345E-E20A1A254A3E24A5).

———. 2018. *Global Wealth Databook 2018.* Zurich: Credit Suisse Research Institute. Accessed January 12, 2019 (https://publications.credit-suisse.com/tasks/render/file/index.cfm?fileid=777FDF0E-E060-F608-52DAF97E062CC35B).

Shostak, Arthur B. 2002. "Clinical Sociology and the Art of Peace Promotion: Earning a World Without War." Pp. 325–345 in *Using Sociology: An Introduction from the Applied and Clinical Perspectives,* ed. Roger A. Straus. Lanham, MD: Rowman & Littlefield.

Showden, Carisa R. 2009. "What's Political About the New Feminisms?" *Frontiers: A Journal of Women Studies* 30 (2): 166–198.

Shrivastava, Bhuma, and Anto Antony. 2015. "Mumbai Is Overflowing with Garbage." Live Mint, July 27. Accessed June 2, 2017 (www.livemint.com/Politics/XUNshUdRrpzuHsV9HDd1TO/Mumbai-is-overflowing-with-garbage.html).

Silva, Tony. 2016. "Bud-Sex: Constructing Normative Masculinity among Rural Straight Men that Have Sex with Men." *Gender & Society* 31(1): 51–73.

Silver, Ira. 1996. "Role Transitions, Objects, and Identity." *Symbolic Interaction* 10 (1): 1–20.

Silver, Laura and Courtney Johnson. 2018. "Internet Connectivity Seen as Having Positive Impact on Life in Sub-Saharan Africa." Global Attitudes & Trends, Pew Research Center October 9. Accessed November 20, 2018 (www.pewglobal.org/2018/10/09/internet-connectivity-seen-as-having-positive-impact-on-life-in-sub-saharan-africa/).

Silver, Nate. 2015. "The Most Diverse Cities Are often the Most Segregated." *FiveThirtyEight,* May 1. Accessed February 4, 2017 (https://fivethirtyeight.com/features/the-most-diverse-cities-are-often-the-most-segregated/).

———. 2016. "Who Will Win the Presidency?" *FiveThirtyEight,* November 8. Accessed December 13, 2016 (http://projects.fivethirtyeight.com/2016-election-forecast/).

———. 2016b. "Why FiveThirtyEight Gave Trump a Better Chance Than Almost Anyone Else." FiveThirtyEight, November 11. Accessed November 6, 2018 (https://fivethirtyeight.com/features/why-fivethirtyeight-gave-trump-a-better-chance-than-almost-anyone-else/).

Simmons, Tavia, and Martin O'Connell. 2003. "Married-Couple and Unmarried-Partner Households: 2000." *Census 2000 Special Reports,* CENBR-5. Washington, DC: U.S. Government Printing Office.

Simons, Gary F. and Charles D. Fennig, eds. 2018. *Ethnologue: Languages of the World,* 21st edition. Dallas, Texas: SIL International. Accessed November 13, 2018 (www.ethnologue.com/statistics).

Sims, Alexandra. 2016. "Denmark's Bizarre Series of Sex Campaigns Lead to Baby Boom." *The Independent,* June 2. Accessed November 3, 2018 (www.independent.co.uk/news/world/europe/denmark-s-bizarre-series-of-sex-campaigns-lead-to-baby-boom-a7062466.html).

Singel, Ryan. 2008. "FBI Tried to Cover Patriot Act Abuses with Flawed, Retroactive Subpoenas, Audit Finds." *Wired,* March 13. Accessed June 30, 2009 (www.wired.com/threatlevel/2008/03/fbi-tried-to-co).

Sklar, Robert. 1994. *Movie-Made America: A Cultural History of American Movies.* Revised and Updated. New York: Vintage Books.

Sluiter, Engel. 1997. "New Light on the 20. and Odd Negroes Arriving in Virginia, August 1619." *The William and Mary Quarterly* 54: 395–398.

Small Arms Survey. 2011. "Estimating Civilian Owned Firearms." Graduate Institute of International and Development Studies, Geneva, Switzerland, *Research Note* 9 (September). Accessed May 23, 2013 (www.smallarmssurvey.org/fileadmin/docs/H-Research_Notes/SAS-Research-Note-9.pdf).

Smarsh, Sarah. 2018. *Heartland: A Memoir of Working Hard and Being Broke in the Richest Country on Earth.* London: Scribe Publications, 88.

Smelser, Neil J. 1962. *Theory of Collective Behavior.* New York: The Free Press.

Smiley, Tavis, and Cornel West. 2012. "America's New Working Poor." *Salon,* May 1. Accessed May 22, 2012 (www.salon.com/2012/05/01/working_in_poverty/).

Smith, Aaron. 2016. "15% of American Adults Have Used Online Dating Sites or Mobile Dating Apps." Pew Research Center February 11. Accessed November 18, 2016 (www.pewinternet.org/files/2016/02/PI_2016.02.11_Online-Dating_FINAL.pdf).

Smith, Aaron, and Janna Anderson. 2014. "AI, Robotics, and the Future of Jobs." Pew Research Center, Internet, Science & Tech, August 6. Accessed March 18, 2015 (www.pewinternet.org/files/2014/08/Future-of-AI-Robotics-and-Jobs.pdf).

Smith, Adam. [1776] 2003. *The Wealth of Nations.* New York: Bantam Classics.

Smith, Dorothy E. 1987. *The Everyday World as Problematic: A Feminist Sociology.* Boston: Northeastern University Press.

Smith, Erica L., and Alexia Cooper. 2013. "Homicide in the U.S. Known to Law Enforcement, 2011." Bureau of Justice Statistics, December, NCJ 24035. Accessed February 19, 2015 (www.bjs.gov/content/pub/pdf/hus11.pdf).

Smith, Stacy L., Marc Choueiti, Katherine Pieper, Ariana Case, and Angel Choi. 2018. "Inequality in 1,100 Popular Films: Examining Portrayals of Gender, Race/Ethnicity, LGBT, & Disability from 2007–2017." Media, Diversity, & Social Change Initiative, Annenberg School of Communication & Journalism, July. Accessed June 10, 2019 (http://assets.uscannenberg.org/docs/inequality-in-1100-popular-films.pdf).

Smith, Tom W. 2004. "Coming of Age in Twenty-first Century America: Public Attitudes Towards the Importance and Timing of Transitions to Adulthood." *Ageing International* 29 (2): 136–148.

————. 2006. "American Sexual Behavior: Trends, Socio-Demographic Differences, and Risk Behavior." National Opinion Research Center, University of Chicago, GSS Topical Report No. 25. Updated March, 2006. Accessed May 12, 2010 (www.norc.org/NR/rdonlyres/2663F09F-2E74-436E-AC81-6FFBF288E183/0/AmericanSexualBehavior2006.pdf).

————. 2011. "Public Attitudes toward Homosexuality." NORC/University of Chicago, September 2011. Accessed May 26, 2012 (www.norc.org/PDFs/2011%20GSS%20Reports/GSS_Public%20Attitudes%20Toward%20Homosexuality_Sept2011.pdf).

Smith, Tom W., Michael Davern, Jeremy Freese, and Michael Hout. 2018. *General Social Surveys, 1972–2016.* Chicago: NORC at the University of Chicago.

Smith, Tom W., Peter Marsden, Michael Hout, and Jibum Kim. 2014. *General Social Surveys, 1972–2012.* Chicago: National Opinion Research Center.

Social Security Administration. 2016. *Fast Facts & Figures about Social Security, 2016.* Office of Retirement and Disability Policy, Office of Research, Evaluation, and Statistics, Washington, DC, SSA Publication No. 13-11785, August. Accessed October 25, 2016 (www.ssa.gov/policy/docs/chartbooks/fast_facts/2016/fast_facts16.pdf).

————. 2017. *Fast Facts & Figures about Social Security, 2017.* Office of Retirement and Disability Policy, Office of Research, Evaluation, and Statistics, Washington, DC, SSA Publication No. 13-11785, September. Accessed November 20, 2018 (www.ssa.gov/policy/docs/chartbooks/fast_facts/2017/fast_facts17.pdf).

————. 2018. "Popular Baby Names." Accessed November 11, 2018 (www.ssa.gov/OACT/babynames/index.html).

Soderstrom, Melanie. 2007. "Beyond Babytalk: Re-evaluating the Nature and Content of Speech Input to Preverbal Infants." *Developmental Review* 27: 501–532.

Sollors, Werner. 1986. *Beyond Ethnicity: Consent and Descent in America.* New York: Oxford University Press.

Solomon, Andrew. 2016. "'The Good Death,' 'When Breath Becomes Air,' and More." *The New York Times,* February 8. Accessed October 25, 2016 (www.nytimes.com/2016/02/14/books/review/the-good-death-when-breath-becomes-air-and-more.html).

Solove, Daniel J. 2008. "Do Social Networks Bring the End of Privacy?" *Scientific American* 299 (September): 100–106.

Accessed June 30, 2009 (www.scientificamerican.com/article.cfm?id5do-social-networks-bring).

Sorokin, Pitirim A. [1927] 1959. *Social and Cultural Mobility.* New York: Free Press.

Spalter-Roth, Roberta, and Nicole Van Vooren. 2008. "What Are They Doing with a Bachelor's Degree in Sociology?" American Sociological Association Department of Research and Development. Washington, DC: ASA. Accessed March 25, 2010 (www.asanet.org/images/research/docs/pdf/What%20Are%20They%20Doing%20with%20BA%20in%20Soc.pdf).

————. 2009. "Idealists vs. Careerists: Graduate School Choices of Sociology Majors." American Sociological Association Department of Research and Development. Washington, DC: ASA. Accessed March 25, 2010 (www.asanet.org/images/research/docs/pdf/Idealist%20vs%20Careerisst.pdf).

————. 2010. "Mixed Success: Four Years of Experiences of 2005 Sociology Graduates." American Sociological Association Department of Research and Development. Washington, DC: American Sociological Association. Accessed May 5, 2011 (www.asanet.org/research/BBMixedSuccessBrief.pdf).

Spalter-Roth, Roberta, Nicole Van Vooren, Michael Kisielewski, and Mary S. Senter. 2012. "Recruiting Sociology Majors: What Are the Effects of the Great Recession?" American Sociological Association, Department of Research & Development, November. Accessed April 26, 2013 (www.asanet.org/documents/research/pdfs/Bachelors_and_Beyond_2012_Brief2_Recruiting.pdf).

Spangler, Todd. 2016. "Man Who Pirated 'The Revenant' Ordered to Pay $1.1 Million to 20th Century Fox." *Variety,* September 30. Accessed November 11, 2016 (http://variety.com/2016/digital/news/revenant-peanuts-movie-piracy-1-1-million-20th-century-fox-1201874892/).

————. 2018. "Global Piracy in 2017: TV and Music Illegal Activity Rose, While Film Declined." *Variety,* March 21. Accessed December 2, 2018 (https://variety.com/2018/digital/news/piracy-global-2017-tv-music-film-illegal-streaming-1202731243/).

Spaulding, John A., George Simpson, and Émile Durkheim. 2010. *Suicide.* Simon and Schuster, 208.

Sperling, Katrin. 2016. "Game of Tongues—The Invented Languages of Game of Thrones." *Babbel Magazine,* April 13. Accessed November 15, 2018 (www.babbel.com/en/magazine/the-invented-languages-in-game-of-thrones/).

Spores, John C. 1988. *Running Amok: An Historical Inquiry.* Athens: Ohio University Press.

Sprague, Joey. 2005————. *Feminist Methodologies for Critical Research: Bridging Differences.* Lanham, MD: AltaMira Press.

Springsteen, Bruce. 2016. "On Jersey, Masculinity and Wishing to Be His Stage Persona." Interview by Terry Gross. *NPR Fresh Air* October 4. Accessed October 31, 2016 (www.npr.org/2016/10/05/496639696/bruce-springsteen-on-jersey-masculinity-and-wishing-to-be-his-stage-persona).

Sreenivasan, Hari. 2018. "Parkland Shooting Survivors Push for Gun Control." *PBS News Hour,* February 18. Accessed January 28, 2019 (www.pbs.org/newshour/show/parkland-shooting-survivors-push-for-gun-reform).

Srinivas, M. N. 1956. "A Note on Sanskritization and Westernization." *The Far Eastern Quarterly* 15: 481–496.

St. Clair, Kassia. 2017. *The Secret Lives of Color.* New York: Penguin Books.

St. Vil, Noelle M., Katrina Bell McDonald, and Caitlin Cross-Barnet. 2018. "A Qualitative Study of Black Married Couples' Relationships with Their Extended Family Networks." *Families in Society* 99(1): 56–66.

Staal, J. F. 1963. "Sanskrit and Sanskritization." *Journal of Asian Studies* 22: 261–275.

Staats, Cheryl, Kelly Capatosto, Robin A. Wright, and Victoria W. Jackson. 2016. *State of the Science: Implicit Bias Review,* 2016 Edition. Columbus, OH: Kirwan Institute for the Study of Race and Ethnicity, The Ohio State University. Accessed October 21, 2016 (http://kirwaninstitute.osu.edu/my-product_category/implicit-bias/).

Stack, Carol. 1974. *All Our Kin: Strategies for Survival in a Black Community.* New York: Harper & Row.

Standish, Peter, and Steven Bell. 2004. *Culture and Customs of Mexico.* Santa Barbara, CA: Greenwood Press.

Stanton, Elizabeth Cady. 1848. Elizabeth Cady Stanton Addresses a Women's Rights Convention in 1848, Digital History.

Stapleton, AnneClair, and Ralph Ellis. 2016. "Timeline of Orlando Nightclub Shooting." *CNN,* June 17. Accessed November 3, 2016 (www.cnn.com/2016/06/12/us/orlando-shooting-timeline/).

Stark, Rodney, and William Sims Bainbridge. 1979. "Of Churches, Sects, and Cults: Preliminary Concepts for a Theory of Religious Movements." *Journal for the Scientific Study of Religion* 18 (June): 117–131.

———. 1980. "Networks of Faith: Interpersonal Bonds and Recruitment to Cults and Sects." *American Journal of Sociology* 85(6): 1376–1395.

———. 1985. *The Future of Religion.* Berkeley: University of California Press.

Starr, Paul. 1982. *The Social Transformation of American Medicine.* New York: Basic Books.

Steele, Jonathan. 2005. "Annan Attacks Britain and U.S. over Erosion of Human Rights." *Guardian Weekly,* March 16, p. 1.

Steiblin, Caroline, and Frank-Stephan Graef. 2015. *Prices and Earnings 2015: Do I Earn Enough for the Life I Want?* Zurich: UBS Switzerland AG. Accessed January 18, 2017 (www.ubs.com/microsites/prices-earnings/prices-earnings.html).

Steidle, Brian. 2007. *The Devil Came on Horseback: Bearing Witness to the Genocide in Darfur.* New York: PublicAffairs.

Stenning, Derrick J. 1958. "Household Viability Among the Pastoral Fulani." Pp. 92–119 in *The Developmental Cycle in Domestic Groups,* ed. John R. Goody. Cambridge, UK: Cambridge University Press.

Stepler, Renee. 2017a. "Number of U.S. Adults Cohabiting with a Partner Continues to Rise, Especially among Those 50 and Older." Pew Research Center, April 6. Accessed December 16, 2018 (www.pewresearch.org/fact-tank/2017/04/06/number-of-u-s-adults-cohabiting-with-a-partner-continues-to-rise-especially-among-those-50-and-older/).

———. 2017b. "Led by Baby Boomers, Divorce Rates Climb for America's 501 Population." Pew Research Center, March 9. Accessed December 17, 2018 (www.pewresearch.org/fact-tank/2017/03/09/led-by-baby-boomers-divorce-rates-climb-for-americas-50-population/).

Stepler, Renee, and Anna Brown. 2016. "Statistical Portrait of Hispanics in the United States." Pew Research Center, Hispanic Trends April 19. Accessed February 6, 2017 (www.pewhispanic.org/2016/04/19/statistical-portrait-of-hispanics-in-the-united-states/).

Stern, Alexandra Minna. 2011. "From Legislation to Lived Experience: Eugenic Sterilization in California and Indiana, 1907–79." Pp. 95–116 in *A Century of Eugenics in America: From the Indiana Experiment to the Human Genome Era,* ed. Paul A. Lombardo. Bloomington, IN: Indiana University Press.

———. 2016. *Eugenic Nation: Faults and Frontiers of Better Breeding in Modern America,* 2nd ed. Oakland, CA: University of California Press.

Stevenson, Mark. 2011. "Money Sent Home by Mexican Migrants Holds Steady." *Chron,* February 1. Accessed June 13, 2011 (www.chron.com/disp/story.mpl/business/7408082.html).

Steverman, Ben. 2016. "Boomers Are Making Sure the Divorces Keep Coming." *Bloomberg,* June 17. Accessed November 23, 2016 (www.bloomberg.com/news/articles/2016-06-17/boomers-are-making-sure-the-divorces-keep-coming).

Stewart, Matthew. 2018. "The 9.9 Percent Is the New American Aristocracy, The Birth of a New American Aristocracy." *The Atlantic,* June 2018. www.theatlantic.com

Stewart, Quincy Thomas. 2006. "Reinvigorating Relative Deprivation: A New Measure for a Classic Concept." *Social Science Research* 35 (3): 779–802.

Stewart, Susan D. 2007. *Brave New Stepfamilies: Diverse Paths Toward Stepfamily Living.* Thousand Oaks, CA: Sage.

Stoeckel, Luke E., Lori S. Palley, Randy L. Gollub, Steven M. Niemi, and Anne Eden Evins. 2014. "Patterns of Brain Activation When Mothers View Their Own Child and Dog: An fMRI Study." *PLos*

ONE 9 (10): e107205. Accessed February 26, 2015 (http://journals.plos.org/plosone/article?id = 10.1371/journal.pone.0107205).

Stolzenberg, Ellen Bara, Kevin Eagan, Melissa C. Aragon, Natacha M. Cesar-Davis, Sidronio Jacobo, Victoria Couch, and Cecilia Rios-Aguilar. 2019. *The American Freshman: National Norms Fall 2017.* Los Angeles: Higher Education Research Institute, UCLA. Accessed April 8, 2019 (https://heri.ucla.edu/publications-tfs/).

Stone, Deborah M., Thomas R. Simon, Katherine A. Fowler, Scott R. Kegler, Keming Yuan, Dristin M. Holland, Asha Z. Ivey-Stephenson, and Alex E. Crosby. 2018. "Vital Signs: Trends in State Suicide Rates—United States, 1999–2016 and Circumstances Contributing to Suicide—27 States, 2015." *MMWR Morbidity and Mortality Weekly Report* 67: 617–624. Accessed October 30, 2018 (https://stacks.cdc.gov/view/cdc/55794).

Strassman, Beverly I. 1999. "Menstrual Synchrony Pheromones: Cause for Doubt." *Human Reproduction* 14 (3): 579–580.

Stratton, Terry D., and Jennifer L. McGivern-Snofsky. 2008. "Toward a Sociological Understanding of Complementary and Alternative Medicine Use." *Journal of Alternative and Complementary Medicine* 14 (6): 777–783.

Streib, Jessi. 2011. "Class Reproduction by Four-Year-Olds." *Qualitative Sociology* 34 (2): 337–352.

Strochlic, Nina. 2018. "An Artist Finds True Skin Colors in a Diverse Palette." *National Geographic,* April. Accessed July 26, 2018 (www.nationalgeographic.com/magazine/2018/04/race-pantone-color-angelica-dass-portrait-photography/).

Strogatz, Steven. 2012. "Friends You Can Count On." *The New York Times,* September 17. Accessed February 11, 2015 (http://opinionator.blogs.nytimes.com/2012/09/17/friends-you-can-count-on/).

Stuckert, Robert P. 1958. "African Ancestry of the White American Population." *The Ohio Journal of Science* 53(3): 155–160.

Stulberg, Lisa M., and Anthony S. Chen. 2014. "The Origins of Race-Conscious Affirmative Action in Undergraduate Admissions: A Comparative Analysis of Institutional Change in Higher Education." *Sociology of Education* 87(1): 36–52.

Suellentrop, Chris. 2016. "Who Says Games Need to Be Fair?" *Slate,* October 14. Accessed October 27, 2016 (www.slate.com/articles/technology/gaming/2016/10/really_bad_chess_proves_that_games_don_t_need_to_be_fair.html).

Sullivan, Kevin. 2006. "In War-Torn Congo, Going Wireless to Reach Home." *The Washington Post,* July 9. Accessed May 6, 2009 (www.washingtonpost.com/wp-dyn/content/article/2006/07/08/AR2006070801063.html).

Sumner, William G. 1906. *Folkways.* New York: Ginn.

Sun, Yongmin, and Yuanzhang Li. 2008. "Stable Postdivorce Family Structures During Late Adolescence and Socioeconomic Consequences in Adulthood." *Journal of Marriage and Family* 70 (1): 129–143.

Surowiecki, James. 2004. *The Wisdom of Crowds.* New York: Anchor Books.

Susen, Simon. 2015. *The 'Postmodern Turn' in the Social Sciences.* London: Palgrave Macmillan.

Susskind, Richard, and Daniel Susskind. 2015. *The Future of Professions: How Technology Will Transform the Work of Human Experts.* New York: Oxford University Press.

Sutherland, Edwin H. 1940. "White-Collar Criminality." *American Sociological Review* 5 (February): 1–11.

———. 1949. *White Collar Crime.* New York: Dryden.

———. 1983. *White Collar Crime: The Uncut Version.* New Haven, CT: Yale University Press.

Sutherland, Edwin H., Donald R. Cressey, and David F. Luckenbill. 1992. *Principles of Criminology,* 11th ed. New York: Rowman & Littlefield.

Suzuki, Toru. 2009. "Fertility Decline and Governmental Interventions in Eastern Asian Advanced Countries." *Japanese Journal of Population* 7 (1): 47–56.

Swatos, William H., Jr. 2011. "Encyclopedia of Religion and Society." Hartford Institute for Religion Research, Hartford Seminary, Hartford, Connecticut. Accessed June 6, 2011 (http://hirr.hartsem.edu/ency/).

Swatos, William H., Jr., ed. 1998. *Encyclopedia of Religion and Society.* Lanham, MD: AltaMira Press.

Sweet, Stephen, and Peter Meiksins. 2017. *Changing Contours of Work: Jobs and Opportunities in the New Economy,* 3rd ed. Thousand Oaks, CA: Sage Publications, Inc.

Sweig, Julia E. 2016. *Cuba: What Everyone Needs to Know.* New York: Oxford University Press.

Swidler, Ann. 1986. "Culture in Action: Symbols and Strategies." *American Sociological Review* 51 (April): 273–286.

Szasz, Thomas S. 1971. "The Same Slave: An Historical Note on the Use of Medical Diagnosis as Justificatory Rhetoric." *American Journal of Psychotherapy* 25 (April): 228–239.

T

Tafur, Maritza Montiel, Terry K. Crowe, and Eliseo Torres. 2009. "A Review of Curanderismo and Healing Practices Among Mexicans and Mexican Americans." *Occupational Therapy International* 16 (1): 82–88.

Tajfel, Henri. 1981. *Human Groups and Social Categories: Studies in Social Psychology.* Cambridge: Cambridge University Press.

Tajfel, Henri and John Turner. 1979. "An Integrative Theory of Intergroup Conflict." Pp. 33–47 in *The Social Psychology of Intergroup Relations,* ed. W. G. Austin, & S. Worchel. Monterey, CA: Brooks/Cole.

Talbot, Margaret. 2018. "The Extraordinary Inclusiveness of the March for Our Lives." *The New Yorker,* March 24. Accessed January 30, 2019 (www.newyorker.com/news/news-desk/the-extraordinary-inclusiveness-of-the-march-for-our-lives).

Tate, Charlotte Chuck, Jay N. Ledbetter, and Cris P. Youssef. 2013. "A Two-Question Method for Assessing Gender Categories in the Social and Medical Sciences." *Journal of Sex Research* 50(8): 767–776.

Tate, Charlotte Chuck, Cris P. Youssef, and Jay N. Bettergarcia. 2014. "Integrating the Study of Transgender Spectrum and Cisgender Experiences of Self-Categorization From a Personality Perspective." *Review of General Psychology* 18(4):302-312.

Tate, Shirley Anne. 2009. *Black Beauty: Aesthetics, Stylization, Politics.* Burlington, VT: Ashgate.

Tattersall, Ian, and Rob DeSalle. 2011. *Race?: Debunking a Scientific Myth.* College Station: Texas A&M University Press.

Tatum, Beverly Daniel. 2017. *Why Are All the Black Kids Sitting Together in the Cafeteria?: And Other Conversations about Race.* New York: Basic Books.

Taylor, Frederick Winslow. 1911. *The Principles of Scientific Management.* New York: Harper & Brothers.

Taylor, Jonathan B., and Joseph P. Kalt. 2005. *American Indians on Reservations: A Data Book of Socioeconomic Change Between the 1990 and 2000 Censuses.* Cambridge, MA: Harvard Project on American Indian Development.

Taylor, Paul, Rich Morin, Kim Parker, D'Vera Cohn, and Wendy Wang. 2009. *Growing Old in America: Expectations vs. Reality.* Pew Research Center Social & Demographic Trends Project, January. Accessed April 5, 2010 (http://pewsocialtrends.org/assets/pdf/Getting-Old-in-America.pdf).

Taylor, Verta. 1999. "Gender and Social Movements: Gender Processes in Womens Self-Help Movements." *Gender and Society* 13: 8–33.

———. 2004. "Social Movements and Gender." Pp. 14348–14352 in *International Encyclopedia of the Social and Behavioral Sciences,* ed. Neil J. Smelser and Paul B. Baltes. New York: Elsevier.

Tejada-Vera, Betzaida, and Paul D. Sutton. 2010. "Births, Marriages, Divorces, and Deaths: Provisional Data for 2009." *National Vital Statistics Reports* 58 (25). Hyattsville, MD: National Center for Health Statistics. Accessed May 28, 2011 (www.cdc.gov/nchs/data/nvsr/nvsr58/nvsr58_25.pdf).

Terkel, Studs. 2003. *Hope Dies Last: Keeping the Faith in Difficult Times.* New York: New Press.

Tertilt, Michèle. 2005. "Polygyny, Fertility, and Savings." *Journal of Political Economy* 113 (6): 1341–1370.

Thomas, Gordon, and Max Morgan-Witts. 2010. *Voyage of the Damned: A Shocking True Story of Hope, Betrayal, and Nazi Terror.* New York: Skyhorse Publishing.

Thomas, William I., and Dorothy Swain Thomas. 1928. *The Child in America: Behavior Problems and Programs.* New York: Knopf.

Thompson, Derek. 2018. "American Meritocracy Is Killing Youth Sports." *The Atlantic* November 6. Accessed January 13, 2019 (www.theatlantic.com/ideas/archive/2018/11/income-inequality-explains-decline-youth-sports/574975/).

Thompson, Warren S. 1929. "Population." *American Journal of Sociology* 34 (6): 959–975.

———. 1948. *Plenty of People: The World's Population Pressures, Problems and Policies and How They Concern Us,* rev. ed. New York: Ronald Press.

Thomson, Elizabeth, and Eva Bernhardt. 2010. "Education, Values, and Cohabitation in Sweden." *Marriage & Family Review* 46 (1/2): 1–21.

Thornton, John. 1998. "The African Experience of the 20. and Odd Negroes Arriving in Virginia in 1619." *The William and Mary Quarterly* 55: 421–434.

Tierney, John. 2003. "Iraqi Family Ties Complicate American Efforts for Change." *The New York Times,* September 28, pp. A1, A22.

Tilley, Cristen. 2018. "Book Week: Analysis of Bestsellers Suggests Kids' Bookshelves Are on a Lean." Australian Broadcasting Corporation News August 21. Accessed January 23, 2019 (www.abc.net.au/news/2018-08-22/kids-book-top-100-analysis/10042904).

Tilly, Charles. 1993. *Popular Contention in Great Britain 1758-1834.* Cambridge, MA: Harvard University Press.

———. 2004. *Social Movements, 1768-2004.* Boulder, CO: Paradigm.

Timmerman, Kelsey. 2012. *Where Am I Wearing?: A Global Tour of the Countries, Factories, and People That Make Our Clothes,* 2nd ed. Hoboken, NJ: John Wiley & Sons, Inc.

Titlow, John Paul. 2016. "How to Get a Match, According to Tinder's Sociologist." *Fast Company* August 3. Accessed November 19, 2016 (www.fastcompany.com/3062454/how-to-get-a-match-according-to-tinders-sociologist).

Tolbert, Kathryn. 2000. "In Japan, Traveling Alone Begins at Age 6." *The Washington Post National Weekly Edition* 17, May 15, p. 17.

Tonkinson, Robert. 1978. *The Mardudjara Aborigines.* New York: Henry Holt.

Tönnies, Ferdinand. [1887] 1988. *Community and Society.* New Brunswick, NJ: Transaction.

Toossi, Mitra. 2004. "Labor Force Projections to 2012: The Graying of the U.S. Workforce." *Monthly Labor Review,* February: 37–57.

———. 2015. "Labor Force Projections to 2024: The Labor Force Is Growing, But Slowly." *Monthly Labor Review,* Bureau of Labor Statistics, U.S. Department of Labor, December. Accessed October 25, 2016 (www.bls.gov/opub/mlr/2015/article/labor-force-projections-to-2024.htm).

Torgler, Benno, and Christoph Schaltegger. 2014. "Suicide and Religion: New Evidence on the Differences Between Protestantism and Catholicism." *Journal for the Scientific Study of Religion* 53(2): 316–340.

Torres, Jose. 2015. "Race/Ethnicity and Stop-and-Frisk: Past, Present, Future." *Sociology Compass* 9(11): 931–939.

Tully, Shawn. 2012. "The 2011 Fortune 500: The Big Boys Rack Up Record-Setting Profits." *CNNMoney,* May 7. Accessed May 22, 2012 (www.dailyfinance.com/2012/05/07/the-2011-fortune-500-the-big-boys-rack-up-record-setting-profit/).

Ture, Kwame, and Charles Hamilton. 1992. *Black Power: The Politics of Liberation,* rev. ed. New York: Vintage Books.

Turner, Ani. 2013. "The Business Case for Racial Equity." Altarum Institute and W.K. Kellogg Foundation, October. Accessed February 4, 2017 (http://altarum.org/sites/default/files/uploaded-publication-files/The%20Business%20Case%20for%20Racial%20Equity%20FINAL.pdf).

Turner, Ralph H. and Lewis M. Killian. 1957. *Collective Behavior.* Englewood Cliffs, NJ: Prentice-Hall.

Tuttle, Hudson. 1866. *The Origin and Antiquity of Physical Man Scientifically Considered.* Boston: William White & Company.

Twain, Mark. 1909. *The Complete Works of Mark Twain [pseud.] Mark Twains Notebook.* New York: Harper & Bros.

Twitchell, James B. 2000. "The Stone Age." pp. 44–48 in *Do Americans Shop Too Much?*, ed. Juliet Schor. Boston: Beacon Press.

Tyson, Alec. 2018. "The 2018 Midterm Vote: Divisions by Race, Gender, Education." Pew Research Center November 8. Accessed January 8, 2019 (www.pewresearch.org/fact-tank/2018/11/08/the-2018-midterm-vote-divisions-by-race-gender-education/).

Tyson, Gareth, Vasile C. Perta, Hamed Haddadi, and Michael C. Seto. 2016. "A First Look at User Activity on Tinder." *arXiv* 1607.01952. Accessed November 18, 2016 (https://arxiv.org/abs/1607.01952).

Tyson, Neil de Grasse. 2016. Twitter. February 5, 2016.

U

Ullah, Faiz, and Shilpa Phadke. 2016. "How the Deonar Garbage-Dump Fire Exposed the Self-Centredness of Mumbai's Elite." *Scroll.In*, February 5. Accessed January 16, 2017 (http://scroll.in/a/803040).

UNAIDS. 2018a. *Global AIDS Update 2018: Miles to Go*. Geneva: Joint United Nations Programme on HIV/AIDS. Accessed January 26, 2019 (www.unaids.org/sites/default/files/media_asset/miles-to-go_en.pdf).

_____. 2018b. *UNAIDS Data 2018*. Geneva: Joint United Nations Programme on HIV/AIDS. Accessed January 26, 2019 (www.unaids.org/sites/default/files/media_asset/unaids-data-2018_en.pdf).

UNESCO. 1950. *The Race Question*. Publication 791. Accessed August 26, 2018 (http://unesdoc.unesco.org/images/0012/001282/128291eo.pdf).

United Nations. 1999. "The World at Six Billion." Population Division, Department of Economic and Social Affairs, United Nations Secretariat, October. Accessed June 28, 2011 (www.un.org/esa/population/publications/sixbillion/sixbillion.htm).

_____. 2000. "United Nations Millennium Declaration." United Nations General Assembly, A/RES/55/2, September 8. Accessed January 20, 2017 (www.un.org/millennium/declaration/ares552e.htm/).

_____. 2014a. *The Millennium Development Goals Report 2014*. New York: United Nations. Accessed April 14, 2015 (www.un.org/millenniumgoals/2014%20MDG%20report/MDG%202014%20English%20web.pdf).

_____. 2015a. *World Marriage Data 2015. Department of Economic and Social Affairs*. Accessed November 21, 2016 (www.un.org/en/development/desa/population/theme/marriage-unions/WMD2015.shtml).

_____. 2016b. International Migration Report 2015. Department of Economic and Social Affairs, Population Division, September. Accessed February 6, 2017 (www.un.org/en/development/desa/population/migration/publications/migrationreport/docs/MigrationReport2015.pdf).

_____. 2016c. "Summary of the Paris Agreement." Climate: Get the Big Picture. Framework Convention on Climate Change. Accessed February 13, 2017 (http://bigpicture.unfccc.int/#content-the-paris-agreemen).

_____. 2016d. "Total Population—Both Sexes." *World Population Prospects: The 2017*. Department of Economic and Social Affairs, Population Division. Accessed July 17, 2017 (https://esa.un.org/unpd/wpp/Download/Standard/Population/).

_____. 2017a. *International Migration Report 2017*. Department of Economic and Social Affairs, Population Division, December. Accessed October 10, 2018 (www.un.org/en/development/desa/population/migration/publications/migrationreport/docs/MigrationReport2017.pdf).

_____. 2017b. "Net Number of Migrants: 1950–2100." *World Population Prospect: The 2017 Revision*. Department of Economic and Social Affairs, Population Division. Accessed January 25, 2019 (https://esa.un.org/unpd/wpp/Download/Standard/Migration/).

_____. 2017c. "Annual Rate of Population Change: 1950–2100." *World Population Prospect: The 2017 Revision*. Department of Economic and Social Affairs, Population Division. Accessed January 25, 2019 (https://esa.un.org/unpd/wpp/Download/Standard/Population/).

_____. 2017d. "Total Population - Both Sexes: 1950–2100." *World Population Prospect: The 2017 Revision*. Department of Economic

and Social Affairs, Population Division. Accessed January 25, 2019 (https://esa.un.org/unpd/wpp/Download/Standard/Population/).

_____. 2017e. "Population by Age Groups." *World Population Prospect: The 2017 Revision*. Department of Economic and Social Affairs, Population Division. Accessed January 25, 2019 (https://esa.un.org/unpd/wpp/Download/Standard/Population/).

_____. 2018a. "Estimates and Projections of Family Planning Indicators 2018." Department of Economic and Social Affairs, Population Division. Accessed January 25, 2019 (www.un.org/en/development/desa/population/theme/family-planning/cp_model.shtml).

_____. 2018b. "Contemporary Forms of Slavery, Including Its Causes and Consequences." United Nations General Assembly, 73rd Session, July 10. Accessed June 4, 2019 (www.un.org/en/ga/search/view_doc.asp?symbol=A/73/139).

United Nations Development Programme. 2000. *Poverty Report 2000: Overcoming Human Poverty*. Washington, DC: UNDP.

_____. 2018. *Human Development Indices and Indicators: 2018 Statistical Update*. New York: The United Nations Development Programme. Accessed January 16, 2019 (www.hdr.undp.org/sites/default/files/2018_human_development_statistical_update.pdf).

United Nations Environment Programme. 2014. "Air Pollution: World's Worst Environmental Health Risk." Pp. 42–47 in *UNEP Year Book 2014: Emerging Issues in Our Environment*. Nairobi: UNEP Division of Early Warning and Assessment. Accessed February 13, 2017 (www.unep.org/yearbook/2014/PDF/UNEP_YearBook_2014.pdf).

_____. 2018. *Air Pollution in Asia and the Pacific: Science Based Solutions*. Accessed January 26, 2019 (http://ccacoalition.org/en/file/5688/download?token=uZkCuXot).

United Nations Framework Convention on Climate Change. 2015a. "Kyoto Protocol." Accessed May 3, 2015 (http://unfccc.int/kyoto_protocol/items/2830.php).

_____. 2015b. "Status of Ratification of the Kyoto Protocol." Accessed May 3, 2015 (http://unfccc.int/kyoto_protocol/status_of_ratification/items/2613.php).

United Nations High Commission for Refugees. 2018. "Syria Regional Refugee Response." Information Sharing Portal hosted by UNHCR, September 24. Accessed September 29, 2018 (http://data.unhcr.org/syrianrefugees/regional.php).

UN News Service. 2010. "Darfur: Security Council Warned of Significant Challenges to Peace Process." UN News Centre, May 20. Accessed May 28, 2010 (www.un.org/apps/news/story.asp?NewsID534761&Cr5&Crl5).

United States Climate Alliance. 2018. *"Fighting for Our Future: 2018 Annual Report."* Accessed January 26, 2019 (www.usclimatealliance.org/annual-report/).

United States Sentencing Commission. 2016. *Guidelines Manual*. November. Accessed November 10, 2016 (www.ussc.gov/sites/default/files/pdf/guidelines-manual/2016/GLMFull.pdf).

UNODC. 2014. *Global Study on Homicide 2013: Trends, Contexts, Data*. United Nations Office on Drugs and Crime, 14.IV.1. Accessed February 19, 2015 (www.unodc.org/documents/gsh/pdfs/2014_GLOBAL_HOMICIDE_BOOK_web.pdf).

_____. 2018a. "Transnational Organized Crime." United Nations Office on Drugs and Crime. Accessed December 4, 2018 (http://www.unodc.org/toc/).

_____. 2018b. "Crime and Criminal Justice Statistics: Statistics on Crime." United Nations Office on Drugs and Crime. Accessed November 15, 2016 (www.unodc.org/unodc/en/data-and-analysis/crime-and-criminal-justice.html).

UNOG. 2018. "Remarks by the Secretary-General to the Pledging Conference on Yemen." The United Nations Office at Geneva, April 3. Accessed January 22, 2019 (www.unog.ch/unog/website/news_media.nsf/(httpNewsByYear_en)/27F6CCAD7178F3E9C1258264003311FA).

U.S. Census Bureau. 1975. *Historical Statistics of the United States, Colonial Times to 1970*. Washington, DC: U.S. Government Printing Office.

_____. 2010a. "Historical Income Tables—Households." Accessed June 9, 2011 (www.census.gov/hhes/www/income/data/historical/household/index.html).

_____. 2010c. "The Questions on the Form." Accessed May 16, 2010 (http://2010.census.gov/2010census/pdf/2010_Questionnaire_Info.pdf).

_____. 2012. "Selected Population Profile in the United States—2011 American Community Survey 1-Year Estimates." American FactFinder. Accessed June 6, 2013 (http://factfinder2.census.gov/faces/nav/jsf/pages/searchresults.xhtml).

_____. 2013a. "Services (Main)." Accessed March 17, 2015 (www.census.gov/econ/services.html).

_____. 2013b. "Detailed Tables on Wealth and Asset Ownership: 2011." Accessed June 3, 2013 (www.census.gov/people/wealth/data/dtables.html).

_____. 2015b. "American Community Survey 5-Year Estimates: 2010–2014." American FactFinder. Accessed December 2, 2016 (http://factfinder.census.gov/faces/nav/jsf/pages/searchresults.xhtml).

_____. 2016a. "Current Population Survey Tables for Personal Income." Washington, DC: U.S. Census Bureau. Accessed September 22, 2016 (www.census.gov/data/tables/time-series/demo/income-poverty/cps-pinc.html).

_____. 2016g. "Families and Living Arrangements: Children." Washington, DC: U.S. Census Bureau. Accessed November 22, 2016 (www.census.gov/hhes/families/data/cps2016C.html).

_____. 2016l. "American Indian and Alaska Native Heritage Month: November 2016." Profile America Facts for Features, CB16-FF.22, November 2. Accessed February 6, 2017 (www.census.gov/newsroom/facts-for-features/2016/cb16-ff22.html).

_____. 2017a. "World Vital Events per Time Unit: 2017." World Vital Events, International Data Base. Accessed February 8, 2017 (www.census.gov/population/international/data/idb/worldvitalevents.php).

_____. 2017b. "Voting in America: A Look at the 2016 Presidential Election." Random Samplings, Census Blogs, May 10. Accessed June 2, 2017 (www.census.gov/newsroom/blogs/random-samplings/2017/05/voting_in_america.html).

_____. 2017c. "Industry and Occupation: Occupation." Accessed November 27, 2018 (www.census.gov/topics/employment/industry-occupation/about/occupation.html).

_____. 2017d. "Voting and Registration in the Election of November 2016." Accessed January 8, 2019 (www.census.gov/data/tables/time-series/demo/voting-and-registration/p20-580.html).

_____. 2018a. "American Community Survey 1-Year Estimates: 2017." American FactFinder. Accessed October 6, 2018 (http://factfinder.census.gov/faces/nav/jsf/pages/searchresults.xhtml).

_____. 2018b. "Current Population Survey Tables for Personal Income." Washington, DC: U.S. Census Bureau. Accessed November 10, 2018 (www.census.gov/data/tables/time-series/demo/income-poverty/cps-pinc.html).

_____. 2018c. "Historical Poverty Tables: People and Families—1959 to 2017." Poverty Data Tables. Accessed November 20, 2018 (www.census.gov/data/tables/time-series/demo/income-poverty/historical-poverty-people.html).

_____. 2018d. "Historical Household Tables." Washington, DC: U.S. Census Bureau. Accessed December 14, 2018 (www.census.gov/data/tables/time-series/demo/families/households.html).

_____. 2018e. "Historical Family Tables." Washington, DC: U.S. Census Bureau. Accessed December 14, 2018 (www.census.gov/data/tables/time-series/demo/families/families.html).

_____. 2018f. "Historical Marital Status Tables." Washington, DC: U.S. Census Bureau. Accessed December 14, 2018 (www.census.gov/data/tables/time-series/demo/families/marital.html).

_____. 2018g. "America's Families and Living Arrangements: 2018." Washington, DC: U.S. Census Bureau. Accessed December 14, 2018 (www.census.gov/data/tables/2018/demo/families/cps-2018.html).

_____. 2018h. "Historical Living Arrangements of Children." Washington, DC: U.S. Census Bureau. Accessed December 14, 2018 (www.census.gov/data/tables/time-series/demo/families/children.html).

_____. 2018i. "Historical Living Arrangements of Adults." Washington, DC: U.S. Census Bureau. Accessed December 16, 2018 (www.census.gov/data/tables/time-series/demo/families/adults.html).

_____. 2018j. "Fertility of Women in the United States: 2016." Washington, DC: U.S. Census Bureau. Accessed December 16, 2018 (www.census.gov/data/tables/2016/demo/fertility/women-fertility.html).

_____. 2019a. "U.S. and World Population Clock." Accessed January 25, 2019 (www.census.gov/popclock/).

U.S. Commission on Civil Rights. 1976. _A Guide to Federal Laws and Regulations Prohibiting Sex Discrimination._ Washington, DC: U.S. Government Printing Office.

_____. 2009. "Racial Categorization in the 2010 Census: A Briefing Before the United States Commission on Civil Rights Held in Washington, DC, April 7, 2006." Briefing Report. Accessed May 16, 2010 (www.usccr.gov/pubs/RC2010Web_Version.pdf).

U.S. Copyright Office. 2016. "Fiscal 2015 Annual Report." Library of Congress, Washington, D.C. Accessed February 14, 2017 (www.copyright.gov/reports/annual/2015/ar2015.pdf).

U.S. Customs Border and Border Protection. 2016a. "United States Border Patrol: Southwest Border Sectors—Southwest Border Deaths by Fiscal Year (Oct. 1st through Sept. 30th)." Accessed January 20, 2017 (www.cbp.gov/sites/default/files/assets/documents/2016-Oct/BP%20Southwest%20Border%20Sector%20Deaths%20FY1998%20-%20FY2016.pdf).

_____. 2018a. "United States Border Patrol: Apprehensions by Sector FY2018." Department of Homeland Security. Accessed January 22, 2019 (www.cbp.gov/newsroom/stats/usbp-sw-border-apprehensions).

_____. 2018b. "United States Border Patrol Nationwide Apprehensions by Citizenship and Sector." Department of Homeland Security. Accessed January 22, 2019 (www.cbp.gov/sites/default/files/assets/documents/2018-Jul/usbp-nationwide-apps-sector-citizenship-fy07-fy17.pdf).

_____. 2018c. "United States Border Patrol: Southwest Border Deaths by Fiscal Year." Department of Homeland Security. Accessed January 22, 2019 (www.cbp.gov/newsroom/stats/usbp-sw-border-apprehensions).

U.S. Department of Agriculture. 2018. "Real Per Capita GDP (2010 Dollars) Historical." International Macroeconomic Data Set, Economic Research Service, Washington, D.C. Accessed December January 5, 2019 (http://ers.usda.gov/data-products/international-macroeconomic-data-set.aspx).

U.S. Department of Education. 2015. "List of 2014 Digest Tables." Washington, DC: Institute of Education Services, U.S. Department of Education. Accessed March 10, 2015 (http://nces.ed.gov/programs/digest/2014menu_tables.asp).

_____. 2016. "Most Current Digest Tables." _Digest of Education Statistics._ Washington, DC: Institute of Education Services, U.S. Department of Education. Accessed July 17, 2017(https://nces.ed.gov/programs/digest/current_tables.asp).

U.S. Department of Education. 1972. "Title IX and Sex Discrimination," Title IX of the Education Amendments of 1972, Office for Civil Rights.

U.S. Department of Health and Human Services. 2016. "The AFCARS Report." Administration for Children and Families, Administration on Children, Youth and Families, Children's Bureau, June, No. 23. Accessed November 22, 2016 (www.acf.hhs.gov/cb/research-data-technology/statistics-research/afcars).

U.S. Department of Homeland Security. 2016. _Yearbook of Immigration Statistics: 2015._ Washington, DC: Office of Immigration Statistics. Accessed January 20, 2017 (www.dhs.gov/immigration-statistics/yearbook).

_____. 2017. _Yearbook of Immigration Statistics: 2016._ Washington, DC: Office of Immigration Statistics. Accessed January 25, 2019 (www.dhs.gov/immigration-statistics/yearbook).

_____. 2018. *Yearbook of Immigration Statistics: 2017.* Washington, DC: Office of Immigration Statistics. Accessed October 11, 2018 (www.dhs.gov/immigration-statistics/yearbook).

U.S. Department of Justice. 1999. "Ten-Year Program to Compensate Japanese Americans Interned During World War II Closes Its Doors." Press release No. 059, February 19. Accessed June 3, 2010 (www.justice.gov/opa/pr/1999/February/059cr.htm).

_____. 2015a. "Justice Department Announces Findings of Two Civil Rights Investigations in Ferguson, Missouri." Office of Public Affairs, March 4. Accessed April 26, 2015 (www.justice.gov/opa/pr/justice-department-announces-findings-two-civil-rights-investigations-ferguson-missouri).

_____. 2015b. "Investigation of the Ferguson Police Department." Civil Rights Division, March 4. Accessed April 27, 2015 (www.justice.gov/sites/default/files/opa/press-releases/attachments/2015/03/04/ferguson_police_department_report.pdf).

_____. 2016d. "Hate Crime Statistics 2015." *Crime in the United States, 2015.* Washington, DC: U.S. Department of Justice, Federal Bureau of Investigation. Accessed January 31, 2017 (https://ucr.fbi.gov/hate-crime/2015).

_____. 2017a. "Hate Crime Statistics 2016." *Crime in the United States, 2016.* Washington, DC: U.S. Department of Justice, Federal Bureau of Investigation. Accessed September 16, 2018 (https://ucr.fbi.gov/hate-crime/2016).

_____. 2018a. "Offenses Known to Law Enforcement." *Crime in the United States, 2017.* Washington, DC: U.S. Department of Justice, Federal Bureau of Investigation. Accessed December 4, 2018 (https://ucr.fbi.gov/crime-in-the-u.s/2017/crime-in-the-u.s.-2017/topic-pages/offenses-known-to-law-enforcement).

_____. 2018b. "2017 Crime Clock Statistics." *Crime in the United States, 2016.* Washington, DC: U.S. Department of Justice, Federal Bureau of Investigation. Accessed December 4, 2018 (https://ucr.fbi.gov/crime-in-the-u.s/2017/crime-in-the-u.s.-2017/topic-pages/crime-clock).

_____. 2018c. "Persons Arrested." *Crime in the United States, 2017.* Washington, DC: U.S. Department of Justice, Federal Bureau of Investigation. Accessed December 4, 2018 (https://ucr.fbi.gov/crime-in-the-u.s/2017/crime-in-the-u.s.-2017/topic-pages/persons-arrested).

_____. 2018d. "Expanded Homicide." *Crime in the United States, 2017.* Washington, DC: U.S. Department of Justice, Federal Bureau of Investigation. Accessed January 25, 2019 (https://ucr.fbi.gov/crime-in-the-u.s/2017/crime-in-the-u.s.-2017/topic-pages/expanded-homicide).

U.S. Department of State. 2018a. "FY 2017 Annual Report on Inter-country Adoption." U.S. Department of State, Washington, DC. Accessed December 15, 2018 (https://travel.state.gov/content/adoptionsabroad/en/about-us/publications.html).

U.S. Department of State. 2018b. *Trafficking in Persons Report: June 2018.* Washington, DC. Accessed January 22, 2019 (www.state.gov/j/tip/rls/tiprpt/).

The U.S. National Archives and Records Administration. 1776. *Declaration of Independence: A Transcription, The unanimous declaration of the thirteen united States of America.* July 4, 1776.

U.S. Patent and Trademark Office. 2016. "U.S. Patent Statistics Chart: Calendar Years 1963–2015." Patent Technology Monitoring Team. Accessed February 14, 2017 (www.uspto.gov/web/offices/ac/ido/oeip/taf/us_stat.htm).

V

Valtin, Heinz. 2002. "'Drink at Least Eight Glasses of Water a Day.' Really? Is There Scientific Evidence for '8 x 8.'" *American Journal of Physiology—Regulatory, Integrative and Comparative Physiology* 283 (5): R993–R1004

Van Dam, Andrew. 2018. "It's Better to Be Born Rich than Gifted." *The Washington Post,* October 9. Accessed January 13, 2019 (www.washingtonpost.com/business/2018/10/09/its-better-be-born-rich-than-talented/).

van den Bergh, Linda, Eddie Denessen, Lisette Hornstra, Marinus Voeten, and Rob W. Holland. 2010. "The Implicit Prejudiced Attitudes of Teachers: Relations to Teacher Expectations and the Ethnic Achievement Gap." *American Educational Research Journal,* January. doi: 10.3102/0002831209353594.

_____. 2017. "All Oscar Nominees Are Available on Pirate Sites." TorrentFreak, February 25. Accessed May 25, 2017 (https://torrentfreak.com/all-oscar-nominees-are-available-on-pirate-sites-170225/).

Vanderstraeten, Raf. 2007. "Professions in Organizations, Professional Work in Education." *British Journal of Sociology of Education* 28 (5): 621–635.

Veblen, Thorstein. [1899] 1964. *Theory of the Leisure Class.* New York: Macmillan.

_____. 1919. *The Vested Interests and the State of the Industrial Arts.* New York: Huebsch.

Venkatesh, Sudhir. 2006. *Off the Books: The Underground Economy of the Urban Poor.* Cambridge, MA: Harvard University Press.

Venter, Craig. 2000. "Remarks at the Human Genome Announcement, at the White House." Accessed June 30, 2008 (www.celera.com/celera/pr_1056647999).

Ventriglio, Antonio, Oyedeji Ayonrinde, and Dinesh Bhugra. 2016. "Relevance of Culture-Bound Syndromes in the 21st Century." *Psychiatry and Clinical Neurosciences* 79: 3–6.

Vespa, Jonathan. 2017. "The Changing Economics and Demographics of Young Adulthood: 1975–2016." *Current Population Reports* April P20-579. Accessed December 17, 2018 (www.census.gov/content/dam/Census/library/publications/2017/demo/p20-579.pdf).

Vigo, Julian. 2019. "The Ecological and Human Rights Impacts of New Technology." *Forbes,* January 12. Accessed January 20, 2019 (www.forbes.com/sites/julianvigo/2019/01/12/the-ecological-and-human-rights-impacts-of-new-technology/).

Vitto, Laura. 2017. "Tinder's In-House Sociologist Explains How to Score a Date for Valentine's Day." *Mashable,* February 10. Accessed December 13, 2018 (https://mashable.com/2017/02/10/tinder-sociologist-profile-tips/#tO9uSuZWYkqP).

Volokh, Eugene. 2015. "Prof. Alice Goffman, 'On the Run,' and Driving a Gang Member Around, Looking for a Mutual Friend's Killer." *The Washington Post,* June 2. Accessed April 1, 2019 (www.washingtonpost.com/news/volokh-conspiracy/wp/2015/06/02/prof-alice-goffman-on-the-run-and-driving-a-gang-member-around-looking-for-a-mutual-friends-killer/).

Vowell, Paul R., and Jieming Chen. 2004. "Predicting Academic Misconduct: A Comparative Test of Four Sociological Explanations." *Sociological Inquiry* 74 (2): 226–249.

W

Wakefield, Sara, and Christopher Uggen. 2010. "Incarceration and Stratification." *Annual Review of Sociology* 36: 387–406.

Walker, Iain, and Heather J. Smith, eds. 2002. *Relative Deprivation: Specification, Development, and Integration.* New York: Cambridge University Press.

Walker, Rebecca. 1995. *To Be Real: Telling the Truth and Changing the Face of Feminism.* Berkeley: University of California Press.

Wallenstein, Peter. 2014. *Race, Sex, and the Freedom to Marry: Loving v. Virginia.* Lawrence, KS: The University Press of Kansas.

Wallerstein, Immanuel. 1974. *The Modern World System.* New York: Academic Press.

_____. 1979. *The End of the World as We Know It: Social Science for the Twenty-first Century.* Minneapolis: University of Minnesota Press.

_____. 2000. *The Essential Wallerstein.* New York: New Press.

_____. 2004. *World-Systems Analysis: An Introduction.* Durham, NC: Duke University Press.

_____. 2010. "Structural Crises." *New Left Review* 62 (March/April): 133–142.

Wallerstein, Judith S., Julia M. Lewis, and Sandra Blakeslee. 2000. *The Unexpected Legacy of Divorce: A 25-Year Landmark Study.* New York: Basic Books.

Wallis, Claudia. 2008. "How to Make Great Teachers." *Time,* February 25, pp. 28–34.

Walmart. 2016. "Only Walmart: 2016 Annual Report." Bentonville, AR: Wal-Mart Stores, Inc. Accessed December 15, 2016 (http://s2.q4cdn.com/056532643/files/doc_financials/2016/annual/2016-Annual-Report-PDF.pdf).

Walsh, Flora. 2016a. "Part I: The Politics of Pink." *Varsity* October 28. Accessed January 30, 2017 (www.varsity.co.uk/fashion/11099).

———. 2016b. "Part II: The Sociology of Pink." *Varsity* November 15. Accessed January 30, 2017 (www.varsity.co.uk/fashion/11290).

Walsh, Froma. 2009a. "Human Animal Bonds I: The Relational Significance of Companion Animals." *Family Process* 48: 462–480.

———. 2009b. "Human Animal Bonds II: The Role of Pets in Family Systems and Family Therapy." *Family Process* 48: 481–499.

Wang, Wendy. 2012. "The Rise of Intermarriage: Rates, Characteristics Vary by Race and Gender." A Social & Demographic Trends Report, Pew Research Center, February 16. Accessed May 8, 2012 (www.pewsocialtrends.org/files/2012/02/SDT-Intermarriage-II.pdf).

Wang, Wendy, and Kim Parker. 2014. "Record Share of Americans Have Never Married." Pew Research Center, Social & Demographic Trends, November 20. Accessed February 26, 2015 (www.pewsocialtrends.org/files/2014/09/2014-09-24_Never-Married-Americans.pdf).

Ward, Audrey. 2016. "A Life in the Day of Nita Ambani." *The Times,* August 21. Accessed January 14, 2017 (www.thetimes.co.uk/article/a-life-in-the-day-of-nita-ambani-bq0cr2wf0).

Ward, Brian W., Tainya C. Clark, Colleen N. Nugent, and Jeannine S. Schiller. 2016. "Early Release of Selected Estimates Based on Data from the 2015 National Health Interview Survey." National Center for Health Statistics, May. Accessed February 12, 2017 (www.cdc.gov/nchs/data/nhis/earlyrelease/earlyrelease201605.pdf).

Ward, Jane. 2015. *Not Gay: Sex between Straight White Men.* New York: New York University Press.

Warner, Michael. 1993. *Fear of a Queer Planet: Queer Politics and Social Theory.* Minneapolis, MN: University of Minnesota Press.

Warner, R. Stephen. 2005. *A Church of Our Own: Disestablishment and Diversity in American Religion.* New Brunswick, NJ: Rutgers University Press.

———. 2007. "The Role of Religion in the Process of Segmented Assimilation." *Annals of the American Academy of Political and Social Science* 612 (1): 100–115.

Warner, W. Lloyd, and Paul S. Lunt. 1941. *The Social Life of a Modern Community.* Volume I, Yankee City Series. New Haven, CT: Yale University Press.

Warren, Patricia, Donald Tomaskovic-Devey, William Smith, Matthew Zingraff, and Marcinda Mason. 2006. "Driving While Black: Bias Processes and Racial Disparity in Police Stops." *Criminology* 44 (3): 709–738.

Wasike, Ben. 2017. "Jocks versus Jockettes: An Analysis of the Visual Portrayal of Male and Female Cover Models on Sports Magazines." *Journalism* (https://journals.sagepub.com/doi.org/10.1177/1464884917716818).

Wasserman, David. 2016. "2016 National Popular Vote Tracker." *The Cook Political Report,* December 7. Accessed December 14, 2016 (http://cookpolitical.com/story/10174).

———. 2019. "2018 National Popular Vote Tracker." *The Cook Political Report,* January 10. Accessed June 6, 2019 (https://cookpolitical.com/analysis/house/house-charts/2018-house-popular-vote-tracker).

Watercutter, Angela. 2017. "*Wonder Woman* and the Importance of the Female Hero Moment." *Wired,* June 6. Accessed January 23, 2019 (www.wired.com/2017/06/wonder-woman-hero-moment/).

Waters, Mary C. 1990. *Ethnic Options: Choosing Identities in America.* Berkeley, CA: University of California Press.

———. 2009. "Social Science and Ethnic Options." *Ethnicities* 9 (1): 130–135.

Watters, Ethan. 2010a. *Crazy Like Us: The Globalization of the American Psyche.* New York: Free Press.

———. 2010b. "The Americanization of Mental Illness." *The New York Times Magazine,* January 8. Accessed February 10, 2017 (www.nytimes.com/2010/01/10/magazine/10psyche-t.html).

Watts, Duncan J. 2007. "Is Justin Timberlake a Product of Cumulative Advantage?" *The New York Times,* April 15. Accessed February 2, 2015 (www.nytimes.com/2007/04/15/magazine/15wwlnidealab.t.html).

———. 2011. *Everything Is Obvious: Once You Know the Answer.* New York: Crown Business.

Weber, Jonetta D., and Robert M. Carini. 2013. "Where Are the Female Athletes in *Sports Illustrated?* A Content Analysis of Covers (2000–2011)." *International Review for the Sociology of Sport* 48 (2): 196–203.

Weber, Max. [1913–1922] 1947. *The Theory of Social and Economic Organization,* trans. A. Henderson and T. Parsons. New York: Free Press.

———. [1904] 1949. *Methodology of the Social Sciences,* trans. Edward A. Shils and Henry A. Finch. Glencoe, IL: Free Press.

———. [1904] 2009. *The Protestant Ethic and the Spirit of Capitalism,* trans. Talcott Parsons. New York: Scribner.

———. [1916] 1958a. "Class, Status, Party." Pp. 180–195 in *From Max Weber: Essays in Sociology,* ed. H. H. Gerth and C. Wright Mills. New York: Oxford University Press.

———. [1916] 1958b. *The Religion of India: The Sociology of Hinduism and Buddhism.* New York: Free Press.

———. [1921] 1958c. "Bureaucracy." Pp. 196–244 in *From Max Weber: Essays in Sociology,* ed. H. H. Gerth and C. Wright Mills. New York: Oxford University Press.

———. [1922] 1958d. "The Social Psychology of the World Religions." Pp. 267–301 in *From Max Weber: Essays in Sociology,* ed. H. H. Gerth and C. Wright Mills. New York: Oxford University Press.

Wedge, Marilyn. 2012. "Why French Kids Don't Have ADHD." *Psychology Today,* March 8. Accessed June 7, 2013 (www.psychologytoday.com/blog/suffer-the-children/201203/why-french-kids-dont-have-adhd).

Weiss, Kenneth M., and Stephanie M. Fullerton. 2005. "Racing Around, Getting Nowhere." *Evolutionary Anthropology* 14: 165–169.

Weiss, Richard. 1969. *The American Myth of Success.* New York: Basic Books.

Wellman, David T. 1993. *Portraits of White Racism,* 2nd ed. New York: Cambridge University Press.

Wells-Barnett, Ida B. [1928] 1970. *Crusade for Justice: The Autobiography of Ida B. Wells,* ed. Alfreda M. Duster. Chicago: University of Chicago Press.

Werner, Carrie A. 2011. "The Older Population: 2010." 2010 Census Briefs C2010BR-09. Washington, DC: U.S. Government Printing Office. Accessed April 6, 2012 (www.census.gov/prod/cen2010/briefs/c2010br-09.pdf).

West, Candace, and Don H. Zimmerman. 1987. "Doing Gender." *Gender and Society* 1 (June): 125–151.

West, Cornel. 2009. Twitter.

Wethington, Elaine. 2000. "Expecting Stress: Americans and the Midlife Crisis." *Motivation & Emotion* 24 (2): 85–103.

Whorton, James C. 2002. *Nature Cures: The History of Alternative Medicine in America.* New York: Oxford University Press.

Wickman, Peter M. 1991. "Deviance." Pp. 85–87 in *Encyclopedic Dictionary of Sociology,* 4th ed., ed. Dushkin Publishing Group. Guilford, CT: Dushkin.

WID.world. 2017. "Average National Income per Adult." World Wealth & Income Database. Accessed January 18, 2017 (http://wid.world/world/#anninc_pall_992_i/WO/2015/us/k/p/yearly/a/false/5554.8875/20000/curve/false).

Wiencek, Henry. 2003. *An Imperfect God: George Washington, His Slaves, and the Creation of America.* New York: Farrar, Straus, and Giroux.

Wierzbicka, Anna. 2008. "Why There Are No Colour Universals in Language and Thought." *Journal of the Royal Anthropological Institute* 14 (2): 407–425.

Wike, Richard, Bruce Stokes, and Jacob Poushter. 2016. "Global Publics Back U.S. on Fighting ISIS, but Are Critical of Post-9/11 Torture." Pew Research Center, Global Attitudes and Trends June 23. Accessed November 1, 2016 (www.pewglobal.org/2015/06/23/global-publics-back-u-s-on-fighting-isis-but-are-critical-of-post-911-torture/).

Wike, Richard, Bruce Stokes, Jacob Poushter, Laura Silver, Janell Fetterolf, and Kat Devlin. 2018. "Trump's International

Ratings Remain Low, Especially Among Key Allies." Pew Research Center, Global Attitudes & Trends October 1. Accessed November 27, 2018 (www.pewglobal.org/2018/10/01/trumps-international-ratings-remain-low-especially-among-key-allies/).

Wilde Oscar. 1890. "The Picture of Dorian Gray." *Lippincott's Monthly Magazine,* July 1890.

Wilford, John Noble. 1997. "New Clues Show Where People Made the Great Leap to Agriculture." *The New York Times,* November 18, pp. B9, B12.

Williams, Alicia, John Fries, Jean Koppen, and Robert Prisuta. 2010. *Connecting and Giving: A Report on How Midlife and Older Americans Spend Their Time, Make Connections and Build Communities.* Washington, DC: AARP.

Williams, Caroline. 2013. "Health Myths: Drink Eight Glasses of Water per Day." *New Scientist,* August 21. Accessed September 12, 2016 (www.newscientist.com/article/mg21929310.700-health-myths-drink-eight-glasses-of-water-per-day).

Williams, Kristine N., and Carol A. B. Warren. 2009. "Communication in Assisted Living." *Journal of Aging Studies* 23 (1): 24–36.

Williams, Robin M., Jr. 1970. *American Society,* 3rd ed. New York: Knopf.

Williamson, Thomas. 2007. "Communicating Amok in Malaysia." *Identities* 14(3): 341–365.

Wills, Jeremiah B., and Barbara J. Risman. 2006. "The Visibility of Feminist Thought in Family Studies." *Journal of Marriage and Family* 68 (August): 690–700.

Wilson, A. N. 1999. *God's Funeral: The Decline of Faith in Western Civilization.* New York: W. W. Norton & Company.

Wilson, Carl. 2007. *Lets Talk About Love: A Journey to the End of Taste.* New York: Continuum.

Wilson, James Q., and George Kelling. 1982. "The Police and Neighborhood Safety: Broken Windows." *The Atlantic Monthly* 127:29–38.

Wilson, William Julius. 1999. *The Bridge over the Racial Divide: Rising Inequality and Coalition Politics.* Berkeley: University of California Press.

Winters, Kelley. 2012. "An Update on Gender Diagnoses, as the DSM-5 Goes to Press." GID Reform Weblog, December 5. Accessed June 5, 2013 (http://gidreform.wordpress.com/2012/12/05/an-update-on-gender-diagnoses-as-the-dsm-5-goes-to-press/).

The Wire. 2002. "Lesson." Home Box Office, Inc., Season 1, Episode 8, July 28, 2002.

Wirth, Louis. 1931. "Clinical Sociology." *American Journal of Sociology* 37 (July): 49–60.

Witsman, Katherine, and Ryan Baugh. 2016. "U.S. Naturalizations: 2015." Annual Flow Report, Homeland Security, November. Accessed January 20, 2017 (www.dhs.gov/immigration-statistics/naturalizations).

Witt, Emily. 2018. "How the Survivors of Parkland Began the Never Again Movement." *The New Yorker,* February 19. Accessed December 1, 2018 (www.newyorker.com/news/news-desk/how-the-survivors-of-parkland-began-the-never-again-movement).

Wolf, Naomi. 1992. *The Beauty Myth: How Images of Beauty Are Used Against Women.* New York: Anchor.

Wolff, Edward N. 2016. "Household Wealth Trends in the United States from 1962 to 2013: What Happened over the Great Recession?" *RSF: The Russell Sage Foundation Journal of the Social Sciences* 2(6): 24–43. Accessed December 22, 2016 (www.rsfjournal.org/doi/abs/10.7758/RSF.2016.2.6.02).

Wolraich, Mark L., David B. Wilson, and Wade White. 1995. "The Effect of Sugar on Behavior or Cognition in Children: A Meta-Analysis." *JAMA* 274 (20): 1617–1621.

Wolraich, Mark L., Scott D. Lindgren, Phyllis J. Stumbo, Lewis D. Stegnik, Mark I. Applebaum, and Mary C. Kiritsy. 1994. "Effects of Diets High in Sucrose or Aspartame on the Behavior and Cognitive Performance of Children." *The New England Journal of Medicine* 330 (5): 301–307.

Wong, Natalie W. M. 2016. "Environmental Protests and NIMBY Activism: Local Politics and Waste Management in Beijing and Guangzhou." *China Information* 30(2): 143–164.

Wonjun, Chung, Jinbong Choi, Chang Wan Woo, Soobum Lee, and Christina E. Saindon. 2016. "Community Relations Dealing with a Not in My Back Yard (NIMBY) Context." *International Journal of Conflict Management* 27(3): 424–452.

Wood, Betty. 1997. *The Origins of American Slavery: Freedom and Bondage in the English Colonies.* New York: Hill and Wang.

Woolgar, Steve. 1988. *Science: The Very Idea.* New York: Tavistock Publications.

Woolley, Benjamin. 2007. *Savage Kingdom: Virginia and the Founding of English America.* New York: HarperPress.

Word, David L., Charles D. Coleman, Robert Nunziator, and Robert Kominski. 2007. "Demographic Aspects of Surnames from Census 2000." Accessed January 2, 2008 (www.census.gov/genealogy/www/surnames.pdf).

World Bank. 2016b. "Health Expenditure, Public (Percent of Total Health Expenditure)." *World Development Indicators,* Databank. Assessed December 22, 2016 (http://data.worldbank.org/indicator/SH.XPD.PUBL).

———. 2016c. *Poverty and Shared Prosperity 2016: Taking on Inequality.* Washington, DC: World Bank. Accessed January 17, 2017 (www.worldbank.org/en/publication/poverty-and-shared-prosperity).

———. 2016d. "GNI per Capita, Atlas Method (Current US$)." *World Development Indicators.* Accessed January 17, 2017 (http://data.worldbank.org/indicator/NY.GNP.PCAP.CD).

———. 2018a. "Bilateral Remittance Matrix, 2017." Migration & Remittances Data. Accessed October 11, 2018 (www.worldbank.org/en/topic/migrationremittancesdiasporaissues/brief/migration-remittances-data).

———. 2018b. "Life Expectancy at Birth, Total (Years)." *World Development Indicators.* Accessed November 20, 2018 (https://data.worldbank.org/indicator/SP.DYN.LE00.IN).

———. 2018c. "Fertility Rate, Total (Births per Woman)." *World Development Indicators.* Accessed December 15, 2018 (https://data.worldbank.org/indicator/SP.DYN.TFRT.IN).

———. 2018d. "Domestic general government health expenditure (% of current health expenditure)." World Development Indicators Databank, Accessed January 13, 2019 (https://data.worldbank.org/indicator/SH.XPD.GHED.CH.ZS).

———. 2018e. *Poverty and Shared Prosperity 2018: Piecing Together the Poverty Puzzle.* Washington, DC: World Bank. Accessed January 17, 2019 (www.worldbank.org/en/publication/poverty-and-shared-prosperity).

———. 2018f. "GDP (current US$)." *World Development Indicators.* Accessed January 20, 2019 (http://data.worldbank.org/indicator/NY.GDP.MKTP.CD).

———. 2018g. "GNI per Capita, Atlas Method (Current US$)." *World Development Indicators.* Accessed January 20, 2019 (http://data.worldbank.org/indicator/NY.GNP.PCAP.CD).

———. 2018h. "Income Share Held by Highest 20%." *World Development Indicators.* Accessed January 20, 2019 (http://data.worldbank.org/indicator/SI.DST.05TH.20).

———. 2018i. "Income Share Held by Lowest 20%." *World Development Indicators.* Accessed January 20, 2019 (http://data.worldbank.org/indicator/SI.DST.FRST.20).

———. 2018j. "Labor Force, Female (% of Total Labor Force)." *World Development Indicators.* Accessed January 20, 2019 (https://data.worldbank.org/indicator/SL.TLF.TOTL.FE.ZS).

———. 2018k. *Atlas of Sustainable Development Goals 2018.* Washington, DC: The World Bank. Accessed January 21, 2019 (https://openknowledge.worldbank.org/handle/10986/29788).

———. 2018l. "Poverty Headcount Ratio at National Poverty Lines (% of Population)." *World Development Indicators.* Accessed January 22, 2019 (https://data.worldbank.org/indicator/SL.TLF.TOTL.FE.ZS).

———. 2018m. "Labor Force, Female (% of Total Labor Force)." *World Development Indicators.* Accessed January 22, 2019 (http://data.worldbank.org/indicator/SL.TLF.TOTL.FE.ZS).

———. 2018n. "Bilateral Remittance Matrix, 2017." Migration & Remittances Data. Accessed January 22, 2019 (www.worldbank.org/en/topic/migrationremittancesdiasporaissues/brief/migration-remittances-data).

References

_____. 2018o. "Birth Rate, Crude (per 1,000 People)." *World Development Indicators,* Databank. Accessed January 25, 2019 (http://data.worldbank.org/indicator/SP.DYN.CBRT.IN).

_____. 2018p. "Fertility Rate, Total (Births per Woman)." *World Development Indicators,* Databank. January 25, 2019 (http://data.worldbank.org/indicator/SP.DYN.TFRT.IN).

_____. 2018q. "Death Rate, Crude (per 1,000 People)." *World Development Indicators,* Databank. Accessed January 25, 2019 (http://data.worldbank.org/indicator/SP.DYN.CDRT.IN).

_____. 2018r. "Mortality rate, infant (per 1,000 live births)." *World Development Indicators,* Databank. Accessed January 25, 2019 (https://data.worldbank.org/indicator/SP.DYN.IMRT.IN).

_____. 2018s. "Life Expectancy at Birth, Total (Years)." *World Development Indicators,* Databank. January 25, 2019 (http://data.worldbank.org/indicator/SP.DYN.LE00.IN).

_____. 2018t. "Current Health Expenditure (% of GDP)." *World Development Indicators,* Databank. Accessed January 26, 2019 (https://data.worldbank.org/indicator/SH.XPD.CHEX.GD.ZS).

_____. 2018u. "CO_2 Emissions (Metric Tons per Capita)." *World Development Indicators,* Databank. Accessed January 26, 2019 (http://data.worldbank.org/indicator/EN.ATM.CO2E.PC).

World Economic Forum. 2018. *The Global Gender Gap Report 2018.* Geneva: World Economic Forum. Accessed January 22, 2019 (www.weforum.org/reports/the-global-gender-gap-report-2018).

World Health Organization. 1948. "Preamble to the Constitution of the World Health Organization." Adopted by the International Health Conference, New York, June 19–July 22, 1946; entered into force on April 7, 1948. Accessed June 30, 2011 (http://whqlibdoc.who.int/hist/official_records/constitution.pdf).

_____. 2005. *WHO Global Atlas of Traditional, Complementary, and Alternative Medicine.* Geneva: WHO Press.

_____. 2013a. *WHO Traditional Medicine Strategy: 2014–2023.* Geneva: World Health Organization. Accessed February 13, 2017 (http://apps.who.int/iris/bitstream/10665/92455/1/9789241506090_eng.pdf).

_____. 2013b. *Global and Regional Estimates of Violence Against Women: Prevalence and Health Effects of Intimate Partner Violence and Non-Partner Sexual Violence.* Geneva: World Health Organization. Accessed April 21, 2015 (http://apps.who.int/iris/bitstream/10665/85239/1/9789241564625_eng.pdf).

_____. 2018a. "Female Genital Mutilation." January 31. Accessed January 22, 2019 (www.who.int/news-room/fact-sheets/detail/female-genital-mutilation).

_____. 2018b. *World Health Statistics, 2018: Monitoring the SDGs, Sustainable Development Goals.* Geneva: WHO Press. Accessed January 26, 2019 (https://apps.who.int/iris/bitstream/handle/10665/272596/9789241565585-eng.pdf).

_____. 2018c. "Skilled Health Professionals Density (per 10,000 Population)." Global Health Observatory Indicator Views. Accessed January 26, 2019 (http://apps.who.int/gho/data/node.imr.SDGSHP?).

_____. 2018d. "Ambient (Outdoor) Air Quality and Health." Fact Sheet May 2. Accessed January 26, 2019 (www.who.int/en/news-room/fact-sheets/detail/ambient-(outdoor)-air-quality-and-health).

_____. 2018e. "Drinking-Water." Fact Sheet February 7. Accessed January 26, 2019 (www.who.int/en/news-room/fact-sheets/detail/drinking-water).

_____. 2018f. "Sanitation." Fact Sheet February 19. Accessed January 26, 2019 (www.who.int/en/news-room/fact-sheets/detail/sanitation).

World Values Survey. 2015. "World Values Survey Wave 6: 2010–2014." Online Data Analysis Tool. Accessed March 10, 2015 (www.worldvaluessurvey.org/WVSOnline.jsp).

Worth, Robert F. 2016. *A Rage for Order: The Middle East in Turmoil, from Tahrir Square to Isis.* New York: Farrar, Straus, and Giroux.

Wotipka, Crystal D., and Andrew C. High. 2016. "An Idealized Self or the Real Me? Predicting Attraction to Online Dating Profiles Using Selective Self-Presentation and Warranting." *Communication Monographs* 83(3): 281–302.

Wyatt, Edward. 2012. "Use of Conflict Minerals Gets More Scrutiny from U.S." *The New York Times,* March 19. Accessed May 18, 2012 (www.nytimes.com/2012/03/20/business/use-of-conflict-minerals-gets-more-scrutiny.html).

X

Xu, Jiaquan, Sherry L. Murphy, Kenneth D. Kochanek, Brigham Bastian, and Elizabeth Arias. 2018. "Deaths: Final Data for 2016." *National Vital Statistics Reports* 67 (5). Hyattsville, MD: National Center for Health Statistics. Accessed October 30, 2018 (www.cdc.gov/nchs/data/nvsr/nvsr67/nvsr67_05.pdf).

Y

Yang, Heream. 2018. "Tinder Troubles or Bumble Blues? Just ask Dr. Jess." *Vanderbilt Hustler,* April 2. Accessed December 13, 2018 (https://vanderbilthustler.com/featured/tinder-troubles-or-bumble-blues-just-ask-dr-jess.html).

Yang, Zhengwei, and Jeffrey C. Schank. 2006. "Women Do Not Synchronize Their Menstrual Cycles." *Human Nature* 17 (4): 433–447.

Yinger, J. Milton. 1970. *The Scientific Study of Religion.* New York: Macmillan.

Yogyakartaprinciples.org. 2007. *The Yogyakarta Principles: Principles on the Application of International Human Rights Law in Relation to Sexual Orientation and Gender Identity.* Accessed May 11, 2010 (www.yogyakartaprinciples.org/principles_en.pdf).

Yoshinaga, Kendra. 2016. "Babies of Color Are Now the Majority, Census Says." *NPR Ed,* July 1. Accessed February 4, 2017 (www.npr.org/sections/ed/2016/07/01/484325664/babies-of-color-are-now-the-majority-census-says).

Z

Zainulbhai, Hani. 2016. "Strong Global Support for Gender Equality, Especially Among Women." Pew Research Center, March 8. Accessed February 2, 2017 (www.pewresearch.org/fact-tank/2016/03/08/strong-global-support-for-gender-equality-especially-among-women/).

Zangwill, Israel. 1909. *The Melting-Pot: Drama in Four Acts.* New York: The Macmillan Company.

Zarembo, Alan. 2004. "A Theater of Inquiry and Evil." *Los Angeles Times,* July 15, pp. A1, A24, A25.

Zimbardo, Philip G. 2007. *The Lucifer Effect: Understanding How Good People Turn Evil.* New York: Random House.

Zimmer, Ben. 2015. "'Cisgender,' a Gender-Issues Buzzword, Takes Off." *The Wall Street Journal,* March 13. Accessed January 31, 2017 (www.wsj.com/articles/cisgender-a-gender-issues-buzzword-takes-off-1426278662).

Zimmerman, Amber Lynn, M. Joan McDermott, and Christina M. Gould. 2009. "The Local Is Global: Third Wave Feminism, Peace, and Social Justice." *Contemporary Justice Review* 12 (1): 77–90.

Ziomkiewicz, Anna. 2006. "Menstrual Synchrony: Fact or Artifact?" *Human Nature* 17 (4): 419–432.

Zola, Irving K. 1972. "Medicine as an Institution of Social Control." *Sociological Review* 20 (November): 487–504.

_____. 1983. *Socio-Medical Inquiries.* Philadelphia: Temple University Press.

Zuckerman, Ezra W., and John T. Jost. 2001. "What Makes You Think You're So Popular?: Self-Evaluation Maintenance and the Subjective Side of the Friendship Paradox." *Social Psychology Quarterly* 64: 201–223.

Zweigenhaft, Richard L., and G. William Domhoff. 2006. *Diversity in the Power Elite: How It Happened, Why It Matters,* 2nd ed. New York: Rowman & Littlefield.